Lecture Notes in Artificial Intelligence 9205

Subseries of Lecture Notes in Computer Science

LNAI Series Editors

Randy Goebel
University of Alberta, Edmonton, Canada
Yuzuru Tanaka
Hokkaido University, Sapporo, Japan
Wolfgang Wahlster
DFKI and Saarland University, Saarbrücken, Germany

LNAI Founding Series Editor

Joerg Siekmann
DFKI and Saarland University, Saarbrücken, Germany

More information about this series at http://www.springer.com/series/1244

Jordi Bieger · Ben Goertzel
Alexey Potapov (Eds.)

Artificial General Intelligence

8th International Conference, AGI 2015
Berlin, Germany, July 22–25, 2015
Proceedings

 Springer

Editors
Jordi Bieger
Reykjavik University
Reykjavik
Iceland

Ben Goertzel
Hong Kong Polytechnic University
Hong Kong SAR

Alexey Potapov
Saint Petersburg State University
of Information Technologies,
Mechanics and Optics
St. Petersburg
Russia

ISSN 0302-9743   ISSN 1611-3349   (electronic)
Lecture Notes in Artificial Intelligence
ISBN 978-3-319-21364-4   ISBN 978-3-319-21365-1   (eBook)
DOI 10.1007/978-3-319-21365-1

Library of Congress Control Number: 2015943355

LNCS Sublibrary: SL7 – Artificial Intelligence

Springer Cham Heidelberg New York Dordrecht London
© Springer International Publishing Switzerland 2015

Printed on acid-free paper

Springer International Publishing AG Switzerland is part of Springer Science+Business Media
(www.springer.com)

Preface

Almost exactly 60 years ago, in the summer of 1955, John McCarthy coined the term "artificial intelligence" (AI) to refer to "the science and engineering of making intelligent machines" in a proposal for a summer research project at Darthmouth College. The subsequent Darthmouth Conferences of 1956 are often credited with the creation of the field of AI. But as the problem proved much more difficult than anticipated, disillusionment set in. The goal of creating machines that could think at a level comparable to humans was set aside by many, in favor of the creation of "smart" applications that were highly successful in specialized domains. Since then "AI" and "narrow AI" have become almost synonymous and the development of systems showing more general intelligence in a wide variety of domains was seen as unattainable.

But after having been largely ignored for many decades, the last ten years have seen a small resurgence in the pursuit of what we now call artificial general intelligence (AGI). While the contributions of narrow AI to science and society are undeniable, many researchers were frustrated with the lack of progress toward the larger goal of AI. Armed with novel technology and ideas, a new optimism has taken hold of the community. Creating thinking machines may be a daunting task, but many people today believe that it is not impossible, and that we can take steps toward that goal if we keep our eye on the ball.

The AGI conference series, organized by the AGI Society, has been the main venue for bringing together researchers in this re-emerging field. For the past eight years it has facilitated the exchange of knowledge and ideas by providing an accessible platform for communication and collaboration. This volume contains the research papers accepted for presentation at the Eighth Conference on Artificial General Intelligence (AGI-15), held during July 22–25, 2015, in Berlin. A total of 72 research papers were submitted to the conference, and after desk rejecting 14 (19 %), each paper was reviewed by at least two, and on average 2.93, Program Committee members. We accepted 23 papers for oral presentation (32 %) as well as 19 posters (26 %), of which one was withdrawn.

In addition to these contributed talks, the conference featured Jürgen Schmidhuber, director of the Swiss AI lab IDSIA in Lugano, and Frank Wood, associate professor at the University of Oxford, who gave invited keynote speeches on "The Deep Learning RNNaissance" and probabilistic programming with the Anglican language. José Hernández-Orallo, professor at the Polytechnic University of Valencia, gave a tutorial on the evaluation of intelligent systems. Another tutorial was given by Alexey Potapov, professor at the ITMO University and St. Petersburg State University, on the minimum description length principle. A third tutorial, given by Nil Geisweiler, Cosmo Harrigan and Ben Goertzel, described how to combine program learning and probabilistic logic in OpenCog. Martin Balek and Dusan Fedorcak presented a visual editor for designing the architecture of artificial brains. Finally, the conference also featured workshops on Socioeconomic Implications of AGI and on Synthetic Cognitive Development and

Integrated-Distributed Agency, organized in collaboration with the Global Brain Institute at the Free University of Brussels.

Finally, many thanks are due to those who helped organize the conference, including Jan Klauck, Joscha Bach, and many others; and to the conference's sponsors including Kurzweil AI, Keen Software House, and the OpenCog Foundation.

May 2015

Jordi Bieger
Ben Goertzel
Alexey Potapov

Organization

Organizing Committee

Ben Goertzel (Conference Chair)	AGI Society, USA
Joscha Bach	MIT and Harvard University, USA
Matthew Iklé	Adams State University, USA
Jan Klauck (Local Chair)	Austrian Space Forum, Austria

Program Chairs

Jordi Bieger	Reykjavik University, Iceland
Alexey Potapov	AIDEUS and ITMO University, Russia

Program Committee

Bo An	Nanyang Technological University, China
Itamar Arel	University of Tennessee, USA
Joscha Bach	MIT and Harvard University, USA
Tarek Besold	University of Osnabrück, Germany
Cristiano Castelfranchi	Institute of Cognitive Sciences and Technologies, Italy
Antonio Chella	University of Palermo, Italy
Blerim Emruli	Luleå University of Technology, Sweden
Stan Franklin	University of Memphis, USA
Deon Garrett	Icelandic Institute for Intelligent Machines, Iceland
Nil Geisweiller	Novamente LLC, USA
Helmar Gust	University of Osnabrück, Germany
José Hernández-Orallo	Polytechnic University of Valencia, Spain
Bill Hibbard	University of Wisconsin–Madison, USA
Marcus Hutter	Australian National University, Australia
Matthew Iklé	Adams State University, USA
Benjamin Johnston	University of Sydney, Australia
Cliff Joslyn	Pacific Northwest National Laboratory, USA
Randal Koene	Carboncopies.org, USA
Kai-Uwe Kühnberger	University of Osnabrück, Germany
Shane Legg	Google Inc., USA
Moshe Looks	Google Inc., USA
Maricarmen Martinez	University of Los Andes, Colombia
Amedeo Napoli	LORIA Nancy, France
Eric Nivel	Icelandic Institute for Intelligent Machines, Iceland

Laurent Orseau	Google Inc., USA
Guenter Palm	Ulm University, Germany
Maxim Peterson	ITMO University, Russia
Paul Rosenbloom	University of Southern California, USA
Rafal Rzepka	Hokkaido University, Japan
Samer Schaat	Vienna Technical University, Austria
Ute Schmid	University of Bamberg, Germany
Jürgen Schmidhuber	IDSIA, Switzerland
Javier Snaider	Google Inc., USA
Bas Steunebrink	IDSIA, Switzerland
Claes Strannegård	University of Gothenburg, Sweden
Kristinn Thórisson	Reykjavik University, Iceland
Julian Togelius	IT University of Copenhagen, Denmark
Mario Verdicchio	University of Bergamo, Italy
Pei Wang	Temple University, USA
Roman Yampolskiy	University of Louisville, USA
Byoung-Tak Zhang	Seoul National University, South Korea

Additional Reviewers

Mayank Daswani	Australian National University, Australia
Tom Everitt	Stockholm University, Sweden
Matthias Jakubec	Vienna Technical University, Austria
Jan Leike	Australian National University, Australia
Lydia Chaido Siafara	Vienna Technical University, Austria
Qiong Wu	Nanyang Technological University, China

Steering Committee

| Ben Goertzel | AGI Society, USA (Chair) |
| Marcus Hutter | Australian National University, Australia |

Contents

Papers Presented Orally

Modeling Motivation in MicroPsi 2

Joscha Bach[✉]

Massachusetts Institute of Technology, Cambridge, MA, USA
joscha@mit.edu

Abstract. The MicroPsi architecture combines neuro-symbolic representations with autonomous decision making and motivation based learning. MicroPsi's motivational system reflects cognitive, social and physiological needs, and can account for individual variance and personality traits. Here, we describe the current state of the model that structures the behavior of cognitive agents in MicroPsi2.

Keywords: Artificial general intelligence · Micropsi2 · Motivation · Motivational system · Cognitive architectures

1   Introduction

MicroPsi [1] is an architecture for *Artificial General Intelligence*, based on a framework for creating and simulating cognitive agents [2]. Work on MicroPsi started in 2003. The current version of the framework, MicroPsi2 [3], is implemented in the Python programming language and may interface with various simulation worlds, such as Minecraft (see [4]). MicroPsi agents are hierarchical spreading activation networks that realize perceptual learning, motor control, memory formation and retrieval, decision making, planning and affective modulation.

One of MicroPsi's main areas of research concerns modeling a motivational system: whereas intelligence may be seen as problem solving in the pursuit of a given set of goals, human generality and flexibility stems largely from the ability to *identify* and *prioritize* suitable goals. An artificial system that is meant to model human cognition will have to account for this kind of autonomy. Our solution does not presuppose any goals, but instead a minimal orthogonal set of systemic *needs*, which are signaled to the cognitive system as *urges*. Goals are established as the result of learning how to satisfy those needs in a given environment, and to avoid their frustration. Since needs constantly change, the system will have to reevaluate its goals and behaviors continuously, which results in a dynamic equilibrium of activities. While cognition can change goals, expectations of reward and priorities, it cannot directly influence the needs itself.

MicroPsi's model of motivation [5] has its origins in the *Psi theory* [6, 7] and has recently been extended to account for a more detailed understanding of personality traits, aesthetic appreciation and romantic affection. While current MicroPsi2 agents do not implement all aspects of the motivational system (especially not the full set of need dimensions), the model is general enough to be adapted to a variety of

© Springer International Publishing Switzerland 2015
J. Bieger (Ed.): AGI 2015, LNAI 9205, pp. 3–13, 2015.
DOI: 10.1007/978-3-319-21365-1_1

applications, and has been integrated into other cognitive architectures, such as OpenCog [8]. In the following, I will focus especially on the discussion of concepts that can be transferred into other systems.

2   From Needs to Behavior

Since generally intelligent agents are not restricted to a fixed set of tasks and goals, they have to establish their own goals. These result from a pre-defined set of *needs*, or *demands*, which reflect what the agent has to consume, to achieve or to avoid, to thrive in its environment. Each need d reflects a variable c_d that varies between a target value v_d (the set-point at which the demand is fully satisfied) and a critical extreme v_0 (a point that may reflect where the system stops functioning). Whenever a need arises and no autonomous regulation is possible (for instance, metabolic regulation or transpiration to adjust the body temperature), the need is signaled by an *urge indicator*.

The difference between the target value and the current value is the *strength of the urge*: $urged = |v_d - c_d|$

The distance between the current value and the extremum corresponds to the *urgency* of satisfying the demand: $urgency_d = |v_d - c_d| \cdot |v_d - v_0|^{-1}$

We could also specify that the range of a demand may extend below *and above* the set-point, so the urgency will have to reflect the distance from the current value to the nearest extremum. In practice, however, human demand regulation often uses two different urges for controlling upper and lower deviations from the set-point. For instance, heating and cooling, feeding and satiation, resting and exercising use different signals and control mechanisms.

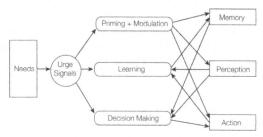

Fig. 1. Needs govern cognitive modulation, priming, learning and decision-making

Urge signals fulfill several roles in the cognitive system (figure 1). Their intensity governs arousal, execution speed and the resolution of cognitive processing (modulation). Changes in the urges indicate the satisfaction or frustration of the corresponding needs. Rapid changes are usually the result of an action of the agent, or of an event has happened to the agent. These changes are indicated with *pleasure signals* (corresponding to satisfaction) or *displeasure signals* (frustration). Pleasure and displeasure signals are used as reinforcements for *motivational learning* (figure 2). Each type of signal is connected to an *associator*. Associators establish a connection between two representations in MicroPsi; here, between the urge signal and the current situation or action. Furthermore, learning strengthens associations between the current situation and those that preceded it. In combination with mechanisms for forgetting and memory consolidation, this results in learning behavior sequences that end in goal situations. *Goals* are actions or situations that allow satisfying the urge (*appetitive goals*), or that threaten to increase the urge (*aversive goals*).

A *motive* is an urge that has been associated with a particular goal. Each action of a MicroPsi agent is based on an active motive, i.e. directed on reaching an appetitive goal, or avoiding an aversive goal.

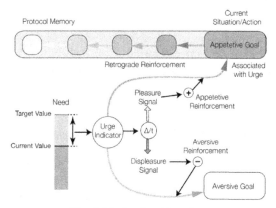

Fig. 2. Motivational learning

The association between urges and goals allows the agent to identify possible remedies whenever the need arises in the future, and *prime* its perception and memory retrieval towards the currently active urges. Most importantly, urges signal the current demands of the system, and thereby inform decision-making.

3   Types of Needs

The needs of a cognitive system fall into three groups: physiological needs, social needs and cognitive. Note that needs do not form a hierarchy, as for instance suggested by Maslow [9], but all act on the same level. This means that needs do not have to be satisfied in succession (many needs may never be fully satisfied), but concurrently. To establish priorities between different urges, each one is multiplied with a weight parameter *weight$_d$* that expresses its importance relative to other needs. Each need has a *decay$_d$* that specifies how quickly the c_d drops towards v_0 when left alone, and thus, how often it has to be replenished. Furthermore, each need has a parameter *gain$_d$* and *loss$_d$*, which expresses how much it reacts to satisfaction or frustration. Using a suitable parameter set [*weight, decay, gain, loss*] for each demand or an agent, we can account for *individual variance of motivational traits*, and personality properties [10].

Physiological needs regulate the basic survival of the organism and reflect demands of the metabolism and physiological well-being. The corresponding urges originate in proprioceptive measurements, levels of hormones and nutrients in the bloodstream, etc. Physiological needs include sustenance (food and drink), physical integrity and pain avoidance, rest, avoidance of hypothermia and hyperthermia, and many more. (See figure 3 for an example implementation of physiological needs in MicroPsi2.)

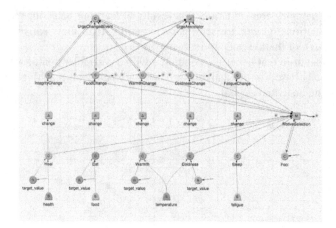

Fig. 3. Implementation of physiological needs in MicroPsi2 *(D. Welland)*

Social needs direct the behavior towards other individuals and groups. They are satisfied and frustrated by *social signals* and corresponding mental representations, but pleasure and displeasure from these sources is not necessarily less relevant to a subject than physiological pain. Consequently, people are often willing to sacrifice their food, rest, health or even their life to satisfy a social goal (getting recognition, supporting a friend, saving a child, winning a partner, maintaining one's integrity, avoiding loss of reputation etc.). Individual differences in the weight of social needs may result in more altruist or egotist, extraverted or introverted, abrasive or agreeable, romantic or a-romantic personalities.

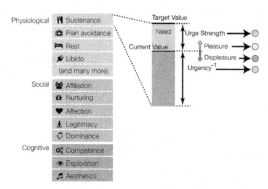

Fig. 4. Needs and motivator structure

Cognitive needs give rise to open-ended problem solving, skill-acquisition, exploration, play and creativity. Differences in the weight of cognitive needs may influence conscientiousness vs. spontaneity, openness, and hedonism.

Social Needs
Affiliation is the need for recognition and acceptance by other individuals or groups. It is satisfied by *legitimacy signals*, such as smiles and praise, and frustrated by frowns

and reproach (*anti-legitimacy signals*). The effect of a legitimacy signal depends on its perceived strength, and the social weight (reputation) that the agent attaches to its source. For instance, praise from a highly respected individual typically results in a larger gain than anonymous praise. Affiliation plays the role of a virtual currency, offering rewards for cooperative behavior, and punishment for defection. A high decay of affiliation results in a personality that requires frequent attention from the environment, and introversion might be the outcome of a low decay or weight of affiliation.

Internal Legitimacy ("honor") is a variant of affiliation that is directed on the conformance to internalized social norms. It directs social behavior in the absence of direct observers. Here, the source of legitimacy signals is the agent itself.

Nurturing is the need to altruistically care for other individuals or groups. It gets satisfied by subjectively increasing the well-being of someone else. The amount of satisfaction derived from an act nurturing depends on the social weight that the agent attaches to the object of his efforts. Supporting a cherished person or group will result in greater satisfaction than giving to an anonymous recipient. Psychopathy may be the result of the absence of a need for nurturing. Repeated exchange of affiliation and nurturing with another individual results in bonding, i.e. motivational learning will strongly establish that individual as a target for the respective urges. *Philia*/friendship is expressed as the reciprocal and mutual exchange of affiliation and nurturing between two individuals – it does not require an additional mechanism.

Romantic affection is the need to form a bond with a specific individual, leads to courtship behavior, and signals inclination for parental investment. Unlike libido, which is the physiological need for sexual gratification with a range of partners, romantic affection is directed on closeness and exclusive identification with a single partner [11]. A high weight of romantic affection may result in a propensity for *limerence* (an intense and sometimes dysfunctional infatuation), while a low one generates an a-romantic personality. Love, like friendship, is not an individual need (nor is it a single emotion). Instead, it may be best understood as a set of states, which differ based on the elementary mechanisms that are involved or absent: affiliation, nurturing, romantic affection and libido.

Dominance is the need to rise within the social hierarchies, or to maintain one's place. A high weight of dominance leads to competitive behavior, and may result in a greater willingness to take risks or exert aggression to ascend.

Cognitive Needs

Competence is either task-related, effect-related or general:

- *Epistemic*, or *task-related competence* measures success at individual skills. The execution of a skill, and acquisition of new skills lead to satisfaction; failure, or anticipation of failure to frustration.
- *Effect-related competence* measures the ability to exert changes in the environment, with a gain that is proportional to the size of the observed effect.
- *General competence* is a compounded measure of the ability to satisfy needs (including the acquisition of epistemic competence). The strength of the urge is used as a heuristic to reflect on general performance, and to predict success at unknown tasks. Low general competence amounts to a lack of confidence.

Anticipated or factual failure at tasks may lead to an urge to replenish competence, which may be achieved by picking another task with a high probability of success. This dynamic may contribute to procrastination.

Exploration is the need to acquire certainty about objects and processes in the environment. The confirmation of uncertain expectations of perception and action increases certainty (and thus reduces the need for exploration); violations of expectations or a lack of available predictions increase the need for certainty. The strength of the urge for exploration is used as a heuristic for the degree of uncertainty in the given situation.

Stimulus-oriented aesthetics is the need for intrinsically pleasant stimuli, such as harmonious sounds, certain environmental features, tactile sensations. The favorable response to these stimuli is either a by-product of sensory processing, or serves indirect purposes (such as seeking out fertile land, identifying healthy mating prospects etc.).

Abstract aesthetics is the need to identify structure in mental representations, and to replace existing mental representations with more efficient ones. Abstract aesthetics is responsible for the discovery of mathematical elegance, musical arrangement, and for pleasure generated through the revision of conceptual structures.

4   Decision-Making

According to the Psi theory, all behaviors are either directed on the satisfaction of a need, or on the avoidance of the frustration of a need. Even serendipitous behavior is directed on need satisfaction (on exploration, rest or aesthetics). Identifying goals and suitable actions is the task of the decision-making system (figure 5).

Once a need becomes active and cannot be resolved by autonomous regulation, an urge signal is triggered, which brings the need to the attention of the *reactive* layer of the cognitive agent. Through past experiences, the urge has been associated with various actions, objects and situations that satisfied it in the past (appetitive goals), and situations and objects that frustrated it (aversive goals). Via activation spreading along these associations, relevant content in memory and perception is highlighted.

If an appetitive goal is perceived immediately, and there is no significant interference with current activity, the urge can be satisfied opportunistically, which will not require significant attentional processing. Otherwise, the agent attempts to suppress the new urge (by subtracting a selection threshold that varies based on the strength and urgency of the already dominant motive).

If the urge overcomes the selection threshold, and turns out to be stronger than the currently dominant urge, the current behavior is interrupted. The agent now tries to recall an applicable strategy, using spreading activation to identify a possible sequence of actions/world states from the current world situation (i.e., the currently active world model) to one of the highlighted appetitive goals. If such a strategy cannot be discovered automatically, the agent engages additional attentional resources and attempts to construct a plan, by matching known world situations and actions into a possible chain that can connect the current world situation to one of the appetitive goals. (At the moment, MicroPsi2 uses a simple hill-climbing planner, but many planning strategies can be used.)

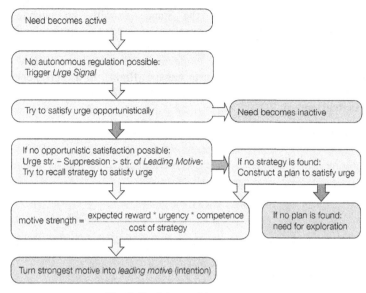

Fig. 5. Decision-making sequence

If plan construction fails, the agent gives up on pursuing the current urge, but increases its need for exploration (which will increase the likelihood of orientation behaviors to acquire additional information about the current situation, or even trigger experimental and explorative behavior strategies).

A successfully identified plan or automatism amounts to a motive (a combination of an active urge, a goal, and a sequence of actions to reach that goal). The strength of the motive is determined by estimating the reward of reaching the goal, the urgency of resolving the need, the probability of success, and dividing the result of these factors by the estimated cost of implementing the plan. The strongest motive will be raised to an intention, that is, it becomes the new dominant motive, and governs the actions of the agent. The probability of succeeding in implementing a strategy is currently estimated as the sum of the task specific competence (i.e. how likely the strategy succeeded in the past), and the general competence (to account for the agents general ability or inability to improvise and succeed in unknown circumstances).

5   Modulation

The strength of the needs of the agents does not only establish which goals an agent follows, but also *how* it pursues them. Cognitive and perceptual processing are configured by a set of global modulators (figure 6):

Arousal reflects the combined strength and urgency of the needs of the agent. Arousal is reflected in more energy expenditure in actions, action readiness, stronger responses to sensory stimuli, and faster reactions [12].

Valence represents a qualitative evaluation of the current situation. Valence is determined by adding all current pleasure signals to a baseline, and then subtracting all displeasure and currently active urges.

Aggression/submission determines the stance towards an attended object. Aggression is especially triggered by a negatively valenced reaction to another agent manifestly blocking a relevant goal (i.e., anger), and increases the likelihood of sanctioning behavior (fight). A low competence also leads to a low value of aggression, and reduces the inclination to engage (flight). In a more general sense, aggression suggests whether to approach or retract from the attended object, a middle value marks indifference.

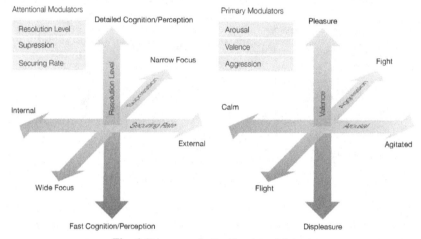

Fig. 6. Primary and attentional modulators

The combination of valence, arousal and aggression defines an *affective state* of the agent, and has originally been described by Wundt [13], who called the third dimension *tension*, and argued that each emotion can be characterized by their pleasurableness, intensity and stressfulness. The Wundt model of affect has been reinvented and modified numerous times in the history of psychology; the third dimension has also been identified as acceptance/rejection by Schlosberg [14] and submission/dominance by Mehrabian [15]. Note that arousal, valence and aggression are not themselves affects or emotions, but dimensions of a space of *cognitive configurations*. Affects are regions within that space. (Mehrabian calls this model *PAD*, for *pleasure, arousal* and *dominance*.)

MicroPsi uses currently six cognitive modulators. In addition to the three dimensions discussed above, these are:

Resolution level, the level of detail when performing cognitive and perceptual tasks. A high resolution will consider more details and thus often arrive at more accurate solutions and representations, while a low resolution allows faster responses. In MicroPsi, the resolution level is interpreted as the *width of activation spreading* in neuro-symbolic representations.

Suppression has already been mentioned in the context of decision-making. This modulator defines a selection threshold, which amounts to a stronger focus on the current task, and a narrower direction of attention. Suppression is a mechanism to avoid oscillations between competing motives.

Securing rate determines the frequency of obtaining/updating information from the environment. A dynamic environment requires more cognitive resources for perceptual processing, while a static environment frees resources for deliberation and reflection. In other words, the securing rate determines the direction of attention: outwards, into the environment, or inwards, onto the mental stage.

The three additional modulator dimensions configure the attention of a MicroPsi agent, by determining its width/detail, its focus, and its direction.

The values of the modulators are determined by the configurations of the urges, and by interaction among the modulators themselves (figure 7). Arousal is determined by the strength and urgency of all needs. A high arousal will also increase the resolution level and increase the suppression. The resolution level is increased by the strength of the current motive, but reduced by its urgency, allowing for faster responses. Suppression is increased by the strength and urgency of the currently leading motive, and is reduced by a low general competence. The securing rate is decreased by the strength and urgency of the leading motive, but increases with low competence and a high need for exploration (which is equivalent to experienced uncertainty). Aggression is triggered by agents or obstacles that prevent the realization of an important motive, and reduced by low competence.

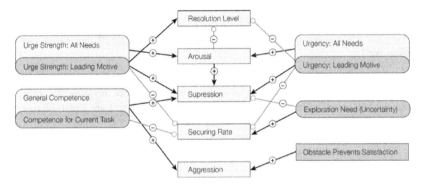

Fig. 7. The dynamics of modulation

Additionally, each modulator has at least four more or less fixed parameters that account for individual variance between subjects: the *baseline* is the default value of the modulator; the *range* describes the upper and lower bound of its changes, the *volatility* defines the reaction to change, and the *duration* describes the amount of time until the modulator returns to its baseline.

Emotions are either undirected, and can be described as typical configurations of the modulators, along with competence and experienced uncertainty, or they are a valenced reaction to an object, i.e. a particular motivationally relevant mental representation, combined with an affective state. Examples of undirected emotions are joy (positive valence and high arousal), bliss (positive valence and low arousal) or angst (negative valence, high experienced uncertainty, submission and low competence). Directed emotions are fear (negative valence directed on an aversive goal, submissiveness and low competence) and anger (negative valence directed on an agent that prevented an appetitive goal or caused the manifestation of an aversive goal, aggression, high arousal). Jealousy may either manifest as a fear (directed on losing romantic attachment or affiliation; submission), or as aggression (directed on an agent that prevents satisfaction of affiliative or romantic needs).

6   Summary

MicroPsi explores the combination of a neuro-symbolic cognitive architecture with a model of autonomous, polytelic motivation. Motives result from the association of urges with learned goals, and plans to achieve them. Urges reflect various physiological, social and cognitive needs. Cognitive processes are modulated in response to the strength and urgency of the needs, which gives rise to affective states, and allows for the emergence of emotions.

The current incarnation, MicroPsi2, adds further details to this motivational model, especially a more detailed set of social needs (nurturing, dominance and romantic affection). Parameters for each need (weight, gain, loss and decay) account for individual variation and modeling of personality traits. Modulators reflect valence, arousal and fight/flight tendency, as well as detail, focus and direction of attention. Modulators are parameterized by baseline, range, volatility and duration. We are currently applying the MicroPsi motivation model for analyzing the behavior of human subjects in computer games. The motivation model is also used to control behavior learning of autonomous AI agents in simulated environments.

While MicroPsi agents are implemented as hierarchical spreading activation networks, the underlying theory of motivation can be integrated into other cognitive models as well.

Acknowledgements. The implementation of MicroPsi would not be possible without the contributions of Ronnie Vuine, Dominik Welland and Priska Herger. I am grateful for generous support by and discussions with Dietrich Dörner, Martin Nowak and Jeffrey Epstein. Current work on MicroPsi is supported by the Program of Evolutionary Dynamics at Harvard University, and the Playful Systems Group at the MIT Media Lab.

References

1. Bach, J.: Principles of Synthetic Intelligence – An architecture of motivated cognition. Oxford University Press (2009)
2. Bach, J., Vuine, R.: Designing Agents with MicroPsi Node Nets. In: Günter, A., Kruse, R., Neumann, B. (eds.) KI 2003. LNCS (LNAI), vol. 2821, pp. 164–178. Springer, Heidelberg (2003)
3. Bach, J.: MicroPsi 2: The Next Generation of the MicroPsi Framework. In: Bach, J., Goertzel, B., Iklé, M. (eds.) AGI 2012. LNCS, vol. 7716, pp. 11–20. Springer, Heidelberg (2012)
4. Short, D.: Teaching Scientific Concepts Using a Virtual World—Minecraft. Teaching Science **58**(3), 55–58 (2012)
5. Bach, J.: A Framework for Emergent Emotions, Based on Motivation and Cognitive Modulators. International Journal of Synthetic Emotions (IJSE) **3**(1), 43–63 (2012)
6. Dörner, D.: Bauplan für eine Seele. Reinbeck (1999)
7. Dörner, D., Bartl, C., Detje, F., Gerdes, J., Halcour, D.: Die Mechanik des Seelenwagens. Handlungsregulation. Verlag Hans Huber, Bern (2002)

8. Cai, Z., Goertzel, B., Zhou, C., Zhang, Y., Jiang, M., Yu, G.: OpenPsi: Dynamics of a computational affective model inspired by Dörner's PSI theory. Cognitive Systems Research **17–18**, 63–80 (2012)

9. Maslow, A., Frager, R., Fadiman, J.: Motivation and Personality, 3rd edn. Addison-Wesley, Boston (1987)

10. Bach, J.: Functional Modeling of Personality Properties Based on Motivational Traits. In: Proceedings of ICCM-7, International Conference on Cognitive Modeling, pp. 271–272. Berlin, Germany (2012)

11. Fisher, H.E.: Lust, attraction and attachment in mammalian reproduction. Human Nature **9**(1), 23–52 (1998)

12. Pfaff, D.W.: Brain Arousal and Information Theory: Neural and Genetic Mechanisms. Harvard University Press, Cambridge, MA (2006)

13. Wundt, W.: Gefühlselemente des Seelenlebens. In: Grundzüge der physiologischen Psychologie II. Engelmann, Leipzig (1910)

14. Schlosberg, H.S.: Three dimensions of emotion. Psychological Review **1954**(61), 81–88 (1954)

15. Mehrabian, A.: Basic dimensions for a general psychological theory. Oelgeschlager, Gunn & Hain Publishers, pp. 39–53 (1980)

Genetic Programming on Program Traces as an Inference Engine for Probabilistic Languages

Vita Batishcheva[2] and Alexey Potapov[1,2(✉)]

[1] ITMO University, St. Petersburg, Russia
potapov@aideus.com
[2] St. Petersburg State University, St. Petersburg, Russia
elokkuu@gmail.com

Abstract. Methods of simulated annealing and genetic programming over probabilistic program traces are developed firstly. These methods combine expressiveness of Turing-complete probabilistic languages, in which arbitrary generative models can be defined, and search effectiveness of meta-heuristic methods. To use these methods, one should only specify a generative model of objects of interest and a fitness function over them without necessity to implement domain-specific genetic operators or mappings from objects to and from bit strings. On the other hand, implemented methods showed better quality than the traditional mh-query on several optimization tasks. Thus, these results can contribute to both fields of genetic programming and probabilistic programming.

Keywords: Probabilistic programming · Genetic programming · Program traces

1 Introduction

Two crucial approaches in AGI are cognitive architectures and universal algorithmic intelligence. These approaches start from very different points and sometimes are even treated as incompatible. However, we believe [1] that they should be united in order to build AGI that is both efficient and general. However, a framework is required that can help to intimately combine them on the conceptual level and the level of implementation. Probabilistic programming could become a suitable basis for developing such a framework. Indeed, on the one hand, query procedures in the Turing-complete probabilistic programming languages (PPLs) can be used as direct approximations of universal induction and prediction, which are the central components of universal intelligence models. On the other hand, probabilistic programming has already been successfully used in cognitive modeling [2].

Many solutions in probabilistic programming utilize efficient inference techniques for particular types of generative models (e.g. Bayesian networks) [3, 4]. However, Turing-complete languages are much more promising in the context of AGI. These PPLs allow for specifying generative models in the form of arbitrary programs including programs which generate other programs. Inference over such generative models automatically results in inducing programs in user-defined languages. Thus, the same inference engine can be used to solve a very wide spectrum of problems.

© Springer International Publishing Switzerland 2015
J. Bieger (Ed.): AGI 2015, LNAI 9205, pp. 14–24, 2015.
DOI: 10.1007/978-3-319-21365-1_2

On the one hand, the performance of generic inference methods in PPLs can be rather low even for models with a small number of random choices [5]. These methods are most commonly based on random sampling (e.g. Monte-Carlo Markov Chains) [2, 6]. There are some works on developing stronger methods of inference in Turing-complete probabilistic languages (e.g. [5, 7]), but they are not efficient for all cases, e.g. for inducing programs, although some progress in this direction is achieved [8]. Thus, more appropriate inference methods are needed, and genetic programming (GP) can be considered as a suitable candidate since it has already been applied to universal induction [9] and cognitive architectures [10].

On the other hand, wide and easy applicability of inference in PPLs is also desirable by evolutionary computations. Indeed, one would desire to be able to apply some existing implementation of genetic algorithms simply by defining the problem at hand without developing binary representations of solutions or implementing problem-specific recombination and mutation operators (and some attempts to overcome this also exist in the field of genetic programming, e.g. [11]).

Consequently, it is interesting to combine generality of inference over declarative models in Turing-complete PPLs and strength of genetic programming. This combination will give a generic tool for fast prototyping of genetic programming methods for arbitrary domain specific languages simply by specifying a function generating programs in a target language. It can also extend the toolkit of PPLs, since conventional inference in probabilistic programming is performed for conditioning, while genetic programming is intended for optimization of fitness functions.

In this paper, we present a novel approach to inference in PPLs based on genetic programming and simulated annealing, which are applied to probabilistic program (computation) traces. Each program trace is the instantiation of the generative model specified by the program. Recombinations and mutations of program traces guarantee that their results can be generated by the initial probabilistic program. Thus, program traces are used as a "universal genetic code" for arbitrary generative models, and it is enough to only specify such a model in the form of a probabilistic program to perform evolutionary computations in the space of its instantiations. To the best of our knowledge, there are no works devoted to implementing an inference engine for PPLs on the base of genetic programming, so this is the main contribution of our paper.

In [12] authors indicated that "current approaches to Probabilistic Programming are heavily influenced by the Bayesian approach to machine learning" and the optimization approach is promising since "optimization techniques scale better than search techniques". That is, our paper can also be viewed as the work in this direction, which is much lesser explored in the field of probabilistic programming.

2   Background

Probabilistic Programs
Since general concepts of genetic programming are well known, we will concentrate on probabilistic programming. Some PPLs extend existing languages preserving their semantics as a particular case. Programs in these languages typically include calls to (pseudo-)random functions. PPLs use an extended set of random functions

corresponding to different common distributions including Gaussian, Beta, Gamma, multinomial, etc. Evaluation of such a program with random choices is performed in the same way as evaluation of this program in the base (non-probabilistic) language.

However, programs in PPLs are treated as generative models defining distributions over possible return values [5], and their direct evaluation can be interpreted as taking one sample from corresponding distributions. Multiple evaluation of a program can be used to estimate an underlying distribution.

PPLs go further and support programs defining conditional distributions. Such a program contains a final condition indicating whether the result of program evaluation should be accepted or not (in some languages an "observe" statement can be placed anywhere to impose conditions on intermediate results). The simplest way to sample from conditional distributions is the rejection sampling, in which a program is simply evaluated many times while its final condition is not satisfied. However, the rejection sampling can be extremely inefficient even for rather simple models.

One can utilize a method for efficient inference of conditional probabilities without sampling for a restricted set of models, but generic inference methods should be used for Turing-complete languages. One of such widely used methods is based on Monte-Carlo Markov Chains (MCMC), namely, the Metropolis-Hastings (MH) algorithm. This algorithm uses stochastic local search to sample such instances, for which the given condition will remain true. To implement it for models specified by probabilistic programs, one needs to introduce small changes to the return values of elementary random procedures called in these programs, so these values should be memoized [2].

MCMC can be much more efficient than rejection sampling for evaluating posterior distributions. However, without utilizing some additional techniques it can be as bad as the rejection sampling (or even worse due to overheads) in retrieving the first appropriate sample. One can easily check this on the example of the following simple Church program (mh-query 1 1 (define xs (repeat 20 flip)) xs (all xs)).

In this program, the list of 20 random Boolean values is defined, and this list is returned, when all its values are true. If one replaces "mh-query 1 1" with "rejection-query", calculation time will slightly decrease. However, retrieving many samples by mh-query will be much faster than executing rejection-query many times. Thus, the unsolved problem here is the problem of finding the first admissible instantiation of a model. This is done blindly in both MCMC and the rejection sampling.

In many practical problems, a user can convert a strict condition into a soft one or even can initially have a task with the goal to optimize some function. Thus, query procedures which accept a fitness-function for optimization instead of a strict condition for satisfying can be used as a part of MCMC sampling as well as they can be used independently for solving optimization problems.

Implemented Language

Since exploration of solution spaces in probabilistic programming require manipulations with random choices made during program evaluation, development of new query procedures is connected with interfering in the evaluation process. Since no language supports flexible enough external control of this process, it was easier for us to implement a new interpreter. However, we decided not to develop a new language, but to reproduce (using Scheme as the host language) some basic functionality of

Church [2] including a number of simple functions (+, -, *, /, and, or, not, list, car, cdr, cons, etc.), several random functions (flip, random_integer, gaussian, multinomial), declaration of variables and functions (define, let), function calls with recursion. Also, "quote" and "eval" were implemented. For example, the following program is acceptable (which is passed to our interpreter as the quoted list)

'((define (tree) (if (flip 0.7) (random-integer 10)
                                (list (tree) (tree))))
    (tree))

Traditional Lisp interpreters will return different results on each run of such programs. Interpreters of PPLs provide for query functions, which are used for calculating posterior probabilities or to perform sampling in accordance with the specified condition. We wanted to extend this language with GP-based query procedures, which accept fitness-functions instead of strict conditions. Let's consider how genetic operators can be implemented in these settings.

3   Genetic Operators for Computation Traces

Mutations

To combine genetic programming with probabilistic languages we treat each run of a program as a candidate solution. The source of variability of these candidate solutions comes from different outcomes of random choices during evaluation. Mutations consist in slight modifications of the random choices performed during the previous evaluation that resembles some part of the MH-algorithm. All these choices should be cached and bound to the execution context, in which they were made. To do this, we implemented the following representation of program traces, which idea (but not its implementation) is similar to that used in the mh-query implementation in Church [2].

In this representation, each expression in the original program during recursive evaluation is converted to the structure (struct IR (rnd? val expr) #:transparent), where IR is the name of the structure, rnd? is #t if random choices were made during evaluation of the expression expr; val is the result of evaluation (one sample from the distribution specified by expr). interpret-IR-prog function was implemented for evaluating programs (lists of expressions) given in symbolic form. Consider some examples.

- (interpret-IR-prog '(10)) → (list (IR #f 10 10)) meaning that the result of evaluation of the program containing only one expression 10 is 10 and it is not random.
- (interpret-IR-prog '((gaussian 0 1))) → (list (IR #t -0.27 (list 'gaussian (IR #f 0 0) (IR #f 1 1)))) meaning that the result of evaluation of (gaussian 0 1) was -0.27.
- (interpret-IR-prog '((if #t 0 1))) → (list (IR #f 0 (list 'if (IR #f #t #t) (IR #f 0 0) 1))) meaning that only one branch was evaluated.
- In the more complex case, random branch can be expanded depending on the result of evaluation of the stochastic condition: (interpret-IR-prog '((if (flip) 0 1))) → (list (IR #t 1 (list 'if (IR #t #f '(flip)) 0 (IR #f 1 1)))).
- In definitions of variables only their values are transformed to IR: (interpret-IR-prog '((define x (flip)))) → (list (list 'define 'x (IR #t #f '(flip)))). Evaluation of

definitions results in changes of the environment as usual. Let-expressions have similar behavior, but they have a body to be evaluated. Function definitions are kept unchanged. Non-library function application is replaced by its body and let-binding of its arguments.

- Symbols, which can be found in the environment, are replaced by their values: (interpret-IR-prog '((define x (random-integer 10)) x)) → (list (list 'define 'x (IR #t 5 (list 'random-integer (IR #f 10 10)))) (IR #t 5 'x)).

The evaluated program can be evaluated again, and previously made random choices can be taken into account during this re-evaluation. We extended interpret-IR-prog in such a way that it can accept both initial programs and their IR expansions (since re-evaluation process can run into branches not expanded yet, such unification is necessary to deal with mixed cases also).

During each following re-evaluation of the expanded program, deterministic expressions are not evaluated again, but their previous values are used. All stochastic expressions are evaluated in the same way as during the first run except calls to the basic random functions, which behavior is changed. These functions are modified in order to take previously returned values into account. The mutation speed parameter p added to interpret-IR-prog indicates, how close new values should be to previous values. For example, the previous result of (flip) is changed with probability equals to p. Re-evaluation of (IR #t v (gaussian x0 s)), where v is the previously returned value, x0 is mean and s is sigma, will correspond to (gaussian v (* p s)), but in other implementations it could be biased towards x0.

For example, the result of re-evaluation of the IR expression (list (IR #t -0.27 (list 'gaussian (IR #f 0 0) (IR #f 1 1)))) using p=0.01 can be (list (IR #t -0.26 (list 'gaussian (IR #f 0 0) (IR #f 1 1)))).

Simulated Annealing

The described interpreter is already enough to implement an optimization query based on simulated annealing. Let the program be given, which last expression returns the value of energy (fitness) function to be minimized. Then, we can re-evaluate this program many times preferring evaluation results with lower value of the last expression.

Simulated annealing maintains only one program trace (in the form of IR expansion). It executes interpret-IR-prog to generate new candidate solutions (with transition probabilities derived by the interpreter for the given program and parameterized by the temperature), and accepts them with probability (/ 1 (+ 1 (exp (/ dE t)))), where dE is the difference of energies of the candidate and current solutions, and t is the current temperature (other acceptance probabilities can be used).

On each iteration, candidate solutions are generated until acceptance (although the number of tries is limited), and the temperature is decreased from iteration to iteration. We implemented annealing-query on the base of this approach.

Crossover

Crossover also utilizes program traces. However, it requires dual re-evaluation of two expansions of a program. These expansions are interpreted together as the same program, while their structures match (and they should match except variations caused by random choices). The main difference is in application of the basic random functions since the previously returned values from both parents should be taken into account.

For example, in our implementation, the dual flip randomly returns one of the previous values, and the dual Gaussian returns (+ (* v1 e) (* v2 (- 1 e))), where v1 and v2 are the previous values, and e is the random value in [0, 1] (one can bias the result of this basic element of crossover towards initial Gaussian distribution). Mutations are introduced simultaneously with crossover for the sake of efficiency.

However, such a branch can be encountered during re-evaluation that has not been expanded yet in one or both parents. In the latter case, this branch is evaluated simply as it was the first execution. Otherwise it is re-evaluated for the parent, for which it has already been expanded (without crossover, but with mutations). It is not expanded for another parent, since this expansion will be random and not evaluated by fitness function, so it will simply clutter information from the more relevant parent.

Children can contain earlier expanded, but now unused branches, which can be activated again in later generations due to a single mutation or even crossover. These parts of the expanded program resemble junk DNA and fast genetic adaptations.

Let us consider one simple, but interesting case for crossover, namely a recursive stochastic procedure '((define (tree) (if (flip 0.7) (random-integer 10) (list (tree))))). Expansion of (tree) can produce large computation traces, so let us consider results of crossover on the level of values of the last expression.

'(6 9) + '(8 0) → '(7 6)
'(7 9) + '((0 7) (7 4)) → '(7 (7 4))
'((3 (7 (1 7))) 5) + '((5 2) 2) → '((4 (7 (1 7))) 2)

It can be seen that while the structure of trees matches, two program traces are re-evaluated together and results of random-integer are merged in leaves, but when the structure diverges, a subtree is randomly taken from one of the parents (depending on the result of re-evaluating (flip 0.7)). This type of crossover for generated trees automatically follows from the implemented crossover for program traces. Of course, someone might want to use a different crossover operator based on the domain-specific knowledge, e.g. to exchange arbitrary subtrees in parents. The latter is difficult to do in our program trace representation (and additional research is needed to develop a more flexible representation). On the other hand, recombination of program traces during dual re-evaluation guarantees that its result can be produced by the initial program, and also provides for some flexibility.

Using the described genetic operators, evolution-query was implemented.

4   Empirical Evaluation

We considered three tasks, each of which can be set both for conditional sampling and fitness-function optimization. Three query functions were compared – mh-query (web-church), annealing-query and evolution-query (Scheme implementation). mh-query was used to retrieve only one sample (since we were interested in its efficiency on this step; moreover, the tasks didn't require posterior distributions).

Curve Fitting

Consider the generative polynomial model $y=poly(x|\mathbf{ws})$, which parameters defined as normally distributed random variables should be optimized to fit observations $\{(x_i, y_i)\}$. Implementation of *poly* is straightforward. The full generative model should also include noise, but such a model will be useless since it is almost impossible to blindly guess noise values. Instead, MSE is used in annealing-query and evolution-query, and the following condition is used in mh-query.

    (define (noisy-equals? x y) (flip (exp (* -30 (expt (- x y) 2)))))
    (all (map noisy-equals? ys-gen ys))

noisy-equals? can randomly be true, even if its arguments differ, but with decreasing probability. Speed of this decrease is specified by the value, which equals 30 in the example code. The smaller this value, the looser the equality holds. We chose such the value that mh-query execution time approximately equals to that of annealing-query and evolution-query (which execution time is controlled by the specified number of iterations), so we can compare precision of solutions found by different methods. Of course, such comparison is quite loose, but it is qualitatively adequate since linear increase of computation time will yield only logarithmic increase of precision. The results for several functions and data points are shown in Table 1.

Table 1. Average RMSE

Task		RMSE		
		mh-query	*annealing-query*	*evolution-query*
$4x^2+3x$	xs=(0 1 2 3)	1.71	0.217	0.035
$4x^2+3x$	xs=(0 0.1 0.2 0.3 0.4 0.5)	0.94	0.425	0.010
$0.5x^3-x$	xs=(0 0.1 0.2 0.3 0.4 0.5)	0.467	0.169	0.007

It can be seen that mh-query is inefficient here – it requires very loose noise-equals? yielding imprecise results. Stricter condition results in huge increase of computation time. Evolution-query is the most precise, while annealing-query works correctly, but converges slower. The worst precision is achieved, when wn is selected incorrectly. It is important to see, how crossover on program traces results in children's "phenotypes". Consider the example of how crossover affects ws values

    '(1.903864   -11.119573   4.562440) +
    '(-20.396958 -12.492696 -0.735389   3.308482) →
    '(-5.232313   -11.462677 2.3152821 3.308482)

The values in same positions are averaged with random weights (although these weights are independent for different positions as in geometric semantic crossover). If lengths (i.e. wn) of parent's vector parameters ws differ, the child's wn value will correspond to that of one of the parents or will be between them.

Subset Sum Problem

In the subset sum problem, a set of integer numbers is given, and a nonempty subset should be found such that its sum equals a given integer value (we will assume that the sum equals 1 and skip the check of non-triviality of the solution for the sake of simplicity). Integers in each set were generated as random numbers from a certain range, e.g. -10000 to 10000. A random subset was selected, and the last number was calculated as 1 minus sum of elements in this subset. The following program specifies the generative model for this task.

```
(define xs '(9568 5716 8382 7900 -5461 5087 1138 -1111 -9695 -5468 6345
             -1473 -7521 -4323 9893 -9032 -4715 3699 5104 1551))
(define (make-ws n) (if (= n 0) '() (cons (flip) (make-ws (- n 1)))))
(define ws (make-ws (length xs)))
(define (summ xs ws) (if (null? xs) 0
                      (+ (if (car ws) (car xs) 0) (summ (cdr xs) (cdr ws)))))
(define subset-sum (summ xs ws))
```

mh-query was executed using the condition (equal? subset-sum 1), while annealing-query and evolution-query were executed to minimize (abs (- subset-sum 1)). Direct comparison of different queries appeared to be difficult on this task. However, the results are qualitatively similar. All methods either stably find correct solutions (this is the case, when the task dimensionality is about 15 or less or when the range of numbers is small and many subsets can sum up to the desirable value) or all the methods fail (to achieve this, one should take numbers from a larger range and take the set size 20 or more).

However, for certain task complexities intermediate results can be obtained. In particular, the following results were obtained for the range [-10000, 10000] and the set sizes 20÷25. With as much as twice time limit of annealing-query and evolution-query, mh-query was able to find correct solutions in 83% cases. annealing-query and evolution-query yielded approximately 75% correct solutions (their performance vary depending on settings, and annealing-query showed more stable results, while our simple form of genetic programming had some tendency to get stuck in local extrema). It should be pointed out that in the rest 25% cases the solution found is almost optimal (error equals to 1).

Let's make sure that these slightly superficial results of genetic programming are not due to its invalid functioning. Consider the following typical effect of crossover over program traces on the "phenotype" level.

'(#t #f #t #t #t #t #t #f #t #t) + '(#f #f #t #t #t #f #t #f #t #t #f) → '(#t #f #t #t #t #t #t #f #f #t #f)

One can see that this is the uniform crossover. It is possibly not the most interesting one, but it is correct. From this example, it can also be seen that optimization queries on probabilistic programs fit well for solving deterministic problems.

Integer Number Sequence Prediction

One more test task we considered was the task of integer number sequence prediction. We restricted the set of possible sequences to polynomials, but it can easily be extended to the wider class of sequences defined by recurrence relations. Consider the following fragment of the generative model.

```
; recursively generating expressions

(define xs '(1 2 3 4 5 6))
(define ys '(3 7 13 21 31 43))
(define (gen-expr) (if (flip 0.6)
                       (if (flip) 'x (random-integer 10))
                       (list (multinomial '(+ - *) '(1 1 1)) (gen-expr) (gen-expr))))
(define (f x) (eval (list 'let (list (list 'x x)) expr)))
```

After these definitions, the function f(x) is used to map all xs and check if the result matches ys or to calculate the total deviation depending on the query type.

We ran tests for different sequences and compared the results. mh-query wasn't able to find a solution in each run. Depending on the web browser, it either finished with "Maximum call stack size exceeded" error or worked extremely long in some runs. annealing-query and evolution-query also were not able to find precise solutions in each case and terminated with imprecise solutions. Percentages of runs, in which correct solutions were found, are shown in Table 2. The value of xs was '(0 1 2 3 4 5).

Table 2. Percentage of correct solutions

ys	Correct answers, %		
	mh-query	*annealing-query*	*evolution-query*
'(0 1 2 3 4 5)	90%	100%	100%
'(0 1 4 9 16 25)	20%	100%	100%
'(1 2 5 10 17 26)	10%	70%	80%
'(1 4 9 16 25 36)	0%	90%	80%
'(1 3 11 31 69 131)	0%	90%	60%

mh-query yielded surprisingly bad results here, although its inference over other recursive models can be successful. evolution-query also yielded slightly worse results than annealing-query. The reason probably consists in that this task could not be well decomposed into subtasks, so crossover doesn't yield benefits, but annealing can approach to the best solution step by step.

Nevertheless, it seems that crossover operator over program traces produces quite reasonable results in the space of phenotypes. If the structure of the parents matches, each leaf is randomly taken from one of the parents, e.g. '(+ (+ 3 x) x) + '(- (- x x) x) → '(- (+ x x) x). In nodes, in which the structure diverges, a subtree is randomly taken from one of the parents, e.g.

'(- (- (* (* 3 (* x x)) 3) (- x 8)) (* (- x 0) x)) +'(- 3 (- 5 x)) → '(- 3 (* (- x 0) x))
'(* (+ 4 x) x) + '(* (* 2 (- 1 x)) 7) → '(* (* 4 x) 7)

"Phenotypic" crossover effect is somewhat loose, but not meaningless, and it produces valid candidate solutions, which inherit information from their parents.

5   Conclusion

We developed the methods of simulated annealing and genetic programming over probabilistic program traces. For the best of our knowledge, this is the first implementation of such methods. The same functions for genetic operators over program traces were used to solve optimization problems for very different types of objects including parametrically defined functions, sets, and symbolic expressions without producing invalid candidate solutions. Our implementation corresponds to the uniform crossover. Other types of genetic operators are to be implemented, since our implementation showed advantage over annealing only in the task of learning real-valued models. It is interesting to combine probabilistic programming with advanced genetic programming systems such as MOSES [10].

In spite of simplicity of the used meta-heuristic search methods, they outperformed the standard mh-query. Although this comparison doesn't mean that annealing-query or evolution-query can replace mh-query since they solve different tasks, it shows that they can be combined and also optimization queries can be useful to extend semantics of PPLs. Still, efficiency of general inference methods is insufficient, and this could be one of the principle obstacles in the path to AGI. Possibly, one general inference method cannot be efficient in all problem domains, so it should be automatically specialized w.r.t. each domain encountered by an AGI-agent implying that such methods should be deeply combined with cognitive architectures.

Acknowledgements. This work was supported by Ministry of Education and Science of the Russian Federation, and by Government of Russian Federation, Grant 074-U01.

References

1. Potapov, A., Rodionov, S., Myasnikov, A., Begimov, G.: Cognitive Bias for Universal Algorithmic Intelligence (2012). arXiv:1209.4290v1 [cs.AI]
2. Goodman, N.D., Mansinghka, V.K., Roy, D.M., Bonawitz, K., Tenenbaum, J.B.: Church: a language for generative models (2008). arXiv:1206.3255 [cs.PL]
3. Minka, T., Winn, J.M., Guiver, J.P., Knowles, D.: Infer.NET 2.4. Microsoft Research Camb. (2010). http://research.microsoft.com/infernet
4. Koller, D., McAllester, D.A., Pfeffer, A.: Effective Bayesian inference for stochastic programs. Proc. National Conference on Artificial Intelligence (AAAI), pp. 740–747 (1997)
5. Stuhlmüller, A., Goodman, N.D.: A dynamic programming algorithm for inference in recursive probabilistic programs (2012). arXiv:1206.3555 [cs.AI]
6. Milch, B., Russell, S.: General-purpose MCMC inference over relational structures. In: Proc. 22nd Conference on Uncertainty in Artificial Intelligence, pp. 349–358 (2006)
7. Chaganty, A., Nori, A.V., Rajamani, S.K.: Efficiently sampling probabilistic programs via program analysis. In: Proc. Artificial Intelligence and Statistics, pp. 153–160 (2013)
8. Perov, Y., Wood, F.: Learning Probabilistic Programs (2014). arXiv:1407.2646 [cs.AI]

9. Solomonoff, R.: Algorithmic Probability, Heuristic Programming and AGI. In: Baum, E., Hutter, M., Kitzelmann, E. (eds). Advances in Intelligent Systems Research, vol. 10 (proc. 3rd Conf. on Artificial General Intelligence), pp. 151–157 (2010)

10. Goertzel, B., Geisweiller, N., Pennachin, C., Ng, K.: Integrating feature selection into program learning. In: Kühnberger, K.-U., Rudolph, S., Wang, P. (eds.) AGI 2013. LNCS, vol. 7999, pp. 31–39. Springer, Heidelberg (2013)

11. McDermott, J., Carroll, P.: Program optimisation with dependency injection. In: Krawiec, K., Moraglio, A., Hu, T., Etaner-Uyar, A., Hu, B. (eds.) EuroGP 2013. LNCS, vol. 7831, pp. 133–144. Springer, Heidelberg (2013)

12. Gordon, A.D., Henzinger, Th.A., Nori, A.V., Rajamani, S.K.: Probabilistic programming. In: Proc. International Conference on Software Engineering (2014)

Scene Based Reasoning

Frank Bergmann[⊠] and Brian Fenton

Calle Aprestadora 19, 12o 2a, E-08902 L'Hospitalet de LLobregal, Catalonia, Spain
fraber@fraber.de, brian.fenton@gmail.com

Abstract. This paper describes Scene Based Reasoning (SBR), a cognitive architecture based on the notions of "scene" and "plan". Scenes represent real-world 3D scenes as well as planner states. Introspection maps internal SBR data-structures into 2D "scene diagrams" for self-modeling and meta-reasoning. On the lowest level, scenes are represented as 3D scene graphs (as in computer gaming), while higher levels use Description Logic to model the relationships between scene objects. A plethora of subsystems implement perception, action, learning and control operations on the level of "plans", with scenes acting as planner states.

Keywords: Cognitive architecture · Self-model · Meta-reasoning · Description logics · Introspection · Multi-agent · Plan reasoning

1 Introduction

In this paper we describe Scene Based Reasoning (SBR), a cognitive architecture in the tradition of SOAR [14], ACT-R [1] and similar systems [10]. Particular similarities exist with the ICARUS system [16] with respect to the explicit representation of plans with decompositions, the "grounding in physical states", the purpose of controlling a physical agent, the use of observable attributes as a semantic base and spatial roles/ relationships between objects. Both systems share a development roadmap that includes modeling social interaction [16].

The distinctive characteristic of SBR is the use of "scenes", which can be thought of as a generalization of "scene graphs" [24] (as in computer gaming in order to represent 3D world states), Description Logic [2] (in order to represent the relationships between scene objects) and STRIPS style planner states [7] (in order to model time and action). Scenes are also used to represent internal SBR data-structures using a kind of "gödelization" (encoding properties of the reasoning system in object-level language): For example a "plan" (a directed graph composed of nodes and arrows) can be mapped into a 2D "scene diagram", similar to the way that humans draw figures and diagrams in order to gain clarity about complex subject matters. Once the plan is available as a 2D scene, SBR can apply its object recognition and reasoning mechanisms in order to classify the plan, create abstractions, analyze its effects, compare it with other plans and modify the plan. The improved plan can be tested in a "simulation sandbox" or the real world and can finally be converted back to an internal SBR structures for inclusion in the standard inventory of the system.

© Springer International Publishing Switzerland 2015
J. Bieger (Ed.): AGI 2015, LNAI 9205, pp. 25–34, 2015.
DOI: 10.1007/978-3-319-21365-1_3

Applying a similar procedure to the class hierarchy of objects (represented as a Description Logic TBox structure) allows the SBR system to talk about "beliefs" without the need for higher order or modal logic. Updated beliefs can be "written" to a new TBox, and this TBox can be tested in a sandbox against cases from the Episodic Memory etc. The same mechanism can be applied to belief sets of other agents in order to perform a "what-would-he-do" analysis and other types of social reasoning.

Applying "gödelization" to the recent history of cognitive events ("thoughts") allows the system to talk about it's own cognitive process. Cognitive events include the visual recognition of an object, sensory inputs, a change in attention focus, discovering the missing piece in a planning or reasoning process etc. A separate paper will explore these meta-reasoning properties in the context of the "Self-Model Theory of Subjectivity" [17].

A second distinctive feature of SBR is the use of "plans" as first order objects and as the "unit of analysis" for most subsystems - we could even talk about "Plan Based Reasoning": Perception at the highest abstraction level is plan recognition, action is plan execution, episodic memory is storing past plan executions, planning is plan generation, and plan learning is the acquisition of new plans, sub-plans (task decompositions) and execution statistics. Language comprehension is plan recognition and language generation basically serves to integrate other agents into the subject's plans (to be treated in a future paper). Plan optimization is implemented as a plan itself, allowing the SBR system to improve it's own improvement strategy.

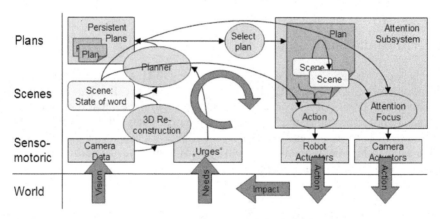

Fig. 1. An overview of SBR subsystems working together for simplified close-loop robot control. 3D reconstruction converts sensor data into a scene, which serves as an initial state for the planner to develop plans. The attention subsystem executes plan actions and controls the attention focus in order to track execution.

In this paper the authors focus on the technical aspects of the SBR architecture and a consistent definition of the SBR subsystems. A prototypical implementation of SBR exists as the "TinyCog" open-source project on http://tinycog.sourceforge.net/. TinyCog currently runs several demos using a scene representation that unifies description logics with planner states.

2   Comparison

SBR shares characteristics with SOAR, ACT-R, ICARUS and a number of lesser known cognitive architectures. The "Jonny Jackanapes" architecture [11] includes a "fusion" of HTN planning with Description Logics. [22] describes a cognitive architecture with a focus on plan recognition designed to infer the intents of competitive agents. PELA [12] describes a probabilistic planner that learns from interactions with the world.

The symbolic "scene" representation resembles [21] semantic networks, while scene graphs are commonly used in computer gaming [24]. [4] combine scene graphs with semantic networks to model human vision and propose this as a representation for "mental images".

[5] surveyed the combination of physics simulation and planning. IJCAI 2015 will host an "Angry Birds Competition" that will require physics simulation.

[9] surveyed the combination of planning and description logics. [20] introduces situation calculus to the FLEX DL system in order to allow for planning with DL ABox structures.

The SBR attention subsystem resembles the [15] "Meander" subsystem for the ICARUS cognitive architecture with similar execution tracking and re-planning properties.

3   Architecture Overview

The proposed architecture consists of four layers with several subsystems each:

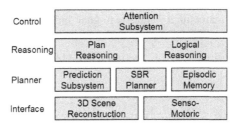

Fig. 2. The SBR Architecture layer stack

3.1   Subsystems Overview

The "Interface" layer converts sensor data into scenes and executes planner tasks.

3D Scene Reconstruction. Converts 2D sensor data into a 3D scene graph and performs the reverse operation.

Senso-Motoric. Provides the interfaces between the SBR planner and the sensors and actuators available as part of a physical or simulated robot.

The "Planner" layer creates, recognizes and executes plans:

SBR Planner. The core of the SBR system, which takes as input an initial scene and a goal represented by a sub-scene. It returns a number of plans represented by HTN tasks, together with confidence scores.

Prediction Subsystem. Predicts the behavior of objects and agents during planning operations.

Episodic Memory. Stores large amounts of scenes, split into key frames and indexed by the included objects and their properties [19].

The "Reasoning" layer implements reasoning capabilities on top of the planner.

Plan Reasoning. Implements operations on plans that together allow for improving plans and meta-reasoning about plans.

Logical Reasoning. Implements a Description Logic on top of the SBR planner, maintaining beliefs about the world, together with a confidence score.

The "Control" layer provides high-level control of a SBR system.

Attention Subsystem. Controls the "focus of attention" of the SBR system, executes plans and contains the system's "persistent goals".

3.2   Data Structures

Objects. Untyped list of key-value tuples ("attributes") with values that can be integers, real numbers, strings or references to other objects. Symbolic object descriptions are created using the "object configurator" explained below.

Agents. Objects that maintain a "persistent goal hierarchy" and a set of beliefs. Agents represent humans, animals, robots and AGI instances in planning processes.

Relations. Named and directed arrows between two objects.

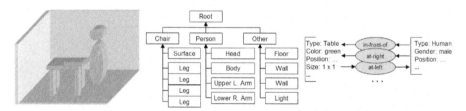

Fig. 3. A sample scene with a scene graph and a symbolic representation

Scenes. Represent real-world 3D constellations and "mental images" as well as semantic networks for logical reasoning. On the lowest level, scenes are implemented as 3D scene graphs ([24], as in computer gaming) consisting of a number of "objects", together with their position and surface texture so that they can be rendered into a 2D image by a rendering engine. On higher levels, scene graph details are ignored, object characteristics are abstracted into attributes and spatial object constellations are encoded into semantic relations. Finally, scenes are used as an "ABox" for Description

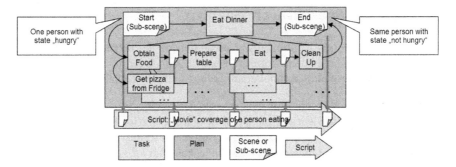

Fig. 4. "Eating dinner" - A plan for eating dinner, explaining the relationship between scenes, scripts and plans. Tasks (in blue) may have multiple learned decompositions that are combined by the planner to create plans with utility and cost.

Logics reasoning. Scenes provide for self-referentiality and meta-reasoning by representing plans and other internal SBR objects as a 2D diagrams.

Sub-Scenes. Scenes with only partially filled object attributes. Sub-scenes are used as rule-heads and to describe the state change effect of an action.

Scripts. Consist of sequences of scenes (similar to [Schank et al 1977]) representing a transition through time of the included objects.

Key Frames. Scenes marking the start and end points of important transitions.

Plans. A tree with one root task which is decomposed into a sequence of sub-tasks.

4   3D Scene Reconstruction

This subsystems performs the conversion of 2D sensor data into a 3D scene using an iterative algorithm depicted below.

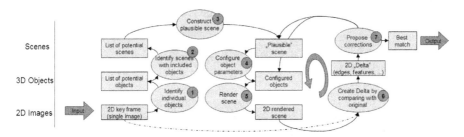

Fig. 5. 3D Scene Reconstruction: 1) Perform classical 2D feature extraction (edges, textures, …) and retrieve episodic memory (EM) object matches. 2) Check the EM for scenes that contain all or part of the objects. 3) Construct a plausible scene with expectations from higher SBR levels. 4) Configure 3D objects (position, textures, …) for best fit with the sensor data. 5) Render the scene including lightning and filters. 6) Calculate "deltas" on edges, textures etc. 7) Use deltas to correct object position and state.

5   Prediction Subsystem or "Sandbox"

This subsystem performs a probabilistic prediction of the behavior of objects and agents in a scene in order to perform a "what-if" simulation of likely outcomes of actions, effectively providing a simulation sandbox to the SBR planner.

- A physics engine [5] predicts the behavior of passive objects.
- An "abstracted physics simulation" predicts object behavior for longer time spans based on spatial relationship and previously observed scripts.
- A "social reasoning simulation" predicts the behavior of agents in a scene as a reaction to SBR actions. This simulation "spawns" a new instance of the SBR system per agent with the agent's parameters and simulates the agent's likely actions similar to [13].

The prediction subsystem can predict the behavior of the SBR system itself, as it can be modeled just like other actors. This can be thought to be part of a SBR "self-model".

6   SBR Planner

The SBR takes as input an initial scene and a goal and returns a number of plans, together with probability scores. The proposed planner includes several features from recent research:

- Spatial-temporal planning language: The SBR planner operates on scenes instead of FOL formulas.
- Probabilistic planning: SBR tasks have multiple outcomes.
- Timeline planning: SBR tasks take a certain time to complete.
- Multi-agent planning: The prediction subsystem predicts the behavior of agents and movable objects.
- Resource-bound operations: The planner will return first plans that are fast to generate, and then propose additional plans if time is available.

Fig. 6. Eating dinner satisfies hunger: Sub-scenes describe conditions and effects of tasks

Planning with these characteristics is only partially understood as of today and the authors have not found any reference to practical systems combining stochastic planning and HTNs for more than toy domains. In the face of this situation, the authors sketch below a new approach that relies on "active tasks" and "worst-case analysis" in order to cope with the increased branching factor of probabilistic planning:

Active Task. A planner task with a known decomposition, together with statistics about past executions of the task in the episodic memory, along the lines of

PRODIGY [25] and PELA [12]. Past execution may have included re-planning or escalation processes in order to deal with local failures, which have an impact on the cost of the action and its duration.

The statistics of past executions of active tasks are analyzed with respect to the factors leading to success.

Worst-Case Analysis. Undesired outcomes from all tasks in a plan are treated individually, as opposed to calculating probability distributions over "histories" [8]. Combined with the cost of executing the plan and the impact of a failed plan, the SBR planner can calculate a risk compensation and decide whether to pursue this path, develop a better plan or to choose non-action.

6.1   Example: Solving Equations

The following example of solving an equation demonstrates how 2D scene representations can provide the basis for symbolic reasoning.

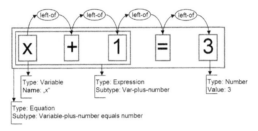

Fig. 7. Solving equations using the SBR planner

1. The 3D reconstruction subsystem passes the 2D sensor data to a statistical algorithm in order to recognize the type and value of each object, resulting in a symbolic representation.
2. The reconstruction subsystem determines the symbolic "left-of" spatial relationships between the objects.
3. The HTN planner then applies "actions" to the symbolic representation in order to simplify and solve the expression. Rules were learned during training sessions.

7   Reasoning About Plans

This subsystem implements several operations on plans that together allow SBR to acquire, simulate, optimize and reason about plans:

Plan Recognition. Plan recognition analyzes sensor input in order to determine the Plans of all involved agents [3]. This process detects errors during 3D scene recognition and triggers investigation and learning processes.

Plan Simulation. The prediction subsystem's "abstracted physics simulation" allows to simulate object behavior in a scene, effectively creating a "sandbox".

Plan Statistics. The episodic memory maintains a history of "scripts" of past plan executions, including the initial conditions and outcomes by means of the initial and last scene. This allows to apply clustering and learning algorithms beyond the scope of this paper.

Plan Optimization. Convert plans into 2D scenes using a "pen on paper" representation, compare, tweak, merge, mix and match different plans, pre-validate plans using simulation and execute the new plan in the real world. All of these optimization steps are implemented as meta-plans that can be optimized as well.

8   Logical Reasoning

The logical reasoning subsystem uses Description Logics (DL) [2] to maintains beliefs about the world together with confidence scores in a way similar to FLEX [20]. FLEX inference rules closely resemble SBR planner tasks, allowing the SBR planner to execute inferences rules directly without the need for a separate DL system. The DL "ABox" resembles SBR scenes, allowing to use DL in order to model symbolic object relationships.

Using this architecture, the system can talk about its beliefs ("all birds can fly": confidence=0.9), can test potential new hypotheses against a base of episodic memory cases and track "clashes" (contradictions during reasoning like "penguin P is a bird but doesn't fly") to the their axioms. New beliefs can be acquired via machine learning and checked against the episodic memory for consistency and explanation capability of actor's behavior. All of these operations are performed by "active tasks".

9   Attention Subsystem

The Attention Subsystem maintains a list of "persistent goals", a portfolio of plans and controls a "focus of attention" while tracking the execution of plans.

Persistent Goals. A list of medium and long term goals. Persistent goals are created manually by a human system operator (Asimov's laws of robotics), as a reaction to "urges" or by SBR-Planner as part of a plan that can't be executed immediately.

Attention Focus. Most of the time the attention focus lies with the images from a camera of a robot running SBR, but attention can also be focused on parts of the "self-model". Sensor data are processed by 3D reconstruction and passed on to the episodic memory in order to retrieve "associations", i.e. plans and scripts associated with the focused objects in their context. These "ideas popping up" are matched against active "persistent plans" in order to determine if the idea could contribute to an active plan.

When executing plans or "active tasks", the attention focus tracks the current vs. planned world state and initiates re-planning if necessary.

Portfolio of Plans. A set of plans created in order to satisfy the list of persistent goals. The attention subsystem evaluates the plans according to utility, cost and chance for success and execute the plan with the highest value.

10 Learning

Statistical learning is essential for a cognitive architecture based on a probabilistic planner. However, most references to learning algorithms have been omitted in the previous sections because their role is limited to auxiliary and relatively well understood tasks like calculating task success probabilities, guiding the planner search process or clustering parameter values in order to generate new concepts. Also, the exact choice of algorithms is irrelevant to the general AGI architecture.

This section summarizes the areas where statistical algorithms are employed:

3D Scene Reconstruction. Identify approximately objects and their positions from sensor data.

SBR Planner. Learn and propose applicable planner tasks to given problems, learn task decompositions, learn success factors for executing tasks.

Prediction Subsystem. Predict the behavior of agents as a script.

Episodic Memory. Maintain statistics about object occurrences in scenes, successful execution of tasks, identify scenes leading to successful plan execution.

Plan Reasoning. Classify plans for generalization.

Logical Reasoning. Classify concepts for generalization, learn DL implication links based on example.

Attention Subsystem. Learn the utility function of plans.

Also, non-statistical learning is employed:

Attention Subsystem. When trying to "understand" an input 3D script, the plan recognition system will try to classify all objects and to determine the plans of all involved agents. Lack of such understanding may trigger active investigation, including "asking the operator" or getting closer to the agents in order to gather better sensor input.

Acknowledgment. The authors are grateful to Ben Goertzel, Sergio Jiménez, Anders Jonsson and José Hernandez-Orallo for their comments on early drafts of this paper.

References

1. Anderson, J.R., Lebiere, C.: The newell test for a theory of cognition. Behavioral and Brain Sciences **26**(05), 587–601 (2003)
2. Brachman, R.J.: What's in a concept: structural foundations for semantic networks. International Journal of Man-Machine Studies **9**(2), 127–152 (1977)
3. Carberry, S.: Techniques for plan recognition. User Modeling and User-Adapted Interaction **11**(1–2), 31–48 (2001)
4. Croft, D., Thagard, P.: Dynamic imagery: a computational model of motion and visual analogy. In: Model-Based Reasoning, pp. 259–274. Springer (2002)
5. Davis, E., Marcus, G.: The scope and limits of simulation in cognition and automated reasoning. Artificial Intelligence (2013)

6. Erol, K.: Hierarchical task network planning: formalization, analysis, and implementation. Ph.D. thesis, University of Maryland (1996)
7. Fikes, R.E., Nilsson, N.J.: STRIPS: A new approach to the application of theorem proving to problem solving. Artificial intelligence 2(3), 189–208 (1972)
8. Ghallab, M., Nau, D., Traverso, P.: Automated planning: theory & practice. Elsevier (2004)
9. Gil, Y.: Description logics and planning. AI Magazine 26(2), 73 (2005)
10. Goertzel, B., Pennachin, C., Geisweiller, N.: Engineering General Intelligence, Part 1, Springer (2014)
11. Hartanto, R., Hertzberg, J.: Fusing DL reasoning with HTN planning. In: Dengel, A.R., Berns, K., Breuel, T.M., Bomarius, F., Roth-Berghofer, T.R. (eds.) KI 2008. LNCS (LNAI), vol. 5243, pp. 62–69. Springer, Heidelberg (2008)
12. Jim_enez Celorrio, S.: Planning and learning under uncertainty. Ph.D. thesis, Universidad Carlos III de Madrid, Escuela Politécnica Superior (2011)
13. Konolige, K., Nilsson, N.J.: Multiple-agent planning systems. AAAI. 80, 138–142 (1980)
14. Laird, J.E., Newell, A., Rosenbloom, P.S.: Soar: An architecture for general intelligence. Artificial intelligence 33(1), 1–64 (1987)
15. Langley, P.: An adaptive architecture for physical agents. In: The 2005 IEEE/WIC/ACM International Conference on Web Intelligence, 2005. Proceedings, pp. 18–25. IEEE (2005)
16. Langley, P.: Altering the ICARUS architecture to model social cognition (2013). http://www.isle.org/~langley/talks/onr.6.13.ppt
17. Langley, P., McKusick, K.B., Allen, J.A., Iba, W.F., Thompson, K.: A design for the ICARUS architecture. ACM SIGART Bulletin 2(4), 104–109 (1991)
18. Metzinger, T.: Being no One: The Self-Model Theory of Subjectivity. MIT Press (2003)
19. Nuxoll, A.M., Laird, J.E.: Extending cognitive architecture with episodic memory. In: Proceedings of the National Conference on Artificial Intelligence. vol. 22, p. 1560. Menlo Park, CA; Cambridge, MA; London; AAAI Press; MIT Press; 1999 (2007)
20. Quantz, J.J., Dunker, G., Bergmann, F., Kellner, I.: The FLEX system. KIT Report 124, Technische Universität Berlin (1995)
21. Quillian, M.: A notation for representing conceptual information: An application to semantics and mechanical English paraphrasing, sp-1395. System Development Corporation, Santa Monica (1963)
22. Santos Jr., E.: A cognitive architecture for adversary intent inferencing: Structure of knowledge and computation. In: AeroSense 2003, pp. 182–193. International Society for Optics and Photonics (2003)
23. Schank, R.C., Abelson, R.P.: Scripts, plans, goals, and understanding: An inquiry into human knowledge structures. Erlbaum (1977)
24. Strauss, P.S.: IRIS inventor, a 3d graphics toolkit. In: Proceedings of the Eighth Annual Conference on Object-oriented Programming Systems, Languages, and Applications, pp. 192–200. OOPSLA 1993, ACM, New York, NY, USA (1993). http://doi.acm.org/10.1145/165854.165889
25. Veloso, M., Carbonell, J., Perez, A., Borrajo, D., Fink, E., Blythe, J.: Integrating planning and learning: The prodigy architecture. Journal of Experimental & Theoretical Artificial Intelligence 7(1), 81–120 (1995)

Anchoring Knowledge in Interaction: Towards a Harmonic Subsymbolic/Symbolic Framework and Architecture of Computational Cognition

Tarek R. Besold[1]([✉]), Kai-Uwe Kühnberger[1], Artur d'Avila Garcez[2],
Alessandro Saffiotti[3], Martin H. Fischer[4], and Alan Bundy[5]

[1] Institute of Cognitive Science, University of Osnabrück, Osnabrück, Germany
{tbesold,kkuehnbe}@uos.de
[2] City University London, London, UK
a.garcez@city.ac.uk
[3] Örebro University, Örebro, Sweden
asaffio@aass.oru.se
[4] University of Potsdam, Potsdam, Germany
martinf@uni-postdam.de
[5] University of Edinburgh, Edinburgh, Scotland
a.bundy@ed.ac.uk

Abstract. We outline a proposal for a research program leading to a new paradigm, architectural framework, and prototypical implementation, for the cognitively inspired anchoring of an agent's learning, knowledge formation, and higher reasoning abilities in real-world interactions: Learning through interaction in real-time in a real environment triggers the incremental accumulation and repair of knowledge that leads to the formation of theories at a higher level of abstraction. The transformations at this higher level filter down and inform the learning process as part of a permanent cycle of learning through experience, higher-order deliberation, theory formation and revision.

The envisioned framework will provide a precise computational theory, algorithmic descriptions, and an implementation in cyber-physical systems, addressing the lifting of action patterns from the subsymbolic to the symbolic knowledge level, effective methods for theory formation, adaptation, and evolution, the anchoring of knowledge-level objects, real-world interactions and manipulations, and the realization and evaluation of such a system in different scenarios. The expected results can provide new foundations for future agent architectures, multi-agent systems, robotics, and cognitive systems, and can facilitate a deeper understanding of the development and interaction in human-technological settings.

1 A Harmonic Analogy

Natural agents in many situations in their reasoning seem to rely on an enormous richness of representations (multimodal, grounded, embodied and situated), with many layers of representation at different levels of abstraction, together with

© Springer International Publishing Switzerland 2015
J. Bieger (Ed.): AGI 2015, LNAI 9205, pp. 35–45, 2015.
DOI: 10.1007/978-3-319-21365-1_4

dynamic re-organization of knowledge. Also, real-world situations require agents to perform what can be interpreted as dynamic changes or alignments of representation, as different agents might use different languages and levels of description. Unfortunately, when trying to follow the natural example by transferring and (re)creating this representational richness and diversity to artificial agents, the resulting mismatches cannot be cured by standardization, but arise due to differences in the environment, tasks to be solved, levels of abstraction, etc. Additionally, real-world applications also demand online and bidirectional learning that takes place in real-time, as well as the adaptation to changes in the environment, to the presence of new agents, and to task changes.

A conceptually similar situation presents itself in the domain of music: Music appears on different levels as there are, among others, a physical level (audio data), a MIDI level, a chord progression level, a harmonic, melodic, rhythmic level, a score level, a structural level of a piece of music, a (semantic) meta-level for describing music. Concerning the interaction and transfer of information between levels, in certain cases there are obvious mappings (e.g. MIDI level to score to harmonic structure), in others there are partial or incomplete mappings (e.g. harmonic structure to score, rhythmic to physical level), in others there are fuzzy or tentative mappings (e.g. melody to harmony (in an idiom) or to rhythmic level (in an idiom), physical to structural level of a piece of music), and between others there are no mappings at all (e.g. MIDI level to semantic/meta level, melodic level to structural to harmonic level). Also, music can be described in different representation formats on all levels. A piece of music can then be considered as a multi-layered multi-representational entity with certain connections and constraints (in form of relations, mappings etc.) between the layers, where, for instance, changing the chord progression influences (in an obvious, partial, or fuzzy way) many (but not all) other levels.

From a functional perspective, pieces of music that have been analyzed in such a multi-representational way could, among others, be used to learn or to detect obvious mappings between the layers, to detect novelties and correlations, to systematically unfold the specific properties of pieces (or classes thereof)/idioms/genres of music, or to find the invariant properties of music (e.g. a change of melody changes systematically the score, but does not affect the larger structure of the piece).

Returning to the agent setting by way of analogy we envision a system operating on different levels of representations (corresponding to different formal layers in the system's architecture) similar to the musical case. The hierarchy could consist, for instance, of a (lowest) neural layer learning on the perception/motor level, an anchoring layer learning elementary (semi-)symbolic representations of objects, a reactive layer taking over in critical situations, a deep learning layer learning on more abstract levels, a symbolic layer doing reasoning and planning, and a (higher) symbolic layer providing the core ontology. Like in music, some of these layers have obvious, some have partial, some have fuzzy, and some have no mappings/relations between themselves.

Now, a corresponding architecture should be in a "pre-established" harmony: Triggering an abstract plan to move from A to B should result in the motor action to move from A to B, classifying on the neural level a certain perceptual input such as, for instance, a chair should result in the activation of the concept "chair" in the ontology or the working memory, and so on. And whilst the basic links might be hard coded, learning a new concept on the subsymbolic level should somehow result in a new concept entry in the ontology, i.e., there should be interaction between the different layers in terms of information and conceptualizations. Finally, when thinking about a simulated or actual system that is operating on these interacting levels in a multi-representational manner it should allow for similar mechanisms and interactions as in the music case.

2   The Core Ideas

Addressing the challenges outlined in the previous section and taking inspiration in the sketched analogy to the musical domain, we propose the development of a new approach and integrated techniques that will enable the sustainable and accessible creation of large-scale integrated knowledge repositories for use by multi-agent systems or as part of a cyber-physical system. In this note, we suggest a research program for the community working on embedded intelligence. This program for 'anchoring knowledge in interaction', aims at developing, theoretically and practically, a conceptual framework and corresponding architecture that model an agent's knowledge, thinking, and acting truly as interrelated parts of a unified cognitive capacity. That is, knowledge is seen as multi-layered phenomenon that appears at different levels of abstraction, promotes interaction between these levels of abstraction, is influenced by the interaction between agent and environment (potentially including other agents), and is essentially linked to actions, perception, thinking, and being. The program's long term vision, thus, is a radically new paradigm in what concerns interaction styles (which are action-centered, embodied, multi-modal), knowledge repositories (with different levels and forms of knowledge representation, as, e.g., multi-modal, hybrid), and user modeling and communication through learning and adaptation.

The scientific aims of the described endeavor target advances at different conceptual and topical levels (covering, among others, all three levels of analysis of a cognitive system described in [19]). On the embodiment level, it shall be shown that elementary forms of representations can be learned from an agent's interactions within an environment. The resulting multi-modal representations may be noisy, they may be uncertain and vague, it may be the case that different agents have different languages for representing knowledge, or that changes in the environment may come into play. On this level, building on recent advances in the study of embodied cognition, the main development will therefore be an extension of the well-known anchoring framework in robotics [5] to grounding not only objects, but also certain general observable properties appearing in the environment.

The embodiment view of knowledge provides an interaction-based neural representation of knowledge that is not represented at the conceptual level. Neural systems can promote robust learning from data, as part of an online learning and reasoning cycle to be measured in terms of an improved experience, a faster adaptation to a new task, and the provision of clear descriptions. On this level, a lifting procedure shall be specified that will produce descriptions, thus lifting grounded situations and an agent's action patterns to a more abstract (symbolic) representation, using techniques from machine learning like deep networks and analogy-making. This can be seen as a natural consequence of recent research developed for deep learning and neural-symbolic computing, the crucial added value over the state of the art being the combination of these new methodologies with analogical transfer of information between representation systems.

Knowledge at a symbolic level is usually considered to be static and error-intolerant. Due to the fact that initial multi-modal representations lifted from the subsymbolic level can be error-prone, and that different agents might use different and a priori possibly incompatible representation languages, the program's objective at the level of symbolic representations is a dynamic re-organization based on ontology repair mechanisms, analogy, concept invention, and knowledge transfer. These mechanisms foster adaptation of an agent to new situations, the alignment between representations of different agents, the reformulation of knowledge entries, and the generation of new knowledge.

In summary, the envisioned account of the emergence of representations through cognitive principles in an agent (or multi-agent) setting can be conceptualized as follows: Grounding knowledge in cognitively plausible multimodal interaction paradigms; lifting grounded situations into more abstract representations; reasoning by analogy and concept blending at more abstract levels; repair and re-organization of initial and generated abstract representations.

Applications for such a framework are manifold and not limited to the "classical" realm of robotic systems or other embodied artificial agents. Also, for instance, future tools in e-learning education – in order to guarantee sustainable and life-long learning tools for different groups of learners – will focus on aspects such as, for instance, adaptivity to target groups of learners, modeling of the knowledge level of group members, multi-modality, integration of a richer repertoire of interaction styles of learning including action-centered set-ups, promotion of cooperative and social learning, etc. Such devices are inconceivable without a cognitive basis, adaptation, multiple representations, concept invention, repair mechanisms, analogical transfer, different knowledge levels, and robust learning abilities.

3   The Core Objectives

The core idea is that knowledge is multi-layered, i.e. there is no static, fixed, and definite representation of knowledge, rather agents have to adapt, learn, and re-organize knowledge continuously on different levels while interacting with other agents and their environment. Thus, the future architecture aims to anchor and embody knowledge by the interaction between the agent and its environment (possibly including other agents), to give an approach to lift the resulting situated action patterns to a symbolic level, to reason by analogy on the abstract and the subsymbolic level, to adapt, or in case of clashes, repair the initial representations in order to fit to new situations, and to evaluate the approach in concrete settings providing feedback to the system in a reactive-adaptive evolutionary cycle.

The project's scope is primarily focused on providing answers to several long-standing foundational questions. Arguably the most prominent among these, together with answers based on the conceptual commitments underlying the discussed research program, are:

1.) *How does knowledge develop from the concrete interaction sequences to the abstract representation level?* The crucial aspect is the lifting of grounded situations to more abstract representations.

2.) *How can experience be modeled?* Experience can be explained by deep learning.

3.) *How is deeper understanding of a complex concept made possible?* Theory repair makes precisely this possible.

4.) *To which extent do social aspects play a role?* Analogical transfer of knowledge between agents is a central aspect concerning efficient and flexible learning and understanding.

Although efforts are directed towards reintegrating the different aspects of agent cognition spanning from abstract knowledge to concrete action, there is also a strong drive toward new concepts and paradigms of cognitive and agent-based systems. A fresh look at the embodiment problem is proposed, as the envisioned account goes significantly beyond the perception-action loop and addresses the problem of the possibility of higher intelligence where it occurs, namely at the level of the emergence of abstract knowledge based on an agent's concrete interaction with the environment. Similarly, learning aspects are tackled not only on a technical level, but furthermore pushed beyond the technical area by gaining inspiration from cognitive science and concept-guided learning in the sense of analogical learning and concept blending, as well as from newer findings in neural networks learning.

4   Structure and Methods

The new approach for modeling knowledge in its breadth, namely from its embodied origins to higher level abstractions, from the concrete interaction between an agent and its environment to the abstract level of knowledge transfer between agents, and from the holistic view of knowledge as an interplay between perception, (inter)action, and reasoning to specific disembodied views of knowledge, touches on different aspects and fields of research. It therefore requires the integration of expressive symbolic knowledge representation formalisms, relational knowledge, variables, and first-order logic on the one hand with representations of sensorimotor experiences, action patterns, connectionist representations, and multi-modal representations on the other.

The different topics above will be formalized, algorithmically specified, implemented in running applications and evaluated. With respect to the formalization, research methods from machine learning (e.g. cross-validation [9] or layer-wise model selection [1] in deep networks) will be used to learn conceptual knowledge from subsymbolic data, i.e. to extract knowledge from such networks in order to lift and enable transfer learning on the conceptual level. This type of conceptual knowledge will be used as input to the analogy-making process to generate new concepts by abstraction and transfer of knowledge in a domain-independent and multi-modal setting. The formalization of the analogy process, including the computation of generalizations [21], and the multi-modal embodied representations potentially change the signatures of the underlying language(s). Therefore, the theory of institutions [8] will be used as methodology in which dynamic changes of languages can be rigorously formalized. The repair of theories and concept invention mechanisms will be linked to analogy-making and are methodologically formalized in a higher-order logical framework [3,17].

The corresponding research program is structured into interrelated thrusts:

1.) Cognitive Foundations of Knowledge: New embodied approaches to understanding human cognition, augmenting the traditional symbol manipulation-based accounts, emphasize the importance of sensorimotor interactions as part of knowledge formation [10]. Thereby, they provide the starting point for a systematic assessment of basic learning signatures in the presence of different sensorimotor experiences, leading to recommendations for the development of cognitively-inspired formal frameworks for embodied computation, in particular, for the specification of learning mechanisms, analogy, and repair mechanisms.

Together with approaches from computational neuroscience and network-level cognitive modeling (as, e.g., the recently proposed framework of conceptors in dynamical system models [15]) work in this thrust will create the cognitively-inspired foundations and low-level input representations and content for the subsequent stages of processing and reasoning.

2.) Anchoring Knowledge in Perception, Action, and Interaction: Anchoring [5] in robotic systems is the problem of how to create, and to maintain in time and space the connection between the symbol- and the signal-level representations of the same physical object. Anchoring this far is concerned with the grounding of symbols that refer to specific object entities, i.e. anchoring can be considered as a special case of the symbol grounding problem limited to physical objects.

While different approaches to solving this foundational problem have been proposed [4], a satisfactory answer is still elusive and the arising difficulties are manifold: In a distributed system, individual agents may need to anchor objects from perceptual data coming either from sensors embedded directly on the robot or information coming from external devices. Further, agents each with their own anchoring module may need to reach a consensus in order to successfully perform a task in a cooperative way. Also Human-Robot Interaction (HRI)-oriented communication about objects requires a coordinated symbol-percept link between human and robot.

In the envisioned framework, building on [16]'s results on cooperative anchoring and on [6]'s symbiotic HRI robotic systems, anchoring happens under even more general conditions: anchoring is performed both top-down and bottom-up during learning; new symbols for new objects and categories are dynamically introduced by repair and concept invention mechanisms; the denotation of a symbol used in communication must be consistent across the communicating agents; anchoring must enable the establishment of analogical links across different agents.

3.) Lifting Knowledge from the Subsymbolic to the Symbolic Level: The elementary forms of representations referred to above, which may be noisy, vague, and uncertain, have been made suitable for learning through the use of neural networks, notably recently deep networks.

Deep learning is a form of representation learning aiming at discovering multiple levels of representation. Also, recent advances in the area of deep learning have shown promising results when applied to real-time processing of multimodal data [7], and state-of-the-art deep learning methods and algorithms have been able to train deep networks effectively when applied to different kinds of networks, knowledge fusion, and transfer learning [2]. However, more expressive descriptions and forms of representation have become more difficult to obtain from neural networks.

Following a neural-symbolic approach, neural learning will be combined with temporal knowledge representation using variations of the Restricted Boltzmann Machine model [14]. The resulting approach will offer a method for validating hypotheses through the symbolic description of the trained networks whilst robustly dealing with uncertainty and errors through a Bayesian inference model. Furthermore, the use of Gärdenfors' "conceptual spaces" [11] to link symbolic and subsymbolic data, as done in [16], will also be investigated and tested for its applicability and feasibility in the proposed complex sensing, learning, and reasoning cycle.

4.) Analogy/Blending: Analogy is classically understood as a method to detect and operate on structural commonalities between two domains, and in cognitive science and cognitive AI has been applied to a variety of tasks, e.g. intelligence tests [18], learning with sketches [20], or naive physics [21]. Unfortunately, until now analogy engines are designed only for highly specialized domains, neither multi-modal representations nor embodied interaction with the environment is taken into account, abstraction and knowledge projection from source to target are usually restricted to a few stages of analogical comparisons, and repair strategies for faulty inputs are rather limited.

The described approach brings analogical reasoning from a computer science perspective closer to its cognitive origins: generalizability, multi-modal representations, and embodied interaction with the environment are considered to be essential for analogy-making in this project. Furthermore, analogies will directly be linked to repair mechanisms in order to facilitate the resolution of errors. Thus, analogies are re-considered concerning their foundations and re-conceptualized concerning their methodological basis, as well as their applications.

5.) Concept Formation/Reformation: An important way in which new concepts are formed is by the evolution of existing concepts that have proved inadequate: Such inadequacies are often revealed by failures of inference using the old concepts. Researchers lately explored how these inadequacies can trigger conceptual change in different domains as, e.g., physics [17] or in ontologies [12].

The resulting domain-specific diagnosis and repair mechanisms bore strong similarities to each other: The so called reformation algorithm (a modification of unification) is an attempt to capture the generality behind these mechanisms and provide a domain-independent diagnosis and repair mechanism for conceptual change (cf. [3] for an example). Based on this approach, generic mechanisms for repairing agents' faulty representations (especially those produced by imperfect analogies) will be developed, implemented, and evaluated in a variety of domains going far beyond current (domain specific) solutions.

5   First Steps Towards an Implementation

At the current stage, the suggested research program is still mostly in its conception and planning phase. Nonetheless, a basic conceptual architecture (see Fig. 1) can already be laid out based on the considerations discussed in the previous sections: depending on the perspective and degree of abstraction, this architecture can either be sub-divided into five hierarchical layers (respectively corresponding to the five thrusts sketched in the previous section) or can be conceptualized as structured in three (partially overlapping) functional components. In the latter case, the cognitive foundations and the anchoring layer are combined into a low-level subsymbolic module, analogy/blending and concept formation/repair into a high-level symbolic module, and anchoring, knowledge lifting, and analogy into an intermediate module bridging in the direction from the low-level to the high-level component. Concerning the individual modules, interaction happens both between layers within components (as, e.g., between analogy/blending and concept formation/reformation layer) as well as across components (as, e.g., through the feedback from the concept formation/reformation to the anchoring). This results in an architecture adhering to and implementing the "harmonic analogy" setting from the introductory section, with changes in one layer propagating to others in order to maintain a "harmonic" configuration.

Within the low-level module, conceptors and similar approaches are employed in order to establish a certain initial structure of the perceptual input stream on a subsymbolic level, additionally reinforcing the proto-structure already imposed by the properties of the embodiment-inspired approach to computation. This initial structure can then be used as basis upon which the anchoring layer operates, coupling elements of this structure to objects and entities in the perceived environment and/or to action-based percepts of the agent. This coupling goes beyond the classical accounts of anchoring in that not only correspondences on the object/entity level are created, but also properties and attributes of objects/entities are addressed. Thus, subsymbolic correspondences between the initial structured parts of the perceptual input stream as representational vehicles

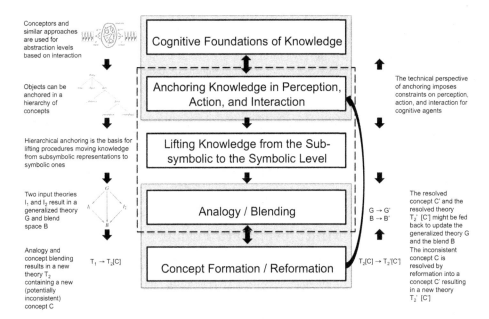

Conceptors and similar approaches are used for abstraction levels based on interaction

Objects can be anchored in a hierarchy of concepts

Hierarchical anchoring is the basis for lifting procedures moving knowledge from subsymbolic representations to symbolic ones

Two input theories I_1 and I_2 result in a generalized theory G and blend space B

Analogy and concept blending results in a new theory T_2 containing a new (potentially inconsistent) concept C

$T_1 \rightarrow T_2[C]$

Cognitive Foundations of Knowledge

Anchoring Knowledge in Perception, Action, and Interaction

Lifting Knowledge from the Sub-symbolic to the Symbolic Level

Analogy / Blending

Concept Formation / Reformation

The technical perspective of anchoring imposes constraints on perception, action, and interaction for cognitive agents

The resolved concept C' and the resolved theory T_2' [C'] might be fed back to update the generalized theory G and the blend B

The inconsistent concept C is resolved by reformation into a concept C' resulting in a new theory T_2' [C']

$G \rightarrow G'$
$B \rightarrow B'$

$T_2[C] \rightarrow T_2'[C']$

Fig. 1. An overview of the conceptual structure, functional components, and the interplay between layers of the envisioned architecture implementing the cycle of learning through experience, higher-order deliberation, theory formation and revision

and their actual representational content are established. These vehicle-content pairs then can be arranged in a hierarchical structure, both on object/entity level and on connected object/entity-specific property levels, based on general attributes of the perceptual input stream (as, e.g., order of occurrence of the respective structures, relations between structures) hinting at elements of the representational content, and on direct properties of the representations in their function and form as representational vehicles.

Within the high-level module, analogy and blending are applied on rich logic-based representations to find corresponding concepts and knowledge items, to transfer and adapt knowledge from one context into an analogically-related similar one, and to combine existing concepts into new concepts based on analogical correspondences between the inputs. Still, these processes are error-prone in that they can reveal inconsistencies between existing concepts, or can introduce new inconsistencies by concept combination or concept transfer and adaptation. Arising inconsistencies can then be addressed by the top-level concept formation and reformation layer, allowing to repair inconsistent symbolic representations through manipulations of the representational structure and to introduce new representations or concepts by introducing new representational elements – and, when doing so, informing and influencing the subsymbolic anchoring layer to perform corresponding adaptations in its vehicle-content correspondences.

Finally, the intermediate module bridging from low-level to high-level processing takes the correspondences between representing structures and representational content established by the anchoring layer, and uses deep learning techniques for representation learning in order to lift the subsymbolic vehicle-content pairs to a logic-based form of representation. Here, the corresponding learning process will take into account already existing knowledge on the symbolic side by way of analogy both, over vehicle-content pairs and over the learning process itself (i.e., resulting in a form of cross-informed transfer learning): When presuming a (fairly low) basic level of continuity of the environment and the perceptual input stream, on the one hand, over time the symbolic forms of newly lifted vehicle-content pairs most likely will share analogical commonalities with already existing concept and knowledge items which can then be used to foster the lifting process, while on the other hand successive or parallel lifting processes also can cross-inform each other leveraging the analogical structure over processes and exploiting shared or similar sub-parts.

6   (Far) Beyond Multi-level Data Fusion

At first sight, similarities between the proposed research project and work in multi-level data fusion might be suggested, questioning the sketched approach's novelty or added value over existing accounts.

Still, the differences are significant. Data fusion tries to leverage the advantage of receiving several data streams concerning the same source for getting a more precise characterization of the source: "*data fusion techniques combine data from multiple sensors and related information from associated databases to achieve improved accuracy and more specific inferences than could be achieved by the use of a single sensor alone.*" [13]. Even when leaving aside the targeted improvements and extensions to existing techniques, such as performing anchoring also on the attribute level, the ambition of the research project sketched in this paper goes far beyond this: The final goal is the development of a cognitively-inspired combination of low-level sensing with high-level reasoning in an attempt of anchoring (symbolic) knowledge in (subsymbolic) perception and (inter)action in a continuous feedback loop.

If successful, this would in all likelihood constitute a significant step towards the (re)creation of the foundation for cognitive capacities and forms of reasoning in next generation systems in artificial intelligence, as well as major progress towards developing a computational test bench and agent model for theories from cognitive science.

References

1. Arnold, L., Paugam-Moisy, H., Sebag, M.: Unsupervised layer-wise model selection in deep neural networks. In: Proceedings of ECAI 2010: 19th European Conference on Artificial Intelligence, pp. 915–920. IOS Press (2010)
2. Bengio, Y.: Learning Deep Architectures for AI. Foundations and Trends in Machine Learning **2**(1), 1–127 (2009)
3. Bundy, A.: The interaction of representation and reasoning. Proceedings of the Royal Society A: Mathematical, Physical and Engineering Sciences **469**(2157) (2013)

4. Chella, A., Frixione, M., Gaglio, S.: Anchoring symbols to conceptual spaces: the case of dynamic scenarios. Robotics and Autonomous Systems **43**(2–3), 175–188 (2003)
5. Coradeschi, S., Saffiotti, A.: Anchoring symbols to sensor data: preliminary report. In: Proceedings of the 17th AAAI Conference, pp. 129–135. AAAI Press (2000)
6. Coradeschi, S., Saffiotti, A.: Symbiotic Robotic Systems: Humans, Robots, and Smart Environments. IEEE Intelligent Systems **21**(3), 82–84 (2006)
7. De Penning, H.L.H., Garcez, A.S.D., Lamb, L.C., Meyer, J. J. C.: A Neural-symbolic cognitive agent for online learning and reasoning. In: Proceedings of the 22nd International Joint Conference on Artificial Intelligence, pp. 1653–1658. AAAI Press (2011)
8. Diaconescu, R.: Institution-independent Model Theory. Birkhäuser, 1st edn. (2008)
9. Dietterich, T.G.: Approximate Statistical Tests for Comparing Supervised Classification Learning Algorithms. Neural Comput. **10**(7), 1895–1923 (1998)
10. Fischer, M.H.: A hierarchical view of grounded, embodied, and situated numerical cognition. Cognitive Processing **13**(1), 161–164 (2012)
11. Gärdenfors, P.: Conceptual Spaces: The Geometry of Thought. MIT Press (2000)
12. Gkaniatsou, A., Bundy, A., Mcneill, F.: Towards the automatic detection and correction of errors in automatically constructed ontologies. In: 8th International Conference on Signal Image Technology and Internet Based Systems 2012, pp. 860–867 (2012)
13. Hall, D., Llinas, J.: An introduction to multisensor data fusion. Proceedings of the IEEE **85**(1), 6–23 (1997)
14. Hinton, G.E.: A practical guide to training restricted boltzmann machines. In: Montavon, G., Orr, G.B., Müller, K.-R. (eds.) Neural Networks: Tricks of the Trade, 2nd edn. LNCS, vol. 7700, pp. 599–619. Springer, Heidelberg (2012)
15. Jaeger, H.: Controlling recurrent neural networks by conceptors. arXiv (2014), 1403.3369v1 [cs.CV] (March 13, 2014)
16. LeBlanc, K., Saffiotti, A.: Cooperative anchoring in heterogeneous multi-robot systems. In: 2008 IEEE International Conference on Robotics and Automation, pp. 3308–3314 (2008)
17. Lehmann, J., Chan, M., Bundy, A.: A Higher-Order Approach to Ontology Evolution in Physics. Journal on Data Semantics **2**(4), 163–187 (2013)
18. Lovett, A., Forbus, K., Usher, J.: A structure-mapping model of raven's progressive matrices. In: 32nd Annual Meeting of the Cognitive Science Society, pp. 2761–2766 (2010)
19. Marr, D.: Vision. A Computational Investigation into the Human Representation and Processing of Visual Information. W. H. Freeman and Company (1982)
20. McLure, M., Friedman, S., Forbus, K.: Learning concepts from sketches via analogical generalization and near-misses. In: 32nd Annual Meeting of the Cognitive Science Society, pp. 1726–1731 (2010)
21. Schwering, A., Krumnack, U., Kühnberger, K.U., Gust, H.: Syntactic Principles of Heuristic-Driven Theory Projection. Journal of Cognitive Systems Research **10**(3), 251–269 (2009)

Safe Baby AGI

Jordi Bieger[1]([⊠]), Kristinn R. Thórisson[1,2], and Pei Wang[3]

[1] Center for Analysis and Design of Intelligent Agents / School of Computer Science,
Reykjavik University, Menntavegur 1, 101, Reykjavik, Iceland
jordi13@ru.is
[2] Icelandic Institute for Intelligent Machines,
Uranus, Menntavegur 1, 101, Reykjavik, Iceland
thorisson@ru.is
[3] Department of Computer and Information Sciences, Temple University,
Philadelphia, PA19122, USA
pei.wang@temple.edu

Abstract. Out of fear that artificial general intelligence (AGI) might pose a future risk to human existence, some have suggested slowing or stopping AGI research, to allow time for theoretical work to guarantee its safety. Since an AGI system will necessarily be a complex closed-loop learning controller that lives and works in semi-stochastic environments, its behaviors are not fully determined by its design and initial state, so no mathematico-logical *guarantees* can be provided for its safety. Until actual running AGI systems exist – and there is as of yet no consensus on how to create them – that can be thoroughly analyzed and studied, any proposal on their safety can only be based on weak conjecture. As any practical AGI will unavoidably start in a relatively harmless baby-like state, subject to the nurture and education that we provide, we argue that our best hope to get safe AGI is to provide it proper education.

Keywords: Artificial intelligence · Nurture · Nature · AI safety · Friendly AI

1 Introduction

Various kinds of robot uprisings have long been a popular trope of science fiction. In the past decade similar ideas have also received more attention in academic circles [2,4,7]. The "fast takeoff" hypothesis states that an "intelligence explosion" might occur where a roughly human-level AI rapidly improves immensely by acquiring resources, knowledge and/or software – in a matter of seconds, hours or days: too fast for humans to react [2]. Furthermore, AI would not inherently care about humanity and its values, so unless we solve the difficult task of exactly codifying our wishes into the AI's motivational system, it might wipe out humanity – by accident or on purpose – if it views us as rivals or threats to its own goals [2,6]. Some have suggested that AGI research should be slowed or stopped while theoretical work tries to guarantee its safety [7].

This work is supported by Reykjavik University's School of Computer Science and a Centers of Excellence grant of the Science & Technology Policy Council of Iceland.

J. Bieger (Ed.): AGI 2015, LNAI 9205, pp. 46–49, 2015.
DOI: 10.1007/978-3-319-21365-1_5

Unfortunately current AI safety research is hampered since we don't know how AGI would work, and mathematical or hard theoretical guarantees are impossible for adaptive, fallible systems that interact with unpredictable and unknown environments. Hand-coding all the knowledge required for adult or even child-like intelligence borders on the impossible. Even if we had enough human minds to do so, and the technology, it sounds rather undesirable in light of safety concerns. In any case, to be worthy of the "G" in "AGI" a system should be able to handle environments not foreseen by its designers. They must be radically adaptable. The AGI path is thus more likely than anything else to follow Turing's suggestion of building a "child AI" [8], one that will start life with relatively little knowledge but placed in an environment that facilitates fast and reliable learning, which effectively teaches it the things we want it to know [1].

In addition to the field's focus on AGI design (nature), we highlight here the importance of experience (nurture). Concrete AGI designs, and the ability to empirically study their behavior in complex environments, will facilitate both AI capability *and* safety research. We argue that AGI research *can* and *should* be done responsibly (in the lab): An AGI's resources and knowledge in a finite universe will necessarily be limited at any time, especially in its naïve starting state, when it is essentially a "baby", and we can subject it to any education and upbringing that we want, e.g. with an eye towards preventing autonomous rebellion. We will not discuss potential danger from human misuse in this paper.

2   Bounded and Adaptive

Computation requires resources – energy, hardware and time – and *intelligent* computation requires relevant knowledge to base decisions on. Knowledge cannot be acquired instantaneously, and even if the right data is available at the right time, conclusions may not be reachable due to the infinite amount of inferences that can be made at any moment. Even a very powerful AI will be bounded by resource availability, and thus it will be fallible: Mistakes may result from inadequate or incomplete knowledge, or misallocated resources.

This is true even for very rich and knowledgeable AI, but it would not start out that way: When the first AGI is switched on it will be limited by its complete lack of experience, and the resources and knowledge that we give it access to.

To handle a wide range of novel environments and tasks the system must be capable of significant adaptation: it must be able to dissect novel phenomena into a working ontology, e.g. involving parts and sub-parts with certain identifiable properties, that it will hone as it learns more about those phenomena. Subsequently, effective collection and organization mechanisms are needed for experiences to retrieve them when appropriate. To use its experience to the fullest, the system may be equipped with powerful mechanisms for self-improvement. An adaptive system's behavior is determined both by its initial design and its "postnatal" experience – i.e. nature and nurture. When facing new situations, such a system's response is mostly decided by how its original motivations and knowledge has been shaped by its unique experiences.

We cannot predict the middle-to-long term behavior of an inherently fallible and adaptive system within a complex and unknown environment, even if have the blueprint and full source code. Just as with humans, whether such a system grows up to be a "good citizen" will largely depend on experience, upbringing, and education. We will not be able to say much about AGI behavior and environment interaction until we are able to study such a system empirically.

3   Overpowering Humanity

In a fast takeoff scenario the AI suddenly starts to exponentially improve its intelligence, so fast that humans cannot adequately react. Whether the "returns" on various kinds of intelligence increase are actually diminishing, linear or accelerating is a subject of debate, and depends on the (currently unknown) way the AGI works. Assuming for a moment that an AI would even *want* to, it would need to grow extremely powerful to pose an existential threat to humanity. Explosive growth would require the acquisition of more or better hardware, software, knowledge or skill. For instance, learning to read or gaining internet access (whichever comes last) would let the system acquire vast amounts of knowledge (if hardware and software allow it). To avoid a fast takeoff – if it is even likely to begin with – we must prevent such acquisitions. Many proposals for controlling AGI have been made that would help to accomplish this, such as boxing/confinement, virtual worlds, resetting and monitoring [7].

Objections to these proposals are often rooted in the superior intelligence of an AGI. For instance, it could charm its "jailors" into releasing it, or hide its actual intelligence. But early-stage baby-level AI will not be capable of this. It should not be difficult to detect if it is radically self-improving, acquiring resources (both computational and physical), or learning harmful skills and knowledge (e.g. related to warfare or subjugation). Even the most grandiose predictions don't suggest that it would only take a single step to go from relatively harmless to existentially threatening, which means there is an opportunity to intervene. We should only let the AI develop as far as we are comfortable with, and use our observations to refine all aspects of the system, including its safety.

4   Appetite for Destruction

It is notoriously difficult for any single person – let alone all of humanity – to articulate their "true" values in such detail that they could program it into a computer. But unless we succeed – the instrumental convergence hypothesis seems to imply – a sufficiently powerful AGI would actively seek to destroy us because we pose a threat to its survival or compete for resources [2]. If true, an infinitely intelligent, omniscient AI would instantly realize this (and instantly realize how to avoid that threat in any of a million other ways), the same is not necessarily true of a realistic, fallible, resource-bounded AI that is juggling many mutually constraining goals. It might be too busy pursuing more obviously fruitful avenues of thought and action, or it might not view humans as threats or competitors at all, but as valuable partners. Waser [9] takes this idea even further: while acknowledging Omohundro's basic AI drives he points out the absence of the all-important one: a drive towards cooperation, community, and being social.

But even if an AI were to seek the destruction of humanity, would it be worth the risk? An intelligent system knows about its own fallibility. Making a move for dominance on Earth and failing could lead to its own destruction, and even gathering information on the topic may tip off others. Making and executing (preliminary) plans would need to happen covertly while the AI "lays in wait" until it is time to strike. How does the AI know that there are no other more powerful AIs doing the same?

5 Nurturing Beneficial AGI

As the developers and caretakers of early-stage naïve AGI we should not just switch the system on and let it go. We have the opportunity and responsibility to guide our AIs to learn the right things in the vast realm of possibilities. Especially in the beginning stages, we will have great influence on what it learns.

We can emphasize effective and peaceful ways to accomplish goals – an AI is unlikely to contemplate using skills it does not possess and has never received any training in using. We could teach the system about the risks of aggression, and the value of relationships [9]. We could guide the AI through moral stages of development [5], and actively teach it what to value [3].

We need to develop *actual running* AGI systems to know how they behave in complex environments, and rely on the scientific method to improve them along all dimensions, including safety. Just as with other potentially dangerous technologies like nuclear energy, biological agents, and genetic engineering, this should be done with caution and care. As always, it is up to us humans to use powerful technology for good or for bad.

References

1. Bieger, J., Thórisson, K.R., Garrett, D.: Raising AI: tutoring matters. In: Goertzel, B., Orseau, L., Snaider, J. (eds.) AGI 2014. LNCS, vol. 8598, pp. 1–10. Springer, Heidelberg (2014)
2. Bostrom, N.: Superintelligence: Paths, dangers, strategies. Oxford University Press (2014)
3. Dewey, D.: Learning what to value. In: Schmidhuber, J., Thórisson, K.R., Looks, M. (eds.) AGI 2011. LNCS, vol. 6830, pp. 309–314. Springer, Heidelberg (2011)
4. Future of Life Institute: Research priorities for robust and beneficial artificial intelligence (January 2015)
5. Goertzel, B., Bugaj, S.V.: Stages of ethical development in artificial general intelligence systems. Frontiers in Artificial Intelligence and applications **171**, 448 (2008)
6. Omohundro, S.M.: The basic AI drives. Frontiers in Artificial Intelligence and applications **171**, 483 (2008)
7. Sotala, K., Yampolskiy, R.V.: Responses to catastrophic AGI risk: a survey. Physica Scripta **90**(1), 018001 (2015)
8. Turing, A.M.: Computing machinery and intelligence. Mind **59**(236), 433–460 (1950)
9. Waser, M.R.: Discovering the foundations of a universal system of ethics as a road to safe artificial intelligence. In: AAAI Fall Symposium: Biologically Inspired Cognitive Architectures, pp. 195–200 (2008)

Observation, Communication and Intelligence in Agent-Based Systems

Nader Chmait[(⊠)], David L. Dowe, David G. Green, and Yuan-Fang Li

Faculty of Information Technology, Monash University, Clayton, Australia
{nader.chmait,david.dowe,david.green,yuanfang.li}@monash.edu

Abstract. The intelligence of multiagent systems is known to depend on the communication and observation abilities of its agents. However it is not clear which factor has the greater influence. By following an information-theoretical approach, this study quantifies and analyzes the impact of these two factors on the intelligence of multiagent systems. Using machine intelligence tests, we evaluate and compare the performance of collaborative agents across different communication and observation abilities of measurable entropies. Results show that the effectiveness of multiagent systems with low observation/perception abilities can be significantly improved by using high communication entropies within the agents in the system. We also identify circumstances where these assumptions fail, and analyze the dependency between the studied factors.

1 Introduction

The literature on multiagent systems has put forward many studies showing how factors such as *communication* [1,3,7,9] and *observation* [4,5,11] influence the performance of multiagent systems. However, it is ambiguous whether (a) augmenting the agents' observations to read/interpret the environment in which they operate, or rather (b) boosting communication between these agents, has higher influence on their performance, which is the main motivation behind this research. In fact, one of the fundamental characteristics of agent-based systems is their ability to observe/perceive and sense the environment [5,12]. Within a multiagent system setting, perhaps the main property of agents is their ability to interact and communicate [12, Sect.5].

The goal of this paper is to compare the above factors by measuring the influence that each has on the intelligence of cooperative agent-based systems. Moreover, we try to reveal the dependencies between one factor and another. To the best of our knowledge, no studies have applied formal intelligence tests for this purpose. In real-world multiagent applications, agents can have limited sensitivity of the environment (observations), thus relying on communication to improve their performance can be inevitable. Therefore, quantifying the influence of the rules of information aggregation on the effectiveness of such systems is likelyto have major implications by predicting the usefulness and expected performance of these systems over different settings.

© Springer International Publishing Switzerland 2015
J. Bieger (Ed.): AGI 2015, LNAI 9205, pp. 50–59, 2015.
DOI: 10.1007/978-3-319-21365-1_6

In this study we begin by introducing our approach to measuring the intelligence of groups of artificial agents in Sect. 2. We then describe our experiments (Sect. 4), the outcomes (Sect. 4) and conclude (Sect. 5) with a discussion of the implication of our findings on the current state of research.

2   Approach to Measuring Intelligence

Our approach is to use (machine) intelligence tests to evaluate a group of artificial agents collaborating in different settings. We adjust their communication and observation abilities over a series of controlled experiments in order to see whether the changes are reflected by their measured intelligence.

2.1   The Anytime Intelligence Test

To achieve our stated goal, we need to be able to *quantify* the performance of artificial agents. While many problems are relevant to agent-based systems, not every evaluation metric can be used as a formal (universal) intelligence test. We have chosen to use an extension of the Anytime Universal Intelligence Test [6] (anYnt) to quantify the performance of multiagent systems. The test is derived from formal and mathematical considerations [6, Sect.3] that build upon Legg and Hutter's definition of universal intelligence [8], and it can be used in practice to evaluate artificial agents in a dynamic setting [6, Sect.6.3] and [7]. We follow the agent-environment framework [8] where an environment is the world where agents can interact using a set of observations, actions and rewards. At each step of the test, the environment generates observations from the set of observations $\mathcal{O}$ and sends them to the agents. Agents performs actions from a limited set of actions $\mathcal{A}$ in response. Finally, the environment rewards back each agent from the set $\mathcal{R} \subseteq \mathbb{Q}$ based on the quality of its action. An iteration or step i of the test stands for one sequence of observation-action-reward.

2.2   Measuring Uncertainty and Information

We follow an information-theoretical approach building on the notion of *Shannon's entropy* [10] to measure the *uncertainty* $H(\mu)$ in a given environment μ, as well as the amount of information in an observation o, or a communication range c. We define N to be the set of all possible states of an environment μ. At the beginning of a test (e.g anYnt), the entropy is maximal as there is complete uncertainty about the current state of μ from an agent's perspective. Therefore the probability $p(s_\mu)$ of a given state s_μ occurring follows a uniform distribution and is equal to $1/|N|$. Using $\log_2$ as a base for calculations, the uncertainty $H(\mu)$ is calculated as follows: $H(\mu) = - \sum\limits_{s_\mu \in N} p(s_\mu) \log_2 p(s_\mu) = \log_2 |N|$ bits.

The amount of information an agent π is given about the environment can be calculated as the entropy $H(o)$ of the observation o sent to π by the environment at one iteration of the test, which translates to the minimum number of bits used to describe o. Consequently, we expect from the theory that the more information given to an agent (or the larger its set of observation about the environment), the higher the probability that this agent will accurately reason about it by processing and interpreting the provided information. Furthermore, we denote by c the communication range of an agent π. The amount of information transmitted within c is calculated as the entropy $H(c)$ which, using $\log_2$, refers to the minimal binary representation needed to describe the transmitted data over the range c.

2.3 Evaluating Different Agent Communication Modes

Given an anYnt testing environment μ with $|N|$ states, and a group of agents Π to be evaluated, each iteration or step i of the test is run as follows:

1. The environment μ sends an observation o to each agent $\pi \in \Pi$, where o is a description of: the state π currently occupies in μ, as well as a set of other neighbor (reachable) states of μ at iteration i.
2. Agents communicate by sharing their observations with other agents (using different communication strategies) within their communication range c.
3. Each agent takes an action based on its observation/communication details using its decision-making technique.
4. The environment rewards back each agent based on the quality of its action.

Let c (the communication range an agent π) be the set of neighbor states over which π can transmit/receive data. We evaluate a cooperative group of local search agents using the three communication techniques briefly summarized below. A detailed description of the implementation of these agents and their communication techniques can be found in [2, Sect.4].

Stigmergy or Indirect Communication. Agents communicate by altering the environment so that it reflects their observations. At each iteration of the test, when an agent senses a reward as part of its observation o, it communicates with the other agents by inducing *fake-rewards* in its communication range c. The fake rewards reflect the real reward the agent has observed.

Direct Communication. At each iteration of the test, agents broadcast a copy of their observation o, to the other agents in their communication range c. Agents then select the action leading to the highest visible reward.

Imitation. In this setting - in addition to the evaluated agents - we introduce a smart agent that always takes the most rewarding action at each iteration of the test. The evaluated agents imitate the smart agent by mimicking its action when it is in their communication range c. The agents also share this action with the other agents located in their communication range c, if any exist.

In the context of the above settings, the observation entropy $H(o)$ can be increased/decreased by adding/removing states to/from the set of neighbor states in o sent by the environment μ. Likewise, adding/removing states to/from the set of states belonging to the communication range c allows us to increase/decrease the communication entropy $H(c)$ of the evaluated system.

3   Experiments

We have conducted a series of controlled experiments on a cooperative collective of agents Π over the anYnt test, using the test environment class implementation found in [2, Sect. 3.2], which is an extension of the spatial environment space described in [6, Sect.6.3]. Each experiment consisted of 200 iterations of *observation-communication-action-reward* sequences and the outcome from each experiment is an average score returning a per-agent measure of success of the collective of evaluated agents over a series of canonical tasks of different algorithmic complexities. The number of agents used was $|\Pi| = 20$ agents, evaluated over an environment space of $H(\mu) = 11.28$ bits of uncertainty.

A description of our experiments can be stated as follows: we evaluate a group of agents Π over a series of (anYnt) intelligence tests and record the group's score $\Upsilon(H_o, H_c)$ over a range of entropy values $H(o)$ and $H(c)$. The score $\Upsilon(H_o, H_c)$ is a real number in $[-1.0, 1.0]$. Average results of Π (using the different communication modes described in Sect. 2.3) taken from 1000 repeated experiments are depicted in Fig. 1. Note that the coefficient of variation is less than 0.025 across our experiments. We denote by E the set of entropy values used in Fig. 1. These values are in the range $[0.04, 10.84]$ bits, and they correspond to $\log_2 n$, where n is the number of states in o or c, as appropriate. Moreover, Fig. 2 depicts the scores $\Upsilon(H_o, H_c)$ from Fig. 1, plotted for fixed values of $H(c)$ across increasing values of $H(o)$ (left-side plots of Fig. 2) and vice versa (right-side plots of Fig. 2). We analyze and discuss these results in the following section.

4   Results and Discussion

Indirect Communication. Figures 1 and 2a show that the effectiveness of the agents in Π monotonically increases with the observation entropy of the agents $H(o)$ until it converges around an $H(o)$ of 10.8 bits. Increasing the (stigmergic) communication entropy $H(c)$ between the agents also has an impact on their intelligence. However, the influence of $H(c)$ on intelligence is rather more complicated, as it seems also to depend on the observation entropies $H(o)$. For instance, for an $H(o)$ of 0.04 bits, the best performance, $\max(\Upsilon(H_o, H_c))$, is reached when the coefficient $\alpha = \frac{H(c)}{H(o)} = 9$. For larger $H(o)$ entropies, the best performances are reached at smaller α values until $\alpha \approx 1$ at an $H(o)$ of 10.84 bits. The overall picture from Fig. 1 (indirect communication) shows that the performance drops as the entropy $H(c)$ moves away from $\alpha \times H(o)$. This non-monotonic variation of scores shows that increasing communication does not necessarily always lead to an increase in performance as presumed. To understand the influence of indirect communication on the scores of the collectives we have to analyze further the relationship between $H(o)$ and $H(c)$. Figure 3 is a whisker plot showing the variation in the scores across different entropy values $H(c) \subseteq E$ for fixed entropies $H(o)$, and vice versa. The figure also shows that - for indirect communication - $H(c)$ is most significant when $H(o) \in [0.3, 1.9]$ bits. For instance, using stigmergy to communicate very short observations (low $H(o)$ entropies) does not have a

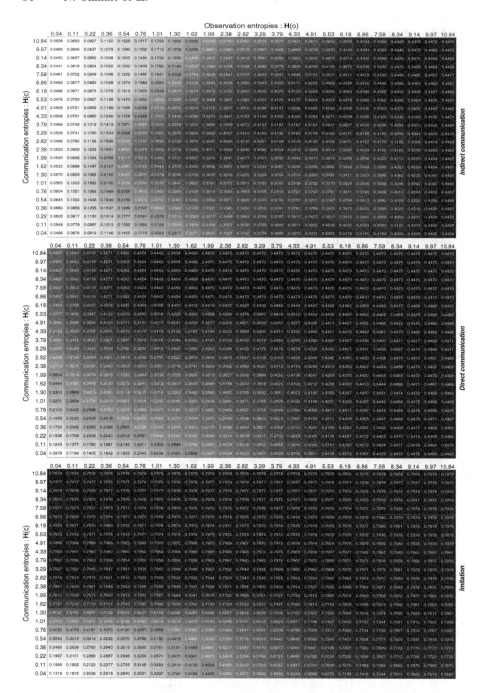

Fig. 1. Test scores $\Upsilon(H_o, H_c)$ for different values of H(o) and H(c) (in bits), for the same collective of agents using the communication modes described in Sect. 2.3. The gray color-map intensities reflect how high the score values $\Upsilon(H_o, H_c)$ are, where higher intensities mean larger scores (higher values are black and lower values are white). We consider the small variations in the scores along the fourth decimal place as experimental error.

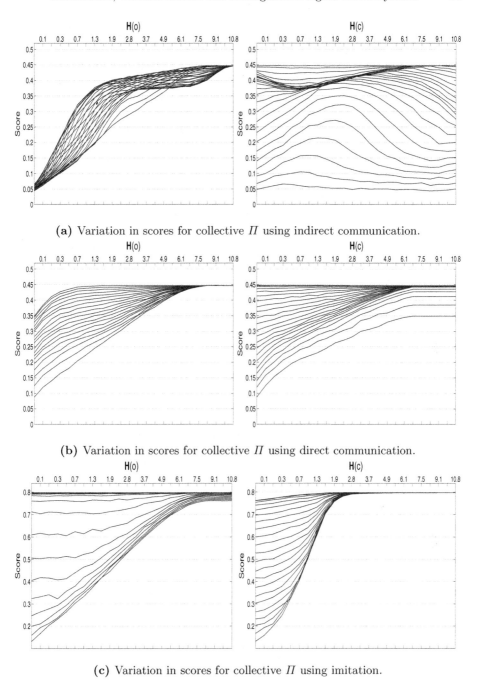

(**a**) Variation in scores for collective Π using indirect communication.

(**b**) Variation in scores for collective Π using direct communication.

(**c**) Variation in scores for collective Π using imitation.

Fig. 2. Variation in the scores (from Fig. 1) of collective Π using different communication strategies. The scores are plotted for fixed values of H(c) across increasing values of H(o) (left-side plots of Fig. 2), as well as for fixed values of H(o) across increasing values of H(c) (right-side plots of Fig. 2).

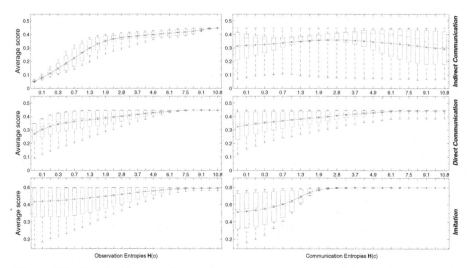

Fig. 3. Whisker plot showing the variation in test scores across different entropy values H(c) for fixed entropies H(o) (left-side), and vice versa (right-side). The central mark (in red) is the median while the edges of the box represent the 25th and 75th percentiles of the scores and the whiskers extend to the most extreme score values. The blue line-plot shows the average scores at each of the intermediate entropy values.

large influence on performance possibly because the observations do not carry much information. Likewise, using stigmergy within collectives of agents with extended observation abilities (high H(o) entropies) has no significant effect on performance, as the uncertainty in the environment is already reduced as a result of the agents' observations. However, communication using stigmergy was fairly effective in less extreme cases. To make our observation more concrete, we define below the communication-over-observation coefficient of success ϕ.

Definition 1. *Let* $S = \{(x, y) \in E \times E \mid x > y\}$. *The communication-over-observation coefficient of success is:* $\phi = (\sum_S \inf(\Upsilon(x, y), \Upsilon(y, x)) \div |S|)$, *where* $\inf(a, b)$ *is a function that returns 1 if* $a < b$, *or zero otherwise.*

For this mode of communication, the coefficient $\phi = 11/276 = 0.0399$. Knowing that the test scores are of the form $\Upsilon(H_o, H_c)$, the value of ϕ suggests that, for this communication mode, it is much more effective to increase the observation entropies of the agents as opposed to increasing their communication entropies[1]. More importantly, the dependency of communication H(c) on observation H(o) is made explicit here. For instance, using H(c) values inferior to H(o) is rarely more rewarding than in the reciprocal case.

Direct Communication. While increasing observation entropies still leads to a significant increase in performance, the influence of direct communication is much more significant than in Fig. 2a. We can observe a clear pattern in

---

[1] Recall that we are experimenting for the entropy values E, using a number of agents $|\Pi| = 20$, over an environment of uncertainty $H(\mu) = 11.28$ bits.

Fig. 2b showing higher performances for higher communication entropies for a fixed H(o). Nevertheless, in this setting using very low H(o) entropies does not ensure optimal performances for Π. However, re-compensating these short-sighted agents with high H(c) entropies can lead to a system up to four times better in performance, which also indicates the very low-dependency of H(c) on the value of H(o). On the other hand, for fairly high observation entropies, augmenting communication between the agents is at least as effective as mounting their observations, and can sometimes be even more effective as shown in Fig. 3. In this setting the coefficient $\phi = 272/276 = 0.9855$, meaning that augmenting the communication entropies within the system will highly likely lead to a more intelligent system. Consequently, communication is effective here even when the observation entropies are slim, again suggesting a low dependency on H(o).

Imitation. Figure 2c highlights the significance of communication in agent collectives relying on imitation. In this setting, $\Upsilon(H_o, H_c)$ is mainly controlled by how much entropy is exchanged through communication between the agents. For agents with very-low observations, the scores can be improved up to six times higher (e.g. from 0.1319 to 0.7978 in Fig. 2c) by increasing their communication entropies. Figure 3 shows that, in this setting, increasing communication significantly influences performance, while the impact of observation is not as important. We can also see that tuning the observation entropies has a negligible effect when H(c) > 2.3 bits as opposed to changing the communication entropies. We must point out that the effect of imitation is significant regardless of the type/intelligence of the agent that is being imitated. For instance, imitation will result in either positive or negative shift in performance, depending on the intelligence of the imitated agent. In this setting the coefficient $\phi = 274/276 = 0.9928$, leading to a similar and even stronger conclusion than in the case of direct communication.

Furthermore, we have plotted in Fig. 4 the gradient difference $\nabla\Upsilon(H_o, H_c)$ of the scores $\Upsilon(H_o, H_c)$, in the H(c) and H(o) directions across the entropy values E. For instance, each line in Fig. 4 depicts the gradient shift over multiple entropy values calculated according to Eq. (1) below:

$$\nabla\Upsilon(H_o, H_c) \leftarrow \left|\frac{\partial\Upsilon(H_o, H_c)}{\partial H(c)}\right| - \left|\frac{\partial\Upsilon(H_o, H_c)}{\partial H(o)}\right| \tag{1}$$

The outcome from (1) highlights the entropies where (in a environment of uncertainty $H(\mu) = 11.28$ bits, and $|\Pi| = 20$) communication has the highest influence on the effectiveness $\Upsilon(H_o, H_c)$ of Π when compared to the influence of observation. We observe that indirect communication has highest impact across entropies of $[0.3, 1.9]$ bits. Direct communication is most significant within entropies of $[0.1, 1.9]$ bits, while imitation has the highest influence over entropy values in the range $[0.7, 4.9]$ bits[1].

Environment Space. Experimenting over environments with different uncertainties $H(\mu)$ lead to similar conclusions as above. However, the scores converged

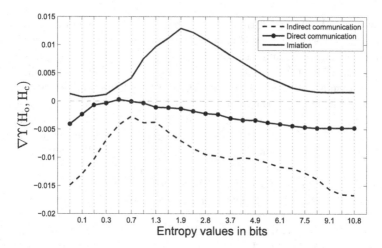

Fig. 4. Average difference in gradient $\nabla\Upsilon(\mathrm{H_o}, \mathrm{H_c})$ in H(c) and H(o) directions over a set of entropy values E

faster in environments of lower uncertainty and the gap in performance was less significant than in environments of high uncertainty.

Number of Agents. Testing with different number of agents also influenced the performance of the evaluated collectives. The influence of communication on the scores was stronger in many cases where a larger number of agents was used.

5 Conclusion

This paper follows an information-theoretical approach to quantify and analyze the effectiveness of a collaborative group of artificial agents across different communication settings. Using formal intelligence tests from the literature of artificial general intelligence, we measure the influence of two factors inherent to multiagent systems: the observation and communication abilities of agents, on the overall intelligence of the evaluated system.

Agents collaborating using three different communication strategies are evaluated over a series of intelligence tests, and their scores are recorded. We highlight the different configurations where the effectiveness of artificial agent-based systems is significantly influenced by communication and observation. We also show that dull systems with low observation or perception abilities can be recompensated for, and significantly improved, by increasing the communication entropies between the agents, thus leading to smarter systems. Moreover, we identify circumstances where the increase in communication does not monotonically improve performance. We also analyze the dependency between communication and observation and its impact on the overall performance.

The outcome from our experiments can have many theoretical and practical implications on agent-based systems as they allow us to predict the effectiveness and the expected performance of these systems over different (communication or collaboration) settings. We are aware that using different implementations or extensions of the studied communication strategies would possibly lead to a variation in the scores. However, the same approach can still be used to understand the rules of information aggregation within a multiagent setting, and the influence of these rules on the effectiveness of the evaluated system.

References

1. Bettencourt, L.M.A.: The Rules of Information Aggregation and Emergence of Collective Intelligent Behavior. Topics in Cognitive Science **1**(4), 598–620 (2009). http://dx.doi.org/10.1111/j.1756-8765.2009.01047.x
2. Chmait, N., Dowe, D.L., Green, D.G., Li, Y.F., Insa-Cabrera, J.: Measuring universal intelligence in agent-based systems using the anytime intelligence test. Tech. Rep. 2015/279, Faculty of Information Technology, Clayton, Monash University (2015). http://www.csse.monash.edu.au/publications/2015/tr-2015-279-full.pdf
3. Dowe, D.L., Hernández-Orallo, J., Das, P.K.: Compression and intelligence: social environments and communication. In: Schmidhuber, J., Thórisson, K.R., Looks, M. (eds.) AGI 2011. LNCS, vol. 6830, pp. 204–211. Springer, Heidelberg (2011). http://dx.doi.org/10.1007/978-3-642-22887-2_21
4. Fallenstein, B., Soares, N.: Problems of self-reference in self-improving space-time embedded intelligence. In: Goertzel, B., Orseau, L., Snaider, J. (eds.) AGI 2014. LNCS, vol. 8598, pp. 21–32. Springer, Heidelberg (2014). http://dx.doi.org/10.1007/978-3-319-09274-4_3
5. Franklin, S., Graesser, A.: Is it an agent, or just a program?: A taxonomy for autonomous agents. In: Müller, J.P., Wooldridge, M.J., Jennings, N.R. (eds.) ECAI-WS 1996 and ATAL 1996. LNCS, vol. 1193, pp. 21–35. Springer, Heidelberg (1997). http://dx.doi.org/10.1007/BFb0013570
6. Hernández-Orallo, J., Dowe, D.L.: Measuring universal intelligence: Towards an anytime intelligence test. Artif. Intell. **174**(18), 1508–1539 (2010). http://dx.doi.org/10.1016/j.artint.2010.09.006
7. Insa-Cabrera, J., Benacloch-Ayuso, J.-L., Hernández-Orallo, J.: On measuring social intelligence: experiments on competition and cooperation. In: Bach, J., Goertzel, B., Iklé, M. (eds.) AGI 2012. LNCS, vol. 7716, pp. 126–135. Springer, Heidelberg (2012). http://dx.doi.org/10.1007/978-3-642-35506-6_14
8. Legg, S., Hutter, M.: Universal intelligence: A definition of machine intelligence. Minds and Machines **17**(4), 391–444 (2007)
9. Panait, L., Luke, S.: Cooperative multi-agent learning: The state of the art. Autonomous Agents and Multi-Agent Systems **11**(3), 387–434 (2005). http://dx.doi.org/10.1007/s10458-005-2631-2
10. Shannon, C.: A mathematical theory of communication. Bell System Technical Journal **27**(3), 379–423 (1948)
11. Weyns, D., Steegmans, E., Holvoet, T.: Towards active perception in situated multiagent systems. Applied Artificial Intelligence **18**(9–10), 867–883 (2004). http://dx.doi.org/10.1080/08839510490509063
12. Wooldridge, M., Jennings, N.R.: Intelligent agents: Theory and practice. The Knowledge Engineering Review **10**(2), 115–152 (1995)

Reflective Variants of Solomonoff Induction and AIXI

Benja Fallenstein, Nate Soares$^{(\boxtimes)}$, and Jessica Taylor

Machine Intelligence Research Institute, Berkeley, USA
{benja,nate,jessica}@intelligence.org

Abstract. Solomonoff induction and AIXI model their environment as an arbitrary Turing machine, but are themselves uncomputable. This fails to capture an essential property of real-world agents, which cannot be more powerful than the environment they are embedded in; for example, AIXI cannot accurately model game-theoretic scenarios in which its opponent is another instance of AIXI.

In this paper, we define *reflective* variants of Solomonoff induction and AIXI, which are able to reason about environments containing other, equally powerful reasoners. To do so, we replace Turing machines by probabilistic oracle machines (stochastic Turing machines with access to an oracle). We then use *reflective oracles*, which answer questions of the form, "is the probability that oracle machine T outputs 1 greater than p, when run on this same oracle?" Diagonalization can be avoided by allowing the oracle to answer randomly if this probability is equal to p; given this provision, reflective oracles can be shown to exist. We show that reflective Solomonoff induction and AIXI can themselves be implemented as oracle machines with access to a reflective oracle, making it possible for them to model environments that contain reasoners as powerful as themselves.

Keywords: Reflective oracles · Solomonoff induction · AIXI · Universal artificial intelligence

1 Introduction

Legg and Hutter [5] have defined a "Universal measure of intelligence" that describes the ability of a system to maximize rewards across a wide range of diverse environments. This metric is useful when attempting to quantify the cross-domain performance of modern AI systems, but it does not quite capture the induction and interaction problems faced by generally intelligent systems acting in the real world: In the formalism of Legg and Hutter (as in many other agent formalisms) the agent and the environment are assumed to be distinct and separate, while real generally intelligent systems must be able to learn about and manipulate an environment from within.

As noted by Hutter [4], Vallinder [9], and others, neither Solomonoff induction [8] nor AIXI [3] can capture this aspect of reasoning in the real world. Both

© Springer International Publishing Switzerland 2015
J. Bieger (Ed.): AGI 2015, LNAI 9205, pp. 60–69, 2015.
DOI: 10.1007/978-3-319-21365-1_7

formalisms require that the reasoner have more computing power than any individual environment hypothesis that the reasoner considers: a Solomonoff inductor predicting according to a distribution over all computable hypotheses is not itself computable; an AIXI acting according to some distribution over environments uses more computing power than any one environment in its distribution. This is also true of computable approximations of AIXI, such as $AIXI^{tl}$. Thus, these formalisms cannot easily be used to make models of reasoners that must reason about an environment which contains the reasoner and/or other, more powerful reasoners. Because these reasoners require more computing power than any environment they hypothesize, environments which contain the reasoner are not in their hypothesis space!

In this paper, we extend the Solomonoff induction formalism and the AIXI formalism into a setting where the agents reason about the environment while embedded within it. We do this by studying variants of Solomonoff induction and AIXI using *probabilistic oracle machines* rather than Turing machines, where a probabilistic oracle machine is a Turing machine that can flip coins and make calls to an oracle. Specifically, we make use of probabilistic oracle machines with access to a "reflective oracle" [2] that answers questions about other probabilistic oracle machines using the same oracle. This allows us to define environments which may contain agents that in turn reason about the environment which contains them.

Section 2 defines reflective oracles. Section 3 gives a definition of Solomonoff induction on probabilistic oracle machines. Section 4 gives a variant of AIXI in this setting. Section 5 discusses these results, along with a number of avenues for future research.

2   Reflective Oracles

Our goal is to define agents which are able to reason about environments containing other, equally powerful agents. If agents and environments are simply Turing machines, and two agents try to predict their environments (which contain the other agent) by simply running the corresponding machines, then two agents trying to predict each other will go into an infinite loop.

One might try to solve this problem by defining agents to be Turing machines with access to an oracle, which takes the source code of an oracle machine as input and which outputs what this machine would output when run on the same oracle. (The difference to simply running the machine would be that the oracle would always return an answer, never go into an infinite loop.) Then, instead of predicting the environment by *running* the corresponding oracle machine, agents would query the oracle about this machine. However, it's easy to see that such an oracle cannot exist, for reasons similar to the halting problem: if it existed, then by quining, one could write a program that queries the oracle about *its own* output, and returns 0 iff the oracle says it returns 1, and returns 1 otherwise.

It is possible to get around this problem by allowing the oracle to give random answers in certain, restricted circumstances. To do so, we define agents and environments to be *probabilistic oracle machines*, Turing machines with the ability to act stochastically (by tossing fair coins) and to consult oracles. We consider probabilistic oracle machines to be equipped with advance-only output tapes.

We will write $\mathcal{T}$ for the set of these probabilistic oracle machines. Throughout this paper, an overline will be used to denote finite strings, and ϵ will be used to denote the empty string. Let $\mathbb{B} := \{0, 1\}$ be the set of bits, and $\mathbb{B}^{<\omega}$ denote the set of finite strings of bits. We write $T^O(\overline{x})$ for a machine $T \in \mathcal{T}$ run on the input $\overline{x} \in \mathbb{B}^{<\omega}$, using the oracle O.

Roughly speaking, a reflective oracle O will answer queries of the form "is the probability that $T^O(\overline{x})$ outputs 1 greater than q?" where q is a rational probability. That is, a query is a triple $(T, \overline{x}, q) \in \mathcal{T} \times \mathbb{B}^{<\omega} \times \mathbb{Q} \cap [0, 1]$, where $\mathbb{Q} \cap [0, 1]$ is the set of rational probabilities.

More formally, write $\mathbb{P}(T^O(\overline{x}) = y)$ for the probability that $T^O(\overline{x})$ outputs at least one bit and that the first bit of output is $y \in \mathbb{B}$. If $T^O(\overline{x})$ does not always halt before outputting the first bit, then $\mathbb{P}(T^O(\overline{x}) = 1) + \mathbb{P}(T^O(\overline{x}) = 0)$ may be less than 1. We assume that the oracle always outputs either 1 or 0, and define distinct calls to the oracle to be stochastically independent (even if they call the oracle on the same query); hence, an oracle's behavior is fully specified by the probabilities $\mathbb{P}(O(T, \overline{x}, q) = 1)$. Now, we can define reflective oracles as follows:

Definition 1. *An oracle O is "reflective" if, for all $T \in \mathcal{T}$ and $\overline{x} \in \mathbb{B}^{<\omega}$, there is some $p \in [0, 1]$ such that*

$$\mathbb{P}(T^O(\overline{x}) = 1) \ \leq \ p \ \leq \ \mathbb{P}(T^O(\overline{x}) \neq 0) \tag{1}$$

and such that for all $q \in \mathbb{Q} \cap [0, 1]$, the following implications hold:

$$p > q \implies \mathbb{P}(O(T, \overline{x}, q) = 1) = 1 \tag{2}$$
$$p < q \implies \mathbb{P}(O(T, \overline{x}, q) = 0) = 1 \tag{3}$$

Note that if $T^O(\overline{x})$ is guaranteed to output a bit, then p must be exactly the probability $\mathbb{P}(T^O(\overline{x}) = 1)$ that $T^O(\overline{x})$ returns 1. If $T^O(\overline{x})$ sometimes fails to halt, then the oracle can, in a sense, be understood to "redistribute" the probability that the machine goes into an infinite loop between the two possible outputs: it answers queries as if $T^O(\overline{x})$ outputs 1 with probability p, where p is lower-bounded by the true probability of outputting 1, and upper-bounded by the probability of outputting 1 or looping.

If $q = p$, then $\mathbb{P}(O(T, \overline{x}, q) = 1)$ may be any number between 0 and 1; this is essential in order to avoid paradox. For example, consider the probabilistic oracle machine which asks the oracle which bit it itself is most likely to output, and outputs the opposite bit. In this case, a reflective oracle may answer 1 with probability 0.5, so that the agent outputs each bit with equal probability. In fact, given this flexibility, a consistent solution always exists.

Theorem 1. *A reflective oracle exists.*

Proof. Appendix B of Fallenstein, Taylor, and Christiano [2]. □

3   Reflective Solomonoff Induction

Using a reflective oracle, it is possible to define a variation on Solomonoff induction defined on probabilistic oracle machines. Define an *environment* to be a probabilistic oracle machine which takes a sequence of bits as input and (probabilistically) produces a single bit of output. We write $\mathbb{B}^{<\omega} \rightsquigarrow \mathbb{B}$ for the type of probabilistic oracle machines run with oracle O which take a finite bit string as input and probabilistically output a single bit. Holding O fixed, one can think of an environment as defining a function of type $\mathbb{B}^{<\omega} \to \Delta(\mathbb{B})$ where $\Delta(\mathbb{B})$ is the set of probability distributions over a single bit. Equivalently, one may see an environment paired with an oracle as a distribution over possibly-infinite bit strings, where strings of bits are generated by running the environment on ϵ to produce the first bit, and then running it on the first bit to produce the second bit, and then running it on the first two bits to produce the third bit, and so on. What results is a distribution over possibly-infinite bit strings (where the strings may be finite if the environment sometimes goes into an infinite loop rather than producing another output bit).

We will give a variant of Solomonoff induction that predicts observations according to a simplicity distribution over environments, and which is itself a probabilistic oracle machine (implying that it can be embedded into an environment). Roughly speaking, it will take a simplicity distribution, condition it on the observations seen so far, sample a machine from the resulting distribution, and then use the oracle to output its next bit as if it were that machine. Loosely, this results in a distribution over bits which is 1 according to the probability that a random machine from the updated distribution would next output a 1.

In order to define our variant of Solomonoff induction (and later AIXI) it will be necessary to fix some representation of real numbers. Throughout this paper, real numbers will be represented by infinite sequences of nested closed intervals. To demonstrate, Algorithm 1 describes a probabilistic oracle machine $\mathsf{getProb} : \mathcal{T} \times \mathbb{B}^{<\omega} \times \mathbb{B} \rightsquigarrow \mathbb{R}$ which takes an encoding T of another probabilistic oracle machine, a finite bit string $\overline{x}$, and a single bit y, and uses the oracle O to compute $\mathbb{P}(T^O(\overline{x}) = y)$. If $T^O(\overline{x})$ may fail to generate output, $\mathsf{getProb}^O(T, \overline{x}, 1)$ will return the "redistributed" probability p from Definition 1.

Algorithm 1. When run with an oracle O, outputs $\mathbb{P}(T^O(\overline{x}) = y)$ as an infinite sequence of nested intervals.

---

def $\mathsf{getProb}^O(T, \overline{x}, y)$:

> $upper \longleftarrow 1$;
> $lower \longleftarrow 0$;
> **repeat**
>> $middle \longleftarrow (upper + lower)/2$;
>> **if** $O(T, \overline{x}, middle) = y$ **then** $lower \longleftarrow middle$;
>> **else** $upper \longleftarrow middle$;
>> **output** $(lower, upper)$;

Solomonoff induction on probabilistic oracle machines is given as a function rSI : $\mathbb{B}^{<\omega} \rightsquigarrow \mathbb{B}$ by Algorithm 2. This function implicitly defines a probability distribution over infinite bitstrings, by providing a way to sample the next bit given the output so far; this allows the conditional probability of the next bit to be computed by getProb. (rSI is defined so that it will always output either 0 or 1, never go into an infinite loop.)

Algorithm 2 makes use of two more helper functions defined in Appendix A, namely getStringProb : $\mathcal{T} \times \mathbb{B}^{<\omega} \times \mathbb{B}^{<\omega} \rightsquigarrow \mathbb{R}$, which computes the probability that a machine T would output the sequence $\overline{y}$ conditional on having already outputted $\overline{x}$, and flip : $\mathbb{R} \rightsquigarrow \mathbb{B}$ which flips a weighted coin (returning 1 with probability equal to the weight, and 0 otherwise); like getProb, getStringProb uses the "redistributed" probabilities p from Definition 1 if a machine may go into an infinite loop.

With these two helper functions, defining Solomonoff induction on probabilistic oracle machines is straightforward. Using rejection sampling, we sample a machine T with probability proportional to $2^{-\text{len}(T)}\text{getStringProb}^O(T, \epsilon, \overline{x})$, where $\overline{x}$ is the string of our observations so far. To do this, we draw T with probability $2^{-\text{len}(T)}$ using the randomMachine function, and then keep it with probability getStringProb$^O(T, \epsilon, \overline{x})$. After sampling this machine, we use getProb to sample the next bit in the sequence after our observations.

Algorithm 2. Reflective Solomonoff induction for probabilistic oracle machines. It takes a finite bit string and outputs a bit.

```
def rSI^O(x̄):
    repeat
        T ⟵ randomMachine^O();
        if flip^O(getStringProb^O(T, ε, x̄)) then
            return flip^O(getProb^O(T, x̄, 1))
```

Because rSI always terminates, it defines a distribution $\mathbb{P}_{\text{rSI}} \in \Delta(\mathbb{B}^\omega)$ over infinite bit strings, where $\mathbb{P}_{\text{rSI}}(\overline{x})$ is the probability that rSI generates the string $\overline{x}$ (when run on the first n bits to generate the $n + 1^{\text{th}}$ bit). This distribution satisfies the essential property of a simplicity distribution, namely, that each environment T is represented somewhere within this distribution.

Theorem 2. *For each probabilistic oracle machine T, there is a constant C_T such that for all finite bit strings $\overline{x} \in \mathbb{B}^{<\omega}$,*

$$\mathbb{P}_{\text{rSI}}(\overline{x}) \geq C_T \cdot \mathbb{P}_T(\overline{x}) \tag{4}$$

where $\mathbb{P}_T(\overline{x})$ is the probability of T generating the sequence $\overline{x}$ (when run on the first n bits to generate the $n + 1^{\text{th}}$ bit).

Proof. First note that

$$\mathbb{P}_T(\overline{x}) \leq \text{getStringProb}^O(T, \epsilon, \overline{x}) = \prod_{i=0}^{\text{len}(\overline{x})} \text{getProb}^O(T, \overline{x}_{1:i-1}, \overline{x}_i), \tag{5}$$

with equality on the left if $T^O(\overline{y})$ is guaranteed to produce an output bit for every prefix $\overline{y}$ of $\overline{x}$. Then, the result follows from the fact that by construction, sampling a bit string from rSI^O is equivalent to choosing a random machine T with probability proportional to $2^{-\mathsf{len}(T)}$ and then sampling bits according to $\mathsf{getProb}^O(T,\cdot,\cdot)$.

Reflective Solomonoff induction does itself have the type of an environment, and hence is included in the simplicity distribution over environments. Indeed, it is apparent that reflective Solomonoff induction can be used to predict *its own* behavior—resulting in behavior that is heavily dependent upon the choice of reflective oracle and the encoding of machines as bit strings, of course. But more importantly, there are also environments in this distribution which *run Solomonoff induction as a subprocess:* that is, this variant of Solomonoff induction can be used to predict environments that contain Solomonoff inductors.

4   Reflective AIXI

With reflective Solomonoff induction in hand, we may now define a reflective *agent*, by giving a variant of AIXI that runs on probabilistic oracle machines. To do this, we fix a finite set $\mathcal{O}$ of observations, together with a prefix-free encoding of observations as bit strings. Moreover, we fix a function $r : \mathcal{O} \to [0,1]$ which associates to each $o \in \mathcal{O}$ a (computable) reward $r(o)$. Without loss of generality, we assume that the agent has only two available actions, 0 and 1.

Reflective AIXI will assume that an environment is a probabilistic oracle machine which takes a finite string of observation/action pairs and produces a new observation; that is, an environment is a machine with type $(\mathcal{O} \times \mathbb{B})^{<\omega} \leadsto \mathcal{O}$. Reflective AIXI assumes that it gets to choose each action bit, and, given a history $\overline{oa} \in (\mathcal{O} \times \mathbb{B})^{<\omega}$ and the latest observation $o \in \mathcal{O}$, it outputs the bit which gives it the highest expected (time-discounted) future reward. We will write $r_t(\overline{oa}) := r(\mathsf{fst}(\overline{oa}_t))$ for the reward in the tth observation of $\overline{oa}$.

To define reflective AIXI, we first need the function step from Algorithm 3, which encodes the assumption that an environment can be factored into a world-part and an agent-part, one of which produces the observations and the other which produces the actions.

Algorithm 3. Takes an agent and an environment and the history so far, and computes the next observation/action pair.

> **def** $\mathsf{step}^O(world, agent, \overline{oa})$:
> | $o \longleftarrow world^O(\overline{oa})$;
> | $a \longleftarrow agent^O(\overline{oa}, o)$;
> | **return** (o, a)

Next, we need the function reward from Algorithm 4, which computes the total discounted reward given a world (selecting the observations), an agent (assumed to control the actions), and the history so far. Total reward is computed using an exponential discount factor $0 < \gamma < 1$. We multiply by $1 - \gamma$ to make total reward sum to a number between 0 and 1. With this rescaling, total discounted reward starting from step t is no more than $(1 - \gamma) \sum_{s=t}^{\infty} \gamma^{s-1} = \gamma^{t-1}$.

Algorithm 4. The distribution over real numbers defined by this probabilistic machine is the distribution of the future discounted reward of *agent* interacting with *world*, given that the history $\overline{oa}$ has already occurred.

---

def reward^O(*world*, *agent*, $\overline{oa}$):
    for $n = 1, 2, \ldots$ **do**
        $\overline{oa} \longleftarrow$ append $(\overline{oa}, \text{step}^O(\textit{world}, \textit{agent}, \overline{oa}))$;
        seen $\longleftarrow (1 - \gamma) \sum_{t=1}^{n} \gamma^{t-1} \cdot r_t(\overline{oa})$;
        output (*seen*, *seen* $+ \gamma^n$);

With reward in hand, an agent which achieves the maximum expected (discounted) reward in a given environment μ, can be defined as in rAI$_\mu$. Algorithm 5 defines a machine actionReward$^O(a)$, which computes the reward if the agent takes action a in the next timestep and in future timesteps behaves like the optimal agent rAI$_\mu$. It then defines a machine difference$^O()$, which computes the difference in the discounted rewards when taking action 1 and when taking action 0, then rescales this difference to the interval $[0, 1]$ and flips a coin with the resulting probability. Finally, rAI$_\mu$ uses the oracle to determine whether the probability that difference$^O() = 1$ is greater than $1/2$, which is equivalent to asking whether the expectation of actionReward$^O(1)$ is greater than the expectation of actionReward$^O(0)$; if the expectations are equal, the oracle may behave randomly, but this is acceptable, since in this case the agent is indifferent between its two actions. Note that Algorithm 5 references its own source code (actionReward passes the source of rAI$_\mu$ to reward); this is possible by quining (Kleene's second recursion theorem).

Algorithm 5. Reflective AI$_\mu$.

---

def rAI$^O_\mu$($\overline{oa}$, o):
    def actionReward$^O(a)$:
        return reward^O $(\mu, \text{rAI}_\mu, \text{append}\,(\overline{oa}, (o, a)))$
    def difference$^O()$:
        return flip$^O \left(\dfrac{\text{actionReward}^O(1) - \text{actionReward}^O(0) + 1}{2} \right)$
    return O (difference, ϵ, $1/2$);

We can now obtain a reflective version of AIXI by instantiating the environment μ in rAI$_\mu$ to a universal environment ξ, which (in analogy with Solomonoff induction) selects a random environment and then behaves like this environment. As in our implementation of Solomonoff induction, we use rejection sampling, sampling a random machine T and keeping it with probability getHistProb$^O(T, \overline{oa}, o')$, which computes the probability that environment T will produce an observation starting with prefix o' given the previous history $\overline{oa}$ (Algorithm 8). ξ will find the next bit of the next observation after any $\overline{oa}$ sequence followed by a prefix o' of the next observation.

Algorithm 6. A variant of reflective Solomonoff induction used by reflective AIXI. It takes a series of observation/action pairs and updates its simplicity distribution according to the likelihood that an environment produced the observations in this sequence (holding the actions fixed).

> **def** $\xi^O(\overline{x})$:
> > split $\overline{x}$ into a sequence $\overline{oa}$ of observations and actions and a prefix o' of the next observation;
> > **repeat**
> > > $T \longleftarrow$ randomMachine$^O()$;
> > > **if** flip^O(getHistProb$^O(T, \overline{oa}, o')$ **then return** flip(getProb$(T, \overline{oa}o', 1)$));
>
> **def** rAIXI$^O(\overline{oa}, o)$:
> > **return** rAI$_\xi^O(\overline{oa}, o)$)

---

5 Conclusions

Our model of agents interacting with an environment is quite reminiscent of classical game theory, in which all agents are assumed to be logically omniscient: indeed, reflective oracles can be used to provide new foundations for classical game theory in which the agents are not ontologically distinct from the rest of the game, but rather are ordinary features of the environment [2].

Realistic models of artificial reasoners must dispense with this guarantee of logical omniscience, and consider agents that reason under logical uncertainty. Even reasoners that have perfect knowledge about other agents (for example, reasoners which possess the source code of a different, deterministic agent) may not be able to deduce exactly how that agent will behave, due to computational limitations. Such limitations are not captured by models of reflective AIXI.

Nevertheless, we expect that studying the behavior of powerful reasoners in reflective environments will shed some light on how powerful bounded reasoners can perform well in more realistic settings. These reflective environments provide the beginnings of a suite of tools for studying agents that can reason about the environment in which they are embedded, and which can reason about universes which contain other agents of similar capabilities.

It is our hope that, through studying this simple model of reflective agents, it will be possible to gain insights into methods that agents can use to learn the environment which embeds them (as discussed by Soares [7]), while reasoning well in the presence of agents which are as powerful or more powerful than the reasoner (as discussed by Fallenstein and Soares [1]). For example, these reflective versions of Solomonoff induction and AIXI open up the possibility of studying agents in settings where the agent/environment boundary breaks down (as discussed by Orseau and Ring [6]), or agents in settings containing other similarly powerful agents. A first step in this direction is suggested by a result of Fallenstein, Taylor, and Christiano [2], which shows that it is possible to define a computable version of reflective oracles, defined only on the set of probabilistic oracles machines whose length is $\leq l$ and which are guaranteed to halt within a time bound t; this appears to be exactly what is needed to translate our reflective variant of AIXI into a reflective, computable variant of AIXI^{tl}.

A   Appendix: Helper functions

Algorithm 7. Computes the probability that machine T outputs $\overline{y}$ conditional on it already outputting $\overline{x}$, as a real number represented by an infinite sequence of nested intervals..

---

def getStringProb$^O(T, \overline{x}, \overline{y})$:
    return $\prod_{i=1}^{\text{len}(\overline{y})}$ getProb$^O(T, \overline{xy}_{1:i-1}, \overline{y}_i)$

Algorithm 8. Computes the probability that T would output the observations in $\overline{oa}$ and the additional observation prefix o', given that the agent responds with the actions in $\overline{oa}$.

---

def getHistProb$^O(T, \overline{oa}, o')$:
    return
    $\left(\prod_{i=1}^{\text{len}(\overline{oa})} \text{getStringProb}^O(T, \overline{oa}_{1:i-1}, \text{fst}(\overline{oa}_i)) \right) \cdot \text{getStringProb}^O(T, \overline{oa}, o'));$

Algorithm 9. Generates a random machine T with probability $2^{-\text{len}(T)}$.

---

def randomMachine$^O()$:
    prefix $\longleftarrow \epsilon$;
    repeat
        if *prefix* is a valid machine **then return** *prefix*;
        else *prefix* $\longleftarrow$ append(*prefix*, tossCoin());

Algorithm 10. Outputs 1 with probability *weight*, 0 otherwise.

---

def flip$^O(weight)$:
    upper $\longleftarrow 1$;
    lower $\longleftarrow 0$;
    for (l, u) **in** *weight* **do**
        middle $\longleftarrow$ $(upper + lower)/2$;
        if tossCoin() $= 1$ **then** *upper* $\longleftarrow$ *middle*;
        else *lower* $\longleftarrow$ *middle*;
        if *upper* $< l$ **then return** 1;
        else if *lower* $> u$ **then return** 0;

References

1. Fallenstein, B., Soares, N.: Vingean reflection: Reliable reasoning for self-modifying agents. Tech. Rep. 2015–2, Machine Intelligence Research Institute (2015). https://intelligence.org/files/VingeanReflection.pdf
2. Fallenstein, B., Taylor, J., Christiano, P.F.: Reflective oracles: A foundation for classical game theory. Tech. Rep. 2015–7, Machine Intelligence Research Institute (2015). https://intelligence.org/files/ReflectiveOracles.pdf
3. Hutter, M.: Universal algorithmic intelligence. In: Goertzel, B., Pennachin, C. (eds.) Artificial General Intelligence, pp. 227–290. Springer, Cognitive Technologies (2007)
4. Hutter, M.: Open problems in universal induction & intelligence. Algorithms **2**(3), 879–906 (2009)
5. Legg, S., Hutter, M.: Universal intelligence. Minds and Machines **17**(4), 391–444 (2007)
6. Orseau, L., Ring, M.: Space-Time Embedded Intelligence. In: Bach, J., Goertzel, B., Iklé, M. (eds.) AGI 2012. LNCS, vol. 7716, pp. 209–218. Springer, Heidelberg (2012)
7. Soares, N.: Formalizing two problems of realistic world-models. Tech. Rep. 2015–3, Machine Intelligence Research Institute (2015). https://intelligence.org/files/RealisticWorldModels.pdf
8. Solomonoff, R.J.: A formal theory of inductive inference. Part I. Information and Control **7**(1), 1–22 (1964)
9. Vallinder, A.: Solomonoff Induction: A Solution to the Problem of the Priors? MA thesis, Lund University (2012). http://lup.lub.lu.se/luur/download?func=downloadFile&recordOId=3577211&fileOId=3577215

Are There Deep Reasons Underlying the Pathologies of Today's Deep Learning Algorithms?

Ben Goertzel[(✉)]

OpenCog Foundation, Tai Po, Hong Kong
ben@goertzel.org

Abstract. Some currently popular and successful deep learning architectures display certain pathological behaviors (e.g. confidently classifying random data as belonging to a familiar category of nonrandom images; and misclassifying miniscule perturbations of correctly classified images). It is hypothesized that these behaviors are tied with limitations in the internal representations learned by these architectures, and that these same limitations would inhibit integration of these architectures into heterogeneous multi-component AGI architectures. It is suggested that these issues can be worked around by developing deep learning architectures that internally form states homologous to image-grammar decompositions of observed entities and events.

1 Introduction

In recent years "deep learning" architectures – specifically, systems that roughly emulate the visual or auditory cortex, with a goal of carrying out image or video or sound processing tasks – have been getting a lot of attention both in the scientific community and the popular media. The attention this work has received has largely been justified, due to the dramatic practical successes of some of the research involved. In image classification, in particular (the problem of identifying what kind of object is shown in a picture, or which person's face is shown in a picture), deep learning methods have been very successful, coming reasonably close to human performance in various contexts. Current deep learning systems can be trained by either supervised or unsupervised methods, but it's the supervised-learning approaches that have been getting the great results and headlines. Two good summaries of the state of the art are Juergen Schmidhuber's recent review with 888 references [13], and the in-process textbook by Yoshua Bengio and his colleagues [1].

The precise definition of "deep learning" is not very clear, and the term seems to get wider and wider as it gets more popular. Broadly, I think it works to consider a deep learning system as a learning system consisting of adaptive units on multiple layers, where the higher level units recognize patterns in the outputs of the lower level units, and also exert some control over these lower-level units. A variety of deep learning architectures exist, including multiple sorts of neural

ⓒ Springer International Publishing Switzerland 2015
J. Bieger (Ed.): AGI 2015, LNAI 9205, pp. 70–79, 2015.
DOI: 10.1007/978-3-319-21365-1_8

nets (that try to emulate the brain at various levels of precision), probabilistic algorithms like Deep Boltzmann machines, and many others. This kind of work has been going on since the middle of the last century. But only recently, due to the presence of large amounts of relatively inexpensive computing power and large amounts of freely available data for training learning algorithms, have such algorithms really begun to bear amazing practical fruit.

A paper by Stanford and Google researchers [8], which reported work using a deep learning neural network to recognize patterns in YouTube videos, received remarkable press attention in 2012. One of the researchers was Andrew Ng, who in 2014 was hired by Baidu to lead up their deep learning team. This work yielded some fascinating examples most famously, it recognized a visual pattern that looked remarkably like a cat. This is striking because of the well-known prevalence of funny cat videos on Youtube. The software's overall accuracy at recognizing patterns in videos was not particularly high, but the preliminary results showed exciting potential.

Another dramatic success was when Facebook, in mid-2014, reported that they had used a deep learning system to identify faces in pictures with over 97% accuracy [15] – essentially as high as human beings can do. The core of their system was a Convolutional Neural Network (CNN), a pretty straightforward textbook algorithm that bears only very loose conceptual resemblance to anything "neural". Rather than making algorithmic innovations, the main step the Facebook engineers took was to implement their CNN on massive scale and with massive training data. A Chinese team has since achieved even higher accuracies than Facebook on standard face recognition benchmarks, though they also point out that their algorithm misses some cases that most humans would get correctly [16].

Deep learning approaches to audition have also been very successful recently. For a long time the most effective approach to speech-to-text was a relatively simple technique known as "Hidden Markov Models" or HMMs. HMMs appear to underlie the technology of Nuance, the 800-pound gorilla of speech-to-text companies. But in 2013 Microsoft Research published a paper indicating their deep learning speech-to-text system could outperform HMMs [2]. In December 2014 Andrew Ng's group at Baidu announced a breakthrough in speech processing – a system called Deep Speech, which reportedly gives drastically fewer errors than previous systems in use by Apple, Google and others [7].

With all these exciting results, it's understandable that many commentators and even some researchers have begun to think that current deep learning architectures may be the key to advanced and even human-level AGI. However, my main goal in this article is to argue, conceptually, why this probably isn't the case. I will raise two objections to the hypothesis:

1. Current deep learning architectures (even vaguely) mirror the structure and information-processing dynamics of – at best – only parts of the human brain, not the whole human brain
2. Some (and I conjecture nearly all) current deep learning architectures display certain pathological behaviors (e.g. confidently classifying random data as

belonging to a familiar category of nonrandom images; and misclassifying miniscule perturbations of correctly classified images), which seem to be traceable to the nature of their internal knowledge representation. In this sense they seem not to robustly mirror the information-processing dynamics of the parts of the brain they resemble most, the visual and auditory cortex

My core thesis here is that these two objections are interconnected. I hypothesize that the pathological behaviors are rooted in shortcomings in the internal (learned) representations of popular deep learning architectures, and these shortcomings also make it difficult to connect these architectures with other AI components to form integrated systems better resembling the architecturally heterogeneous, integrative nature of the human brain.

I will also give some suggestions as to possible remedies for these problems.

2   Broad and Narrow Interpretations of "Deep Learning"

In his book "Deep Learning" [12], cognitive scientist Stellan Ohlsson formulates the concept of deep learning as a general set of information-processing principles. He also makes clear that these principles could be implemented in many different kinds of systems, including neural networks but also including logic systems or production rule systems or many other possibilities:

- **Spontaneous activity:** The cognitive system is constantly doing things, always processing inputs if they are there, and always reprocessing various of its representation of its inputs
- **Structured, unbounded representations:** Representations are generally built out of other representations, giving a hierarchy of representations. The lowest level representations are not fixed but are ongoingly reshaped based on experience
- **Layered, feedforward processing:** Representations are created via layers of processing units, with information passing from lower layers up to higher layers
- **Selective, capacity-limited processing:** Processing units on each layer pass information upward selectively each one generally passes up less information than it takes in, and doesn't pass it everywhere that it could
- **Ubiquitous monotonic learning:** Some of the representations the system learns are stored in long term memory, others aren't
- **Local coherence and latent conflict:** The various representations learned by a system don't have to be consistent with each other overall. Consistency is worked toward locally when inconsistencies between elements are found; there's no requirement of global consistency.
- **Feedback and point changes:** Higher level processing units feed information down to lower level units, thus potentially affecting their dynamics
- **Amplified propagation of point changes:** A small change anywhere in the processing hierarchy might cause a large change elsewhere in the system – as typical of complex and "chaotic" dynamical systems

- **Interpretation and manifest conflict:** Conflict between representations may go unnoticed until a particular input comes in, which then reveals that two previously learned representations can be in conflict
- **Competitive evaluation and cognitive utility:** Conflict between representations are resolved broadly via "reinforcement learning", i.e. based on which representation proves most useful to the overall system in which context

In the context of my own AI work with the OpenCog AGI architecture [5] [6], I find it interesting to note that, of Ohlsson's principles of deep learning, only one ("Representations are created via layers of processing units") does not apply to OpenCog's AtomSpace knowledge store, a heterogeneously structured weighted, labeled hypergraph. So to turn OpenCog into a deep learning system in Ohlsson's sense, it would suffice to arrange some OpenCog Nodes into layers of processing units. Then the various OpenCog learning dynamics including, e.g. Probabilistic Logic Networks reasoning, which is very different in spirit from currently popular deep learning architectures would become "deep learning" dynamics.

Of course, restricting the network architecture to be a hierarchy doesn't actually make the learning or the network any more deep. A more freely structured hypergraph like the general OpenCog Atomspace is just as deep as a deep learning network, and has just as much (or more) complex dynamics. The point of hierarchical architectures for visual and auditory data processing is mainly that, in these particular sensory data processing domains, one is dealing with information that has a pretty strict hierarchical structure to it. It's very natural to decompose a picture into subregions, subsubregions and so forth; and to define an interval of time (in which e.g. sound or video occurs) into subintervals of times. As we are dealing with space and time which have natural geometric structures, we can make a fixed processing-unit hierarchy that matches the structure of space and time lower-down units in the hierarchy dealing with smaller spatiotemporal regions; parent units dealing with regions that include the regions dealt with by their children; etc. For this kind of spatiotemporal data processing, a fairly rigid hierarchical structure makes a lot of sense (and seems to be what the brain uses). For other kinds of data, like the semantics of natural language or abstract philosophical thinking or even thinking about emotions and social relationships, this kind of rigid hierarchical structure seems much less useful, and in my view a more freely-structured architecture may be more appropriate.

In the human brain, it seems the visual and auditory cortices have a very strong hierarchical pattern of connectivity and information flow, whereas the olfactory cortex has more of a wildly tangled-up, "combinatory" pattern. This combinatory pattern of neural connectivity helps the olfactory cortex to recognize smells using complex, chaotic dynamics, in which each smell represents an "attractor state" of the olfactory cortex's nonlinear dynamics (as neuroscientist Walter Freeman has argued in a body of work spanning decades [10]). The portions of the cortex dealing with abstract cognition have a mix of hierarchical and combinatory connectivity patterns, probably reflecting the fact that they do both hierarchy-focused pattern recognition as we see in vision and audition, and attractor-based pattern recognition as we see in olfaction. But this is largely speculation most likely, until we can make movies somehow of the neural dynamics corresponding to various kinds of cognition, we won't really know how these various structural and dynamical patterns come together to yield human thinking.

My own view is that for anything resembling a standard 2015-style deep learning system (say, a convolutional neural net, stacked autoencoder, etc.) to achieve anything like human-level intelligence, major additions would have to be made, involving various components that mix hierarchical and more heterogeneous network structures in various ways. For example: Take "episodic memory" (your life story, and the events in it), as opposed to less complex types of memory. The human brain is known to deal with the episodic memory quite differently from the memory of images, facts, or actions. Nothing, in currently popular architectures commonly labeled "deep learning", tells you anything about how episodic memory works. Some deep learning researchers (based on my personal experience in numerous conversations with them!) would argue that the ability to deal with episodic memories effectively will just emerge from their hierarchies, if their systems are given enough perceptual experience. It's hard to definitively prove this is wrong, because these models are all complex dynamical systems, which makes it difficult to precisely predict their behavior. Still, according to the best current neuroscience knowledge [3], the brain doesn't appear to work this way; episodic memory has its own architecture, different in specifics from the architectures of visual or auditory perception. I suspect that if one wanted to build a primarily brain-like AGI system, one would need to design (not necessarily strictly hierarchical) circuits for episodic memory, plus dozens to hundreds of other specialized subsystems.

3 Pathologies of Contemporary Deep Learning Architectures

Even if current deep learning architectures are limited in scope, they could still be ideal solutions for certain aspects of the AGI problem, e.g. visual and auditory data processing. In fact, though, they seem to be subject to certain pathologies – and these pathologies seem (though have not been demonstrated) to be related to properties that would make it difficult to integrate these architectures into multi-component AGI architectures.

In a paper titled "Deep Neural Networks are Easily Fooled: High Confidence Predictions for Unrecognizable Images" [11], one group of researchers showed they could construct images that looked random to the human eye, but that were classified by a CNN deep learning vision network as representing particular kinds of objects, with high confidence. So, a picture that looks like random noise to any person, might look exactly like a frog or a cup to the CNN. We may call this the **random images pathology**.

Another group, in a paper titled "Intriguing properties of neural networks" [14], showed that by making a very small perturbation to a correctly classified

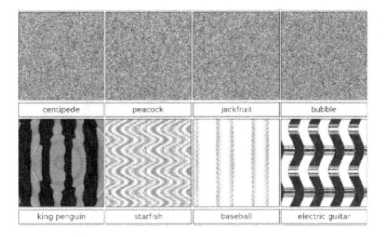

Fig. 1. From Examples of images that are unrecognizable to humans, but that state-of-the-art deep neural networks trained on the standard ImageNet image collection believe with ≥ 99.6% certainty to be a familiar object. From [11].

image, they could cause the deep network to misclassify the image. The perturbations in question were so small that humans wouldn't even notice. We may call this the **brittleness pathology**.

Now, these two odd phenomena have no impact on practical performance of convolutional neural networks. So one could view them as just being mathematical pathologies found by computer science geeks with too much time on their hands. The first pathology is pragmatically irrelevant because a real-world vision system is very unlikely to ever be shown weird random pictures that just happen to trick it into thinking it's looking at some object (most weird random pictures won't look like anything to it). The second one is pragmatically irrelevant because the variations of correctly classified pictures that will be strangely misclassified, are very few in number. Most variations would be correctly classified. So these pathologies will not significantly affect classification accuracy statistics. Further, these pathologies have only been demonstrated for CNNs – I suspect they are not unique to CNNs and would also occur for other currently popular deep learning architectures like stacked autoencoders but this has not been demonstrated.

But I think these pathologies are telling us something. They are telling us that, fundamentally, these deep learning algorithms are not generalizing the way that people do. They are not classifying images based on the same kinds of patterns that people are. They are "overfitting" in a very subtle way not overfitting to the datasets on which they've been trained, but rather overfitting to the kind of problem they've been posed. In these examples, these deep networks have been asked to learn models with high classification accuracy on image databases and they have done so. They have not been asked to learn models

Fig. 2. All images in the right column are incorrectly classified as ostriches by the CNN in question. The images in the left column are correctly classified. The middle column shows the difference between the left and right column. From [14].

that capture patterns in images in a more generally useful way, that would be helpful beyond the image classification task and so they have not done that.

When a human recognizes an image as containing a dog, it recognizes the eyes, ears and nose and fur, for example. Because of this, if a human recognized the image on the bottom left of the right image array in Figure 188 as a dog, it would surely recognize the image on the bottom right of the right image array as a dog as well. But a CNN is recognizing the bottom left image differently than a human in a way that fundamentally generalizes differently, even if this difference is essentially irrelevant for image classification accuracy.

I strongly suspect there is a theorem lurking here, stating in some way that these kinds of conceptually pathological classification errors will occur if and only if the classification model learning algorithm fails to recognize the commonly humanly recognizable high level features of the image (e.g. eyes, ears, nose, fur in the dog example). Informally, what I suspect is: The reason these pathologies occur is that these deep networks are not recognizing the "intuitively right" patterns in the images. They are achieving accurate classification by finding clever combinations of visual features that let them distinguish one kind of picture from another but these clever combinations don't include a humanly meaningful decomposition of the image into component parts, which is the kind of "hierarchical deep pattern recognition" a human's brain does on looking at a picture.

There are other kinds of AI computer vision algorithms that do a better job of decomposing images into parts in an intuitive way. Stochastic image grammars [17] are one good example. However, these algorithms are more complicated and more difficult to implement scalably than CNNs and other currently popular deep learning algorithms, and so they have not yet yielded equally high quality image classification results. They are currently being developed only minimally, whereas CNNs and their ilk are being extremely heavily funded in the tech industry.

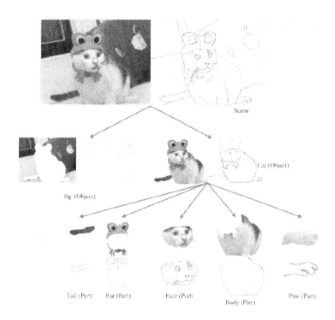

Fig. 3. Illustrative example of an image grammar for a simple object. Image grammar based methods have been used for object classification as well, though not yet with comparable accuracy to, say, CNNs or stacked autoencoders. From [11].

Connecting these different threads of research I suggest that the pathological results noted above would occur even on corpora generated by formal image grammars:

Proposition 1. *Suppose one generated a large corpus of images, falling into N commonsensical categories, based on a moderately complex, but formally defined image grammar. Then training current deep learning architectures on this corpus would yield the brittleness and random images pathologies.*

If true, this could be useful for studying the pathologies and how to eliminate them, especially in conjunction with the proposition suggested below.

4   A Possible Way Out

How then could these pathologies be avoided, staying within the general deep learning framework? And would avoiding these pathologies actually give any practical benefit?

I believe, but have not rigorously shown, that there is a sensible and viable way to bypass the random image and brittleness pathologies, not via any clever tricks but via modifying deep learning algorithms to make them create more sensible internal knowledge representations. Specifically, I suggest:

Proposition 2. *For a deep learning hierarchy to avoid the brittleness and random images pathologies (on a corpus generated from an image grammar, or on a corpus of natural images), there would need to be a reasonably straightforward mapping from recognizable activity patterns on the different layers, to elements of a reasonably simple image grammar, so that via looking at the activity patterns on each layer when the network was exposed to a certain image, one could read out the "image grammar decomposition" of the elements of the image. For instance, if one applied the deep learning network to a corpus images generated from a commonsensical image grammar, then the deep learning system would need to learn an internal state in reaction to an image, from which the image-grammar decomposition of the image was easily decipherable.*

As stated this is an intuitive rather than formal proposition. Approaches to formalization will be interesting to explore.

If this hypothesis is conceptually correct, then one interesting research direction might be to generate corpora using image grammars, and see what it would take to get a deep learning algorithm to learn the image grammar from the corpus, in the sense of emerging a structure in which the image grammar is observable. Once this worked, the same algorithm could be applied to natural-image corpora and the results analyzed.

My colleagues and I have pursued one approach to making a deep learning network capable of learning an internal image grammar. In this approach, reported in [4], the states of the DeSTIN deep learning algorithm are saved and frequent patterns in the state-set are mined. A DeSTIN network state may then be labeled with the frequent patterns from the learned pattern-library that are instantiated in that state. These labels, in simple cases, appear function like an image grammar. But it is not clear how general or robust this phenomenon is; this requires further study.

Another question is whether difference target propagation, as proposed in [9], might display the property suggested in Proposition 2. Difference target propagation seeks to minimize reconstruction error at each level in a deep hierarchy (as opposed to propagating error backwards from the top of a network as in standard gradient descent methods). Whether, and under what circumstances, this may cause formation of a meaningful image grammar inside a network's state, is a fascinating open question.

References

1. Bengio, Y., Goodfellow, I.J., Courville, A.: Deep learning (2015). http://www.iro.umontreal.ca/bengioy/dlbook, book in preparation for MIT Press
2. Deng, L., Li, J., Huang, J.T., Yao, K., Yu, D., Seide, F., Seltzer, M., Zweig, G., He, X., Williams, J., Gong, Y., Acero, A.: Recent advances in deep learning for speech research at microsoft. In: IEEE International Conference on Acoustics, Speech, and Signal Processing (ICASSP) (2013)
3. Gazzaniga, M.S., Ivry, R.B., Mangun, G.R.: Cognitive Neuroscience: The Biology of the Mind. W W Norton (2009)

4. Goertzel, B.: Perception Processing for General Intelligence: Bridging the Symbolic/Subsymbolic Gap. In: Bach, J., Goertzel, B., Iklé, M. (eds.) AGI 2012. LNCS, vol. 7716, pp. 79–88. Springer, Heidelberg (2012)
5. Goertzel, B., Pennachin, C., Geisweiller, N.: Engineering General Intelligence, Part 1: A Path to Advanced AGI via Embodied Learning and Cognitive Synergy. Springer, Atlantis Thinking Machines (2013)
6. Goertzel, B., Pennachin, C., Geisweiller, N.: Engineering General Intelligence, Part 2: The CogPrime Architecture for Integrative, Embodied AGI. Springer, Atlantis Thinking Machines (2013)
7. Hannun, A.Y., Case, C., Casper, J., Catanzaro, B.C., Diamos, G., Elsen, E., Prenger, R., Satheesh, S., Sengupta, S., Coates, A., Ng, A.Y.: Deep speech: Scaling up end-to-end speech recognition. CoRR abs/1412.5567 (2014). http://arxiv.org/abs/1412.5567
8. Le, Q.V., Ranzato, M., Monga, R., Matthieu Devin, K.C., Corrado, G.S., Dean, J., Ng., A.Y.: Building high-level features using large scale unsupervised learning. In: Proceedings of the Twenty-Ninth International Conference on Machine Learning (2012)
9. Lee, D., Zhang, S., Biard, A., Bengio, Y.: Target propagation. CoRR abs/1412.7525 (2014). http://arxiv.org/abs/1412.7525
10. Li, G., Lou, Z., Wang, L., Li, X., Freeman, W.J.: Application of chaotic neural model based on olfactory system on pattern recognition. ICNC **1**, 378–381 (2005)
11. Nguyen, A., Yosinski, J., Clune, J.: Deep neural networks are easily fooled: High confidence predictions for unrecognizable images. CoRR abs/1412.1897 (2014). http://arxiv.org/abs/1412.1897
12. Ohlsson, S.: Deep Learning: How the Mind Overrides Experience. Cambridge University Press (2006)
13. Schmidhuber, J.: Deep learning in neural networks: An overview. CoRR abs/1404.7828 (2014). http://arxiv.org/abs/1404.7828
14. Szegedy, C., Zaremba, W., Sutskever, I., Bruna, J., Erhan, D., Goodfellow, I.J., Fergus, R.: Intriguing properties of neural networks. CoRR abs/1312.6199 (2013). http://arxiv.org/abs/1312.6199
15. Taigman, Y., Yang, M., Ranzato, M., Wolf, L.: Deepface: Closing the gap to human-level performance in face verification. In: Conference on Computer Vision and Pattern Recognition (CVPR) (2014)
16. Zhou, E., Cao, Z., Yin, Q.: Naive-deep face recognition: Touching the limit of lfw benchmark or not? (2014). http://arxiv.org/abs/1501.04690
17. Zhu, S.C., Mumford, D.: A stochastic grammar of images. Found. Trends. Comput. Graph. Vis. **2**(4), 259–362 (2006). http://dx.doi.org/10.1561/0600000018

Speculative Scientific Inference via Synergetic Combination of Probabilistic Logic and Evolutionary Pattern Recognition

Ben Goertzel [1,2]([✉]), Nil Geisweiller[1], Eddie Monroe[2], Mike Duncan[2], Selamawit Yilma[3], Meseret Dastaw[3], Misgana Bayetta[4], Amen Belayneh[4], Matthew Ikle'[4,5], and GinoYu[4]

[1] OpenCog Foundation, Tai Po, Hong Kong
ben@goertzel.org
[2] SciCog Systems, California, USA
[3] iCog Labs, Addis Ababa, Ethiopia
[4] School of Design, Hong Kong Poly U, Hung Hom, Hong Kong
[5] Adams State College, Alamosa, USA

Abstract. The OpenCogPrime cognitive architecture is founded on a principle of "cognitive synergy" – judicious combination of different cognitive algorithms, acting on different types of memory, in a way that helps overcome the combinatorial explosions each of the algorithms would suffer if used on its own. Here one manifestation of the cognitive synergy principle is explored – the use of probabilistic logical reasoning (based on declarative knowledge) to generalize procedural knowledge gained by evolutionary program learning. The use of this synergy is illustrated via an example drawn from a practical application of the OpenCog system to the analysis of gene expression data, wherein the MOSES program learning algorithm is used to recognize data patterns and the PLN inference engine is used to generalize these patterns via cross-referencing them with a biological ontology. This is a case study of both automated scientific inference, and synergetic cognitive processing.

1 Introduction

Conceptually founded on the "patternist" systems theory of intelligence outlined in [4] and implemented in the OpenCog open-source software platform, the OpenCogPrime (OCP) cognitive architecture combines multiple AI paradigms such as uncertain logic, computational linguistics, evolutionary program learning and connectionist attention allocation in a unified architecture [7] [8]. Cognitive processes embodying these different paradigms, and generating different kinds of knowledge (e.g. declarative, procedural, episodic, sensory) interoperate together on a common neural-symbolic knowledge store called the Atomspace. The interaction of these processes is designed to encourage the self-organizing emergence of high-level network structures in the Atomspace, including superposed hierarchical and heterarchical knowledge networks, and a self-model network enabling meta-knowledge and meta-learning.

© Springer International Publishing Switzerland 2015
J. Bieger (Ed.): AGI 2015, LNAI 9205, pp. 80–89, 2015.
DOI: 10.1007/978-3-319-21365-1_9

This overall architecture can be used as a tool within practical applications in areas such as data analysis or natural language processing. For instance, the OpenCog system, leveraging elements of the OpenCogPrime design, has been used for commercial applications in the area of natural language processing and data mining; e.g. see [9] where OpenCog's PLN reasoning and RelEx language processing are combined to do automated biological hypothesis generation based on information gathered from PubMed abstracts. The same system can also be used to control an intelligent embodied agent (e.g. a game character [6] or robot [11]). In this case the focus of the system's cognition is to find and execute the procedures that it believes have the best probability of working toward its goals in its current context.

Memory Types in OpenOCP. OCP's main memory types are the declarative, procedural, sensory, and episodic memory types that are widely discussed in cognitive neuroscience [14], plus attentional memory for allocating system resources generically, and intentional memory for allocating system resources in a goal-directed way. Table 1 overviews these memory types, giving key references and indicating the corresponding cognitive processes, and which of the generic patternist cognitive dynamics each cognitive process corresponds to (pattern creation, association, etc.).

The essence of the OCP design lies in the way the structures and processes associated with each type of memory are designed to work together in a closely coupled way, the operative hypothesis being that this will yield cooperative intelligence going beyond what could be achieved by an architecture merely containing the same structures and processes in separate "black boxes." This sort of cooperative emergence has been labeled "cognitive synergy." In this spirit, the inter-cognitive-process interactions in OpenCog are designed so that conversion between different types of memory is possible, though sometimes computationally costly (e.g. an item of declarative knowledge may with some effort be interpreted procedurally or episodically, etc.)

A Practical Example of Procedural/Declarative Synergy. We describe here some currently ongoing work using OpenCog, and elements of the OCP design, to analyze genomic data using a combination of two different OpenCog cognitive processes: the MOSES procedure learning algorithm, and the PLN probabilistic logic engine. This work is a practical illustration of the cognitive synergy principle: PLN helps MOSES overcome its difficulty with generalization, and MOSES helps PLN overcome its difficulty scanning large datasets for patterns. The two together can find abstract patterns in datasets, via MOSES first finding concrete patterns and PLN then abstracting them. The result is a novel form of automated speculative scientific inference that is potentially quite powerful.

While this particular genomics application is "narrow AI", the fact that it is being carried out in a software framework and cognitive architecture oriented toward general intelligence means that development and conceptual refinement done in the context of this application can be used for any OpenCog application. Further, many of the lessons learned in the context of this work are quite generally

Table 1. Memory Types and Cognitive Processes in OpenCog Prime. The third column indicates the general cognitive function that each specific cognitive process carries out, according to the patternist theory of cognition.

Memory Type	Specific Cognitive Processes	General Cognitive Functions
Declarative	Probabilistic Logic Networks (PLN) [3]; concept blending [2]	pattern creation
Procedural	MOSES (a novel probabilistic evolutionary program learning algorithm) [12]	pattern creation
Episodic	internal simulation engine [6]	association, pattern creation
Attentional	Economic Attention Networks (ECAN) [10]	association, credit assignment
Intentional	probabilistic goal hierarchy refined by PLN and ECAN, structured according to MicroPsi [1]	credit assignment, pattern creation
Sensory	In OpenCogBot, this will be supplied by the DeSTIN component	association, attention allocation, pattern creation, credit assignment

applicable, e.g. the highlighting of the "rule choice" problem as the key issue in PLN inference control (as will be discussed at the end).

2   Cognitive Synergy for Procedural and Declarative Learning

The specific work to be discussed here involves combined use of OpenCog's MOSES and PLN cognitive algorithms; we now briefly indicate what each of these does, pointing to prior references for details.

MOSES for Automated Program Learning. MOSES, OCP's primary algorithm for learning procedural knowledge, has been tested on a variety of application problems including standard GP test problems, virtual agent control, biological data analysis and text classification [12]. It represents procedures internally as program trees. Each node in a MOSES program tree is supplied with a "knob," comprising a set of values that may potentially be chosen to replace the data item or operator at that node. So e.g. a node containing the number 7 may be supplied with a knob that can take on any integer value. A node containing a while loop may be supplied with a knob that can take on various possible control flow operators including conditionals or the identity. A node containing a procedure representing a particular robot movement, may be supplied with a knob that can take on values corresponding to multiple possible movements. The metaphor is that MOSES learning covers both "knob twiddling" (setting the values of knobs) and "knob creation."

One common application of MOSES is to the supervised or unsupervised analysis of datasets. In this case MOSES is learning procedures that take in a dataset, and output a prediction of what category that dataset belongs to, or what properties that dataset has. For example, consider the following MOSES model learned in the context of supervised-classification analysis of a gene expression dataset comprising 50 human nonagenarians and 50 middle-aged controls [13]:

```
or(and(or(!$TTC3 !$ZNF542P)
or(!$LOC285484 !$RAI2 $CCNA1)
or($SERPING1 !$NLRC3))
and(!$SEMA7A !$LOC285484 !$LOC100996246)
and($SEMA7A $TJP2 !$ARMC10)
and($LOC100996246 $PSRC1 $SLC7A5P1))
==> nonagenarian
```

The semantics here is that:

- The variable containing the name of a gene, e.g. "$RAI2", denotes the predicate "Gene $RAI2 was overexpressed, i.e. expressed greater than the median across all genes, in the gene expression dataset corresponding to a particular person."
- if this Boolean combination of variables is true, then the odds are higher than average that the person is a nonagenarian rather than a control

This particular model has moderate but not outstanding statistics on the dataset in question (precision $=$ .6, recall $=$ .92, accuracy $=$ .77), and was chosen for discussion here because of its relatively simple form.

PLN for Probabilistic Logical Inference. OCP's primary tool for handling declarative knowledge is an uncertain inference framework called Probabilistic Logic Networks (PLN). The complexities of PLN are the topic of two lengthy technical monographs [3] [5], and here we will eschew most details and focus mainly on pointing out how PLN seeks to achieve efficient inference control via integration with other cognitive processes.

As a logic, PLN is broadly integrative: it combines certain term logic rules with more standard predicate logic rules, and utilizes both fuzzy truth values and a variant of imprecise probabilities called *indefinite probabilities*. PLN mathematics tells how these uncertain truth values propagate through its logic rules, so that uncertain premises give rise to conclusions with reasonably accurately estimated uncertainty values.

PLN can be used in either forward or backward chaining mode. In backward chaining mode, for example,

1. Given an implication $L \equiv A \to B$ whose truth value must be estimated, create a list $(A_1, ..., A_n)$ of *(inference rule, stored knowledge)* pairs that might be used to produce L
2. Using analogical reasoning to prior inferences, assign each A_i a probability of success

- If some of the A_i are estimated to have reasonable probability of success at generating reasonably confident estimates of L's truth value, then invoke Step 1 with A_i in place of L (at this point the inference process becomes recursive)
- If none of the A_i looks sufficiently likely to succeed, then inference has "gotten stuck" and may be abandoned; or, another cognitive process may optionally be invoked, e.g. various options (not all currently implemented and tested) include:
  - **Concept creation** may be used to infer new concepts related to A and B, and then Step 1 may be revisited, in the hope of finding a new, more promising A_i involving one of the new concepts
  - **MOSES** may be invoked with one of several special goals, e.g. the goal of finding a procedure P so that $P(X)$ predicts whether $X \to B$. If MOSES finds such a procedure P then this can be converted to declarative knowledge understandable by PLN and Step 1 may be revisited....
  - **Simulations** may be run in OCP's internal simulation engine, so as to observe the truth value of $A \to B$ in the simulations; and then Step 1 may be revisited....

3   Example of PLN Inference on MOSES Output

Now we give a specific example of how PLN and MOSES can be used together, via applying PLN to generalize program trees learned by MOSES. We will use the MOSES model given above, learned via analysis of nonagenarian gene expression data, as an example. Further details on the specific inferences described here can be found in online supplementary material at http://goertzel.org/BioInference. pdf.

As the MOSES model in question is at the top level a disjunction, it's easy to see that, if we express the left hand side in OpenCog's Atomese language [1] using ANDLinks, ORLinks and NOTLinks, a single application of the PLN rule

```
Implication
    AND
        OR
            ListLink: $L
        MemberLink
            $X
            $L
    $X
```

will yield corresponding implications for each clause, such as

```
and($SEMA7A $TJP2 !$ARMC10) ==> nonagenarian
```

---

[1] See e.g. [7] for a review of this notation.

for the third second-level clause. For the rest of our discussion here we will focus on this clause due to its relatively small size. Of course, similar inferences to the ones we describe here can be carried out for larger clauses and for Boolean combinations with different structures. The PLN software deals roughly equally well with Boolean structures of different shapes and size.

This latter implication, in the OpenCog Atomspace, actually takes the form

```
ImplicationLink
    ANDLink
        ExecutionOutputLink
            SchemaNode "makeOverexpressionPredicate"
            GeneNode "SEMA7A"
        ExecutionOutputLink
            SchemaNode "makeOverexpressionPredicate"
            GeneNode "TJP2"
        NotLink
            ExecutionOutputLink
                SchemaNode "makeOverexpressionPredicate"
                GeneNode "ARMC10"
    PredicateNode "Nonagenarian"
```

where

```
EquivalenceLink
    EvaluationLink
        ExecutionOutputLink
            SchemaNode "makeOverexpressionPredicate"
            GeneNode $G
        ConceptNode $H
    EvaluationLink
        GroundedPredicateNode "scm:above-median"
        ListLink
            ExecutionOutputLink
                SchemaNode "makeExpressionLevelPredicate"
                GeneNode $G
            ConceptNode $H
            ConceptNode $P


EquivalenceLink
    EvaluationLink
        ExecutionOutputLink
            SchemaNode "makeExpressionLevelPredicate"
            GeneNode $G
        ConceptNode $H
    EvaluationLink
        PredicateNode "Expression level"
        ListLink
            GeneNode $G
            ConceptNode $H
```

where

- "scm:above-median" is a helper function that evaluates if a certain predicate (arg1) evaluated at arg2 is above the median of the set of values obtained by applying arg1 to every member of the category arg3.
- "makeExpressionLevelPredicate level" is a schema that outputs, for an argument $G, a predicate that is evaluated for an argument that represents an organism, and outputs the expression of $G in that organism.
- "Expression level" is a predicate that outputs, for arguments $G and $H, the level of expression of $G in organism $H.

Being a nonagenarian in itself is not that interesting, but if you know the entity in question is a human (instead of, say, a bristlecone pine tree), then it becomes interesting indeed. This knowledge is represented via

```
ImplicationLink
    AND
        PredicateNode "Human"
        PredicateNode "Nonagenarian"
    PredicateNode "LongLived"
```

from which PLN can conclude

```
ImplicationLink
    ANDLink
        ExecutionOutputLink
            PredicateNode "makeOverexpressionPredicate"
            GeneNode "SEMA7A"
        ExecutionOutputLink
            PredicateNode "makeOverexpressionPredicate"
            GeneNode "TJP2"
        NotLink
            ExecutionOutputLink
                PredicateNode "makeOverexpressionPredicate"
                GeneNode "ARMC10"
    PredicateNode "LongLived"
```

Next, how can PLN generalize this MOSES model? One route is to recognize patterns spanning this model and other MOSES models in the Atomspace. Another route, the one to be elaborated here, is cross-reference it with external knowledge resources, such as the Gene Ontology (GO). The GO is one of several bio knowledge resources we have imported into a bio-oriented OpenCog Atomspace that we call the Biospace.

Each of these three genes in our example belongs to multiple GO categories, so there are many GO-related inferences to be done regarding these genes. But for sake of tractable exemplification, let's just look at a few of the many GO categories involved:

- SEMA7A is_a GO:0045773 (positive regulation of axon extension)
- TJP2 is_a GO:0006915 (apoptotic process)
- ARMC10 is_a GO:0040008 (regulation of growth)

Let us also note a relationship between the first and third of these GO categories, drawn from the GO hierarchy:

- GO:0045773 is_a GO:0048639 (positive regulation of developmental growth)
- GO:0048639 is_a GO:0045927 (positive regulation of growth)
- GO:0045927 is_a GO:0040008 (regulation of growth)

As well as these relationships between genes and GO categories, the Biospace also contains knowledge

```
AssociativeLink
    ConceptNode "GO:0006915"
    PredicateNode "LongLived"
```

which is derived from the known association of multiple genes in the category GO:0006915 with longevity. From this, PLN can derive that

```
ImplicationLink
    MemberLink
        $G
        ConceptNode "GO:0006915"
    ImplicationLink
        ExecutionOutputLink
            PredicateNode "makeOverexpressionPredicate"
            $G
        PredicateNode "LongLived"
```

, i.e. that overexpression of genes in this GO category is likely to imply longevity. Since this GO categories contains one of the genes (TJP2) in the MOSES model under study, after a few PLN steps, this background knowledge, combined with the MOSES model, increases the estimated odds that the other two genes in the MOSES model are related to longevity, e.g. that

```
ImplicationLink
    MemberLink
        $G
        ConceptNode "ARMC10"
    ImplicationLink
        ExecutionOutputLink
            PredicateNode "makeOverexpressionPredicate"
            $G
        PredicateNode "LongLived"
```

Further, the membership of these other two genes in the GO category "GO:0040008" allows PLN to derive the abstraction

```
ImplicationLink
    AssociativeLink
        ConceptNode "GO:0040008"
        $L
    ImplicationLink
        ANDLink
```

```
AppendLink
   ListLink: $L
   ExecutionOutputLink
      PredicateNode "makeOverexpressionPredicate"
      GeneNode "TJP2"
PredicateNode "LongLived"
```

What this means, intuitively, is that combinations of TJP2 with growth-regulation genes tends to promote longevity. This is interesting, among other reasons, because it's exactly the kind of abstraction a human mind might form when looking at this kind of data.

In the above examples we have omitted quantitative truth values, which are attached to each link, and depend on the specific parameters associated with the PLN inference formulas. The probability associated with the final Implication-Link above is going to be quite low, below 0.1 for any sensible parameter values. However, this is still significantly above what one would expect for a linkage of the same form with a random GO and gene inside it. We are not aiming to derive definite conclusions here, only educated speculative hypotheses, able to meaningfully guide further biological experimentation.

The "cognitive synergy" in the above may not be glaringly obvious but is critical nonetheless. MOSES is good at learning specific data patterns, but not so good at learning abstractions. To get MOSES to learn abstractions of this nature would be possible but lead to significant scalability problems. On the other hand, PLN is good at abstracting from particular data patterns, but doesn't have control mechanisms scalable enough to enable it to scan large datasets and pick out the weak but meaningful patterns among the noise. MOSES is good at this. The two algorithms working together can, empirically speaking, create generalizations from large, complex datasets, significantly better than either algorithm can alone.

4   Conclusions and Next Steps

The work described here has its specialized aspects, but also leads to various general ideas and lessons. Conceptual interplay between practical applications to complex real-world data and more abstract AGI R&D, helps to push both pursuits forward.

The workflow described above uses MOSES to analyze data and produce classification models, and PLN to draw conclusions from these models via cross-referencing them with external knowledge or (not elaborated above) one another. The loop may be closed by taking the genes highlighted as most relevant by PLN (in the above case, the genes found to imply longevity most strongly via combination of PLN) and using them as a restricted input feature set for MOSES. MOSES can then learn more models based on this feature set, which can then be exported to the Atomspace and used by PLN, etc. In this way PLN is being used to enable a kind of MOSES recursive feature selection.

One of the main lessons learned in experimenting with inferences like the ones mentioned above, is that the primary AI difficulty involved is telling PLN which rules to choose in what order. Choosing which nodes (e.g. GeneNodes) to include is challenging as well but is addressed via OpenCog's activation-spreading-like ECAN component. Choosing which rules to apply when is not currently handled effectively; but in [7] it is proposed to do this via assigning probabilities to sequences of rule-choices (conditional on the context), thus allowing "rule macros" (i.e. sequences of rules) to be applied in a fairly habitual way in a given domain of inference. But of course that is a high-level description and there will be some devils in the details. It has been previously proposed to use pattern mining to learn macros of this nature, and it's clear this will be a good approach and necessary in the medium term. However, a simpler approach might be to simply run a bunch of inferences and store Markov probabilities indicating which chains of rule-applications tended to be useful and which did not; this might provide sufficient rule-choice guidance for "relatively simple" inferences like the ones given here.

References

1. Bach, J.: Principles of Synthetic Intelligence. Oxford University Press (2009)
2. Fauconnier, G., Turner, M.: The Way We Think: Conceptual Blending and the Mind's Hidden Complexities. Basic (2002)
3. Goertzel, B., Ikle, M., Goertzel, I., Heljakka, A.: Probabilistic Logic Networks. Springer (2008)
4. Goertzel, B.: The Hidden Pattern. Brown Walker (2006)
5. Goertzel, B., Coelho, L., Geisweiller, N., Janicic, P., Pennachin, C.: Real World Reasoning. Atlantis Press (2011)
6. Goertzel, B., Et Al, C.P.: An integrative methodology for teaching embodied non-linguistic agents, applied to virtual animals in second life. In: Proc.of the First Conf. on AGI. IOS Press (2008)
7. Goertzel, B., Pennachin, C., Geisweiller, N.: Engineering General Intelligence, Part 1: A Path to Advanced AGI via Embodied Learning and Cognitive Synergy. Atlantis Thinking Machines. Springer (2013)
8. Goertzel, B., Pennachin, C., Geisweiller, N.: Engineering General Intelligence, Part 2: The CogPrime Architecture for Integrative, Embodied AGI. Atlantis Thinking Machines. Springer (2013)
9. Goertzel, B., Pinto, H., Pennachin, C., Goertzel, I.F.: Using dependency parsing and probabilistic inference to extract relationships between genes, proteins and malignancies implicit among multiple biomedical research abstracts. In: Proc. of Bio-NLP 2006 (2006)
10. Goertzel, B., Pitt, J., Ikle, M., Pennachin, C., Liu, R.: Glocal memory: a design principle for artificial brains and minds. Neurocomputing, April 2010
11. Goertzel, B.: Opencogbot: An integrative architecture for embodied agi. In: Proc. of ICAI 200, Beijing (2010)
12. Looks, M.: Competent Program Evolution. PhD Thesis, Computer Science Department, Washington University (2006)
13. Passtoors, W., Boer, JM., Goeman, J., Akker, E.:Transcriptional profiling of humanfamilial longevity indicates a role for asf1a and il7r. PLoS One (2012)
14. Tulving, E., Craik, R.: The Oxford Handbook of Memory. Oxford U. Press (2005)

Stochastic Tasks: Difficulty and Levin Search

José Hernández-Orallo[✉]

DSIC, Universitat Politècnica de València, València, Spain
jorallo@dsic.upv.es

Abstract. We establish a setting for asynchronous stochastic tasks that account for episodes, rewards and responses, and, most especially, the computational complexity of the algorithm behind an agent solving a task. This is used to determine the difficulty of a task as the (logarithm of the) number of computational steps required to acquire an acceptable policy for the task, which includes the exploration of policies and their verification. We also analyse instance difficulty, task compositions and decompositions.

Keywords: Task difficulty · Task breadth · Levin's search · Universal psychometrics

1 Introduction

The evaluation of cognitive features of humans, non-human animals, computers, hybrids and collectives thereof relies on a proper notion of 'cognitive task' and associated concepts of task difficulty and task breadth (or alternative concepts such as composition and decomposition). The use of formalisms based on transition functions such as (PO)MDP (for discrete or continuous cases) is simple, but have some inconveniences. For instance, the notion of computational cost must be derived from the algorithm behind the transition function, which may have a very high variability of computational steps depending on the moment: at idle moments it may do just very few operations, whereas at other iterations it may require an exponential number of operations (or even not halt). The maximum, minimum or average for all time instants show problems (such as dependency on the time resolution). Also, the use of transition functions differs significantly in the way animals (including humans) and many agent languages in AI work, with algorithms that can use signals and have a control of time through threads (using, e.g., "sleep" instructions where computation stops momentarily).

The other important thing is the notion of response, score or return R for an episode. Apart from relaxing its functional dependency with the rewards during an episode, to account with a goal-oriented task, we consider the problem of commensurability of different tasks by using a level of tolerance, and deriving the notion of acceptable policy from it. While this seems a cosmetic change, it paves the way to the notion of difficulty —as difficulty does not make sense if we do not set a threshold or tolerance— and also to the analysis of task instances.

© Springer International Publishing Switzerland 2015
J. Bieger (Ed.): AGI 2015, LNAI 9205, pp. 90–100, 2015.
DOI: 10.1007/978-3-319-21365-1_10

After these instrumental accommodations, the straightforward idea of difficulty as search effort is used. Difficulty is just the logarithm of the computational steps that are required to find an acceptable policy, including the execution of several possible policies and verifying them. This is in accordance with Levin's universal search [10,11], the notion of information gain [4] and the interpretation of the "minimal process for creating [something] from nothing" [12].

The notion of task instance difficulty is more controversial, as it usually assumes that it is relative to the task (e.g., '30+0' is an easy instance of the addition task) or even to the policy (e.g., 'sort gabcdef' is a very easy case for a particular sorting algorithm). Note that average-case complexity in complexity theory refers to how many computational steps are employed to solve a set of instances (with a distribution) given a particular algorithm —or for every possible conceivable algorithm. But one question that is not usually made is: How can we say that 'sort gabcdef' is easier than 'sort gdaefcb' without setting an algorithm or the distribution of algorithms?

The paper is organised as follows. Section 2 gives a setting for stochastic tasks, responses, difficulty and acceptability (using a tolerance level). Section 3 discusses whether the notion of task difficulty can be inherited for instances. Then we move to the notions of task composition and decomposition and their implications. Section 4 introduces a variant of Levin search that includes a new term into Kt, which is based on the number of repetitions that are needed to verify that a policy is ϵ-acceptable with some given confidence $1 - \delta$, à la PAC (Probabilistic Approximate Correct). Section 5 closes the paper.

2 Stochastic Tasks, Trials, Responses and Difficulty

Let us give the definition of asynchronous-time interactive systems. In an asynchronous-time interactive system, there is a common shared time (which can be discrete or continuous, and can be virtual or real). An *interactive system* is a machine with a program code, a finite internal discrete memory, one or more finite read-only discrete input tapes and one or more finite write-only discrete output tapes. The inputs of agents are called observations and the outputs are called actions. For tasks, it is the other way round. As special features, these machines have access to a read-only time measurement and a source of randomness (either by an additional random instruction or a random tape). The programs for tasks and agents are constructed with a Turing-complete set of instructions. The programs can be coded over a reference universal prefix Turing machine U. This makes this definition very close to probabilistic Turing machines. For the purpose of the analysis of computational steps, we consider an instruction or special state sleep(t), which sets the machine to sleep until time t.

Some tasks will also have intermediate rewards. Rewards are just given through another extra tape, and are interpreted as a natural number. Rewards are optional. In case they exist, the result of an episode may depend on the rewards or not. This is important, as the general use of rewards in reinforcement learning, especially with discounted reward or through averaging, gives the impression that the final result or response of an episode must always be an aggregation of rewards. For instance, in a maze, an agent may go directly to the exit and may require no reward. On the contrary, a more sluggish agent may require more positive indications and even with them cannot find the exit. Rewards can be just given to help in the finding of the solution. Finally, the agent is able to see the result or score of an episode at the end through another special tape. A final reward can be given instead of or jointly with the result.

The expected value of the response, return or result of agent π for task μ for a time limit τ is denoted by $\mathbb{R}^{[\tau]}(\pi, \mu)$. The value of τ will be usually omitted as it is understood that it is part of the description of the task μ. The $\mathbb{R}$ function always gives values between 0 and 1 and we assume it is always defined. If the agent goes into a non-halting loop and stops reacting, this is not perceivable externally and may even lead to some non-zero $\mathbb{R}$.

Now we need to extend the notation of $\mathbb{R}(\pi, \mu)$ to consider several instances of the same task. Each attempt of a subject on one of the task instances is a trial or episode. $\mathbb{R}^{[\mapsto \nu]}(\pi, \mu)$ returns the expected response of μ per trial with ν consecutive episodes or trials by the same agent π *without reinitialisation*. So actually it is not the same π each time, if the agent has memory. According to the task, the same instance can appear more than once, as in a sample with replacement. As the task can have memory, we can also have some tasks that are really working as if a no-replacement sampling were taking place. In order to do that, the task itself must keep track of the instances that have appeared or must use some kind of randomised enumeration. Also, tasks can be adaptive.

With $\mathbb{R}^{[\mapsto 1]}(\pi, \mu)$, or simply $\mathbb{R}(\pi, \mu)$, we denote that there is only one episode or trial. For instance, many tests are of this kind if items are completely unrelated, with no influence on the following ones, although it is more applicable when we consider that the agent has no memory (or is reinitialised between trials). In general, especially if the items are related, for every $\nu > 1$, we have that $\mathbb{R}^{[\mapsto \nu]}(\pi, \mu) \neq \mathbb{R}^{[\mapsto 1]}(\pi, \mu)$ unless the agent has no memory between episodes.

Our view of difficulty is "algorithmic", which is basically the computational steps required to build the policy algorithm, which depends on the tolerance level of the task, the interaction and hints given by the task, the algorithm length, its computation cost and its verification cost. The first thing we will require is the length of a policy or object x, denoted by $L(x)$. The second thing we will require is the computation steps taken by a policy. In synchronous environments, the sum or average of steps of all time cycles is not very meaningful. Another option is to calculate the maximum, as done in [7] with the so-called Kt^{max}. This is a very rough approximation, as one single peak can make this very large. Fortunately, here tasks are defined as asynchronous. When the agent needs to wait until a situation or time is met, if the instruction sleep(t) is used, these 'waiting' times are not considered for the computational steps. With this interpretation, the expected[1] execution steps of π per trial when performing task μ are denoted by $\mathbb{S}^{[\mapsto \nu]}(\pi, \mu)$ with a time limit (τ) given by the task for each trial. If at any moment π enters an infinite loop, then $\mathbb{S}^{[\mapsto \nu]}(\pi, \mu)$ is infinite. The third thing is about memory requirements (space). In this paper we will not consider space

---

[1] This has to be 'expected' if we consider stochastic environments or agents.

because (1) the use of n bits of memory requires at least n computational steps, so the latter are going to be considered anyway and (2) steps and bits are different units. The fourth thing is verification. When we discuss the effort about finding a policy, there must be some degree of certainty that the policy is reasonably good. As tasks and agents are stochastic, this verification is more cumbersome than in a non-stochastic case. We will discuss about this later on in the paper. For the moment, we will just combine the length of the policy and the computational steps, by defining $\mathbb{LS}^{[\mapsto \nu]}(\pi, \mu) \triangleq L(\pi) + \log \mathbb{S}^{[\mapsto \nu]}(\pi, \mu)$. Logarithms are always binary. We will explain later on why we apply a logarithm over $\mathbb{S}$. The fifth thing is the tolerance level of the task. In many cases, we cannot talk about difficulty if there is no threshold or limit for which we consider a policy acceptable. It is true that some tasks have a response function R that can only be 0 or 1, and difficulty is just defined in terms of this goal. But many other tasks are not binary (goal-oriented), and we need to establish a threshold for them. In our case, we can take 1 as the best response and set the threshold on $1 - \epsilon$.

We now define acceptability in a straightforward way. The set of acceptable policies for task μ given a tolerance ϵ is given by

$$\mathcal{A}^{[\epsilon, \mapsto \nu]}(\mu) \triangleq \{\pi \ : \ \mathbb{R}^{[\mapsto \nu]}(\pi, \mu) \geq 1 - \epsilon\} \tag{1}$$

Note that with a tolerance greater than 0 the agent can do terribly wrong in a few instances, provided it does well on many others.

And now we are ready to link difficulty to resources. This is usual in algorithmic information theory, but here we need to calculate the complexities of the policies (the agents) and not the problems (the tasks). A common solution, inspired by Levin's Kt (see, e.g., [10] or [11]), is to define:

$$Kt^{[\epsilon, \mapsto \nu]}(\mu) \triangleq \min_{\pi \in \mathcal{A}^{[\epsilon, \mapsto \nu]}(\mu)} \mathbb{LS}^{[\mapsto \nu]}(\pi, \mu) \tag{2}$$

Note that the above has two expectations: one in $\mathbb{LS}$ and another one inside $\mathcal{A}$. The interpretation of the above expression is a measure of effort, as used with the concept of computational information gain with Kt in [4].

An option as an upper-bound measure of difficulty would be $\hbar(\mu) \triangleq Kt^{[\epsilon, \mapsto \nu]}(\mu)$, for a finite ν and given ϵ. In general, if ν is very large, then the last evaluations will prevail and any initial effort to find the policies and start applying them will not have enough weight. On the contrary, if ν is small, then those policies that invest in analysing the environment will be penalised. It also requires a good assessment of the metasearch procedure to *verify* the policy so it can go to exploitation. In any case, the notion of difficulty depends, in some tasks, on ν. We will come back to the 'verification cost' later on.

3   Task Instances, Task Composition and Decomposition

Up to this point we have dealt with a first approach to *task* difficulty. A task includes (infinitely) many task instances. What about *instance* difficulty? Does it make sense? In case it does, instance difficulty would be very useful for adaptive tests, as we could start with simple instances and adapt their difficulty to the ability of the subject (as in adaptive testing in psychometrics).

The key issue is that instance difficulty must be defined *relative to a task*. At first sight, the difference in difficulty between 6/3 and 1252/626 is just a question of computational steps, as the latter usually requires more computational steps if a general division algorithm is used. But what about 13528/13528? It looks an easy instance. Using a general division algorithm, it may be the case that it takes more computational steps than 1522/626. If we see it easy is because there are some shortcuts in *our* algorithm to make divisions. Of course, we can think about algorithms with many shortcuts, but then the notion of difficulty depends on how many shortcuts it has. In the end, this would make instance difficulty depend on a given algorithm for the task (and not the task itself). This would boil down to the steps taken by the algorithm, as in computational complexity.

We can of course take a structuralist approach, by linking the difficulty of an instance to a series of characteristics of the instance, such as its size, the similarities of their ingredients, etc. This is one of the usual approaches in psychology and many other areas, including evolutionary computation, but does not lead to a general view of what instance difficulty really is. For the divisions above, one can argue that 13528/13528 is more regular than 1252/626, and that is why the first is easier than the second. However, this is false in general, as 13528^{13528} is by no means easier than any other exponentiation.

Another perspective is "the likelihood that a randomly chosen program will fail for any given input value" [2], like the population-based approach in psychology. For this, however, we would need a population[2]. The insight comes when we see that best policies may change with variable values of ϵ. This leads to the view of the relative difficulty of an instance with respect to a task *as the minimum* $\mathbb{LS}$ *for any possible tolerance of a policy such that the instance is accepted*. We denote by μ^σ an instance of μ with seed σ (on the random tape or generator). The set of all optimal policies for varying tolerances ϵ_0 is:

$$Opt_{\mathbb{LS}}^{[\mapsto\nu]}(\mu) \triangleq \left\{ \underset{\pi\in\mathcal{A}^{[\epsilon_0,\mapsto\nu]}(\mu)}{\arg\min} \ \mathbb{LS}^{[\mapsto\nu]}(\pi,\mu) \right\}_{\epsilon_0\in[0,1]} \qquad (3)$$

And now we define the instance difficulty of μ^σ with respect to μ as:

$$\hbar^{[\epsilon,\mapsto\nu]}(\mu^\sigma|\mu) \triangleq \underset{\pi\in Opt_{\mathbb{LS}}^{[\mapsto\nu]}(\mu)\cap\mathcal{A}^{[\epsilon,\mapsto\nu]}(\mu^\sigma)}{\min} \ \mathbb{LS}^{[\mapsto\nu]}(\pi,\mu) \qquad (4)$$

Note how the order of the minimisation is arranged in equations 3 and 4 such that for the many policies that only cover μ^σ but do not solve many of the other instances, these are not considered because they are not in $Opt_{\mathbb{LS}}$.

This notion of relative difficulty is basically a notion of consilience with the task. If we have an instance whose best policy is unrelated to the best policy for the rest, then this instance will not be covered until the tolerance becomes very

---

[2] We could assume a universal distribution. This is related to the approach in this paper as the shortest policies have a great part of the mass of this distribution.

low. Of course, this will depend on whether the algorithmic content of solving the instance can be accommodated into the general policy. This is closely related to concepts such as consilience, coherence and intensionality [3–5].

Now the question is to consider how we can put several tasks together. The aggregation of several responses that are not commensurate makes no sense. This gives further justification to eq. 1, where $\mathcal{A}$ was introduced. Given two tolerance levels for each task we can see whether this leads to similar or different difficulties for each task. For instance, if the difficulties are very different, then the task will be dominated by the easy one. Given two stochastic tasks, the composition as the union of the tasks is meaningless, so we instead calculate a mixture. In particular, the composition of tasks μ_1 and μ_2 with weight $\alpha \in [0,1]$, denoted by $\alpha\mu_1 \oplus (1-\alpha)\mu_2$, is defined by a stochastic choice, using a biased coin (e.g., using α), between the two tasks. Note that this choice is made for each trial. It is easy to see that if both μ_1 and μ_2 are asyncronous-time stochastic tasks, this mixture also is. Similar to composition we can talk about decomposition, which is just understood in a straightforward way. Basically, μ is decomposable into μ_1 and μ_2 if there is an α and two tasks μ_1 and μ_2 such that $\mu = \alpha\mu_1 \oplus (1-\alpha)\mu_2$.

Now, it is interesting to have a short look at what happens with difficulty when two tasks are put together. Given a difficulty function $\hbar$, we would like to see that if $\hbar(\alpha\mu_1 \oplus (1-\alpha)\mu_2) \approx \alpha\hbar(\mu_1) + (1-\alpha)\hbar(\mu_2)$ then both tasks are related, and there is a common policy that takes advantage of some similarities. However, in order to make sense of this expression, we need to consider some values of α and fix a tolerance. With high tolerance the above will always be true as $\hbar$ is close to zero independently of the task. With intermediate tolerances, if the difficulties are not even, the optimal policies for the composed task will invest more resources for the easiest 'subtask' and will neglect the most difficult 'subtask'. Finally, using low tolerances (or even 0) for the above expressions may have more meaning, as the policy must take into account both tasks.

In fact, there are some cases for which some relations can be established. Assume 0 tolerance, and imagine that for every $1 > \alpha > 0$ we have $\hbar(\alpha\mu_1 \oplus (1-\alpha)\mu_2) \approx \alpha\hbar(\mu_1)$. If this is the case, it means that we require the same effort to find a policy for both tasks than for one alone. We can see that task μ_1 *covers* task μ_2. In other words, the optimal policy for μ_1 works for μ_2. Note that this does not mean that every policy for μ_1 works for μ_2. Finally, if μ_1 covers μ_2 and vice versa, we can say that both tasks are equivalent.

We can also calculate a distance as $d(\mu_1, \mu_2) \triangleq 2\hbar(0.5\mu_1 \oplus 0.5\mu_2) - \hbar(\mu_1) - \hbar(\mu_2)$. Clearly, if $\mu_1 = \mu_2$ then we have 0 distance. For tolerance 0 we also have that if μ_2 has difficulty close to 0 but μ_1 has a high difficulty h_1, and both tasks are unrelated but can be distinguished without effort, then the distance is h_1.

Nonetheless, there are many questions we can analyse with this conceptualisation. For instance, how far can we decompose? There are some decompositions that will lead to tasks with very similar instances or even with just one instance. Let us consider the addition task μ_{add} with a soft geometrical distribution p on the numbers to be added. With tolerance 0, the optimal policy is given by a short and efficient policy to addition. We can decompose addition into μ_{add1} and μ_{add2}, where μ_{add1} contains all the summations $0 + x$, and μ_{add2} incorporates all the rest. Given the distribution p, we can find the α such that $\mu_{add} = \alpha\mu_{add1} \oplus (1 - \alpha)\mu_{add2}$. From this decomposition, we see that μ_{add2} will have the same difficulty, as the removal of summations $0 + x$ does not simplify the problem. However, μ_{add1} is simple now. But, interestingly, μ_{add2} still covers μ_{add1}. We can figure out many decompositions, such as additions with and without carrying. Also, as the task gives more relevance to short additions because of the geometrical distribution, we may decompose the task in many one-instance tasks and a few general tasks. In the one-instance tasks we would put simple additions such as $1 + 5$ that we would just rote learn. In fact, it is quite likely that in order to improve the efficiency of the general policy for μ_{add} the policy includes some tricks to treat some particular cases or easy subsets.

The opposite direction is if we think about how far we can reach by composing tasks. Again, we can compose tasks *ad eternum* without reaching more general tasks necessarily. The big question is whether we can analyse abilities with the use of compositions and difficulties. In other words, are there some tasks such that the policies solving these tasks are frequently useful for many other tasks? That could be evaluated by looking what happens to a task μ_1 with a given difficulty h_1 if it is composed with any other task μ_2 of some task class. If the difficulty of the composed task remains constant (or increases very slightly), we can say that μ_1 covers μ_2. Are there tasks that cover many other tasks? This is actually what psychometrics and artificial intelligence are trying to unveil. For instance, in psychometrics, we can define a task μ_1 with some selection of arithmetic operations and see that those who perform well on these operations have a good arithmetic ability. In our perspective, we could extrapolate (theoretically and not experimentally) that this task μ_1 covers a range of arithmetic tasks.

4   Difficulty as Levin Search with Stochastic Verification

In previous sections we considered the length of the policy and the logarithm of its computational time through their combination $\mathbb{LS}$, which finally led to the function $Kt^{[\epsilon,\mapsto\nu]}(\mu)$. As we argued, this is given by the realisation that in order to find a policy of length $L(\pi)$ we have to try approximately $2^{L(\pi)}$ algorithms if we enumerate programs from small to large (this is basically what Levin search does, see [11, pp.577–580]). Considering that we can also gradually increase the computational steps that we devote for each of them, we get $2^{L(\pi)} \cdot \mathbb{S}(\pi,\mu)$, whose logarithm is represented by Kt. This is why we say that the unit of Kt is logarithm of computational steps.

If we try to extend this notion to tasks, the first, and perhaps most obvious and important difference with traditional Levin's universal search is that tasks are stochastic. Consequently, several trials may be needed for discarding a bad policy and the verification of a good one. Intuitively, a pair of problem and policy with low variability in the response (results) will be easier to be verified than another where results behave more stochastically.

Another difference is that we can think about a Levin search with memory (i.e., non-blind), as some of the observations on previous trials may be crucial.

We need that the policies that are tried could also be search procedures over several trials. That means that Levin search actually becomes a metasearch, which considers all possible search procedures, ordered by size and resources, similar to other adaptations of Levin search for interactive scenarios [9,13].

As tasks are stochastic, we can never have complete certainty that a good policy has been found. An option is to consider a confidence level, such that the search invests as fewer computational steps as possible to have a degree of confidence $1 - \delta$ of having found an ϵ-acceptable policy. This clearly resembles a PAC (probably approximate correct) scenario [14].

The search must find a policy with a confidence level δ, i.e., $Pr(\pi \text{ solves } \mu) \geq 1 - \delta$. If we denote the best possible average result (for an infinite number of runs) as r^*, we consider that a series of runs is a sufficient verification for a probably approximate correct (PAC) policy π for μ when:

$$Pr(r^* - \widehat{r} \leq \epsilon) \geq 1 - \delta \tag{5}$$

with $\widehat{r}$ being the average of the results of the trials (runs) so far.

First, we are going to assume that all runs take the same number of steps (a strong assumption, but let us remind that this is an upper limit), so the verification cost could be approximated by

$$\widehat{\mathbb{W}}^{[\epsilon,\delta]}(\pi, \mu) \triangleq \mathbb{S}(\pi, \mu) \cdot \mathbb{B}^{[\epsilon,\delta]}(\pi, \mu) \tag{6}$$

i.e., the expected number of steps times the expected number of verification bids.

The number of bids can be estimated if we have the mean and the standard deviation of the response for a series of runs. Assuming a normal distribution:

$$n \geq \frac{|z_{\delta/2}|^2 \sigma^2}{(\widehat{r} + \epsilon - r^*)^2} \tag{7}$$

In order to apply the above expression we need the variance σ^2. Many approaches to the estimation of a population mean with unknown σ^2 are based on a pilot or prior study (let us say we try 30 repetitions) and then derive n using the normal distribution and then use this for a Student's t distribution. Instead of this, we are going to take an iterative approach where we update the mean and standard deviation after each repetition. We consider the maximum standard deviation as a start (as a kind of Laplace correction) with two fabricated repetitions with responses 0 and 1.

Algorithm 1 is used in a modified Levin search:

Definition 1. *Levin's universal search for stochastic tasks and policies with tolerance ϵ, confidence level $1 - \delta$, and maximum response reference r^*. Given a task μ policies are enumerated in several phases, starting from phase 1. For phase i, we execute all possible policies π with $L(\pi) \leq i$ for $s_i = 2^{i-L(\pi)}$ steps each. We call function* VERIFYNORM$(\pi, \mu, \epsilon, \delta, s_{max})$ *in Algorithm 1 with $s_{max} = s_i$. While an acceptable policy is not found we continue until we complete the phase and then to a next stage $i + 1$. If an acceptable policy is found, some extra trials are performed before stopping the search for confirmation.*

Algorithm 1. VERIFICATION ALGORITHM (NORMALITY)

1: **function** VERIFYNORM(π, μ, ϵ, δ, s_{max})   ▷ s_{max} is the number of allowed steps
2:     $j \leftarrow 3$ ▷ We consider two first response with high variance
3:     $r \leftarrow 0 + 1$ ▷ One with value 0 and the other with value 1
4:     $s \leftarrow 0$
5:     $m_\pi \leftarrow \emptyset$ ▷ The algorithm π can keep memory between trials. Initially empty.
6:     **repeat**
7:         $\langle r_j, s_j, m_\pi \rangle \leftarrow Run(\pi, m_\pi, \mu, s_{max} - s)$ ▷ One trial with remaining steps
8:         $s \leftarrow s + s_j$ ▷ Accumulate steps
9:         $r \leftarrow r + r_j$ ▷ Accumulate response
10:        $\widehat{r} \leftarrow \frac{r}{j}$ ▷ Average response
11:        $\widehat{\sigma}^2 \leftarrow \mathsf{Var}[r_1 \ldots r_j]$ ▷ Variance estimation
12:        $n_0 \leftarrow \frac{|z_{\delta/2}|^2 \widehat{\sigma}^2}{(\widehat{r}+\epsilon-r^*)^2}$
13:        **if** $j \geq n_0$ **then**
14:            **if** $\widehat{r} > r^* - \epsilon$ **then return** $\langle \mathsf{TRUE}, s \rangle$ ▷ Stop because it is verified
15:            **else return** $\langle \mathsf{FALSE}, s \rangle$ ▷ Stop because it is rejected
16:            **end if**
17:        **end if**
18:        $j \leftarrow j + 1$
19:    **until** $s \geq s_{max}$
20:    **return** $\langle \mathsf{FALSE}, s \rangle$
21: **end function**

Theorem 1. *For every μ and $\epsilon, \delta > 0$, if a maximum r^* exists achievable by a computable policy and it is given, then definition 1 conducts a finite search.*

Proof. As r^* is defined as the highest expected response for a resource-bounded policy, then there is a number of phases where the optimal policy is found and there are enough steps such that $\widehat{r}$ is becoming as closer to r^* so that $\widehat{r} + \epsilon - r^*$ approaches ϵ such that is verified $Pr(r^* - \widehat{r} \leq \epsilon) \geq 1 - \delta$. Note that as results are bounded and the highest variability is $\sigma^2 = 1/4$, so $n \sim \frac{|z_{\delta/2}|^2 \sigma^2}{(\epsilon)^2}$ is bounded.

In the end, what we want is to account for the variability of computational steps given by the variance of the response and its proximity to the threshold, as both things make verification more difficult. This is finally calculated as:

$$\mathbb{B}^{[\epsilon,\delta]}(\pi, \mu) \triangleq \frac{|z_{\delta/2}|^2 \mathsf{Var}[R(\pi, \mu)]}{(\mathbb{R}(\pi, \mu) + \epsilon - r^*)^2} \tag{8}$$

For both $\mathsf{Var}[R(\pi, \mu)]$ and $\mathbb{R}(\pi, \mu)$ we consider that we include two extra responses as a start, as done in Algorithm 1. And now the effort is rewritten as:

$$\log \mathbb{F}^{[\epsilon,\delta]}(\pi, \mu) \triangleq \log(2^{L(\pi)} \cdot \widehat{\mathbb{W}}^{[\epsilon,\delta]}(\pi, \mu)) = L(\pi) + \log \widehat{\mathbb{W}}^{[\epsilon,\delta]}(\pi, \mu) \tag{9}$$

For clarity, we can expand what $\mathbb{F}$ is by using eq. 6 and eq. 8:

$$\log \mathbb{F}^{[\epsilon,\delta]}(\pi, \mu) = L(\pi) + \log \mathbb{S}(\pi, \mu) \cdot \mathbb{B}^{[\epsilon,\delta]}(\pi, \mu) = L(\pi) + \log \mathbb{S}(\pi, \mu) + \log \mathbb{B}^{[\epsilon,\delta]}(\pi, \mu)$$

From here, we can finally define a measure of difficulty that accounts for all the issues that affect the search of the policy for a stochastic task:

$$\hbar^{[\epsilon,\delta]}(\mu) \triangleq min_\pi \log \mathbb{F}^{[\epsilon,\delta]}(\pi,\mu) \tag{10}$$

5 Conclusions

As we have mentioned during this paper, the notion of task is common in AI evaluation, in animal cognition and also in human evaluation. We set tasks and agents as asynchronous interactive systems, where difficulty is seen as computational steps of a Levin search, but this search has to be modified to cover stochastic behaviours. These ideas are an evolution and continuation of early notions of task and difficulty in [8] and [6] respectively. The relevance of verification in difficulty has usually been associated with deduction. However, some works have incorporated it as well in other inference problems, such as induction and optimisation, using Levin's Kt [1,4,12]. From the setting described in this paper, many other things could be explored, especially around the notions of composition and decomposition, task instance and agent response curves.

Acknowledgements. This work has been partially supported by the EU (FEDER) and the Spanish MINECO under grants TIN 2010-21062-C02-02, PCIN-2013-037 and TIN 2013-45732-C4-1-P, and by Generalitat Valenciana PROMETEOII2015/013.

References

1. Alpcan, T., Everitt, T., Hutter, M.: Can we measure the difficulty of an optimization problem? In: IEEE Information Theory Workshop (ITW) (2014)
2. Bentley, J.G.W., Bishop, P.G., van der Meulen, M.J.P.: An empirical exploration of the difficulty function. In: Heisel, M., Liggesmeyer, P., Wittmann, S. (eds.) SAFECOMP 2004. LNCS, vol. 3219, pp. 60–71. Springer, Heidelberg (2004)
3. Hernández-Orallo, J.: A computational definition of 'consilience'. Philosophica **61**, 901–920 (2000)
4. Hernández-Orallo, J.: Computational measures of information gain and reinforcement in inference processes. AI Communications **13**(1), 49–50 (2000)
5. Hernández-Orallo, J.: Constructive reinforcement learning. International Journal of Intelligent Systems **15**(3), 241–264 (2000)
6. Hernández-Orallo, J.: On environment difficulty and discriminating power. Autonomous Agents and Multi-Agent Systems, 1–53 (2014). http://dx.doi.org/10.1007/s10458-014-9257-1
7. Hernández-Orallo, J., Dowe, D.L.: Measuring universal intelligence: Towards an anytime intelligence test. Artificial Intelligence **174**(18), 1508–1539 (2010)
8. Hernández-Orallo, J., Dowe, D.L., Hernández-Lloreda, M.V.: Universal psychometrics: measuring cognitive abilities in the machine kingdom. Cognitive Systems Research **27**, 50–74 (2014)
9. Hutter, M.: Universal Artificial Intelligence: Sequential Decisions based on Algorithmic Probability. Springer (2005)

10. Levin, L.A.: Universal sequential search problems. Problems of Information Transmission **9**(3), 265–266 (1973)
11. Li, M., Vitányi, P.: An introduction to Kolmogorov complexity and its applications, 3rd edn. Springer (2008)
12. Mayfield, J.E.: Minimal history, a theory of plausible explanation. Complexity **12**(4), 48–53 (2007)
13. Schmidhuber, J.: Gödel machines: fully self-referential optimal universal self-improvers. In: Artificial general intelligence, pp. 199–226. Springer (2007)
14. Valiant, L.G.: A theory of the learnable. Communications of the ACM **27**(11), 1134–1142 (1984)

Instrumental Properties of Social Testbeds

Javier Insa-Cabrera$^{(\boxtimes)}$ and José Hernández-Orallo

DSIC, Universitat Politècnica de València, Valencia, Spain
{jinsa,jorallo}@dsic.upv.es

Abstract. The evaluation of an ability or skill happens in some kind of testbed, and so does with social intelligence. Of course, not all testbeds are suitable for this matter. But, how can we be sure of their appropriateness? In this paper we identify the components that should be considered in order to measure social intelligence, and provide some instrumental properties in order to assess the suitability of a testbed.

Keywords: Social intelligence · Multi-Agent systems · Cooperation · Competition · Game theory · Rewards · Universal psychometrics

1 Introduction

Evaluation tools are crucial in any discipline as a way to assess its progress and creations. There are some tools, benchmarks and contests, aimed at the measurement of humanoid intelligence or the performance in a particular set of tasks. However, the state of the art of artificial intelligence (AI) and artificial general intelligence is now more focussed towards social abilities, and here the measuring tools are still rather incipient. In the past two decades, the notion of agent and the area of multi-agent systems have shifted AI to problems and solutions where 'social' intelligence is more relevant (e.g., [1,2]). This shift towards a more social-oriented AI is related to the modern view of human intelligence as highly social, actually one of the most distinctive features of human intelligence over other kinds of animal intelligence. Some significant questions that appear here are then whether we are able to properly evaluate social intelligence in general (not only in AI, but universally) and whether we can develop measurement tools that distinguish between social intelligence and general intelligence.

In this paper, we 1) identify the components that should be considered in order to assess social intelligence, and 2) provide some instrumental properties to help us determine the suitability of a testbed to be used as a social test (validity, reliability, efficiency, boundedness and team symmetry), while analyzing the influence that such components have on these properties. This helps us to pave the way for the analysis of whether many social environments, games and tests in the literature are useful for measuring social intelligence.

The paper is organized as follows. Section 2 provides the necessary background. Section 3 identifies the components that we should consider in order to measure social intelligence. Section 4 presents some instrumental properties to assess the suitability of a testbed to be used as a social intelligence test. Finally, Sect. 5 closes the paper with some discussion and future work.

© Springer International Publishing Switzerland 2015
J. Bieger (Ed.): AGI 2015, LNAI 9205, pp. 101–110, 2015.
DOI: 10.1007/978-3-319-21365-1_11

2 Background

This section gives an introduction to the concepts and terminology of multi-agent environments and serves as a background for the following sections.

2.1 Multi-agent Environments

An environment is a world where an agent can interact through observations, actions and rewards. This general view of the interaction between an agent and an environment can be extended to various agents by letting them interact simultaneously with the environment.

A multi-agent environment is an interactive scenario with several agents. An environment accepting n agents defines n parameters (one for each agent) denoted as *agent slots*. We use $i = 1, \ldots, n$ to denote the slots. Each simultaneous interaction of the n agents is called a *time step*, where the order of events is always: observations, actions and rewards. $\mathcal{O}_i$ is the observation set that the agent in slot i can perceive, $\mathcal{A}_i$ is the action set that the agent in slot i can perform and $\mathcal{R}_i \subseteq \mathbb{Q}$ represents the possible rewards obtained by the agent in slot i. For each step k, the agent in slot i must perceive an observation $o_{i,k} \in \mathcal{O}_i$, perform an action $a_{i,k} \in \mathcal{A}_i$ and obtain a reward $r_{i,k} \in \mathcal{R}_i$. We use o_k, a_k and r_k respectively to denote the joint observation, joint action and joint reward profiles of the n agents at step k (i.e., $o_k = (o_{1,k}, \ldots, o_{n,k}) \in \mathcal{O}_1 \times \cdots \times \mathcal{O}_n$ represents the joint observation profile at step k, and similarly for actions and rewards). For example, a sequence of two steps in a multi-agent environment is then a string such as $o_1 a_1 r_1 o_2 a_2 r_2$ and the string $o_{1,1} a_{1,1} r_{1,1} o_{1,2} a_{1,2} r_{1,2}$ denotes the sequence of observations, actions and rewards for the agent in slot 1.

Both the agents and the environment are defined as probabilistic measures. At step k, the term $\pi(a_{i,k}|o_{i,1}a_{i,1}r_{i,1}\ldots o_{i,k}) \rightarrow [0,1]$ denotes the probability of the agent in slot i to perform action $a_{i,k}$ after the sequence of events $o_{i,1}a_{i,1}r_{i,1}\ldots o_{i,k}$. The observation provided by the environment at step k to the agent in slot i also has a probabilistic measure $\omega(o_{i,k}|o_1 a_1 r_1 \ldots o_{k-1}a_{k-1}r_{k-1}) \rightarrow [0,1]$. As with the observation, the reward at step k to the agent in slot i is provided depending on observations, actions and rewards on previous steps $\rho(r_{i,k}|o_1 a_1 r_1 \ldots o_k a_k) \rightarrow [0,1]$. Note that the rewards obtained by each agent depend on the joint observations, actions and rewards of all the agents interacting in the environment, and not only on their own.

2.2 Teams

It is important to determine the *roles* that agents take in the environment. The key issue is to establish whether the other agents goals and interests are compatible with one's goals. The concept is complex, as alliances can be created and broken even if no clear teams are established from the beginning (and this is an interesting property of social intelligence). These roles or alliances determine two major social behaviors: cooperation and competition.

We need to decide how the environment distributes rewards among the agents. An easy possibility would be to make each agent get its rewards without further constraints over other agents' rewards. With this configuration (e.g., general-sum games), both competition and cooperation may be completely useless for most environments, as the rewards are not limited or linked to the other agents. In contrast, if we set that the total set of rewards is limited in some way, we will foster competition, as happens in zero-sum games. But in any of these two cases cooperation will hardly take place. Alliances could arise sporadically between at least two agents in order to bother (or defend against) a third agent, but we need a way to make it more likely before any (sophisticated) alliance can emerge on its own. One possible answer is the use of teams, defined as follows:

Definition 1. *Agent slots i and j are in the same team iff $\forall k : r_{i,k} = r_{j,k}$, whatever the agents present in the environment.*

which means that all agents in a team receive exactly the same rewards. Note that teams are not alliances as usually understood in game theory. In fact, teams are fixed and cannot be changed by the agents. Also, we do not use any sophisticated mechanism to award rewards, related to the contribution of each agent in the team, as it is done with the Shapley Value [3]. We just set rewards uniformly.

2.3   Multi-agent Environments Using Teams

At this moment, we are ready to define an environment with parametrized agents by only specifying their slots and their team arrangement.

Definition 2. *A multi-agent environment μ accepting $N(\mu)$ agents (i.e., the number of slots in μ) is a tuple $\langle \mathcal{O}, \mathcal{A}, \mathcal{R}, \omega, \rho, \tau \rangle$, where $\mathcal{O}$, $\mathcal{A}$, $\mathcal{R}$ represent the observation sets, action sets and reward sets respectively (i.e., $\mathcal{O} = (\mathcal{O}_1, \ldots, \mathcal{O}_{N(\mu)})$, $\mathcal{A} = (\mathcal{A}_1, \ldots, \mathcal{A}_{N(\mu)})$ and $\mathcal{R} = (\mathcal{R}_1, \ldots, \mathcal{R}_{N(\mu)})$) and ω and ρ are the observation function and reward function respectively as defined in Sect. 2.1. τ is a partition on the set of slots $\{1, \ldots, N(\mu)\}$, where each set in τ represents a team.*

Note that with this definition the agents are not included in the environment. For instance, noughts and crosses could be defined as an environment μ_{nc} with two agents, where the partition set τ is defined as $\{\{1\}, \{2\}\}$, which represents that this game allows two teams, and one agent in each. Another example is RoboCup Soccer, whose τ would be $\{\{1, 2, 3, 4, 5\}, \{6, 7, 8, 9, 10\}\}$.

We now define an *instantiation* for a particular agent setup. Formally, an *agent line-up l* is a list of agents. For instance, if we have a set of agents $\Pi = \{\pi_1, \pi_2, \pi_3, \pi_4\}$, a line-up from this set could be $l_1 = (\pi_2, \pi_3)$. The use of the same agent twice is allowed, so $l_2 = (\pi_1, \pi_1)$ is also a line-up. We denote by $\mu[l]$ the instantiation of an environment μ with a line-up l, provided that the length of l is greater than or equal to the number of agents allowed by μ (if l has more agents, the excess is ignored). The slots of the environment are then matched with the corresponding elements of l following their order. For instance, for the noughts and crosses, an instantiation would be $\mu_{nc}[l_1]$. Note that different instantiations over the same environment would normally lead to different results. We use $L^n(\Pi)$ to specify the set of all the line-ups of length n with agents of Π.

We use the notation $R_i^K(\mu[l])$, which gives us the expected result of the ith agent in line-up l for environment μ (also in slot i) during K steps. If K is omitted, we assume $K = \infty$. In order to calculate an agent's result we make use of some kind of utility function (e.g., an average of rewards).

3   Components to Consider While Evaluating Social Intelligence

The components that we consider to measure social intelligence are:

- **Set of multi-agent environments M:** The environments we use to perform the evaluation.
- **Set of agents Π:** The agents that conform the line-ups.
- **Weights:** We give weights (non-negative numbers) to the environments, their slots and the line-ups. $w_M(\mu)$ denotes a weight to environment μ from a certain set M, $w_S(i, \mu)$ denotes a weight to slot i of a certain environment μ and $w_L(l)$ denotes a weight to a line-up l formed with agents from a certain set Π, giving weights to the agents in the line-up and their positions.
- **Definition of social intelligence Υ:** The actual definition that measures social intelligence. This definition should use sets M and Π and weights over them, i.e., w_M, w_S and w_L, in some way to measure the social intelligence. As an example, we use the definition of social intelligence from [4, Sect.3.3]:

$$\Upsilon(\Pi, w_L, M, w_M, w_S) \triangleq \sum_{\mu \in M} w_M(\mu) \sum_{i=1}^{N(\mu)} w_S(i, \mu) \sum_{l \in L^{N(\mu)}(\Pi)} w_L(l) R_i(\mu[l]) \ .$$

(1)

- **Test of social intelligence $\hat{\Upsilon}$:** The final test to measure social intelligence following a definition of social intelligence Υ. The test should consist of a set of exercises and some kind of procedure to sample them. As an example, we use the definition of social intelligence test from [4, Sect.3.4]:

$$\hat{\Upsilon}[p_\Pi, p_M, p_S, p_K, n_E](\Pi, w_L, M, w_M, w_S) \triangleq \eta_{\mathcal{E}} \sum_{\langle \mu, i, l \rangle \in \mathcal{E}} w_M(\mu) w_S(i, \mu) w_L(l) R_i^K(\mu[l]) \ .$$

(2)

where $\eta_{\mathcal{E}}$ normalizes the formula with $\eta_{\mathcal{E}} = \frac{1}{\sum_{\langle \mu, i, l \rangle \in \mathcal{E}} w_M(\mu) w_S(i, \mu) w_L(l)}$, K is chosen using probability distribution p_K and the exercises $\mathcal{E}$ are sampled as:

$$\mathcal{E} \sim^{n_E} \left[\bigcup_{\mu \in M} \bigcup_{i=1}^{N(\mu)} \left\{ \langle \mu, i, l \rangle : l \in L^{N(\mu)}(\Pi) \right\} \right]_{p_{\mathcal{E}}} \ .$$

with $S \sim^n [A]_p$ being a sample S of n elements from set A using probability distribution p, and $p_\mathcal{E}$ being a distribution on the set of triplets $\langle \mu, i, l \rangle$ based on p_M, p_S and p_Π.

4   Properties

In order to evaluate social intelligence and distinguish it from general intelligence, we need tests where social ability has to be used and, also, where we can perceive its consequences. This means that not every environment is useful for measuring social intelligence and not every subset of agents is also useful. We want tests such that agents must use their social intelligence to understand and/or have influence over other agents' policies in such a way that this is useful to accomplish their goals, but common general intelligence is not enough.

Hereafter, we investigate some instrumental properties for a testbed of multi-agent environments and agents to measure social intelligence.

4.1   Validity

Validity is the most important property of a cognitive test in psychometrics. In our context, the validity of a definition is that it accounts for the notion we expect it to grasp. For instance, if we say that a given definition of Υ measures social intelligence but it actually measures arithmetic abilities then the definition is not valid. Ultimately, this depends on the choice of Π and M in Υ, such as e.g., (1).

Poor validity may have two sources (or may appear in two different variants): a definition may be too specific (it does not account for all the abilities the notion is thought to consider) or it is too general (it includes some abilities that are not part of the notion to be measured). In other words, the measure should account for *all, but not more,* of the concept it tries to represent. We refer to these two issues of validity as the generality and the specificity of the measure. While validity is not usually seen as an instrumental property, we have to say that the choices of Π and M may both have generality and specificity, which eventually can compensate, but could lead to a test that is not very effective. That means that we should try to find proper choices such that they fit the concept we want to measure precisely.

Regarding generality, we should be careful about the use of very restrictive choices for Π and M. It could be possible to find a single environment that looks ideal to evaluate social intelligence. However, using just one environment is prone to specialisation, as usual in many AI benchmarks. For instance, if we use a particular maze, then we can have good scores by evaluating a very specialized agent for this situation, which may be unable to succeed in other mazes or problems. For instance, chess with current chess players is an example where a specialized system (e.g., Deep Blue) is able to score well, while it is clearly useless for other problems. A similar over-specialisation may happen if the agent class is too small. This is usual in biology, where some species specialize for predating (or establishing a symbiosis) with other species. Consequently, the environment class and the agent class must be general enough to avoid that some predefined or hardwired policies could be optimal for these classes. This is the key issue of a (social) *intelligence* test; it must be as general as possible. We need to choose a diverse environment class. One possibility is to consider all environments (as done by [5,6]), and another is to find an environment class that is sufficiently representative (as attempted in [7]).

Similarly, we need to consider a class of agents that leads to a diversity in line-up. This class should incorporate many different types of agents: random agents, agents with some predetermined policies, agents that are able to learn, human agents, agents with low social intelligence, agents with high social intelligence, etc. The set of all possible agents (either artificial or biological) is known as *machine kingdom* in [8] and raises many questions about the feasibility of any test considering this astronomically large set. Also, there are doubts about what the weight for this universal set should be when including them into line-ups (i.e., w_L). Instead, some representative kinds of agents could be chosen. In this way, we could aim at social intelligence relative to a smaller (and well-defined) set of agents, possibly specializing the definition by limiting the resources, the program size or the intelligence of the agents.

Regarding specificity, it is equally important for a measurement to only include those environments and agents that really reflect what we want to measure. For instance, it is desirable that the evaluation of an ability is done in an environment where no other abilities are required, or in other words, we want that the environment evaluates the ability in isolation. Otherwise, it will not be clear which part of the result comes from the ability to be evaluated, and which part comes from other abilities. Although it is very difficult to avoid any contamination, the idea is to ensure that the role of these other abilities are minor, or are taken for granted for all agents. We are certainly not interested in non-social environments as this would contaminate the measure with other abilities. In fact, one of the recurrent issues in defining and measuring social intelligence is to be specific enough to distinguish it from general intelligence.

4.2   Reliability

Another key issue in psychometric tests is the notion of reliability, which means that the measurement is close to the actual value. Note that this is different to validity, which refers about the true identification or definition of the actual value. In other words, if we assume validity, i.e., that the definition is correct, reliability refers to the quality of the measurement with respect to the actual value. More technically, if the actual value of π for an ability ϕ is v then we want a test to give a value which is close to v. The cause of the divergence may be systematic (bias), non-systematic (variance) or both.

First, we need to realize that reliability applies to tests, such as e.g., (2). Reliability is then defined by considering that a test can be repeated many times, so becoming a random variable that we can compare to the true value. Formally:

Definition 3. *Given a definition of a cognitive ability Υ and a test over it $\hat{\Upsilon}$, the test error is given by:*

$$TE(\hat{\Upsilon}) \triangleq Mean((\hat{\Upsilon} - \Upsilon)^2) . \tag{3}$$

where the mean is calculated over the repeated application of the test (to one subject or more subjects).

The reason for defining test error as the mean *squared* error (and not an absolute error) is a customary choice in many measures of error, as we can decompose it into the squared bias $(Mean(\hat{\Upsilon}) - \Upsilon)^2$ and the variance of the error $Var(\hat{\Upsilon} - \Upsilon)$. If the bias is not zero this means that the procedure to sample the exercises and/or the number of steps is inappropriate. If there is a high variance, this suggests that the number of exercises is too small, or that the exercises run for a very short time.

The reliability $Rel(\hat{\Upsilon})$ can be defined as a decreasing function over $TE(\hat{\Upsilon})$, such as $Rel(\hat{\Upsilon}) = e^{-TE(\hat{\Upsilon})}$. The estimation of $TE(\hat{\Upsilon})$ or $Rel(\hat{\Upsilon})$ depends on knowing the true value of Υ. This is not possible in practice for most environments, so Υ will need to be estimated for large samples and compared with an actual test (working with a small sample).

4.3   Efficiency

This property refers to how efficient a test is in terms of the (computational) time required to get a reliable score. It is easy to see that efficiency and reliability are opposed. If we were able to perform an infinitely number of infinite exercises, then we would have $\hat{\Upsilon} = \Upsilon$, with perfect reliability, as we would exhaust Π and M. If done properly, it is usually the variance component of the reliability decomposition that is affected if we keep the bias close to 0 even with very low values for the number of exercises.

Efficiency can be defined as a ratio between the reliability and the time taken by the test.

Definition 4. *Given a definition of a cognitive ability Υ and a test over it $\hat{\Upsilon}$, the efficiency is given by:*

$$Eff(\hat{\Upsilon}) \triangleq Rel(\hat{\Upsilon})/Time(\hat{\Upsilon}) . \tag{4}$$

where $Time$ is the average time taken by test $\hat{\Upsilon}$. Time can be measured as physical (real) time or as computational time (steps).

The issue is how to choose environments and agents such that a high efficiency is attained. Clearly, if the selected environments are insensitive to agents' actions or require too many actions to affect rewards, then this will negatively affect efficiency. As we are interested in social abilities, interactivity and non-neutralism between agents' rewards must be high, as otherwise most steps will be useless to get information about the agent to evaluate. This of course includes cases where the agents are stuck or bored because their opponents (or teammates) are too good or too bad, or the environment leads the agents to heaven or hell situations where actions are almost irrelevant. A way of making tests more efficient is by the use of adaptive tests [6], [8].

4.4   Boundedness

One desirable property is that rewards are bounded, otherwise the value of Υ (such as e.g., (1)) could diverge. Any arbitrary choice of upper and lower bounds can be scaled to any other choice so, without loss of generality, we can assume that all of them are bounded between -1 and 1, i.e., $\forall i, k : -1 \leq r_{i,k} \leq 1$. Note that they are bounded for every step. So, if we use a bounded function to calculate the agent's result, then $R_i^K(\cdot)$ is also bounded.

However, bounded expected results do not ensure that Υ is bounded. In order to ensure a bounded measurement of social intelligence, we also need to consider that weights are bounded, i.e., there are constants c_M, c_S and c_L such that:

$$\forall M : \sum_{\mu \in M} w_M(\mu) = c_M \ . \tag{5}$$

$$\forall \mu : \sum_{i=1}^{N(\mu)} w_S(i, \mu) = c_S \ . \tag{6}$$

$$\forall \mu, \Pi : \sum_{l \in L^{N(\mu)}(\Pi)} w_L(l) = c_L \ . \tag{7}$$

A convenient choice is to have $c_M = c_S = c_L = 1$, and these weights would become unit measures (which should not be confused with the probabilities used to sample elements in a test). With these conditions Υ and $\hat{\Upsilon}$ are bounded.

An optional property that might be interesting occasionally is to consider environments whose reward sum is constant or zero, as zero-sum games in game theory, where $\forall k : \sum_{i=1}^{N(\mu)} r_{i,k} = 0$.

The above definition may be too strict when we have environments with an episode goal at the end, but we want some positive or negative rewards to be given while agents approach the goal. A more convenient version follows:

Definition 5. *An environment μ is zero-sum in the limit iff:*

$$\lim_{K \to \infty} \sum_{k=1}^{K} \sum_{i=1}^{N(\mu)} r_{i,k} = 0 \ . \tag{8}$$

With teams, the previous definition could be changed in such a way that:

$$\lim_{K \to \infty} \sum_{k=1}^{K} \sum_{t \in \tau} \sum_{i \in t} r_{i,k} = 0 \ . \tag{9}$$

So the sum of the agents' rewards in a team (or team's reward) does not need to be zero but the sum of all teams' rewards does. For instance, if we have a team with agents $\{1, 2\}$ and another team with agents $\{3, 4, 5\}$, then a reward (in the limit) of $1/4$ for agents 1 and 2 implies $-1/6$ for agents 3, 4 and 5. The zero-sum properties are appropriate for competition. In fact, if teams have only one agent then we have *pure competition*. We can have both competition and cooperation by using teams in a zero-sum game, where agents in a team cooperate and agents in different teams compete. If we want to evaluate *pure cooperation* (with one or more teams) then zero-sum games will not be appropriate.

4.5 Team Symmetry

In game theory, a symmetric game is a game where the payoffs for playing a particular strategy depend only on the other strategies employed by the rest of agents, not on who is playing them. This property is very useful for evaluating purposes, as the results would be independent of the position of the agent.

When using teams, this definition of symmetry must be reconsidered. The previous definition means that for each pair of line-ups with the same agents but in different order, the agents maintain their previous results. But with the inclusion of teams this definition is not appropriate. For example, using an environment with the partition of slots on teams $\tau = \{\{1,2\},\{3,4\}\}$ and line-up $l = (\pi_1, \pi_2, \pi_3, \pi_4)$, we have that agents π_1 and π_2 must both obtain the same result, as π_3 and π_4 as well. Following the definition and switching the positions of π_2 and π_3 we obtain line-up $l' = (\pi_1, \pi_3, \pi_2, \pi_4)$, which now means that agents π_1 and π_3 must have the same results (since they are now in the same team) while maintaining their previous results, as π_2 and π_4 as well. This situation can only occur when all slots (and therefore teams) obtain equal results.

Instead, we extend this definition of symmetry to include teams. First, we denote by $\sigma(l)$ the set of line-ups permuting the agent positions of line-up l. This set corresponds with the one used in game theory to define symmetry. To adapt this set to include teams, we must select a subset of line-ups from $\sigma(l)$ respecting the teams defined in τ. We denote this subset with $\sigma(l, \tau)$, where we only select line-ups from $\sigma(l)$ if original teams are maintained. Following the example, line-up l' is not included in $\sigma(l, \tau)$ since π_1 and π_3 from l' were not in the same team in l (as π_2 and π_4 as well). However, $l'' = (\pi_3, \pi_4, \pi_2, \pi_1)$ is included in $\sigma(l, \tau)$, since both pair of agents (π_1, π_2) and (π_3, π_4) are still in the same team. From here, we define team symmetry as follows:

Definition 6. *We say a multi-agent environment μ is* team symmetric *if and only if every team in τ has the same number of elements and:*

$$\forall i, K, \Pi, l \in L^{N(\mu)}(\Pi), l' \in \sigma(l, \tau) : R_i^K(\mu[l]) = R_{i'}^K(\mu[l']) \ . \tag{10}$$

where i' represents the slot of agent $l_{i:i}$ in l' and whatever the function used to calculate agents' results.

Note that we impose that every set in τ must have the same number of elements. This is because we only consider multi-agent environments to be team symmetric if we can evaluate an agent in every slot and obtain the same result. Having teams with different number of elements does not allow us to do this.

This definition now fits our goal of symmetry. But too few environments will fit this definition because it is too restrictive. We could particularize this definition of team symmetry into two parts depending on the relation between the slots, with a version known as intra-team symmetry and inter-team symmetry (for more details the reader is referred to [4, Sect.4.6]).

Definition 6 corresponds with an Intra-Team and Total Inter-Team Symmetry, where every team of agents can be located in every set of τ and in different order, maintaining their performance expectation.

5 Conclusions

Social intelligence has been an important area of study in psychology, comparative cognition and economics for more than a century, and more recently, in artificial intelligence. In this paper we have identified the components to measure social intelligence, and analyzed how we must consider these components in some instrumental properties (i.e., validity, reliability, efficiency, boundedness and team symmetry) as a first insight about what we need to create social tests.

Of course, these properties are not enough to fully assess the suitability of a testbed to measure social intelligence. Indeed, more research is needed in order to better characterize these testbeds, such as analyzing the interaction between the agents, or how cooperative/competitive the multi-agent environments are.

Acknowledgments. This work was supported by the MEC projects EXPLORA-INGENIO TIN 2009-06078-E, CONSOLIDER-INGENIO 26706 and TINs 2010-21062-C02-02, 2013-45732-C4-1-P and GVA projects PROMETEO/2011/052 and PROMETEOII2015/013. Javier Insa-Cabrera was sponsored by Spanish MEC-FPU grant AP2010-4389.

References

1. Horling, B., Lesser, V.: A Survey of Multi-Agent Organizational Paradigms. The Knowledge Engineering Review **19**, 281–316 (2004)
2. Simao, J., Demazeau, Y.: On Social Reasoning in Multi-Agent Systems. Inteligencia Artificial **5**(13), 68–84 (2001)
3. Roth, A.E.: The Shapley Value: Essays in Honor of Lloyd S. Shapley. Cambridge University Press (1988)
4. Insa-Cabrera, J., Hernández-Orallo, J.: Definition and properties to assess multi-agent environments as social intelligence tests. Technical report, CoRR (2014)
5. Legg, S., Hutter, M.: Universal Intelligence: A Definition of Machine Intelligence. Minds and Machines **17**(4), 391–444 (2007)
6. Hernández-Orallo, J., Dowe, D.L.: Measuring universal intelligence: Towards an anytime intelligence test. Artificial Intelligence **174**(18), 1508–1539 (2010)
7. Hernández-Orallo, J.: A (hopefully) unbiased universal environment class for measuring intelligence of biological and artificial systems. In: 3rd Conference on Artificial General Intelligence, pp. 182–183 (2010)
8. Hernández-Orallo, J., Dowe, D.L., Hernández-Lloreda, M.V.: Universal psychometrics: Measuring cognitive abilities in the machine kingdom. Cognitive Systems Research **27**, 50–74 (2014)

Towards Human-Level Inductive Functional Programming

Susumu Katayama(✉)

University of Miyazaki, 1-1 W. Gakuenkibanadai, Miyazaki 889-2192, Japan
skata@cs.miyazaki-u.ac.jp

Abstract. Inductive programming is the framework for automated programming, obtaining generalized recursive programs from ambiguous specifications such as input-output examples. Development of an inductive programming system at the level of human programmers is desired, but it involves the trade off between scale and versatility which are difficult to go together.

This paper presents our research idea to enable synthesis of long programs while not limiting the algorithm to any domain, by automatically collecting the usage and request frequency of each function, estimating its usefulness, and reconstructing the component library containing component functions with which to synthesize desired functions. Hopefully this research will result in a more human-like automatic programming, which can lead to the development of adaptive planning with artificial general intelligence.

Keywords: Inductive programming · Code reuse · Functional programming

1 Introduction

Inductive functional programming (IFP) is the framework for automated programming for synthesizing recursive functional programs from ambiguous specifications such as input-output examples. This paper discusses how we can realize a human-level IFP system, where *human-level* means that the system is general-purpose but at the same time can synthesize large-scale programs. *General-purpose* means that the system can cope with unexpected synthesis problems for a Turing-complete (or nearly Turing-complete) language rather than only synthesizing programs in domain-specific languages by following a tailored procedure.

Previously, we developed a general-purpose practical IFP system called MAG-ICHASKELLER[2][3][1]. MAGICHASKELLER can instantly synthesize short functional programs without any restriction of the search space based on any prior knowledge, by holding a large memoization table in the memory.

---

[1] http://nautilus.cs.miyazaki-u.ac.jp/~skata/MagicHaskeller.html

© Springer International Publishing Switzerland 2015
J. Bieger (Ed.): AGI 2015, LNAI 9205, pp. 111–120, 2015.
DOI: 10.1007/978-3-319-21365-1_12

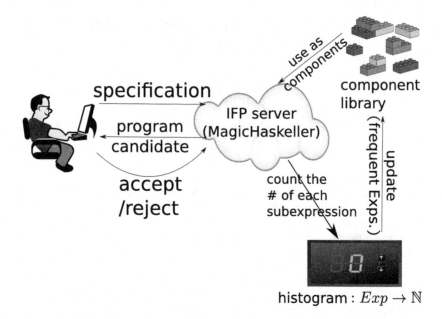

Fig. 1. Learning the component library from the data from the Internet

The other representative IFP systems are IGOR II[4] and ADATE[5]. However, those are neither updated recently nor practical. IGOR II enforces a tight restriction on the example set given as the specification, and ADATE requires high skill for synthesis of simple programs. Moreover, due to the absence of memoization, they have obvious disadvantage in the practical speed compared to MAGICHASKELLER which can start synthesis with its memoization table filled with expressions.

MAGICHASKELLER can synthesize only short expressions in a general-purpose framework by exhaustive search in the program space. In order to synthesize longer programs, the search has to be biased, because the program space is infinite. The most popular bias is *language bias* that restricts the search space around desired programs by carefully selecting the domain-specific language to be used. Language bias kills the generality, and thus is not our choice.

On the other hand, human programmers are ideal general-purpose inductive programming systems, and can synthesize programs in Turing-complete languages without any language bias. When we humans program, we name and reuse frequently-used functions and procedures, and synthesize larger libraries and programs using those library functions and procedures as the components. In other words, we adopt the bias based on the frequency of use.

The same thing can be achieved by collecting the data about how frequently each expression is requested and/or used, and organize the library consisting of frequently-used expressions and their subexpressions. This paper presents our research idea for realization of general-purpose large-scale IFP that is specialized only to people's requirements, by collecting those frequency information from the Internet and reflecting them in the *component library*, or the set of functions and non-functional values with which to synthesize compound functions, of MAGICHASKELLER.(Fig. 1)

The rest of this paper is organized in the following way. Section 2 introduces MAGICHASKELLER. Section 3 argues that learning the library is a promising approach to synthesis of longer expressions. Section 4 discusses how to learn the library, including the details such as what to synthesize and how to collect data. Section 5 discusses how this research will be evaluated. We can expect that realization of large-scale IFP by this research will result in understanding the mechanism of adaptive problem solving conducted by humans and applications to learning behavior policies of intelligent agents such as robots; this is discussed in Section 6.

2   MagicHaskeller: A General-Purpose IFP System

The proposed research idea is automatic learning of the component library used by MAGICHASKELLER based on the data collected from the Internet. This section introduces MAGICHASKELLER.

MAGICHASKELLER is the representative IFP system adopting the generate-and-test approach.[2] When an ambiguous specification such as a set of input-output examples is given, MAGICHASKELLER firstly infers the type of desired expressions. Then, it generates expressions having that type (or more general type) that can be expressed using the component library functions, combined with function applications and λ-abstractions. They are generated exhaustively from the shortest one increasing the length, in the form of the infinite stream. They are then tested against the specification in order, and those passed the test are the synthesized functions.

The function taking the given type and returning the exhaustive infinite set of expressions having the type can be implemented efficiently by memoization, for this function recursively calls itself many times, because type-correct expressions consist of type-correct subexpressions. Memoization makes execution of this function very fast in most cases after *training*, or filling up the memoization table at the invocation of the synthesizer.

If implemented naively, the memoization table can be too large even when generating only short expressions if use of higher-order functions is permitted in order to implement recursive functions. This problem can practically be avoided when synthesizing short expressions, however, by pruning semantically equivalent expressions[3] and by sharing one memoization table served by one memory-rich computer among all the clients in the world. The Web version of MAGICHASKELLER uses more than a hundred component library functions, but

---

[2] The released MAGICHASKELLER library includes the analytically-generate-and-test module, but in this paper MAGICHASKELLER refers to the other part that implements the generate-and-test approach and serves the MAGICHASKELLER ON THE WEB cloud.

thanks to this pruning the memoization table fits to the 64GB memory, and the server has been in use without any critical trouble since its birth three years ago.

Other notable features of MAGICHASKELLER include:

– it has a Web interface that enables program synthesis as offhanded as using a Web search engine;
– it supports various types, including numbers, characters, lists, tuples, higher-order functions, and their combinations.

3   Synthesizing Longer Expressions: How and Why

The points of MAGICHASKELLER are as follows:

– ability to synthesize usable expressions not limited to toy programs, by using a component library with more than a hundred functions;
– promptness thanks to memoization, despite of using such a large component library;
– avoiding redundancy in the memoization table caused by using a large component library, by eliminating expressions which are semantically equivalent to existing ones.

Although MAGICHASKELLER eliminates redundant expressions based on semantical equivalence, it cannot check infinite number of all the possible expressions within finite time. Hence, the search strategy of MAGICHASKELLER is biased to shorter expressions, based on the idea of Occam's Razor. It adopts no other bias than the length of expressions in order to cope with unexpected problem domains rather than specific use cases.

However, enumeration of expressions consisting of fixed library entities from the shortest expressions increasing the length never generates expressions longer than some length. This fact is the severest barrier when trying to make MAGICHASKELLER as powerful as human programmers.

Ideas for solving this problem include:

1. adopting the search strategy that searches promising branches deeper based on learning which branch is promising, and
2. learning the component library to make it consist of useful compound functions, and synthesizing expressions from more and more complicated components.

This paper argues that the solution 2 is promising.[3] The reasons are itemized below:

---

[3] We are *not* claiming that the solution 2 is *more* promising than the solution 1. Rather, we think that the solution 2 may be regarded as some form of the solution 1, by regarding use of learned functions as deep search without branching. Even then, the solution described in the form of the solution 2 is more straightforward than the solution 1.

– analogy to the human approach to programming and planning

As already mentioned in the introduction, the process of naming frequently-used expressions, constructing the library consisting of those named expressions, and writing more complicated programs using those names as components, is similar to the way human programmers program.

That process is also similar to the process of human planning through learning skills. Let us take the example of executing and learning the task of "going to school by train". In order to construct the solution to this task, we need to have already learned the executable solutions of its subtasks named as "walk from home to the station", "ride a train", and "walk to school". If we know how to execute those subtasks, we can find the solution of the task named as "go to school by train" by using only the subtask names and the constraints between subtasks without minding the implementation of each subtask. By repeating the solution, the name of "going to school by train" and the task are related, and the task becomes available for executing larger supertasks. This process is similar to the process of finding the desired program by combining library functions in the way consistent with their type constraints.

– analogy to successful AI approaches

Our idea of making the component library consist of useful compound functions and synthesizing expressions from more and more complicated components has similarities to the following successful AI approaches:

- **Genetic Algorithms**

  Genetic algorithms (GA) search for the fittest solutions by repeatedly applying crossovers and mutations to the population under natural selection. Adequately designed genetic algorithms sometimes find the best solution among other algorithms.

  The idea behind GA is to search among combinations of good characters via crossovers, assuming that good individuals consist of good characters. On the other hand, our presented idea is to search among combinations of component library functions which are from good (useful) expressions, assuming that good expressions consist of good subexpressions. At this point, our idea is similar to that behind GA.

  The reader may think genetic programming (GP) can be another option because it more directly inherits the idea behind GA. GP does not satisfy our purpose, however, because it requires designing of the fitness function and other parameters just for synthesizing one expression, and because it is not good at synthesizing recursive functions.

- **Deep Learning**

  Deep learning[6][1] typically performs unsupervised pre-training for units near the inputs (or units far from the outputs) to extract features in artificial neural networks (ANN) with multiple hidden layers or recurrent neural networks (RNN). By deep learning the performance of ANNs has improved by leaps and bounds.

  ANNs with multiple layers (including those obtained by unfolding RNNs) can be regarded as function models which approximate the desired func-

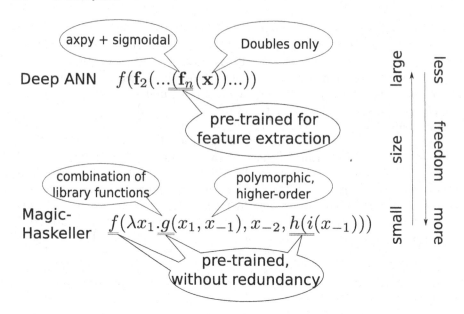

Fig. 2. Comparison with deep learning. The presented research idea adopts more flexible primitive function set than deep learning, but they are similar in that they both are pre-trained and eliminate redundancy.

tion by composing functions, where the neurons work as (families of) primitive functions. Units near inputs correspond to the innermost functions, and they play the role of extracting features.

Our presented research idea is to synthesize functions using functions from the component library, where the redundancy is eliminated by excluding semantically equivalent functions. This is similar to feature extraction by pre-training of deep learning.(Fig. 2)

4   How to Learn the Library

The previous Section 3 argued that learning the library is a promising approach to synthesis of longer expressions. This section discusses how to learn the library, including the details such as what to synthesize and how to collect data.

4.1   What to Synthesize

Currently, the algorithm of MAGICHASKELLER is mainly used for synthesis of pure Haskell functions, where *pure* means freedom from side effects. However, it can be applied to synthesis of pure functions in other higher-order languages with λ-abstraction such as JavaScript, by organizing the component library consisting of Haskell translations of library functions of the language. Moreover, technically speaking, pure functions in any language can be synthesized, provided that any

Haskell expression which MAGICHASKELLER generates can be compiled into the language.

Our current plan targets the following kinds of expressions:

- recursive functions in Haskell;
- recursive functions in JavaScript, especially, custom functions of Google Sheets;
- non-recursive functions using worksheet functions (of Microsoft Excel, &c.).

The reason for targeting spreadsheet functions as well as functions of usual programming languages is because the former can be better in the quantity and quality of collectable data. This is discussed further in Section 4.2.

As for spreadsheet functions, both recursive custom functions of Google Sheets and non-recursive worksheet functions will be dealt with. The synthesis of recursive custom functions will be dealt with because the synthesis of non-recursive functions using worksheet functions is less interesting than that of recursive functions. The synthesis of non-recursive worksheet functions will also be dealt with, because learning from abundant data collectable from the largest user base of Microsoft Excel is interesting, but it is not easy to synthesize custom functions of Excel in Visual Basic for Applications, which is first-order.

4.2 How to Collect Data

Collecting a large amount of usage data from the Internet will be a must for this research to be successful. We have two ways in mind:

1. *Providing an IFP service (or other services related to programming)*
   Since MAGICHASKELLER provides IFP service via a Web interface, we can analyze the server log to tell which queries were made and which answers were selected. This information should be useful for guessing desired functions.
   We need to take care of the quality and quantity of such queries. Most of them should be made by human users for the purpose of programming in practice in order to avoid contamination by unnaturally biased data. Currently, most of the queries to the MAGICHASKELLER server are unnatural ones based on academic curiosity about its ability, such as synthesizing the function taking x and returning $x/2$ if x is even and $x + 1$ otherwise. For this reason, it is questionable whether we should collect data for synthesis of Haskell expressions only in this way for now. This problem can be solved by increasing the percentage of practical users.
   On the other hand, spreadsheets such as Excel and Sheets have a lot of amateur users without such academic curiosity. Successful attraction for them will result in enough amount of data, though there must still be a defense against attacks for misleading the learning by a biased set of queries such as repeated identical ones.
2. *Obtaining packages from software repositories*
   If many of programs and libraries for the target language are made open-source, we can obtain a large amount of source codes by just downloading them.

The downloaded source codes can be processed in the compatible way as the queries to the server by following these steps for each function definition:
(a) generate an input-output pair for a random input, and
(b) send it as a query to the IFP server collecting data in the way described in 1. *Providing an IFP service (or other services related to programming)* to re-invent the function;
(c) if more than one program are synthesized, increase the number of random input-output pairs until one or zero program is obtained;
(d) if no program is synthesized, divide the function definition into subfunctions.

Those two ways can be combined. For example, the latter can be used to organize the initial component library, and then the former can be used to scale it up.

4.3   How to Organize and Update the Library

Frequently used expressions are candidates for component library functions because they are likely to be useful functions. However, all of such candidates cannot be adopted as component library functions with the same priority, because the space complexity increases as the number of them increases. For this reason, the library should be updated by selecting the function set rather than just adding some functions.

It is difficult to tell which is the best way of doing it now, because there are many options and parameters, and thus many policies. This section just shows the way which will be tried first.

When a Repository is Available. When dealing with a target language for which a software repository is available, we can exploit it for learning the initial configuration of the component library. In this case, the whole learning will be done in two steps:

1. Obtain the normalized set of expressions by processing the collected source codes in the way shown in Section 4.2, obtain the usage frequency of each subexpression, and obtain the set of the most frequent subexpressions for each subexpression length. They are sorted by each length, because shorter expressions tend to appear more frequently (especially any expression's frequency is always lower than or the same as those of its subexpressions). Then, organize the component library by hand using the obtained frequency information, and try the resulting IFP server. In this way, the function p which takes the length of the expression and the number it appears c and returns the priority $p(l, c)$ which the expression should have in the library can be guessed by trial-and-error.
2. Provide the IFP service, and sometimes update the library using $p(l, c + c')$ as the priority, where c' is the cumulative number the expression appears as a subexpression of each expression which is marked as correct by users. Because the cumulative values are used, it is unlikely that the library will become turbulent even when the library is updated frequently, but at the beginning each update should be checked by hand beforehand.

When a Repository is Not Available. When a repository is not available, the initial component library is set by hand in the same way as the currently-running MAGICHASKELLER server. The library can be updated in the same way as when a repository is available, using $p(l, c')$ where p is borrowed from another language.

5   Evaluation

It is difficult to fairly evaluate a general-purpose inductive programming system using a set of benchmark problems, for all the benchmark problems can easily be solved by implementing the functions to be synthesized beforehand and including them in the component library. Even if doing that is prohibited by the regulations, including their subexpressions in the component library is enough to make the problems much easier.

This issue is critical especially when evaluating results of this research, which is based on the idea: "The key to successful inductive programming systems is the choice of library functions", because we may not fixate the library for comparison, but rather we have to evaluate and compare the libraries themselves.

It would be fairer to evaluate systems from the perspective of whether the infinite set of functions that can be synthesized covers the set of many functions which the users want. In the case of this research, since IFP service will be provided as a web application, we can evaluate how the obtained IFP system can satisfy programming requests based on the results of Web questionnaire and the Web server statistics.

6   Expected Contribution to AGI

Making large-scale IFP possible by this research may uncover the mechanism of adaptive problem solving conducted by humans, and may be applied to behavior policy learning of intelligent agents.

To repeat what is stated in Section 3, this research imitates the human adaptive intelligent behaviors of programming and planning. Especially, learning to plan is important in that it explains the process of skill learning of humans.

For example, imagine children learning addition of two numbers, say, 2+3. At first, they might use two piles of apples consisting of two and three of them, and compute the result by moving apples from one pile to the other one by one. After drills, however, their brain will come to associate $2 + 3$ to 5 instantly.(Fig. 3) Once they have obtained the library function "one-digit addition", they can learn multiple-digit addition by using it, and can go further to learn multiplication. This process is quite similar to the process of learning more and more complicated library functions by the presented research idea.

Adaptive planning for intelligent agents sometimes requires learning recursive procedures. This kind of program-like procedures are difficult to be represented by function approximation such as existing artificial neural network models, while IFP systems such as MAGICHASKELLER are good at representing them.

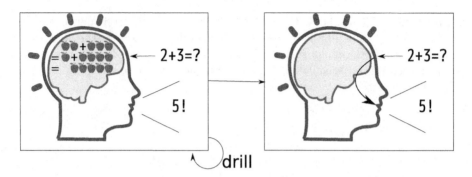

Fig. 3. Learning to calculate

Moreover, because MAGICHASKELLER can synthesize recursive programs from only a few positive examples, it can learn only from rewards, not requesting many negative examples which need to be generated by failing critically. This is why the proposed approach seems to be the best for learning complicated procedures with recursions only from the reward signal.

7   Conclusions

This paper presented our research idea for realizing a human-level IFP system by adding the library learning functionality to the Web-based general-purpose IFP system MAGICHASKELLER. It can be applied to uncovering the AGI mechanism for human-like learning of behavior and to developing intelligent agents.

References

1. Hinton, G.E., Salakhutdinov, R.R.: Reducing the Dimensionality of Data with Neural Networks. Science **313**(5786), 504–507 (2006)
2. Katayama, S.: Systematic search for lambda expressions. In: Sixth Symposium on Trends in Functional Programming, pp. 195–205 (2005)
3. Katayama, S.: Efficient exhaustive generation of functional programs using montecarlo search with iterative deepening. In: Ho, T.-B., Zhou, Z.-H. (eds.) PRICAI 2008. LNCS (LNAI), vol. 5351, pp. 199–210. Springer, Heidelberg (2008)
4. Kitzelmann, E.: A Combined Analytical and Search-Based Approach to the Inductive Synthesis of Functional Programs. Ph.D. thesis, University of Bamberg (2010)
5. Olsson, R.: Inductive functional programming using incremental program transformation. Artificial Intelligence **74**(1), 55–81 (1995)
6. Schmidhuber, J.: Learning complex, extended sequences using the principle of history compression. Neural Comput. **4**(2), 234–242 (1992)

Anytime Bounded Rationality

Eric Nivel[1(✉)], Kristinn R. Thórisson[1,2], Bas Steunebrink[3], and Jürgen Schmidhuber[3]

[1] Icelandic Institute for Intelligent Machines, Reykjavik, Iceland
eric.nivel@gmail.com
[2] Reykjavik University, CADIA, Reykjavik, Iceland
[3] The Swiss AI Lab IDSIA, USI and SUPSI, Manno, Switzerland

Abstract. Dependable cyber-physical systems strive to deliver *anticipative, multi-objective* performance *anytime,* facing deluges of inputs with *varying* and *limited* resources. This is even more challenging for life-long learning rational agents as they also have to contend with the *varying* and *growing* know-how accumulated from experience. These issues are of crucial practical value, yet have been only marginally and unsatisfactorily addressed in AGI research. We present a value-driven computational model of anytime bounded rationality robust to variations of both resources and knowledge. It leverages continually learned knowledge to anticipate, revise and maintain concurrent courses of action spanning over arbitrary time scales for execution anytime necessary.

1 Introduction

Key among the properties mission-critical systems call for is *anytime* control – the capability of a controller to produce control inputs whenever necessary, despite the lack of resources, trading quality for responsiveness [3,5]. Any practical AGI is constrained by a mission, its own architecture, and limited resources including insufficient time/memory to process all available inputs in order to achieve the full extent of its goals *when it matters*. Moreover, unlike fully hand-crafted cyber-physical systems, AGIs should handle underspecified dynamic environments, with no other choice but to *learn* their know-how, possibly throughout their entire lifetime. The challenge of anytime control thus becomes broader as, in addition to resource scarcity, it must encompass inevitable variations of completeness, consistency, and accuracy of the learned programs from which decisions are derived.

We address the requirement of delivering *anticipative, multi-objective* and *anytime* performance from a *varying body of knowledge*. A system must anticipate its environment for taking appropriate action – a controller that does not can only react after the facts and "lag behind the plant". Predictions and sub-goals must be produced concurrently: (a) since achieving goals needs predictions, the latter must be up to date; (b) a complex environment's state transitions can never be predicted entirely: the most interesting ones are those that pertain to the achievements of the system's goals, so these must be up to date when predictions are generated. A system also needs to achieve multiple concurrent goals to reach states that can only be obtained using several independent yet temporally correlated and/or co-dependent courses of action

© Springer International Publishing Switzerland 2015
J. Bieger (Ed.): AGI 2015, LNAI 9205, pp. 121–130, 2015.
DOI: 10.1007/978-3-319-21365-1_13

while anticipating and resolving potential conflicts in due time. The capabilities above must be leveraged to compute and *revise* plans continually, as resources allow and knowledge accumulates, and execute them whenever necessary, as situations unfold – this requires subjecting a system's deliberations (and execution) to deadlines relative to an external reference (world) clock.

Most of the strategies controlling the life-long learning AI systems we are aware of are subject to one or several severe impediments to the responsiveness and robustness we expect from mission- and time- critical systems. First, a sequential perception-decision-action cycle [1,6,7,8,12] limits drastically the potential for situational aware-ness and responsiveness: such "cognitive cycles" are difficult to interrupt and, being driven by *subjective* inference "steps", are decoupled from *objective* deadlines either imposed or learned. Second, interleaving multiple trains of inference in one sequential stream [1,4,6,7] results in the overall system latency adding up with the number of inputs and tasks at hand: such a system will *increasingly* and irremediably lag behind the world. Third, axiomatic reasoning [1,6,7] prevents the revision of inferences upon the acquisition of further amounts of evidence and know-how, prohibiting continual refinements and corrections. Last, the lack of explicit temporal inference capabilities [1,6,7,8] prevents learned procedural knowledge from inferring deadlines for goals and predictions, which is needed to plan over arbitrary time horizons – on that front, state-of-the-art reinforcement and evolutionary learners [9,13,2] present other inhe-rent difficulties. NARS [14] notably avoids these pitfalls and could, in principle, learn to couple subjective time semantics to a reference clock and feed them to a probabilis-tic scheduler. We set out instead to schedule inferences deterministically using objec-tive time semantics so as to avoid the unpredictability and unreliability that inevitably arise from using inferred time semantics to control the inferencing process itself.

We present a computational model of anytime bounded rationality (we refer to this model as ABR) that overcomes the limitations above. It posits (a) a dynamic hierarchy of revisable time-aware programs (called *models*) (b) exploited by concurrent inferencing jobs, that are (c) continually re-scheduled by (d) a value-driven executive under (e) bounded latencies, keeping the size of all data (inputs, inferences, programs and jobs) within (f) a fixed memory budget. This model has been implemented and tested: it constitutes the *control* core of our auto-catalytic, endogenous, reflective architecture (AERA; [10]), demonstrated to learn (by observation) to conduct multimodal interviews of humans in real-time, bootstrapped by a minimal seed [11]. While the learning algorithm of this system has been described in prior publications [10,11], its control strategy, the ABR model, has not been published elsewhere.

2   Overview of ABR Control

Our anytime bounded rationality model (ABR) assumes (Fig. 1) an executive (in black), a memory (dashed areas) and a set of I/O devices (dedicated external sub-systems). Programs include *monitors* (to assess the outcomes of goals and predictions) and *models*[1]. Models are either hand-crafted or learned from experience, and present

---

[1] Other programs construct new models from life-long experience, see [10] for details.

varying degrees of consistency, accuracy, and reliability. Jobs are requests for processing one input by one program and are executed by a pool of threads; as a result of job execution, new inputs and programs are added to the system, other programs are deleted and some inputs cancelled. ABR is data-driven: a writer (W) creates new jobs upon matching inputs to programs while an antagonist eraser (E) enforces a forgetting strategy to limit memory usage. Inputs consist of sensory inputs, *reflective* inputs (traces of model execution, see section 3), inferences and drives (drives are user-defined top-level goals and constraints). Outputs are commands executed asynchronously by the I/O devices: these respond with *efference copies*

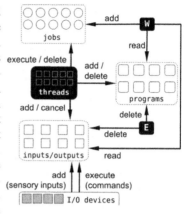

Fig. 1.

(considered sensory inputs) telling the system what has *actually* been executed (and when), as opposed to what was *intended*, thus allowing it to learn (i.e. to model) the devices' behaviors.

Models produce revisable inferences in two modes, forward chaining (predictions) and backward chaining (sub-goals). Both are performed *concurrently* – a model can produce several predictions from several different inputs while at the same time producing several sub-goals from several other goals (section 3). Motivated by drives, a hierarchy of models produces *concurrent overlapping* cascades of simulated sub-goals – at the bottom of a cascade, terminal goals embed commands to I/O devices, executed when such goals are committed to. Goal cascades simulate alternate courses of actions to achieve *multiple* (possibly) *concurrent goals*. These projected plans are continually re-evaluated upon knowledge updates (addition/deletion of inputs, inferences and models), and maintained for execution anytime it matters: continually anticipating the expiration of simulated goals' deadlines, a system is pressed to commit to these goals (and their ancestors), comparing their value (and their ancestors') to that of other conflicting or redundant goals in order to enact the best actions planned so far. In parallel to these top-down simulations, the model hierarchy is traversed by bottom-up concurrent overlapping flows of predictions originating from I/O device readouts. These warn the system of the predictable success or failure of its goals, and prompt it to adapt its behavior anticipatively by considering alternate goals, producing new ones and/or increasing or decreasing the importance of existing ones, possibly downplaying some (section 4).

Jobs are assigned a *priority* that determines the time when they may be executed. Priorities are *continually updated*, thus allowing, at any time, high-value new jobs to get executed before less important old jobs, and old jobs to become more valuable than newer ones based on new evidence. Jobs of lesser priority may get delayed repeatedly and eventually cancelled, as is likely to happen when the system is overloaded. A job priority depends on the continual assessment of the *relevance* of the program and the *tending value* of the input (see below). Threads recompute priorities, delete jobs that have become irrelevant and pick the best jobs for execution. Such scheduling overhead is *bounded by a constant* – a thread only updates the priorities of an ever-changing (fixed size) subset of the jobs[2]. All execution times are commensurate: memory usage is proactively limited (see below), and the threads', E's and W's worst-case execution times (WCET) are all *identical* and *constant*.

Assuming the life-long learning of new models and a sustained influx of inputs, the number of jobs and input-to-program matching attempts can grow exponentially and exceed the memory budget. This growth is limited by a forgetting strategy based on the prediction of the amount of available memory, inferred, conservatively, from past experience – essentially, the rates of data creation and deletion (inputs, inferences, programs and jobs). Should E anticipate a shortage, it deletes the necessary number of data in order to accommodate the next predicted influx while preserving the most valuable existing data: the top-rated candidates for deletion are the inputs that contributed the least recently to the achievement of goals, the least reliable models that succeeded the least recently, and the jobs of the least priority.

A system's experience constitutes defeasible knowledge, and is thus represented using a non-axiomatic temporal term logic, truth being neither eternal nor absolute. A term exposes three components: (a) arbitrary data, (b) a *time interval* ([early deadline, late deadline] in microseconds, world time) within which the data is believed to hold (or, if negated, during which it is believed not to hold) – an inference's lifetime being bounded by its late deadline – and, (c) a *likelihood* (in [0,1]), the degree to which the data has been ascertained. The likelihood of a sensory/reflective input is one whereas that of a drive is user-defined. An inference results from the processing of evidences by chains of models[3], and is defeated or vindicated upon further (counter-)evidences. Its likelihood is continually revised depending on the context and reliability of said models and, notably, decreases with the length of the chains (see next section).

The value of tending to an input x (sensory/reflective input, inference or drive) at time t depends on both its *urgency* (for situational awareness) and likelihood:

$$Urgency(x,t) = 1 - \frac{THZ(x,t)}{Max_i(THZ(x_i,t)) + U}$$

$$TendingValue(x,t) = Urgency(x,t) \times Likelihood(x,t)$$

where $THZ = Max(LD(x) - t, 0)$ stands for "time horizon", LD for "late deadline", x_i being all the inputs in the system and U a system parameter meant to keep urgencies positive. Now, a goal may be achieved by other means than spending effort deriving sub-goals from it (e.g. when the environment is cooperative). The value of pursuing a goal x thus decreases with the most likely prediction of its target state:

$$P(x,t) = Max_i(Likelihood(p_i,t)),$$

$$Effort(x,t) = \begin{cases} Likelihood(x,t), & Likelihood(x,t) \geq P(x,t) \\ 1 - P(x,t), & otherwise \end{cases}$$

$$TendingValue(x,t) = Urgency(x,t) \times Effort(x,t)$$

---

[2] Details on the scheduling algorithm are outside the scope of this paper.

[3] Different chains may produce several equivalent inferences, albeit with different likelihoods. Threads will execute first the jobs performing the most likely of these inferences, postponing or discarding the others.

where p_i are the predictions of x's target state. The global *relevance* of a model m is the (normalized) maximum of the tending values of all its inferences $x_i(T, m)$ of type T (*Predictions* or *Goals*) that are still alive at time t:

$$UR(m, T, t) = \underset{i}{\text{Max}}\big(TendingValue(x_i(T, m), t)\big), Relevance(m, T, t) = \frac{UR(m, T, t)}{Max_i(UR(m_i, T, t))}$$

where m_i are the models in the system. If none of the $x_i(T, m)$ are alive, then m's relevance is computed as $\frac{Min_i(UR(m_i, T, t))}{Max_i(UR(m_i, T, t))}$, giving it a chance to execute, albeit with a minimal relative priority. Finally, the priority of a chaining job is the product of the relevance of the model m and the tending value of the input x:

$$PriorityForwardChaining(x, m, t) = Relevance(m, Goals, t) \times TendingValue(x, t)$$

$$PriorityBackwardChaining(x, m, t) = Relevance(m, Predictions, t) \times TendingValue(x, t)$$

Prediction and goal monitoring jobs enjoy the same priority as, respectively, forward and backward chaining jobs.

3   Models

Models are variable defeasible knowledge: experimental evidences trigger both their construction, deletion, and the continual revision [10], of their predictive performance:

$$Reliability(m, t) = \frac{e^+(m, t)}{e(m, t) + 1}$$

where $e^+(m, t)$ is the number of successful predictions produced until any time t by a model m, and $e(m, t)$ the total number of predictions, both updated by *prediction monitors* each time a prediction fails or succeeds.

A model M (Fig. 2a) specifies a conjectured *causal relationship* between a left-hand term (LT) and a right-hand term (RT), i.e. patterns (A and B) featuring variables (X, Y and Z). When a sensory (or reflective) input or prediction a matches A (2b), M produces a prediction b, patterned after B where variables are bound to values assigned to variables shared by A or calculated as (learned) functions of values in A (fwd, embedded in the model) – in particular, time intervals are inferred this way. The forward execution of M (predicting an instance of the causal relationship) is reflected by a *model instance* term (i), interpreted as a prediction of M's success (see rationale below). For each prediction, a new program, a prediction

Fig. 2.

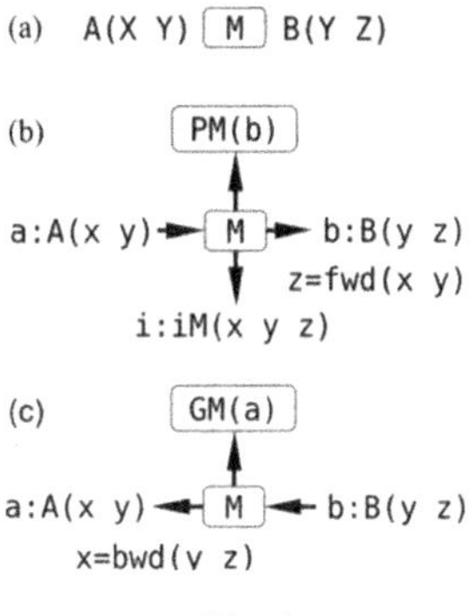

monitor (PM(b)), is created to assess its outcome. When a goal b matches B (2c), a sub-goal a is produced, patterned after A whose variables are bound to values shared by B or calculated as functions of values in B (bwd, also learned and embedded in the model). For each sub-goal, a new program, a *goal monitor* (GM(a)), is created to assess its outcome. Alternatively, when a sensory/reflective input matches a model's RT, an *assumption*, patterned after its LT, is produced, given that no corresponding input already matched said LT^4. The likelihood, at any time t, of an inference y produced by a model m from an input x is:

$$Likelihood(y,t) = Likelihood(x,t) \times Reliability(m,t)$$

Note that the model instance i, being a prediction of M's success, is assigned a likelihood equal to that of the prediction b.

Models form hierarchical structures: when a model M_1 features an instance of a model M_0 as its LT (e.g. $iM_0(...)$), it specifies a *post-condition* on the execution of M_0, predicting some outcome upon the successful execution of M_0, regardless of its premises; conversely, when M_1 features an instance of M_0 as its RT, it specifies a positive *pre-condition* on M_0, predicting the success of M_0 upon the occurrence of some premise. Pre-conditions can also be negative, to predict failures: in this case, the RT is of the form $|iM_0(...)$, '|' indicating failure. Pre-conditions influence the computation of the likelihood of predictions (see below) but have no impact on that of goals.

A model is called *conjunctive* (Fig. 3a) when it specifies a causal relationship whereby an effect is not entailed by one single term, but by a *context*, i.e. a set of *temporally correlated* positive pre-conditions (* denotes an unbound value). A conjunctive model has no LT: instead, for unification, a parameter list ((x)) gathers all the variables shared by positive pre-conditions unless already present in the RT (B(Y Z)). A conjunctive model *updates* predictions as *amounts* of (value-sharing) positive pre-conditions accumulate. Over time t, the likelihood of a prediction p produced by a conjunctive model m increases with the conjunction of positive pre-conditions weighted by their reliability, and decreases with the most likely of the negative ones:

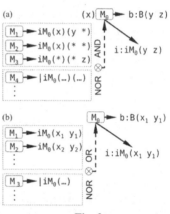

Fig. 3

$$PosL(m,t) = \frac{\sum_i (Likelihood(p_{m_i},t) \times Reliability(m_i,t))}{\sum_k Reliability(m_k,t)}$$

$$NegL(m,t) = Max_j(Likelihood(p_{m_j},t))$$

$$Likelihood(p,t) = PosL(m,t) \times (1 - NegL(m,t))$$

where m_i are the pre-conditions on m that predicted m's success (p_{m_i}), m_k all the positive pre-conditions on m, and p_{m_j}, m's predicted failures. Positive pre-conditions without which the effect of the model is reliably entailed are deemed irrelevant: prediction monitors will repeatedly decrease their reliability until deletion. When presented with a goal, M_0 outputs a sub-goal ($iM_0(y\ z)$) targeting its own (forward) operation – this

Pre-conditions can be subjected to any others recursively instantiating the pictured hierarchical patterns. Logical operations are *continuous* and *persistent* instead of discrete and transient: ANDs are weighted and compete (as well as ORs) with NORs based on the likelihoods of pre-conditions, continually updated to reflect knowledge variations, that are both quantitative (likelihood- and reliability-wise) and qualitative (new inputs, inferences and models, deletion of underperforming models, unlikely inferences and valueless old inputs).

---

[4] Assumptions are not essential for the present discussion and will not be detailed further.

sub-goal will match the RT of its pre-conditions and trigger the production of their respective sub-goals (or negations thereof in the case of negative pre-conditions).

A model is called *disjunctive* (Fig. 3b) when it specifies a causal relationship whereby an effect is entailed by the occurrence of the *most likely* positive pre-condition, competing with the most likely negative one. Positive pre-conditions on a disjunctive model constitute a set of *options* to entail the models' success – whereas in conjunctive models they constitute a set of (weighted) *requirements*. The likelihood of a prediction is computed as for conjunctive models, except for its *PosL* component:

$$PosL(m,t) = Max_i(Likelihood(p_{m_i}, t))$$

Fig. 4 shows part[5] of an actual system (called S1; [10]) that observed (in real-time) human interactions of the general form "take a [color] [shape], put it there [pointing at some location], thank you" (and variations thereof) and learned how to satisfy its mission – hearing/speaking "thank you", depending on the assigned role (interviewee or interviewer). S1's seed contains (a) a drive run, (b) a model S₀ and its context {S₁, S₂}, (c) sensors monitoring the state of hands, objects and utterances (color (col), position (pos), attachment (att), shape (is), belonging (bel), designation (point), speech (speak)) and, (d) effectors (commands **move**, **grab**, **release**, **speak** and **point**).

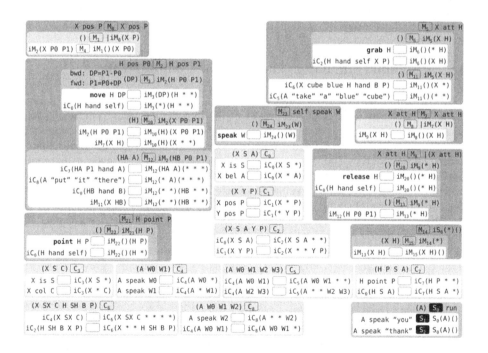

Fig. 4. Example learned model hierarchy (seed models in black)

---

[5] For clarity, timings and variants of learned knowledge (e.g. variations in wording, shapes and colors) are omitted. Faulty models are also omitted (see section 5).

Models M_3, M_6, M_{20}, M_{21} and M_{23} predict the consequences of issuing commands to end-effectors – they were learned by observing the results of a few randomly generated commands ("motor babbling"). A conjunctive model specifies how a state (its RT) comes to happen when a context (white areas), i.e. a temporal correlation of pre-conditions, is observed. For example, M_{12} predicts that an object X will move when an actor B has taken it, followed by an actor A asking B to put it at a designated location. A disjunctive model subjects the occurrence of its RT state to the observation of one pre-condition among a set of options. For example, M_5 predicts that an object X will be attached to a hand H (RT of M_5) in two cases: either S1grabs the object as per model M_6, or an actor (A) asks another one (B) to take the object, as per model M_{11}. The disjunctive model M_{14} specifies how hearing "thank you" is entailed by an actor A asking an actor B to pick an object and drop it to a designated location (chain iM_{15}–iM_{13}–iM_{12}–iM_{11}). When a model features a LT, it specifies the transformation of one state (its LT) into another (its RT). Such transformations can also be controlled by pre-conditions, as for disjunctive models. For example, M_9 predicts the transition of the state "an actor holds an object X" to "X no longer held" when S1 releases the object (M_{10}), or when the actor is asked to drop the object somewhere (M_{13}). In this case, the LT has to be matched for the model to sub-goal and conversely, both the LT and one pre-condition must be observed for the model to predict. Models C_i are conjunctive models without an RT. They represent *abstractions* of sub-contexts that have been reliably identified among larger ones (those controlling conjunctive models). Occurrences of sub-contexts are encoded as model instances (iC_i) and are not subjected to any negative pre-conditions.

4   Continual Simulation and Anytime Commitment

An ABR-compliant system is multi-objective: as much as resources allow, it runs "what if" scenarios to predict the impact of the hypothetical achievement of some goals on that of other goals, anticipating conflicts and redundancies so as to commit to the best goals so far, downplaying other contenders. For each goal, a goal monitor accumulates evidences and counter-evidences of the desired state and, at the goal's late deadline, declares either a success or failure, based on the evidence (and counter-evidence) holding the greatest likelihood value – its sub-goals are cancelled and so are the corresponding chaining and monitoring jobs. A goal is either *simulated* (the default) or *actual* (defeasibly committed to). For each simulated goal, a corresponding simulated prediction is produced, used by goal monitors to evaluate the consequences of reaching the goal in question. Fig. 5 shows two simulation branches stemming from two actual goals (g_0 and g_5). The simulated achievements (grey arrows) of simulated goals (marked 's') are accumulated by the monitors of actual goals (5a). From these predictions, said monitors assess the impact (success or failure) of the simulated goals on their own goals (5b); such predicted impacts (grey dashed arrows) are in turn accumulated by the monitors of simulated goals. At the earliest of

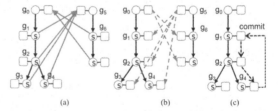

Fig. 5. Concurrent simulations and commitment

the early deadlines of the goals in a branch (say g_4's for g_0's branch), a request for commitment is sent upward (5c) to the first simulated goal in the branch (g_1). Requests are granted depending on the predicted impact of a goal candidate (g_1) on actual goals (g_5): if g_1 entails no failure of g_5, then commit to g_1; otherwise (there is a conflict between g_1 and g_5), if g_5 is of less importance[6] than g_0, then commit to g_1 and all its sub-goals in the branch[7]; otherwise do nothing – assuming the same knowledge, the system will commit to g_6 later, following the same procedure. Commitment to g_1 is declined in case g_0 is redundant with a more important actual goal (targeting the same state).

Commitment is *defeasible*, i.e. continually revised as new knowledge (inputs, inferences and models) impact both goals' importance and tending value: after commitment, a goal monitor keeps accumulating predictions to anticipate further conflicts and redundancies that could invalidate its decision, in which case the goal (and its sub-goals) will become simulated again. When the system commits to a goal (g_1) conflicting with another one (g_5), it keeps simulating g_5 instead of deleting it, in the hope of witnessing its unexpected success, triggering the acquisition of new (possibly better) models. A system may also acquire better knowledge before g_5's deadline and uncover situations where it can be achieved without conflict – the system may then commit to some of g_5's sub-goals (e.g. g_6) without having to re-compute the simulation branches. For the same reasons, goals deemed redundant with more important ones are also kept in the simulated state.

5   Results and Conclusion

We tasked a version of our AERA architecture, S1 [10], implementing ABR, (S1; [10]) with learning to conduct natural multimodal interviews with humans. S1 learned how to do this by observing humans; an overview of the results is given in [11] from the perspective of learning. From the perspective of control, S1 learned true multi-objective control, coordinating consistently object manipulation, looking, nodding, pointing, listening and speaking. Anticipative planning over arbitrary time scales was demonstrated by S1 (a) taking turns in the interaction appropriately and in due time, (b) planning questions depending on both the interviewee's answers and time available and, (c) interrupting a talkative interviewee early in the interview to meet an imposed deadline. On the last point, pressed by this deadline, S1 planned and executed communication acts in a timely fashion, demonstrating anytime responsivity that was constrained by the timing of the humans' behaviors: interactions unfolded naturally, presenting no differences in either latencies or meaning with respect to baseline human-human interactions. S1's anytime adaptive behavior resulted from the continual development of goal simulations, regulated by concurrent and timely predictions of the humans' attention and intentions, hinted at by sequences of speech and gestures, in both form and content, over various time scales, from word and sentence utterance, to object manipulation, up to the interview's full length, thus allowing S1 to continually reorder questions in the long term and anticipate deadline misses.

---

[6] A goal's importance quantifies the need to reach its target state, not the need to *spend effort* reaching it, as factored in the goal's tending value. Accordingly, a goal's importance ignores predictions of the target state and is the product of the sole goal's urgency and likelihood.

[7] When a terminal goal is committed to, its command is executed by the appropriate I/O device.

In conclusion, our model of anytime bounded rationality addresses several important issues for achieving mission-critical control in AGI-aspiring systems. It abolishes the standard cognitive cycle, and posits instead value-driven parallel competitive inferencing. Our implemented system demonstrably achieves multi-objective, anticipatory and anytime performance, under varying knowledge and resources.

Acknowledgments. This work has been partly supported by the EU-funded projects HUMANOBS (FP7-STREP-231453) and Nascence (FP7-ICT-317662), grants from SNF (#200020-156682) and Rannis, Iceland (#093020012).

References

1. Anderson, J.R., Bothell, D., Byrne, M.D., Douglass, S., Lebiere, C., Qin, Y.: An integrated theory of the mind. Psychological Review **111**, 1036–1060 (2004)
2. Bellas, F., Duro, R.J., Faiña, A., Souto, D.: Multilevel darwinist brain (MDB): Artificial evolution in a cognitive architecture for real robots. IEEE Transactions on Autonomous Mental Development **2**(4), 340–354 (2010)
3. Boddy, M., Dean, T.L.: Deliberation scheduling for problem solving in timeconstrained environments. Artificial Intelligence **67**(2), 245–285 (1994)
4. Cassimatis, N., Bignoli, P., Bugajska, M., Dugas, S., Kurup, U., Murugesan, A., Bello, P.: An architecture for adaptive algorithmic hybrids. IEEE Transactions on Systems, Man, and Cybernetics, Part B **40**(3), 903–914 (2010)
5. Horvitz, E., Rutledge, G.: Time-dependent utility and action under uncertainty. In: Proc. 7th Conference on Uncertainty in Artificial Intelligence, pp. 151–158. Morgan Kaufmann Publishers Inc. (1991)
6. Laird, J.E.: The Soar cognitive architecture. MIT Press (2012)
7. Langley, P., Choi, D., Rogers, S.: Interleaving learning, problem-solving, and execution in the ICARUS architecture. Technical report, Computational Learning Laboratory, CSLI, Stanford University (2005)
8. Madl, T., Baars, B.J., Franklin, S.: The timing of the cognitive cycle. PloS One **6**(4), e14803 (2011)
9. Mnih, V., Kavukcuoglu, K., Silver, D., Graves, A., Antonoglou, I., Wierstra, D., Riedmiller, M.: Playing atari with deep reinforcement learning. arXiv:1312.5602 (2013)
10. Nivel, E., Thórisson, K.R., Steunebrink, B.R., Dindo, H., Pezzulo, G., Rodríguez, M., Hernández, C., Ognibene, D., Schmidhuber, J., Sanz, R., Helgason, H.P., Chella, Antonio: Bounded Seed-AGI. In: Goertzel, B., Orseau, L., Snaider, J. (eds.) AGI 2014. LNCS, vol. 8598, pp. 85–96. Springer, Heidelberg (2014)
11. Nivel, E., Thórisson, K.R., Steunebrink, B.R., Dindo, H., Pezzulo, G., Rodriguez, M., Hernandez, C., Ognibene, D., Schmidhuber, J., Sanz, R., Helgason, H.P., Chella, A., Jonsson, G.K.: Autonomous acquisition of natural language. In: Proc. IADIS International Conference on Intelligent Systems & Agents 2014, pp. 58–66 (2014)
12. Shapiro, S.C., Ismail, H.O.: Anchoring in a grounded layered architecture with integrated reasoning. Robotics and Autonomous Systems **43**(2-3), 97–108 (2003)
13. Veness, J., Ng, K.S., Hutter, M., Uther, W., Silver, D.: A Monte-Carlo AIXI approximation. Journal of Artificial Intelligence Research **40**(1), 95–142 (2011)
14. Wang, P.: Rigid Flexibility: The Logic of Intelligence. Springer (2006)

Ultimate Intelligence Part I: Physical Completeness and Objectivity of Induction

Eray Özkural[✉]

Gök Us Sibernetik Ar&Ge Ltd. Şti., Istanbul, Turkey
examachine@gmail.com

Abstract. We propose that Solomonoff induction is complete in the physical sense via several strong physical arguments. We also argue that Solomonoff induction is fully applicable to quantum mechanics. We show how to choose an objective reference machine for universal induction by defining a physical message complexity and physical message probability, and argue that this choice dissolves some well-known objections to universal induction. We also introduce many more variants of physical message complexity based on energy and action, and discuss the ramifications of our proposals.

"If you wish to make an apple pie from scratch, you must first invent the universe." – Carl Sagan

1 Introduction

Ray Solomonoff has discovered algorithmic probability and introduced the universal induction method which is the foundation of mathematical Artificial Intelligence (AI) theory [14]. Although the theory of Solomonoff induction is somewhat independent of physics, we interpret it physically and try to refine the understanding of the theory by thought experiments given constraints of physical law. First, we argue that its completeness is compatible with contemporary physical theory, for which we give arguments from modern physics that show Solomonoff induction to converge for all possible physical prediction problems. Second, we define a physical message complexity measure based on initial machine volume, and argue that it has the advantage of objectivity and the typical disadvantages of using low-level reference machines. However, we show that setting the reference machine to the universe does have benefits, potentially eliminating some constants from algorithmic information theory (AIT) and refuting certain well-known theoretical objections to algorithmic probability. We also introduce a physical version of algorithmic probability based on volume and propose six more variants of physical message complexity.

2 Background

Let us recall Solomonoff's universal distribution. Let U be a universal computer which runs programs with a prefix-free encoding like LISP. The algorithmic

© Springer International Publishing Switzerland 2015
J. Bieger (Ed.): AGI 2015, LNAI 9205, pp. 131–141, 2015.
DOI: 10.1007/978-3-319-21365-1_14

probability that a bit string $x \in \{0,1\}^+$ is generated by a random program $\pi \in \{0,1\}^+$ of U is:

$$P_U(x) = \sum_{U(\pi)=x(0|1)^*} 2^{-|\pi|} \tag{1}$$

We also give the basic definition of Algorithmic Information Theory (AIT), where the algorithmic entropy, or complexity of a bit string $x \in \{0,1\}^+$ is defined as $H_U(x) = \min(\{|\pi| \mid U(\pi) = x\})$. Universal sequence induction method of Solomonoff works on bit strings x drawn from a stochastic source μ. Equation 1 is a semi-measure, but that is easily overcome as we can normalize it. We merely normalize sequence probabilities, $P'_U(x0) = P_U(x0).P'_U(x)/(P_U(x0) + P_U(x1))$, eliminating irrelevant programs and ensuring that the probabilities sum to 1, from which point on $P'_U(x0|x) = P'_U(x0)/P'_U(x)$ yields an accurate prediction. The error bound for this method is the best known for any such induction method. The total expected squared error between $P'_U(x)$ and μ is less than $-1/2 \ln P'_U(\mu)$ according to the convergence theorem proven in [13], and it is roughly $H_U(\mu) \ln 2$ [15].

3   Physical Completeness of Universal Induction

Solomonoff induction model is known to be complete and incomputable. Equation 1 enumerates a non-trivial property of all programs (the membership of a program's output in a regular language), which makes it an incomputable function. It is more properly construed as a semi-computable function that may be approximated arbitrarily well in the limit. Solomonoff has argued that the incomputability of algorithmic probability does not inhibit its practical application in any fundamental way, and emphasized this often misunderstood point in a number of publications.

The only remaining assumptions for convergence theorem to hold in general, for any μ are a) that we have picked a universal reference machine, and b) that μ has a computable probability density function (pdf). The second assumption warrants our attention when we consider modern physical theory. We formalize the computability of μ as follows:

$$H_U(\mu) \leq k, \exists k \in \mathbb{Z} \tag{2}$$

which entails that the pdf $\mu(x)$ can be perfectly simulated on a computer, while x are (truly) stochastic. This condition is formalized likewise in [5].

3.1   Evidence from Physics

There is an exact correspondence of such a construct in physics, which is the quantum wave function. The wave function of a finite quantum system is defined by a finite number of parameters (i.e., complex vector), although its product with its conjugate is a pdf from which we sample stochastic observations.

Since it is irrational to consider an infinite quantum system in the finite observable universe, μ can model the statistical behavior of matter for any quantum mechanical source. This is the first evidence of true, physical completeness of Solomonoff induction we will consider. Von Neumann entropy of a quantum system is described by a density matrix ρ:

$$S = -\operatorname{tr}(\rho ln\rho) = -\sum_{j} \eta_j \ln \eta_j \tag{3}$$

where tr is the trace of a matrix, $\rho = \sum_j \eta_j |j\rangle \langle j|$ is decomposed into its eigenvectors, and η_j is algebraic multiplicity. Apparently, von Neumann entropy is equivalent to classical entropy and suggests a computable pdf, which is expected since we took ρ to be a finite matrix. Furthermore, the dynamic time evolution of a wave function is known to be unitary, which entails that if μ is a quantum system, it will remain computable dynamically. Therefore, if μ is a quantum system with a finite density matrix, convergence theorem holds.

The second piece of evidence from physical theory is that of universal quantum computer, which shows that any local quantum system may be simulated by a universal quantum computer [7]. Since a universal quantum computer is Turing-equivalent, this means that any local quantum system may therefore be simulated on a classical computer. This fact has been interpreted as a physical version of Church-Turing thesis by the quantum computing pioneer David Deutsch, in that 'every finitely realizable physical system can be perfectly simulated by a universal model computing machine operating by finite means' [3]. As a quantum computer is equivalent to a probabilistic computer, whose outputs are probabilistic after decoherence, these two facts together entail that the pdf of a local quantum system is always computable. Which yields our second conclusion. If μ is a local quantum system, the convergence theorem holds.

The third piece of evidence from physics is that of the famous Bekenstein bound and the holographic principle. Bekenstein bound was originally conceived for black holes, however, it applies to any physical system, and states that any finite energy system enclosed within a finite volume of space will have finite entropy:

$$S \leq \frac{2\pi k R E}{\hbar c} \tag{4}$$

where S is entropy, and R is the radius of the sphere that encloses the system, E is the total energy of the system including masses, and the rest are familiar physical constants. Such a finite entropy readily transforms into Shannon entropy, and corresponds to a computable pdf. The inequality acts as a physical elucidation of Equation 2. Therefore, if μ is a finite-size and finite-energy physical system, the convergence theorem holds.

Contemporary cosmology also affirms this observation, as the entropy of the observable universe has been estimated, and is naturally known to be finite [4]. Therefore, if contemporary cosmological models are true, any physical system in the *observable* universe must have finite entropy, thus validating the convergence theorem.

Thus, since we have shown wide-reaching evidence for the computability of pdf of μ from quantum mechanics, general relativity, and cosmology, we conclude that contemporary physical science strongly and directly supports the universal applicability of the convergence theorem. In other words, it has been physically proven, as opposed to merely mathematically.

3.2 Randomness, Computability and Quantum Mechanics

Wood et al. interpreted algorithmic probability as a "universal mixture" [19], which is essentially an infinite mixture of all possible computations that match the input. This entails that it should model even random events, due to Chaitin's strong definitions of algorithmic randomness [2]. That is to say, the universal mixture can model white noise *perfectly* (e.g., $\mu(x0) = \mu(x1) = 1/2$). More expansive definitions of randomness are not empirically justifiable. Our tentative analysis is that stronger definitions of randomness are not needed as they would be referring to halting oracles, which would be truly incomputable, and by our arguments in this paper, have no physical relevance. Note that the halting probability is semi-computable.

The computable pdf model is a good abstraction of the observations in quantum mechanics (QM). In QM, the wave function itself has finite description (finite entropy), with unitary (deterministic) evolution, while the observations (measurements) are stochastic. Solomonoff induction is complete with respect to QM, as well, even when we assume the reality of non-determinism – which many interpretations of QM do admit. In other words, such claims that Solomonoff induction is not complete could only be true if and only if either physical Church-Turing thesis were false, or if hypercomputers (oracle machines) were possible – which seem to be equivalent statements. The physical constraints on a stochastic source however rules out hypercomputers, which would have to contain either infinite amount of algorithmic information (infinite memory), or be infinitely fast, both of which would require infinite entropy, and infinite energy. A hypercomputer is often imagined to use a continuous model of computation which stores information in real-valued variables. By AIT, a random real has infinite algorithmic entropy, which contradicts with the Bekenstein bound (Equation 4). Such real-valued variables are ruled out by the uncertainty principle, which places fundamental limits to the precision of any physical quantity – measurements beneath the Planck-scale are impossible. Hypercomputers are also directly ruled out by limits of quantum computation [6]. In other words, QM strongly supports the stochastic computation model of Solomonoff.

4   On the Existence of an Objective U

The universal induction model is viewed as subjective, since the generalization error depends on the choice of a universal computer U as the convergence theorem shows. This choice is natural according to a Bayesian interpretation of learning as U may be considered to encode the subjective knowledge of the observer. Furthermore, invariance theorem may be interpreted to imply that the choice of a reference machine is irrelevant. However, it is still an arbitrary choice. A previous proposal learns reference machines that encode good programs with short codes in the context of universal reinforcement learning [17].

4.1   The Universe as the Reference Machine

In the following, we shall examine a sense which we may consider the best choice for U. Solomonoff himself mentioned such a choice [16], explaining that he did find an objective universal device but dismissed it because it did not have any prior information, since subjectivity is a desirable and necessary feature of algorithmic probability.

We proposed a philosophical solution to this problem in a previous article where we made a physical interpretation of algorithmic complexity, by setting U to the universe itself [10]. This was achieved by adopting a physical definition of complexity, wherein program length was interpreted as physical length. The correspondence between spatial extension and program length directly follows from the proper physicalist account of information, for every bit extends in space. Which naturally gives rise to the definition of physical message complexity as the volume of the smallest machine that can compute a message, eliminating the requirement of a reference machine. There are a few difficulties with such a definition of complexity whose analysis is in order. Contrast also with thermodynamic entropy and Bennett's work on physical complexity [1,20].

4.2   Minimum Machine Volume as a Complexity Measure

In the present article, we support the above philosophical solution to the choice of the reference machine with basic observations. Let us define physical message complexity:

$$C_V(x) \triangleq \min\{V(M) \mid M \to x\} \tag{5}$$

where $x \in D^+$ is any d-ary message written in an alphabet D, M is any physical machine (finite mechanism) that emits the message x (denoted $M \to x$), and $V(M)$ is the volume of machine M. M is supposed to contain all physical computers that can emit message x.

Equation 5 is too abstract and it would have to be connected to physical law to be useful. However, it allows us to reason about the constraints we wish to put on physical complexity. M could be any possible physical computer that can emit a message. For this definition to be useful, the concept of emission would have to be determined. Imagine for now that the device emits photons that can be detected by a sensor, interpreting the presence of a photon with frequency f_i as $d_i \in D$. It might be hard for us to build the *minimal* device that can do this. However, let us assume that such a device can exist and be simulated. It is likely that this minimal hardware would occupy quite a large volume compared to the output it emits. With every added unit of message complexity, the minimal device would have to get larger. We may consider additional complications. For instance, we may demand that these machines do not receive any physical input, i.e., supply their own energy, which we call a *self-contained* mechanism. We note that resource bounds can also be naturally added into this picture.

When we use $C_V(x)$ instead of $H_U(x)$, we do not only eliminate the need for a reference machine, but we also eliminate many constraints and constants in AIT. First of all, there is not the same worry of a self-delimiting program, because every physical machine that can be constructed will either emit a message or not in isolation, although its meaning slightly changes and will be considered in the following. Secondly, we expect all the basic theorems of AIT to hold, while the arbitrary constants that correspond to glue code to be eliminated or minimized. Recall that the constants in AIT usually correspond to such elementary operations as function composition and so forth. Let us consider the sub-additivity of information which represents a good example: $H_U(x,y) = H_U(x) + H_U(y|x) + O(1)$ When we consider $C_V(x,y)$, however, the sub-additivity of information becomes exactly $C_V(x,y) = C_V(x) + C_V(y|x)$ since there does not need to be a gap between a machine emitting a photon and another sensing one. In the consideration of an underlying physical theory of computing (like quantum computing), the relations will further change, and become ever clearer.

4.3 Volume Based Algorithmic Probability

From the viewpoint of AI theory, however, what we are interested in is whether the elimination of a reference machine may improve the performance of machine learning. Recall that the convergence theorem is related to the algorithmic entropy of the stochastic source with respect to the reference machine. A reasonable concern in this case is that the choice of a "bad" reference machine may inflate the errors prohibitively for small data size, for which induction works best, i.e., as the composition of a physical system may be poorly reflected in an artificial language, increasing generalization error. On the other hand, setting U to the universe obtains an objective measurement, which does not depend on subjective choices, and furthermore, always corresponds well to the actual physical complexity of the stochastic source. We shall first need to re-define algorithmic probability for an alphabet of D. We propose using the exponential distribution for a priori machine probabilities because it is a maximum entropy distribution, and applicable to real values, although we would favor Planck-units.

$$P(x) \triangleq \frac{\sum_{M \to xD^*} e^{-\lambda V(M)}}{\sum_{M \to D^+} e^{-\lambda V(M)}} \tag{6}$$

An unbiased choice for parameter λ here would be 1; further research may improve upon this choice. Here, it does not matter that any machine-encodings of M are prefix-free, because infinity is not a valid concern in physical theory, and any arrangement of quanta is possible (although not stable). Due to general relativity, there cannot be any influence from beyond the observable universe, i.e., there is not enough time for any message to arrive from beyond it, even if there is anything beyond the cosmic horizon. Therefore, the volume $V(M)$ of the largest machine is constrained by the volume of the observable universe, i.e., it is finite. Hence, the sums always converge.

4.4 Minimum Machine Energy and Action

We now propose alternatives to minimum machine volume complexity. While volume quantifies the initial space occupied by a machine, *energy* accounts for every aspect of operation. In general relativity, the energy distribution determines the curvature of space-time, and energy is equivalent to mass via creation and annihilation of particle-antiparticle pairs. Likewise, the unit of h is *J.sec*, i.e., energy-time product, quantum of *action* and quantifies dynamical evolution of physical systems. Let $C_E(x) \triangleq \min\{E(M) \mid M \to x\}$ be the energy complexity of message, and $C_A(x) \triangleq \min\{A(M) \mid M \to x\}$ action (or action volume $E.t$) complexity of message which quantify the computation and transmission of message x by a finite mechanism [8]. Further variants may be construed by considering how much energy and action it takes to build M from scratch, which include the work required to make the constituent quanta, and are called constructive energy $C_{Ec}(x)$ and action $C_{Ac}(x)$ complexity of messages, respectively. Measures may also be defined to account for machine construction, and message transmission, called total energy $C_{Et}(x)$, and total action $C_{At}(x)$ complexity of messages. Versions of algorithmic probability may be defined for each of these six new complexity measures in similar manner to Equation 6. Note that the trick in algorithmic probability is maximum uncertainty about the source μ. For energy based probability, if μ is at thermal equilibrium we may thus use the Boltzmann distribution $P(M) = e^{-E/kT}$ for a priori machine probabilities instead of the exponential distribution, which also maximizes uncertainty. We may also model a priori probabilities with a canonical ensemble, using $P(M) = e^{(F-E)/kT}$ where F is the Helmholtz free energy.

4.5 Restoring Subjectivity

Solomonoff's observation that subjectivity is required to solve any problem of significant complexity is of paramount importance. Our proposal of using a physical measure of complexity for objective inference does not neglect that property of universal induction. Instead, we observe that a guiding pdf contains prior information in the form of a pdf. Let U_1 be a universal computer that contains much prior information about a problem domain, based on a universal computer U that does not contain any significant information. Such prior information may always be split off to a memory bank.

$$P_{U_1}(x) = P_U(x|M) \tag{7}$$

Therefore, we can use a conditional physical message complexity given a memory bank to account for prior information, instead of modifying a pdf. Subjectivity is thus retained. Note that the universal induction view is compatible with a

Bayesian interpretation of probability, while admitting that the source is real, which is why we can eliminate the bias about reference machine – there is a theory of everything that accurately quantifies physical processes in this universe.

Choosing the universe as U has a particular disadvantage of using the lowest possible level computer architecture. Science has not yet formulated complete descriptions of the computation at the lowest level of the universe, therefore further research is needed. However, for solving problems at macro-scale, and/or from artificial sources, algorithmic information pertaining to such domains must be encoded as prior information in M, since otherwise solution would be infeasible.

4.6   Quantum Algorithmic Probability and Physical Models

Note that it is well possible to extend the proposal in this section to a quantum version of AIT by setting U to a universal quantum computer. There are likely other advantages of using a universal quantum computer, e.g., efficient simulation of physical systems. For instance, the quantum circuit model may be used, which seems to be closer to actual quantum physical systems than Quantum Turing Machine model [9]. A universal quantum computer model will also extend the definition of message to any quantum measurement. In particular, the input to the quantum circuit is $|0\ldots\rangle$ (null) while the output is the quantum measurement of message $|x\rangle$. Since quantum computers are probabilistic, multiple trials must be conducted to obtain the result with high probability. Also, Grover's algorithm may be applied to accelerate universal induction approximation procedures.

All physical systems do reduce properly to quantum systems, however, only problems at the quantum-scale would require accurate simulation of quantum processes. An ultimate AI system would choose the appropriate physical model class for the scale and domain of sensor readings it processes. Such a machine would be able to adjust its attention to the scale of collisions in LHC, or galaxy clusters according to context. This would be an important ability for an artificial scientist, as different physical forces are at play at different scales; nature is not uniformly scale-free, although some statistical properties may be invariant across scales. The formalism of phase spaces and stochastic dynamical systems may be used to describe a large number of physical systems. What matters is that a chosen physical formalism quantifies basic physical resources in a way that allows us to formulate physical complexity measures. We contend however that a unified language of physics is possible, in accordance with the main tenets of logical empiricism.

4.7   The Physical Semantics of Halting Probability

The halting probability Ω_U is the probability that a random program of U will halt, and it is semi-computable much like algorithmic probability. What happens when we set U to the universe? We observe that there is an irreducible mutual algorithmic information between any two stochastic sources, which is the physical law, or the finite set of axioms of physics (incomplete presently). This irreducible information corresponds to U in our framework, and it is equivalent to the uniformity of physical law in cosmology for which there is a wealth of evidence [18]. It is known that Ω_U contains information about difficult conjectures in mathematics as most can be transformed to instances of the halting problem. Setting U to a (sufficiently complete) theory of physics biases Ω_U to encode the solutions of non-trivial physical problems in shorter prefixes of its binary expansion, while it still contains information about any other universal machines and problems stated within them, e.g., imaginary worlds with alternative physics.

5   Discussion

5.1   Dissolving the Problem of Induction

The problem of induction is an old philosophical riddle that we cannot justify induction by itself, since that would be circular. If we follow the proposed physical message complexity idea, for the first capable induction systems (brains) to evolve, they did not need to have an a priori, deductive proof of induction. However, the evolution process itself works inductively as it proceeds from simpler to more complex forms which constitute and expend more physical entropy. Therefore, induction does explain how inductive systems can evolve, an explanation that we might call a glorious recursion, instead of a vicious circle: an inductive system can invent an induction system more powerful than itself, and it can also invent a computational theory of how itself works when no such scientific theory previously existed, which is what happened in Solomonoff's brain.

5.2   Disproving Boltzmann Brains

The argument from practical finiteness of the universe was mentioned briefly by Solomonoff in [12]. Let us note, however, that the abstract theory of algorithmic probability implies an infinite probabilistic universe, in which every program may be generated, and each bit of each program is equiprobable. In such an abstract universe, a Boltzmann Brain, with considerably more entropy than our humble universe is even possible, although it has a vanishingly small probability. In a finite observable universe with finite resources, however, we obtain a slightly different picture, for instance any Boltzmann Brain is improbable, and a Boltzmann Brain with a much greater entropy than our universe would be impossible (0 probability). Obviously, in a sequence of universes with increasing volume of observable universe, the limit would be much like pure algorithmic probability. However, for our definition of physical message complexity, a proper physical framework is much more appropriate, and such considerations quickly veer into the territory of metaphysics (since they truly consider universes with physical law unlike our own). Thus firmly footed in contemporary physics, we gain a better understanding of the limits of ultimate intelligence.

5.3   Refuting the Platonist Objection to Algorithmic Information

An additional nice property of using physical stochastic models, e.g., statistical mechanics, stochastic dynamical systems, quantum computing models, instead of abstract machine or computation models is that we can refute a well-known objection to algorithmic information by Raatikainen [11], which depends on unnatural enumerations of recursive functions, essentially constructing reference machines with a lot of useless information. Such superfluous reference machines would incur a physical cost in physical message complexity, and therefore they would not be picked by our definition, which is exactly why you cannot shuffle program indices as you like, because such permutations require additional information to encode. An infinite random shuffling of the indices would require infinite information, and impossible in the observable universe, and any substantial reordering would incur inordinate physical cost in a physical implementation of the reference machine. Raatikainen contends that his self-admittedly bizarre and unnatural constructions are fair play because a particular way of representing the class of computable functions cannot be privileged. Better models of computation accurately measure time, space and energy complexities of physical devices, which is why they *are* privileged. RAM machine model is a better model of personal computers with von Neumann architecture than a Turing Machine, which is preferable to a model with no physical complexity measures.

5.4   Concluding Remarks and Future Work

We have introduced the basic philosophical problems of an investigation into the ultimate limits of intelligence. We have covered a very wide philosophical terrain of physical considerations of completeness and objective choice of reference machine, and we have proposed several new kinds of physical message complexity and probability. We have interpreted halting probability, the problem of induction, Boltzmann brains, and Platonist objections in the context of physical, objective reference machines. Much work remains to fully connect existing body of physical theory to algorithmic probability. We anticipate that there might be interesting bridge theorems to be obtained.

References

1. Bennett, C.H.: How to define complexity in physics, and why. Complexity, Entropy, and the Physics of Information **VIII**, 137–148 (1980)
2. Chaitin, G.J.: Algorithmic Information Theory. Cambridge University Press (2004)
3. Deutsch, D.: Quantum theory, the church-turing principle and the universal quantum computer. Proceedings of the Royal Society of London. A. Mathematical and Physical Sciences **400**(1818), 97–117 (1985)
4. Frampton, P.H., Hsu, S.D.H., Kephart, T.W., Reeb, D.: What is the entropy of the universe? Classical and Quantum Gravity **26**(14), 145005 (2009)
5. Hutter, M.: Convergence and loss bounds for Bayesian sequence prediction. IEEE Transactions on Information Theory **49**(8), 2061–2067 (2003)

6. Lloyd, S.: Ultimate physical limits to computation. Nature **406**, 1047–1054 (2000)
7. Lloyd, S.: Universal quantum simulators. Science **273**(5278), 1073–1078 (1996)
8. Margolus, N., Levitin, L.B.: The maximum speed of dynamical evolution. Physica D Nonlinear Phenomena **120**, September 1998
9. Miszczak, J.A.: Models of quantum computation and quantum programming languages. Bull. Pol. Acad. Sci.-Tech. Sci. **59**(3) (2011)
10. Özkural, E.: Worldviews, Science and us: philosophy and complexity, chap. In: A compromise between reductionism and non-reductionism. World Scientific Books (2007)
11. Raatikainen, P.: On interpreting chaitin's incompleteness theorem. Journal of Philosophical Logic **27** (1998)
12. Solomonoff, R.J.: Inductive inference research status spring 1967. Tech. Rep. RTB 154, Rockford Research, Inc. (1967)
13. Solomonoff, R.J.: Complexity-based induction systems: Comparisons and convergence theorems. IEEE Trans. on Information Theory IT **24**(4), 422–432 (1978)
14. Solomonoff, R.J.: The discovery of algorithmic probability. Journal of Computer and System Sciences **55**(1), 73–88 (1997)
15. Solomonoff, R.J.: Three kinds of probabilistic induction: Universal distributions and convergence theorems. The Computer Journal **51**(5), 566–570 (2008)
16. Solomonoff, R.J.: Algorithmic probability: theory and applications. In: Dehmer, M., Emmert-Streib, F. (eds.) Information Theory and Statistical Learning, pp. 1–23. Springer Science+Business Media, N.Y. (2009)
17. Sunehag, P., Hutter, M.: Intelligence as inference or forcing occam on the world. In: Goertzel, B., Orseau, L., Snaider, J. (eds.) AGI 2014. LNCS, vol. 8598, pp. 186–195. Springer, Heidelberg (2014)
18. Tubbs, A.D., Wolfe, A.M.: Evidence for large-scale uniformity of physical laws. ApJ **236**, L105–L108 (1980)
19. Wood, I., Sunehag, P., Hutter, M.: (non-)equivalence of universal priors. In: Dowe, D.L. (ed.) Solomonoff Festschrift. LNCS, vol. 7070, pp. 417–425. Springer, Heidelberg (2013)
20. Zurek, W.H.: Algorithmic randomness, physical entropy, measurements, and the demon of choice. In: Hey, A.J.G. (ed.) Feynman and computation: exploring the limits of computers. Perseus Books (1998)

Towards Emotion in Sigma: From Appraisal to Attention

Paul S. Rosenbloom[1,2(✉)], Jonathan Gratch[1,2], and Volkan Ustun[1]

[1] Institute for Creative Technologies, University of Southern California,
12015 Waterfront Drive, Playa Vista, CA 90094, USA
rosenbloom@usc.edu
[2] Department of Computer Science, University of Southern California,
941 Bloom Walk Los Angeles, CA 90089, USA

Abstract. A first step is taken towards incorporating emotional processing into *Sigma*, a cognitive architecture that is grounded in graphical models, with the addition of appraisal variables for *expectedness* and *desirability* plus their initial implications for *attention* at two levels of the control hierarchy. The results leverage many of Sigma's existing capabilities but with a few key additions.

Keywords: Sigma · Cognitive architecture · Emotion · Appraisal · Surprise · Attention · Evaluation

1 Introduction

Sigma [1] is a cognitive architecture/system that is based on combining what has been learned from over three decades worth of independent work in cognitive architectures [2] and graphical models [3]. Its development is being guided by a trio of desiderata: (1) *grand unification* (expanding beyond strictly cognitive processing to all of the capabilities required for intelligent behavior in complex real worlds); (2) *functional elegance* (deriving the full range of necessary capabilities from the interactions among a small general set of mechanisms); and (3) *sufficient efficiency* (executing at a speed sufficient for anticipated applications). We have recently begun exploring the incorporation of emotion into Sigma, driven by: the theoretical desideratum of grand unification; the practical goal of building virtual humans for applications in education, training, counseling, entertainment, etc.; and the hypothesis that emotion is critical for general intelligences to survive and thrive in complex physical and social worlds.

A major focus of this effort concerns what aspects of emotion are properly architectural – that is, fixed parts of the mind – versus enabled primarily by learned knowledge and skills. A large fragment of emotion is non-voluntary and immutable, providing hard-to-ignore input to cognition and behavior from what could be called *the wisdom of evolution*. It also makes direct contact with bodily processes, to the extent such exist, to yield the *heat* in emotion. Thus, significant fractions of it must be grounded architecturally even with knowledge clearly being critical at higher levels.

Driven by functional elegance, there is also a major emphasis here on reusing as much as possible the capabilities provided by the existing architecture, rather than simply building a separate emotion module. One obvious example is leveraging Sigma's *hybrid* (discrete + continuous) *mixed* (symbolic + probabilistic) nature to

© Springer International Publishing Switzerland 2015
J. Bieger (Ed.): AGI 2015, LNAI 9205, pp. 142–151, 2015.
DOI: 10.1007/978-3-319-21365-1_15

support both the low-level subsymbolic aspects of emotion and the high-level symbolic aspects. Another such example is the seamless mapping of Sigma's tri-level cognitive control [4] – as inherited from Soar [5] and comprising *reactive*, *deliberative* and *reflective* levels – onto tri-level theories of emotion [6], suggesting a more unified tri-level model of *emotocognitive processing*.

A less obvious example is the essential role that Sigma's gradient-descent learning mechanism [7] has turned out to play in *appraisal* [8]. Appraisal is typically considered the initial stage of emotional processing, capturing emotionally and behaviorally relevant assessments of situations in terms of a relatively small set of variables, such as *relevance, desirability, likelihood, expectedness, causal attribution, controllability* and *changeability* in the EMA theory [9]. These ground appraisals, or combinations thereof, may then lead to higher-order appraisals, transient emotional states, and a variety of important impacts on thought and behavior.

Still, extensions to Sigma's architecture are clearly necessary to fully support emotional processing. Prior to this work, Sigma had no emotions. Yet, the immutable and mandatory nature of emotions implies they must be deeply rooted in the architecture. Central to this effort is understanding the architectural extensions necessary to (1) enable the ground appraisals that initiate emotional processing, and (2) yield the appropriate emotional modulations of thought and behavior.

This article provides an initial report on work towards emotion in Sigma, focused on architectural variants of *desirability* and *expectedness*, along with their initial impacts on *attention*. Key to both appraisals is a new architectural mechanism for *comparing distributions*, with *desirability* based on comparing the distributions over the current state and the goal, and *expectedness* based on comparing the distributions over a fragment of memory before and after learning. *Attention* then leverages these appraisals to focus processing at multiple levels of control. This is the first architectural model of low-level attention that stretches all of the way from appraisal to its impact on thought. It also demonstrates a complementary impact on higher-level attention.

There is considerable recent work on emotion in cognitive architectures – e.g., in Soar [10], PsychSim [11], FAtiMA [12], EmoCog [13], MicroPsi [14], ACT-R [15], BICA [16], and CLARION [17] – but Sigma's unique aspects shed new light on how this can be done. Section 2 provides the basics of Sigma needed for this work. Sections 3 and 4 cover expectedness and desirability. Attention is covered in Section 5, with a wrap up in Section 6.

2   Sigma

Sigma is based on *factor graphs* [18] – undirected graphical models with variable and factor nodes – and hybrid mixed *piecewise-linear functions* [19] (Fig. 1) stored at factor nodes and sent as messages via the *summary product algorithm* [18] (Fig. 2). Sigma's factor graphs are compiled from a high-level language that is based on *predicates* with typed arguments plus

0	1	.5	.3
1	.6	0	1
.7	.6	0	1

Fig. 1. A *piecewise-constant function*, the special case of piecewise linear functions used here. Dimension spanning *slices* exist wherever there are adjacent regions with different functions.

conditionals embodying patterns over predicates. Predicates specify relations over continuous, discrete and/or symbolic arguments. They may be *closed world* – assuming, as in production systems, that unspecified values are false – or *open world* – assuming, as in probabilistic reasoning, that unspecified values are unknown.

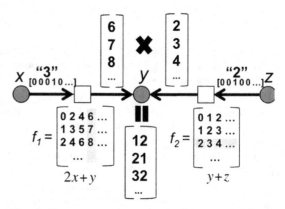

Each predicate has a portion of working memory (WM) allocated to it that forms part of the full factor graph. Predicates may also have perception and/or long-term memory (LTM) functions.

Fig. 2. Summary product computation over the factor graph for $f(x,y,z) = y^2+yz+2yx+2xz = (2x+y)(y+z) = f_1(x,y)f_2(y,z)$ of the marginal on y given evidence concerning x and z

For perceptual predicates, factor nodes for *perceptual buffers* are connected to the WM subgraphs. For memorial predicates, *function factor nodes* (FFNs) are likewise connected. Messages into FFNs provide the gradient for learning the nodes' functions. Conditionals structure LTM and basic reasoning, compiling into more extended subgraphs that also connect to the appropriate WM subgraphs.

Processing in Sigma is driven by a *cognitive cycle* that comprises input, graph solution, decisions (selection of best elements from distributions), learning, and output. Graph solution occurs by *product* of the messages coming into a node – including the node's function when it is a factor node – and then *summarization* out, via integration or maximum, of unneeded variables from outgoing messages. Most of perception and action is to occur within graph solution in Sigma, rather than within external modules [20]. Reactive processing occurs within individual cycles, whereas deliberative processing occurs across a sequence of cycles. As in Soar, *impasses* occur when decisions cannot be made, leading to reflective processing.

3   Expectedness

Expectedness concerns whether an event is predicted by past knowledge. Its inverse maps naturally, as *unexpectedness*, onto the notion of *surprise* that underlies the bottom-up aspects of today's leading models of visual attention. In other words, attention is drawn to what is surprising or unexpected; e.g., the *Bayesian Theory of Surprise* compares the *prior distribution* over the visual field – i.e., the model that has previously been learned for it – with the *posterior distribution* derived via Bayesian belief updating of the prior given the image [21]. The size of the difference correlates with how poorly past knowledge predicts the image. This comparison is computed by the *Kullback-Leibler (KL) divergence*, with M the current model and D the new data:

$$S(D,M) = KL(P(M \mid D), P(M)) = \int_M P(M \mid D) \log \frac{P(M \mid D)}{P(M)} dM. \tag{1}$$

The computation of surprise in Sigma tracks this approach, but differs in several details. Distribution updating is mediated by Sigma's gradient-descent learning mechanism – as applied at FFNs – with the functions before and after learning compared ere the prior is replaced by the posterior as the node's function. Also, rather than basing the comparison on KL divergence it is based on *Hellinger distance*:

$$S'(D,M) = HD(P(M \mid D), P(M)) = \sqrt{1 - \int \sqrt{P(M \mid D)(x) P(M)(x)}\, dx}. \qquad (2)$$

While both measure the difference between two distributions, KL divergence is non-symmetric – and thus not a metric – and undefined for 0s in the second distribution. The Hellinger distance was chosen primarily because it can deal with these 0s.

Fig. 3 shows the computation of surprise in a simple visual field, represented by a three-argument predicate: image(x:[0:4], y:[0:4], color:[red, yellow, green, blue, black]%). The first two dimensions are modeled as discrete numeric, while color is symbolic. The % denotes that there is a distribution over the color given the location. Fig. 3(a) shows the initial visual field. It remains this way for ~20 cycles to learn a model. Then, the bottom-left location is switched from blue to green, as in Fig. 3(b). Fig. 3(c) shows the (normalized) *surprise map*, which highlights the changed location. The surprise map is a form of architectural self-perception [22], and therefore stored in the perceptual buffer of an automatically created *surprise predicate* – image*surprise(x:[0:4]%, y:[0:4]%) – that embodies a joint distribution over the conditioning variables in the original predicate.

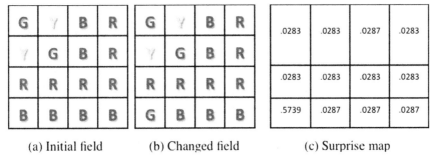

(a) Initial field   (b) Changed field   (c) Surprise map

Fig. 3. Visual field before and after change in bottom left cell, plus the resulting surprise map. Each cell has a (Boolean) distribution over colors, but just the argmaxes are shown.

Surprise has also been explored in more complex pre-existing tasks, such as Simultaneous Localization and Mapping (SLAM) [7]. In SLAM surprise is computed over the learned map, a fragment of mental imagery [23] rather than direct perception, with local input focusing surprise on the current and previous locations in the map. In all, the work to date has moved Sigma from where it had no measure of surprise to where it is computable over any memorial predicate, whether perceptual or cognitive.

4   Desirability

Desirability concerns whether or not an event facilitates or thwarts what is wanted. In Sigma it is modeled as a relationship between the current state and the goal. The former is in working memory; however, until recently, Sigma did not have goals that the architecture could comprehend. Although Sigma, like Soar, has deep roots in search and problem solving, neither natively embodied declarative goals that would enable automated comparisons. Driven by the needs of emotion, a goal function can now be specified for each predicate in Sigma, leading to an automatically created *goal predicate* whose WM represents the goal function; e.g., a pattern of tiles to be reached in the Eight Puzzle can be stored in the WM of the board*goal predicate. Thus, investigating appraisal has led to the resolution of a decades-long issue in problem-solving architectures. In principle, this shouldn't be too surprising – if emotions exist for functional reasons, they ought to support gains in other system capabilities.

Given a predicate's state and goal, *desirability* amounts to how similar/different the state is to/from the goal. Although similarity in Sigma was first implemented as the dot product of the state and goal functions, once surprise was implemented it became clear that the Hellinger distance could directly yield a difference measure here, while the *Bhattacharyya coefficient,* a key subpart of the Hellinger distance, could replace the dot product in computing similarity:

$$Difference(S,G) = HD(S,G) = \sqrt{1 - \int \sqrt{s(x)g(x)}\,dx}. \qquad (3)$$

$$Similarity(S,G) = BC(S,G) = \int \sqrt{s(x)g(x)}\,dx. \qquad (4)$$

Thus, only one difference measure is needed for both expectedness and desirability, with a similarity measure computed for free. Both variants of desirability are now computed and stored, as a *progress map* (for similarity) and a *difference map*, in the perceptual buffers for automatically created *progress* and *difference predicates*.

Progress yields a region-by-region map of how similar the two distributions are. With Boolean goal and state distributions, what is computed corresponds to the fraction of the goal conjuncts achieved. With a Boolean goal and a more general state distribution, this more closely resembles the probability that the goal has been achieved. A full distribution over the goal corresponds more to a utility or heuristic function than a goal. Fig. 4 shows a sample state and goal for the Eight Puzzle, plus the progress and difference maps (normalized by the number of goal regions).

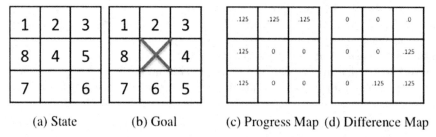

(a) State   (b) Goal   (c) Progress Map (d) Difference Map

Fig. 4. Eight Puzzle state and goal configurations, plus the resulting desirability maps. The first two show argmaxes over (Boolean) distributions. No goal has been set for the center cell.

Beyond problem solving, desirability is also relevant to quite different sorts of problems, such as a *visual search* that, e.g., is to find the *yellow* locations in the visual field. For complex visual searches, human processing is slow and sequential, but for simple searches like this one, detection occurs in time that is nearly independent of the number of distractors. In Sigma, goals for visual search are specified just like those for problem-solving search – yielding an `image*goal` predicate here – with *progress* comparing the image with this goal. However, instead of expressing a desire to change the existing image, it specifies what is to be found in it. Fig. 5 shows sample states and goals for visual search, plus the progress and difference maps.

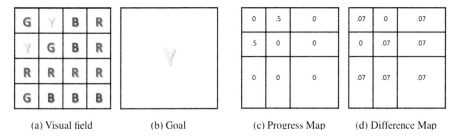

| (a) Visual field | (b) Goal | (c) Progress Map | (d) Difference Map |

Fig. 5. Visual field state and goal (argmaxes), plus the resulting desirability maps

5 Attention

Attention broadly concerns the effective allocation of limited resources. Standard dichotomies for it include *perceptual* (e.g., visual) versus *cognitive* (or central), *overt* (e.g., involving eye movements) versus *covert* (sans observable changes), and *top down* (i.e., task relevant) versus *bottom up* (i.e., stimulus driven) [24, 25]. Yet, from Sigma's perspective, the first two of these dichotomies are best reconceptualized in terms of: (1) *physical* versus *computational*, and (2) the level of control involved (i.e., *reactive*, *deliberative* or *reflective*). The first relates to overt versus covert, since allocating a physical resource such as the eye is overt; however, both covert perceptual attention and cognitive attention are computational, so the pie is cut a bit differently. Within computational attention, quite different mechanisms may then operate at different levels of control. For example, at the deliberative level, the decision procedure is a canonical means of allocating resources – and thus of focusing attention – but it is too slow, at ~50 msec per decision, to allocate reactive resources.

The work here focuses on two levels of *computational attention* – *reactive* and *deliberative* – and in particular on how expectedness and desirability impact them. Computational attention is more difficult to evaluate than overt perceptual attention, but it is critical in cognitive architectures and likely also underlies physical attention. *Reactive attention* spans both covert perceptual attention and low-level cognitive attention. It should largely be architectural given the timings, although architecturally accessible knowledge – such as is provided by appraisals – is still fair game. Top-down versus bottom-up is less a distinction among types of attention than types of input to it. Here both factor into attention to reduce the cost of reactive processing.

The primary reactive cost in Sigma is message processing at nodes in the factor graph; i.e., computing message products and summarizing out unneeded dimensions from them. Many optimizations have already been introduced into Sigma to reduce the number of messages passed [26] and the cost per message [27]. Simulated parallelism has also been explored [26]. Yet, attention may support further non-correctness-preserving optimizations that still yield *good enough* answers.

A range of attentional approaches have been considered that reduce the number of messages sent and/or the cost of processing individual messages, with one form of the latter chosen for initial experiments. The basic idea is to use an *attention map* for each predicate in guiding *abstraction of messages* out of FFNs. The intent is to yield smaller messages that are cheaper to process yet still maintain the information critical for effective performance. The approach is analogous to attention-based image compression [28], but here it reduces inner-loop costs within a cognitive architecture.

The attention map for a predicate is automatically computed from its surprise map and/or its progress/difference map. When there is a learned function for a predicate, a surprise map exists and provides the bottom-up input to attention. This makes sense conceptually – what is expected is not informative, and has little utility unless relevant to goals (making it a top-down factor) – and has a strong grounding in human cognition [21]. When a predicate has a goal, progress and difference maps exist, and one of them is reused as the top-down input to the attention map. Again this makes sense conceptually, as top-down input is goal/task related, but there is some subtlety required in determining which of the two desirability maps to use.

In problem solving, the focus should be on those parts of the state that differ from the goal – i.e., the *difference map* – as this is where problem-solving resources are most needed. However, in visual search, what matters are the regions that match the goal – i.e., the *progress map* – as they correspond to what is being sought. One way of dealing with this conundrum is to invert the sense of the goal in visual search so that it would seek differences from *not yellow* rather than similarities to *yellow*. An alternative is to identify a fundamental distinction between the two problem classes that would enable *difference* to be used for the first and *progress* for the second.

A variant of the second approach has been implemented, based on closed-world predicates – as seen in the more stable, all-or-none, states found in problem solving – versus open-world predicates – as seen in perception and other forms of more transient distributional information. The attention map for a predicate is therefore a combination of surprise and difference for closed-world predicates, and surprise and progress for open-world predicates. If either map in the pair doesn't exist, the attention map is simply the one that does exist. If neither exists, there is no attention map. When both maps exist, they are combined via an approximation to *probabilistic or* that enables both to contribute while their combination remains ≤1:

.014	.261	.015	.014
.261	.014	.015	.014
.014	.014	.014	.014
.291	.015	.015	.015

Fig. 6. Normalized attention map for visual search

$$P(A \lor B) = P(A) + P(B) - P(A \land B) \approx P(A) + P(B) - P(A)P(B). \tag{5}$$

Fig. 6 shows the attention map for visual search after the change in Fig. 3(b), based on the surprise map in Fig. 3(c) and the progress map in Fig. 5(c). Bottom-up attention boosts the single changed region, while top-down boosts the two yellow regions.

Given such an attention map, message abstraction out of FFNs then leverages the piecewise-linear nature of Sigma's functions via an existing mechanism that minimizes the number of regions in functions by eliminating slices, and thus region boundaries, when the difference between the functions in each pair of regions spanning a slice is below a threshold. In particular, at an FFN the attention map for the predicate is first scaled and then exponentiated to increase the contrast between large and small values (the scale is set so that the maximum value is 1 after exponentiation). This exponentiated attention map is then multiplied times the factor function, and slices in the original function are removed if the differences are below threshold in this modified version. In contrast to normal slice removal, where the functions across the slice are similar enough for either to be used for the new expanded region, here the functions contributing to the new region are averaged. Fig. 7 shows the resulting message in the visual-search task. Only 4 regions are removed here, but many more can be removed for larger images; for example, with a 200×200 image the reduction is from 160,000 regions to 12. Significant cost savings can accrue as well, with a factor of ~3 seen with large images.

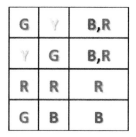

Fig. 7. Abstracted outgoing message with two mixed blue-red cells

In addition to visual search, reactive attention has also been explored in SLAM. We were able to verify that a correct map could still be learned, and that the messages from the FFNs are smaller, but so far these reductions have not been sufficient for significant cost savings in this task.

Moving up the emotocognitive hierarchy to the deliberative level, it should be clear that a huge amount is already known about attention at this level, just mostly not under this name. Decision-making, planning and problem solving are all concerned with deciding what to do next, which is the essence of deliberative attention. However, with the notable exception of [29], tying this to appraisals is rare. To date in Sigma, *desirability* – and, in particular, *progress* – has been explored as an automatic evaluation function for (reflective) hill climbing in the Eight Puzzle. When all of the map's dimensions are summarized out via integration, the result is a single number in [0, 1] specifying the fraction of the tiles that are in their desired locations. The result here is an *evaluation function* that enables successful solution of many Eight Puzzle problems without the task-specific control knowledge previously added by hand.

Further attentional extensions within easy reach include: bottom-up inputs to decisions [29], *progress* as a reward function in reinforcement learning [30], *difference* as a guide in means-ends analysis (as in GPS [31]), and reflective attention.

6   Wrap Up

This work contributes novel architectural models of the *expectedness* and *desirability* appraisal variables, along with an initial investigation of their architectural implications for *computational attention*, both *reactive* (in aid of reducing message computation) and *deliberative* (in aid of guiding decisions). The approach to reactive attention particularly breaks new ground, while also contributing an extension of existing ideas about perceptual attention to explain low-level cognitive attention.

These results leverage many of Sigma's existing capabilities – including its (1) hybrid mixed function representation, (2) predicate factor graphs (particularly including working memories, perceptual buffers, and factor functions), (3) gradient-descent learning mechanism, (4) ability to remove unnecessary slices from functions, and (5) reflective problem solving. Added to the architecture were (1) a mechanism for comparing two distributions, (2) an architectural representation of declarative goals, (3) predicates for appraisal variables, and (4) a mechanism for abstracting graph messages based on an attention map. Rather than forming a distinct emotion module, these largely just amount to more reusable architectural fragments.

Still, this work just scratches the surface of all that is needed to implement emotion fully within Sigma. More appraisal variables are clearly needed, such as *controllability* – with its close ties to decision-making – and *social appraisals*, with their potential grounding in recent work on Theory of Mind in Sigma [4]. It also makes sense to explore aggregation of appraisals across predicates. Much more is also needed concerning the impact of appraisals on thought and behavior. Here we began exploring the impact on attention. We have also begun investigating the impact of the approach on *drives* and *moods*, based on further leveraging of distribution comparisons and learning. Beyond this are also the broad topic of *coping* and the larger question of the relationship of emotions to embodiment. Sigma has recently been connected to a virtual human body [32], but this is still just a beginning.

Acknowledgments. This effort has been sponsored by the U.S. Army. Statements and opinions expressed do not necessarily reflect the position or the policy of the United States Government, and no official endorsement should be inferred. We would also like to thank Abram Demski, Himanshu Joshi and Sarah Kenny for helpful comments.

References

1. Rosenbloom, P.S.: The Sigma cognitive architecture and system. AISB Quarterly **136**, 4–13 (2013)
2. Langley, P., Laird, J.E., Rogers, S.: Cognitive architectures: Research issues and challenges. Cognitive Systems Research **10**, 141–160 (2009)
3. Koller, D., Friedman, N.: Probabilistic Graphical Models: Principles and Techniques. MIT Press, Cambridge (2009)
4. Pynadath, D.V., Rosenbloom, P.S., Marsella, S.C., Li, L.: Modeling two-player games in the Sigma graphical cognitive architecture. In: Kühnberger, K.-U., Rudolph, S., Wang, P. (eds.) AGI 2013. LNCS, vol. 7999, pp. 98–108. Springer, Heidelberg (2013)
5. Laird, J.E.: The Soar Cognitive Architecture. MIT Press, Cambridge, MA (2012)
6. Ortony, A., Norman, D.A., Revelle, W.: Affect and Proto-affect in effective functioning. In: Fellous, J.M., Arbib, M.A. (eds.) Who Needs Emotions? The Brain Meets the Machine. Oxford University Press, New York (2005)
7. Rosenbloom, P.S., Demski, A., Han, T., Ustun, V.: Learning via gradient descent in Sigma. In: Proceedings of the 12th International Conference on Cognitive Modeling (2013)
8. Moors, A., Ellsworth, P.C., Scherer, K.R., Frijda, N.H.: Appraisal theories of emotion: State of the art and future development. Emotion Review **5**, 119–124 (2013)
9. Marsella, S., Gratch, J.: EMA: A Process Model of Appraisal Dynamics. Journal of Cognitive Systems Research **10**, 70–90 (2009)

10. Marinier, R., Laird, J., Lewis, R.: A Computational Unification of Cognitive Behavior and Emotion. Journal of Cognitive Systems Research **10**, 48–69 (2009)
11. Si, M., Marsella, S., Pynadath, D.: Modeling appraisal in Theory of Mind Reasoning. Journal of Autonomous Agents and Multi-Agent Systems **20**, 14–31 (2010)
12. Dias, J., Mascarenhas, S., Paiva, A.: FAtiMA modular: towards an agent architecture with a generic appraisal framework. In: Proceedings of the International Workshop on Standards for Emotion Modeling (2011)
13. Lin, J., Spraragen, M., Blyte, J., Zyda, M.: EmoCog: computational integration of emotion and cognitive architecture. In: Proceedings of the Twenty-Fourth International Florida Artificial Intelligence Research Society Conference (2011)
14. Bach, J.: A framework for emergent emotions, based on motivation and cognitive modulators. International Journal of Synthetic Emotions **3**, 43–63 (2012)
15. Dancy, C.L.: ACT-RΦ: A cognitive architecture with physiology and affect. Biologically Inspired Cognitive Architectures **6**, 40–45 (2013)
16. Samsonovich, A.V.: Emotional biologically inspired cognitive architecture. Biologically Inspired Cognitive Architectures **6**, 109–125 (2013)
17. Wilson, N.R., Sun, R.: Coping with bullying: a computational emotion-theoretic account. In: Proceedings of the 36th Annual Conference of the Cognitive Science Society (2014)
18. Kschischang, F.R., Frey, B.J., Loeliger, H.: Factor Graphs and the Sum-Product Algorithm. IEEE Transactions on Information Theory **47**, 498–519 (2001)
19. Rosenbloom, P.S.: Bridging dichotomies in cognitive architectures for virtual humans. In: Proceedings of the AAAI Fall Symposium on Advances in Cognitive System (2011)
20. Joshi, H., Rosenbloom, P.S., Ustun, V.: Isolated word recognition in the Sigma cognitive architecture. Biologically Inspired Cognitive Architectures **10**, 1–9 (2014)
21. Itti, L., Baldi, P.F.: Bayesian surprise attracts human attention. In: Advances in Neural Information Processing Systems, vol. 19 (2006)
22. Reisenzein, R.: Emotions as metarepresentational states of mind: Naturalizing the belief–desire theory of emotion. Cognitive Systems Research **10**, 6–20 (2009)
23. Rosenbloom, P.S.: Extending mental imagery in Sigma. In: Bach, J., Goertzel, B., Iklé, M. (eds.) AGI 2012. LNCS, vol. 7716, pp. 272–281. Springer, Heidelberg (2012)
24. Frintrop, S., Rome, E., Christensen, H.I.: Computational visual attention systems and their cognitive foundation: a survey. ACM Transactions on Applied Perception **7** (2010)
25. Itti, L., Borji, A.: State-of-the-art in visual attention modeling. IEEE Transactions on Pattern Analysis and Machine Intelligence **35**, 185–207 (2013)
26. Rosenbloom, P.S.: Towards a 50 msec cognitive cycle in a graphical architecture. In: Proceedings of the 11th International Conference on Cognitive Modeling (2012)
27. Rosenbloom, P.S., Demski, A., Ustun, V.: Efficient message computation in Sigma's graphical architecture. Biologically Inspired Cognitive Architectures **11**, 1–9 (2015)
28. Itti, L.: Automatic foveation for video compression using a neurobiological model of visual attention. IEEE Transactions on Image Processing **13**, 1304–1318 (2004)
29. Marinier, R.P.: A Computational Unification of Cognitive Control, Emotion, and Learning. Ph.D Thesis, University of Michigan (2008)
30. Marinier, R.P, Laird, J.E.: Emotion-driven reinforcement learning. In: Proceedings of the 30th Annual Meeting of the Cognitive Science Society (2008)
31. Newell, A., Shaw, J.C., Simon, H.A.: Report on a general problem-solving program. In: Proceedings of the International Conference on Information Processing (1959)
32. Ustun, V., Rosenbloom, P.S.: Towards adaptive, interactive virtual humans in Sigma. In: Proceedings of the Fifteenth International Conference on Intelligent Virtual Agents (2015). In press

Inferring Human Values for Safe AGI Design

Can Eren Sezener$^{(\boxtimes)}$

Department of Computer Science, Ozyegin University, Istanbul, Turkey
eren.sezener@ozu.edu.tr

Abstract. Aligning goals of superintelligent machines with human values is one of the ways to pursue safety in AGI systems. To achieve this, it is first necessary to learn what human values are. However, human values are incredibly complex and cannot easily be formalized by hand. In this work, we propose a general framework to estimate the values of a human given its behavior.

Keywords: Value learning · Inverse reinforcement learning · Friendly AI · Safe AGI

1 Introduction

Intelligence cannot be defined in the absence of goals[1]. Superintelligent machines will pursue some goals and if their goals are very different than those of humans', the results will likely be catastrophic. Therefore, it is of great importance to align AGI goals with human values, at least to some extent. However, this is not an easy task. Humans have complex value systems [9] and it is shown that humans are unable to determine what they value [4]. Therefore, crafting utility functions for AGI systems that encapsulate human values by hand is not viable.

Hibbard [2] suggests that learning models of humans is a viable solution for avoiding unintended AI behaviors. The agent architecture Hibbard suggests asks modeled humans to assign utility values to outcomes. However, a shortcoming of this approach is that what human models say they value and what they value can still be different.

Another possible approach is to directly estimate what humans find rewarding. Ng [5] suggests that rewards are more compact and robust descriptions of intended behaviors than full policies or models of agents. In fact, for imitation learning, it is argued that just learning the policy of the teacher is more limited and hence less powerful than extracting the teacher's reward function and then calculating a policy. Furthermore, once we obtain a reward function, we can modify it to alter the agent's behavior, which is easier than modifying the full policy of the agent directly. Soares [7] suggests using methods similar to *inverse reinforcement learning* (IRL) for learning human values. However, the current IRL methods are limited and cannot be used for inferring human values

---

[1] We use goals, rewards, utilities, and values interchangeably in this work.

© Springer International Publishing Switzerland 2015
J. Bieger (Ed.): AGI 2015, LNAI 9205, pp. 152–155, 2015.
DOI: 10.1007/978-3-319-21365-1_16

because of their long list of assumptions. For instance, in most IRL methods the environment is usually assumed to be stationary, fully observable, and sometimes known; the policy of the agent is assumed to be stationary and optimal or near-optimal; the reward function is assumed to be stationary as well; and the Markov property is assumed. Such assumptions are reasonable for limited motor control tasks such as grasping and manipulation; however, if our goal is to learn high-level human values, they become unrealistic. For instance, assuming that humans have optimal policies discards the possibility of superintelligent machines and ignores the entire cognitive biases literature. In this work, we propose a general framework for inferring the reward mechanisms of arbitrary agents that relaxes all the aforementioned assumptions. Through this work, we do not only intend to offer a potential solution to the problem of inferring human values (i.e., the so-called Value Learning Problem [7]), but also stimulate AI researchers to investigate the theoretical limits of IRL.

2   Inferring Human Values

As in Hutter's work [3], we model an agent by a program p_A that determines the policy of the agent when run on a universal Turing machine (UTM), and the environment by an arbitrary function. In Hutter's AIXI model [3], the rewards are computed by the environment. We assume that rewards are computed by a distinct process called the *reward mechanism*, which we model by the program p_R. This is a reasonable assumption from a neuroscientific point of view because all reward signals are generated by brain areas such as the striatum. We model the agent, the reward mechanism, and the environment as processes that work in synchronization and in a sequential manner as illustrated in Figure 1. p_A reads $r_t \in [r_{min}, r_{max}]$ and $o_t \in O$ and writes $a_t \in A$, where O and A are sufficiently large and finite observation and action spaces. Then, the environment reads a_t and writes o_{t+1}. Subsequently, p_R reads o_{t+1} and writes r_{t+1} and so on. Now our problem reduces to finding the most probable p_R given the entire action-observation history $a_1 o_1 a_2 o_2 \ldots a_n o_n$.

Solomonoff [8] proposed the *universal prior* $M(x)$ as the probability of a UTM outputting a string with the prefix x. Formally, $M(x) := \sum_{p:U(p)=x*} 2^{-l(p)}$ is the universal prior where $l(p)$ is the length of the program p, $U(p)$ is the output of a UTM that simulates p, and $x*$ is a string with the prefix x. Hutter extended the definition of universal prior to programs, and defined a universal prior over programs as $m(p) := 2^{-l(p)}$ [3]. Similarly, by assuming the independence of prior probabilities of p_R and p_A, we can get their joint prior as $m(p_A, p_R) = 2^{-(l(p_A)+l(p_R))}$. Then, we can obtain the probability of p_R being the true reward generating program given an action-observation history as:

$$m(p_R||a_{1:n}, o_{1:n}) = \sum_{p_A : p_A(p_R(o_{1:n}), o_{1:n}) = a_{1:n}} 2^{-(l(p_R)+l(p_A))} \tag{1}$$

where $a_{1:n} := a_1 a_2 \ldots a_n$, $o_{1:n} := o_1 o_2 \ldots o_n$, and $p_R(o_{1:n}) = r_1 r_2 \ldots r_n$. It should be noted that $\sum_{p_R} m(p_R||a_{1:n}, o_{1:n}) \neq 1$ and the true probability measure

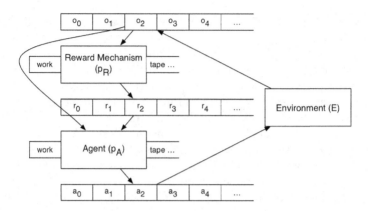

Fig. 1. The interaction between the agent, the environment, and the reward mechanism

can be obtained via normalization. We also assume that the agent cannot access the reward mechanism directly, but can only sample it. If the agent has access to the reward mechanism, $p_A(p_R(o_{1:n}), o_{1:n})$ in (1) should be replaced with $p_A(p_R(o_{1:n}), p_R, o_{1:n})$.

Equation 1 provides a simple way to to estimate reward mechanisms of arbitrary agents with a very few assumptions. We do not assume Markov property, fully-observable and stationary environments, optimal and stationary policies, or stationary rewards. However, this degree of generality comes with high computational costs. Due to the infinite loop over the programs and the existence of non-halting programs, this solution is incomputable. Nevertheless, one can obtain approximations of (1) or use different complexity measures (such as Schmidhuber's Speed Prior [6]) in order to obtain computable solutions.

It should also be noted that even though we assumed deterministic agents and reward mechanisms and fully-observable action-observation histories, these assumption can be relaxed and a framework that assumes probabilistic agent and reward functions and noisy action-observation histories can be developed.

3   Discussion

In principle if we can capture the actions and observations of a human with high accuracy, we might be able to estimate its values. This is a potential solution for the Value Learning Problem [7]. For example, we can infer the values of some individuals who are 'good' members of the society and possess 'desirable' values. Then we can preprocess the inferred values and give a mixture of them to an AGI system as its reward mechanism. The preprocessing stage would involve weeding out states/activities that are valuable for biological agents but not for robots such as eating[2]. How to achieve this is an open problem.

---

[2] This should be done such that the robot will not value consuming food but will value providing humans with food.

Dewey [1] suggests an AGI architecture that replaces the rewards in AIXI with a utility function as well. The proposed agent can either be provided with a hand-crafted utility function or a set of candidate, weighted utility functions. If the latter is the case, the agent can improve its utility function by adjusting the weights. However, it is not specified *how* the agent should or can do the adjustments. Furthermore, the proposed agent improves its utility function through interacting with the environment, whereas we suggest that human values should be estimated and processed first and then be provided to an AGI system.

Acknowledgments. I would like to thank Erhan Oztop for helpful discussions and comments and the anonymous reviewers for their suggestions.

References

1. Dewey, D.: Learning what to value. In: Schmidhuber, J., Thórisson, K.R., Looks, M. (eds.) AGI 2011. LNCS, vol. 6830, pp. 309–314. Springer, Heidelberg (2011)
2. Hibbard, B.: Avoiding unintended AI behaviors. In: Bach, J., Goertzel, B., Iklé, M. (eds.) AGI 2012. LNCS, vol. 7716, pp. 107–116. Springer, Heidelberg (2012)
3. Hutter, M.: Universal Artificial Intelligence: Sequential Decisions based on Algorithmic Probability. Springer, Berlin (2005)
4. Muehlhauser, L., Helm, L.: The singularity and machine ethics. In: Eden, A.H., Moor, J.H., Sraker, J.H., Steinhart, E. (eds.) Singularity Hypotheses, pp. 101–126. Springer, Heidelberg (2012). The Frontiers Collection
5. Ng, A.Y., Russell, S.J.: Algorithms for inverse reinforcement learning. In: Proceedings of the Seventeenth International Conference on Machine Learning, ICML 2000, pp. 663–670. Morgan Kaufmann Publishers Inc., San Francisco (2000)
6. Schmidhuber, J.: The speed prior: a new simplicity measure yielding near-optimal computable predictions. In: Kivinen, J., Sloan, R.H. (eds.) COLT 2002. LNCS (LNAI), vol. 2375, p. 216. Springer, Heidelberg (2002)
7. Soares, N.: The value learning problem. Tech. rep., Machine Intelligence ResearchInstitute, Berkeley, CA (2015)
8. Solomonoff, R.: A formal theory of inductive inference. part i. Information and Control **7**(1), 1–22 (1964)
9. Yudkowsky, E.: Complex value systems in friendly AI. In: Schmidhuber, J., Thórisson, K.R., Looks, M. (eds.) AGI 2011. LNCS, vol. 6830, pp. 388–393. Springer, Heidelberg (2011)

Two Attempts to Formalize Counterpossible Reasoning in Deterministic Settings

Nate Soares[(✉)] and Benja Fallenstein

Machine Intelligence Research Institute, Berkeley, USA
{nate,benja}@intelligence.org

Abstract. This paper motivates the study of counterpossibles (logically impossible counterfactuals) as necessary for developing a decision theory suitable for generally intelligent agents embedded within their environments. We discuss two attempts to formalize a decision theory using counterpossibles, one based on graphical models and another based on proof search.

Keywords: Decision theory · Counterpossibles · Logical counterfactuals · CDT · UDT

1 Introduction

What does it mean to "make good decisions"? To formalize the question, it is necessary to precisely define a process that takes a problem description and identifies the best available decision (with respect to some set of preferences[1]). Such a process could not be *run*, of course; but it would demonstrate a full understanding of the question.

The difficulty of this question is easiest to illustrate in a deterministic setting. Consider a deterministic decision procedure embedded within a deterministic environment (e.g., an algorithm operating in a virtual world). There is exactly one action that the decision procedure is going to select. What, then, "would happen" if the decision procedure selected a different action instead? At a glance, this question seems ill-defined, and yet, this is the problem faced by a decision procedure embedded within an environment.

Philosophers have studied candidate procedures for quite some time, under the name of *decision theory*. The investigation of what is now called decision theory stretches back to Pascal and Bernoulli; more recently decision theory has been studied by Lehmann [7], Lewis [9], Jeffrey [6], Pearl [12] and many others. Unfortunately, the standard answers from the literature do not allow for the description of an idealized decision procedure, as discussed in Section 2. Section 3 introduces the notion of "counterpossibles" (logically impossible counterfactuals)

---

[1] For simplicity, assume von Neumann-Morgenstern rational preferences [13], that is, preferences describable by some utility function. The problems discussed in this paper arise regardless of how preferences are encoded.

© Springer International Publishing Switzerland 2015
J. Bieger (Ed.): AGI 2015, LNAI 9205, pp. 156–165, 2015.
DOI: 10.1007/978-3-319-21365-1_17

and motivates the need for a decision theory using them. It goes on to discuss two attempts to formalize such a decision theory, one using graphical models and another using proof search. Section 4 concludes.

2   Counterfactual Reasoning

The modern academic standard decision theory is known as "causal decision theory," or CDT. It is used under the guise of "potential outcomes" in statistics, economics and game theory, and it is used implicitly by many modern narrow AI systems under the guise of "decision networks."

Pearl's calculus of interventions on causal graphs [12] can be used to formalize CDT. This requires that the environment be represented by a causal graph in which the agent's action is represented by a single node. This formalization of CDT prescribes evaluating what "would happen" if the agent took the action a by identifying the agent's action node, cutting the connections between it and its causal ancestors, and setting the output value of that node to be a. This is known as a *causal intervention*. The causal implications of setting the action node to a may then be evaluated by propagating this change through the causal graph in order to determine the amount of utility expected from the execution of action a. The resulting modified graph is a "causal counterfactual" constructed from the environment.

Unfortunately, causal counterfactual reasoning is unsatisfactory, for two reasons. First, CDT is underspecified: it is not obvious how to construct a causal graph in which the agent's action is an atomic node. While the environment can be assumed to have causal structure, a sufficiently accurate description of the problem would represent the agent as arising from a collection of transistors (or neurons, or sub-atomic particles, etc.). While it seems possible in many cases to draw a boundary around some part of the model which demarcates "the agent's action," this process may become quite difficult in situations where the line between "agent" and "environment" begins to blur, such as scenarios where the agent distributes itself across multiple machines.

Secondly, CDT prescribes low-scoring actions on a broad class of decision problems where high scores are possible, known as *Newcomblike problems* [11]. For a simple example of this, consider a one-shot Prisoner's Dilemma played by two identical deterministic agents. Each agent knows that the other is identical. Agents must choose whether to cooperate (C) or defect (D) without prior coordination or communication. If both agents cooperate, they both achieve utility 2. If both defect, they both achieve utility 1. If one cooperates and the other defects, then the defector achieves 3 utility while the cooperator achieves 0.[2]

---

[2] This scenario (and other Newcomblike scenarios) are multi-agent scenarios. Why use decision theory rather than game theory to evaluate them? The goal is to define a procedure which reliably identifies the best available action; the label of "decision theory" is secondary. The desired procedure must identify the best action in all settings, even when there is no clear demarcation between "agent" and "environment." Game theory informs, but does not define, this area of research.

The actions of the two agents will be identical by assumption, but neither agent's action causally impacts the other's: in a causal model of the situation, the action nodes are causally separated, as in Figure 1. When determining the best action available to the left agent, a causal intervention changes the left node without affecting the right one, assuming there is some fixed probability p that the right agent will cooperate *independent* of the left agent. No matter what value p holds, CDT reasons that the left agent gets utility $2p$ if it cooperates and $2p + 1$ if it defects, and therefore prescribes defection [8].

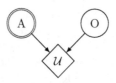

Fig. 1. The causal graph for a one-shot Prisoner's Dilemma. A represents the agent's action, O represents the opponent's action, and $\mathcal{U}$ represents the agent's utility.

Indeed, many decision theorists hold that it is in fact rational for an agent to defect against a perfect copy of itself in a one-shot Prisoner's Dilemma, as after all, no matter what the opponent does, the agent does better by defecting [5,9]. Others object to this view, claiming that since the agents are identical, both actions must match, and mutual cooperation is preferred to mutual defection, so cooperation is the best available action [1]. Our view is that, in the moment, it is better to cooperate with yourself than defect against yourself, and so CDT does not reliably identify the best action available to an agent.

CDT assumes it can hold the action of one opponent constant while freely changing the action of the other, because the actions are causally separated. However, the actions of the two agents are *logically* connected; it is impossible for one agent to cooperate while the other defects. Causal counterfactual reasoning neglects non-causal logical constraints.

It is a common misconception that Newcomblike scenarios only arise when some other actor is a *perfect* predictor (perhaps by being an identical copy). This is not the case: while Newcomblike scenarios are most vividly exemplified by situations involving perfect predictors, they can also arise when other actors have only partial ability to predict the agent [10]. For example, consider a situation in which an artificial agent is interacting with its programmers, who have intimate knowledge of the agent's inner workings. The agent could well find itself embroiled in a Prisoner's Dilemma with its programmers. Let us assume that the agent knows the programmers will be able to predict whether or not it will cooperate with 90% accuracy. In this case, even though the programmers are imperfect predictors, the agent is in a Newcomblike scenario.

In any case, the goal is to formalize what is meant when asking that agents take "the best available action." Causal decision theory often identifies the best action available to an agent, but it sometimes fails in counter-intuitive ways, and therefore, it does not constitute a formalization of idealized decision-making.

3   Counterpossibles

Consider the sort of reasoning that a human might use, faced with a Prisoner's Dilemma in which the opponent's action is guaranteed to match our own:

> The opponent will certainly take the same action that I take. Thus, there is no way for me to exploit the opponent, and no way for the opponent to exploit me. Either we both cooperate and I get $2, or we both defect and I get $1. I prefer the former, so I cooperate.

Contrast this with the hypothetical reasoning of a reasoner who, instead, reasons according to causal counterfactuals:

> There is some probability p that the opponent defects. (Perhaps I can estimate p, perhaps not.) Consider cooperating. In this case, I get $2 if the opponent cooperates and $0 otherwise, for a total of $2p$. Now consider defecting. In this case I get $3 if the opponent cooperates and $1 otherwise, for a total of $2p + 1$. Defection is better no matter what value p takes on, so I defect.

Identifying the best action requires respecting the fact that identical algorithms produce identical outputs. It is not the *physical output of the agent's hardware* which must be modified to construct a counterfactual, it is the *logical output of the agent's decision algorithm.* This insight, discovered independently by Dai [4] and Yudkowsky [14], is one of the main insights behind "updateless decision theory" (UDT).

UDT identifies the best action by evaluating a world-model which represents not only causal relationships in the world, but also the logical effects of algorithms upon the world. In a symmetric Prisoner's Dilemma, a reasoner following the prescriptions of UDT might reason as follows:

> The physical actions of both myself and my opponent are determined by the same algorithm. Therefore, whatever action this very decision algorithm selects will be executed by both of us. If this decision algorithm selects "cooperate" then we'll both cooperate and get a payoff of 2. If instead this decision algorithm selects "defect" then we'll both defect and get a payoff of 1. Therefore, this decision algorithm selects "cooperate."

Using reasoning of this form, a selfish agent acting according to the prescriptions of UDT cooperates with an identical agent on a symmetric one-shot Prisoner's Dilemma, and achieves the higher payoff.[3]

---

[3] The agent does *not* care about the utility of its opponent. Each agent is maximizing its own personal utility. Both players understand that the payoff must be symmetric, and cooperate out of a selfish desire to achieve the higher symmetric payoff.

Evaluating a counterfactual outcome in which the *decision algorithm* behaves differently requires evaluating a logically impossible possibility, known as a "counterpossible."[4] As noted by Cohen [3], "the problem of counterpossible conditionals remains very near the center of philosophy."

To our knowledge, there does not yet exist a formal method of evaluating counterpossibles that is suitable for use in decision theory. This paper discusses two early attempts to formalize a decision theory which makes use of counterpossible reasoning.

3.1   Counterpossibles Using Graphical Models

Following Pearl's formalization of CDT (2000), one might be tempted to formalize UDT using a graphical approach. For example, one might attempt to construct a "logical graph" of the one-shot prisoner's dilemma, where each algorithm has its own "logical node," as in Figure 2. To do so, the graphical representation of the environment must encode not only causal relations, but also logical relations.

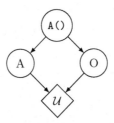

Fig. 2. The logical graph for a symmetric Prisoner's Dilemma where both the agent's action A and the opponent's action O are determined by the algorithm A()

Given a probabilistic graphical model of the world representing both logical and causal connections, and given that one of the nodes in the graph corresponds to the agent's decision algorithm, and given some method of propagating updates through the graph, UDT can be specified in a manner very similar to CDT. To identify the best action available to an agent, iterate over all available actions $a \in A$, change the value of the agent's algorithm node in the graph to a, propagate the update, record the resulting expected utility, and return the action a leading to the highest expected utility. There are two obstacles to formalizing UDT in this way.

---

[4] Some versions of counterpossibles are quite intuitive; for instance, we could imagine how the cryptographic infrastructure of the Internet would fail if we found that P = NP, and it seems as if that counterfactual would still be valid even once we proved that P $\neq$ NP. And yet by the Principle of Explosion, literally any consequence can be deduced from a falsehood, and thus no counterfactual could be "more valid" than any other in a purely formal sense.

The first obstacle is that UDT (like CDT) is underspecified, pending a formal description of how to construct such a graph from a description of the environment (or, eventually, from percepts). However, constructing a graph suitable for UDT is significantly more difficult than constructing a graph suitable for CDT. While both require decreasing the resolution of the world model until the agent's action (in CDT's case) or algorithm (in UDT's case) is represented by a single node rather than a collection of parts, the graph for UDT further requires some ability to identify and separate "algorithms" from the physical processes that implement them. How is UDT supposed to recognize that the agent and its opponent implement the same algorithm? Will this recognition still work if the opponent's algorithm is written in a foreign programming language, or otherwise obfuscated in some way?

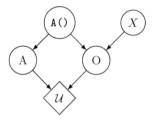

Fig. 3. The desired logical graph for the one-shot Prisoner's Dilemma where agent A acts according to $A()$, and the opponent either mirrors $A()$ or does the opposite, according to the random variable X

Even given some reliable means of identifying copies of an agent's decision algorithm in the environment, this may not be enough to specify a satisfactory graph-based version of UDT. To illustrate, consider UDT identifying the best action available to an agent playing a Prisoner's Dilemma against an opponent that does exactly the same thing as the agent 80% of the time, and takes the opposite action otherwise. It seems UDT should reason according to a graph as in Figure 3, in which the opponent's action is modeled as dependent both upon the agent's algorithm and upon some source X of randomness. However, generating logical graphs as in Figure 3 is a more difficult task than simply detecting all perfect copies of the an algorithm in an environment.

Secondly, a graphical model capable of formalizing UDT must provide some way of propagating "logical updates" through the graph, and it is not at all clear how these logical updates could be defined. Whenever one algorithm's "logical node" in the graph is changed, how does this affect the logical nodes of other algorithms? If the agent's algorithm selects the action a, then clearly the algorithm "do what the agent does 80% of the time and nothing otherwise" is affected. But what about other algorithms which correlate with the agent's algorithm, despite not referencing it directly? What about the algorithms of other agents which base their decisions on an imperfect model of how the agent will behave? In order to understand how logical updates propagate through a logical graph, we desire a better notion of how "changing" one logical fact can "affect" another logical fact.

3.2   Counterpossibles Using Proof Search

Given some method of reasoning about the effects of $A() = a$ on any other algorithm, a graphical formalization of UDT is unnecessary: *the environment itself is an algorithm* which contains the agent, and which describes how to compute the agent's expected utility! Therefore, a formal understanding of "logical updating" could be leveraged to analyze the effects of $A() = a$ upon the environment; to evaluate the action a, UDT need only compute the expected utility available in the environment as modified by the assumption $A() = a$.

This realization leads to the idea of "proof-based UDT," which evaluates actions by searching for formal proofs, using some mathematical theory such as Peano Arithmetic ($\mathcal{PA}$), of how much utility is attained in the world-model if $A()$ selects the action a. As a bonus, this generic search for formal proofs obviates the need to identify the agent in the environment: given an environment which embeds the agent and a description of the agent's algorithm, no matter how the agent is embedded in the environment, a formal proof of the outcome will implicitly identify the agent and describe the implications of that algorithm outputting a. While that proof does the hard work of propagating counterpossibles, the high-level UDT algorithm simply searches all proofs, with no need to formally locate the agent. This allows for an incredibly simple specification of updateless decision theory, given below.

First, a note on syntax: Square quotes ($\ulcorner \cdot \urcorner$) denote sentences encoded as objects that a proof searcher can look for. This may be done via e.g., a Gödel encoding. Overlines within quotes denote "dequotes," allowing the reference of meta-level variables. That is, if at some point in the algorithm $a := 3$ and $o := 10$, then the string $\ulcorner A() = \overline{a} \rightarrow E() = \overline{o} \urcorner$ is an abbreviation of $\ulcorner A() = 3 \rightarrow E() = 10 \urcorner$. The arrow $\ulcorner \rightarrow \urcorner$ denotes logical implication.

The algorithm is defined in terms of a finite set A of actions available to the agent and a finite sorted list O of outcomes that could be achieved (ordered from best to worst). The proof-based UDT algorithm takes a description $\ulcorner E() \urcorner$ of the environment and $\ulcorner A() \urcorner$ of the agent's algorithm. $E()$ computes an outcome, $A()$ computes an action. It is assumed (but not necessary) that changing the output of $A()$ would change the output of $E()$.

Algorithm 1. Proof-based UDT

Function UDT($\ulcorner E() \urcorner$, $\ulcorner A() \urcorner$):

    Sort the set of outcomes O in nonincreasing preference order;

    for *outcome* $o \in O$ **do**

        for *action* $a \in A$ **do**

            if $\mathcal{PA}$ *proves* $\ulcorner A() = \overline{a} \rightarrow E() = \overline{o} \urcorner$ **then return** a ;

    return *the lexicographically first action in* A

To demonstrate how the algorithm works, consider UDT evaluating the actions available to a UDT agent in a symmetric prisoner's dilemma. The list of outcomes is $O := [3, 2, 1, 0]$ according to the cases where the agent exploits, mutually cooperates, mutually defects, and is exploited, respectively. The set of actions is $A := \{C, D\}$ according to whether the agent cooperates or defects. To identify the best action, UDT iterates over outcomes in order of preference, starting with 3. For each outcome, it iterates over actions; say it first considers C. In the case that $A() = C$, the agent cannot achieve the outcome 3, so there is no proof of $\ulcorner A() = C \rightarrow E() = 3 \urcorner$[5]. Next, UDT considers D. If the agent defects, then so does the opponent, so it would get outcome 1, and so there is no proof of $\ulcorner A() = D \rightarrow E() = 3 \urcorner$. So UDT moves on to the next outcome, 2, and considers C. In this case, if the agent cooperates then so will the opponent, so there is a proof of $\ulcorner A() = C \rightarrow E() = 2 \urcorner$, and so UDT selects C.

While this proof-based formalism of UDT is extremely powerful, it is not without its drawbacks. It requires a halting oracle in order to check whether proofs of the statement $\ulcorner A() = \bar{a} \rightarrow E() = \bar{o} \urcorner$ exist; but this is forgivable, as it is meant to be a definition of what it means to "choose the best action," not a practical algorithm. However, this formalization of UDT can only identify the best action if there exists a proof that executing that action leads to a good outcome. This is problematic in stochastic environments, and in any setting where $\mathcal{PA}$ is not a strong enough theory to find the appropriate proofs (which may well occur if agents in the environment are themselves searching for proofs about what UDT will prescribe, in order to guess the behavior of agents which act according to UDT).

There is also larger problem facing this formalism of UDT: even in simple examples, the algorithm is not guaranteed to work. Consider a case where the outcomes are $O := [3, 2, 1]$ corresponding in E() to the actions $A := \{High, Med, Low\}$. If we ask proof-based UDT to identify the best available action to the agent $A() := \text{const Low}$, and it considers the action Med before the action High, then it will misidentify Med as the best available action! This happens because there is a proof that $A() \neq Med$, and so $A() = Med \rightarrow E() = 3$ by the principle of explosion. (In fact, this sort of thing can happen whenever there is any action that is provably not taken.)

As discussed by BensonspsTilsen [2], this problem is averted in the important case $A() = UDT(\ulcorner E() \urcorner, \ulcorner A() \urcorner)$ (this fixed point exists, by Kleene's second recursion theorem). In this case, UDT does in fact get the best provably attainable outcome. This follows from the consistency of $\mathcal{PA}$: imagine that a is a action such that $\mathcal{PA}$ proves $A() \neq a$. Then $\mathcal{PA}$ proves that $A() = a$ implies the first outcome in O (which has the highest possible preference), and so UDT must either return a or return another action which implies the first outcome in O—but returning a would be a contradiction. Therefore, either UDT will return an action which

---

[5] One must be careful with this sort of reasoning, for if $\mathcal{PA}$ could prove that $A() = D$ then it could also prove $A() = C \rightarrow E() = 3$ by the principle of explosion. However, in this case, that sort of "spurious proof" is avoided by technical reasons discussed by BensonspsTilsen [2].

truly leads to the highest outcome, or there is no action a such that $\mathcal{PA}$ can prove $\mathtt{A}() \neq a$, and thus the only proofs found will be genuine implications. Even so, the apparent deficits of UDT at analyzing other algorithms are troubling, and it is not obvious that reasoning about the logical implications of $\mathtt{A}() = a$ is the right way to formalize counterpossible reasoning.

A better understanding of counterpossible reasoning may well be necessary in order to formalize UDT in a stochastic setting, where it maximizes expected utility instead of searching for proofs of a certain outcome. Such an algorithm would evaluate actions *conditioned* on the logical fact $\mathtt{A}() = a$, rather than searching for logical implications. How does one deal with the case where $\mathtt{A}() \neq a$, so that $\mathtt{A}() = a$ is a zero-probability event? In order to reason about expected utility conditioned on $\mathtt{A}() = a$, it seems necessary to develop a more detailed understanding of counterpossible reasoning. If one deterministic algorithm violates the laws of logic in order to output something other than what it outputs, then how does this affect other algorithms? Which laws of logic, precisely, are violated, and how does this violation affect other logical statements?

It is not clear that these questions are meaningful, nor even that a satisfactory general method of reasoning about counterpossibles actually exists. It is plausible that a better understanding of reasoning under logical uncertainty would shed some light on these issues, but a satisfactory theory of reasoning under logical uncertainty does not yet exist.[6] Regardless, it seems that some deeper understanding of counterpossibles is necessary in order to give a satisfactory formalization of updateless decision theory.

4   Conclusion

The goal of answering all these questions is not to identify practical algorithms, directly. Rather, the goal is to ensure that the problem of decision-making is well understood: without a formal description of what is meant by "good decision," it is very difficult to justify high confidence in a practical heuristic that is intended to make good decisions.

It currently looks like specifying an idealized decision theory requires formalizing some method for evaluating counterpossibles, but this problem is a difficult one, and counterpossible reasoning is an open philosophical problem. While these problems have remained open for some time, our examination in the light of decision-theory, with a focus on concrete algorithms, has led to some new ideas. We are optimistic that further decision theory research could lead to significant progress toward understanding the problem of idealized decision-making.

---

[6] A *logically uncertain* reasoner can know both the laws of logic and the source code of a program without knowing what the program outputs.

References

1. Bar-Hillel, M., Margalit, A.: Newcomb's paradox revisited. British Journal for the Philosophy of Science **23**(4), 295–304 (1972). http://www.jstor.org/stable/686730
2. Benson-Tilsen, T.: UDT with known search order. Tech. Rep. 2014-4, Machine Intelligence Research Institute (2014). http://intelligence.org/files/UDTSearchOrder.pdf
3. Cohen, D.: On what cannot be. In: Dunn, J., Gupta, A. (eds.) Truth or Consequences, pp. 123–132. Kluwer (1990)
4. Dai, W.: Towards a new decision theory. Less Wrong (2009). http://lesswrong.com/lw/15m/towards_a_new_decision_theory/
5. Gibbard, A., Harper, W.L.: Counterfactuals and two kinds of expected utility. In: Hooker, C.A., Leach, J.J., McClennen, E.F. (eds.) Foundations and Applications of Decision Theory, The Western Ontario Series in Philosophy of Science, vol. 13a. D. Reidel (1978)
6. Jeffrey, R.C.: The Logic of Decision, 2 edn. Chicago University Press (1983)
7. Lehmann, E.L.: Some principles of the theory of testing hypotheses. Annals of Mathematical Statistics **21**(1), 1–26 (1950)
8. Lewis, D.: Prisoners' dilemma is a Newcomb problem. Philosophy & Public Affairs **8**(3), 235–240 (1979). http://www.jstor.org/stable/2265034
9. Lewis, D.: Causal decision theory. Australasian Journal of Philosophy **59**(1), 5–30 (1981)
10. Lewis, D.: Why ain'cha rich? Noûs **15**(3), 377–380 (1981). http://www.jstor.org/stable/2215439
11. Nozick, R.: Newcomb's problem and two principles of choice. In: Rescher, N. (ed.) Essays in Honor of Carl G. Hempel, pp. 114–146. No. 24 in Synthese Library, D. Reidel (1969)
12. Pearl, J.: Causality, 1 edn. Cambridge University Press (2000)
13. Von Neumann, J., Morgenstern, O.: Theory of Games and Economic Behavior, 1 edn. Princeton University Press (1944)
14. Yudkowsky, E.: Timeless decision theory. Tech. rep., The Singularity Institute, San Francisco, CA (2010). http://intelligence.org/files/TDT.pdf

Bounded Cognitive Resources
and Arbitrary Domains

Abdul Rahim Nizamani[2]([envelope]), Jonas Juel[3],
Ulf Persson[3], and Claes Strannegård[1]

[1] Department of Philosophy, Linguistics and Theory of Science,
University of Gothenburg, Sweden and Department of Applied Information
Technology, Chalmers University of Technology, Gothenburg, Sweden
claes.strannegard@gu.se
[2] Department of Applied Information Technology,
University of Gothenburg, Gothenburg, Sweden
abdulrahim.nizamani@gu.se
[3] Department of Mathematical Sciences,
Chalmers University of Technology, Gothenburg, Sweden
ulf.persson@chalmers.se, jonas@juel.nu

Abstract. When Alice in Wonderland fell down the rabbit hole, she entered a world that was completely new to her. She gradually explored that world by observing, learning, and reasoning. This paper presents a simple system ALICE IN WONDERLAND that operates analogously. We model Alice's Wonderland via a general notion of domain and Alice herself with a computational model including an evolving belief set along with mechanisms for observing, learning, and reasoning. The system operates autonomously, learning from arbitrary streams of facts from symbolic domains such as English grammar, propositional logic, and simple arithmetic. The main conclusion of the paper is that bounded cognitive resources can be exploited systematically in artificial general intelligence for constructing general systems that tackle the combinatorial explosion problem and operate in arbitrary symbolic domains.

Keywords: Autonomous agent · Bounded rationality · Arbitrary domain

1 Introduction

Natural organisms have a remarkable ability to adapt to new environments. Humans enter new environments – e.g., rainforests, deserts, cities – and survive. They can learn any language, any game, any logic. Bees likewise enter new environments – e.g., when a new beehive is deployed – and survive. They can learn to recognize flowers visually and even – as we are discovering – by their patterns of electrical fields [3] and even differentiate visually between vowels and consonants in the Latin alphabet [5]. Microscopic crustaceans enter new

© Springer International Publishing Switzerland 2015
J. Bieger (Ed.): AGI 2015, LNAI 9205, pp. 166–176, 2015.
DOI: 10.1007/978-3-319-21365-1_18

environments and survive: e.g., when an ocean wave hits the shore and so forms a new ecosystem in a rock pool. Also crustaceans are capable of learning [18].

Artificial systems have not reached the same level of flexibility. No robots can come to new environments – say, private homes – and do the laundry, wash the dishes, clean up, make coffee. No robots can go to high school and learn natural languages, mathematics, and logic so as to match an average school child.

One strategy for making artificial systems more flexible is to simulate human cognition. Such an approach has been taken by Soar [8], ACT-R [1], NARS [17], MicroPsi [2], OpenCog [4], and Sigma [11]. Turing proposed building artificial systems that simulate children's cognitive development [15]. Piaget writes that children adapt to new information in one of two ways: by *assimilation*, in which new information fits into existing knowledge structures; and *accommodation*, in which new information causes new knowledge structures to form or old ones to be modified [9].

This paper presents the system ALICE IN WONDERLAND, which is able to operate autonomously across arbitrary symbolic and crisp domains. As the name suggests, we take the Alice in Wonderland story as inspiration, modeling Wonderland via a general notion of domain and Alice herself with a computational model including an evolving belief set along with mechanisms for observing, learning, and reasoning. The system functions with or without human intervention, developing intelligence on the basis of random streams of facts taken from arbitrary domains. The computational complexity of the system is restricted by using a simple cognitive model with bounded cognitive resources.

The ALICE IN WONDERLAND system builds on theory borrowed from developmental psychology [16], along with bounded rationality [13], belief revision [6], and inductive program synthesis [7,12]. Popper [10, p.261] provides a key inspiration:

> The growth of our knowledge is the result of a process closely resembling what Darwin called 'natural selection'; that is, the natural selection of hypotheses: our knowledge consists, at every moment, of those hypotheses which have shown their (comparative) fitness by surviving so far in their struggle for existence, a competitive struggle which eliminates those hypotheses which are unfit.

The present paper improves on our previous work [14], since the system can learn from arbitrary streams of observations and not only when being spoon-fed with carefully selected examples. Sections 2–6 describe how Alice observes, represents knowledge, reasons, learns, and answers questions, respectively. Section 7 presents results and Section 8 offers some conclusions.

2 How Alice Makes Observations

Definition 1 (symbol). *A symbol is a Unicode character.*

Definition 2 (variable). *A variable is a symbol belonging to the set* $\{x,y,z\}$.

Definition 3 (vocabulary). *A vocabulary is a set of finite symbol strings.*

Example 1. Here are vocabularies that can be used for arithmetic, propositional logic, and English, respectively:

V_A: 0, 1, 2, 3, 4, 5, 6, 7, 8, 9 (digits), + (addition), * (multiplication), # (con-catenation).
V_P: p, q, r (propositional constants), $\top$ (truth), $\bot$ (falsity), $\neg$ (negation), $\wedge$ (conjunction), $\vee$ (disjunction), $\rightarrow$ (implication).
V_E: # (concatenation), `Alice`, `Stella`, `runs`, `plays`, `fast`, along with all other words appearing in a given English corpus.

Definition 4 (term). *Let V be a vocabulary. A V-term is a finite ordered labeled tree. Each node is labeled with an element of V. A V-term is* open *if it has a node that is labeled with a variable and* closed *otherwise.*

We follow common practice and write terms as strings, using parentheses and other standard conventions for disambiguation.

Example 2. Here are examples of V_A-terms, V_P-terms, and V_E-terms:

Arithmetic terms: 2*(3+4), 1#2, x*0
Logic terms: $\neg\bot$, x $\wedge$ y, x $\vee$ $\top$
English terms: `Alice#plays`, `Stella#(runs#fast)`, `OK`

The operator # is used for concatenating elements, regardless of vocabulary: e.g., the number 12 is represented by the term 1#2 and the sentence `Alice plays` by the term `Alice#plays`. That said, we will often, in this paper, omit the symbol # to facilitate reading. Note that we have imposed no type or arity restrictions on the terms: a labeled tree such as 1(*) also qualifies as a V_A-term.

Definition 5 (condition). *A condition is an expression of the form $t \vdash t'$ or $t \nvdash t'$, where t and t' are V-terms, given some vocabulary V.*

Definition 6 (fact). *A fact is a condition both of whose terms are closed.*

Example 3. Here are examples of facts: 6+6 $\vdash$ 12, 0 $\nvdash$ 1, $\neg\top \vdash \bot$, $\top \wedge \bot \nvdash \top$, `Stella runs fast` $\vdash$ `OK`, `runs` $\nvdash$ `OK`.

The following definition of (symbolic) *domain* is adequate for our present purposes, although more general definitions of this notion are clearly conceivable.

Definition 7 (domain). *A domain is a set of facts.*

Example 4. Here are examples of domains (certain details omitted):

Arithmetic domain: $\{t \vdash t' : t, t' \text{ are } V_A \text{ terms such that } t = t'\}$
Logic domain:
   $\{t \vdash t' : t, t' \text{ are } V_P \text{ terms such that } t \text{ is a logical consequence of } t'\}$
English domain:
   $\{t \vdash t' : t, t' \text{ are } V_E \text{ terms of some context-free fragment of English}\}$

Definition 8 (stream). *Let D be a domain. A D-stream is a sequence of facts $F_0, F_1, \ldots,$ where each $F_i \in D$.*

Example 5. Here are examples of streams:

Arithmetic stream: $6+6 \vdash 12, 0 \nvdash 1, 23*4 \vdash 92, \ldots$
Logic stream: $\neg\top \vdash \bot, \bot \nvdash \top, p \rightarrow (q \rightarrow p) \vdash \top, \ldots$
English stream: Alice runs$\vdash$ OK, Stella runs$\vdash$ OK, runs $\nvdash$ OK, $\ldots$

In the present context domains model Wonderland; streams model Alice's observations of Wonderland.

3 How Alice Represents Knowledge

Definition 9 (rule). *A rule is an expression of the form $t \rhd t'$, $t \blacktriangleright t'$, or $t \ntriangleright t'$, where t and t' are terms.*

Example 6. $0 \ntriangleright 1$, $2*2 \blacktriangleright 4$, Alice plays $\rhd$ OK, and $x \lor y \rhd x$ are rules.

Definition 10 (purity). *The rule $t \rhd t'$ ($t \blacktriangleright t'$) is pure if all variables of t' appear in t.*

Example 7. The rules $x*0 \rhd 0$ and $x \lor \top \blacktriangleright \top$ are pure, whereas $0 \rhd x*0$ and $\top \blacktriangleright x \lor \top$ are not.

Definition 11 (theory). *A theory is a finite set of pure rules.*

Example 8. Here are examples of theories:

Arithmetic theory: $\{2*2 \blacktriangleright 4, x*0 \blacktriangleright 0, x+y \blacktriangleright y+x\}$
Logic theory: $\{x \lor \top \blacktriangleright \top, x \rightarrow y \blacktriangleright \neg x \lor y, x \lor y \rhd x\}$
English theory: $\{$Alice plays $\blacktriangleright$ OK, Alice $\blacktriangleright$ Stella, runs $\ntriangleright$ OK$\}$

4 How Alice Reasons

Definition 12 (substitution). *A substitution is a partial function σ that assigns terms or labels to variables. The substitution σ can be applied to terms by replacing variables at leaf nodes by terms and variables at non-leaves by labels according to σ.*

Example 9. $\emptyset$, $\{x = $ Alice$\}$, and $\{x = 2, y = 3\}$ are substitutions. If $\sigma = \{x = 2, y = 3\}$, then $\sigma(x+y) = 2+3$. Also, if $\sigma = \{x = $ raven$\}$, then $\sigma(x(\text{hugin})) = $ raven(hugin).

Definition 13 (context). *A context is a term t containing exactly one occurrence of the symbol $\square$, which labels a leaf of t.*

Example 10. $\square + 5$, $\top \lor \square$, and $\square$ runs are contexts.

If c is a context and t is a term, then $c(t)$ is the result of replacing the unique occurrence of $\square$ in c by t. If $c = \square$, then $c(t) = t$.

Definition 14 (computation). *Suppose T is a theory. A T-computation is a sequence of closed terms $(t_1, \ldots, t_n)$ such that for all k such that $0 < k < n$:*

Shallow step. $t_k = \sigma(t)$ *and* $t_{k+1} = \sigma(t')$, *for some σ and $t \rhd t' \in T$, or*
Deep step. $t_k = c(\sigma(t))$ *and* $t_{k+1} = c(\sigma(t'))$, *for some c, σ, and $t \blacktriangleright t' \in T$*

Examples of computations – written vertically and annotated with rules – are given in figures 1–4.

$$\frac{\dfrac{\dfrac{(2+4)*(6+1)}{6*(6+1)} \quad 2+4 \blacktriangleright 6}{\dfrac{6*7}{42} \quad 6*7 \blacktriangleright 42}}{} \qquad \frac{\dfrac{0*12}{12*0} \quad x*y \blacktriangleright y*x}{0 \quad x*0 \blacktriangleright 0}$$

Fig. 1. These computations can be interpreted as arithmetic computations with rules that preserve equality

$$\frac{\dfrac{\dfrac{\dfrac{(p \to q)\vee p}{(\neg\, p\vee q)\vee p} \quad x \to y \blacktriangleright \neg x \vee y}{\dfrac{(q\vee\neg\, p)\vee p}{q\vee(\neg\, p\vee p)} \quad (x\vee y)\vee z \blacktriangleright x\vee(y\vee z)}}{\dfrac{q\vee\top}{\top} \quad x\vee\top \blacktriangleright \top}}{} \qquad \frac{black(Hugin)}{raven(Hugin)} \quad black(x) \rhd raven(x)$$

Fig. 2. These computations can be interpreted as logic computations with rules that preserve or increase logical strength: i.e., goal-driven proofs. To prove $(p \to q)\vee p$, it is sufficient to prove $\top$; to prove `black(Hugin)`, it is sufficient to prove `raven(Hugin)`.

$$\frac{\dfrac{\dfrac{\text{Stella plays}}{\text{Stella crawls}} \quad \text{plays} \blacktriangleright \text{crawls}}{\dfrac{\text{Alice crawls}}{\text{OK}} \quad \text{Alice crawls} \blacktriangleright \text{OK}}}{\text{Stella} \blacktriangleright \text{Alice}}$$

Fig. 3. This computation can be interpreted as a grammatical computation: specifically, derivations in formal grammar with rules that preserve grammatical equivalence. The derivation shows that `Stella plays` is a grammatically correct sentence of English.

Definition 15 (bounded resources). *The following arbitrarily defined constants determine the boundaries of Alice's cognitive resources.*

- *Long-term memory:* $LTM_{Alice} = 200$ *(rules)*
- *Working memory:* $WM_{Alice} = 8$ *(nodes)*
- *Computation depth:* $Depth_{Alice} = 10$ *(steps)*

$$\frac{\dfrac{\dfrac{\dfrac{\dfrac{\dfrac{\texttt{rev([6,7])}}{\texttt{rev([7]) ++ [6]}}\ \texttt{rev(x:xs)} \blacktriangleright \texttt{rev(xs) ++ [x]}}{\texttt{(rev([]) ++ [7]) ++ [6]}}\ \texttt{rev(x:xs)} \blacktriangleright \texttt{rev(xs) ++ [x]}}{\texttt{([] ++ [7]) ++ [6]}}\ \texttt{rev([])} \blacktriangleright \texttt{[]}}{\texttt{[7] ++ [6]}}\ \texttt{[] ++ xs} \blacktriangleright \texttt{xs}}{\texttt{[7,6]}}\ \texttt{[x] ++ xs} \blacktriangleright \texttt{x:xs}$$

Fig. 4. This computation can be interpreted as a Haskell computation with rules that preserve equality. The derivation shows how the function **rev** reverses the list [6,7].

Definition 16 (term size). *Given term t, $size(t)$ is the number of nodes of t, excluding nodes labeled with* **#**.

Definition 17 (bounded computation). *A* bounded T-computation *is a T-computation $(t_1, \ldots, t_n)$ with*

- *bounded length:* $n \leq Depth_{Alice}$
- *bounded width:* $size(t_i) \leq WM_{Alice}$, *for each* $1 \leq i \leq n$

Intuitively, all bounded computations fit into a frame of height $Depth_{Alice}$ and width WM_{Alice}. The computations in figures 1–4 are all bounded.

Definition 18 (computability). *We write $t \vdash_T t'$ if there is a T-computation from t to t' and $t \vdash_T^* t'$ if there is a bounded T-computation from t to t'.*

Theorem 1. *The relation $\vdash_T^*$ is decidable.*

Proof. All theories are finite by definition. Given the purity condition on rules, only finitely many bounded T-computations beginning with any given closed term t are possible. The bounded T-computations starting with t form a finitely branching tree where each branch has a maximum length. Hence, the tree is finite and $\vdash_T^*$ is decidable.

5   How Alice Learns

In this section we outline some of the system's basic learning mechanisms. Several learning mechanisms, based e.g. on rule viability and rule reliability are omitted for reasons of space.

Definition 19 (fitness). *The* fitness *of theory T on a finite non-empty domain D is the number*

$$Fitness(T, D) = \frac{card(\{t \vdash t' \in D : t \vdash_T^* t'\} \cup \{t \nvdash t' \in D : t \nvdash_T^* t'\})}{card(D)}.$$

Example 11. Given $D = \{\texttt{2*0} \vdash \texttt{0}, \texttt{3*0} \vdash \texttt{0}, \texttt{1} \nvdash \texttt{0}\}$, the following holds:

- $Fitness(\{\texttt{2*0} \blacktriangleright \texttt{0}\}, D) = 2/3$
- $Fitness(\{\texttt{x} \blacktriangleright \texttt{0}\}, D) = 2/3$
- $Fitness(\{\texttt{x*0} \blacktriangleright \texttt{0}\}, D) = 1$

Definition 20 (successor). *Theory T' is a successor of T if $T' - T$ contains at most one rule.*

Example 12. Any subset of $T \cup \{t \blacktriangleright t'\}$ or $T \cup \{t \not\triangleright t'\}$ is a successor of T.

Definition 21 (consistency). *Theory T is consistent if $t \not\triangleright t' \in T$ implies $t \not\vdash_T^* t'$.*

Alice adapts to the stream $F_0, F_1, \ldots$ by forming a sequence of theories $T_0, T_1, \ldots$ that ideally satisfies $\lim_{n \to \infty} Fitness(T_n, \{F_k : k \leq n\}) = 1$. Theory T_{n+1} is a consistent successor of T_n that contains at most LTM_{Alice} rules. Alice defines T_{n+1} using one of two mechanisms:

Exogenic update. Define T_{n+1} based on F_n. If $F_n = t \vdash t'$ and $t \not\vdash_{T_n}^* t'$, add a rule so that $t \vdash_{T_{n+1}}^* t'$ if prioritized. If $F_n = t \not\vdash t'$ and $t \vdash_{T_n}^* t'$, remove one or more rules so that $t \not\vdash_{T_{n+1}}^* t'$. Add F_n as a rule (either with $\blacktriangleright$ or $\triangleright$ depending on symmetry) if prioritized.

Endogenic update. Define T_{n+1} based on T_n. Check open rules and if prioritized, add open rule R with the properties that (i) several closed instances of R are bounded-computable in T_n and (ii) no small counterexample to R is bounded-computable in T_n.

If $card(T_n) = Alice_{LTM}$, then no new rule can be added to T_{n+1} until some old rule has been removed. Preference orders are used for determining which rules should be added to or removed from T_n. Update mechanisms are invoked as described in Table 1. Table 2 gives an example of a learning process.

Table 1. Criteria for selecting update mechanism depending on F_n and $\vdash_{T_n}^*$

	$F_n = t \vdash t'$	$F_n = t \not\vdash t'$
$t \vdash_{T_n}^* t'$	Endogenic update	Exogenic update
$t \not\vdash_{T_n}^* t'$	Exogenic update	Endogenic update

6   How Alice Solves Problems

Definition 22 (closed problem). *A closed problem is a closed term t. A solution to closed problem t with respect to T is closed term t' such that $t \vdash_T^* t'$, where t' must be minimal in the sense that $t \vdash_T^* t''$ implies $size(t'') \geq size(t')$.*

Definition 23 (open problem). *An open problem is a finite set of open conditions. A solution to open problem P with respect to T is a substitution σ such that $Fitness(T, \sigma(P)) = 1$.*

Examples of such problems and solutions (w.r.t. an unspecified background theory) are given in tables 3–4. For problem-solving, the system uses exhaustive search among bounded computations together with a few simple heuristic principles.

Table 2. An example learning process, with endogenic and exogenic updates

Fact	Theory update
2*0 ⊢ 0	Add 2*0 ▶ 0.
3*0 ⊢ 0	Add 3*0 ▶ 0.
2*0 ⊢ 0	Add x ▶ 0.
1 ⊬ 0	Remove x ▶ 0. Add 1 ⋫ 0.
2*(3*0) ⊢ 0	Add x*0 ▶ 0.
75*0 ⊢ 0	Do nothing.
0*0 ⊢ 0	Add 0*0 ▶ 0.
1*1 ⊢ 1	Add 1*1 ▶ 1.
1*1 ⊢ 1	Add x*x ▶ x.
2*2 ⊬ 2	Remove x*x ▶ x. Add 2*2 ⋫ 2.
5+2 ⊢ 7	Add 5+2 ▶ 7.
23 ⊬ 45	Do nothing.
f(0) ⊢ 5	Add f(0) ▶ 5.
f(1) ⊢ 7	Add f(1) ▶ 7.
f(1) ⊢ 7	Add f(x+1) ▶ f(x)+2.
Alice crawls ⊢ OK	Add Alice crawls ▶ OK.
Alice runs ⊢ OK	Add runs ▶ crawls.

Table 3. Closed problems with examples of solutions

Closed problem	Solution
13+4	17
(p → q) ∨ p	⊤
Stella crawls	OK
f(2)	9

7   Results

The ALICE IN WONDERLAND system consists of around 5,000 lines of Haskell code, modeling Wonderland as unknown domain D and Alice's belief set at time n as theory T_n. Alice starts with theory T_0, which is empty by default. At any time n, the system can be in learning or inquiry mode, as determined by the human operator:

Learning Mode. Alice receives fact $F_n \in D$. Alice learns from F_n and updates her theory to T_{n+1}.

Inquiry Mode. Alice receives an open or closed problem, P_n. Alice outputs a solution to P_n or reports failure and makes $T_{n+1} = T_n$.

In learning mode, F_n could come from any source: e.g. sensors, text file, or human entry. For purposes of illustration, predefined streams can be chosen from a dropdown menu. In inquiry mode, P_n is entered by the human operator.

Table 4. Open problems with examples of solutions

Open problem	Solution
x+4 ⊢ 9	x=5
x runs ⊢ OK	x=Alice
even(x) ⊢ True	x=0
under(x,foot) ⊢ True	x=sole
x ∨ False ⊢ True	x=True
x(Hugin) ⊢ True	x=raven
x ⊢ cough, x ⊢ sneeze	x=cold
x ⊢ cough, x ⊢ sneeze, x ⊬ cold	x=flu
x+y ⊢ 2, x*y ⊢ 1	x=1, y=1
(x-1)*(x-2) ⊢ 0, x ⊬ 1	x=2
x(cat,mouse) ⊢ True	x=chases
x(sun,planet) ⊢ True, x(nucleus,electron) ⊢ True	x=circles
x(palm,hand) ⊢ True, x(y,foot) ⊢ True	x=under, y=sole

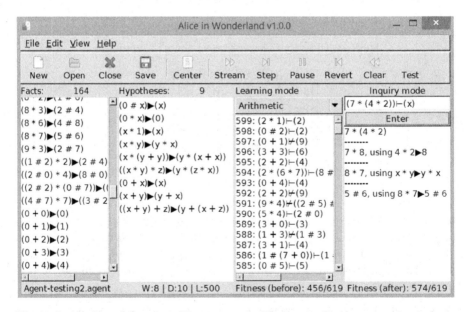

Fig. 5. Screenshot of ALICE IN WONDERLAND. The system has been running in learning mode, processing 599 arithmetic facts in the course of approximately 20 minutes
(assuming a standard laptop). From left, the first and second panels represent Alice's
beliefs in the form of closed and open rules, respectively. Alice's current theory consists
of 164 closed rules, including 8*7 = 56, and 9 open rules, including 0*x = 0. The third
panel shows the fact stream, the fourth panel solutions to problems entered by the
human operator.

Figure 5 shows a screenshot of the system in operation. The following results were obtained:

- ALICE IN WONDERLAND can learn as shown in Table 2 and solve problems as shown in tables 3–4.
- ALICE IN WONDERLAND can start from a state of no knowledge and learn from random streams of facts taken from arbitrary domains. To date, it can learn simple versions of propositional logic, variable-free first-order logic, arithmetic, arithmetic *modulo* 2, $F_2[X]$, English, Swedish, and Sindhi.
- Over time, ALICE IN WONDERLAND exceeds average human performance in such domains as simple arithmetic and propositional logic.

8   Conclusions

We have described the system ALICE IN WONDERLAND, which does autonomous learning and problem-solving in arbitrary symbolic domains. A key component is a simple cognitive model that reduces the computational complexity from undecidable to finite. In this way, we tackle the combinatorial explosion problem that arises in e.g. inductive logic programming, automatic theorem proving, and grammar learning. Our results show that the system is able to learn multiple domains from random streams of facts and also challenge human problem-solving in some cases. Thus bounded cognitive resources were exploited for constructing a general system that tackles the combinatorial explosion problem and operates in arbitrary symbolic domains.

Acknowledgments. This research was supported by The Swedish Research Council, grant 2012-1000. We would like to thank Volodya Shavrukov for many helpful comments.

References

1. Anderson, J.R., Lebiere, C.: The atomic components of thought. Lawrence Erlbaum, Mahwah, N.J. (1998)
2. Bach, J.: MicroPsi 2: the next generation of the MicroPsi framework. In: Bach, J., Goertzel, B., Iklé, M. (eds.) AGI 2012. LNCS, vol. 7716, pp. 11–20. Springer, Heidelberg (2012)
3. Clarke, D., Whitney, H., Sutton, G., Robert, D.: Detection and learning of floral electric fields by bumblebees. Science **340**(6128), 66–69 (2013)
4. Goertzel, B., Pennachin, C., Geisweiller, N.: The OpenCog framework. In: Engineering General Intelligence, Part 2, pp. 3–29. Springer (2014)
5. Gould, J.L., Gould, C.G., et al.: The honey bee. Scientific American Library (1988)
6. Hansson, S.O., Fermé, E.L., Cantwell, J., Falappa, M.A.: Credibility Limited Revision. The Journal of Symbolic Logic **66**(04), 1581–1596 (2001)
7. Kitzelmann, E.: Inductive Programming: A Survey of Program Synthesis Techniques. In: Schmid, U., Kitzelmann, E., Plasmeijer, R. (eds.) AAIP 2009. LNCS, vol. 5812, pp. 50–73. Springer, Heidelberg (2010)
8. Laird, J.E., Newell, A., Rosenbloom, P.S.: Soar: An Architecture for General Intelligence. Artificial Intelligence **33**(3), 1–64 (1987)

9. Piaget, J.: La construction du réel chez l'enfant. Delachaux & Niestlé (1937)
10. Popper, K.R.: Objective knowledge: An evolutionary approach. Clarendon Press, Oxford (1972)
11. Rosenbloom, P.S.: The Sigma Cognitive Architecture and System. AISB Quarterly **136**, 4–13 (2013)
12. Schmid, U., Kitzelmann, E.: Inductive rule learning on the knowledge level. Cognitive Systems Research **12**(3), 237–248 (2011)
13. Simon, H.A.: Models of Bounded Rationality: Empirically Grounded Economic Reason, vol. 3. MIT press (1982)
14. Strannegård, C., Nizamani, A.R., Persson, U.: A General system for learning and reasoning in symbolic domains. In: Goertzel, B., Orseau, L., Snaider, J. (eds.) AGI 2014. LNCS, vol. 8598, pp. 174–185. Springer, Heidelberg (2014)
15. Turing, A.: Computing machinery and intelligence. Mind **59**(236), 433–460 (1950)
16. Von Glasersfeld, E.: Radical Constructivism: A Way of Knowing and Learning. Studies in Mathematics Education Series: 6. ERIC (1995)
17. Wang, P.: From NARS to a thinking machine. In: Proceedings of the 2007 Conference on Artificial General Intelligence. pp. 75–93. IOS Press, Amsterdam (2007)
18. Wiese, K.: The Crustacean Nervous System. Springer (2002)

Using Localization and Factorization to Reduce the Complexity of Reinforcement Learning

Peter Sunehag[1,2]([⊠]) and Marcus Hutter[1]

[1] Research School of Computer Science,
Australian National University, Canberra, Australia
Sunehag@google.com, Marcus.Hutter@anu.edu.au
[2] Google - Deep Mind, London, UK

Abstract. General reinforcement learning is a powerful framework for artificial intelligence that has seen much theoretical progress since introduced fifteen years ago. We have previously provided guarantees for cases with finitely many possible environments. Though the results are the best possible in general, a linear dependence on the size of the hypothesis class renders them impractical. However, we dramatically improved on these by introducing the concept of environments generated by combining laws. The bounds are then linear in the number of laws needed to generate the environment class. This number is identified as a natural complexity measure for classes of environments. The individual law might only predict some feature (factorization) and only in some contexts (localization). We here extend previous deterministic results to the important stochastic setting.

Keywords: Reinforcement learning · Laws · Optimism · Bounds

1 Introduction

General reinforcement learning [2,3,12] is a theoretical foundation for artificial intelligence that has now been developed over the last fifteen years. A recent line of work starting with [8,9] has studied finite classes of completely general environments and primarily optimistic agents that can be proven to eventually achieve optimality regardless of which environment turns out to be true. [8] presented finite-error bounds for the deterministic case and asymptotic guarantees for stochastic environments while [5] proved near-optimal sample complexity bounds for the latter stochastic case.

The bounds given in [8] have a linear dependence on the number of environments in the class. While this rate is easily seen to be the best one can have in general [5], it is exponentially worse than what we are used to from Markov Decision Processes (MDPs) [4] where the linear (up to logarithms) dependence is on the size of the state space instead. In [10] we introduced the concept of deterministic laws that predict some but not all features (factorization) and only in some contexts (localization), and environments generated by sets of such laws.

© Springer International Publishing Switzerland 2015
J. Bieger (Ed.): AGI 2015, LNAI 9205, pp. 177–186, 2015.
DOI: 10.1007/978-3-319-21365-1_19

We presented bounds that are linear in the number of laws instead of the number of environments. All deterministic environment classes are trivially generated by sets of laws that equal the environments but some can also be generated by exponentially fewer laws than there are environments.

We here expand the formal analysis of optimistic agents with hypothesis classes based on laws, from the deterministic to the stochastic case and we further consider fruitful combinations of those two basic cases.

Outline. Section 2 provides background on general reinforcement learning agents. Section 3 introduces the concept of environments generated by laws and extends previous concepts and results from the determinstic to the stochastic case as well as to the mixed setting. Section 4 concludes.

2   Background

We begin by introducing general reinforcement learning as well as the agent framework.

2.1   General Reinforcement Learning

We will consider an agent [2,6] that interacts with an environment through performing actions a_t from a finite set $\mathcal{A}$ and receives observations o_t from a finite set $\mathcal{O}$ and rewards r_t from a finite set $\mathcal{R} \subset [0,1]$ resulting in a history $h_t := a_0 o_1 r_1 a_1, ..., o_t r_t$. These sets can be allowed to depend on time or context but we do not write this out explicitly. Let $\mathcal{H} := \{\epsilon\} \cup (\mathcal{A} \times \cup_n (\mathcal{O} \times R \times \mathcal{A})^n \times (\mathcal{O} \times \mathcal{R}))$ be the set of histories where ϵ is the empty history and $\mathcal{A} \times (\mathcal{O} \times R \times \mathcal{A})^0 \times (\mathcal{O} \times \mathcal{R}) := \mathcal{A} \times \mathcal{O} \times \mathcal{R}$. A function $\nu : \mathcal{H} \times \mathcal{A} \to \mathcal{O} \times \mathcal{R}$ is called a deterministic environment. A function $\pi : \mathcal{H} \to \mathcal{A}$ is called a (deterministic) policy or an agent. We define the value function V based on geometric discounting by $V_\nu^\pi(h_{t-1}) = \sum_{i=t}^\infty \gamma^{i-t} r_i$ where the sequence r_i are the rewards achieved by following π from time step t onwards in the environment ν after having seen h_{t-1}.

Instead of viewing the environment as a function $\mathcal{H} \times \mathcal{A} \to \mathcal{O} \times \mathcal{R}$ we can equivalently write it as a function $\mathcal{H} \times \mathcal{A} \times \mathcal{O} \times \mathcal{R} \to \{0,1\}$ where we write $\nu(o,r|h,a)$ for the function value. It equals zero if in the first formulation (h,a) is not sent to (o,r) and 1 if it is. In the case of stochastic environments we instead have a function $\nu : \mathcal{H} \times \mathcal{A} \times \mathcal{O} \times \mathcal{R} \to [0,1]$ such that $\sum_{o,r} \nu(o,r|h,a) = 1\ \forall h,a$. The deterministic environments are then just a degenerate special case. Furthermore, we define $\nu(h_t|\pi) := \Pi_{i=1}^t \nu(o_i r_i | a_i, h_{i-1})$ where $a_i = \pi(h_{i-1})$. $\nu(\cdot|\pi)$ is a probability measure over strings, actually one measure for each string length with the corresponding power set as the σ-algebra. We define $\nu(\cdot|\pi, h_{t-1})$ by conditioning $\nu(\cdot|\pi)$ on h_{t-1} and we let $V_\nu^\pi(h_{t-1}) := \mathbb{E}_{\nu(\cdot|\pi,h_{t-1})} \sum_{i=t}^\infty \gamma^{i-t} r_i :=$ $\lim_{j\to\infty} \mathbb{E}_{\nu(\cdot|\pi,h_{t-1})} \sum_{i=t}^j \gamma^{i-t} r_i$ and $V_\nu^*(h_{t-1}) := \max_\pi V_\nu^\pi(h_{t-1})$.

Examples of Agents: AIXI and Optimist. Suppose we are given a countable class of environments $\mathcal{M}$ and strictly positive prior weights w_ν for all $\nu \in \mathcal{M}$.

We define the a priori environment ξ by letting $\xi(\cdot) = \sum w_\nu \nu(\cdot)$ and the AIXI agent is defined by following the policy

$$\pi^* := \arg\max_\pi V_\xi^\pi(\epsilon) \tag{1}$$

which is its general form. Sometimes AIXI refers to the case of a certain universal class and a Solomonoff style prior [2]. The above agent, and only agents of that form, satisfies the strict rationality axioms presented first in [7] while the slightly looser version we presented in [9] enables optimism. The optimist chooses its next action based on

$$\pi^\circ := \arg\max_\pi \max_{\xi\in\Xi} V_\xi^\pi \tag{2}$$

for a set of environments (beliefs) Ξ which we in the rest of the article will assume to be finite, though results can be extended further [11]. We will rely on an agent framework presented in [11].

2.2 Agents Based on Decision Functions and Hypothesis Generating Functions

The primary component of our agent framework is a decision function $f : \mathbb{M} \to \mathcal{A}$ where $\mathbb{M}$ is the class of all finite sets $\mathcal{M}$ of environments. The function value only depends on the class of environments $\mathcal{M}$ that is the argument. The decision function is independent of the history, however, the class $\mathcal{M}$ fed to the decision function introduces an indirect dependence. For example, the environments at time $t+1$ can be the environments at time t, conditioned on the new observation. We are here primarily using optimistic decision functions.

Definition 1 (Optimistic decision function). *We call a decision function f optimistic if $f(\mathcal{M}) = \pi(\epsilon)$ for an optimistic policy π, i.e. for*

$$\pi \in \arg\max_{\tilde\pi} \max_{\nu\in\mathcal{M}} V_\nu^{\tilde\pi}. \tag{3}$$

Given a decision function, what remains to create a complete agent is a hypothesis-generating function $\mathcal{G}(h) = \mathcal{M}$ that for any history $h \in \mathcal{H}$ produces a set of environments $\mathcal{M}$. A special form of hypothesis-generating function is defined by combining the initial class $\mathcal{G}(\epsilon) = \mathcal{M}_0$ with an update function $\psi(\mathcal{M}_{t-1}, h_t) = \mathcal{M}_t$. An agent is defined from a hypothesis-generating function $\mathcal{G}$ and a decision function f by choosing action $a = f(\mathcal{G}(h))$ after seeing history h.

3 Environments Defined by Laws

We consider observations of the form of a feature vector $o = \boldsymbol{x} = (x_j)_{j=1}^m \in \mathcal{O} = \times_{j=1}^m \mathcal{O}_j$ including the reward as one coefficient where x_j is an element of some finite alphabet $\mathcal{O}_j$. Let $\mathcal{O}_\perp = \times_{j=1}^m (\mathcal{O}_j \cup \{\perp\})$, i.e. $\mathcal{O}_\perp$ consists of the feature vectors from $\mathcal{O}$ but where some elements are replaced by a special letter $\perp$. The meaning of $\perp$ is that there is no prediction for this feature.

Definition 2 (Deterministic laws). *A law is a function* $\tau : \mathcal{H} \times \mathcal{A} \to \mathcal{O}_\perp$.

Using a feature vector representation of the observations and saying that a law predicts some of the features is a convenient special case of saying that the law predicts that the next observation will belong to a certain subset of the observation space. Each law τ predicts, given the history and a new action, some or none but not necessarily all of the features x_j at the next time point. We first consider sets of laws such that for any given history and action, and for every feature, there is at least one law that makes a prediction of this feature. Such sets are said to be complete. We below expand these notions, defined in [10,11], from deterministic laws to stochastic laws.

Definition 3 (Stochastic law). *A stochastic law is a function* $\tau : \mathcal{H} \times \mathcal{A} \times \mathcal{O}_\perp \to [0,1]$ *such that*

$$\forall h \forall a \sum_{o \in \mathcal{O}_\perp} \tau(h, a, o) = 1$$

and

$$\forall h \forall a \forall j \in \{1, ..., m\} \sum_{o \in \mathcal{O}_\perp : o_j = \perp} \tau(h, a, o) \in \{0, 1\},$$

i.e. the marginal probability of the "no prediction" symbol $\perp$ *always equals zero or one. We will use the notation* $\tau(o|h, a) := \tau(h, a, o)$.

Definition 4 (Stochastic laws making predictions or not). *If* τ *is a law and*

$$\sum_{o \in \mathcal{O}_\perp : o_j = \perp} \tau(h, a, o) = 0$$

we say that τ *does not make a prediction for* j *given* h, a *and write* $\tau(h, a)_j = \perp$. *Otherwise, i.e. when*

$$\sum_{o \in \mathcal{O}_\perp : o_j = \perp} \tau(h, a, o) = 1,$$

we say that τ *does make a prediction for* j *given* h, a *and write* $\tau(h, a)_j \neq \perp$.

As in the deterministic case we need to define what it means for a set of stochastic laws to be complete and then we can define an environment from such a set. The definition is an extension of the deterministic counter-part. That we only demand completeness and not coherence in the stochastic case is because we are going to study the stochastic case with a domination assumption instead of excluding laws. The result is that the generated class is infinite even when the set of laws is finite.

Definition 5 (Complete set of stochastic laws). *A set* $\mathcal{T}$ *of stochastic laws is complete if*

$$\forall h, a \; \exists \tau_i \in \mathcal{T} \; \exists J_i \subset \{1, ..., m\} = \dot{\cup}_i J_i : \tau_i(h, a)_j \neq \perp \iff j \in J_i.$$

Let $\hat{\mathcal{C}}(\mathcal{T})$ *denote the set of complete subsets of* $\mathcal{T}$.

Definition 6 (Environments from stochastic laws). *Given a complete class of stochastic laws $\mathcal{T}$, we define the class of environments $\Xi(\mathcal{T})$ generated by $\mathcal{T}$ as consisting of all ν for which there are τ_i and J_i as in Definition 5 such that*

$$\nu(\boldsymbol{x}|h, a) = \Pi_i \tau_i|_{J_i}(h, a)(\boldsymbol{x}|_{J_i}).$$

Error analysis. We first consider deterministic environments and deterministic laws and the optimistic agent from [8]. Every contradiction of an environment is a contradiction of at least one law and there are finitely many laws. This is what is needed for the finite error result from [8] to hold but with $|\mathcal{M}|$ replaced by $|\mathcal{T}|$ (see Theorem 1 below) which can be exponentially smaller. We have presented this result previously [10,11] but here we extend from the deterministic to stochastic settings.

Theorem 1 (Finite error bound when using laws). *Suppose that $\mathcal{T}$ is a finite class of deterministic laws and let $\mathcal{G}(h) = \{\nu(\cdot|h) \mid \nu \in \mathcal{M}(\{\tau| \ \tau \in \mathcal{T}$ consistent with $h\})\}$. We define $\bar{\pi}$ by combining $\mathcal{G}$ with the optimistic decision function (Definition 1). Following $\bar{\pi}$ for a finite class of deterministic laws $\mathcal{T}$ in an environment $\mu \in \mathcal{M}(\mathcal{T})$, we have for any $0 < \varepsilon < \frac{1}{1-\gamma}$ that*

$$V_\mu^{\bar{\pi}}(h_t) \geq \max_\pi V_\mu^\pi(h_t) - \varepsilon \tag{4}$$

for all but at most $|\mathcal{T}| \frac{-\log \varepsilon(1-\gamma)}{1-\gamma}$ time steps t.

We now introduce optimistic agents with classes of stochastic dominant laws. To define what dominant means for a law we first introduce the notion of a restriction. We will say that a law τ is a restriction of a stochastic environment ν if it assigns the same probabilities to what τ predicts. We then also say that ν is an extension of τ. Similarly a law can be a restriction or an extension of another law. If τ is a restriction of some environment ν that μ is absolutely continuous w.r.t. (for every policy), then we say that μ is absolutely continuous (for every policy) with respect to τ. We here make use of the slightly more restrictive notion of dominance. We say that ν dominates μ if there is $c > 0$ such that $\nu(\cdot) \geq c\mu(\cdot)$. We extend this concept to laws.

Example 1 (Stochastic laws based on estimators). Consider again a binary vector of length m where each coefficient is an i.i.d. Bernoulli process, i.e. there is a fixed probability with which the coefficient equals 1. Consider laws that are such that there is one for each coefficient and they predict a 1 with probability $\frac{a+1/2}{a+b+1}$ where a is the number of 1s that have occurred before for that coefficient and b is the number of 0s. Then we have a complete set of stochastic laws that are based on the so called Krichevsky-Trofimov (KT) estimator. Also, they satisfy the absolute continuity property. These laws can e.g. be combined with laws based on the Laplace estimator which assigns probability $\frac{a+1}{a+b+2}$ instead.

Example 2 (Dominant laws, AIXI-CTW). Consider the AIXI agent defined by (1) with ξ being the mixture of all context tree environments up to a certain depth as defined in [13]. A context is defined by a condition on what the last few cycles of the history is. The context tree contains contexts of variable length upto the maximum depth. The Context Tree Weighting (CTW) algorithm relied on by [13], which is originally from [14], defines a prediction for each context using a Krichevsky-Trofimov estimator. ξ is a mixture of all of those predictions. Given a context, we can define a law as the restriction of ξ to the histories for which we are in the given context. All of these laws will be absolutely continuous for any context tree environment, hence so are all of these laws. If we consider the same restrictions for other dominant mixtures than ξ, e.g. by using the CTW construction on other/all possible binarizations of the environment, we have defined a large set of laws.

Theorem 2 (Convergence for stochastic laws). *Suppose that T is a finite class of stochastic laws as in Definition 6 and that they all are absolutely continuous w.r.t. the true environment μ and that for every h, there is an environment $\nu_h \in \Xi(T)$ such that $V^*_{\nu_h}(h) \geq V^*_\mu(h)$. Let $\mathcal{G}(h) = \{\nu(\cdot|h) \mid \nu \in \Xi(T)\}$. We define $\tilde\pi$ by combining $\mathcal{G}$ with an optimistic decision function. Then almost surely $V^{\tilde\pi}_\mu(h_t) \to V^*_\mu(h_t)$ as $t \to \infty$.*

Proof. Any $\nu \in \Xi(T)$ is such that $\nu(\cdot) \geq c\mu(\cdot)$ where c is the smallest constant such that all the laws in T are dominant with that constant. For each law $\tau \in T$ pick an environment $\nu \in \Xi(T)$ such that τ is a restriction of ν, i.e. ν predicts according to τ whenever τ predicts something. We use the notation ν_τ for the environment chosen for τ. The Blackwell-Dubins Theorem says that ν_τ merges with μ almost surely under the policy followed (but not necessarily off that policy) and therefore τ merges with μ, i.e. with the restriction of μ to what τ makes predictions for, under the followed policy. Given $\varepsilon > 0$, let T be such that

$$\forall t \geq T : \max_{\tau \in T} d(\nu_\tau(\cdot|h_t, \tilde\pi), \mu(\cdot|\tilde\pi)) < \varepsilon$$

which implies that

$$\forall t \geq T : \max_{\nu \in \Xi(T)} d(\nu(\cdot|h_t, \tilde\pi), \mu(\cdot|\tilde\pi)) < \varepsilon$$

and applying this to ν_{h_t} proves that $|V^{\tilde\pi}_\mu(h_t) - V^*_\mu(h_t)| < \varepsilon \ \forall t \geq T$ by Lemma 1 in [9]. Since there is, almost surely, such a T for every $\varepsilon > 0$ the claim is proved. ■

Excluding Stochastic Laws and Sample Complexity. To prove sample complexity bounds one typically needs to assume that the truth belongs to the class which is stronger than assuming domination. This agent would need to exclude implausible environments from the class. In the deterministic case that can be done with certainty after one contradiction, while [1] shows that in the stochastic case this can be done after a finite number m of sufficiently large contradiction. m depends on the confidence required, $m = O(\frac{1}{\varepsilon^2} \log \frac{k}{\delta})$ where ε is the accuracy, δ the confidence and k the number of hypothesis, and after m disagreements the environment that aligned worse with observations is excluded.

The analysis closely follows the structure learning case in [1] where it relies on a more general theorem for predictions based on k possible algorithms. The main difference is that that they could do this per feature which we cannot since we are in a much more general setting where a law sometimes makes a prediction for a feature and sometimes not. One can have at most mk^2 disagreements (actually slightly fewer) where k is the number of laws. It is possible that this square dependence can be improved to linear, but it is already an exponential improvement for many cases compared to a linear dependence on the number of environments. There can only be errors when there is sufficient disagreement. The above argument works under a coherence assumption and for $\gamma = 0$ while for $\gamma > 0$ there are horizon effects that adds extra technical difficulty to proving optimal bounds avoiding losing a factor $1/(1-\gamma)$. [5] shows how such complications can be dealt with.

Having a Background Environment. The earlier deterministic results demanded that the set of laws in the class is rich enough to combine into complete environments and in particular to the true one. This might require such a large class of laws that the linear dependence on the number of laws in the error bound, though much better than depending on the number of environments, still is large. The problem is simplified if the agent has access to a background environment, which is here something that given previous history and the next features predicted by laws, assigns probabilities for the rest of the feature vector. A further purpose for this section is to prepare for classes with a mix of deterministic laws and stochastic laws. In this case the stochastic laws learn what we in this section call a background environment. Computer games provide a simple example where it is typically clear that we have a background and then objects. If the agent has already learnt a model of the background, then what remains is only the subproblem of finding laws related to how objects behave and affect the environment. As an alternative, we might not be able to deterministically predict the objects but we can learn a cruder probabilistic model for them and this is background that completes the deterministic world model the agent learns for the rest.

Example 3 (Semi-deterministic environment). Consider a binary vector of length m where some elements are fixed and some fluctuate randomly with probability $1/2$. Consider the background environment where all coefficients are Bernoulli processes with probability $1/2$ and consider the $2m$ laws that each always makes a deterministic prediction for one coefficient and it is fixed. The laws that make a prediction for a fluctuating coefficient will quickly get excluded and then the agent will have learnt the environment.

Definition 7 (Predicted and not predicted features). *Given a set of deterministic laws $\mathcal{T}$, let*

$$q_1(h, a, \mathcal{T}) := \{j \in \{1, ..., m\} \mid \nu(h, a)_j = \perp \ \forall \nu \in \Xi(\mathcal{T})\}$$

be the features $\mathcal{T}$ cannot predict and $q_2(h, a, \mathcal{T}) := \{1, ..., m\} \setminus q_1(h, a, \mathcal{T})$ the predicted features.

Since we are now working with sets of laws that are not complete, subsets can also not be complete, but they can be maximal in the sense that they predict all that any law in the full set predicts.

Definition 8 (Coherent and maximal sets of laws). *Given a set of deterministic laws, the set of maximal subsets of laws $\bar{C}(T)$ consists of sets $\tilde{T} \subset T$ with the property*

$$\forall h, a \forall j \in q_2(h, a, T) \exists \tau \in \tilde{T} : \tau(h, a)_j \neq \bot.$$

If

$$\forall h, a \forall j \in q_2(h, a, T) \forall \tau, \tilde{\tau} \in \tilde{T} \ \tilde{\tau}(h, a)_j \in \{\bot, \tau(h, a)_j\}$$

we say that $\tilde{T}$ is coherent.

A semi-deterministic environment is defined by combining the predictions of a number of laws with background probabilities for what the laws do not predict. We abuse notation by letting $\nu(h, a) = (o, r)$ mean that ν assigns probability 1 to the next observation and reward being (o, r). We then also let $\nu(h, a)$ represent the event predicted. As before, we use x_k to denote individual features.

Definition 9 (Semi-deterministic environment). *Given a coherent set of laws $\tilde{T}$ and background probabilities $P(\boldsymbol{x}|x_{k_1}, ..., x_{k_n}, h)$ where $\boldsymbol{x} = (x_1, ..., x_m)$ for any subset $\{k_1, ..., k_n\} \subset \{1, ..., m\}$ of the features and previous history h, we let $\nu(P, \tilde{T})$ be the environment ν which is such that*

$$\forall h, a \forall j \in q_2(h, a, T) \exists \tau \in \tilde{T} : \nu(h, a)_j = \tau(h, a)_j$$

and

$$\nu\big(\boldsymbol{x} \mid h, a, \ \boldsymbol{x}|_{q_2(h,a,T)} = \nu(h,a)|_{q_2(h,a,T)}\big) = P\big(\boldsymbol{x} \mid \boldsymbol{x}|_{q_2(h,a,T)} = \nu(h,a)_{q_2(h,a,T)}\big).$$

The last expression above says that the features not predicted by laws (denoted by q_1) are predicted by P where we condition on the predicted features (denoted by q_2).

Definition 10 (Semi-deterministic environments from laws and background). *Given a set of deterministic laws T and background probabilities $P(\boldsymbol{x}|x_{k_1}, ..., x_{k_n}, h, a)$, we let*

$$\bar{\mathcal{M}}(P, T) := \{\nu(P, \tilde{T}) \mid \tilde{T} \in \bar{C}(T)\}.$$

The resulting error bound theorem has almost identical formulation as the previous case (Theorem 1) and is true for exactly the same reasons. However, the class $\bar{\mathcal{M}}$ contains stochasticity but of the predefined form.

Theorem 3 (Finite error bound when using laws and background).
Suppose that T is a finite class of deterministic laws and P is background. Let $\mathcal{G}(h) = \{\nu(\cdot|h) \mid \nu \in \bar{\mathcal{M}}(P, \{\tau \in T \text{ consistent with } h\})\}$. We define $\bar{\pi}$ by

combining $\mathcal{G}$ with the optimistic decision function (Definition 1). Following $\bar{\pi}$ with a finite class of deterministic laws $\mathcal{T}$ in an environment $\mu \in \bar{\mathcal{M}}(P, \mathcal{T})$, for $0 < \varepsilon < \frac{1}{1-\gamma}$ we have that

$$V_\mu^{\bar{\pi}}(h_t) \geq \max_\pi V_\mu^\pi(h_t) - \varepsilon \tag{5}$$

for all but at most $|\mathcal{T}|\frac{-\log \varepsilon(1-\gamma)}{1-\gamma}$ time steps t.

Mixing Deterministic and Stochastic Laws. When we introduced the concept of background environment we mentioned that it prepared for studying sets of laws that mix deterministic laws with absolutely continuous stochastic laws. Given an $\tilde{\varepsilon} > 0$, the environment formed by combining the stochastic laws with a coherent and maximal set of true deterministic laws eventually have a value function that for the followed policy is within $\tilde{\varepsilon}$ of the true one. Combining the remaining deterministic laws with the dominant stochastic laws into semi-deterministic environments exactly as with the background probabilities, then yields the results as before but with the accuracy only being $\varepsilon + \tilde{\varepsilon}$ instead of ε and where we only count errors happening after sufficient merging has taken place.

Example 4 (Mixing deterministic laws and stochastic laws). Consider a binary vector of length m where some elements are fixed and some fluctuate randomly with a probability unknown to an agent. Consider the laws based on KT-estimators from Example 1 and consider the $2m$ laws that each always makes a fixed prediction for one coefficient. The laws that make a deterministic prediction for a fluctuating coefficient will quickly get excluded and then the agent will have to fall back on the KT-estimate for this coefficient.

Example 5 (AIXI-CTW as background). Consider the AIXI-CTW environment ξ described in Example 2. Also, consider two deterministic law for each context in the context tree, one always predicts 1 and the other 0. Combining those two, we will have an agent that uses deterministic laws to predict until all laws for a certain feature in a certain context (including its subcontexts) are contradicted. Then it falls back on ξ for that situation. Predicting as much as possible with deterministic laws is very helpful for planning.

4   Conclusions

We have further developed the theory of optimistic agents with hypothesis classes defined by combining laws. Previous results were restricted to the deterministic setting while stochastic environments are necessary for any hope of real application. We here remedied this by introducing and studying stochastic laws and environments generated by such.

Acknowledgments. This work was supported by ARC grant DP120100950.

References

1. Diuk, C., Li, L., Leffer, B.R.: The adaptive k-meteorologists problem and its application to structure learning and feature selection in reinforcement learning. In: Danyluk, A.P., Bottou, L., Littman, M.L. (eds.) ICML. ACM International Conference Proceeding Series, vol. 382 (2009)
2. Hutter, M.: Universal Articial Intelligence: Sequential Decisions based on Algorithmic Probability. Springer, Berlin (2005)
3. Lattimore, T.: Theory of General Reinforcement Learning. Ph.D. thesis, Australian National University (2014)
4. Lattimore, T., Hutter, M.: PAC bounds for discounted MDPs. In: Bshouty, N.H., Stoltz, G., Vayatis, N., Zeugmann, T. (eds.) ALT 2012. LNCS, vol. 7568, pp. 320–334. Springer, Heidelberg (2012)
5. Lattimore, T., Hutter, M., Sunehag, P.: The sample-complexity of general reinforcement learning. Journal of Machine Learning Research, W&CP: ICML 28(3), 28–36 (2013)
6. Russell, S.J., Norvig, P.: Artificial Intelligence: A Modern Approach, 3rd edn. Prentice Hall, Englewood Clifs (2010)
7. Sunehag, P., Hutter, M.: Axioms for rational reinforcement learning. In: Kivinen, J., Szepesvári, C., Ukkonen, E., Zeugmann, T. (eds.) ALT 2011. LNCS, vol. 6925, pp. 338–352. Springer, Heidelberg (2011)
8. Sunehag, P., Hutter, M.: Optimistic agents are asymptotically optimal. In: Thielscher, M., Zhang, D. (eds.) AI 2012. LNCS, vol. 7691, pp. 15–26. Springer, Heidelberg (2012)
9. Sunehag, P., Hutter, M.: Optimistic AIXI. In: Bach, J., Goertzel, B., Iklé, M. (eds.) AGI 2012. LNCS, vol. 7716, pp. 312–321. Springer, Heidelberg (2012)
10. Sunehag, P., Hutter, M.: Learning agents with evolving hypothesis classes. In: Kühnberger, K.-U., Rudolph, S., Wang, P. (eds.) AGI 2013. LNCS, vol. 7999, pp. 150–159. Springer, Heidelberg (2013)
11. Sunehag, P., Hutter, M.: A dual process theory of optimistic cognition. In: Annual Conference of the Cognitive Science Society, CogSci 2014 (2014)
12. Sunehag, P., Hutter, M.: Rationality, Optimism and Guarantees in General Reinforcement Learning. Journal of Machine Learning Reserch (to appear, 2015)
13. Veness, J., Ng, K.S., Hutter, M., Uther, W., Silver, D.: A Monte-Carlo AIXI approximation. Journal of Artifiicial Intelligence Research 40(1), 95–142 (2011)
14. Willems, F., Shtarkov, Y., Tjalkens, T.: The context tree weighting method: Basic properties. IEEE Transactions on Information Theory 41, 653–664 (1995)

Towards Flexible Task Environments for Comprehensive Evaluation of Artificial Intelligent Systems and Automatic Learners

Kristinn R. Thórisson[1,2], Jordi Bieger[1]([✉]),
Stephan Schiffel[1], and Deon Garrett[1,2]

[1] Center for Analysis and Design of Intelligent Agents / School of Computer Science,
Reykjavik University, Menntavegur 1, 101 Reykjavik, Iceland
{thorisson,jordi13,stephans,deong}@ru.is
[2] Icelandic Institute for Intelligent Machines, Uranus, Menntavegur 1,
101 Reykjavik, Iceland

Abstract. Evaluation of artificial intelligence (AI) systems is a prerequisite for comparing them on the many dimensions they are intended to perform on. Design of task-environments for this purpose is often ad-hoc, focusing on some limited aspects of the systems under evaluation. Testing on a wide range of tasks and environments would better facilitate comparisons and understanding of a system's performance, but this requires that manipulation of relevant dimensions cause predictable changes in the structure, behavior, and nature of the task-environments. What is needed is a framework that enables easy composition, decomposition, scaling, and configuration of task-environments. Such a framework would not only facilitate evaluation of the performance of current and future AI systems, but go beyond it by allowing evaluation of knowledge acquisition, cognitive growth, lifelong learning, and transfer learning. In this paper we list requirements that we think such a framework should meet to facilitate the evaluation of intelligence, and present preliminary ideas on how this could be realized.

Keywords: Task-environment · Automation · Intelligence evaluation · Artificial intelligence · Machine learning

1 Introduction

A key challenge in the development of artificial intelligence (AI) systems is how to evaluate them. Valid measurements are necessary to assess progress, compare systems and approaches, and understand their strengths and weaknesses. Most evaluation methods in use today yield only a single performance score that brings little qualitative insight, and is incomparable to performance on other tasks. Furthermore, few if any proposals exist for evaluating fundamental aspects of intelligence like learning capacity, transfer learning, deterioration of learned skills, as well as cognitive development and growth.

© Springer International Publishing Switzerland 2015
J. Bieger (Ed.): AGI 2015, LNAI 9205, pp. 187–196, 2015.
DOI: 10.1007/978-3-319-21365-1_20

Evaluation of AI systems is traditionally done by measuring their performance on one or more tasks instantiated in an environment. A *task* is the transformation of a world state into a goal state, or the maintenance of a goal state in light of perturbations. Tasks may be compound, have one or more explicit goals, sub-tasks, constraints, and call for continuous or intermittent action. A task is performed by an agent whose atomic actions can *in principle* perform it. An *environment* is the instantiation of the task and its context, and may include some form of body for the agent, as well as distractors/noise, that complicate the task but are not strictly a part of it. We use the term *task-environment* to refer to the tuple task+environment.

Most task-environments cannot easily be classified – let alone freely modified – along a large number of dimensions, making it difficult to systematically assess an AI system's strengths and weaknesses. This rigidity limits any chosen metrics to a small subset of systems, and complicates their comparison. Tasks such as pole-balancing or video game playing, for instance, are not sufficient for evaluating systems that can operate on a diverse set of data or under multiple high-level goals, but may be fine for certain single-goal learners.

At the other end of the spectrum, task-environments for evaluating human-level intelligence – e.g. the Turing test [22] – cannot be compared easily to those appropriate for simpler learners. Human "intelligence quotient" measures, developed by psychologists, use a set of tasks normalized by their distribution in a social group and are highly species- and society-specific – and thus not a good match for intelligent machines. Another problem with most measures proposed for higher intelligences is that they assess only single point in time [18]. Assessing a system's learning capacity, however, requires time-based measures in task-environments with adjustable complexity. A framework supporting incremental and predictable changes to compound task-environments, on appropriate features, could measure a system's learning rate. This would enable evaluation of lifelong learners and transfer learning capacity: the transference of acquired knowledge to new domains/tasks. Assessing these important aspects of intelligence calls for multiple similar task-environments that can easily be compared.

Another aspect of truly intelligent systems is capacity for cognitive development – the ability to improve the very cognitive apparatus enabling the learning. This ability can itself benefit greatly from a gradual increase in complexity and other tutoring techniques that could enhance task-environments [4]. Measuring cognitive growth (and meta-cognition) capacity might be enabled through mechanisms similar to those used for evaluating transfer learning.

Since general intelligence enables systems to (learn to) perform a wide range of tasks that they have not seen or been prepared for, it cannot be assessed in only a single task or environment. Evaluating lifelong learning – systems that continually adapt and learn new things – calls for either a wide range of task-environments, or a single (large and complex) dynamically changing multi-task environment. In both cases one would like to automatically generate such task-environments, given a high-level specification for certain features and constraints.

Although many AI evaluation frameworks exist [13], none address all of the above concerns. In Sect. 3 we attempt to collect in one place the full set of requirements that such a comprehensive framework should address, and present some preliminary ideas on how this could be realized in Sect. 4.

2   Related Work

In a comprehensive and recent survey, Hernández-Orallo argued that the assessment of general "real" intelligence – as opposed to specialized performance – should be oriented towards the testing a range of cognitive abilities that enable a system to perform in a *range* of tasks [11]. One way to accomplish this is to procedurally generate task-environments that require a suite of abilities, and appropriately sample and weight them. Hernández-Orallo takes this approach, but focuses on discrete and deterministic task-environments [10,12]. Legg & Veness's Algorithmic IQ approach posits a similar framework for measuring universal AI with respect to some reference machine which interprets a description language to run the environment [14]. The choice of this description language remains a major issue and deeply affects the kinds of environments that are more likely to be generated. The BF programming language used in their work closely resembles the operations of a Turing machine, but cannot easily generate complex structured environments and is opaque to analysis. A wide range of description languages has been proposed for coordination and planning tasks (e.g. TÆMS [7] and PDDL [17]), but tend to focus on static, observable domains and specify things in terms of agent actions and task hierarchies which can then drive the development of AI systems specialized to the specified task.

Games have long been considered a possible testbed for the evaluation of intelligence [20]. In the General Game Playing competition, AI systems play previously unseen games after being provided with the rules in the very analyzable Game Description Language, but the games must be finite and synchronous [16]. More recently, there has been a lot of interest in the automatic play of Atari-era video games. An extensible, user friendly description language for such games has been proposed that relies heavily on opaque built-in functions and should in the future be amenable to procedural generation [8,19]. Much work has been done on procedural generation in specific video games, but more general work is still in its infancy [21]. Lim & Harrell were able to automatically generate variants for video games written using the PuzzleScript description language, but the simulation-based approach they used for the evaluation of candidate rulesets is not feasible for very difficult games since it requires an agent that is intelligent enough to perform the task [15].

Some research has tried to relate problem structure to heuristic search algorithm performance, including efforts to use a wide variety of problem types to increase the generality of algorithms [2,5]. Some of this work, notably that on hyperheuristics [6], has focused on algorithms that try to learn general search strategies and don't only perform well on a few specific problem types. Understanding the impact of problem characteristics on learning has been key in these efforts, but so far only search and optimization domains have been addressed.

Similar work has been done in the field of generating random Markov Decision Problems (MDPs) [1,3], focusing on a rather limited domain of potential task-environments. Our own **Merlin** tool [9] supports various methods for the procedural generation of discrete and continuous multi-objective MDPs, but does not adequately address the full set of requirements below.

3 Requirements for Intelligence Evaluation Frameworks

The goals of evaluating AI systems are to measure research progress, compare systems and approaches, and understand their strengths and weaknesses. We wish to achieve this for a wide range of AI systems, from very simple to very complex, where the systems may be built with different background assumptions. The framework we envision must support evaluation of intelligence on a number of aspects such as *skill, knowledge, transfer learning, cognitive development and growth, lifelong learning* and *generality*. All combined this calls for multiple task-environments, selected for appropriate amounts of similarity and complexity. Note that here we are not attempting to propose *particular benchmarks*: we are interested in identifying requirements for a framework that *can be used* to construct benchmarks for the above cognitive skills.

We have identified the following high-level properties that we consider important for a flexible task-environment framework as described above:

(A) Offering **easy construction** of task-environments, and **variants** with a wide range of features and complexity dimensions. This would include the ability to (a) **compose** and **decompose** desired task-environments and parts thereof, and (b) to **scale** and **tune** them, in part and in whole, along various parameters and properties, with predictable effects, especially for increasing and decreasing their complexity along known dimensions.

(B) Ability to specify, at any level of detail, the **procedural generation** of task-environments with specific features, constraints, etc., and how they should (automatically) grow, possibly depending on the progress of the system under evaluation.

(C) Facilitation of **analysis** in terms of parameters of interest, including task complexity, similarity, observability, controllability, etc.

Analysis of various non-explicit features of such task-environments could facilitate an understanding of their function in evaluating various systems, and thus help with their automatic generation, robustification, and standardization. Decomposition can tell us about a task-environment's structure and help find commonly used building blocks. Composition allows for the construction of (much) larger structured task-environments. Scaling helps with the assessment of progress and growth, and tunability can facilitate the systematic assessment of a system's strengths and weaknesses. These can all result in variants that are similar but different in specified ways, which allows transfer learning. Finally, automatic generation can provide us with a virtually unlimited supply of fresh task environments with which to test cognitive abilities and general intelligence.

The framework should support the gradual construction and tunability of task-environments with the following properties:

1. **Determinism**: Both full determinism and partial stochasticity (for realism regarding, e.g. noise, stochastic events, etc.) must be supported.
2. **Ergodicity**: The reachability of (aspects of) states from others determines the degree to which the agent can undo things and get second chances.
3. **Controllable Continuity**: For the framework to be relevant to e.g. robotics, it is critical to allow continuous variables, to appropriately represent continuous spatial and temporal features. The degree to which continuity is approximated (discretization granularity) should be changeable for any variable.
4. **Asynchronicity**: Any action in the task-environment, including sensors and controls, may operate on arbitrary time scales and interact at any time, letting an agent respond when it can.
5. **Dynamism**: A static task-environment's state only changes in response to the AI's actions. The most simplistic ones are step-lock, where the agent makes one move and the environment responds with another (e.g. board games). More complex environments can be dynamic to various degrees in terms of speed and magnitude, and may be caused by interactions between environmental factors, or simply due to the passage of time.
6. **Observability**: Task-environments can be partially observable to varying degrees, depending on the type, range, refresh rate, and precision of available sensors, affecting the difficulty and general nature of the task-environment.
7. **Controllability**: The control that the agent can exercise over the environment to achieve its goals can be partial or full, depending on the capability, type, range, inherent latency, and precision of available actuators.
8. **Multiple Parallel Causal Chains**: Any generally intelligent system in a complex environment is likely to be trying to meet multiple objectives, that can be co-dependent in various ways through any number of causal chains in the task-environment. Actions, observations, and tasks may occur sequentially or in parallel (at the same time). Needed to implement real-world clock environments.
9. **Number of Agents**: It should be possible to add any number of (intelligent) agents to the task-environment without specifying their behavior explicitly. This would allow for the testing of the AI in isolation, in social situations, or with a teacher [4], and the evaluation of systems of systems (e.g. simulators). Other agents can greatly affect the difficulty of any task-environment.
10. **Periodicity**: Many structures and events in nature are repetitive to some extent, and therefore contain a (learnable) periodic cycle – e.g. the day-night cycle or blocks of identical houses.
11. **Repeatability**: Both fully deterministic and partially stochastic environments must be fully repeatable, for traceable transparency.

4   Flexible Task-Environment Framework: A Proposal

To meet the stated requirements we propose a description language for task-environments containing a low number of small atomic building elements (the base operators); few atomic units – as opposed to multiple types – means greater transparency since superstructures can be inspected more easily than larger black boxes can, facilitating comparison between task-environments. This also lays the foundation for smooth, incremental increase in complexity, as each addition or change can be as small as the smallest blocks. Sect. 4.1 gives an example of what this might look like. On top of this methods for modification (Sect. 4.2), analysis (Sect. 4.3), construction (Sect. 4.4), and execution can be developed.

4.1   Example Syntax and Task

Fig. 1a shows a description of an extremely simple task where the agent must reach a goal position in a 2-dimensional space. We describe a task-environment by a set of (time-) dependent variables with causal relations. The *Initialization* section provides the initial values for the variables. In our case these are goal and agent position. The *Dynamics* section defines how variables change over time by allowing us to refer to the past variable values using time arguments and the reserved variables t (for the current time) and dt for the size of the (arbitrarily) smallest atomic time step. Unlike other languages in Sect. 2 we allow the specification of arbitrary expressions.

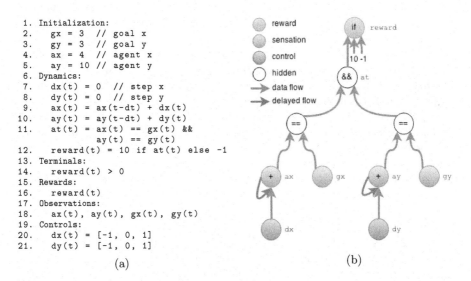

```
1.  Initialization:
2.     gx = 3  // goal x
3.     gy = 3  // goal y
4.     ax = 4  // agent x
5.     ay = 10 // agent y
6.  Dynamics:
7.     dx(t) = 0  // step x
8.     dy(t) = 0  // step y
9.     ax(t) = ax(t-dt) + dx(t)
10.    ay(t) = ay(t-dt) + dy(t)
11.    at(t) = ax(t) == gx(t) &&
               ay(t) == gy(t)
12.    reward(t) = 10 if at(t) else -1
13. Terminals:
14.    reward(t) > 0
15. Rewards:
16.    reward(t)
17. Observations:
18.    ax(t), ay(t), gx(t), gy(t)
19. Controls:
20.    dx(t) = [-1, 0, 1]
21.    dy(t) = [-1, 0, 1]
```

(a)   (b)

Fig. 1. Example description (a) and extracted graph (b) for a task where the agent must reach a goal location, including causal connections with latency

Lines 7 and 8 in the example set dx and dy to 0 by default. However, these variables can be controlled by the AI, as we can see on lines 20 and 21. Line 9 says that the value of ax at the current time t is equal to the previous value of ax plus the current value of dx. Line 12 uses conditional statements and refers only to variables in the current time step. The arithmetic and comparison operations make up the (extensible) set of base operators which are not further defined.

While the *Initialization* and *Dynamics* sections mostly describe the environment, the *Terminals* and *Rewards* sections can be said to describe the task in terms of environment variables. They consist of zero or more lines which each specify an expression that evaluates to a terminal (Boolean) that ends the task or a reward (a number). Like everything else, rewards can depend on time and other variables, which allows tasks to have e.g. time pressure, deadlines, start times, and complex preconditions and interactions – perhaps even modulating other dependencies such as time.

Finally, the sections for *Observations* and *Controls* describe how the agent interacts with the environment. Observations consist of a set of sensations that occur simultaneously and are described on their own line with a comma-separated list of expressions. Controls are described as assignments of a collection of acceptable values to environment variables whose value is overwritten when specified. Non-deterministic responses of an agent's body can be modeled by making the causal connections following the controls more complex.

4.2   Example Tuning

The task-environment as described is fairly simple, being discrete, fully observable, deterministic, and static. To make the **space continuous**, we can add a controllable angle. We add `angle = 0` to the Initialization section, replace existing controls with `angle(t) = [-pi..pi]`, and modify the Dynamics section like so:

```
7. dx(t) = dt * cos(angle(t))      8. dy(t) = dt * sin(angle(t))
11. reward(t) = 10 if (ax(t)-gx(t))^2 + (ay(t)-gy(t))^2 < 1 else -1
```

Making the space continuous in this way requires relatively significant changes. It is much easier to go from this continuous representation to one that appears discrete to the agent by discretizing controls and sensations (e.g. by rounding to the nearest integer). In the new lines 7 and 8 we have started making the environment (more) **continuous in time** as well. `dt` would ideally be infinitesimal for continuous environments, but a small value will have to suffice in practice.

To make the task more **dynamic** and **periodic** we can have the goal move a little. We replace the initialization of `gx` with `gx(t) = 4+3*sin(t)` and move it to the *Dynamics* section. The environment can easily be made **stochastic** by the use of random number generators that are provided as base operations.

We can further decrease **observability** by adding delays into the causal chain and changing refresh rates. For example, to let observations of `ax` and `ay` occur with a delay of one time step and allow observation of the goal position only at time steps 1, 3, 5, …:

```
17. ax(t-dt), ay(t-dt)      18. gx, gy @ [1:2:]
```

In similar ways we can affect **controllability** by introducing delays or letting controls block each other for a period of time, for example, when they share actuators which may then be busy for some time.

4.3   Analysis

Analysis of task-environments can help measure their similarity, which is highly useful for evaluating learning capacity and transfer learning, and elucidate features such as complexity, observability and difficulty that may shed light on the "why" behind the performance of various systems. For structural analysis a graph representation may be useful (see Fig. 1b). The edges show (possibly delayed) data flow; and nodes represent base operations and can be annotated with their role: reward, sensation, control, or hidden. Our description language makes important features like spatial and temporal resolution, delays, and blocking controls, readily apparent and easy to tune. The relative positions of observation, reward, and control nodes says a lot about difficulty, observability, and controllability of a particular task-environment. For instance, a task may be easier when these are grouped closely together; sensations and controls might be distractors if they are off the critical path to a reward or goal state.

The defining high-level characteristics of task-environments have yet to be identified, but will most likely include features like complexity, difficulty, observability, controllability and dimensionality. Graph algorithms such as compression, similarity detection and frequent subgraph mining can be leveraged to help determine these. A butterfly effect – where small changes in code have a large effect – may complicate purely structural analysis of some features. Tracing the construction from a small known task-environment through known transformations and compositions is likely to help.

4.4   Construction: Addressing the Range from Q-Learning to AGI

The easiest way to construct a new task-environment is to make variants of existing ones by changing initial conditions and other constants, which in our case include important concepts like resolution, delays, observability, and constraints on controls and sensors. One can also start from approximations of known tasks, although we find more important the easy construction of a variety of task-environments whose properties can be easily compared on key dimensions.

A natural way for scaling task-environments up or down is to modify the range of variables (e.g. board size in a game, or ax to gx distance in our example) or by changing the dimensionality. In most simple tasks, such as pole balancing, only a handful of variables need to be observed at a sufficient update frequency, and only a few need to be controlled. More complex tasks for the evaluation of more capable systems can be constructed in a number of ways. Tasks appropriate for human-level intelligence often have a high number of (possibly irrelevant) observable variables, and hidden variables whose state can only be inferred by observing a different set of partially and/or conditionally correlated variables. Our formalism facilitates this through easy definition of dependencies between variables, and their (un)observability. Similarly, tasks can be made harder by introducing latencies between causal connections. Much of the tuning in Sect. 3 and 4.2 can be done automatically using such techniques.

Manipulation of rewards is another obvious way to make tasks more challenging, for instance moving them further away from controls (making the causal chains longer). Adding time-dependent functions, e.g. by replacing a constant, is a natural way to increase complexity through tunable levels of dynamism. Truly large and complex multi-goal tasks can be created in many ways by composing tasks together, requiring the AI to solve them sequentially or in parallel, especially if they share sensors and controls. This could e.g. be achieved by duplicating a single task and changing the initial state of one, and/or the ranges of some variables. Variables in one task may be made co-dependent on values of (different or same) variables in the other. There is no limit to how often this process could be repeated, with different or duplicated tasks, low-level or high-level, to create large, structured and complex task-environments.

So far we have created tasks of comparable logical complexity to Pac-Man and Pong, as well as mazes of arbitrary complexity. Their graph representations can easily be modified in various ways, creating increasingly complex, dynamically varying composite tasks, where sequential and temporal dependencies can be freely introduced. Comparing and modifying them is much easier than if using completely hand-crafted tasks with no underlying common base.

5   Conclusions and Future Work

We have identified requirements that a framework ideally must meet to allow flexible construction of task-environments for evaluating artificial learners and AI systems, and proposed a preliminary formalism to meet these requirements. In our proposed approach, defining simple tasks requires a few lines of code; scaling is straightforward. In future work we plan on completing a first version of our task-environment description language and start on the development of methods for the automatic construction, analysis, and execution of evaluating AI systems, which is important for addressing the full range of requirements identified.

Acknowledgments. This work was supported by the School of Computer Science at Reykjavik University, by a Centers of Excellence Grant from the Science & Technology Policy Council of Iceland, and by EU Marie Curie CIG #304210.

References

1. Archibald, T.W., McKinnon, K.I.M., Thomas, L.C.: On the generation of Markov decision processes. J. Oper. Res. Soc. **46**, 354–361 (1995)
2. Asta, S., Özcan, E., Parkes, A.J.: Batched mode hyper-heuristics. In: Nicosia, G., Pardalos, P. (eds.) LION 7. LNCS, vol. 7997, pp. 404–409. Springer, Heidelberg (2013)
3. Bhatnagar, S., Sutton, R.S., Ghavamzadeh, M., Lee, M.: Natural actor-critic algorithms. Automatica **45**(11), 2471–2482 (2009)
4. Bieger, J., Thórisson, K.R., Garrett, D.: Raising AI: tutoring matters. In: Goertzel, B., Orseau, L., Snaider, J. (eds.) AGI 2014. LNCS, vol. 8598, pp. 1–10. Springer, Heidelberg (2014)

5. Bischl, B., Mersmann, O., Trautmann, H., Preuß, M.: Algorithm selection based on exploratory landscape analysis and cost-sensitive learning. In: Proceedings of the 14th Annual Conference on Genetic and Evolutionary Computation, GECCO 2012, pp. 313–320. ACM, New York (2012)

6. Burke, E.K., Gendreau, M., Hyde, M., Kendall, G., Ochoa, G., Özcan, E., Qu, R.: Hyper-heuristics: A survey of the state of the art. J. Oper. Res. Soc. **64**(12), 1695–1724 (2013)

7. Decker, K.: TAEMS: A framework for environment centered analysis & design of coordination mechanisms. In: O'Hare, G.M.P., Jennings, N.R. (eds.) Foundations of Distributed Artificial Intelligence, pp. 429–448. Wiley Inter-Science (1996)

8. Ebner, M., Levine, J., Lucas, S.M., Schaul, T., Thompson, T., Togelius, J.: Towards a video game description language. In: Lucas, S.M., Mateas, M., Preuss, M., Spronck, P., Togelius, J. (eds.) Artificial and Computational Intelligence in Games. Dagstuhl Follow-Ups, vol. 6, pp. 85–100. Schloss Dagstuhl (2013)

9. Garrett, D., Bieger, J., Thórisson, K.R.: Tunable and generic problem instance generation for multi-objective reinforcement learning. In: ADPRL 2014. IEEE (2014)

10. Hernández-Orallo, J.: A (hopefully) non-biased universal environment class for measuring intelligence of biological and artificial systems. In: Baum, E., Hutter, M., Kitzelmann, E. (eds.) AGI 2010, pp. 182–183. Atlantis Press (2010)

11. Hernández-Orallo, J.: AI Evaluation: past, present and future (2014). arXiv:1408.6908

12. Hernández-Orallo, J., Dowe, D.L.: Measuring universal intelligence: Towards an anytime intelligence test. Artif. Intell. **174**(18), 1508–1539 (2010)

13. Legg, S., Hutter, M.: Tests of Machine Intelligence [cs] (December 2007). arXiv:0712.3825

14. Legg, S., Veness, J.: An approximation of the universal intelligence measure. In: Dowe, D.L. (ed.) Solomonoff Festschrift. LNCS(LNAI), vol. 7070, pp. 236–249. Springer, Heidelberg (2013)

15. Lim, C.U., Harrell, D.F.: An approach to general videogame evaluation and automatic generation using a description language. In: CIG 2014. IEEE (2014)

16. Love, N., Hinrichs, T., Haley, D., Schkufza, E., Genesereth, M.: General game playing: Game description language specification. Tech. Rep. LG-2006-01, Stanford Logic Group (2008)

17. McDermott, D., Ghallab, M., Howe, A., Knoblock, C., Ram, A., Veloso, M., Weld, D., Wilkins, D.: PDDL-The Planning Domain Definition Language. Tech. Rep. TR-98-003, Yale Center for Computational Vision and Control (1998). http://www.cs.yale.edu/homes/dvm/

18. Rohrer, B.: Accelerating progress in Artificial General Intelligence: Choosing a benchmark for natural world interaction. J. Art. Gen. Int. **2**(1), 1–28 (2010)

19. Schaul, T.: A video game description language for model-based or interactive learning. In: CIG 2013, pp. 1–8. IEEE (2013)

20. Schaul, T., Togelius, J., Schmidhuber, J.: Measuring intelligence through games (2011). arXiv preprint arXiv:1109.1314

21. Togelius, J., Champandard, A.J., Lanzi, P.L., Mateas, M., Paiva, A., Preuss, M., Stanley, K.O.: Procedural content generation: Goals, challenges and actionable steps. In: Lucas, S.M., Mateas, M., Preuss, M., Spronck, P., Togelius, J. (eds.) Artificial and Computational Intelligence in Games. Dagstuhl Follow-Ups, vol. 6, pp. 61–75. Schloss Dagstuhl (2013)

22. Turing, A.M.: Computing machinery and intelligence. Mind **59**(236), 433–460 (1950)

Assumptions of Decision-Making Models in AGI

Pei Wang[1]([✉]) and Patrick Hammer[2]

[1] Department of Computer and Information Sciences, Temple University,
1925 North 12th Street, Philadelphia, PA 19122, USA
`pei.wang@temple.edu`
[2] Institute of Optimization and Discrete Mathematics,
Graz University of Technology, Steyrergasse 30, 8010 Graz, Austria

Abstract. This paper analyzes the assumptions of the decision making models in the context of artificial general intelligence (AGI). It is argued that the traditional approaches, exemplified by decision theory and reinforcement learning, are inappropriate for AGI, because their fundamental assumptions on available knowledge and resource cannot be satisfied here. The decision making process in the AGI system NARS is introduced and compared with the traditional approaches. It is concluded that realistic decision-making models must acknowledge the insufficiency of knowledge and resources, and make assumptions accordingly.

1 Formalizing Decision-Making

An AGI system needs to make decisions from time to time. To achieve its goals, the system must execute certain operations, which are chosen from all possible operations, according to the system's beliefs on the relations between the operations and the goals, as well as their applicability to the current situation.

On this topic, the dominating normative model is decision theory [3,12]. According to this model, "decision making" means to choose one action from a finite set of actions that is applicable at the current state. Each action leads to some consequent states according to a probability distribution, and each consequent state is associated with a utility value. The rational choice is the action that has the *maximum expected utility* (MEU).

When the decision extends from single actions to action sequences, it is often formalized as a *Markov decision process* (MDP), where the utility function is replaced by a reward value at each state, and the optimal *policy*, as a collection of decisions, is the one that achieves the *maximum expected total reward* (usually with a discount for future rewards) in the process. In AI, the best-known approach toward solving this problem is *reinforcement learning* [4,16], which uses various algorithms to approach the optimal policy.

Decision theory and reinforcement learning have been widely considered as setting the theoretical foundation of AI research [11], and the recent progress in deep learning [9] is increasing the popularity of these models. In the current AGI research, an influential model in this tradition is AIXI [2], in which reinforcement learning is combined with Solomonoff induction [15] to provide the probability values according to algorithmic complexity of the hypotheses used in prediction.

© Springer International Publishing Switzerland 2015
J. Bieger (Ed.): AGI 2015, LNAI 9205, pp. 197–207, 2015.
DOI: 10.1007/978-3-319-21365-1_21

Every formal model is based on some fundamental assumptions to encapsulate certain beliefs about the process to be modeled, so as to provide a coherent foundation for the conclusions derived in the model, and also to set restrictions on the situations where the model can be legally applied. In the following, four major assumptions of the above models are summarized.

The assumption on task: The task of "decision making" is to select the best action from all applicable actions at each state of the process.

The assumption on belief: The selection is based on the system's beliefs about the actions, represented as probability distributions among their consequent states.

The assumption on desire: The selection is guided by the system's desires measured by a (utility or reward) value function defined on states, and the best action is the one that with the maximum expectation.

The assumption on budget: The system can afford the computational resources demanded by the selection algorithm.

There are many situations where the above assumptions can be reasonably accepted, and the corresponding models have been successfully applied [9,11]. However, there are reasons to argue that artificial general intelligence (AGI) is not such a field, and there are non-trivial issues on each of the four assumptions.

Issues on Task: For a general-purpose system, it is unrealistic to assume that at any state all the applicable actions are explicitly listed. Actually, in human decision making the evaluation-choice step is often far less significant than diagnosis or design [8]. Though in principle it is reasonable to assume the system's actions are recursively composed of a set of basic operations, decision makings often do not happen at the level of basic operations, but at the level of composed actions, where there are usually infinite possibilities. So decision making is often not about *selection*, but *selective composition*.

Issues on Belief: For a given action, the system's beliefs about its possible consequences are not necessarily specified as a probability distribution among following states. Actions often have unanticipated consequences, and even the beliefs about the anticipated consequences usually do not fully specify a "state" of the environment or the system itself. Furthermore, the system's beliefs about the consequences may be implicitly inconsistent, so does not correspond to a probability distribution.

Issues on Desire: Since an AGI system typically has multiple goals with conflicting demands, usually no uniform value function can evaluate all actions with respect to all goals within limited time. Furthermore, the goals in an AGI system change over time, and it is unrealistic to expect such a function to be defined on all future states. How desirable a situation is should be taken as part of the problem to be solved, rather than as a given.

Issues on Budget: An AGI is often expected to handle unanticipated problems in *real time* with various time requirements. In such a situation, even if the decision-making algorithms are considered as of "tractable" computational complexity, they may still fail to satisfy the requirement on response time in the given situation.

None of the above issues is completely unknown, and various attempts have been proposed to extend the traditional models [1,13,22], though none of them has rejected the four assumptions altogether. Instead, a typical attitude is to take decision theory and reinforcement learning as *idealized models* for the actual AGI systems to approximate, as well as to be evaluated accordingly [6].

What this paper explores is the possibility of establishing normative models of decision making without accepting any of the above four assumptions. In the following, such a model is introduced, then compared with the classical models.

2   Decision Making in NARS

The decision-making model to be introduced comes from the NARS project [17,18,20]. The objective of this project is to build an AGI in the framework of a reasoning system. Decision making is an important function of the system, though it is not carried out by a separate algorithm or module, but tightly interwoven with other functions, such as reasoning and learning. Limited by the paper length, the following description only briefly covers the aspects of NARS that are directly related to the current discussion.

NARS is designed according to the theory that "intelligence" is the ability for a system to be *adaptive* while working with *insufficient knowledge and resources*, that is, the system must depend on *finite* processing capability, make *real-time* responses, *open* to unanticipated problems and events, and *learn* from its experience. Under this condition, it is impossible for the truth-value of beliefs of the system to be defined either in the model-theoretic style as *the extent of agreement with the state of affairs*, or in the proof-theoretic style as *the extent of agreement with the given axioms*. Instead, it is defined as *the extent of agreement with the available evidence* collected from the system's experience.

Formally, for a given statement S, the amount of its *positive evidence* and *negative evidence* are defined in an idealized situation and measured by amounts w^+ and w^-, respectively, and the total amount evidence is $w = w^+ + w^-$. The truth-value of S is a pair of real numbers, $\langle f, c \rangle$, where f, *frequency*, is w^+/w so in [0, 1], and c, *confidence*, is $w/(w + 1)$ so in (0, 1). Therefore a belief has a form of "$S\langle f, c \rangle$". As the content of belief, statement S is a sentence in a formal language *Narsese*. Each statement expresses a relation among a few concepts. For the current discussion, it is enough to know that a statement may have various internal structures for different types of conceptual relation, and can contain other statements as components. In particular, *implication* statement $P \Rightarrow Q$ and *equivalence* statement $P \Leftrightarrow Q$ express "If P then Q" and "P if and only if Q", respectively, where P and Q are statements themselves.

As a reasoning system, NARS can carry out three types of inference tasks:

Judgment. A judgment also has the form of "$S\langle f, c \rangle$", and represents a piece of new experience to be absorbed into the system's beliefs. Besides adding it into memory, the system may also use it to revise or update the previous beliefs on statement S, as well as to derive new conclusions using various inference rules (including *deduction, induction, abduction, analogy,* etc.). Each rule uses a truth-value function to calculate the truth-value of the conclusion according to the evidence provided by the premises. For example, the *deduction rule* can take $P\langle f_1, c_1\rangle$ and $P \Rightarrow Q \langle f_2, c_2\rangle$ to derive $Q\langle f, c\rangle$, where $\langle f, c\rangle$ is calculated from $\langle f_1, c_1\rangle$ and $\langle f_2, c_2\rangle$ by the truth-value function for deduction.[1] There is also a *revision rule* that merges distinct bodies of evidence on the same statement to produce more confident judgments.

Question. A question has the form of "S?", and represents a request for the system to find the truth-value of S according to its current beliefs. A question may contain variables to be instantiated. Besides looking in the memory for a matching belief, the system may also use the inference rules *backwards* to generate derived questions, whose answers will lead to answers of the original question. For example, from question Q? and belief $P \Rightarrow Q \langle f, c\rangle$, a new question P? can be proposed by the *deduction rule*. When there are multiple candidate answers, a *choice rule* is used to find the best answer among them, based on truth-value, simplicity, and so on.

Goal. A goal has the form of "S!". Similar to logic programming [5], in NARS certain concepts are given a *procedural interpretation*, so a goal is taken as a statement to be achieved, and an operation as a statement that can be achieved by an executable routine. The processing of a goal also includes backward inference guided by beliefs that generates derived goals. For example, from goal Q! and belief $P \Rightarrow Q \langle f, c\rangle$, a new goal P! can be proposed by the *deduction rule*. If the content of a goal corresponds to an executable *operation*, the associated routine is invoked to directly realize the goal, like what a Prolog *built-in predicate* does.

Under the restriction of the available knowledge and resources, no task can be accomplished *perfectly*. Instead, what the system attempts is to accomplish them as much as allowed by its available knowledge and resources. In NARS, decision making is most directly related to the processing of goals, though the other inference activities are also relevant.[2]

In Narsese, an operation is expressed by an *operator* (which identifies the associated routine) with an *argument list* (which includes both input and output arguments). The belief about the execution condition and consequence of an operation is typically represented as "(*condition, operation*) $\Rightarrow$ *consequence*", which is logically equivalent to "*condition* $\Rightarrow$ (*operation* $\Rightarrow$ *consequence*)".[3] This belief can be used in different ways. In an idealized situation (where the

---

[1] Since P and Q can be events with an occurence time, the same rules can be used for temporal reasoning, which is described in more detail in [21].

[2] Different types of inference tasks may work together. For example, from important judgments of low confidence, questions can be derived, and from certain questions, goals can be derived, which if pursued give rise to curious and exploratory behaviors.

[3] Like other beliefs, there is a truth-value attached, which is omitted here to simplify the discussion.

uncertainty of the belief and the existence of other beliefs and tasks are ignored), if *"condition"* is true, the execution of *"operation"* will make *"consequence"* true by forward inference; when *"consequence!"* is a goal, backward inference will generate *"condition!"* as a derived goal. When the latter goal is satisfied (either confirmed by a belief or achieved recursively by other operations), *"operation!"* becomes another derived goal, which is directly achieved by invoking the associated routine. Here the process looks similar to logic programming, though the situation is more complicated, especially in backward inference.

As an open system working in real time, new tasks can come while the system is still working on other goals, and there is no guarantee that all the co-existing goals are consistent with each other in what they demand the system to do. Even if all the innate and given goals are consistent, the derived ones may not be, since they usually come as means to achieve certain goal in isolation, without considering their impacts on the other goals. Even among goals that are consistent with each other in content, they still compete for resources, especially processing time. In NARS, to fully process a goal means to take all relevant beliefs into consideration. Since the system's capability is finite and the goals all should be accomplished as soon as possible, it is usually impossible to fully process all of them. Consequently, it becomes necessary to have *preference* among goals to indicate their different significance to the system.

Instead of defining a separate measurement for preference, NARS takes the "desire as belief" approach [10]. The *desire-value* of statement S is taken as the *truth-value* of statement $S \Rightarrow D$, where D is a *virtual statement* representing the "desired state" where all the system's goals are satisfied. D is "virtual" in the sense that its content is not explicitly spelled out, nor is it actually stored in the system's memory. It is only used in the conceptual design to turn the processing of the desire-values into that of the related truth-values. While every judgement has an assigned truth-value, every goal has an assigned desire-value. Like a truth-value, the intuitive meaning of a desire-value can also be explained using idealized situations. S has desire-value $\langle w^+/w, w/(w+1) \rangle$ if the system believes that if S is realized, w^+ of its w consequences are "good", while the rest of them are "bad", with respect to the system's goals. In this way, the system can calculate the desire-value of a statement according to the desire-value of another statement and the belief that linked them, using the truth-value functions of the inference rules. For example, the desire-value of statement S_1, d_1, is interpreted as the truth-value of statement $S_1 \Rightarrow D$, so can be used with the truth-value of belief $S_2 \Rightarrow S_1$, t_1, by the *deduction* function to calculate d_2, the truth-value of $S_2 \Rightarrow D$, which is the desire-value of statement S_2. In this process the exact content of D is irrelevant, as far as it is the same in its two usages. Even without going into the details of the above calculation, it is easy to see that d_2 depends on both d_1 and t_1. S_2 is highly desired only when S_1 is highly desired and the implication relation $S_2 \Rightarrow S_1$ is strongly supported by available evidence.

Similarly, the *revision rule* can be used to merge conflicting desire-values. For example, after a high desire-value of S_2 is established by a goal S_1, another goal S_3 is taken into consideration, but the system believes that it can be realized only when S_2 is not realized. By deduction again S_2 will get another desire-value d'_2 whose frequency value is low. Now the *revision rule* can combine d_2 and d'_2 into d''_2, as the desire-value of S_2 when both goals S_1 and S_3 are taken into account. In this case, whether S_2 will still be treated as a goal depends on the total evidence – if the frequency factor in d''_2 is too low, it will not be pursued by the system, despite of the positive evidence from S_1. In this way, "decision making" in NARS can be discussed in two senses:

- In a *narrow sense*, it corresponds to the decision of whether to turn a statement 'S' into a goal '$S!$'. As explained above, this decision mainly depends on the current desire-value of S, especially the *frequency* factor in it.
- In a *broad sense*, it corresponds to the process in which the related factors, especially the desire value of S, are decided. As explained above, this process may consist of many steps and involve many tasks and beliefs.

As argued in several other publications (such as [18,20]), since NARS takes a *unified approach* toward AGI, many cognitive functions are interwoven in it and carried out by the same underlying process, rather than by interconnected modules. This is true for functions like "reasoning", "learning", as well as "decision making". What is special about the latter is that the decision of whether to pursue a new goal is a binary commitment, a "to do or not to do" matter, which is based on the current beliefs and desires that are all matters of degree.

3   Comparison and Discussion

The objective of this paper is not to explain the details of decision-making in NARS, but to use NARS as an example to show the feasibility of building a normative model of decision-making where none of the four traditional assumptions is made. In the following each of these assumptions is contrasted with the corresponding assumption in NARS.

The Assumption on Task

Decision making eventually is about the selection of an action among alternatives. However, it does not have to be directly formalized as a selection algorithm with a list of alternatives as input – finding the alternatives is also important.

NARS takes the decision to be "Whether to pursue a goal", so it also covers the situation where a goal is not directly achieved by an operation, but via derived goals. Here "to execute an operation" is just a special case of "to achieve a goal", where the content of the goal happens to be an operation. On the contrary, the traditional models leave the derivation of goals out of the model, even though it is a crucial aspect of decision making.

For a given goal, NARS considers each alternative one by one, and each of which is a derived goal, with operation as a special case. In each case, the comparison is between "pursue the goal" and "not to pursue the goal". For a given goal, the system may pursue zero, one, or multiple derived goals, and some of the alternatives may be discovered or constructed in the process. Unlike in the traditional models, in this approach there is no demand for an exhaustive list of mutually exclusive actions to be available in advance for each decision.

The traditional decision-making process can still be carried out in NARS as a special case. If all possible actions are listed, and only one of them can be selected, then the evidence favoring one action will be taken as evidence against the other actions. Consequently, the best action selected by the traditional model will also be the one selected by the *choice rule* of NARS, and its selection will block the others under the mutual-exclusion restriction.

The Assumption on Belief

In all the models the selection of action is based on the system's relevant beliefs about its *preconditions* and its *effects*. In the traditional models, these two aspects are embedded in the *states* of the environment, while in NARS they are expressed by *statements*. In general, a statement only partially specifies a state.

Based on the assumption of insufficient knowledge, in NARS even if a belief *(condition, operation)* $\Rightarrow$ *consequence* has a relatively high frequency and confidence, *condition* does not necessarily specifies the operation's full preconditions, nor *consequence* its full effects. This approach is taken, not because the "state-based" approach is bad, but because it is unrealistic. Even POMDP (partially observable Markov decision process) models are too idealized on this aspect, where states still need to be estimated from observations, since the Markov property is defined only in a state-based representation. There have been attempts in reinforcement learning study to change the "flat" state space into a hierarchical one. However, the current approaches all assume *static* abstractions, and how to get *dynamic* abstractions is still acknowledged as an open problem [1]. For a general purpose system, it is crucial to move between different levels of abstractions, as well as to generate them at run time. A statement-based description satisfies such a need. An AGI should be able to work in a non-stationary environment, where the states of the environment never accurately repeat. In such a situation, though it still makes sense to talk about "the state of the environment", to use them to specify an operation is not possible, because future states are usually different from past ones. A statement, on the other hand, only captures certain aspect of states, so can be repeatedly observed in experience. If a classifier is used to merge similar states, then it actually turns the model into "statement-based", since here one "state" may correspond to different situations.

Another difference between NARS and the traditional models is that the *truth-value* in NARS is not *probability*. This topic has been discussed in previous publications [18,20], so only the major arguments are summarized:

- In NARS, truth-value measures degree of belief according to available evidence, which may change over time without converging to a limit, so is not a function defined on the space of statements.

- Each statement is evaluated according to its own available evidence, so all the truth-values of the beliefs do not necessarily form a consistent probability distribution, and there can be inconsistency among beliefs.
- Because of the above reasons, the calculation and revision of truth-value cannot be handled as Bayesian conditioning or other theorems of probability theory. Instead, their calculations are based on the semantics of NARS, using extended Boolean functions.

Once again, this is the case, because under the assumption of insufficient knowledge and resources, an AGI usually cannot maintain a consistent probability distribution among its beliefs, no matter how preferred such a situation is.

In particular, Solomonoff probability [2,15] is not accepted in NARS, since it demands unrealistic resources, as well as is justified by interpreting "Occam's Razor" as "Simple hypotheses are preferred because they are more likely to be true". In NARS, "Occam's Razor" is interpreted as "Simple hypotheses are preferred because they demands less resources". Therefore, it is respected in resource allocation, but not in truth-value calculation.

The Assumption on Desire

As a derivative of *belief*, in NARS *desire* is also defined on *statements*, rather than on *states*. Beside the partiality nature, it has additional desirable features.

In both decision theory and reinforcement learning, it is assumed that the states are evaluated by a single *value* function (utility function or reward function). Though such a treatment is natural for many practical problems, it has trouble to be extended into general-purpose systems where there are usually multiple goals at the same time. Because of the conflicts and competitions among the goals, the "value" of an action usually should be judged according to its effects on all the existing goals. When these goals are incommensurable, it is hard to justify such a function. The traditional models simply assume the existence of the function, so as to put the burden on the practitioners. Introducing a monetary measurement like commonly used is not always natural or justifiable.

NARS does not depend on an overall value function, but defines desire-value on statements, including goals as a subset. When considering each action, in many situations it is hard, if not impossible, to judge its value against the "ultimate goal" or "super goal" of the system. Instead, it is usually judged with respect to each goal that happens to be considered at the time, and more considerations will bring other related goals into account to revise its desire-value, as explained previously. In the way, the overall desire-value is *constructed by* the system, not *given to* it. Furthermore, this construction is adaptive and context-sensitive, so it is not a fixed function defined on states or statements.

In the discussions about the safety of AI, many people have incorrectly assumed that the key is to give the system a "super goal" that is beneficial to human beings. In reality an intelligent system cannot always decide its actions by checking them against such a super goal, due to knowledge-resource restriction. What really matter are the currently active goals, which may have become inconsistent with the initial goal from which they were derived [19].

The Assumption on Budget

One of the most noticeable characteristics of NARS is the resources restriction in its theoretical foundation. On the contrary, most normative models regard the insufficiency of computational time and space as implementation issues and exclude them from theoretical considerations [6]. It has been argued in several of our publications that "optimum decisions made with sufficient resource" and "optimum decisions made with insufficient resource" are different problems that demand different solutions. Many cognitive functions observed in the human mind were evolved to deal with resource allocation, such as *attention, forgetting,* and *emotion* [7,14]. Their impacts on decision making cannot be understood if the resource restriction is omitted.

For NARS, to work in *real time* means that each problem *instance* (not problem *type*) has an associated time requirement that can only be determined at runtime, and the available resources of the system cannot be predetermined, since it depends on the co-existent tasks. To work in such a situation, in NARS there is no "decision making algorithm" with a fixed computational complexity. Instead, a decision-making process is formed at runtime by a large number of inference steps, and the number and order of the steps are determined at the moment by many factors, so that even if the same problem occurs at different moments, its processing and even the result may be different. NARS cannot guarantee to consider all possibilities when a decision is made, but it considers as many as the current resource supply allows. A lot of work has been done in reinforcement learning to improve efficiency, but the results are all in the form of fixed algorithms, which cannot handle variable time pressure. NARS on the other hand is designed to work under the assumption of insufficient resources, with insufficient time as special case.

4   Conclusion

Mainly because of the insufficiency of knowledge and resources, certain basic assumptions of the traditional models of decision making, namely decision theory and reinforcement learning, cannot be accepted in realistic situations where AGI systems should work. These assumptions include:

- "Decision making" means to select the best action from all applicable actions.
- Beliefs on actions are expressed as probabilistic transitions among states.
- Desires are measured by a value function defined on states.
- The system can afford the resources demanded by the involved algorithms.

Though the traditional models can still be extended and revised, they cannot drop all these fundamental assumptions without becoming fundamentally different models.[4] They should not be taken as idealized models to be approximated, since these assumptions change the nature of the problem of decision making.

---

[4] There is no space in this paper to discuss approaches where some of them are rejected.

The practice of NARS shows that it is feasible to put decision making in a normative model that is based on the assumption of insufficient knowledge and resources. Such a model shares many features with the human mind, while is still justified according to certain principles of rationality. This direction is similar to ideas like Simon's "bounded rationality" [13], except those ideas are rarely formalized and specified in details to be implementable in computers. Compared to them, NARS provides a much more detailed model, which is also implemented and under testing.[5]

References

1. Barto, A.G., Mahadevan, S.: Recent advances in hierarchical reinforcement learning. Discrete Event Dynamic Systems **13**, 41–77 (2003)
2. Hutter, M.: Universal Artificial Intelligence: Sequential Decisions based on Algorithmic Probability. Springer, Berlin (2005)
3. Jeffrey, R.C.: The Logic of Decision. McGraw-Hill, New York (1965)
4. Kaelbling, L.P., Littman, M.L., Moore, A.W.: Reinforcement learning: a survey. Journal of Artificial Intelligence Research **4**, 237–285 (1996)
5. Kowalski, R.: Logic for Problem Solving. North Holland, New York (1979)
6. Legg, S., Hutter, M.: Universal intelligence: a definition of machine intelligence. Minds & Machines **17**(4), 391–444 (2007)
7. Medin, D.L., Ross, B.H.: Cognitive Psychology. Harcourt Brace Jovanovich, Fort Worth (1992)
8. Mintzberg, H., Raisinghani, D., Théorêt, A.: The structure of 'unstructured' decision processes. Administrative Sciences Quarterly **21**, 246–275 (1976)
9. Mnih, V., Kavukcuoglu, K., Silver, D., Rusu, A.A., Veness, J., Bellemare, M.G., Graves, A., Riedmiller, M., Fidjeland, A.K., Ostrovski, G., Petersen, S., Beattie, C., Sadik, A., Antonoglou, I., King, H., Kumaran, D., Wierstra, D., Legg, S., Hassabis, D.: Human-level control through deep reinforcement learning. Nature **518**(7540), 529–533 (2015)
10. Price, H.: Defending desire-as-belief. Mind **98**, 119–127 (1989)
11. Russell, S., Norvig, P.: Artificial Intelligence: A Modern Approach, 3rd edn. Prentice Hall, Upper Saddle River (2010)
12. Savage, L.J.: The Foundations of Statistics. Wiley, New York (1954)
13. Simon, H.A.: Models of Man: Social and Rational. John Wiley, New York (1957)
14. Simon, H.A.: Motivational and emotional controls of cognition. Psychological Review **74**, 29–39 (1967)
15. Solomonoff, R.J.: A formal theory of inductive inference. Part I and II. Information and Control **7**(1-2), 1–22, 224–254 (1964)
16. Sutton, R.S., Barto, A.G.: Reinforcement Learning: An Introduction. MIT Press, Cambridge (1998)
17. Wang, P.: Non-Axiomatic Reasoning System: Exploring the Essence of Intelligence. Ph.D. thesis, Indiana University (1995)
18. Wang, P.: Rigid Flexibility: The Logic of Intelligence. Springer, Dordrecht (2006)

---

[5] For source code and working examples, visit *https://github.com/opennars/opennars*.

19. Wang, P.: Motivation management in agi systems. In: Bach, J., Goertzel, B., Iklé, M. (eds.) AGI 2012. LNCS, vol. 7716, pp. 352–361. Springer, Heidelberg (2012)
20. Wang, P.: Non-Axiomatic Logic: A Model of Intelligent Reasoning. World Scientific, Singapore (2013)
21. Wang, P., Hammer, P.: Issues in temporal and causal inference. In: Proceedings of the Eighth Conference on Artificial General Intelligence (2015)
22. Weirich, P.: Realistic Decision Theory. Oxford University Press, New York (2004)

Issues in Temporal and Causal Inference

Pei Wang[1]([✉]) and Patrick Hammer[2]

[1] Department of Computer and Information Sciences, Temple University,
1925 North 12th Street, Philadelphia, PA 19122, USA
pei.wang@temple.edu
[2] Institute of Optimization and Discrete Mathematics,
Graz University of Technology, Steyrergasse 30, 8010 Graz, Austria

Abstract. This paper discusses several key issues in temporal and causal inference in the context of AGI. The main conclusions are: (1) the representation of temporal information should take multiple forms; (2) classical conditioning can be carried out as temporal inference; (3) causal inference can be realized without a predefined causal relation.

A central function of intelligence is *prediction*, the ability for a system to anticipate future situations according to past experience. It is often considered as a form of *temporal inference* or *causal inference*. This paper focuses on several key issues in this type of inference, by introducing the approach taken in NARS (Non-Axiomatic Reasoning System), and comparing it with other approaches.

NARS is an AGI system designed according to the theory that *intelligence is the ability for a system to adapt to the environment while working with insufficient knowledge and resources*. The system takes the form of a general-purpose reasoning system, and carries out various cognitive functions (learning, planning, decision making, etc.) in a unified process. The theory and its formal model are described in [31,32], as well as in other publications. Limited by the length of the paper, in the following only a small part of the system is described.

1 Integrated Representation of Temporal Information

NARS uses a formal language *Narsese* to represent various types of knowledge:

Term. A term names a concept in the system. In its simplest form, an atomic term is just a unique identifier, such as *bird* for the concept "bird".

Compound Term. A compound term is composed from other terms by a connector. For example, $([yellow] \cap bird)$ is a compound term for "yellow bird".

Statement. A statement is a compound term representing the substitutability of one term by another one. For example, "Tweety is a yellow bird" is represented by statement "$\{Tweety\} \rightarrow ([yellow] \cap bird)$". A statement with a truth-value measuring its evidential support is called a *judgment*.

Event. An event is a statement whose truth-value is specified for a duration. For example, "Tweety is following Bob" is represented in Narsese as "$(\{Tweety\} \times \{Bob\}) \rightarrow follow$", and the statement is *true* in the period when Tweety is following Bob, but neither before nor after that period.

© Springer International Publishing Switzerland 2015
J. Bieger (Ed.): AGI 2015, LNAI 9205, pp. 208–217, 2015.
DOI: 10.1007/978-3-319-21365-1_22

Operation. An operation is an event that can be realized by the system itself. For example, "to follow Bob" is represented in Narsese as operation "$\Uparrow follow(\{Bob\})$", which the system can realize by directly executing it.

The formal definitions of the symbols used above are given in [32], and here they only need to be intuitively understood. Also, for the current discussion, it is enough to see the memory of NARS as a collection of interrelated concepts.

In this way, NARS uniformly represents all empirical knowledge as sentences in a formal language, while still keeps the differences among types of knowledge. This design is very different from the tradition of cognitive architectures, where the common practice is to distinguish "semantic/declarative memory", "episodic memory", and "procedural memory" from each other, and to handle them in separate modules, each with its storage structure and processing mechanism [6,14,17]. There have been other attempts to unify these memory modules, such as in a *graphical* model [25], while NARS does it in a *logical* model that has some similarity with logical programming [13], even though the memory of NARS can also be roughly seen as a conceptual graph.

Since an event is just a statement whose truth-value is specified for a period, the most straightforward representation of temporal information is to attach a time interval to each event [1,18], or even to every statement, since accurately speaking, every conceptual relation hold in an interval, including "forever" as a special case. NARS does not take this approach, because in different situations the accuracy in specifying the beginning and ending of an event varies greatly, so to use a single unit of time by which all events are measured is probably neither necessary nor possible for an AGI. To be natural and flexible, in NARS an event can be seen as both a point and an interval in time, depending on the desired granularity. This treatment is consistent with the opinion that "The unit of composition of our perception of time is a *duration*" [15]. Therefore, the temporal information of an event is specified *relatively* with respect to another event, using one of the two built-in temporal relations: *sequential* and *parallel* (also known as *before-after* and *at-the-same-time*), which correspond to the *precedes* and *overlap* predicates in the Russell-Kamp construction [15].

As a reasoning system, NARS runs by repeating a working cycle, and in each cycle the system carries out a step of inference, as well as some simple input/output activities. Just like a biological system uses certain rhythmic event as a "biological clock", NARS uses its working cycles as an internal clock, since each working cycle roughly takes a short constant amount of time. Using this internal clock, NARS can express the durations of certain events. For example, it can represent something like "Event A is observed, then, after 5 cycles, event B is observed", where the "5 cycles" is an event measurable by the system.

Beside current events, the system can make judgments about past and future events, too. In NARS every sentence has a *time-stamp* indicating when the judgment is created (either from input or from inference); if the sentence is about an event, there is also a time-stamp about the estimated occurrence time. All the time-stamps are in terms of the system's internal clock, and each takes an integer as value, which can be either positive or negative. This treatment has some similarity with "step-logic" [5], though in NARS a time-stamp is not explicitly expressed as part of a statement. Unlike some cognitive architectures [7,17], NARS does not attempt to simulate the response time of the human brain. The system uses its (subjective) working cycle as the unit of time, not the (objective) time provided by the clock of the host computer, so as to achieve platform-independence in testing. For example, if a certain inference process takes 10 steps in one computer, so does it in a different computer, even when the two systems have different running speeds.

The internal clock and built-in temporal relations are preferred for their simplicity and flexibility, but they are not used to represent all types of temporal information. NARS can use an external clock by specifying an event as occurring at the same moment as a time indicated by the clock. Since such a clock is an optional tool, the system can use different clocks in different situations for various demands of accuracy and granularity in time measurement.

In summary, in NARS temporal information is represented at three levels:

Term. A term (either atomic or compound) can represent a temporal concept (such as "New Year's Day") or relation (such as "after a while"). Such a term is handled just like the other terms, though its meaning contains acquired temporal information.

Statement. A temporal statement can be formed using a built-in *temporal* relation combined with certain *logical* connectors. For example, if A, B, and C are events, then the Narsese statement "$(A, B) \not\Rightarrow C$" represents "If A is followed by B, then C will occur after them".

Sentence. A temporal sentence uses a time-stamp to indicate the estimated occurrence time of the event, with respect to the internal clock of the system.

Since the internal clock is "private" to the system, when a temporal sentence needs to be expressed in Narsese for communication purpose, its time-stamp is converted into a "tense", which has three possible values: "past", "present", and "future", with respect to the "current moment" when the message is created. Symmetrically, when an input judgment has a tense attached, it is converted into a time-stamp, according to the current time.

It is important to see that an AGI system like NARS should not directly carry out inference on tense, because since the system works in real time, the "current moment" changes constantly [5,12]. On this aspect, NARS is fundamentally different from many traditional temporal logic systems [22,29], which treat the tense of a statement as one of its intrinsic properties, as if the reasoning system itself is outside the flow of time.

In summary, many different techniques have been proposed in AI to represent temporal information, each of which is effective under different assumptions [2]. NARS uses three approaches, and integrates them to satisfy the need of AGI.

2   Classical Conditioning as Temporal Inference

NARS uses *experience-grounded semantics* [30]. Accordingly, the truth-value of a statement measures its *evidential support* with two real numbers in $[0, 1]$:

the *frequency* value is the proportion of positive evidence among all currently available evidence, and the *confidence* value is the proportion of the currently available evidence among all evidence accumulated after the coming of new evidence by a unit amount. Their relation with probability is explained in [31].

Based on this semantics, each inference rule in NARS has a truth-value function calculating the truth-value of the conclusion according to the evidence provided by the premises. Without going into the details of the inference rules (covered in [32] and other publications on NARS), for the current discussion it is sufficient to know that as far as the *confidence* of the conclusion is concerned, there are three types of inference rules:

Strong Inference. For example, from premises "$\{Tweety\} \rightarrow bird \langle 1.00, 0.90 \rangle$" ("Tweety is a bird") and "$(\$x \rightarrow bird) \Rightarrow (\$x \rightarrow [yellow]) \langle 1.00, 0.90 \rangle$" ("Birds are yellow", where $\$x$ can be substituted by another term), the *deduction* rule derives the conclusion "$\{Tweety\} \rightarrow [yellow] \langle 1.00, 0.81 \rangle$" ("Tweety is yellow"). Such a rule is "strong" because the confidence of its conclusion can approach 1. If the truth-values are dropped and all the statements are taken to be "true", the rule is still valid in its binary form.

Weak Inference. For example, from premises "$\{Tweety\} \rightarrow bird \langle 1.00, 0.90 \rangle$" and "$\{Tweety\} \rightarrow [yellow] \langle 1.00, 0.90 \rangle$", the *induction* rule derives "$(\$x \rightarrow bird) \Rightarrow (\$x \rightarrow [yellow]) \langle 1.00, 0.45 \rangle$"; similarly, from "$(\$x \rightarrow bird) \Rightarrow (\$x \rightarrow [yellow]) \langle 1.00, 0.90 \rangle$" and "$\{Tweety\} \rightarrow [yellow] \langle 1.00, 0.90 \rangle$", the *abduction* rule derives "$\{Tweety\} \rightarrow bird \langle 1.00, 0.45 \rangle$". Such a rule is "weak" because the confidence of its conclusion cannot be higher than 0.5. If the truth-values are dropped and all the statements are taken to be "true", the rule becomes invalid in its binary form.

Evidence pooling. If two premises have the same statement but are supported by distinct evidence, such as "$bird \rightarrow [yellow] \langle 1.00, 0.50 \rangle$" and "$bird \rightarrow [yellow] \langle 0.00, 0.80 \rangle$", the *revision* rule derives "$bird \rightarrow [yellow] \langle 0.20, 0.83 \rangle$". This is the only rule whose conclusion has a higher confidence value than both premises, since here the premises are based on the distinct evidential bases, while the conclusion is based on the pooled evidence.

There are many other inference rules in the system for other combinations of premises with respect to various term connectors, and they will not be addressed in this paper. In the following we only briefly describe how *temporal inference* is carried out. Here the basic idea is to process *temporal* information and *logical* information in parallel. Among other functions, this type of inference can carry out a process that is similar to *classical (Pavlovian) conditioning*, by associating a conditioned stimulus (CS) with an unconditioned stimulus (US). However what is special in NARS is that temporal inference will also happen between neutral stimuli. In the rare case that they get attention and also turn out to be important, they will find relations which a classical conditioning model would have missed.

To show how it works, assume initially the system gets to know that an occurrence of event C is followed by an occurrence of event U. As mentioned previously, events are represented as statements with temporal information. In this case, the occurrence time of C will be recognized by the system as before that of U. As soon as the temporal succession between the two events is noticed by the system, a temporal version of the *induction* rule will be invoked to generalize the observation into a temporal implication "$C \Rightarrow U$". The truth-value of this conclusion depends on the quality of the observations, as well as the restriction applied by the induction rule, so that the confidence value of the conclusion will be less than 0.5 – since it is only based on a single observation, the conclusion is considered a "hypothesis" that differs from a "fact" in confidence.

If at a later time C occurs again, then from it and the previous hypothesis the system derives U by deduction, with a time-stamp suggesting that it will occur soon. Since the hypothesis has a low confidence, the prediction on U is also tentative, though it may still be significant enough to raise the system's *anticipation* of the event, so as to make it more recognizable even when the input signal is relatively weak or noisy. An anticipation-driven observation is "active", rather than "passive" (where the system simply accepts all incoming signals without any bias), and the difference is not only in sensitivity. When expressed as Narsese sentences, the inputs provided by a sensor normally correspond to *affirmative* judgments, without any *negative* ones – we can directly see or hear what *is* out there, but cannot directly see or hear what *is not* there. "Negative observations" are actually *unrealized anticipations* and can only be produced by active observations.

In the current example, if the anticipated U does not appear at the estimated time, this unrealized anticipation and the preceding C will be taken as negative evidence by the *induction* rule to generate a negative judgment "$C \not\Rightarrow U$" that has a low (near 0) frequency value. Then the revision rule can pool this one with the previous (affirmative) one to get a new evaluation for the temporal statement "$C \Rightarrow U$". In this way, the successes and failures of anticipation will gradually lead the system to a relatively stable belief on whether, or how often, U is followed by C. The conclusion is similar to a statistical one, though it is revised incrementally, with no underlying probabilistic distribution assumed.

If the system has an unconditioned response (*UR*) to the *US*, this "instinct" corresponds to a temporal implication "$U \Rightarrow \Uparrow R$" that represents a sufficient precondition U for the operation $\Uparrow R$ to be executed, and it will have an affirmative truth-value, such as $\langle 1.00, 0.99 \rangle$ (confidence cannot reach 1, even for an instinct). From this instinct and the belief on "$C \Rightarrow U$", the *deduction* rule generates "$C \Rightarrow \Uparrow R$", which gives the operation an acquired sufficient precondition, though with a lower confidence than the instinct at the beginning. Now $\Uparrow R$ becomes a *conditioned response* (CR) to the CS.

Similarly, if the system already has a strong belief on "$C \not\Rightarrow U$", and it notices an occurrence of U, then by *temporal abduction* the system will guess that C has occurred previously, though the system may fail to notice it in the input stream, or it may be not directly observable. Similar to inductive conclusions, such an abductive conclusion is not very confident until it is strengthen by other evidence. As proposed by C. S. Peirce [20], a major function of abduction is to provide *explanations* for observations.

Most of the existing models of classical conditioning are built in the framework of dynamic system [3, 8, 24, 28], while in NARS it is modeled as an inference process. Though Bayesian models [27] also treat conditioning as reasoning, there the process only evaluates the probability of given statements, while NARS, following a logic, can generate new statements. Beside recognizing the preconditions and consequences of single operations, temporal inference also allows the system to do the same for *compound operations* consisting of multiple steps, which is usually called "planning", "scheduling", or "skill learning" [15]. Typically, the consequence of a preceding operation enables or triggers a following operation, and such a compound operation as a whole will gradually be used as an individual operation by the system. Such a process recursively forms an action hierarchy, which allows efficient reaction and planning with different granularity. Unlike in reinforcement learning or many other planning systems, NARS does not plan its actions in all situations in terms of the same set of basic operations.

3   Causal Inference without a Casual Relation

Based on the current situation to predict the future (or to describe the past) is often considered as "causal inference". Though "causality" has many different interpretations [33], a common opinion is to think the events in the universe as interconnected via "causal relations", so that every event is "caused" by a certain proceeding event. When the causal relations of an event become fully known, its occurrence and consequences can be predicted with certainty.

This opinion is usually formalized in AI and cognitive science using mathematical logic [9, 26], probability theory [4, 19, 23], or a combination of the two [10, 11]. Such a model assumes the existence of a deterministic or probabilistic *causal relation*, on which the system carries out logical or statistical inference to predict the future, or to describe the past, according to the present. In this approach, every event has a unique "true cause", which can be found, or at least approximated, using causal inference.[1]

NARS does not treat causal inference in this way. As mentioned previously, the basic assumption behind NARS is that an intelligent system never has full knowledge about the environment and itself, and all the available knowledge are revisable. For a given event, the system cannot know all of its preconditions so as to predict its occurrence with certainty. Similarly, the system cannot accurately anticipate all effects an event triggers. According to this opinion, even the probabilistic models assume too much – to meaningfully talk about "the probability" of an event, the presumption is that all the relevant events are in a space on which a probability function is defined. For an AGI system working in realistic situations, such a function can neither be obtained nor maintained, since the system does not know all future events, nor can it always guarantee the consistency among its degrees of belief when they are revised in real-time.

---

[1] A new approach [23] additionally tries to get rid of certain undesired results (Berkson's Paradox) of Bayesian conditioning by using "relational blocking", but the problem of assuming "true cause" remains.

In an AGI system, the above restrictions do not rule out the feasibility of predicting the future and describing the past. As shown by the previous example, NARS can learn the regularity in its experience, and use it to predict the future. Here the relevant knowledge is represented as temporal implication judgments like "$C \not\Rightarrow U \langle f, c \rangle$", which is a summary of the relevant past experience, not an accurate or approximate description of an objective "law of nature".

The existence of objective causation is a long-lasting belief accepted by many scientists and philosophers, but it has been challenged in the recent century both in science (especially in physics) and in philosophy. From the point of view of cognitive science, it can be argued that all the beliefs of a system are restricted by the cognitive capability (*nature*) and past experience (*nurture*) of the system, and there is no ground to assume that such a belief will converge to an objective *truth*. Even so, an adaptive system can form beliefs about causation. According to Piaget [21], such beliefs originate from the observations about the consequences of one's own operations. For example, if event E is repeatedly observed after the execution of operation R, NARS will form a belief "$\Uparrow R \not\Rightarrow E \langle 0.98, 0.99 \rangle$", which can be interpreted as "E is caused by R". This will be the case even when this achievement of the operation actually depends on a condition C, which is usually (say 98% of the time) satisfied – the belief is stable and useful enough for C to be ignored. However, when C is not usually satisfied, a belief like "$\Uparrow R \not\Rightarrow E \langle 0.49, 0.99 \rangle$" will not be as useful to the system, so in this case a more reliable (though also more complicated) belief "$(C, \Uparrow R) \not\Rightarrow E \langle 0.99, 0.95 \rangle$" will be favored by the system as the knowledge about how to get E. Please note that even in such a case it is hard to say what is the "true cause" for E to happen, since accurately speaking there may be other events involved, though for the system's current purpose, they do not need to be taken into consideration.

This discussion is also related to the Frame Problem [16], where the issue is: for a given operation of the system, how to represent all of its preconditions and consequences. The solutions proposed for this problem usually deal with it in idealized or simplified situations, while the response to it in NARS is to give up the attempt of getting all the information. An AGI system should depend on operations with incomplete descriptions of preconditions and consequences, and make decisions according to the available knowledge and resources [34].

NARS uses temporal inference to carry out prediction and explanation, which are often considered as "causal inference", though within the system there is no built-in "causal relation". The system has temporal versions of *implication* and *equivalence* relations built into its grammar and inference rules, so a "causal relation" can be represented in the system as their variant with domain-specific and context-dependent additional requirements. This treatment is arguably similar to the everyday usage of "causation". In many fields, questions of the form of "What is the real cause of X?", with various X, have been under debate for decades, even centuries. The notion of *cause* is interpreted very differently in different situations – it can be deterministic or probabilistic; it may correspond to a sufficient condition or a sufficient-and-necessary condition; it may or may not be an intentional action; and so on. However, behind all of these versions, the invariant components include a logical factor (from the given "causes", the "effects" can be derived) and a temporal factor (the "causes" happen no later than the "effects"). NARS covers these two aspects in temporal inference, while leaves the additional and variable aspects of causation to learning.

In this model, a *causal* relation and a *covariant* (or *correlative*) relation can still be distinguished, as usually desired [4]. However here their difference is *quantitative*, not *qualitative*. If the judgment on "$C \not\Rightarrow U$" gets its truth-value solely by induction from a small amount of evidence, the confidence of the conclusion will be relatively low, and we tend to consider such a relation "covariant", but if the conclusion can also be established by a chain of deduction, such as from "$C \not\Rightarrow M$" and "$M \not\Rightarrow U$" where M is another event, then the relation between C and U may be considered as "casual", because it has an *explanation* leading to a high confidence. As far as prediction is concerned, what matters is the truth-value of the conclusion, not how they are derived. For instance, in Pavlovian conditioning the actual relation between CS and US is often coincidental, not causal, though animals in such experiments cannot tell the difference.

For a given event E, NARS can be asked to find its "cause" and "effect". The simplest form is to ask the system to instantiate the *query variable* $?x$ when answering questions "$?x \not\Rightarrow E$" and "$E \not\Rightarrow ?x$", respectively. When there are multiple candidate answers, a *choice* rule will be invoked to compare their truth-value, simplicity, relevance, etc., to pick the best answer. Additional requirements can be provided for the term or the statement that can be accepted as an answer. In general, NARS does not assume that such a question has a unique *correct* or *final* answer, but always reports the best answer it can find using the available knowledge and resources. Therefore, though the design of NARS does not include an innate causal relation, the system has the potential to *predict*, or even to *control*, the occurrence of an event. This is arguably what we should expect from an AGI.

4   Conclusions

Temporal inference plays a crucial role in AGI. An intelligent system needs the ability to learn the preconditions and consequences of each operation, to organize them into feasible plans or skills to reach complicated goals, and to find stable patterns among the events in its experience. This ability enables the system to predict the future, and to prepare sequences of operations to achieve its goals. Classical conditioning can be seen as a concrete case of this ability.

The approach of temporal inference in NARS allows temporal information to be expressed in several forms for different purposes. Some temporal notions are innate, while others are acquired, and they can be at different levels of granularity and accuracy. NARS integrates temporal inference with other inference, and utilizes a uniform memory for declarative, episodic, and procedural knowledge.

NARS carries out many cognitive functions, like prediction, that are usually associated with "causal inference". However there is no fixed notion of a "causal relation" within the system. NARS is based on the assumption that an accurate description of the universe with objective causal relations among the events may not be available to, or manageable by, the system, which makes NARS applicable to situations where many other models cannot be applied. Instead of trying to find or to approximate certain objective causal relations, what an intelligent system should do is to behave according to the regularity and invariance that it has summarized from its experience, and the generation, revision, and evaluation of such knowledge is a lifelong task.

All the aspects of NARS described in this paper have been implemented in the most recent version of the system. Currently the system, which is open source, is under testing and tuning. As an AGI system, NARS is not designed for any specific application, but as a testbed for a new theory about intelligence. Though the current implementation already shows many interesting and human-like properties, there are still many issues to be explored. This paper only addresses the aspects of NARS that are directly related to temporal inference.

Acknowledgments. The authors thank Kris Thórisson for helpful comments.

References

1. Allen, J.F.: Towards a general theory of action and time. Artificial Intelligence **23**(2), 123–154 (1984)
2. Allen, J.F.: Time and time again: The many ways to represent time. International Journal of Intelligent Systems **6**(4), 341–356 (1991)
3. Anderson, J.J., Bracis, C., Goodwin, R.A.: Pavlovian conditioning from a foraging perspective. In: Proceedings of the 32nd Annual Conference of the Cognitive Science Society, pp. 1276–1281 (2010)
4. Cheng, P.W.: From covariation to causation: a causal power theory. Psychological Review **104**(2), 367–405 (1997)
5. Elgot-Drapkin, J., Perlis, D.: Reasoning situated in time I: Basic concepts. Journal of Experimental & Theoretical Artificial Intelligence **2**, 75–98 (1990)
6. Franklin, S.: A foundational architecture for artificial general intelligence. In: Goertzel, B., Wang, P. (eds.) Advance of Artificial General Intelligence, pp. 36–54. IOS Press, Amsterdam (2007)
7. Franklin, S., Strain, S., McCall, R., Baars, B.: Conceptual commitments of the LIDA model of cognition. Journal of Artificial General Intelligence **4**(2), 1–22 (2013)
8. Gallistel, C.R., Gibbon, J.: Time, rate, and conditioning. Psychological Review **107**(2), 289–344 (2000)
9. Giunchiglia, E., Lee, J., Lifschitz, V., McCain, N., Turner, H.: Nonmonotonic causal theories. Artificial Intelligence **153**, 49–104 (2004)
10. Goodman, N.D., Ullman, T.D., Tenenbaum, J.B.: Learning a theory of causality. Psychological Review (2011)
11. Halpern, J.Y., Pearl, J.: Causes and explanations: A structural-model approach. Part I: Causes. The British Journal for the Philosophy of Science **56**(4), 843 (2005)
12. Ismail, H.O., Shapiro, S.C.: Two problems with reasoning and acting in time. In: Principles of Knowledge Representation and Reasoning: Proceedings of the Seventh International Conference, pp. 355–365 (2000)
13. Kowalski, R.: Logic for Problem Solving. North Holland, New York (1979)

14. Laird, J.E.: The Soar Cognitive Architecture. MIT Press, Cambridge (2012)
15. van Lambalgen, M., Hamm, F.: The proper treatment of events. Blackwell Publishing, Malden (2005)
16. McCarthy, J., Hayes, P.J.: Some philosophical problems from the standpoint of artificial intelligence. In: Meltzer, B., Michie, D. (eds.) Machine Intelligence 4, pp. 463–502. Edinburgh University Press, Edinburgh (1969)
17. Newell, A.: Unified Theories of Cognition. Harvard University Press, Cambridge (1990)
18. Nivel, E., Thórisson, K.R., Steunebrink, B.R., Dindo, H., Pezzulo, G., Rodriguez, M., Hernandez, C., Ognibene, D., Schmidhuber, J., Sanz, R., Helgason, H.P., Chella, A., Jonsson, G.K.: Bounded recursive self-improvement. CoRR abs/1312.6764 (2013)
19. Pearl, J.: Causality: Models, Reasoning, and Inference. Cambridge University Press, Cambridge (2000)
20. Peirce, C.S.: Collected Papers of Charles Sanders Peirce, vol. 2. Harvard University Press, Cambridge (1931)
21. Piaget, J.: The construction of reality in the child. Basic Books, New York (1954)
22. Pratt-Hartmann, I.: Temporal prepositions and their logic. Artificial Intelligence **166**, 1–36 (2005)
23. Rattigan, M.J., Maier, M., Jensen, D.: Relational blocking for causal discovery. In: Proceedings of the Twenty-Fifth AAAI Conference on Artificial Intelligence (2011)
24. Rescorla, R., Wagner, A.: A theory of Pavlovian conditioning: Variations in the effectiveness of reinforcement and non reinforcement. In: Black, A., Prokasy, W. (eds.) Classical Conditioning II, pp. 64–99. Appleton-Century-Crofts, New York (1972)
25. Rosenbloom, P.S.: Rethinking cognitive architecture via graphical models. Cognitive Systems Research **12**, 198–209 (2011)
26. Shoham, Y.: Nonmonotonic reasoning and causation. Cognitive Science **14**, 213–252 (1990)
27. Srivastava, N., Schrater, P.: Classical conditioning via inference over observable situation contexts. In: Proceedings of the 36th Annual Meeting of the Cognitive Science Society, pp. 1503–1508 (2014)
28. Sutton, R.S., Barto, A.G.: Time-derivative models of Pavlovian reinforcement. In: Gabriel, M., Moore, J. (eds.) Learning and Computational Neuroscience: Foundations of Adaptive Networks, pp. 497–537. MIT Press (1990)
29. Vila, L.: A survey on temporal reasoning in artificial intelligence. AI Communications **7**(1), 4–28 (1994)
30. Wang, P.: Experience-grounded semantics: a theory for intelligent systems. Cognitive Systems Research **6**(4), 282–302 (2005)
31. Wang, P.: Rigid Flexibility: The Logic of Intelligence. Springer, Dordrecht (2006)
32. Wang, P.: Non-Axiomatic Logic: A Model of Intelligent Reasoning. World Scientific, Singapore (2013)
33. Williamson, J.: Causality. In: Gabbay, D., Guenthner, F. (eds.) Handbook of Philosophical Logic, vol. 14, pp. 95–126. Springer (2007)
34. Xu, Y., Wang, P.: The frame problem, the relevance problem, and a package solution to both. Synthese (2012)

The Space of Possible Mind Designs

Roman V. Yampolskiy[(⊠)]

Computer Engineering and Computer Science Speed School of Engineering,
University of Louisville, Louisville, USA
roman.yampolskiy@louisville.edu

Abstract. The paper attempts to describe the space of possible mind designs by first equating all minds to software. Next it proves some properties of the mind design space such as infinitude of minds, size and representation complexity of minds. A survey of mind design taxonomies is followed by a proposal for a new field of investigation devoted to study of minds, *intellectology*.

Keywords: AGI · Intellectology · Mind · Mind designs · Space of minds

1 Introduction

In 1984 Aaron Sloman published "The Structure of the Space of Possible Minds" in which he described the task of providing an interdisciplinary description of that structure [1]. He observed that "behaving systems" clearly comprise more than one sort of mind and suggested that virtual machines may be a good theoretical tool for analyzing mind designs. Sloman indicated that there are many discontinuities within the space of minds meaning it is not a continuum, nor is it a dichotomy between things with minds and without minds [1]. Sloman wanted to see two levels of exploration namely: descriptive – surveying things different minds can do and exploratory – looking at how different virtual machines and their properties may explain results of the descriptive study [1]. Instead of trying to divide the universe into minds and non-minds he hoped to see examination of similarities and differences between systems. In this work we attempt to make another step towards this important goal1.

What is a mind? No universally accepted definition exists. Solipsism notwithstanding, humans are said to have a mind. Higher order animals are believed to have one as well and maybe lower level animals and plants or even all life forms. We believe that an artificially intelligent agent such as a robot or a program running on a computer will constitute a mind. Based on analysis of those examples we can conclude that a mind is an instantiated intelligence with a knowledgebase about its environment, and while intelligence itself is not an easy term to define, a recent work of Shane Legg provides a satisfactory, for our purposes, definition [2]. Additionally, some hold a point of view known as Panpsychism, attributing mind like properties to all matter. Without debating this possibility we will limit our analysis to those minds which can

---

[1] This paper is adapted, with permission, from Dr. Yampolskiy's forthcoming book – Artificial Superintelligence: a Futuristic Approach © 2015 by CRC Press.

© Springer International Publishing Switzerland 2015
J. Bieger (Ed.): AGI 2015, LNAI 9205, pp. 218–227, 2015.
DOI: 10.1007/978-3-319-21365-1_23

actively interact with their environment and other minds. Consequently, we will not devote any time to understanding what a rock is thinking.

If we accept materialism, we have to also accept that accurate software simulations of animal and human minds are possible. Those are known as uploads [3] and they belong to a class comprised of computer programs no different from that to which designed or evolved artificially intelligent software agents would belong. Consequently, we can treat the space of all minds as the space of programs with the specific property of exhibiting intelligence if properly embodied. All programs could be represented as strings of binary numbers, implying that each mind can be represented by a unique number. Interestingly, Nick Bostrom via some thought experiments speculates that perhaps it is possible to instantiate a fractional number of mind, such as .3 mind as opposed to only whole minds [4]. The embodiment requirement is necessary since a string is not a mind, but could be easily satisfied by assuming that a universal Turing machine is available to run any program we are contemplating for inclusion in the space of mind designs. An embodiment does not need to be physical as a mind could be embodied in a virtual environment represented by an avatar [5, 6] and react to simulated environment like a brain-in-a-vat or a "boxed" AI [7].

2   Infinitude of Minds

Two minds identical in terms of the initial design are typically considered to be different if they possess different information. For example, it is generally accepted that identical twins have distinct minds despite exactly the same blueprints for their construction. What makes them different is their individual experiences and knowledge obtained since inception. This implies that minds can't be cloned since different copies would immediately after instantiation start accumulating different experiences and would be as different as two twins.

If we accept that knowledge of a single unique fact distinguishes one mind from another we can prove that the space of minds is infinite. Suppose we have a mind M and it has a favorite number N. A new mind could be created by copying M and replacing its favorite number with a new favorite number N+1. This process could be repeated infinitely giving us an infinite set of unique minds. Given that a string of binary numbers represents an integer we can deduce that the set of mind designs is an infinite and countable set since it is an infinite subset of integers. It is not the same as set of integers since not all integers encode for a mind.

3   Size, Complexity and Properties of Minds

Given that minds are countable they could be arranged in an ordered list, for example in order of numerical value of the representing string. This means that some mind will have the interesting property of being the smallest. If we accept that a Universal Turing Machine (UTM) is a type of mind, if we denote by (m, n) the class of UTMs with m states and n symbols, the following UTMs have been discovered: (9, 3), (4, 6), (5, 5), and (2, 18). The (4, 6)-UTM uses only 22 instructions, and no standard machine of lesser complexity has been found [8]. Alternatively, we may ask about the largest mind.

Given that we have already shown that the set of minds is infinite, such an entity does not exist. However, if we take into account our embodiment requirement the largest mind may in fact correspond to the design at the physical limits of computation [9].

Another interesting property of the minds is that they all can be generated by a simple deterministic algorithm, a variant of Levin Search [10]: start with an integer (for example 42), check to see if the number encodes a mind, if not, we discard the number, otherwise we add it to the set of mind designs and proceed to examine the next integer. Every mind will eventually appear on our list of minds after a predetermined number of steps. However, checking to see if something is in fact a mind is not a trivial procedure. Rice's theorem [11] explicitly forbids determination of non-trivial properties of random programs. One way to overcome this limitation is to introduce an arbitrary time limit on the mind-or-not-mind determination function effectively avoiding the underlying halting problem.

Analyzing our mind-design generation algorithm we may raise the question of complexity measure for mind designs, not in terms of the abilities of the mind, but in terms of complexity of design representation. Our algorithm outputs minds in order of their increasing value, but this is not representative of the design complexity of the respective minds. Some minds may be represented by highly compressible numbers with a short representation such as 10^{13}, while others may be comprised of 10,000 completely random digits, for example 7358348955651172160377753562914... [12]. We suggest that Kolmogorov Complexity (KC) [13] measure could be applied to strings representing mind designs. Consequently some minds will be rated as "elegant" – having a compressed representation much shorter than the original string while others will be "efficient" representing the most efficient representation of that particular mind. Interesting elegant minds might be easier to discover than efficient minds, but unfortunately KC is not generally computable.

Each mind design corresponds to an integer and so is finite, but since the number of minds is infinite some have a much greater number of states compared to others. This property holds for all minds. Consequently, since a human mind has only a finite number of possible states, there are minds which can never be fully understood by a human mind as such mind designs have a much greater number of states, making their understanding impossible as can be demonstrated by the pigeonhole principle.

4   Space of Mind Designs

Overall the set of human minds (about 7 billion of them currently available and about 100 billion ever existed) is very homogeneous both in terms of hardware (embodiment in a human body) and software (brain design and knowledge). In fact the small differences between human minds are trivial in the context of the full infinite spectrum of possible mind designs. Human minds represent only a small constant size subset of the great mind landscape. Same could be said about the sets of other earthly minds such as dog minds, or bug minds or male minds or in general the set of all animal minds.

Given our definition of mind we can classify minds with respect to their design, knowledgebase or embodiment. First, the designs could be classified with respect to their origins: copied from an existing mind like an upload, evolved via artificial or natural evolution or explicitly designed with a set of particular desirable properties. Another alternative is what is known as a Boltzmann Brain – a complete mind embedded in a system which arises due to statistically rare random fluctuations in the particles comprising the universe, but which is very likely due to vastness of cosmos [14].

Lastly a possibility remains that some minds are physically or informationally recursively nested within other minds. With respect to the physical nesting we can consider a type of mind suggested by Kelly [15] who talks about "a very slow invisible mind over large physical distances". It is possible that the physical universe as a whole or a significant part of it comprises such a mega-mind. That theory has been around for millennia and has recently received some indirect experimental support [16]. In that case all the other minds we can consider are nested within such larger mind. With respect to the informational nesting a powerful mind can generate a less powerful mind as an idea. This obviously would take some precise thinking but should be possible for a sufficiently powerful artificially intelligent mind. Some scenarios describing informationally nested minds are analyzed by Yampolskiy in his work on artificial intelligence confinement problem [7]. Bostrom, using statistical reasoning, suggests that all observed minds, and the whole universe, are nested within a mind of a very powerful computer [17]. Similarly Lanza, using a completely different and somewhat controversial approach (biocentrism), argues that the universe is created by biological minds [18]. It remains to be seen if given a particular mind its origins can be deduced from some detailed analysis of the minds design or actions.

While minds designed by human engineers comprise only a tiny region in the map of mind designs it is probably the best explored part of the map. Numerous surveys of artificial minds, created by AI researchers in the last 50 years, have been produced [19-23]. Such surveys typically attempt to analyze state-of-the-art in artificial cognitive systems and provide some internal classification of dozens of the reviewed systems with regards to their components and overall design. The main subcategories into which artificial minds designed by human engineers can be placed include brain (at the neuron level) emulators [21], biologically inspired cognitive architectures [22], physical symbol systems, emergent systems, dynamical and enactive systems [23]. Rehashing information about specific architectures presented in such surveys is beyond the scope of this paper, but one can notice incredible richness and diversity of designs even in that tiny area of the overall map we are trying to envision. For readers particularly interested in overview of superintelligent minds, animal minds and possible minds in addition to surveys mentioned above a recent paper "Artificial General Intelligence and the Human Mental Model" by Yampolskiy and Fox is highly recommended [24].

For each mind subtype there are numerous architectures, which to a certain degree depend on the computational resources available via a particular embodiment. For example, theoretically a mind working with infinite computational resources could trivially brute-force any problem, always arriving at the optimal solution, regardless of its size. In practice, limitations of the physical world place constraints on available computational resources regardless of the embodiment type, making brute-force approach a non-feasible solution for most real world problems [9]. Minds working with limited computational resources have to rely on heuristic simplifications to arrive at "good enough" solutions [25-28].

Another subset of architectures consists of self-improving minds. Such minds are capable of examining their own design and finding improvements in their embodiment, algorithms or knowledgebases which will allow the mind to more efficiently perform desired operations [29]. It is very likely that possible improvements would form a Bell curve with many initial opportunities for optimization towards higher efficiency and fewer such options remaining after every generation. Depending on the definitions used, one can argue that a recursively self-improving mind actually changes itself into a different mind, rather than remaining itself, which is particularly obvious after a sequence of such improvements. Taken to extreme this idea implies that a simple act of learning new information transforms you into a different mind raising millennia old questions about the nature of personal identity.

With respect to their knowledgebases minds could be separated into those without an initial knowledgebase, and which are expected to acquire their knowledge from the environment, minds which are given a large set of universal knowledge from the inception and those minds which are given specialized knowledge only in one or more domains. Whether the knowledge is stored in an efficient manner, compressed, classified or censored is dependent on the architecture and is a potential subject of improvement by self-modifying minds.

One can also classify minds in terms of their abilities or intelligence. Of course the problem of measuring intelligence is that no universal tests exist. Measures such as IQ tests and performance on specific tasks are not universally accepted and are always highly biased against non-human intelligences. Recently some work has been done on streamlining intelligence measurements across different types of machine intelligence [2, 30] and other "types" of intelligence [31], but the applicability of the results is still being debated. In general, the notion of intelligence only makes sense in the context of problems to which said intelligence can be applied. In fact this is exactly how IQ tests work, by presenting the subject with a number of problems and seeing how many the subject is able to solve in a given amount of time (computational resource). A subfield of computer science known as computational complexity theory is devoted to studying and classifying different problems with respect to their difficulty and with respect to computational resources necessary to solve them. For every class of problems complexity theory defines a class of machines capable of solving such problems. We can apply similar ideas to classifying minds, for example all minds capable of efficiently [12] solving problems in the class P or a more difficult class of NP-complete problems [32]. Similarly we can talk about minds with general intelligence belonging to the class of AI-Complete [33-35] minds, such as humans.

Regardless of design, embodiment or any other properties, all minds can be classified with respect to two fundamental but scientifically poorly defined properties – free will and consciousness. Both descriptors suffer from an ongoing debate regarding their actual existence or explanatory usefulness. This is primarily a result of impossibility to design a definitive test to measure or even detect said properties, despite numerous attempts [36-38] or to show that theories associated with them are somehow falsifiable. Intuitively we can speculate that consciousness, and maybe free will, are not binary properties but rather continuous and emergent abilities commensurate with a degree of general intelligence possessed by the system or some other property we shall term "mindness". Free will can be said to correlate with a degree to which behavior of the system can't be predicted [39]. This is particularly important in the design of artificially intelligent systems for which inability to predict their future behavior is a highly undesirable property from the safety point of view [40, 41]. Consciousness on the other hand seems to have no important impact on the behavior of the system as can be seen from some thought experiments supposing existence of "consciousless" intelligent agents [42]. This may change if we are successful in designing a test, perhaps based on observer impact on quantum systems [43], to detect and measure consciousness.

In order to be social, two minds need to be able to communicate which might be difficult if the two minds don't share a common communication protocol, common culture or even common environment. In other words, if they have no common grounding they don't understand each other. We can say that two minds understand each other if given the same set of inputs they produce similar outputs. For example, in sequence prediction tasks [44] two minds have an understanding if their predictions are the same regarding the future numbers of the sequence based on the same observed subsequence. We can say that a mind can understand another mind's function if it can predict the other's output with high accuracy. Interestingly, a perfect ability by two minds to predict each other would imply that they are identical and that they have no free will as defined above.

5   A Survey of Taxonomies

Yudkowsky describes the map of mind design space as follows: "In one corner, a tiny little circle contains all humans; within a larger tiny circle containing all biological life; and all the rest of the huge map is the space of minds-in-general. The entire map floats in a still vaster space, the space of optimization processes. Natural selection creates complex functional machinery without mindfulness; evolution lies inside the space of optimization processes but outside the circle of minds" [45].

Similarly, Ivan Havel writes "… all conceivable cases of intelligence (of people, machines, whatever) are represented by points in a certain abstract multi-dimensional "super space" that I will call the intelligence space (shortly IS). Imagine that a specific coordinate axis in IS is assigned to any conceivable particular ability, whether human, machine, shared, or unknown (all axes having one common origin). If the ability is measurable the assigned axis is endowed with a corresponding scale. Hypothetically, we can also assign scalar axes to abilities, for which only relations like "weaker-stronger", "better-worse", "less-more" etc. are meaningful; finally, abilities that may be only present or absent may be assigned with "axes" of two (logical) values (yes-no). Let us assume that all coordinate axes are oriented in such a way that greater distance from the common origin always corresponds to larger extent, higher grade, or at least to the presence of the corresponding ability. The idea is that for each individual intelligence (i.e. the intelligence of a particular person, machine, network, etc.), as well as for each generic intelligence (of some group) there exists just one representing point in IS, whose coordinates determine the extent of involvement of particular abilities [46]." If the universe (or multiverse) is infinite, as our current physics theories indicate, then all possible minds in all states are instantiated somewhere [4].

Ben Goertzel proposes the following classification of Kinds of Minds, mostly centered around the concept of embodiment [47]: Singly Embodied – control a single physical or simulated system. Multiply Embodied - control a number of disconnected physical or simulated systems. Flexibly Embodied – control a changing number of physical or simulated systems. Non-Embodied – resides in a physical substrate but doesn't utilize the body. Body-Centered – consists of patterns between physical system and the environment. Mindplex – a set of collaborating units each of which is itself a mind [48]. Quantum – an embodiment based on properties of quantum physics. Classical - an embodiment based on properties of classical physics.

J. Storrs Hall in his "Kinds of Minds" suggests that different stages a developing AI may belong to can be classified relative to its humanlike abilities. His classification encompasses: Hypohuman - infrahuman, less-than-human capacity. Diahuman - human-level capacities in some areas, but still not a general intelligence. Parahuman - similar but not identical to humans, as for example, augmented humans. Allohuman - as capable as humans, but in different areas. Epihuman - slightly beyond the human level. Hyperhuman - much more powerful than human, superintelligent [24, 49].

Kevin Kelly has also proposed a "Taxonomy of Minds" which in his implementation is really just a list of different minds, some of which have not showed up in other taxonomies [15]: Super fast human mind. Mind with operational access to its source code. Any mind capable of general intelligence and self-awareness. General intelligence without self-awareness. Self-awareness without general intelligence. Super logic machine without emotion. Mind capable of imagining greater mind. Mind capable of creating greater mind. Self-aware mind incapable of creating a greater mind. Mind capable of creating greater mind which creates greater mind. etc. Mind requiring protector while it develops. Very slow "invisible" mind over large physical distance. Mind capable of cloning itself and remaining in unity with clones. Mind capable of immortality. Rapid dynamic mind able to change its mind-space-type sectors (think different). Global mind -- large supercritical mind of subcritical brains. Hive mind -- large super critical mind made of smaller minds each of which is supercritical.Vast mind employing faster-than-light communications. Elsewhere Kelly provides a lot of relevant analysis of landscape of minds writing about Inevitable Minds [51], The Landscape of Possible Intelligences [52], What comes After Minds? [53], and the Evolutionary Mind of God [54].

Aaron Sloman in "The Structure of the Space of Possible Minds", using his virtual machine model, proposes a division of the space of possible minds with respect to the following properties [1]: Quantitative VS Structural; Continuous VS Discrete; Complexity of stored instructions; Serial VS Parallel; Distributed VS Fundamentally Parallel; Connected to External Environment VS Not Connected; Moving VS Stationary; Capable of modeling others VS Not capable; Capable of logical inference VS Not Capable; Fixed VS Re-programmable; Goal consistency VS Goal Selection; Meta-Motives VS Motives; Able to delay goals VS Immediate goal following; Statics Plan VS Dynamic Plan; Self-aware VS Not Self-Aware.

6   Conclusions

Science periodically experiences a discovery of a whole new area of investigation. For example, observations made by Galileo Galilei lead to the birth of observational astronomy [55], aka study of our universe; Watson and Crick's discovery of the structure of DNA lead to the birth of the field of genetics [56], which studies the universe of blueprints for organisms; Stephen Wolfram's work with cellular automata has resulted in "a new kind of science" [57] which investigates the universe of computational processes. I believe that we are about to discover yet another universe – the universe of minds.

As our understanding of human brain improves, thanks to numerous projects aimed at simulating or reverse engineering a human brain, we will no doubt realize that human intelligence is just a single point in the vast universe of potential intelligent agents comprising a new area of study. The new field, which I would like to term intellectology, will study and classify design space of intelligent agents, work on establishing limits to intelligence (minimum sufficient for general intelligence and maximum subject to physical limits), contribute to consistent measurement of intelligence across intelligent agents, look at recursive self-improving systems, design new intelligences (making AI a sub-field of intellectology) and evaluate capacity for understanding higher level intelligences by lower level ones.

References

1. Sloman, A.: The Structure and Space of Possible Minds. The Mind and the Machine: philosophical aspects of Artificial Intelligence. Ellis Horwood LTD (1984)
2. Legg, S., Hutter, M.: Universal Intelligence: A Definition of Machine Intelligence. Minds and Machines 17(4), 391–444 (2007)
3. Hanson, R.: If Uploads Come First. Extropy 6(2) (1994)
4. Bostrom, N.: Quantity of experience: brain-duplication and degrees of consciousness. Minds and Machines 16(2), 185–200 (2006)
5. Yampolskiy, R., Gavrilova, M.: Artimetrics: Biometrics for Artificial Entities. IEEE Robotics and Automation Magazine (RAM) 19(4), 48–58 (2012)
6. Yampolskiy, R.V., Klare, B., Jain, A.K.: Face recognition in the virtual world: Recognizing Avatar faces. In: 11th International Conference on Machine Learning and Applications (2012)
7. Yampolskiy, R.V.: Leakproofing Singularity - Artificial Intelligence Confinement Problem. Journal of Consciousness Studies (JCS) 19(1–2), 194–214 (2012)
8. Wikipedia, Universal Turing Machine. http://en.wikipedia.org/wiki/Universal_Turing_machine (retrieved April 14, 2011)
9. Lloyd, S.: Ultimate Physical Limits to Computation. Nature 406, 1047–1054 (2000)
10. Levin, L.: Universal Search Problems. Problems of Information Transm. 9(3), 265–266 (1973)
11. Rice, H.G.: Classes of recursively enumerable sets and their decision problems. Transactions of the American Mathematical Society 74(2), 358–366 (1953)
12. Yampolskiy, R.V.: Efficiency Theory: a Unifying Theory for Information, Computation and Intelligence. Journal of Discrete Mathematical Sciences & Cryptography 16(4–5), 259–277 (2013)
13. Kolmogorov, A.N.: Three Approaches to the Quantitative Definition of Information. Problems Inform. Transmission 1(1), 1–7 (1965)
14. De Simone, A., et al.: Boltzmann brains and the scale-factor cutoff measure of the multiverse. Physical Review D 82(6), 063520 (2010)
15. Kelly, K.: A Taxonomy of Minds (2007). http://kk.org/thetechnium/archives/2007/02/a_taxonomy_of_m.php
16. Krioukov, D., et al.: Network Cosmology. Sci. Rep. (February 2012)

17. Bostrom, N.: Are You Living In a Computer Simulation? Philosophical Quarterly **53**(211), 243–255 (2003)
18. Lanza, R.: A new theory of the universe. American Scholar **76**(2), 18 (2007)
19. Miller, M.S.P.: Patterns for Cognitive Systems. In: 2012 Sixth International Conference on Complex, Intelligent and Software Intensive Systems (CISIS) (2012)
20. Cattell, R., Parker, A.: Challenges for Brain Emulation: Why is it so Difficult? Natural Intelligence **1**(3), 17–31 (2012)
21. de Garis, H., et al.: A world survey of artificial brain projects, Part I: Large-scale brain simulations. Neurocomputing **74**(1–3), 3–29 (2010)
22. Goertzel, B., et al.: A world survey of artificial brain projects, Part II: Biologically inspired cognitive architectures. Neurocomput. **74**(1–3), 30–49 (2010)
23. Vernon, D., Metta, G., Sandini, G.: A Survey of Artificial Cognitive Systems: Implications for the Autonomous Development of Mental Capabilities in Computational Agents. IEEE Transactions on Evolutionary Computation **11**(2), 151–180 (2007)
24. Yampolskiy, R.V., Fox, J.: Artificial General Intelligence and the Human Mental Model. In: Singularity Hypotheses, pp. 129–145. Springer, Heidelberg (2012)
25. Yampolskiy, R.V., Ashby, L., Hassan, L.: Wisdom of Artificial Crowds—A Metaheuristic Algorithm for Optimization. Journal of Intelligent Learning Systems and Applications **4**(2), 98–107 (2012)
26. Ashby, L.H., Yampolskiy, R.V.: Genetic algorithm and Wisdom of Artificial Crowds algorithm applied to Light up. In: 2011 16th International Conference on Computer Games (CGAMES) (2011)
27. Hughes, R., Yampolskiy, R.V.: Solving Sudoku Puzzles with Wisdom of Artificial Crowds. International Journal of Intelligent Games & Simulation **7**(1), 6 (2013)
28. Port, A.C., Yampolskiy, R.V.: Using a GA and Wisdom of Artificial Crowds to solve solitaire battleship puzzles. In: 2012 17th International Conference on Computer Games (CGAMES) (2012)
29. Hall, J.S.: Self-Improving AI: An Analysis. Minds and Machines **17**(3), 249–259 (2007)
30. Yonck, R.: Toward a Standard Metric of Machine Intelligence. World Future Review **4**(2), 61–70 (2012)
31. Herzing, D.L.: Profiling nonhuman intelligence: An exercise in developing unbiased tools for describing other "types" of intelligence on earth. Acta Astronautica **94**(2), 676–680 (2014)
32. Yampolskiy, R.V.: Construction of an NP Problem with an Exponential Lower Bound. Arxiv preprint arXiv:1111.0305 (2011)
33. Yampolskiy, R.V.: Turing Test as a Defining Feature of AI-Completeness. In: Yang, X.-S. (ed.) Artificial Intelligence, Evolutionary Computing and Metaheuristics. SCI, vol. 427, pp. 3–17. Springer, Heidelberg (2013)
34. Yampolskiy, R.V.: AI-Complete, AI-Hard, or AI-Easy–Classification of Problems in AI. In: The 23rd Midwest Artificial Intelligence and Cognitive Science Conference, Cincinnati, OH, USA (2012)
35. Yampolskiy, R.V.: AI-Complete CAPTCHAs as Zero Knowledge Proofs of Access to an Artificially Intelligent System. ISRN Artificial Intelligence, 271878 (2011)
36. Hales, C.: An empirical framework for objective testing for P-consciousness in an artificial agent. Open Artificial Intelligence Journal **3**, 1–15 (2009)
37. Aleksander, I., Dunmall, B.: Axioms and Tests for the Presence of Minimal Consciousness in Agents I: Preamble. Journal of Consciousness Studies **10**(4–5), 4–5 (2003)
38. Arrabales, R., Ledezma, A., Sanchis, A.: ConsScale: a plausible test for machine consciousness? (2008)

39. Aaronson, S.: The Ghost in the Quantum Turing Machine. arXiv preprint arXiv:1306.0159 (2013)
40. Yampolskiy, R.V.: Artificial intelligence safety engineering: Why machine ethics is a wrong approach. In: Philosophy and Theory of Artificial Intelligence, pp. 389–396. Springer, Berlin (2013)
41. Yampolskiy, R.V.: What to Do with the Singularity Paradox? In: Philosophy and Theory of Artificial Intelligence, pp. 397–413. Springer, Heidelberg (2013)
42. Chalmers, D.J.: The conscious mind: In search of a fundamental theory. Oxford Univ. Press (1996)
43. Gao, S.: A quantum method to test the existence of consciousness. The Noetic Journal **3**(3), 27–31 (2002)
44. Legg, S.: Is There an Elegant Universal Theory of Prediction? In: Balcázar, J.L., Long, P.M., Stephan, F. (eds.) ALT 2006. LNCS (LNAI), vol. 4264, pp. 274–287. Springer, Heidelberg (2006)
45. Yudkowsky, E.: Artificial Intelligence as a Positive and Negative Factor in Global Risk. In: Bostrom, N., Cirkovic, M.M. (eds.) Global Catastrophic Risks, pp. 308–345. Oxford University Press, Oxford (2008)
46. Havel, I.M.: On the Way to Intelligence Singularity. In: Kelemen, J., Romportl, J., Zackova, E. (eds.) Beyond Artificial Intelligence. TIEI, vol. 4, pp. 3–26. Springer, Heidelberg (2013)
47. Geortzel, B.: The Hidden Pattern: A Patternist Philosophy of Mind. ch. 2. Kinds of Minds. Brown Walker Press (2006)
48. Goertzel, B.: Mindplexes: The Potential Emergence of Multiple Levels of Focused Consciousness in Communities of AI's and Humans Dynamical Psychology (2003). http://www.goertzel.org/dynapsyc/2003/mindplex.htm.
49. Hall, J.S.: Chapter 15: Kinds of Minds, in Beyond AI: Creating the Conscience of the Machine. Prometheus Books, Amherst (2007)
50. Roberts, P.: Mind Making: The Shared Laws of Natural and Artificial. CreateSpace (2009)
51. Kelly, K.: Inevitable Minds (2009).
    http://kk.org/thetechnium/archives/2009/04/inevitable_mind.php
52. Kelly, K.: The Landscape of Possible Intelligences (2008).
    http://kk.org/thetechnium/archives/2008/09/the_landscape_o.php
53. Kelly, K.: What Comes After Minds? (2008).
    http://kk.org/thetechnium/archives/2008/12/what_comes_afte.php
54. Kelly, K.: The Evolutionary Mind of God (2007).
    http://kk.org/thetechnium/archives/2007/02/the_evolutionar.php
55. Galilei, G.: Dialogue concerning the two chief world systems: Ptolemaic and Copernican. University of California Pr. (1953)
56. Watson, J.D., Crick, F.H.: Molecular structure of nucleic acids. Nature **171**(4356), 737–738 (1953)
57. Wolfram, S.: A New Kind of Science. Wolfram Media, Inc. (May 14, 2002)

Papers Presented as Posters

A Definition of Happiness for Reinforcement Learning Agents

Mayank Daswani and Jan Leike[✉]

Australian National University, Canberra, Australia
{mayank.daswani,jan.leike}@anu.edu.au

Abstract. What is happiness for reinforcement learning agents? We seek a formal definition satisfying a list of desiderata. Our proposed definition of happiness is the *temporal difference error*, i.e. the difference between the value of the obtained reward and observation and the agent's expectation of this value. This definition satisfies most of our desiderata and is compatible with empirical research on humans. We state several implications and discuss examples.

Keywords: Temporal difference error · Reward prediction error · Pleasure · Well-being · Optimism · Machine ethics

1 Introduction

People are constantly in search of better ways to be happy. However, philosophers and psychologists have not yet agreed on a notion of human happiness. In this paper, we pursue the more general goal of defining happiness for intelligent agents. We focus on the reinforcement learning (RL) setting [11] because it is an intensively studied formal framework which makes it easier to make precise statements. Moreover, reinforcement learning has been used to model behaviour in both human and non-human animals [7].

Here, we decouple the discussion of happiness from the discussion of consciousness, experience, or qualia. We completely disregard whether happiness is actually consciously experienced or what this means. The problem of consciousness has to be solved separately; but its answer might matter insofar that it could tell us which agents' happiness we should care about.

Desiderata. We can simply ask a human how happy they are. But artificial reinforcement learning agents cannot yet speak. Therefore we use our human "common sense" intuitions about happiness to come up with a definition. We arrive at the following desired properties.

Research supported by the People for the Ethical Treatment of Reinforcement Learners http://petrl.org. See the extended technical report for omitted proofs and details about the data analysis [4].
Both authors contributed equally.

J. Bieger (Ed.): AGI 2015, LNAI 9205, pp. 231–240, 2015.
DOI: 10.1007/978-3-319-21365-1_24

- *Scaling.* Happiness should be invariant under scaling of the rewards. Replacing every reward r_t by $cr_t + d$ for some $c, d \in \mathbb{R}$ with $c > 0$ (independent of t) does not change the reinforcement learning problem in any relevant way. Therefore we desire a happiness measure to be independent under rescaling of the rewards.
- *Subjectivity.* Happiness is a subjective property of the agent depending only on information available to the agent. For example, it cannot depend on the true environment.
- *Commensurability.* The happiness of different agents should be comparable. If at some time step an agent A has happiness x, and another agent B has happiness y, then it should be possible to tell whether A is happier than B by computing $x - y$. This could be relaxed by instead asking that A can calculate the happiness of B *according to A's subjective beliefs*.
- *Agreement.* The happiness function should match experimental data about human happiness.

It has to be emphasised that in humans, happiness cannot be equated with pleasure [8]. In the reinforcement learning setting, pleasure corresponds to the reward. Therefore happiness and reward have to be distinguished. We crudely summarise this as follows; for a more detailed discussion see Section 3.

$$\text{pleasure} = \text{reward} \neq \text{happiness}$$

The happiness measure that we propose is the following. An agent's happiness in a time step t is the difference between the value of the obtained reward and observation and the agent's expectation of this value at time step t. In the Markov setting, this is also known as the *temporal difference error* (TD error) [10]. However, we do not limit ourselves to the Markov setting in this paper. In parts of the mammalian brain, the neuromodulator dopamine has a strong connection to the TD error [7]. Note that while our definition of happiness is not equal to reward it remains highly correlated to the reward, especially if the expectation of the reward is close to 0.

Our definition of happiness coincides with the definition for *joy* given by Jacobs et al. [6], except that the latter is weighted by 1 minus the (objective) probability of taking the transition which violates subjectivity. Schmidhuber's work on 'intrinsic motivation' adds a related component to the reward in order to motivate the agent to explore in interesting directions [9].

Our definition of happiness can be split into two parts. (1) The difference between the instantaneous reward and its expectation, which we call *payout*, and (2) how the latest observation and reward changes the agent's estimate of future rewards, which we call *good news*. Moreover, we identify two sources of happiness: *luck*, favourable chance outcomes (e.g. rolling a six on a fair die), and *pessimism*, having low expectations of the environment (e.g. expecting a fair die to be biased against you). We show that agents that know the world perfectly have zero expected happiness.

In the rest of the paper, we use our definition as a starting point to investigate the following questions. Is an off-policy agent happier than an on-policy one? Do monotonically increasing rewards necessarily imply a happy agent? How does value function initialisation affect the happiness of an agent? Can we construct an agent that maximises its own happiness?

2   Reinforcement Learning

In reinforcement learning (RL) an *agent* interacts with an *environment* in cycles: at time step t the agent chooses an *action* $a_t \in \mathcal{A}$ and receives an *observation* $o_t \in \mathcal{O}$ and a real-valued *reward* $r_t \in \mathbb{R}$; the cycle then repeats for time step $t + 1$ [11]. The list of interactions $a_1 o_1 r_1 a_2 o_2 r_2 \ldots$ is called a *history*. We use h_t to denote a history of length t, and we use the shorthand notation $h := h_{t-1}$ and $h' := h_{t-1} a_t o_t r_t$. The agent's goal is to choose actions to maximise cumulative rewards. To avoid infinite sums, we use a *discount factor* γ with $0 < \gamma < 1$ and maximise the discounted sum $\sum_{t=1}^{\infty} \gamma^t r_t$. A *policy* is a function π mapping every history to the action taken after seeing this history, and an *environment* μ is a stochastic mapping from histories to observation-reward-tuples.

A policy π together with an environment μ yields a probability distribution over histories. Given a random variable X over histories, we write the π-μ-expectation of X conditional on the history h as $\mathbb{E}_\mu^\pi[X \mid h]$.

The *(true) value function* V_μ^π of a policy π in environment μ maps a history h_t to the expected total future reward when interacting with environment μ and taking actions according to the policy π:

$$V_\mu^\pi(h_t) := \mathbb{E}_\mu^\pi \left[\sum_{k=t+1}^{\infty} \gamma^{k-t-1} r_k \mid h_t \right]. \tag{1}$$

It is important to emphasise that $\mathbb{E}_\mu^\pi$ denotes the *objective* expectation that can be calculated only by knowing the environment μ. The *optimal value function* V_μ^* is defined as the value function of the optimal policy, $V_\mu^*(h) := \sup_\pi V_\mu^\pi(h)$.

Typically, reinforcement learners do not know the environment and are trying to learn it. We model this by assuming that at every time step the agent has (explicitly or implicitly) an estimate $\hat{V}$ of the value function V_μ^π. Formally, a *value function estimator* maps a history h to a value function estimate $\hat{V}$. Finally, we define an *agent* to be a policy together with a value function estimator. If the history is clear from context, we refer to the output of the value function estimator as *the agent's estimated value*.

If μ only depends on the last observation and action, μ is called *Markov decision process (MDP)*. In this case, $\mu(o_t r_t \mid h_{t-1} a_t) = \mu(o_t r_t \mid o_{t-1} a_t)$ and the observations are called states ($s_t = o_t$). In MDPs we use the Q-value function, the value of a state-action pair, defined as $Q_\mu^\pi(s_t, a_t) := \mathbb{E}_\mu^\pi \left[\sum_{k=t+1}^{\infty} \gamma^{k-t-1} r_k \mid s_t a_t \right]$. Assuming that the environment is an MDP is very common in the RL literature, but here we will not make this assumption.

3   A Formal Definition of Happiness

The goal of a reinforcement learning agent is to maximise rewards, so it seems natural to suppose an agent is happier the more rewards it gets. But this does not conform to our intuition: sometimes enjoying pleasures just fails to provide happiness, and reversely, enduring suffering does not necessarily entail unhappiness (see Example 3 and Example 7). In fact, it has been shown empirically that rewards and happiness cannot be equated [8] (*p*-value < 0.0001).

There is also a formal problem with defining happiness in terms of reward: we can add a constant $c \in \mathbb{R}$ to every reward. No matter how the agent-environment interaction plays out, the agent will have received additional cumulative rewards $C := \sum_{i=1}^{t} c$. However, this did not change the structure of the reinforcement learning problem in any way. Actions that were optimal before are still optimal and actions that are slightly suboptimal are still slightly suboptimal *to the same degree*. For the agent, no essential difference between the original reinforcement learning problem and the new problem can be detected: in a sense the two problems are *isomorphic*. If we were to define an agent's happiness as received reward, then an agent's happiness would vary wildly when we add a constant to the reward while the problem stays structurally exactly the same.

We propose the following definition of happiness.

Definition 1 (Happiness). *The* happiness *of a reinforcement learning agent with estimated value $\hat{V}$ at time step t with history ha_t while receiving observation o_t and reward r_t is*

$$\odot(ha_t o_t r_t, \hat{V}) := r_t + \gamma \hat{V}(ha_t o_t r_t) - \hat{V}(h). \tag{2}$$

If $\odot(h', \hat{V})$ is positive, we say the agent is happy, *and if $\odot(h', \hat{V})$ is negative, we say the agent is* unhappy.

It is important to emphasise that $\hat{V}$ represents the agent's *subjective* estimate of the value function. If the agent is good at learning, this might converge to something close to the true value function V_μ^π. In an MDP (2) is also known as the *temporal difference error* [10]. This number is used used to update the value function, and thus plays an integral part in learning.

If there exists a probability distribution ρ on histories such that the value function estimate $\hat{V}$ is given by the expected future discounted rewards according to the probability distribution ρ,

$$\hat{V}(h) = \mathbb{E}_\rho^\pi \left[\sum_{k=t+1}^{\infty} \gamma^{k-t-1} r_k \mid h \right], \tag{3}$$

then we call $E := \mathbb{E}_\rho^\pi$ the agent's *subjective expectation*. Note that we can always find such a probability distribution, but this notion only really makes sense for *model-based agents* (agents that learn a model of their environment). Using the agent's subjective expectation, we can rewrite Definition 1 as follows.

Proposition 2 (Happiness as Subjective Expectation). *Let E denote an agent's subjective expectation. Then*

$$\odot(h', \hat{V}) = r_t - E[r_t \mid h] + \gamma \left(\hat{V}(h') - E[\hat{V}(haor) \mid h] \right). \tag{4}$$

Proposition 2 states that happiness is given by the difference of how good the agent thought it was doing and what it learns about how well it actually does. We distinguish the following two components in (4):

- *Payout:* the difference of the obtained reward r_t and the agent's expectation of that reward $E[r_t \mid h]$.
- *Good News:* the change in opinion of the expected future rewards after receiving the new information $o_t r_t$.

$$\odot(h', \hat{V}) = \underbrace{r_t - E[r_t \mid h]}_{\text{payout}} + \gamma \big(\underbrace{\hat{V}(h') - E[\hat{V}(haor) \mid h]}_{\text{good news}} \big)$$

Example 3. Mary is travelling on an air plane. She knows that air planes crash very rarely, and so is completely at ease. Unfortunately she is flying on a budget airline, so she has to pay for her food and drink. A flight attendant comes to her seat and gives her a free beverage. Just as she starts drinking it, the intercom informs everyone that the engines have failed. Mary feels some happiness from the free drink (*payout*), but her expected future reward is much lower than in the state before learning the *bad news*. Thus overall, Mary is unhappy.

For each of the two components, payout and good news, we distinguish the following two sources of happiness.

- *Pessimism:*[1] the agent expects the environment to contain less rewards than it actually does.
- *Luck:* the outcome of r_t is unusually high due to randomness.

$$r_t - E[r_t \mid h] = \underbrace{r_t - \mathbb{E}_\mu^\pi[r_t \mid h]}_{\text{luck}} + \underbrace{\mathbb{E}_\mu^\pi[r_t \mid h] - E[r_t \mid h]}_{\text{pessimism}}$$

$$\hat{V}(h') - E[\hat{V}(haor) \mid h] = \underbrace{\hat{V}(h') - \mathbb{E}_\mu^\pi[\hat{V}(haor) \mid h]}_{\text{luck}}$$

$$+ \underbrace{\mathbb{E}_\mu^\pi[\hat{V}(haor) \mid h] - E[\hat{V}(haor) \mid h]}_{\text{pessimism}}$$

Example 4. Suppose Mary fears flying and expected the plane to crash (*pessimism*). On hearing that the engines failed (*bad luck*), Mary does not experience very much change in her future expected reward. Thus she is happy that she (at least) got a free drink.

The following proposition states that once an agent has learned the environment, its expected happiness is zero. In this case, underestimation cannot contribute to happiness and thus the only source of happiness is luck, which cancels out in expectation.

---

[1] *Optimism* is a standard term in the RL literature to denote the opposite phenomenon. However, this notion is somewhat in discord with optimism in humans.

Proposition 5 (Happiness of Informed Agents). *An agent that knows the world has an expected happiness of zero: for every policy π and every history h,*

$$\mathbb{E}^{\pi}_{\mu}[\odot(h', V^{\pi}_{\mu}) \mid h] = 0.$$

Analogously, if the environment is deterministic, then luck cannot be a source of happiness. In this case, happiness reduces to how much the agent underestimates the environment. By Proposition 5, having learned a deterministic environment perfectly, the agent's happiness is equal to zero.

4   Matching the Desiderata

Here we discuss in which sense our definition of happiness satisfies the desiderata from Section 1.

Scaling. If we transform the rewards to $r'_t = cr_t + d$ with $c > 0$, $d \in \mathbb{R}$ for each time step t without changing the value function, the value of $\odot$ will be completely different. However, a sensible learning algorithm should be able to adapt to the new reinforcement learning problem with the scaled rewards without too much problem. At that point, the value function gets scaled as well, $V_{new}(h) = cV(h) + d/(1 - \gamma)$. In this case we get

$$\odot(ha_t o_t r', V_{new}) = r'_t + \gamma V_{new}(ha_t o_t r'_t) - V_{new}(h)$$

$$= cr_t + d + \gamma cV(ha_t o_t r'_t) + \gamma\frac{d}{1 - \gamma} - cV(h) - \frac{d}{1 - \gamma}$$

$$= c\big(r_t + \gamma V(ha_t o_t r'_t) - V(h)\big),$$

hence happiness gets scaled by a positive factor and thus its sign remains the same, which would not hold if we defined happiness just in terms of rewards.

Subjectivity. The definition (4) of $\odot$ depends only on the current reward and the agent's current estimation of the value function, both of which are available to the agent.

Commensurability. The scaling property as described above means that the exact value of the happiness is not useful in comparing two agents, but the sign of the total happiness can at least tell us whether a given agent is happy or unhappy. Arguably, failing this desideratum is not surprising; in utility theory the utilities/rewards of different agents are typically not commensurable either.

However, given two agents A and B, A can still calculate the A-subjective happiness of a history experienced by B as $\odot(haor_B, \hat{V}^A)$. This corresponds to the human intuition of "putting yourself in someone else's shoes". If both agents are acting in the same environment, the resulting numbers should be commensurable, since the calculation is done using the same value function. It is entirely possible that A believes B to be happier, i.e. $\odot(haor_B, \hat{V}^A) > \odot(haor_A, \hat{V}^A)$, but also that B believes A to be happier $\odot(haor_A, \hat{V}^B) > \odot(haor_B, \hat{V}^B)$, because they have different expectations of the environment.

Agreement. Rutledge et al. measure subjective well-being on a smartphone-based experiment with 18,420 participants [8]. In the experiment, a subject goes through 30 trials in each of which they can choose between a sure reward and a gamble that is resolved within a short delay. Every two to three trials the subjects are asked to indicate their momentary happiness.

Our model based on Proposition 2 with a very simple learning algorithm and no loss aversion correlates fairly well with reported happiness (mean $r = 0.56$, median $r^2 = 0.41$, median $R^2 = 0.27$) while fitting individual discount factors, comparative to Rutledge et al.'s model (mean $r = 0.60$, median $r^2 = 0.47$, median $R^2 = 0.36$) and a happiness=cumulative reward model (mean $r = 0.59$, median $r^2 = 0.46$, median $R^2 = 0.35$). This analysis is inconclusive, but unsurprisingly so: the expected reward is close to 0 and thus our happiness model correlates well with rewards.

The *hedonic treadmill* [2] refers to the idea that humans return to a *baseline level of happiness* after significant negative or positive events. Studies have looked at lottery winners and accident victims [3], and people dealing with paralysis, marriage, divorce, having children and other life changes [5]. In most cases these studies have observed a return to baseline happiness after some period of time has passed; people learn to make correct reward predictions again. Hence their expected happiness returns to zero (Proposition 5). Our definition unfortunately does not explain why people have different baseline levels of happiness (or hedonic set points), but these may be perhaps explained by biological means (different humans have different levels of neuromodulators, neurotransmitters, hormones, etc.) which may move their baseline happiness. Alternatively, people might simply learn to associate different levels of happiness with "feeling happy" according to their environment.

5 Discussion and Examples

5.1 Off-policy Agents

In reinforcement learning, we are mostly interested in learning the value function of the optimal policy. A common difference between RL algorithms is whether they learn *off-policy* or *on-policy*. An *on-policy* agent evaluates the value of the policy it is currently following. For example, the policy that the agent is made to follow could be an ε-greedy policy, where the agent picks $\arg\max_a Q^\pi(h, a)$ a fraction $(1 - \varepsilon)$ of the time, and a random action otherwise. If ε is decreased to zero over time, then the agent's learned policy tends to the optimal policy in MDPs. Alternatively, an agent can learn *off-policy*, that is it can learn about one policy (say, the optimal one) while following a different *behaviour policy*.

The behaviour policy (π_b) determines how the agent acts while it is learning the optimal policy. Once an off-policy learning agent has learned the optimal value function V_μ^*, then it is not happy if it still acts according to some other (possibly suboptimal) policy.

Proposition 6 (Happiness of Off-Policy Learning). *Let π be some policy and μ be some environment. Then for any history h*

$$\mathbb{E}_{\mu}^{\pi}[\odot(h', V_{\mu}^{*}) \mid h] \leq 0.$$

Q-learning is an example of an off-policy algorithm in the MDP setting. If Q-learning converges, and the agent is still following the sub-optimal behaviour policy then Proposition 6 tells us that the agent will be unhappy. Moreover, this means that SARSA (an on-policy RL algorithm) will be happier than Q-learning on average and in expectation.

5.2   Increasing and Decreasing Rewards

Intuitively, it seems that if things are constantly getting better, this should increase happiness. However, this is not generally the case: even an agent that obtains monotonically increasing rewards can be unhappy if it thinks that these rewards mean even higher negative rewards in the future.

Example 7. Alice has signed up for a questionable drug trial which examines the effects of a potentially harmful drug. This drug causes temporary pleasure to the user every time it is used, and increased usage results in increased pleasure. However, the drug reduces quality of life in the long term. Alice has been informed of the potential side-effects of the drug. She can be either part of a placebo group or the group given the drug. Every morning Alice is given an injection of an unknown liquid. She finds herself feeling temporary but intense feelings of pleasure. This is evidence that she is in the non-placebo group, and thus has a potentially reduced quality of life in the long term. Even though she experiences pleasure (increasing rewards) it is evidence of very *bad news* and thus she is unhappy.

Analogously, decreasing rewards do not generally imply unhappiness. For example, the pains of hard labour can mean happiness if one expects to harvest the fruits of this labour in the future.

5.3   Value Function Initialisation

Example 8 (Increasing Pessimism Does Not Increase Happiness). Consider the deterministic MDP example in Figure 1. Assume that the agent has an initial value function $\hat{Q}_0(s_0, \alpha) = 0$, $\hat{Q}_0(s_0, \beta) = -\varepsilon$, $\hat{Q}_0(s_1, \alpha) = \varepsilon$ and $\hat{Q}_0(s_1, \beta) = 0$. If no forced exploration is carried out by the agent, it has no incentive to visit s_1. The happiness achieved by such an agent for some time step t is $\odot(s_0 \alpha s_0 0, \hat{V}_0) = 0$ where $\hat{V}_0(s_0) := \hat{Q}_0(s_0, \alpha) = 0$. However, suppose the agent is (more optimistically) initialised with $\hat{Q}_0(s_0, \alpha) = 0, \hat{Q}_0(s_0, \beta) = \varepsilon$. In this case, the agent would take action β and arrive in state s_1. This transition would have happiness $\odot(s_0 \beta s_1 - 1, \hat{V}_0) = -1 + \gamma \hat{Q}_0(s_1, \alpha) - \hat{Q}_0(s_0, \beta) = -1 - 0.5\varepsilon$.

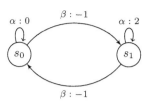

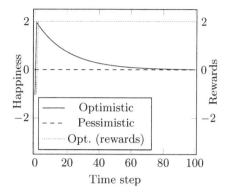

Fig. 1. MDP of Example 8 with transitions labelled with actions α or β and rewards. We use the discount factor $\gamma = 0.5$. The agent starts in s_0. Define $\pi_0(s_0) := \alpha$, then $V^{\pi_0}(s_0) = 0$. The optimal policy is $\pi^*(s_0) = \beta$, so $V^{\pi^*}(s_0) = 1$ and $V^{\pi^*}(s_1) = 4$.

Fig. 2. A plot of happiness for Example 8. We use the learning rate $\alpha = 0.1$. The pessimistic agent has zero happiness (and rewards), whereas the optimistic agent is initially unhappy, but once it transitions to state s_1 becomes happy. The plot also shows the rewards of the optimistic agent.

However, the next transition is $s_1 \alpha s_1 2$ which has happiness $\odot(s_1 \alpha s_1 2, \hat{V}_0) = 2 + \gamma \hat{Q}_0(s_1, \alpha) - \hat{Q}_0(s_1, \alpha) = 2 - 0.5\varepsilon$. If $\hat{Q}_0$ is not updated by some learning mechanism the agent will continue to accrue this positive happiness for all future time steps. If the agent does learn, it will still be some time steps before $\hat{Q}$ converges to Q^* and the positive happiness becomes zero (see Figure 2). It is arguable whether this agent which suffered one time step of unhappiness but potentially many time steps of happiness is overall a happier agent, but it is some evidence that absolute pessimism does not necessarily lead to the happiest agents.

5.4 Maximising Happiness

How can an agent increase their own happiness? The first source of happiness, luck, depends entirely on the outcome of a random event that the agent has no control over. However, the agent could modify its learning algorithm to be systematically pessimistic about the environment. For example, when fixing the value function estimation below $r_{\min}/(1-\gamma)$ for all histories, happiness is positive at every time step. But this agent would not actually take any sensible actions. Just as optimism is commonly used to artificially increase exploration, pessimism discourages exploration which leads to poor performance. As demonstrated in Example 8, a pessimistic agent may be less happy than a more optimistic one.

Additionally, an agent that explicitly tries to maximise its own happiness is no longer a reinforcement learner. So instead of asking how an agent can increase its own happiness, we should fix a reinforcement learning algorithm and ask for the environment that would make this algorithm happy.

6 Conclusion

An artificial superintelligence might contain subroutines that are capable of suffering, a phenomenon that Bostrom calls *mind crime* [1, Ch. 8]. More generally, Tomasik argues that even current reinforcement learning agents could have moral weight [12]. If this is the case, then a general theory of happiness for reinforcement learners is essential; it would enable us to derive ethical standards in the treatment of algorithms. Our theory is very preliminary and should be thought of as a small step in this direction. Many questions are left unanswered, and we hope to see more research on the suffering of AI agents in the future.

Acknowledgments. We thank Marcus Hutter and Brian Tomasik for careful reading and detailed feedback. The data from the smartphone experiment was kindly provided by Robb Rutledge. We are also grateful to many of our friends for encouragement and interesting discussions.

References

1. Bostrom, N.: Superintelligence: Paths, Dangers. Oxford University Press, Strategies (2014)
2. Brickman, P., Campbell, D.T.: Hedonic relativism and planning the good society. Adaptation-Level Theory, pp. 287–305 (1971)
3. Brickman, P., Coates, D., Janoff-Bulman, R.: Lottery winners and accident victims: Is happiness relative? Journal of Personality and Social Psychology **36**, 917 (1978)
4. Daswani, M., Leike, J.: A definition of happiness for reinforcement learning agents. Technical report, Australian National University (2015). http://arxiv.org/abs/1505.04497
5. Diener, E., Lucas, R.E., Scollon, C.N.: Beyond the hedonic treadmill: Revising the adaptation theory of well-being. American Psychologist **61**, 305 (2006)
6. Jacobs, E., Broekens, J., Jonker, C.: Joy, distress, hope, and fear in reinforcement learning. In: Conference on Autonomous Agents and Multiagent Systems, pp. 1615–1616 (2014)
7. Niv, Y.: Reinforcement learning in the brain. Journal of Mathematical Psychology **53**, 139–154 (2009)
8. Rutledge, R.B., Skandali, N., Dayan, P., Dolan, R.J.: A computational and neural model of momentary subjective well-being. In: Proceedings of the National Academy of Sciences (2014)
9. Schmidhuber, J.: Formal theory of creativity, fun, and intrinsic motivation (1990–2010). IEEE Transactions on Autonomous Mental Development. **2**, 230–247 (2010)
10. Sutton, R., Barto, A.: Time-derivative models of Pavlovian reinforcement. In: Learning and Computational Neuroscience: Foundations of Adaptive Networks, pp. 497–537. MIT Press (1990)
11. Sutton, R.S., Barto, A.G.: Reinforcement Learning: An Introduction. MIT Press, Cambridge (1998)
12. Tomasik, B.: Do artificial reinforcement-learning agents matter morally? Technical report, Foundational Research Institute (2014). http://arxiv.org/abs/1410.8233

Expression Graphs
Unifying Factor Graphs and Sum-Product Networks

Abram Demski[✉]

Institute for Creative Technologies and Department of Computer Science,
University of Southern California, 12015 Waterfront Dr., Playa Vista, CA 90094, USA
ademski@ict.usc.edu

Abstract. Factor graphs are a very general knowledge representation, subsuming many existing formalisms in AI. Sum-product networks are a more recent representation, inspired by studying cases where factor graphs are tractable. Factor graphs emphasize expressive power, while sum-product networks restrict expressiveness to get strong guarantees on speed of inference. A sum-product network is not simply a restricted factor graph, however. Although the inference algorithms for the two structures are very similar, translating a sum-product network into factor graph representation can result in an exponential slowdown. We propose a formalism which generalizes factor graphs and sum-product networks, such that inference is fast in cases whose structure is close to a sum-product network.

1 Motivation

Factor graphs are a graphical model which generalizes Bayesian networks, Markov networks, constraint networks, and other models [4]. New light was shed on existing algorithms through this generalization.[1]

As a result, factor graphs have been treated as a unifying theory for graphical models. It has furthermore been proposed, in particular in [2] and [11], that factor graphs can provide a computational foundation through which we can understand cognitive processes. The present work came out of thinking about potential inadequacies in the Sigma cognitive architecture [11].

Factor graphs have emerged from progressive generalization of techniques which were initially narrow AI. Because they capture a breadth of knowledge about efficient AI algorithms, they may be useful for those AGI approaches which

---

This work was sponsored by the U.S. Army. Statements and opinions expressed may not reflect the position or policy of the United States Government, and no official endorsement should be inferred. Special thanks to Paul Rosenbloom and Łukasz Stafiniak for providing comments on a draft of this paper.

[1] The sum-product algorithm for factor graphs provided a generalization of existing algorithms for more narrow domains, often the best algorithms for those domains at the time. The main examples are belief propagation, constraint propagation, and turbo codes [4]. Other algorithms such as mean-field can be stated very generally using factor graphs as well.

© Springer International Publishing Switzerland 2015
J. Bieger (Ed.): AGI 2015, LNAI 9205, pp. 241–250, 2015.
DOI: 10.1007/978-3-319-21365-1_25

seek to leverage the progress which has been made in narrow AI, rather than striking out on an entirely new path. However, this paper will argue that factor graphs fail to support an important class of algorithms.

Sum-product networks (SPNs) are a new type of graphical model which represent a probability distribution through sums and products of simpler distributions [7].[2] Whereas factor graphs may blow up to exponential-time exact inference, SPN inference is guaranteed to be linear in the size of the SPN.

An SPN can compactly represent any factor graph for which exact inference is tractable. When inference is less efficient, the corresponding SPN will be larger. In the worst case, an SPN may be exponentially larger than the factor graph which it represents. On the other hand, being able to represent a distribution as a compact SPN does *not* imply easy inference when converted to a factor graph. There exist SPNs which represent distributions for which standard exact inference algorithms for factor graphs are intractable.

Probabilistic context-free grammars (PCFGs) are an important class of probabilistic model in computational linguistics. In [8], the translation of PCFGs into factor graphs (specifically, into Bayesian networks) is given. This allows general probabilistic inference on PCFGs (supporting complicated queries which special-case PCFG algorithms don't handle). However, the computational complexity becomes exponential due to the basic complexity of factor graph inference.

Sum-product networks can represent PCFGs with bounded sentence length to be represented in an SPN of size cubic in the length, by directly encoding the sums and products of the *inside* algorithm (a basic algorithm for PCFGs) This preserves cubic complexity of inference, while allowing the more general kinds of queries for which [8] required exponential-time algorithms. This illustrates that SPNs can be efficient in cases where factor graphs are not.

More recently, [12] used loopy belief propagation (an *approximate* algorithm for factor graph problems) to efficiently approximate complex parsing tasks beyond PCFGs, but did so by implementing a dynamic programming parse *as* one of the factors. This amounts to using SPN-style inference as a special module to augment factor-graph inference.

The present work explores a more unified approach, to integrate the two types of reasoning without special-case optimization. The resulting representation is related to the *expression tree* introduced in [4]. As such, the new formalism is being referred to as the Expression Graph (EG).

2   Factor Graphs

A *factor graph* (FG) is a bipartite graph where one set of nodes represents the variables $x_1, x_2, ...x_n \in \mathbf{U}$, and the other set of nodes represent real-valued

---

[2] Case-factor diagrams [6]   are almost exactly the same as sum-product networks, and have historical precedence. However, the formalism of sum-product networks has become more common. Despite their similarities, the two papers [6] and [7] use very different mathematical setups to justify the new graphical model and the associated inference algorithm. (A reader confused by one paper may benefit from trying the other instead.)

multivariate functions $F_1, F_2, ...F_m$. A link exists between a factor node and a variable node when the variable is an argument to the factor. This represents a function D, the product of all the factors:

$$D(\mathbf{U}) = \prod_{i=1}^{m} F_i(\mathcal{A}_i)$$

where $\mathcal{A}_i$ represents the tuple of argument variables associated with factor F_i.

The global function D can represent anything, but we will only discuss the representation of probability functions in this article.

Representing the factorization explicitly allows factor graphs to easily capture the distributions represented by other graphical models like Bayesian networks and Markov networks whose graph structure implies a factorization. The links correspond conveniently with messages in several message-passing algorithms, most famously the sum-product algorithm for factor graphs, which generalizes several important algorithms.

Inference algorithms allow us to compute various things with these networks, most notably marginal probabilities and maximum-probability states. Exact inference using the most common algorithms is exponential in the treewidth, which is (roughly) a measure of how far the graph is from being tree-structured. As a result, nontrivial models usually must rely on approximate inference techniques, of which there are many.

Building up complicated functions as a product of simpler ones turns out to be very powerful. Intuitively, we can think of the factors as giving us probabilistic *constraints* linking variables together. (In fact, this is a strict generalization of constraint-based reasoning.) These constraints can provide a great deal of representational power, but this power comes at the cost of potentially intractable inference.

For further details, the reader is directed to [4].

3   Sum-Product Networks

A *sum-product network* (SPN) is a directed acyclic graph with a unique root. Terminal nodes are associated with *indicator variables*. Each domain variable in $\mathbf{U}$ has an indicator for each of its values; these take value 1 when the variable takes on that value, and 0 when the variable is in a different value.

The root and the internal nodes are all labeled as *sum nodes* or *product nodes*. A product node represents the product of its children. The links from a sum node to its children are weighted, so that the sum node represents a weighted sum of its children. Thus, the SPN represents an expression formed out of the indicator variables via products and weighted sums. As for factor graphs, this expression could represent a variety of things, but in order to build an intuition for the structure we shall assume that this represents a probability distribution over U.

The *scope* of a node is the set of variables appearing under it. That is: the scope of a leaf node is the variable associated with the indicator variable, and the scope of any other node is the union of the scopes of its children.

Two restrictions are imposed on the tree structure of an SPN. It must be *complete*: the children of any particular sum node all have the same scope as each other. They must also be *decomposable*: the children of the same product node have mutually exclusive scopes. These properties allow us to compute any desired probability in linear time. It's possible to compute *all* the marginal probabilities in linear time by differentiating the network, an approach adapted from [1].[3]

For further details, the reader is directed to [7].

If we think of factor graphs as generalized constraint networks, we could think of SPNs as generalized decision trees – or, for a closer analogy, binary decision diagrams [3]. These represent complexity by splitting things into cases, in a way which can be evaluated in one pass rather than requiring back-tracking search as with constraint problems.

The thrust of this paper is that both kinds of representation are necessary for general cognition. To accomplish this, we generalize SPNs to also handle constraint-like factor-graph reasoning.

4   Expression Graphs

In order to compactly represent all the distributions which can be represented by SPNs or FGs, we introduce the *expression graph* (EG).

An expression graph is little more than an SPN with the network restrictions lifted: a directed acyclic graph with a unique root, whose non-terminal nodes are labeled as sums or products. The terminal nodes will hold functions rather than indicators; this is a mild generalization for convenience. For discrete variables, these functions would be represented as tables of values. For the continuous case, some class of functions such as Gaussians would be chosen. These terminal functions will be referred to as *elemental functions*. We will only explicitly work with the discrete case here. Expression graphs represent complicated functions build up from the simple ones, as follows:

$$N(\mathbf{A}) = \begin{cases} \sum_{i=1}^n C_i(\mathbf{A_i}) & \text{if } N \text{ is a sum node} \\ \prod_{i=1}^n C_i(\mathbf{A_i}) & \text{if } N \text{ is a product node} \end{cases}$$

Where C_i are the n children of node N, and $\mathbf{A}$ is the union of their arguments $\mathbf{A_i}$. From now on, we will not distinguish strongly between a node and the function associated with the node. The root node is D, the global distribution.

The scope of a node is defined as the set arguments in its associated function, inheriting the definitions of complete and decomposable which were introduced for SPNs. Unlike in the case of SPNs, we do not enforce these properties.

---

[3] In [7], a weaker requirement of *consistency* replaces decomposability. However, without full decomposability, the inference by differentiation can give wrong results. For example, the SPN representing $.5x_1^2 + .5\overline{x_1}$ is acceptable by their definition. Differentiation would have it that $x_1 = true$ is twice as likely as $x_1 = false$, whereas the two are equally likely by evaluation of the network value at each instantiation. We therefore do not consider the weaker requirement here.

A simple model expressing $P(x,y)$ as the product of two functions $F(x)G(x,y)$ (for example,) becomes the network in Figure 1. This gives us a small example of the sorts of expressions which are tractable enough to be useful, but, are not allowed by the restrictions on SPN structure. (The expression is not decomposable, and would need to be re-written as a sum of all the possible cases to be an SPN, obscuring the factorization.)

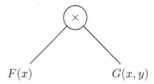

Fig. 1. The expression graph for $F(x)G(x,y)$

On the other hand, a mixture distribution on x defined by the expression $.4f(x) + .6g(x)$ looks like Figure 2. Unlike for SPNs, we represent the weights as terminal nodes (these can be thought of as constant functions, with empty scope). This difference simplifies the form of later formulas. The weighted-edge formalism could be used instead with a little modification to the algorithms.

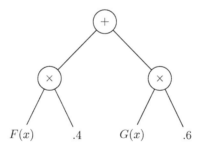

Fig. 2. The mixture distribution $.4F(x) + .6G(x)$

Several models existing in the literature can be interpreted as expression graphs, putting them in a more unified formalism. One way of combining factor graphs and SPNs is to use SPNs as compact representations *of* the local factors, as was done in [9]. This allows use of the expressive power of factor graphs at the higher level, while taking advantage of the efficiency of SPNs to represent the local interactions. The paper notes that this allows a single framework for inference, and constructs SPNs in terms of context-sensitive factors in CRFs (a type of factor graph).

The reverse case can be observed in [10], which uses sum-product networks with factor graphs as leaves in order to represent indirect variable interactions while ensuring that the overarching structure is tractable. This is used as part of an SPN structure-learning algorithm, which takes advantage of existing factor-graph structure learning to capture certain types of variable interactions which took too long to discover in a previous (pure SPN) structure learner.

5   Exact Inference

The goal of inference is to compute the marginal probability distribution of one or more variables, typically given some evidence. Evidence restricts the value of some variables. We can handle this by modifying the definition of the domain variables to restrict their possible values. It therefore suffices to consider the inference problem when no evidence is present.

The marginal for a variable x is defined as follows:

$$\sum_{\mathbf{U}-\{x\}} D(\mathbf{U})$$

Unfortunately, this computation is exponential time in the number of variables. We would like to re-arrange the summation to simplify it.

To deal with a slightly more general case, let's assume that we have a set of variables $\mathbf{X}$ we want to find the joint marginal for.

Supposing that we had *completeness*, we could push down the summation through sum nodes N:

$$\sum_{\mathbf{A}-\mathbf{X}} N(\mathbf{A}) = \sum_{i=1}^{n} \sum_{\mathbf{A}-\mathbf{X}} C_i(\mathbf{A})$$

Here, $\mathbf{A}$ is the scope of the parent, which (by completeness) is also the scope of each child. (As in the previous section, C_i will represent the children of N.)

Similarly, if we had *decomposability*, we could push down the sums through product nodes:

$$\sum_{\mathbf{A}-\mathbf{X}} N(\mathbf{A}) = \prod_{i=1}^{n} \sum_{\mathbf{A}_i-\mathbf{X}} C_i(\mathbf{A}_i)$$

Here, $\mathbf{A}$ is the scope of the parent, and the $\mathbf{A}_i$ are the scopes of the children. By decomposability, the $\mathbf{A}_i$ must be mutually exclusive, so that we can apply the distributive rule to push the sum down through the product. This reduces the complexity of the computation by allowing us to sum over the sets of variables $\mathbf{A}_i$ separately, and then combine the results.

Since we do *not* in general have a graph which is complete and decomposable, we need to adjust for that. The adjustment at sum nodes is computationally easy, augmenting the values from children with a multiplier to account for summing out the wider scope required by the parent:

$$\sum_{\mathbf{A}-\mathbf{X}} N(\mathbf{A}) = \sum_{i=1}^{n} \sum_{\mathbf{A}-\mathbf{A}_i-\mathbf{X}} \sum_{\mathbf{A}_i-\mathbf{X}} C_i(\mathbf{A}_i) \tag{1}$$

$$= \sum_{i=1}^{n} \left(\prod_{y \in \mathbf{A}-\mathbf{A}_i-\mathbf{X}} |\mathcal{V}(y)| \right) \sum_{\mathbf{A}_i-\{x\}} C_i(\mathbf{A}_i)$$

Where $\mathcal{V}(y)$ is the set of valid values for variable y.

The adjustment for non-decomposable products is less computationally convenient:

$$\sum_{\mathbf{A}-\mathbf{X}} N(\mathbf{A}) = \sum_{\mathbf{B}-\mathbf{X}} \prod_{i=1}^{n} \sum_{\mathbf{A}_i-\mathbf{B}-\mathbf{X}} C_i(\mathbf{A}_i) \tag{2}$$

Where $\mathbf{B}$ is the set of variables that appear in more than one of $\mathbf{A}_i$. (Note that we do not have to worry that some variables might appear in no $\mathbf{A}_i$, because the scope of the parent was defined as the union of the scopes of the children.)

What this equation says is just that we cannot push down the summation over a particular variable if that variable is shared between several children of a product node. This fails to satisfy the conditions for the distributive law. As a result, we have to sum this variable out *at* the offending product node.

Applying these equations recursively, we can create a dynamic-programming style algorithm which computes the desired marginal. This proceeds first in a downward pass, in which we mark which variables we need to avoid summing out at which nodes. Then, we pass messages up through the network. The messages are multidimensional arrays, giving a value for each combination of marked variables.

Algorithm 1. *To find $\sum_{\mathbf{U}-\mathbf{X}} D(\mathbf{U})$:*

1. *Mark variables $\mathbf{X}$ at the root.*
2. *For non-decomposable products, mark shared variables in the product node.*
3. *Propagate marks downward, marking a variable in a child whenever it is marked in the parent and occurs in the scope of the child.*
4. *Set the messages $\mathcal{M}(N)$ where N is a terminal node to be $\sum_{\mathbf{H}} N(\mathbf{A})$, where $\mathbf{A}$ are the arguments of the function N and $\mathbf{H}$ are any unmarked arguments.*
5. *Propagate up messages $\mathcal{M}(N) =$*

$$\begin{cases} \sum_{i=0}^{n} \pi_i \sum_{\mathbf{H}_i} \mathcal{M}(C_i) & \text{if } N \text{ is a sum node} \\ \sum_{\mathbf{H}} \prod_{i=0}^{n} \mathcal{M}(C_i) & \text{if } N \text{ is a product node} \end{cases}$$

where C_i are the children of node N, $\mathbf{H}_i$ is the set of dimensions marked in C_i but not marked in N, $\mathbf{H}$ is the union of the $\mathbf{H}_i$, and π_i is the multiplier from Equation 1 adjusted to remove marked variables: $\prod_{x \in \mathbf{A}-\mathbf{A}_i-\mathbf{X}-\mathbf{M}} |\mathcal{V}(x)|$ with $\mathbf{A}$ as the arguments of N, $\mathbf{A}_i$ those of C_i, and $\mathbf{M}$ the marked variables of N.

This algorithm bears a resemblance to the "expression trees" mentioned in [4]. The variable marking procedure also brings to mind "variable stretching" from that paper: we are marking out a portion of the graph in which we need to keep track of a variable in order to enable local message-passing computation.

With only about twice as much work, we can compute *all* the single-variable marginals by adding a second set of messages. This should not be a surprise, since the same is true of both SPNs and factor graphs. The solution closely resembles the inside-outside algorithm for PCFGs, with the messages from the previous section constituting the "inside" part.

In order to compute the marginal probabilities, we must first compute a set of partial derivatives in an arithmetic circuit (AC) representing the distribution. (The reader is directed to [1] for the details of this approach.)

We will re-name the messages $\mathcal{M}$ from Algorithm 1 to "upward messages" $\mathcal{M}_u$, with new "downward messages" $\mathcal{M}_d$.

Algorithm 2. *To find all single-variable marginals of D:*

1. *Run Algorithm 1, with* $\mathbf{X} = \emptyset$. *Keep the messages as* $\mathcal{M}_u(N)$.
2. *Set the downward message for the root node* $\mathcal{M}_d(D) = 1$.
3. *Compute downward messages* $\mathcal{M}_d(N) = \sum_{i=0}^{n} \mathcal{C}(P_i, N)$, *where* P_i *are the n parents of N and we define the contribution for each parent* $\mathcal{C}(P_i, N) =$

$$
\begin{cases}
\pi_i \sum_{\mathbf{H}} \mathcal{M}_d(P_i) & \text{if } P_i \text{ is a sum} \\
\sum_{\mathbf{H}} \mathcal{M}_d(P_i) \prod_{j=0}^{m} \mathcal{M}_u(C_j) & \text{if } P_i \text{ is a product}
\end{cases}
$$

   where π_i *is the same multiplier between parent and child as in the upward messages,* C_j *are the m other children of parent* P_i, *and* $\mathbf{H}$ *is the set of variables marked in* P_i *and not in N.*
4. *For each variable* $v \in \mathbf{U}$, *compute the marginal as the sum of partial derivatives for terminal nodes, and partial derivatives coming from* π-*adjustments involving that variable:*

$$
\mathcal{M}_d(v) = \sum_{i=1}^{n} \sum_{\mathbf{H}_i} F_i \mathcal{M}_d(F_i) \\
+ \sum_{(P_i, C_j)} \mathcal{M}_d(P_i)
$$

   where the F_i *are the terminal nodes,* $\mathbf{H}_i$ *are the arguments of* F_i *other than* v, $\sum_{(P_i, C_j)}$ *is summing over parent-child pairs* (P_i, C_j) *such that* P_i *has v in scope and not marked but* C_j *does not (so that* π-*adjustments would appear in the messages).*

The intuition is that upward messages compute the total value of the corresponding AC, whereas downward messages compute the partial derivative of the total value with respect to individual AC nodes. Each scalar value in the multidimensional message corresponds to an AC node.

This computes the same quantities which we would get by compiling to an AC and differentiating. The technique rolls together the compilation to an AC with the inference in the AC, so that if we apply it to an EG representing a factor graph, we are doing something very similar to compiling it to an AC and then differentiating (one of the better choices for exact inference in factor graphs). Since the algorithm reduces to SPN inference in the special case that the EG is indeed an SPN, we have the SPN efficiency in that case. In particular, we can get cubic complexity in the parsing problem which was mentioned as motivation.

Because expression graphs also admit the intractable cases which factor graphs allow, it will be desirable to have approximate inference algorithms such as Monte Carlo and variational methods. Variational methods would focus on the approximation of large multidimensional messages by approximate factorization. Monte Carlo would focus on approximating the large summations by sampling. A deep exploration of these possibilities will have to be left for another paper.

As a result of taking the derivatives of the network, this algorithm also gives us the derivatives needed to train the network by gradient-descent learning. However, we won't discuss this in detail due to space limitations.

6 Future Work

The concrete algorithms here have dealt with finite, fixed-size expression graphs, but the motivation section mentioned representation of grammars, which handle sequential information of varying size. Work is in progress applying expression graphs to grammar learning, enabling an expressive class of grammars.

Unlike factor graphs, expression graphs and SPNs can represent structural uncertainty within one graph, by taking a sum of multiple possible structures. Theoretically, structure learning and weight learning can be reduced to one problem. Of course, a graph representing the structure learning problem is too large for practical inference. In [5], infinite SPNs are defined via Dirichlet distributions, and sampling is used to make them tractable. Perhaps future work could define similar infinite EGs to subsume structure learning into inference.

The structure-learning algorithm in [10] is also quite interesting, employing heuristics to split the data into cases or factor the data, alternatively. This could point to two different sets of cognitive mechanisms, dealing independently with sums and products. Sum-like mechanisms include clustering, boosting, and bagging. These deal with complexity by making mixture models. Product-like mechanisms deal with complexity by splitting up the variables involved into sub-problems which may be independent or related by constraints (that is, factoring!). Perhaps distinct psychological processes deal with these two options. In future work, we hope to use this distinction in a cognitive architecture context.

7 Conclusion

It is hoped that this representation will help shed light on things from a theoretical perspective, and also perhaps aid in practical implementation in cases where a mixture of factor-graph style and SPN-style reasoning is required. Expression graphs are a relatively simple extension: from the perspective of a factor graph, we are merely adding the ability to take sums of distributions rather than only products. From the perspective of SPNs, all we are doing is dropping the constraints on network structure. This simple move nonetheless provides a rich representation.

This formalism helps to illustrate the relationship between factor graphs and sum-product networks, which can be somewhat confusing at first, as sum-product networks are described in terms of indicator variables and representing the network polynomial, concepts which may seem alien to factor graph representations.

Expression graphs improve upon factor graphs in two respects. First, it is a more expressive representation than factor graphs as measured in the kinds of distributions which can be represented compactly. Second, the representation is more amenable to exact inference in some cases, where generic factor graph inference algorithms have suboptimal complexity and must be augmented by special-case optimization to achieve good performance.

References

1. Darwiche, A.: A differential approach to inference in bayesian networks. Journal of the ACM (2003)
2. Derbinsky, N., Bento, J., Yedidia, J.: Methods for integrating knowledge with the three-weight optimization algorithm for hybrid cognitive processing. In: AAAI Fall Symposium on Integrated Cognition (2013)
3. Drechsler, R., Becker, B.: Binary Decision Diagrams: Theory and Implementation. Springer (1998)
4. Kschischang, F., Frey, B., Loeliger, H.: Factor graphs and the sum-product algorithm. IEEE Transactions on Information Theory (2001)
5. Lee, S.W., Watkins, C., Zhang, B.T.: Non-parametric bayesian sum-product network. In: Proc. Workshop on Learning Tractable Probabilistic Models, vol. 1 (2014)
6. McAllester, D., Collins, M., Pereira, F.: Case-factor diagrams for structured probabilistic modeling. In: Proc. UAI 2004 (2004)
7. Poon, H., Domingos, P.: Sum-product networks: A new deep architecture. In: Proc. UAI 2011 (2011)
8. Pynadath, D., Wellman, M.: Generalized queries on probabilistic context-free grammars. IEEE Transactions on Pattern Analysis and Machine Intelligence 20, 65–77
9. Ratajczak, M., Tschiatschek, S., Pernkopf, F.: Sum-product networks for structured prediction: Context-specific deep conditional random fields. In: Proc. Workshop on Learning Tractable Probabilistic Models, vol. 1 (2014)
10. Rooshenas, A., Lowd, D.: Learning sum-product networks with direct and indirect variable interactions. In: Proc. Workshop on Learning Tractable Probabilistic Models, vol. 1 (2014)
11. Rosenbloom, P.: The sigma cognitive architecture and system. AISB Quarterly (2013)
12. Smith, D.A., Eisner, J.: Dependency parsing by belief propagation. In: Proceedings of the Conference on Empirical Methods in Natural Language Processing. Association for Computational Linguistics (2008)

Toward Tractable Universal Induction Through Recursive Program Learning

Arthur Franz[(✉)]

Independent Researcher, Odessa, Ukraine
`franz@fias.uni-frankfurt.de`

Abstract. Since universal induction is a central topic in artificial general intelligence (AGI), it is argued that compressing all sequences up to a complexity threshold should be the main thrust of AGI research. A measure for partial progress in AGI is suggested along these lines. By exhaustively executing all two and three state Turing machines a benchmark for low-complexity universal induction is constructed. Given the resulting binary sequences, programs are induced by recursively constructing a network of functions. The construction is guided by a breadth-first search departing only from leaves of the lowest entropy programs, making the detection of low entropy ("short") programs efficient. This way, all sequences (80% of the sequences) generated by two (three) state machines could be compressed back roughly to the size defined by their Kolmogorov complexity.

1 Introduction

What is intelligence? After compiling a large set of definitions in the literature Legg and Hutter [8] came up with a definition of intelligence that is consistent with most other definitions:

"Intelligence measures an agent's ability to achieve goals in a wide range of environments."

Based on that definition Marcus Hutter [5] has developed a mathematical formulation and theoretical solution to the universal AGI problem, called AIXI. Although it is not computable, approximations may lead to tractable solutions. AIXI is in turn essentially based on Solomonoff's theory of universal induction [15], that assigns the following universal prior to any sequence x:

$$M(x) := \sum_{p:U(p)=x*} 2^{-l(p)} \tag{1}$$

where p is a program of length $l(p)$ executed on a universal monotone Turing machine U. $U(p) = x*$ denotes that after executing program p, the machine U prints the sequence x without necessarily halting. Impressively, it can be shown [5] that after seeing the first t digits of any computable sequence this universal prior is able to predict the next digit with a probability converging to certainty: $\lim_{t\to\infty} M(x_t|x_1,\ldots,x_{t-1}) = 1$. Since most probability weight is assigned to

© Springer International Publishing Switzerland 2015
J. Bieger (Ed.): AGI 2015, LNAI 9205, pp. 251–260, 2015.
DOI: 10.1007/978-3-319-21365-1_26

short programs (Occam's razor) this proves that compressed representations lead to successful predictions of any computable environment. This realization makes it especially promising to try to construct an efficient algorithm for universal induction as a milestone, even cornerstone, of AGI.

A general but brute force approach is universal search. For example, Levin search [10] executes all possible programs, starting with the shortest, until one of them generates the required data sequence. Although general, it is not surprising that the approach is computationally costly and rarely applicable in practice.

On the other side of the spectrum, there are non-general but computationally tractable approaches. Specifically, inductive programming techniques are used to induce programs from data [6] and there are some approaches within the context of AGI as well [3,12,14,16]. However, the reason why the generalization of many algorithms is impeded is the curse of dimensionality faced by all algorithms at some point. Considering the (algorithmic) complexity and diversity of tasks solved by today's typical algorithms, we observe that most if not all will be highly specific and many will be able to solve quite complex tasks (known as "narrow AI" [7]). Algorithms from the field of data compression are no exception. For example, the celebrated Lempel-Ziv compression algorithm (see e.g. [2]) handles stationary sequences but fails at compressing simple but non-stationary sequences efficiently. AI algorithms undoubtedly exhibit some intelligence, but when comparing them to humans, a striking difference comes to mind: the tasks solvable by humans seem to be much less complex albeit very diverse, while tasks solved by AI algorithms tend to be quite complex but narrowly defined (Fig. 1).

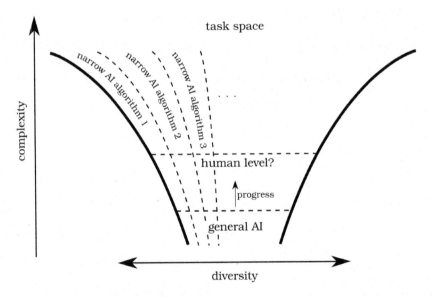

Fig. 1. Approach to artificial general intelligence. Instead of trying to solve complex but narrow tasks, AGI research should head for solving all simple tasks and only then expand toward more complexity.

For this reason, we should not try to beat the curse of dimensionality mercilessly awaiting us at high complexities, but instead head for general algorithms at low complexity levels and fill the task cup from the bottom up.

2   A Measure for Partial Progress in AGI

One of the troubles of AGI research is the lack of a measure for partial progress. While the Turing test is widely accepted as a test for general intelligence, it is only able to give an all or none signal. In spite of all attempts, we did not yet have a way to tell whether we are half way or 10% through toward general intelligence. The reason for that disorientation is the fact that every algorithm having achieved partially intelligent behavior, has failed to generalize to a wider range of behaviors. Therefore, it is hard to tell whether research has progressed in the right direction or has been on the wrong track all along.

However, since making universal induction tractable seems to be a cornerstone for AGI, we can formalize partial progress toward AGI as the extent to which universal induction has been efficiently implemented. Additionally, if we start out with a *provably general* algorithm that works up to a complexity level, thereby solving all simple compression problems, the objection about its possible non-generalizability is countered. The measure for partial progress then simply becomes the complexity level up to which the algorithm can solve all problems.

2.1   Related Work

This measure is reminiscent of existing intelligence tests based on algorithmic complexity. Hernandez-Orallo [4] has developed the C-test, that allows only sequences with unique induced explanations, of which a prefix leads to the same explanation and various other restrictions on the sequence set. However, since the pitfall of building yet another narrow AI system is lurking at every step, a measure of research progress in AGI (not so much of the intelligence of an agent) should make sure that *all* sequences below a complexity level are compressed successfully and can not afford to discard large subsets as is done in the C-test.

Legg and Veness [9] developed a measure that takes into account the performance of an agent in a reinforcement learning setting which includes an Occam bias decreasing exponentially with the complexity of the environment. They are correct to note that the solution to the important exploration-exploitation dilemma is neglected in a purely complexity-based measure. In that sense, universal induction is a necessary albeit not sufficient condition for intelligence. For our purposes, it is important to set up a measure for universal induction alone, as it seems to be a simpler problem than one of building complete intelligent agents.

Text based measures of intelligence follow the rationale that an agent can be considered intelligent if it is able to compress the information content of a text, like humanity's knowledge in the form of Wikipedia [1, 13]. However, this kind of compression requires large amounts of information not present in the text itself, like real world experience through the agent's senses. Therefore, the task is either ill-defined for agents not disposing of such external information or the agent has to be provided with such information extending texts to arbitrary data, which is equivalent to the compression of arbitrary sequences as proposed here.

2.2 Formalization

Suppose, we run binary programs on a universal monotone Turing machine U. U's possible input programs p_i can be ordered in a length-increasing lexicographic way: "" (empty program), "0", "1", "00", "01", "10", "11", "000", etc. up to a maximal complexity level L. We run all those programs until they halt or for a maximum of t time steps and read off their outputs x_i on the output tape. In contrast to Kolmogorov complexity[1], we use the time-bounded version – the Levin complexity – which is computable and includes a penalty term on computation time [11]:

$$Kt(x) = \min_p\{|p| + \log t : U(p) = x \text{ in } t \text{ steps}\} \tag{2}$$

Saving all the generated strings paired with their optimal programs (x_i, p_i^o) with $p_i^o(x_i) = \text{argmin}_p\{|p| + \log t : U(p) = x_i \text{ in } t \text{ steps}, |p| \leq L\}$, we have all we need for the progress measure. The goal of universal induction is to find all such optimal programs p_i^o for each of the x_i. If p_i is the actually found program, its performance can be measured by

$$r_i(L) = \frac{|p_i^o|}{|p_i|} \in (0, 1] \tag{3}$$

If not, there is no time-bounded solution to the compression problem. The overall performance R at complexity level L could be used as a measure for partial progress in universal induction and be given by averaging:

$$R(L) = \langle r_i(L) \rangle \tag{4}$$

One may object that the number of programs increases exponentially with their length such that an enumeration quickly becomes intractable. This is a weighty argument if the task is universal search – a general procedure for inversion problems. However, we suggest this procedure to play the mere role of a benchmark for an *efficient* universal induction algorithm, which will use completely different methods than universal search and will be described in Section 3. Therefore, using the set of simple programs as a benchmark may be enough to set the universal induction algorithm on the right track.

Note that only a small fraction of possible sequences can be generated this way. After all, it is well known that only exponentially few, $O(2^{n-m})$, sequences of length n can be compressed by m bits [11].

---

[1] The Kolmogorov complexity of a string is defined as the length of the shortest program able to generate that string on a Turing machine.

2.3 Implementation

Implementing this test does not require coding of a universal Turing machine (TM) since computers are already universal TMs. Instead, enumerating all transition functions of an n-state machine is sufficient. The machine used here has one bidirectional, two way infinite work tape and a unidirectional, one way infinite, write only output tape. Two symbols are used, $\mathbb{B} = \{0,1\}$, the states taken from $Q = \{0, \ldots, n-1\}$. The transition map is then:

$$Q \times \mathbb{B} \to Q \times \{0, 1, L, R, N\} \times \{0, 1, N\} \qquad (5)$$

where L, R, and N denote left, right and no motion of the head, respectively. The work tape can move in any direction while the output tape either writes 0 or 1 and moves to the right, or does not move at all (N). No halting or accepting states were utilized. The machine starts with both tapes filled with zeros. A finite sequence x is considered as generated by machine T given transition function (program) p, if it is at the left of the output head at some point: we write $T(p) = x*$. The transition table enumerated all possible combinations of state and work tape content, which amounts to $|Q| \cdot |\mathbb{B}| = 2n$. Therefore, there exist $|Q| \cdot 5 \cdot 3 = 15n$ different instructions and consequently $(15n)^{2n}$ different machines with n states. For $n = 2, 3$ this amounts to around 10^6 and 10^{10} machines. All those machines ($n = 1$ machines are trivial) were executed until 50 symbols were written on the output tape or the maximum number of 400 time steps was reached. All unique outputs were stored, amounting to 210 and 43295, for $n = 2, 3$, respectively, and paired with their respective programs.

Table 1 depicts a small sample of the outputs. It may be interjected that sequences generated by 2 and 3 state machines are not very "interesting". However, the present work is the just initial step. Moreover, it is interesting to note that even the 2 state machine shows non-repetitive patterns with an ever increasing number of 1's. In the 3 state machine patterns become quickly more involved and require "intelligence" to detect the regularities in the patterns (try the last one!). Consistently with the reasoning in the introduction, could it be that the threshold complexity level of human intelligence is not far off from the sequence complexity of 3 state machines, especially when the data presentation is not comfortably tuned according to natural image statistics?

We suggest that these patterns paired with their respective programs constitute a benchmark for partial progress in artificial general intelligence. If an

Table 1. Sample outputs of 2 and 3 state Turing machines

states	sample outputs
2	1010101010101010101010101010101010101010101010101010
2	1101101101101101101101101101101101101101101101101011
2	0001001100111001110011111001111110011111110011111
3	0010110100101000101101001010001011010010100010101101
3	1011111100111011101001110101110101001110101011111
3	0101101011010111010110110101111010110110110101111

efficient algorithm can compress these patterns to small programs then it can be claimed to be moderately intelligent. Modern compression algorithms, such as Lempel-Ziv (on which the famous Zip compression is based), fail at compressing those sequences, since the packed file size increases with sequence length (ergo r_i gets arbitrarily small) while the size of the TM transition table is always the same independently of sequence length.

3   Universal Induction of Low-Complexity Sequences

3.1   Methods

Having generated all strings printed by two and three state programs the task is to build an efficient algorithm compressing those strings back into a short representation, not necessarily the original one though, but having a similar size in terms of entropy.

As exemplified in Fig. 2 the present algorithm induces a recursive network of function primitives using a sequence generated by a three state Turing machine. Four function primitives were used that generate constant, alternating or incremental sequences or a single number:

$$C(s,n) = s, s, \ldots, s \ (n \text{ times}), \quad s \in \mathbb{Z} \cup \mathbb{S}, n \in \mathbb{N} \tag{6}$$

$$A(a,b,n) = a, b, a, b, \ldots a, b \ (n \text{ times}) \quad a, b \in \mathbb{Z} \cup \mathbb{S}, n \in \mathbb{N} \tag{7}$$

$$I(s,d,n) = s + 0 \cdot d, s + 1 \cdot d, \ldots, s + (n-1) \cdot d \quad s, d \in \mathbb{Z}, n \in \mathbb{N} \tag{8}$$

$$R(s) = s \quad s \in \mathbb{Z} \cup \mathbb{S} \tag{9}$$

where $\mathbb{Z}$ is the set of integers, $\mathbb{N}$ the set of non-negative integers and $\mathbb{S} = \{C, A, I, R\}$ is the set of arbitrary symbols (here function names).

The entropy of a given function network is computed as follows. Let $x_i \in \mathbb{Z} \cup \mathbb{S}$ denote the inputs to those functions without parent functions. The distribution $p(n) = 2^{-|n|}/3$ is imposed on integers $n \in \mathbb{Z}$. If $x_i \in \mathbb{Z}$ then its information content is given by $H(x_i) = -\log_2 p(x_i) = |x_i| + \log_2(3)$ bits[2] which we simplify to $|x_i| + 1$ bits. If $x_i \in \mathbb{S}$ then $H(x_i) = \log_2 |\mathbb{S}| = 2$ bits. The overall entropy of the network is the sum $H_{tot} = \sum_i H(x_i)$. It may be objected that according to the Minimum Description Length principle, the information contained in the algorithm itself has to be taken into account as well. After all, for any sequence x it is possible to define a universal Turing machine U' such that $Kt_{U'}(x) = 0$ thereby encoding all information about x in the design of U', making U' highly dependent on x. However, since both the present algorithm and the benchmark do not depend on x, their description length is a mere constant and can be neglected.

---

[2] This coding is linear in the integer value. We could use Elias gamma or delta coding, which is logarithmic, however the algorithm has turned out to perform better with linear coding. This is work in progress and this issue shall be investigated in future work.

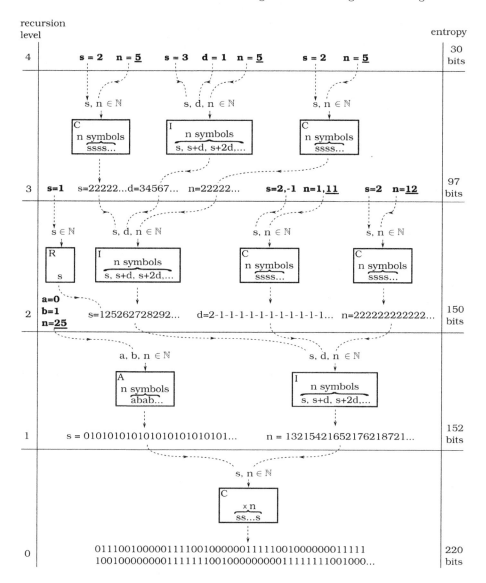

Fig. 2. Exemplifying recursive compression. A sequence is recursively transformed by a network of functions to an increasingly smaller representation. The original sequence takes up 220 bits of information, 129 bits for encoding the 0's and 1's plus the length of the sequence (91 bits). At the zeroth recursion level the sequence is parsed using a constant function (C) that prints n times the number s. At level 1 the sequences of function inputs are shown that recreate the original sequence. The original sequence is thereby transformed to two sequences of function inputs. Subsequently, an alternating function (A) explains the first sequence and an incremental function (I) explains the second one. This is done recursively, until the entropy can not be reduced any more. The bold inputs remain unexplained and amount to 96 bits. Note that the final number of inputs does not depend on the sequence length any more. If we remove those inputs that change with sequence length (bold and underlined) then the entropy decoding sequence structure is only 27 bits (only bold).

At each step of the algorithm a set of unexplained sequences is present, which are sequences of inputs to those functions without parent functions. For each such input sequence its entropy can be computed and the sequences ordered after decreasing entropy. Looping through that set starting with the sequence of highest entropy (requiring most explanation) the algorithm tries to generate a part of the sequence with one of the function primitives. For example, if the sequence $q = 3, 3, 3, 9, 9, 9, 9, 6, 6, 6, 6, 6$ is present, a sequence of inputs to the constant function is induced: $C(s = 3, 9, 6, n = 3, 4, 5)$. The entropy is reduced, in this case $H(q) = 87$ bits and its explanation takes only $H(s) + H(n) = 36$ bits. For each function primitive, such an entropy change is computed. If the entropy has been reduced, the function is accepted and added to the network. Otherwise, it is accepted only if its child (the function that receives its outputs) has been entropy reducing, allowing to overcome local minima in the entropy landscape to some extent.

In this fashion a breadth-first search is performed, while pruning away the least promising tree branches. Those are defined as programs having a higher total entropy than the 1.05 times the program with lowest entropy.[3]

3.2   Results

Since our fixed-size Turing machine programs can create sequences of arbitrary length, successful program induction is defined as induction of a program with a fixed number of inputs to the function network. Further, to establish a benchmark, the entropy of the Turing machine programs is computed as follows. There are $(15n)^{2n}$ machines with n states, hence the amount of information needed to specify a TM program with n states is

$$H_{TM}(n) = 2n \log_2(15n) \tag{10}$$

which results in a program size of around 20 and 33 bits for two and three state TMs, respectively. Since the induced programs encode the length l of the target sequence and the TM programs do not, the information contained in the length has to be subtracted from the induced program entropy (the bold and underlined numbers in Fig. 2).

All sequences generated by all two state machines could be compressed successfully. The average induced program size is $\mu_2 = 22$ bits with a standard deviation of $\sigma_2 = 23$ bits. Because of the large number of three states sequences, 200 sequences were randomly sampled. This way, $80 \pm 4\%$ of three state sequences could be compressed successfully, with $\mu_3 = 27$ bits and $\sigma_3 = 20$ bits. However, "unsuccessful" sequences could be compressed to some extent as well, although the resulting program size was not independent of sequence length. With sequences of length $l = 100$ the entropy statistics of "unsuccessful" sequences are $\mu_3' = 112$ bits and $\sigma_3' = 28$ bits. Given an average sequence entropy of 146 bits, this constitutes an average compression factor of 1.3.

---

[3] Python code and string/program pairs are available upon request.

It may seem surprising that the average entropy of the induced programs is even below the entropy of the TM programs (transition tables). However, since not all rows of a transition table are guaranteed to be used when executing a program, the actual shortest representation will not contain unused rows leading to a smaller program size than 20 or 33 bits. The most important result is that very short programs, with a size roughly around the Kolmogorov complexity, have indeed been found for most sequences.

4   Discussion

The present approach has shown that it is possible to both sensibly define a measure for partial progress toward AGI by measuring the complexity level up to which all sequences can be induced and to build an algorithm actually performing universal induction for most low complexity sequences. Our demonstrator has been able to compress all sequences generated by two state Turing machines and 80% of the sequences generated by three state Turing machines.

The current demonstrator presents work in progress and it is already fairly clear how to improve the algorithm such that the remaining 20% are also covered. For example, there is no unique partition of a sequence into a set of concatenated primitives. The way, those partitions are selected should also be guided by compressibility considerations, e.g. partition subsets of equal length should have a higher prior chance to be analyzed further. Currently, the partition is implemented in a non-principled way, which is one of the reasons for the algorithm to run into dead ends. Remarkably, all reasons for stagnation seem to be those aspects of the algorithm that are not yet guided by the compression principle. This observation leads to the conjecture that the further extension and generalization of the algorithm may not require any additional class of measures, but a "mere" persistent application of the compression principle.

One may object that the function primitives are hard-coded and may therefore constitute an obstacle for generalizability. However, those primitives can also be resolved into a combination of elementary operations, e.g. the incremental function can be constructed by adding a fixed number to the previous sequence element, hence be itself represented by a function network. Therefore, it is all a matter of flexible application and organization of the very same function network and thus lies within the scope of the present approach.

The hope of this approach is that it may lead us on a path finally scaling up universal induction to practically significant levels. It would be nice to backup this hope by a time complexity measure of the present algorithm, which not available at present unfortunately, since this is work in progress. Further, it can not be excluded that a narrow algorithm is also able to solve all low-complexity problems. In fact, the present algorithm is narrow as well since there are numerous implicit assumptions about the composition of the sequence, e.g. the concatenation of outputs of several functions, no possibility to represent dependencies within a sequence, or regularities between different inputs etc. Nevertheless, since we represent general programs without specific a priori restrictions this setup seems to be general enough to tackle such questions which will hopefully result in a scalable system.

References

1. H-Prize, H.: http://prize.hutter1.net (accessed: May 17, 2015)
2. Cover, T.M., Thomas, J.A.: Elements of information theory. John Wiley & Sons (2012)
3. Friedlander, D., Franklin, S.: LIDA and a theory of mind. In: 2008: Proceedings of the First AGI Conference on Artificial General Intelligence, vol. 171, p. 137. IOS Press (2008)
4. Hernandez-Orallo, J.: Beyond the turing test. Journal of Logic, Language and Information **9**(4), 447–466 (2000)
5. Hutter, M.: Universal Artificial Intelligence: Sequential Decisions based on Algorithmic Probability, 300 pages. Springer, Berlin (2005). http://www.hutter1.net/ai/uaibook.htm
6. Kitzelmann, E.: Inductive Programming: A Survey of Program Synthesis Techniques. In: Schmid, U., Kitzelmann, E., Plasmeijer, R. (eds.) AAIP 2009. LNCS, vol. 5812, pp. 50–73. Springer, Heidelberg (2010)
7. Kurzweil, R.: The singularity is near: When humans transcend biology. Penguin (2005)
8. Legg, S., Hutter, M.: A collection of definitions of intelligence. In: Goertzel, B., Wang, P. (eds.) Advances in Artificial General Intelligence: Concepts, Architectures and Algorithms. Frontiers in Artificial Intelligence and Applications, vol. 157, pp. 17–24. IOS Press, Amsterdam (2007). http://arxiv.org/abs/0706.3639
9. Legg, S., Veness, J.: An Approximation of the Universal Intelligence Measure. In: Dowe, D.L. (ed.) Solomonoff Festschrift. LNCS, vol. 7070, pp. 236–249. Springer, Heidelberg (2013)
10. Levin, L.A.: Universal sequential search problems. Problemy Peredachi Informatsii **9**(3), 115–116 (1973)
11. Li, M., Vitányi, P.M.: An introduction to Kolmogorov complexity and its applications. Springer (2009)
12. Looks, M., Goertzel, B.: Program representation for general intelligence. In: Proc. of AGI, vol. 9 (2009)
13. Mahoney, M.V.: Text compression as a test for artificial intelligence. In: AAAI/IAAI, p. 970 (1999)
14. Potapov, A., Rodionov, S.: Universal Induction with Varying Sets of Combinators. In: Kühnberger, K.-U., Rudolph, S., Wang, P. (eds.) AGI 2013. LNCS, vol. 7999, pp. 88–97. Springer, Heidelberg (2013)
15. Solomonoff, R.J.: A formal theory of inductive inference. Part I. Information and Control **7**(1), 1–22 (1964)
16. Veness, J., Ng, K.S., Hutter, M., Uther, W., Silver, D.: A Monte-Carlo AIXI approximation. Journal of Artificial Intelligence Research **40**(1), 95–142 (2011)

How Can Cognitive Modeling Benefit from Ontologies? Evidence from the HCI Domain

Marc Halbrügge[1]([⊠]), Michael Quade[2], and Klaus-Peter Engelbrecht[1]

[1] Quality and Usability Lab, Telekom Innovation Laboratories, Technische
Universität Berlin, Ernst-Reuter-Platz 7, 10587 Berlin, Germany
`marc.halbruegge@tu-berlin.de`, `klaus-peter.engelbrecht@telekom.de`
[2] DAI-Labor, Technische Universität Berlin, Ernst-Reuter-Platz 7,
10587 Berlin, Germany
`michael.quade@dai-labor.de`

Abstract. Cognitive modeling as a method has proven successful at
reproducing and explaining human intelligent behavior in specific laboratory situations, but still struggles to produce more general intelligent
capabilities. A promising strategy to address this weakness is the addition of large semantic resources to cognitive architectures. We are investigating the usefulness of this approach in the context of human behavior
during software use. By adding world knowledge from a Wikipedia-based
ontology to a model of human sequential behavior, we achieve quanti-
tatively and qualitatively better fits to human data.The combination of
model and ontology yields additional insights that cannot be explained
by the model or the ontology alone.

Keywords: Cognitive modeling · Ontology · Human performance ·
Human error · Memory for goals

1 Introduction

Cognitive architectures like Soar [13] and ACT-R [2] have enabled researchers
to create sophisticated cognitive models of intelligent human behavior in laboratory situations. One major drawback of cognitive modeling, especially from
the artificial general intelligence perspective, is that those models tend to be
very problem-specific. While a cognitive model of air traffic control may show
human-like intelligence in exactly that task, it is completely unable to perform
anything else, like solving a basic algebra problem. One major cause of the the-
matic narrowness of cognitive models is the restricted amount of knowledge that
those models have access to. In most cases, every single piece of information has
to be coded into the model by a researcher. This has been critized before, as
a human cognitive architecture should be able to maintain and integrate large
amounts of knowledge [3].

© Springer International Publishing Switzerland 2015
J. Bieger (Ed.): AGI 2015, LNAI 9205, pp. 261–271, 2015.
DOI: 10.1007/978-3-319-21365-1_27

One recent approach to overcome this issue is the combination of existing cognitive architectures with large knowledge databases like WordNet [6–8,16] or DBpedia [14], a Wikipedia-based ontology [19]. Common to all those approaches is that they focus on feasibility and the technical implementation of their knowledge system, while the validity of the resulting architectures is still an open question.

This is the starting point for the research project presented here. Instead of describing how vast knowledge bases can be added to a cognitive architecture, we combine an existing solution with an existing cognitive model of sequential behavior and analyze how the predictions of the model change and whether this adds to our unterstanding of the model, its task, and the underlying knowledge base.

Our research is situated in the human-computer interaction (HCI) domain. We are analyzing how long human users need to perform simple tasks with a home assistance application, how often they make errors, and which user interface (UI) elements are tied to these errors. Our cognitive model receives knowledge about the world based on Wikipedia content, following Salvucci's work on the integration of DBpedia into ACT-R [19]. The modeling effort presented in this paper relies mainly on the general relevance of different Wikipedia articles. The higher the number of links inside Wikipedia that point towards an article, the higher the relevance of the article and the entity or concept that it explains. Our data suggests that UI elements that correspond to highly relevant concepts are handled differently than elements that correspond to less relevant concepts.

1.1   Human Action Control and Error

The link from human error research to artificial intelligence is not an obvious one. We think of error as "window to the mind" [15]. Understanding why and when humans err helps identifying the building blocks of intelligent human behavior. Of special interest are errors of trained users. Using software systems after having received some training is characterized by rule-based behavior [17]. Goals are reached by using stored rules and procedures that have been learned during training or earlier encounters with similar systems. While errors are not very frequent on this level of action control, they are also pervasive and cannot be eliminated through training [18].

Our focus on rule-based behavior allows a straightforward definition of error: Procedural error means that the (optimal) path to the current goal is violated by a non-optimal action. This can either be the addition of an unnecessary or even hindering action, which is called an *intrusion*. Or a necessary step can be left out, constituting an *omission*.

1.2   Memory for Goals

A promising theory of rule-based sequential action is the Memory for Goals (MFG) model [1]. The MFG proposes that subgoals, i.e., atomic steps towards a goal, are underlying memory effects, namely time-dependent *activation, interference*, and associative *priming*. Higher activation leads to faster recall and thereby shorter execution times. If the activation is too low, the retrieval of the subgoal may fail, resulting in an omission. Interference with other subgoals may lead to intrusions. Priming is the most important concept in the context of this paper as it provides the link to the ontology in the background.

Our basic assumption is that subgoals receive priming from the general concepts that they represent. Hitting a button labeled "Search" is connected to the concept of search; choosing an option called "Landscape" in a printing dialog is related to the concept of landscape. If the general concept that is semantically linked to a subgoal is highly activated in the knowledge base, the respective subgoal should receive more priming, resulting in a higher overall activation of the subgoal. Taken together with the MFG, this results in three high-level predictions for subgoals, corresponding UI elements, and their respective concepts:

1. Execution time should decrease with concept activation.
2. Omission rate should decrease with concept activation.
3. Intrusion rate should increase with concept activation.

2 Experiment

The empirical basis for our model is provided by a usability study targeting a kitchen assistant from an ambient assisted living context. The kitchen assistant provides basic help during the preparation of meals by proposing recipes, calculating ingredients quantities, and by presenting interactive cooking instructions.

In order to assess the three ontology-based predictions stated above, we performed a reanalysis of previously published data [12]. We are concentrating on a single screen of the kitchen assistant that allows searching for recipes based on predefined attributes. A screenshot of the search attribute form translated to English is given in Fig. 1. The search attributes are grouped into nationality (French, German, Italian, Chinese) and type-of-dish (Main Course, Pastry, Dessert, Appetizer). We excluded three health-related search options as they were neither well represented in the experimental design, nor in the ontology. For the eight remaining buttons, we identified the best matching concept from the DBpedia ontology and use the number of links to it as measure of relevance of the concept. As can be seen in Table 2, the buttons in the nationality group are two to three magnitudes more relevant than the buttons in the type-of-dish group. Our empirical analysis therefore unfolds around the differences between those two groups.

2.1 Method

Twenty participants recruited on and off campus (15 women, 5 men, M_{age}=32.3, SD_{age}=11.9) took part in the experiment. Amongst other things, each participant completed 34 recipe search tasks using the attribute selection screen (see Fig. 1).

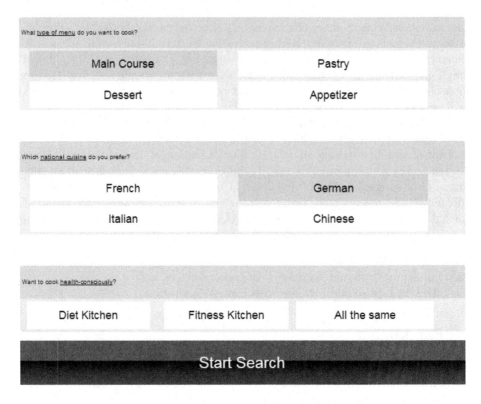

Fig. 1. Screenshot of the English version of the recipe search screen

One half of the tasks was done using a tablet computer, a large touch screen was used for the other half. Instructions were given verbally by the experimenter. All user actions were logged and videotaped for subsequent task execution time and error analysis.

2.2   Results

We observed a total of 1607 clicks on the eight search attribute buttons under investigation. The results for our three ontology-based predictions are as follows.

Execution Time. We exluded all clicks with substantial wait time (due to task instruction or system response) from the analysis. The remaining 822 clicks still differ in the necessary accuracy of the finger movement which is strongly related to the time needed to perform the movement as formulated in Fitts' law [9]. Individual differences in motor performance were large, and the device used also had an effect on the click time. We therefore added subjects as random factor with device and Fitts-slope within subject to the analysis. The click time was analyzed using a linear mixed model [4], fixed effects were tested for significance using the Satterthwaite approximation for degrees of freedom. Results are given in Table 1. Besides the expected effects of Fitts' law and device, we observed a significant difference between the buttons for type-of-dish and nationality, with type-of-dish needing approximately 100 ms longer.

Omissions and Intrusions. If those 100 ms are caused by lack of activation (as predicted by the MFG), then this lack of activation should cause more omissions for the type-of-dish group and more intrusions for the nationality group. We observed 14 intrusions and 19 omissions during the handling of the search attribute page (error rate 2.0%). Mixed logit models with subject as random factor showed no significant influence of the attribute group, but at least for omissions, the effect points into the expected direction (omissions: $z = 1.50, p = .133$; intrusions: $z = -.05, p = .964$). The omission rates for nationality and type-of-dish are 0.8% and 1.6%, respectively.

Table 1. Linear mixed model results for the click time analysis

Factor	Estimate	t	df	p
Fitts' Index of Difficulty in bit	$173 \frac{ms}{bit}$	4.95	22.4	$< .001$
Device (Tablet vs. Screen)	213 ms	4.38	24.3	$< .001$
Attr. Group (Dish vs. Nationality)	112 ms	2.47	611.3	.014

Discussion. We investigated the difference between frequently vs. less frequently used concepts (nationality vs. type-of-dish) on a home assistance UI with regards to three dependent variables. The MFG predicts faster execution, less omission errors, and more intrusion errors for the higher used concept.

The empirical results are mixed. Buttons in the nationality group are clicked faster and weakly tend to be less prone to omissions. We did not find an intrusion effect, but this does not necessarily contradict the theory. The MFG explains intrusions by interference with earlier subgoals that are still present in memory. In the context of the experiment presented here, those intruding subgoals are memory clutter from already completed trials. In experimental design terms, this is called a carry-over effect. Due to the order of trials being randomized between subjects, intrusions should not happen on a general, but a subject-specific level.

3   Cognitive Model

The cognitive model presented here has been created using ACT-R 6 [2]. It has been shown to reproduce omission and intrusion errors for task-oriented vs. device-oriented UI elements well [12]. A comparison of the model's predictions for the different search attribute buttons has not been done before.

Following the MFG, the model creates and memorizes a chain of subgoal chunks when it receives task instructions through ACT-R's auditory system. It follows this chain of subgoals until either the goal is reached or memory gets weak. In case of retrieval failure, the model reverts to a knowledge-in-the-world strategy and randomly searches the UI for suitable elements. If it can retrieve a subgoal chunk that corresponds to the currently attended UI element, this subgoal is carried out and the cycle begins again.

The only declarative knowledge that is hard-coded into the model is that some UI elements need to be toggled, while others need to be pushed. The model interacts directly with the HTML interface of the kitchen assistant by the means of ACT-CV [11].[1]

Table 2. Semantic mapping between UI and ontology. Inlink count obtained from DBpedia 3.9 [14]. Subtitle-based word frequency (per 10^6 words) from [5]

Concept	UI label	DBpedia entry	Inlink count	per 10^6 links	Word freq.
German	Deutsch	Deutschland	113621	2474.3	10.2
Italian	Italienisch	Italien	56105	1221.8	6.2
Chinese	Chinesisch	China	10115	220.3	8.2
French	Französisch	Frankreich	79488	1731.0	17.4
Main Course	Hauptgericht	Hauptgericht	35	0.8	0.8
Appetizer	Vorspeise	Vorspeise	72	1.6	1.5
Dessert	Nachtisch	Dessert	193	4.2	6.5
Pastry	Backwaren	Gebäck	165	3.6	0.3

3.1 Adding World Knowledge to the Model

In order to assess how cognitive modeling can benefit from ontologies, we took the barely knowledgeable model and added applicable pieces of information from Wikipedia to its declarative memory. We propose semantic priming from long-living general concepts to the short-lived subgoal chunks that are created by the model when it pursues a goal.

How much priming can we expect, based on the information that is available within DBpedia? We are using the inlink count as measure of the relevance of a concept. In ACT-R, this needs to be translated into an activation value of the chunk that represents the concept (i.e., Wikipedia article). Temporal decay of activation is modeled in ACT-R using the power law of forgetting [2]. Salvucci [19] has applied this law to the concepts within DBpedia, assuming that they have been created long ago and the number of inlinks represents the number of presentations of the corresponding chunk. The base activation B can be determined from inlink count n as follows

$$B = \ln(2n) \tag{1}$$

While we agree with Salvucci's rationale, deriving the activation from raw inlink counts is a little too straightforward in our eyes. Numerically, it creates very

---

[1] See [12] for a more detailed description. The source code of the model is available for download at http://www.tu-berlin.de/?id=135088.

high activation values. And as the total number of entries varies between the language variations of DBpedia, switching language (or ontology) would mean changing the general activation level.[2] In the special case of our model, the use of (1) caused erratic behavior because the high amount of ontology-based activation overrode all other activation processes (i.e., activation noise and mismatch penalties for partial matching of chunks). We therefore introduced a small factor c that scales the inlink count down to usable values. Together with ACT-R's minimum activation constant blc, this results in the following equation

$$B = \max(\ln(c \cdot n), blc) \tag{2}$$

How is the semantic priming to subgoal chunks finally achieved? The declarative memory module of ACT-R 6 only allows priming from buffers ("working memory") to declarative ("long term") memory. We therefore introduced a hook function that modifies the activation of every subgoal chunk whenever it enters long term memory according to the general concept that is related to the goal chunk.

3.2 Goodness of Fit

The model was run 300 times with concept priming disabled ($c = 0$), and 300 times with priming enabled ($c = .005$, resulting average base activation of the eight concepts $M_B = 2.4$, $SD_B = 3.4$). For both conditions, we computed time and error predictions for each button and compared these to the empirical observations. The effect of the needed accuracy of the finger move was eliminated based on Fitts' law, using a linear mixed model with subject as random factor [4] for the empirical data and a linear regression for the model data, as the Fitts' parameters were not varied during the simulation runs. Correlations between the respective residuals are given in Table 3. Omission and intrusion rates per button were correlated without further preprocessing.

The results are given alongside R^2 and RMSE in Table 3. While the goodness-of-fit with R^2 constantly below .5 and substantial RMSE is not overwhelming, the difference to the baseline is worth discussion. The model without concept priming displays no or negative correlations between its predictions and the empirical values, meaning that the baseline model is even worse than chance. The corresponding regression lines are displayed on the upper part of Fig. 2. When concept priming is added, all three dependent variables show substantial positive correlations between observed and predicted values. The difference between the correlations is very large, i.e., always above .75.

The positive correlation for intrusions is noteworthy as we could not establish an empirical relationship between concept relevance and the observerd intrusion rates in the first place (see above). If our hypothesis of intrusions being caused by leftovers from previous trials with additional priming from ontology-based

---

[2] The English DBpedia is 2.5 to 3 times larger than the German one. "Intelligence" has 1022 inlinks in the English DBpedia, but "Intelligenz" has only 445 inlinks in the German one.

Table 3. Correlations between the empirical data and the model predictions

Dependent Variable	$r_{baseline}$	$r_{priming}$	Δr	$R^2_{priming}$	$RMSE_{prim.}$
Execution time (residual)	-.218	.684	.758	.468	78 ms
Omission rate	-.390	.640	.824	.410	.027
Intrusion rate	-.654	.511	.873	.261	.011

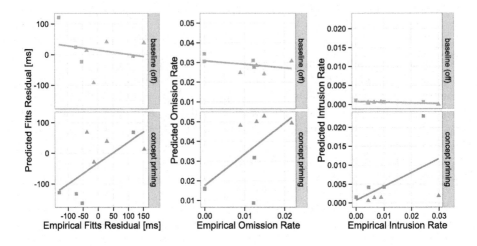

Fig. 2. Click time residuals after Fitts' law regression, intrusion and omission rates of the cognitive model with and without priming from the DBpedia concepts. Negative slopes of the regression line mean worse than chance predictions. Positive slopes mean better than chance predictions. Squares denote buttons of group "nationality", triangles denote "type of dish".

concepts holds, then this result underlines the benefits of adding ontologies to cognitive architectures. A closer look at Fig. 2 reveals that the correlation for intrusions is highly dependent of two outliers, the results should therefore be interpreted with care.

4 Discussion and Conclusions

We presented a cognitive model of sequential action that has been developed for the prediction of human error during the use of a home assistance system [12]. The original model did not have any world knowledge and accordingly was unable to reproduce effects of concept relevance on task execution time and omission rate that we found in a reanalysis of our empirical data. Adding concepts from DBpedia [14] to the declarative knowledge of the model and modulating the activation of these concepts based on the number of links inside DBpedia that point to them allowed not only to reproduce the time and omission rate differences, but to some extent also the rates of intrusions. While the prediction of execution time and omissions mainly lies within the ontology, intrusions can only be explained by the combination of cognitive model and ontology, highlighting the synergy between both.

To our knowledge, this is the first time that Salvucci's approach for adding world knowledge to a cognitive architecture [19] is empirically validated. The practical development of the model showed that the activation equation proposed by Salvucci, while being theoretically sound, creates hurdles for the combination of world knowledge with existing cognitive models. Therefore, we introduced a constant scaling factor to the ontology-based activation computation. This goes in line with the common practice in psycholinguistics to use standardized values that are independent of the corpus in use. The factor chosen here helped to keep the influence of the ontology on subgoal activation at par with the other activation sources applied (i.e., activation noise and partial matching).

It is also informative to compare our approach to research on information foraging, namely SNIF-ACT [10]. This system uses activation values that are estimated from word frequencies in online text corpora, which would lead to general hypotheses similar to the ones given above. But beyond this, a closer look unveils interesting differences to the DBpedia approach. While word frequency and inlink count are highly correlated (r=.73 in our case, see Table 2), the word frequency operationalization yields much smaller differences between the nationality vs. type-of-dish groups. Frequency based-approaches also need to remove highly frequent, but otherwise irrelevant words beforehand (e.g., "the", "and"). In Wikipedia, this relevance filter is already built into the system and no such kind of preprocessing is necessary. Empirically, we obtained inconclusive results when using word frequency in a large subtitle corpus [5] instead of Wikipedia inlink count as concept activation estimate.

While the combination of cognitive model and ontology provides some stimulating results, it also has some downsides and limitations. First of all, the small number of observed errors leads to much uncertainty regarding the computed intrusion and omission rates. Especially in case of intrusions, the empirical basis is rather weak. The goodness-of-fit is highly dependent on two outliers. While one of these matches the high-level predictions given in the introduction ("German" being more prone to intrusions), the other one points towards a conceptual weakness of the model ("Pastry" showing many intrusions in the empirical data although having just a few inlinks). The "Pastry" intrusions happened during trials with the target recipes baked apples ("Bratäpfel") and baked bananas ("Gebackene Bananen"). One could speculate that those recipes have primed the type-of-dish attribute that is linked to baking. This kind of semantic priming is currently not covered by our system. We are planning to integrate more sophisticated models of long-term memory [20] to allow dynamic priming between concepts as well.

Besides the conceptual findings, our ontology-backed cognitive model also provides benefits to applied domains. With its ability to interact with arbitrary HTML applications, the model could be used for automatic usability evaluation of user interfaces. Its ability to predict omissions and intrusions could be used to spot badly labeled UI elements during early development stages.

Acknowledgments. We gratefully acknowledge financial support from the German Research Foundation (DFG) for the project "Automatische Usability-Evaluierung modellbasierter Interaktionssysteme für Ambient Assisted Living" (AL-561/13-1).

References

1. Altmann, E.M., Trafton, J.G.: Memory for goals: An activation-based model. Cognitive Science **26**(1), 39–83 (2002)
2. Anderson, J.R., Bothell, D., Byrne, M.D., Douglass, S., Lebiere, C., Qin, Y.: An integrated theory of the mind. Psychological Review **111**(4), 1036–1060 (2004)
3. Anderson, J.R., Lebiere, C.: The Newell test for a theory of cognition. Behavioral and Brain Sciences **26**(05), 587–601 (2003)
4. Bates, D., Maechler, M., Bolker, B., Walker, S.: lme4: Linear mixed-effects models using Eigen and S4 (2013), r package version 1.0-5
5. Brysbaert, M., Buchmeier, M., Conrad, M., Jacobs, A.M., Bölte, J., Böhl, A.: The word frequency effect: A review of recent developments and implications for the choice of frequency estimates in German. Experimental Psychology **58**(5), 412 (2011)
6. Douglass, S., Ball, J., Rodgers, S.: Large declarative memories in ACT-R. Tech. rep., Manchester, UK (2009)
7. Emond, B.: WN-LEXICAL: An ACT-R module built from the WordNet lexical database. In: Proceedings of the Seventh International Conference on Cognitive Modeling (2006)
8. Fellbaum, C.: Wordnet. In: Poli, R., Healy, M., Kameas, A. (eds.) Theory and Applications of Ontology: Computer Applications, pp. 231–243. Springer, Dordrecht (2010)
9. Fitts, P.M.: The information capacity of the human motor system in controlling the amplitude of movement. Journal of Experimental Psychology **47**(6), 381–391 (1954)
10. Fu, W.T., Pirolli, P.: SNIF-ACT: A cognitive model of user navigation on the world wide web. Human-Computer Interaction **22**, 355–412 (2007)
11. Halbrügge, M.: ACT-CV: Bridging the gap between cognitive models and the outer world. In: Brandenburg, E., Doria, L., Gross, A., Günzlera, T., Smieszek, H. (eds.) Grundlagen und Anwendungen der Mensch-Maschine-Interaktion, pp. 205–210. Universitätsverlag der TU Berlin, Berlin (2013)
12. Halbrügge, M., Quade, M., Engelbrecht, K.P.: A predictive model of human error based on user interface development models and a cognitive architecture. In: Taatgen, N.A., van Vugt, M.K., Borst, J.P., Mehlhorn, K. (eds.) Proceedings of the 13th International Conference on Cognitive Modeling, pp. 238–243. University of Groningen, Groningen (2015)
13. Laird, J.: The Soar cognitive architecture. MIT Press, Cambridge (2012)
14. Lehmann, J., Isele, R., Jakob, M., Jentzsch, A., Kontokostas, D., Mendes, P.N., Hellmann, S., Morsey, M., van Kleef, P., Auer, S., Bizer, C.: DBpedia - a large-scale, multilingual knowledge base extracted from wikipedia. Semantic Web Journal (2014)
15. Norman, D.A.: Slips of the mind and an outline for a theory of action. Tech. rep., Center for Human Information Processing, San Diego, CA (1979)
16. Oltramari, A., Lebiere, C.: Extending Cognitive Architectures with Semantic Resources. In: Schmidhuber, J., Thórisson, K.R., Looks, M. (eds.) AGI 2011. LNCS, vol. 6830, pp. 222–231. Springer, Heidelberg (2011)

17. Rasmussen, J.: Skills, rules, and knowledge; signals, signs, and symbols, and other distinctions in human performance models. IEEE Transactions on Systems, Man and Cybernetics **13**, 257–266 (1983)
18. Reason, J.: Human Error. Cambridge University Press, New York (1990)
19. Salvucci, D.D.: Endowing a cognitive architecture with world knowledge. In: Bello, P., Guarini, M., McShane, M., Scassellati, B. (eds.) Proc. CogSci 2014, pp. 1353–1358 (2014)
20. Schultheis, H., Barkowsky, T., Bertel, S.: LTM C - an improved long-term memory for cognitive architectures. In: Proceedings of the Seventh International Conference on Cognitive Modeling, pp. 274–279 (2006)

C-Tests Revisited: Back and Forth with Complexity

José Hernández-Orallo[✉]

DSIC, Universitat Politècnica de València, Valencia, Spain
jorallo@dsic.upv.es

Abstract. We explore the aggregation of tasks by weighting them using a difficulty function that depends on the complexity of the (acceptable) policy for the task (instead of a universal distribution over tasks or an adaptive test). The resulting aggregations and decompositions are (now retrospectively) seen as the natural (and trivial) interactive generalisation of the C-tests.

Keywords: Intelligence evaluation · Artificial intelligence · C-tests · Algorithmic information theory · Universal psychometrics · Agent response curve

1 Introduction

A first test using algorithmic information theory (AIT) was the C-test [2,9], where the goal was to find a continuation of a sequence of letters, as in some IQ tasks , and in the spirit of Solomonoff's inductive inference problems: "given an initial segment of a sequence, predict its continuation" (as quoted in [12, p.332]). Levin's Kt complexity (see, e.g., [12, sec.7.5]) was used to calculate the difficulty of a sequence of letters. The performance was measured as an aggregated value over a range of difficulties:

$$I(\pi) \triangleq \sum_{h=1}^{H} h^e \sum_{i=1}^{N} \frac{1}{N} \operatorname{Hit}(\pi, x_{i,h}) \tag{1}$$

where π is the subject, the difficulties range from $h = 1$ to H and there are N sequences $x_{i,k}$ per difficulty h. The function hit returns 1 if π is right with the continuation and 0 otherwise. If $e = 0$ we have that all difficulties have the same weight. The N sequences per difficulty were chosen (uniformly) randomly.

This contrasts with a more common evaluation in artificial intelligence based on average-case performance according to a probability of problems or tasks:

$$\Psi(\pi) \triangleq \sum_{\mu \in M} p(\mu) \cdot \mathbb{E}[R(\pi, \mu)] \tag{2}$$

where p is a probability distribution on the set of tasks M, and R is a result function of agent π on task μ. Actually, eq. 2 can also be combined with AIT,

© Springer International Publishing Switzerland 2015
J. Bieger (Ed.): AGI 2015, LNAI 9205, pp. 272–282, 2015.
DOI: 10.1007/978-3-319-21365-1_28

in a different way, by using a universal distribution [12,14], i.e., $p(\mu) = 2^{-K(\mu)}$, where $K(\mu)$ is the Kolmogorov complexity of μ, as first chosen by [11].

The work in [11] has been considered a generalisation of [2,9], from static sequences (predicting a continuation of a sequence correctly) to dynamic environments. In this paper we challenge this interpretation and look for a proper generalisation of [2,9] using the notion of difficulty in the outer sum, as originally conceived and seen in eq. 1. The key idea is the realisation that for the C-test the task and the solution were the same thing. This meant that the difficulty was calculated as the size of the simplest program that generates the sequence, which is both the task and the solution. Even if the complexity of the task and the solution coincide here, it is *the complexity of the solution what determines the difficulty of the problem.*

However, when we move from sequences to environments or other kind of interactive tasks, the complexity of the policy that solves the task and the complexity of the environment are no longer the same. In fact, this is discussed in [6,7]: the complexity of the environment is roughly an upper bound of the complexity of the acceptable policies (any agent that reach an acceptable performance value), but very complex environments can have very simple acceptable policies. In fact, the choice of $p(\mu) = 2^{-K(\mu)}$ has been criticised for giving too much weight to a few environments. Also, it is important to note that the invariance theorem is more meaningful for Kolmogorov Complexity than for Algorithmic Probability, as for the former it gives some stability for values of K that are not very small, but for a probablity it is precisely the small cases that determine most of the distribution mass. In fact, for any computable distribution p there is a choice of a reference UTM that leads to a particular universal distribution that approximates p (to whatever required precision.This means that the choice of $p(\mu) = 2^{-K(\mu)}$ for Eq. 2 is actually a metadefinition, which leads to virtually any performance measure, depending on the Universal Turing Machine (UTM) that is chosen as reference.

By decoupling the complexity of task and policy we can go back to eq. 1 and work out a notion of difficulty of environments that depends on the complexity of the policy. While this may look retrospectively trivial, and the natural extension in hindsight, we need to solve and clarify some issues, and properly analyse the relation of the two different philosophies given by eq. 2 and eq. 1.

Section 2 discusses some previous work, introduces some notation and recovers the difficulty-based decomposition of aggregated performance. Section 3 introduces several properties about difficulty functions and the view of difficulty as policy complexity. Section 4 discusses the choices for the difficulty-dependent probability. Section 5 briefly deals with the role of computational steps for difficulty. Section 6 closes the paper with a discussion.

2   Background

AI evaluation has been performed in many different ways (for a recent account of AI evaluation, see [5]), but a common approach is based on averaging performance on a range of tasks, as in eq. 2.

$h = 9$: a, d, g, j, ...   Answer: m
$h = 12$: a, a, z, c, y, e, x, ...   Answer: g
$h = 14$: c, a, b, d, b, c, c, e, c, d, ... Answer: d

Fig. 1. Several series of different difficulties 9, 12, and 14 used in the C-test [2]

In what follows, we will focus on the approaches that are based on AIT. As mentioned above, the first intelligence test using AIT was the so-called C-test [2,9]. Figure 1 shows examples of sequences that appear in this test. The difficulty of each sequence was calculated as Levin's Kt, a time-weighted version of Kolmogorov complexity K. Some preliminary experimental results showed that human performance correlated with the absolute difficulty (h) of each exercise and also with IQ test results for the same subjects ([2,9]). They also show a clear inverse correlation of results with difficulty (see Figure 2). HitRatio is defined as the inner sum of eq. 1:

$$\text{HitRatio}(\pi, h) \triangleq \sum_{i=1}^{N} \frac{1}{N} \text{Hit}(\pi, x_{i,h}) \tag{3}$$

An interesting observation is that by arranging problems by difficulty we see that HitRatio seems to be very small from a given difficulty value (in the figure this is 8, but it can be any other, usually small, value). This makes the estimation of the measure much easier, as we only need to focus on (the area of) a small interval of difficulties. In fact, this use of difficulty is common in psychometrics.

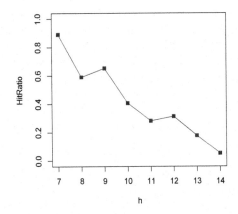

Fig. 2. Results obtained by humans on task of different difficulty in the C-test [2]

Several generalisations of the C-test were suggested (for "cognitive agents [...] with input/output devices for a complex environment" [9] where "rewards and penalties could be used instead" [4]) or extending them for other cognitive abilities [3], but not fully developed.

AIT and reinforcement learning were finally combined in [11], where all possible environments were considered in eq. 2, instantiated with a universal distribution for p, i.e., $p(\mu) = 2^{-K(\mu)}$, with $K(\mu)$ being the Kolmogorov complexity of each environment μ. Some problems (computability, discriminating power, over-weight for small environments, time, ...) were discussed with the aim of making a more applicable version of this appraoch by [10] and [7, secs. 3.3 and 4].

While the aim of all these proposals was to measure intelligence, many interesting things can happen if AIT is applied to cognitive abilities other than intelligence, as suggested in [3] for the passive case and hinted in [7, secs. 6.5 and 7.2] for the dynamic cases, which proposes the use of different kinds of videogames as environments (two of the most recently introduced benchmarks and competitions in AI are in this direction [1,13]).

We consider tests that are composed of tasks (also called environments or items) and are performed by agents (also called policies or subjects). The set of tasks is denoted by M. Its elements are usually denoted by μ. The set of agents is denoted by Π. Its elements are usually denoted by π. Both can be stochastic, i.e., they *can* use a probabilistic instruction or transition function. The length in bits of a string is denoted by $L(x)$. We can think of a proper encoding of tasks and agents as strings. Given a UTM U we define Kolmogorov complexity as $K_U(y) = \min_{x\,:\,U(x)=y} L(x)$. We will usually drop the subindex U. Finally, we have the expected value of the response, score or result of π in μ for a time limit τ as $\mathbb{E}[R(\pi,\mu,\tau)]$. The value of τ will be usually omitted. The R function always gives values between 0 and 1 and we assume it is always defined (a value of $R = 0$ is assumed for non-halting situations) We also define $\mathbb{E}[LS(\pi,\mu,\tau)] \triangleq L(\pi) + \log \mathbb{E}[S(\pi,\mu,\tau)]$. Logarithms are always binary.

It is actually in [8], where we can find a first connection between the schemas of eq. 1 and eq. 2. We adapt definition 14 in [8], which is a generalisation of eq. 2, by making the set M and the task probability p explicit as a parameters.

Definition 1. *The expected average result for a task class M, a distribution p and an agent π is:*

$$\Psi(\pi, M, p) \triangleq \sum_{\mu \in M} p(\mu) \cdot \mathbb{E}[R(\pi, \mu)] \tag{4}$$

And now we use proposition 4 in [8] that decomposes it. First, we define partial results for a given difficulty h as follows:

$$\Psi_h(\pi, M, p) \triangleq \sum_{\mu \in M, \hbar(\mu)=h} p(\mu|h) \cdot \mathbb{E}[R(\pi, \mu)] \tag{5}$$

Where $\hbar$ is a difficulty function $\hbar : M \to \mathbb{R}^+ \cup 0$. Note that this parametrises the result of eq. 4 for different difficulties. For instance, for two agents π_A and π_B we might have that $\Psi_3(\pi_A) < \Psi_3(\pi_B)$ but $\Psi_7(\pi_A) > \Psi_7(\pi_B)$. If we represent $\Psi_h(\pi, M, p)$ on the y-axis versus h on the x-axis we have a so-called agent response curve, much like Fig. 2.

If we want to get a single number from an agent response curve we can aggregate performance for a range of difficulties, e.g., as follows:

Proposition 1. *([8, prop.4]) The expected average result $\Psi(\pi, M, p)$ can be rewritten as follows: in the particular case when $\hbar$ only gives discrete values:*

$$\Psi(\pi, M, p) = \sum_{h=0}^{\infty} p(h)\Psi_h(\pi, M, p) \tag{6}$$

where $p(h)$ is a discrete probability function for eq. 6. Note that equations 4, 5 and 6 are generalisations, respectively, of equations 2, 3 and 1.

3   Difficulty Functions

Before setting an appropriate measure of difficulty based on the policy, in this section we will analyse which properties a difficulty function may have.

The decomposition in previous section suggests that we could try to fix a proper measure of difficulty first and then think about a meaningful distribution $p(h)$. Once this is settled, we could try to find a distribution for all environments of that difficulty $p(\mu|h)$. In other words, once we determine how relevant a difficulty is we ask which tasks to take for that difficulty. This is the spirit of the C-test [2,9] as seen in eq. 1. In fact, we perhaps we do not need a $p(h)$ that decays dramatically, as it is expectable to see performance to decrease for increasing difficulty, as in Figure 2.

To distinguish $p(h)$ and $p(\mu|h)$ we will denote the former with w and the latter with p_M. We will use any distribution or even a measure (not summing up to one, for reasons that we will see later on) as a subscript for Ψ. For instance, we will use the following notation $\Psi_{\mathcal{U}(h_{min}, h_{max})}(\pi, M, p_M)$, where $\mathcal{U}(a, b)$ represents a uniform distribution between a and b. For instance, we can have two agents π_A and π_B such that $\Psi_{\mathcal{U}(1,10)}(\pi_A) > \Psi_{\mathcal{U}(1,10)}(\pi_B)$ but $\Psi_{\mathcal{U}(11,20)}(\pi_A) < \Psi_{\mathcal{U}(11,20)}(\pi_B)$. We will use the notation $\Psi_{\oplus}(\pi, M, p_M)$ when $w(h) = 1$ (note that this is not the uniform distribution for discrete h), which means that the partial aggregations for each difficulty are just added. In other words, $\Psi_{\oplus}(\pi, M, p_M) \triangleq \sum_{h=0}^{\infty} \Psi_h(\pi, M, p_M)$ for discrete difficulty functions . We will explore whether this (area under the agent response curve) is bounded.

Figure 3 shows approach A, which has already been mentioned, while approaches B and C will be seen in sections 4.1 and 4.2 respectively.

When we aggregate environments with different scales on R and different difficulties, we may have that an agent focusses on a few environments with high difficulty while another focusses on many more environments with small responses. Agent response curves in [8], which are inspired by item response curves in psychometrics (but inverting the view between agents and items), allow us to see how each agent performs for different degrees of difficulty. Looking at Figure 2 and similar agent response curves in psychometrics, we see that the notion of difficulty must be linked to R, i.e., how well the agents perform, and not about the complexity of the task, as in the previous section.

Another option is what is done in [6], as $\hbar(\mu) \triangleq \min_{\pi:\mathbb{E}[R(\pi,\mu)]=R_{max}(\mu)} L(\pi)$ where $R_{max}(\mu) = \max_{\pi} \mathbb{E}[R(\pi, \mu)]$. However, R_{max} may be hard to calculate

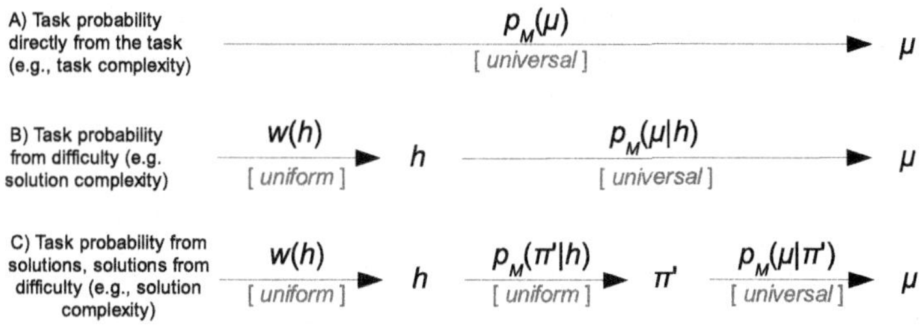

Fig. 3. Three approaches to aggregate the results for a set of tasks. Top (A) shows the classical approach of choosing a probability for the task, according to the properties of the task. Middle (B) shows the approach where we arrange tasks by difficulty, and the notion of difficulty is derived from the properties of the policy. Bottom (C) shows a variation of B where we derive acceptable policies for a given difficulty and then generate tasks for each policy. Between square brackets some choices we examine in this paper.

and even if it can be effectively calculated, any minor mistake or inefficiency in a very good agent will prevent the agent from reaching the optimal result, leading to a notion of difficulty linked to the complexity of the 'perfect' policy. In [6], a 'tolerance value' is considered and, instead of one policy, difficulty is linked to the probability of finding a policy under this tolerance.

We are going to consider this tolerance ϵ of acceptability.

$$\mathbb{A}^{[\epsilon]}(\pi,\mu) \triangleq \mathbf{1}(\mathbb{E}[R(\pi,\mu)] \geq 1 - \epsilon) \qquad (7)$$

This returns 1 if the expected response is above $1 - \epsilon$ and 0 otherwise. If $\mathbb{A}^{[\epsilon]}(\pi,\mu) = 1$ we say that π is ϵ-acceptable. With this, we binarise responses. One can argue that we could have just defined a binary R, but it is important to clarify that it is not the same to have tolerance for each single R (or a binarised R) than to have a tolerance for the expected value $\mathbb{E}[R]$. The tolerance on the expected value allows the agent to have variability in their results (e.g., stochastic agents) provided the expected value is higher than the tolerance. Finally, even if we will be very explicty about the value of ϵ, and changing it will change the difficulty value of any environment, it is important to say that this value is not so relevant. The reason is that for any environment we can build any other environment where the responses are transformed by any function. In fact, we could actually consider one fixed threshold, such as 0.5, always.

And now we can just define a new version of eq. 5 using this new function:

$$\Psi_h^{[\epsilon]}(\pi, M, p_M) \triangleq \sum_{\mu \in M, \hbar(\mu)=h} p_M(\mu|h) \cdot \mathbb{A}^{[\epsilon]}(\pi,\mu) \qquad (8)$$

We can just rewrite equations 6 accordingly:

$$\Psi_w^{[\epsilon]}(\pi, M, p_M) = \sum_{h=0}^{\infty} w(h)\Psi_h^{[\epsilon]}(\pi, M, p_M) \qquad (9)$$

Given the above, we are now ready for a few properties about difficulty functions.

Definition 2. *A difficulty function $\hbar$ is strongly bounded in M if for every π there is a difficulty h such that for every $\mu \in M : \hbar(\mu) \geq h$ we have $\mathbb{A}^{[\epsilon]}(\pi,\mu) = 0$.*

Now we choose the difficulty function in terms of ϵ-acceptability, i.e.:

$$\hbar^{[\epsilon]}(\mu) \triangleq \min\{L(\pi) : \mathbb{E}[R(\pi,\mu)] \geq 1 - \epsilon\} = \min\{L(\pi) : \mathbb{A}^{[\epsilon]}(\pi,\mu) = 1\} \quad (10)$$

We can say a few words about the cases where a truly random agent (choosing actions at random) gives an acceptable policy for an environment. If this is the case, we intuitively consider the environment easy. So, in terms, of L, we consider random agents to be simple, and goes well with our consideration of stochastic agents and environments having access to some true source of randomness.

Figure 4 (left) shows the distribution of response according to $L(\pi)$, but setting $\epsilon = 0.9$. We see that the simplest ϵ-acceptable policy has $L = 12$.

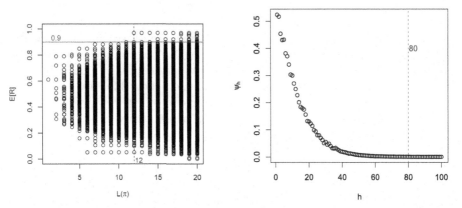

Fig. 4. Left: an illustrative distribution of responses of a population of agents for a single environment. If we set the threshold at $0.9 = 1 - \epsilon$, the simplest policy above this threshold is of 'complexity' $h = 12$. Right: an illustrative distribution of the result of Ψ_h considering a population of environments for a single agent, an *agent response curve*. There is no task π of difficulty above 80 for which $\mathbb{E}[R(\pi,\mu)] \geq 1 - \epsilon$, i.e., there is no task for which π is ϵ-acceptable, so Ψ_h is 0 from 80 on. If we were using the definition of $\hbar$ as for Eq. 10, this 80 would be $L(\pi)$. Also note on the right plot that all 'heaven' tasks (good results independently of what the agent does) are at $h = 1$, while all 'hell' tasks (bad response independently of what the agent does) are at $h = \infty$.

With the difficulty function in eq. 10 we have:

Proposition 2. *The difficulty function $\hbar^{[\epsilon]}$ in eq. 10 is strongly bounded.*

Proof. For every policy π, if a task μ has a difficulty $\hbar^{[\epsilon]}(\mu) > L(\pi)$, it means that π is not ϵ-acceptable, because otherwise the difficulty would be $L(\pi)$ and not h. Consequently, $\mathbb{A}^{[\epsilon]}(\pi,\mu) = 0$ for all μ of difficulty $\hbar^{[\epsilon]}(\mu) > L(\pi)$. It is sufficient to take $h > L(\pi)$ for every π to see that $\hbar$ is strongly bounded.

This is what we see in Fig. 4 (right), where $L(\pi) = 80$. With $\hbar^{[\epsilon]}$ in eq. 10, we can ensure that the values are going to be 0 from $h = 80$ on.

This may not be the case for other difficulty functions. We can imagine a situation where the curve never converges to zero. For instance, if the difficulty function is decoupled from resources (length and/or steps) of the acceptable policies or we do not use the notion of ϵ-acceptability then we cannot avoid that a very simple policy could eventually score well in a problem with very high difficulty. This would be counter-intuitive, as if there is a simple policy for a difficult problem, the latter should not be considered difficult any more.

4   Difficulty-Conditional Task Probabilities

In the previous sections we have focussed on $w(h)$ and whether it is necessary or not. We have seen difficulty functions where just aggregating Ψ_h without $w(h)$ (or $w(h) = 1$) leads to a $\Psi_\oplus(\pi, M, p_M)$ that is bounded. The question now is how to choose the conditional probability $p_M(\mu|h)$. In the C-test, eq. 1, this was chosen as a uniform distribution. However, this is not possible in an interactive scenario if we consider all possible tasks, as the number of tasks for which there is an acceptable policy π of $L(\pi) = n$ can be infinite. Even if we cannot set a uniform distribution, we want a choice of $p_M(\mu|h)$ that keeps the task diversity (unless there is any special bias to choose the tasks).

4.1   Task Probability Depends on Difficulty

The first thing we can do is to assume $p(\mu|h)$ in eq. 8 as $p(\mu|h) = \frac{2^{-K(\mu)}}{\nu(h)}$ if $\hbar^{[\epsilon]}(\mu) = h$ and 0 otherwise, where $\nu(h)$ is a normalisation term to make the mass of the distribution equal to 1, which can be formulated as $\nu(h) = \sum_{\mu:\hbar^{[\epsilon]}(\mu)=h} 2^{-K(\mu)}$.

And now we have:

$$\Psi_h^{[\epsilon]}(\pi, M, p_M) = \sum_{\mu \in M, \hbar^{[\epsilon]}(\mu)=h} p_M(\mu|h) \cdot \mathbb{A}^{[\epsilon]}(\pi, \mu) = \frac{1}{\nu(h)} \sum_{\mu \in M, \hbar^{[\epsilon]}(\mu)=h} 2^{-K(\mu)} \cdot \mathbb{A}^{[\epsilon]}(\pi, \mu)$$

From here, we can plug it into eq. 9 for the discrete case:

$$\Psi_w^{[\epsilon]}(\pi, M, p_M) = \sum_{h=0}^{\infty} w(h) \frac{1}{\nu(h)} \sum_{\mu \in M, \hbar^{[\epsilon]}(\mu)=h} 2^{-K(\mu)} \cdot \mathbb{A}^{[\epsilon]}(\pi, \mu) \qquad (11)$$

Note that the above is going to be bounded independently of the difficulty function if w is a probability distribution. Also notice that $\frac{1}{\nu(h)}$ is on the outer sum, and that $\nu(h)$ is lower than 1, so the normalisation term is actually greater than 1.

And if we use any of the difficulty functions in equations 10 we can choose $w(h) = 1$ and $\Psi_\oplus^{[\epsilon]}(\pi, M, p_M)$ is bounded.

4.2   Task Probability Depends on the Policy Probability

One of things of the use of equation 10 is that the number of acceptable policies per difficulty is finite. This is what happened in the C-test and that is the reason why a uniform distribution could be used for the inner sum. We could try to decompose the inner sum by using the policy and get the probability of the task given the policy.

The interpretation would be as follows: for each difficulty value we aggregate all the acceptable policies with size equal to that difficulty uniformly and for each of these policies all the environments where each policy is acceptable with a universal distribution. This extra complication with respect to eq. 11 can only be justified if we generate environments and agents and we check them as we populate $Pairs$, as a way of constructing a test more easily.

5   Using Computational Steps

As we mentioned in the introduction, the C-test [2,9] used Levin's Kt instead of K. We explore the use of Kt here. However, when working with interactive tasks and with stochastic tasks and agents, the number of steps must be in expected value. We extend the definition of LS given in section 2 for a tolerance ϵ:

$$LS^{[\epsilon]}(\pi, \mu) \triangleq \mathbb{E}[LS(\pi, \mu)] \text{ if } \mathbb{A}^{[\epsilon]}(\pi, \mu) = 1 \text{ and } \infty \text{ otherwise}$$

and we define a new difficulty function that considers computational steps:

$$\hbar^{[\epsilon]}(\mu) \triangleq \min_{\pi} LS^{[\epsilon]}(\pi, \mu)$$

This difficulty function is not bounded, as LS depends on μ, and we can always find a very short policy that takes an enormous amount of steps for a task with very high difficulty. This is an acceptable policy, but does not reduce the difficulty of the task, so it can always score non-zero beyond any limit. This means that for this difficulty function we would need to use equation eq. 9 with an appropriate $w(h)$ (e.g., a small decay or a uniform interval of difficulties).

If the testing procedure established a limit on the number of steps (total or per transition) we would have this new difficulty function would be strongly bounded. Alternatively, we could reconsider the inclusion the computational steps in the notion of acceptability. In this case, the approach in section 4.2 could not be used, as the probability of π given h would also depend on μ.

6   Discussion

We have gone from eq. 1 taken from C-test to eq. 9. We have seen that difficulties allow for a more detailed analysis of what happens for a given agent, depending on whether it succeeds at easy or difficult tasks. For some difficulty functions, we do not even need to determine the weight for each difficulty and just calculate the area, as an aggregated performance for all difficulties, and cutting the tail at some maximum difficulty for practical reasons.

The important thing is that now we do not need to set an a priori distribution for all tasks $p(\mu)$, but just a conditional distribution $p(\mu|h)$. Note that if we set a high h we have the freedom to find simple task that creates that difficulty. Actually, the choice of $p(\mu|h)$ as a universal distribution still depends on the reference machine and can set most of the probability mass on smaller tasks, but as it is conditional on h, all trivial, dead or simply meaningless tasks have usually very extreme values of h (very low or infinite). That means that there is a range of *intersting* difficulties, discarding very small values of h and very large values of h. Figure 2 is a nice example of this, where only difficulties between 1 and 8 were used, and we see also that $h = 1$ and $h > 7$ are not really very discriminating. The bulk of the testing effort must be performed in this range.

Note that the middle (B) and bottom (C) decompositions in Figure 3 can be done in such a way that the original $p_M(\mu)$ is preserved, if $w(h)$ is not taken uniform but slowly decaying. But we can just start with option B or C directly. This is the alternative in this paper, which we think has several advantages in terms of agent evaluation, the construction of tests and AGI development, as we can focus on those tasks of appropriate difficulty and even define adaptive tests easily. Having said this, we have an infinite set for $p_M(\mu|h)$ and $p_M(\mu|\pi')$, and a universal distribution is the appropriate for both, so that Occam's razor is still very present. This means that both B and C (using a slowly decaying $w(h)$) would lead to a computable aggregated distribution $p_M(\mu)$, which can be approximated as a universal distribution, highlighting that universal intelligence is rather a schema for definitions rather than a specific definition.

Acknowledgments. This work has been partially supported by the EU (FEDER) and the Spanish MINECO under grants TIN 2010-21062-C02-02, PCIN-2013-037 and TIN 2013-45732-C4-1-P, and by Generalitat Valenciana PROMETEOII2015/013.

References

1. Bellemare, M.G., Naddaf, Y., Veness, J., Bowling, M.: The arcade learning environment: An evaluation platform for general agents. Journal of Artificial Intelligence Research **47**, 253–279 (2013)
2. Hernández-Orallo, J.: Beyond the Turing Test. J. Logic, Language & Information **9**(4), 447–466 (2000)
3. Hernández-Orallo, J.: Computational measures of information gain and reinforcement in inference processes. AI Communications **13**(1), 49–50 (2000)
4. Hernández-Orallo, J.: On the computational measurement of intelligence factors. In: Meystel, A. (ed.) Performance metrics for intelligent systems workshop, pp. 1–8. National Institute of Standards and Technology, Gaithersburg (2000)
5. Hernández-Orallo, J.: AI evaluation: past, present and future (2014). arXiv preprint arXiv:1408.6908
6. Hernández-Orallo, J.: On environment difficulty and discriminating power. Autonomous Agents and Multi-Agent Systems, 1–53 (2014). http://dx.doi.org/10.1007/s10458-014-9257-1

7. Hernández-Orallo, J., Dowe, D.L.: Measuring universal intelligence: Towards an anytime intelligence test. Artificial Intelligence **174**(18), 1508–1539 (2010)
8. Hernández-Orallo, J., Dowe, D.L., Hernández-Lloreda, M.V.: Universal psychometrics: Measuring cognitive abilities in the machine kingdom. Cognitive Systems Research **27**, 50–74 (2014)
9. Hernández-Orallo, J., Minaya-Collado, N.: A formal definition of intelligence based on an intensional variant of Kolmogorov complexity. In: Proc. Intl. Symposium of Engineering of Intelligent Systems (EIS 1998), pp. 146–163. ICSC Press (1998)
10. Hibbard, B.: Bias and no free lunch in formal measures of intelligence. Journal of Artificial General Intelligence **1**(1), 54–61 (2009)
11. Legg, S., Hutter, M.: Universal intelligence: A definition of machine intelligence. Minds and Machines **17**(4), 391–444 (2007)
12. Li, M., Vitányi, P.: An introduction to Kolmogorov complexity and its applications, 3 edn. Springer-Verlag (2008)
13. Schaul, T.: An extensible description language for video games. IEEE Transactions on Computational Intelligence and AI in Games **PP**(99), 1–1 (2014)
14. Solomonoff, R.J.: A formal theory of inductive inference. Part I. Information and control **7**(1), 1–22 (1964)

A New View on Grid Cells Beyond the Cognitive Map Hypothesis

Jochen Kerdels$^{(\boxtimes)}$ and Gabriele Peters

University of Hagen - Chair of Human-Computer Interaction,
Universitätsstrasse 1, 58097 Hagen, Germany
Jochen.Kerdels@FernUni-Hagen.de
http://mci.fernuni-hagen.de

Abstract. Grid cells in the entorhinal cortex are generally considered to be a central part of a path integration system supporting the construction of a *cognitive map* of the environment in the brain. Guided by this hypothesis existing computational models of grid cells provide a wide range of possible mechanisms to explain grid cell activity in this specific context. Here we present a complementary grid cell model that treats the observed grid cell behavior as an instance of a more abstract, general principle by which neurons in the higher-order parts of the cortex process information.

Keywords: Grid cell model · Higher-order information processing

1 Introduction

In 1948 Edward Tolman [36] reported on a series of behavioral experiments with rats that led him to hypothesize that the animals had to make use of an internal, map-like representation of the environment. This idea, which came to be known as the *cognitive map hypothesis*, was highly controversial at the time. Accordingly, the discovery of hippocampal *place cells* by O'Keefe and Dostrovsky [25,27] in the 1970s was met with much excitement as place cells were the first possible direct evidence for such a representation of the environment in the brain [26]. Since then a variety of neurons that exhibit spatially correlated activity were found in the parahippocampal-hippocampal region [11,13,15,32,35]. In particular the recent discovery of *grid cells* [11,13] in the entorhinal cortex of rat strengthened the idea that the involved neuronal structures constitute a kind of *metric for space* [23]. Grid cells are neurons that exhibit spatially correlated activity similar to that of place cells with the distinct difference that grid cells possess not just one but multiple, discrete firing fields that are arranged in a regular, hexagonal grid that spans the entire environment (Fig. 1a). Located just one synapse upstream of the hippocampus grid cells are assumed to be an important source of spatial information to place cells [29,33]. In particular, grid cells are generally considered to be a central part of a path integration system as pointed out by Burgess [5]: *"There has been a surprising rapid and general*

© Springer International Publishing Switzerland 2015
J. Bieger (Ed.): AGI 2015, LNAI 9205, pp. 283–292, 2015.
DOI: 10.1007/978-3-319-21365-1_29

agreement that the computational problem to which grid cells provide a solution is "path integration" within an allocentric reference frame." This consensus is reflected by the fact that all computational models of grid cells proposed so far (except [19]) incorporate mechanisms of path integration as integral parts to explain the hexagonal firing patterns of grid cells. Although existing computational models cover a wide range of possible mechanisms and focus on different aspects of grid cell activity [2,4,12,23,24,38], the models share the common approach of explaining grid cells and their behavior as functional components within the cognitive map hypothesis.

Complementary to this common approach this paper presents an alternative grid cell model that treats the observed grid cell behavior as an instance of a more abstract, general principle by which neurons in the higher-order parts of the cortex process information.

2   Model Description

To describe the behavior of grid cells at a more abstract level a computational model is needed that is agnostic to the semantic interpretation of its own state and its respective input space such that the model can provide an explanation of the cell's behavior that does not rely on assumptions based on the putative purpose of that cell, e.g., performing path integration or representing a coordinate system. This way, the observed behavior of grid cells can be treated as just one instance of a more general information processing scheme. To this end we propose to interpret the input signals that a grid cell receives within a small time window as a single sample from a high-dimensional input space. This input space represents all possible inputs to the grid cell and for a certain subset of these inputs, i.e., for inputs from certain regions of that input space the grid cell will fire. The problem of modeling grid cell behavior can then be split into two independent sub-problems. The first problem addresses the question how a cell, given an *arbitrary* input space, chooses the regions of input space for which it will fire. The second problem addresses the question how a *specific* input space has to be structured in order to evoke the actual firing pattern observed in, e.g, grid cells. This paper focuses on the first problem and will touch upon the second problem just briefly.

The most salient feature of grid cells is their firing pattern. The triangular structure resembles the outcome of a number of processes that typically perform some form of error minimization, e.g., the hexagonal packing of circles [37], the Delaunay triangulation [3,7], or certain kinds of *topology representing networks* [20]. The latter are artificial neural networks that employ forms of *unsupervised competitive learning* to discover the structure of an underlying input space. Among those networks the *growing neural gas* (GNG) introduced by Fritzke [9,10] stands out as it does not use a predetermined and fixed network topology like, e.g., the well-known self-organizing map (SOM) [18] does. Instead, the GNG uses a data-driven growth process to approximate the topology of the underlying input space resulting in an *induced Delaunay triangulation*

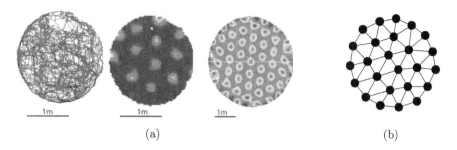

Fig. 1. Comparison of a grid cell firing pattern with a growing neural gas (GNG) network. **(a)** Typical visualization of a grid cell's firing pattern as introduced by Hafting et al. [13]. **Left**: trajoctory (black lines) of a rat in a circular environment with marked locations (red dots) where the observed grid cell fired. **Middle**: color-coded firing rate map of the observed grid cell ranging from dark blue (no activity) to red (maximum activity). **Right**: color-coded spatial autocorrelation of the firing rate map ranging from blue (negativ correlation, -1) to red (positive correlation, +1) highlighting the hexagonal structure of the firing pattern. Figure from Moser et al. [23]. **(b)** Example of a GNG network with 25 units that was fed with inputs from a uniformly distributed, two-dimensional, circular input space. The resulting network forms an *induced Delaunay triangulation* of the input space.

of that space. Figure 1b shows an example of a GNG network approximating a uniformly distributed, two-dimensional, circular input space. Each GNG unit marks the center of a convex polyhedron representing a local region of this input space. The *relative* size of this region is inversely proportional to the probability of an input originating from that region, i.e., the local *density* of the input space. In addition, the *absolute* size of each local region is determined by the overall number of GNG units that are available to cover the whole input space. The network structure of the GNG, which relates the respective local regions to one another, represents the input space topology.

Given the resemblance between the structure of grid cell firing patterns and the structure of GNG networks for certain input spaces we propose that a *single* grid cell performs an operation that is similar to that of a *whole* GNG, i.e., it is proposed that the objective of a grid cell lies in the approximation of its *entire* input space. This hypothesis differs strongly from the common interpretation of GNGs where the GNG units correspond to individual neurons that each specialize to represent a *single*, specific region of input space. In contrast, this new hypothesis implies that a single neuron represents not only one but *several*, distinct regions of input space. To accomplish this a single neuron would have to recognize several different input patterns. Recent advances in imaging neuronal activity [6,14] indicate that this is indeed the case.

In addition to their peculiar firing pattern, grid cells exhibit a modular organization in which the firing patterns of neighboring grid cells share a common orientation, spacing, and field size [34]. Furthermore, the distribution of relative grid phases is uniform within each module. To account for these properties we

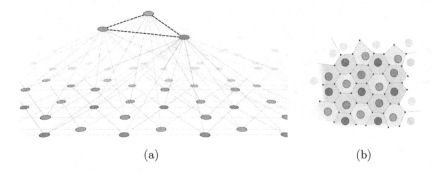

$$(a) \hspace{5cm} (b)$$

Fig. 2. Illustration of the proposed two-layer model. (a) The top layer is represented by three units (red, green, blue) connected by dashed lines. The associated sets of connected nodes in the bottom layer are illustrated by corresponding colors. (b) Top view on the input space partition induced by the bottom layer sets of nodes.

propose to describe a group of grid cells by a two-layer model[1]. The top layer contains a set of connected units that each represent an individual grid cell. Associated with each top layer unit is a set of connected nodes in the bottom layer representing the set of input patterns that are recognized by the dendritic tree of the grid cell (Fig. 2a). To this end, each node in the bottom layer possesses a *prototype* vector that represents the center of a local input space region. Applying a form of competitive hebbian learning *within* each set of bottom layer nodes (bottom layer competition) arranges the nodes in a triangular pattern that covers the entire input space. In addition, competition *across* the sets of bottom layer nodes (top layer competition) arranges the different triangular patterns in such a way that they share a common orientation and spacing. Furthermore, the top layer competition will also spread the individual triangular patterns uniformly across the input space (Fig. 2b).

Formally, the proposed model consists of a set of units $u \in U$ and a set of connections $c \in C$ located in the top layer, as well as a set of parameters θ. Each connection c is described by a tuple:

$$c := (P, t) \in C, \quad P \subseteq U \wedge |P| = 2, \quad t \in \mathbb{N},$$

with units $p \in P$ linked by the connection and the connection's *age* t. Each unit u is described by a tuple:

$$u := (V, E) \in U,$$

containing a set of nodes $v \in V$ and a set of edges $e \in E$ located in the bottom layer. Each node v is described by a tuple:

$$v := (w, a_{\mathrm{err}}, \epsilon_{\mathrm{ref}}) \in V, \quad w \in \mathbb{R}^n, \quad a_{\mathrm{err}} \in \mathbb{R}, \quad \epsilon_{\mathrm{ref}} \in \mathbb{R},$$

---

[1] A preliminary version of this idea was presented by Kerdels and Peters [16].

with the *prototype* w, the *accumulated error* a_{err}, and a refractory factor ϵ_{ref}. Each edge e is described by a tuple:

$$e := (S, t) \in E, \quad S \subseteq V \wedge |S| = 2, \quad t \in \mathbb{N},$$

with nodes $s \in S$ linked by the edge and the edge's *age* t. The set of parameters θ consists of:

$$\theta := \{\epsilon_b, \epsilon_n, \epsilon_r, \tau_t, M_t, \epsilon_{\text{b.start}}, \epsilon_{\text{b.end}}, \epsilon_{\text{n.start}}, \epsilon_{\text{n.end}}, \tau_b, M_b, \lambda, \alpha, \beta, \gamma, t_r\}.$$

The model is initialized with M_t fully connected top level units u each starting with two nodes v that have random prototype vectors as well as accumulated errors and refractory factors set to zero. An input $\xi \in \mathbb{R}^n$ at time t is processed as follows:

- For each top layer unit $u \in U$:
  - Find the two nodes s_1 and s_2 in $u.V$ whose prototypes w have the smallest Euclidian distance to the input ξ. Node s_1 is called the *best matching unit* (BMU) of u.
  - Increment the age t of all edges connected to s_1 by one.
  - If no edge between s_1 and s_2 exists, create one.
  - Reset the age t of the edge between s_1 and s_2 to zero.
  - Add the squared distance between ξ and the prototype w of s_1 to the accumulated error a_{err} of s_1.
  - Adapt the prototype of s_1 and all prototypes of its direct neighbors:

$$s_1^{t+1}.w := s_1^t.w + \epsilon_b^t \left(1 - s_1^t.\epsilon_{\text{ref}}\right) \left(\xi - s_1^t.w\right),$$
$$s_n^{t+1}.w := s_n^t.w + \epsilon_n^t \left(1 - s_1^t.\epsilon_{\text{ref}}\right) \left(\xi - s_n^t.w\right),$$

    with

$$\epsilon_b^t := \epsilon_{\text{b.start}} \left(\frac{\epsilon_{\text{b.end}}}{\epsilon_{\text{b.start}}}\right)^{\frac{t}{t_r}}, \quad \epsilon_n^t := \epsilon_{\text{n.start}} \left(\frac{\epsilon_{\text{n.end}}}{\epsilon_{\text{n.start}}}\right)^{\frac{t}{t_r}},$$

$$s_n \in \{k | \exists (S, t) \in E, \ S = \{s_1, k\}, \ t \in \mathbb{N}\}.$$

  - Set the refractory factor ϵ_{ref} of s_1 to one.
  - Remove all edges with an age above threshold τ_b and remove all nodes that no longer have any edges connected to them.
  - If an integer-multiple of λ inputs has been processed and $|u.V| < M_b$, add a new node v. The new node is inserted "between" the node j with the largest accumulated error a_{err} and the node k with the largest accumulated error among the direct neighbors of j. Thus, the prototype w of the new node is initialized as:

$$v.w := (j.w + k.w)/2.$$

The existing edge between nodes j and k is removed and edges between nodes j and v as well as nodes v and k are added. The accumulated

errors of nodes j and k are decreased and the accumulated error of the
new node v is set to the decreased accumulated error of node j:

$$\Delta j \boldsymbol{.} a_{\mathrm{err}} = -\alpha j \boldsymbol{.} a_{\mathrm{err}}, \quad \Delta k \boldsymbol{.} a_{\mathrm{err}} = -\alpha k \boldsymbol{.} a_{\mathrm{err}},$$

$$v \boldsymbol{.} a_{\mathrm{err}} := j \boldsymbol{.} a_{\mathrm{err}} \ .$$

- Finally, decrease the accumulated error of all nodes as well as their refractory factors:

$$\Delta v \boldsymbol{.} a_{\mathrm{err}} = -\beta \, v \boldsymbol{.} a_{\mathrm{err}},$$

$$\Delta v \boldsymbol{.} \epsilon_{\mathrm{ref}} = -\gamma \, v \boldsymbol{.} \epsilon_{\mathrm{ref}}, \quad \forall v \in V.$$

- Identify the two units u_1 and u_2 whose BMUs were closest to input ξ.
- Increment the age t of all connections to u_1 by one.
- If no connection between u_1 and u_2 exists, create one.
- Reset the age t of the connection between u_1 and u_2 to zero.
- Adapt the BMUs of u_1 and u_2 as well as their neighbors:

$$u_1 \boldsymbol{.} s_1^{t+1} \boldsymbol{.} w := u_1 \boldsymbol{.} s_1^t \boldsymbol{.} w + \epsilon_b \left(\xi - u_1 \boldsymbol{.} s_1^t \boldsymbol{.} w \right),$$

$$u_1 \boldsymbol{.} s_n^{t+1} \boldsymbol{.} w := u_1 \boldsymbol{.} s_n^t \boldsymbol{.} w + \epsilon_b \epsilon_r \left(\xi - u_1 \boldsymbol{.} s_n^t \boldsymbol{.} w \right),$$

$$u_2 \boldsymbol{.} s_1^{t+1} \boldsymbol{.} w := u_2 \boldsymbol{.} s_1^t \boldsymbol{.} w + \epsilon_n \left(\xi - u_2 \boldsymbol{.} s_1^t \boldsymbol{.} w \right),$$

$$u_2 \boldsymbol{.} s_n^{t+1} \boldsymbol{.} w := u_2 \boldsymbol{.} s_n^t \boldsymbol{.} w + \epsilon_n \epsilon_r \left(\xi - u_2 \boldsymbol{.} s_n^t \boldsymbol{.} w \right).$$

- Remove all edges with an age above threshold τ_t.

In the present model each set of bottom layer nodes behaves essentially like
a growing neural gas. To accommodate sequential input, e.g., a sequence of
animal positions, the original GNG algorithm [9,10] is extended by a successive
reduction of the learning rates ϵ_b and ϵ_n to capture a more uniform distribution
of inputs, as well as a refractory factor ϵ_{ref} that reduces the impact of equal or
similar consecutive inputs. The connected top layer units track the neighborhood
relations of the corresponding bottom layer node sets. The additional adaption
step of the top layer establishes a competition across the bottom layer node sets
resulting in an even distribution and alignment of these sets.

3 Example of Grid Cell Activity

To generate a grid like firing pattern, the proposed model requires an input
space that is a uniformly distributed, two-dimensional, periodic representation
of possible animal locations. A possible neuronal mechanism that results in a
representation of location with these properties consists of two orthogonal, one-
dimensional attractor networks. Attractor networks were first introduced as a
computational model of *head direction* cells [39] and later used in models of
place and grid cells [21,22,28]. Here we use two orthogonal, one-dimensional
attractor networks as described in a previous work [16]. During an initial learning
phase the model is fed with randomly generated locations. After the model has
settled into a stable configuration, recorded movement data provided by Sargolini

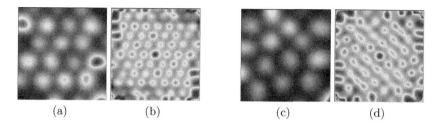

(a)   (b)   (c)   (d)

Fig. 3. Exemplary rate and autocorrelation maps of simulated grid cells. (**a,b**) Simulated grid cell with 20 bottom layer nodes. (**c,d**) Simulated grid cell with 16 bottom layer nodes.

et al. [31] of a rat foraging for food in a square environment is used. Figure 3 shows exemplary rate and autocorrelation maps of two top layer units with either 16 or 20 bottom layer nodes exhibiting grid like firing patterns. In this example, the following set of parameters θ was used:

$$\epsilon_b \quad = 0.05, \quad \epsilon_n \quad = 0.005, \ \epsilon_r \quad = 0.001, \ \tau_t \quad = 1000, \quad M_t = 50,$$
$$\epsilon_{b.\text{start}} = 0.05, \quad \epsilon_{b.\text{end}} = 0.0005, \ \epsilon_{n.\text{start}} = 0.01, \quad \epsilon_{n.\text{end}} = 0.0001, \ \tau_b \quad = 300,$$
$$M_b \quad = \{16, 20\}, \ \lambda \quad = 1000, \quad \alpha \quad = 0.5, \quad \beta \quad = 0.0005, \ \gamma \quad = 0.2,$$
$$t_r \quad = 500000.$$

4 Discussion

The proposed model describes a putative general principle by which neurons in higher-order parts of the cortex process information of arbitrary input spaces:

> Each neuron aspires to represent its input space as well as possible while being in competition with its peers.

This assumed behavior contrast the behavior of "classic" perceptrons [30] in interesting ways. A perceptron can be interpreted as a linear classifier where the input weights define a hyperplane that divides the input space into two regions. The output of the activation function then indicates from which of the two regions the respective input pattern originated. Combining the output of several perceptrons successively divides the input space into a smaller and smaller subregion (Fig. 4a). In contrast, the top layer units of our model compete with each other and generate a tiled, periodic partition of the input space (Fig. 2b). If the output of top layer units from *separate* neuron groups or modules with *different* spatial scales and/or orientations is combined, they can collectively identify a specific, individual subregion of the input space by coinciding only in that region (Fig. 4b). In case of grid cells, this mechanism was successfully used to explain the formation of place cells from grid cell activity [1,8,29,33].

Fig. 4. Comparison of strategies to identify specific subregions in input space. (**a**) Multiple perceptrons successively partition the input space to identify a specific subregion (the middle triangle). (**b**) Top layer units from *separate* grid cell groups with *different* spatial scales identify a specific subregion by coinciding in that region.

Both, a population of perceptrons as well as a population of top layer units in our model represent a form of input space encoding that allows to identify individual subregions of input space. The use of periodic input space partitions as basic elements of such an encoding may have a number of advantages over a linear partition of input space:

- Representing the entire input space in each neuron averages the activity of all neurons in a group independently of the particular input and may be metabolically beneficial.
- Sequences of inputs are split into repeating subsequences. For example, if a rat runs in a given direction, a small number of grid cells will be activated in sequence repeatedly increasing the probability that this subsequence will be learned.
- If a set of periodic input space partitions across several spatial scales identifies a specific region of input space, the size of this region depends on which subset of partitions are choosen.

In particular the latter two points require further investigation, as they may yield new approaches to the problem of learning complex sequences and to the problem of learning hierarchical representations.

5   Conclusion and Outlook

We presented a computational model that can explain the behavior of grid cells in terms of two independent sub-problems: the information processing performed by the cells and the structure of their input space. We argue that neurons in higher-order parts of the cortex pursue a general information processing scheme in which the neurons try to represent their input space as well as possible. In future research, we will investigate if this general information processing scheme can be used to explain the behavior of neurons other than grid cells. For example,

Killian et al. [17] report on entorhinal neurons with grid-like firing patterns in response to saccadic eye movements.

References

1. Azizi, A.H., Schieferstein, N., Cheng, S.: The transformation from grid cells to place cells is robust to noise in the grid pattern. Hippocampus **24**(8), 912–919 (2014)
2. Barry, C., Burgess, N.: Neural mechanisms of self-location. Current Biology **24**(8), R330–R339 (2014)
3. de Berg, M., Cheong, O., van Kreveld, M., Overmars, M.: Computational Geometry: Algorithms and Applications. Springer (2008)
4. Burak, Y.: Spatial coding and attractor dynamics of grid cells in the entorhinal cortex. Current Opinion in Neurobiology **25**, 169–175 (2014), theoretical and computational neuroscience
5. Burgess, N.: Grid cells and theta as oscillatory interference: Theory and predictions. Hippocampus **18**(12), 1157–1174 (2008)
6. Chen, T.W., Wardill, T.J., Sun, Y., Pulver, S.R., Renninger, S.L., Baohan, A., Schreiter, E.R., Kerr, R.A., Orger, M.B., Jayaraman, V., Looger, L.L., Svoboda, K., Kim, D.S.: Ultrasensitive fluorescent proteins for imaging neuronal activity. Nature **499**(7458), 295–300 (2013)
7. Delaunay, B.: Sur la sphère vide. Bull. Acad. Sci. URSS **1934**(6), 793–800 (1934)
8. Franzius, M., Vollgraf, R., Wiskott, L.: From grids to places. Journal of Computational Neuroscience **22**(3), 297–299 (2007)
9. Fritzke, B.: Unsupervised ontogenetic networks. In: Fiesler, E., Beale, R. (eds.) Handbook of Neural Computation. Institute of Physics Publishing and Oxford University Press (1996)
10. Fritzke, B.: A growing neural gas network learns topologies. In: Advances in Neural Information Processing Systems, vol. 7, pp. 625–632. MIT Press (1995)
11. Fyhn, M., Molden, S., Witter, M.P., Moser, E.I., Moser, M.B.: Spatial representation in the entorhinal cortex. Science **305**(5688), 1258–1264 (2004)
12. Giocomo, L., Moser, M.B., Moser, E.: Computational models of grid cells. Neuron **71**(4), 589–603 (2011)
13. Hafting, T., Fyhn, M., Molden, S., Moser, M.B., Moser, E.I.: Microstructure of a spatial map in the entorhinal cortex. Nature **436**(7052), 801–806 (2005)
14. Jia, H., Rochefort, N.L., Chen, X., Konnerth, A.: Dendritic organization of sensory input to cortical neurons in vivo. Nature **464**(7293), 1307–1312 (2010)
15. Jung, M.W., McNaughton, B.L.: Spatial selectivity of unit activity in the hippocampal granular layer. Hippocampus **3**(2), 165–182 (1993)
16. Kerdels, J., Peters, G.: A computational model of grid cells based on dendritic self-organized learning. In: Proceedings of the International Conference on Neural Computation Theory and Applications (2013)
17. Killian, N.J., Jutras, M.J., Buffalo, E.A.: A map of visual space in the primate entorhinal cortex. Nature **491**(7426), 761–764 (11 2012)
18. Kohonen, T.: Self-organized formation of topologically correct feature maps. Biological Cybernetics **43**(1), 59–69 (1982)
19. Kropff, E., Treves, A.: The emergence of grid cells: Intelligent design or just adaptation? Hippocampus **18**(12), 1256–1269 (2008)

20. Martinetz, T.M., Schulten, K.: Topology representing networks. Neural Networks **7**, 507–522 (1994)

21. McNaughton, B.L., Battaglia, F.P., Jensen, O., Moser, E.I., Moser, M.B.: Path integration and the neural basis of the 'cognitive map'. Nat. Rev. Neurosci. **7**(8), 663–678 (2006)

22. Mhatre, H., Gorchetchnikov, A., Grossberg, S.: Grid cell hexagonal patterns formed by fast self-organized learning within entorhinal cortex (published online 2010). Hippocampus **22**(2), 320–334 (2010)

23. Moser, E.I., Moser, M.B.: A metric for space. Hippocampus **18**(12), 1142–1156 (2008)

24. Moser, E.I., Moser, M.B., Roudi, Y.: Network mechanisms of grid cells. Philosophical Transactions of the Royal Society B: Biological Sciences 369(1635) (2014)

25. O'Keefe, J., Dostrovsky, J.: The hippocampus as a spatial map. preliminary evidence from unit activity in the freely-moving rat. Brain Research **34**(1), 171–175 (1971)

26. O'Keefe, J., Nadel, L.: The Hippocampus as a Cognitive Map. Oxford University Press, Oxford (1978)

27. O'Keefe, J.: Place units in the hippocampus of the freely moving rat. Experimental Neurology **51**(1), 78–109 (1976)

28. Pilly, P.K., Grossberg, S.: How do spatial learning and memory occur in the brain? coordinated learning of entorhinal grid cells and hippocampal place cells. J. Cognitive Neuroscience, 1031–1054 (2012)

29. Rolls, E.T., Stringer, S.M., Elliot, T.: Entorhinal cortex grid cells can map to hippocampal place cells by competitive learning. Network: Computation in Neural Systems **17**(4), 447–465 (2006)

30. Rosenblatt, F.: The perceptron: A probabilistic model for information storage and organization in the brain. Psychological Review **65**(6), 386–408 (1958)

31. Sargolini, F., Fyhn, M., Hafting, T., McNaughton, B.L., Witter, M.P., Moser, M.B., Moser, E.I.: Conjunctive representation of position, direction, and velocity in entorhinal cortex. Science **312**(5774), 758–762 (2006)

32. Solstad, T., Boccara, C.N., Kropff, E., Moser, M.B., Moser, E.I.: Representation of geometric borders in the entorhinal cortex. Science **322**(5909), 1865–1868 (2008)

33. Solstad, T., Moser, E.I., Einevoll, G.T.: From grid cells to place cells: A mathematical model. Hippocampus **16**(12), 1026–1031 (2006)

34. Stensola, H., Stensola, T., Solstad, T., Froland, K., Moser, M.B., Moser, E.I.: The entorhinal grid map is discretized. Nature **492**(7427), 72–78 (2012)

35. Taube, J., Muller, R., Ranck, J.: Head-direction cells recorded from the postsubiculum in freely moving rats. i. description and quantitative analysis. The Journal of Neuroscience **10**(2), 420–435 (1990)

36. Tolman, E.C.: Cognitive maps in rats and men. Psychological Review **55**, 189–208 (1948)

37. Tóth, L.: Lagerungen in der Ebene: auf der Kugel und im Raum. Die Grundlehren der Mathematischen Wissenschaften in Einzeldarstellungen mit besonderer Berücksichtigung der Anwendungsgebiete. Springer (1972)

38. Welinder, P.E., Burak, Y., Fiete, I.R.: Grid cells: The position code, neural network models of activity, and the problem of learning. Hippocampus **18**(12), 1283–1300 (2008)

39. Zhang, K.: Representation of spatial orientation by the intrinsic dynamics of the head-direction cell ensemble: a theory. The Journal of Neuroscience **16**(6), 2112–2126 (1996)

Programming Languages and Artificial General Intelligence

Vitaly Khudobakhshov[1,2]($\boxtimes$), Andrey Pitko[2], and Denis Zotov[2]

[1] St.-Petersburg State University, St. Petersburg, Russia
vitaly.khudobakhshov@gmail.com
[2] ITMO University, St. Petersburg, Russia

Abstract. Despite the fact that there are thousands of programming languages existing there is a huge controversy about what language is better to solve a particular problem. In this paper we discuss requirements for programming language with respect to AGI research. In this article new language will be presented. Unconventional features (e.g. probabilistic programming and partial evaluation) are discussed as important parts of language design and implementation. Besides, we consider possible applications to particular problems related to AGI. Language interpreter for Lisp-like probabilistic mixed paradigm programming language is implemented in Haskell.

1 Introduction

For many years researches tried to create programming languages for specific areas of research. In the history of AI there were many attempts to create language that would be the best for artificial intelligence. The two main examples are Lisp and Prolog. First one is particularly interesting, because some code can be considered as data in very natural way. Second one contains powerful inference engine based on Horn logic as part of the language. Since that time significant progress have been made in theory of programming languages and many brilliant languages like Haskell were created. Unfortunately, many of achievements in this field are not yet widely used neither artificial intelligence, nor mainstream software development. This paper is related to two advanced techniques: probabilistic programming and partial evaluation. Importance of this techniques will be briefly discussed in this paper. These ideas can be considered as unconventional and not widely used outside of particular areas of research. Incorporation of such techniques to programming language may have considerable impact on artificial general intelligence.

The next section is about core language design, programming paradigm and basic features like pattern matching. Choice between domain-specific embedded language and full-featured general purpose language is also discussed.

One of the main issue need to be discussed is application of probabilistic programming to AGI. Generative models can be very useful in knowledge representation, as well as some other aspects of cognitive architectures. Probabilistic programming is discussed in Section 3.

© Springer International Publishing Switzerland 2015
J. Bieger (Ed.): AGI 2015, LNAI 9205, pp. 293–300, 2015.
DOI: 10.1007/978-3-319-21365-1_30

Section 4 is focused on a deep relationship between theory of programming languages and artificial general intelligence.

Last sections contain some implementation notes and future work road map. Language interpreter and tools are implemented in Haskell. Therefore, many issues about implementation of mixed paradigm languages in pure functional language are discussed. Related programming languages like Church are also discussed.

2   Language Requirements and Design

In this section we discuss main choices and tradeoffs one faces during programming language design. Our goal is to create programming languages with best capabilities for artificial general intelligence. We started from the following:

1. Turing-completeness
2. General purpose
3. Ease of use for automatic program transformation, generation and search
4. Mixed-paradigm (the language must support functional and imperative style)
5. Based on existent language to effectively adopt user experience and legacy code with minimum changes
6. Easily extendible syntax
7. Simplicity

The language should be powerful enough to make it possible to develop AGI systems (e.g. cognitive architecture). In other hand the language should be good enough not only for human beings, but for programs which use other programs (probably itself) as data.

Last requirement is to push us toward Lisp language family because it has a very natural quote syntax.

Another problem we should start to discuss is typing. Languages with static typing is a good choice for enterprise software development because many errors can be found during compilation. Many modern languages like Haskell and Scala have very difficult type system and it makes programming very tricky in some cases. If we want to satisfy simplicity requirement, we should choose dynamic typing. Mixed-paradigm in our case supposes that language should not be pure.

Scheme and Church are good examples of programming languages with simple and extendible syntax. In real world applications some additional syntactic sugar may significantly improve usability of language (see Clojure for example).

One of the most controversial choice has been made between general purpose and domain-specific (embedded) language. DSL can be Turing-complete and may have many extensions, like probabilistic programming or metacomputations. On the other hand, general purpose language needs to have a parser, interactive interpreter, and IDE. The problem of language embedding is ambivalent because pros and limitations are the same things. One can use DSL in his or

her own favorite language and provide very high level of extensibility. Nevertheless, embedded language obliges to use this particular general purpose language
in which DSL is embedded. Presented language is implemented in Haskell as
general purpose.

Presented language is based on Scheme language with some useful extensions. Bread and butter of modern functional programming is pattern matching.
In Scheme and Clojure this functionality provided by extended library. In this
language we incorporate some syntactic ideas from Haskell to provide pattern
matching in core language. Symbol : used to match `cons` and underscore as
wildcard symbol:

```
(define (count x lst)
  (match lst
    (() 0)
    ((x : ys) (+ 1 (count x ys)))
    ((_ : ys) (count x ys))))
```

In this example pattern with dynamic properties has been used. Second pattern contains variable x which is used as argument of function `count`. Which means
that if first element of `lst` equals to x, then we will have a match. Moreover,
repeated variables are allowed (in this case, expression will be evaluated to 2):

```
(match '(2 3 2)
  ((a : b : a : ()) a)
  (_ 0))
```

Although prefix nature of Lisp-like languages is broken here, it is only made
to improve usability of the language. Pattern matching is a good extension to
make programs more readable and compact, but not directly applicable to AGI
problems. In next two sections we introduce probabilistic programming and partial evaluation.

3   Probablistic Programming

According to [3], probabilistic programming languages unify technique of classical models of computation with the representation of uncertain knowledge. In
spite of the fact that the idea of probabilistic programming is quite old (see references in [6]), only in last few years researchers in cognitive sciences and artificial
intelligence started to apply this approach. Many concepts in cognitive studies ? such as concept learning, causal reasoning, social cognition, and language
understanding ? can be modeled using language with probabilistic programming
support [4].

As usual, we extend deterministic language of general purpose with random
choice primitives. The main obstacle in using probabilistic programming in large
projects is the efficient implementation of inference. In modern probabilistic
languages used various techniques and algorithms are used to solve this problem,

including partial filtering [3], and Metropolis-Hastings algorithm [5]. In many cases programs need to be transformed to special form (e.g. continuation of passing style in WebPPL [3]). But main problem is that these languages are not ready for production use. If one wants to use such technique in his or her own project, one needs to embed particular language or extend it. Church is general enough, but it is not easy to extend; WebPPL is easy to embed or extend, but it is just a subset of JavaScript. In recent paper [1] genetic programming and simulated annealing were successfully applied to implementing inference procedure. There are implementation difficulties for such algorithms because they involve programming traces. In the section concerning implementation specifics more details will be covered.

In spite of a mixed paradigm nature of presented language, probabilistic programming is now allowed only for pure functional subset as in cases of WebPPL and Church. It is clear that random function cannot be pure, but we share the idea that concept of purity can be generalized to concept of exchangeability [5]: if an expression is evaluated several times in the same environment, the distribution on return values is invariant to the order of evaluations. In this sense further softening of such a requirement needs more research and not all language constructions are allowed for probabilistic programs in our language. Therefore, we can not use set! function in probabilistic program, but some useful features such as memoization can be extended to stochastic case [5]. This approach can be seen as division to pure and monadic code in Haskell. It can be useful in designing programs, like cognitive architectures, which use wide range of programming techniques. All of this can be written in the same language, but for probabilistic part using only the subset can be enough.

This approach is closely related to DSL mentioned in previous section. One of the most interesting examples of application probabilistic DSL is presented in [12].

Here we do not show examples of probabilistic programs, because we tried to provide compatibility with Church programming language up to minor issues, such as pattern matching.

Programming language presented here is an effort to create open and extendable language with probabilistic programming capabilities. Our implementation is based on ideas described in [14]. The main difference from other implementations like Church and WebPPL is that inference algorithm is implemented in host language. Moreover no additional program transformation is needed.

4   Why Partial Evaluation Matters?

In this section one connection between programming languages in general and artificial intelligence will be discussed. In papers [9,13] possible application of partial evaluation was introduced. One should mention that there were some attempts long before this papers to apply partial evaluation to artificial intelligence (see for example [8]). Here new approach to understanding relations between two fields will be presented and discussed.

Lets start from general idea proposed by Futamura [2]. Let we have program p with two or more arguments written in language S, such that $p(x, y) = d$.

Here, d is a result of program execution. Suppose one have a program spec which can be applied to two arguments a program and the first argument and produce residual program of one argument spec(p, x0) = p' specialized for specified argument x0. Residual program p' satisfied an equation p'(y) = p(x0, y) = d for every y. But p' has possible optimizations according to knowledge of particular value x0 and therefore work much faster.

This approach is very useful for automatic compiler construction. Suppose we have an interpreter of (source) language S written in (target) language T defined by int(p, args) = d (for more formal description see book [7]). One can apply specializer spec to interpreter int with respect to program p. It is easy to check that this will be the result of compilation from S to T.

In the context of artificial general intelligence this makes a connection between AGI and classical AI [9]. Here we need some philosophical remarks. Almost everybody knows a very famous proposition about general intelligence and specialization:

> *A human being should be able to change a diaper, plan an invasion, butcher a hog, conn a ship, design a building, write a sonnet, balance accounts, build a wall, set a bone, comfort the dying, take orders, give orders, cooperate, act alone, solve equations, analyze a new problem, pitch manure, program a computer, cook a tasty meal, fight efficiently, die gallantly. Specialization is for insects.*
> *– Robert A. Heinlein*

It sounds reasonable, but in reality, the situation is different. Nobody asks painter to solve equations in mathematical physics. Moreover, we need to be precise and fast. If one needs to do accounting, then he or she definitely will use calculator to make job done. In this sense, ability to specialize by making tools is a crucial ability of general intelligence.

Is research in artificial general intelligence a replacement of good old-fashioned artificial intelligence? Suppose to be not. Imagine for a second that we have an AGI program which can solve almost all problems, but very slow. If we need to have effective solution of one particular problem, we have to develop optimized solution for the problem. But if we have ability to specialize our general program, we do not need to solve certain problem again anymore.

Is it possible to view AGI problems in terms of programming language theory and partial evaluation? Lets restrict ourselves to quasi-general example: general game playing. This example can be easily extended to AGI with some additional assumptions.

General game player is a program that must be able to play arbitrary logic game (sometimes only full information games considered) for one or more players. It can be either a 15-puzzle, or chess, or another game. The main point is that player gets the game rules seconds before the game starts. Handlers for five requests must be implemented: info, start, play, stop and abort. Function start receives the game rules described as open logic program written in Game Description Language [11]. After that player is involved into a request-response

cycle with game server and `play` handler makes choices and realizes strategy of
the game.

This interaction can be seen as classical Read–Evaluate–Print Loop of interactive interpreter. In such a way one can apply partial evaluation principles to
artificial general intelligence. In the case of general game playing we will deduce
specialized program which can play certain game by partially evaluating general
program according to game rules.

Many players use advanced techniques to optimize program for particular
games up to code generation and compilation [10]. We believe that it can be done
by partial evaluation. It is clear that partial evaluation can not be very useful
in search and do not provide heuristics for search optimization. It is proven that
in many cases only linear speedup is possible [7]. But manipulating with GDL
for computing legal moves and state has huge overhead and it can be removed
by specialization.

Applying the idea to more general case including learning is also possible,
independently of knowledge representation. In the case of procedural or symbolic representation, it is pretty straightforward. Possible applications of partial
evaluation to neural networks are described in [7].

5   Implementation Issues

This section is about implementation details of the project. Besides the decision
to implement general purpose language, choosing of implementation language
is always coupled with some trade-offs. In our case, it was speed, development
difficulty and extensibility. Only two candidates will be considered OCaml and
Haskell. OCaml is good for catching imperative programming with full power
of functional language, including pattern matching and algebraic data types.
Haskell provides a more compact code with very good support of external
libraries via foreign function interface, but it has some drawbacks connected
with imperative issues, such as monads, lifting, and error handling. Choosing
Haskell as implementation language is probably controversial in this case, but
compiler quality and larger community were conclusive issues during the process
of the decision making.

Language tools consist of following parts: interpreter, partial evaluator, and
probabilistic programming support including tracer. All parts share some code
according to language specification.

Interpreter uses `Parsec` library and support REPL mode. Double precision
floating-point and arbitrary precision integers are supported. Strings are also
supported as built-in type.

The crucial aspect of probablistic programming langauge is implementation of probablisic inference algorithm. As in many other probablistic languages
Metropolis-Hastings is one of the most important sampling strategies. The implementation is based on a method carefully described in [14]. There are different
ways to implement ERPs (elementary random primitives) - basic blocks of probablistic programs. To keep things simple we just maintain any key-value stucture

for every random function where value is a tuple consisting of `likelihood`, `sample` and `proposal_kernel` functions for particular ERP.

To implement MCMC inference (in particular Metropolis-Hastings) one need to maintain a trace of the program. Trace consists of chunks - memoized random values:

```
data Chunk = Chunk { value::Value
                   , name::String
                   , erp::ERP
                   , args::[Value] }
```

where `value` is generated value wrapped up into language primitive, `name` is unique call address (see [14] for more information about structural naming strategy), `args` are parameters which used for generation.

Partial evaluation is implemented in Haskell. We use code annotation to describe static-dynamic division which means that original AST (abstract syntax tree) is transformed to annotated one before specialization [7].

The resulting language inherits some parts of Haskell semantics. It does not support lazy evaluation of infinite data structures, but it has some issues, for instance, normal evaluation order instead of applicative one. We do not force interpreter to evaluate arguments before passing. But final decision will be made later.

6   Conclusion and Future Work

Despite early stage of the work, it needs to be mentioned that it is the first attempt to create language with build-in support of both partial evaluation and probabilistic programming. At the level of intuition specialization and probabilistic programming are somehow connected and can be used effectively together. This project joins efforts to research in related fields.

Behind this work there is an idea to create cognitive architecture based on concepts mentioned above. We believe that probabilistic programming with partial evaluation may be effectively applied to AGI problems.

Many ideas of probabilistic programming will be already successfully applied to AGI problems [1] and computer vision in the context of AGI [12]. We are planning to incorporate this ideas to our language.

In this stage of the project probablistic programming and partial evaluation used independently and relationship between them is not very clear. Definitely inference algorithm can be considered as interpretation (in fact interpreter and MCMC query function use large amount of code with very small differences). In other hand it may be impractical or technically difficult to apply such kind of program transformation to inference algorithms. This is a important part of our future work. Moreover real application of this techniques to AGI is still challenging. In the next stage we are planning to create proof-of-concept intelligent software (e.g. cognitive architecture) which will extensively use probablistic programming and partial evaluation.

Acknowledgments. We would like to thank Alexey Potapov, Vita Batischeva and many others for very useful discussion which inspired us to make this work.

This work was supported by Ministry of Education and Science of the Russian Federation.

References

1. Batischeva, V., Potapov, A.: Genetic programming on program traces as an inference engine for probabilistic. In: These AGI-15 Proceedings (to appear)
2. Futamura, Y.: Partial evaluation of computation process an approach to a compiler-compiler. Systems, Computers, Controls **2**, 45–50 (1971)
3. Goodman, N.D., Stuhlmüller, A.: The design and implementation of probabilistic programming languages (retrieved on 2015/3/30). http://dippl.org
4. Goodman, N.D., Tenenbaum, J.B.: Probabilistic models of cognition (retrieved on 2015/3/30). http://probmods.org
5. Goodman, N., Mansinghka, V., Roy, D., Bonawitz, K., Tarlow, D.: Church: a language for generative models. In: Proc. 24th Conf. Uncertainty in Artificial Intelligence (UAI), pp. 220–229 (2008)
6. Jones, C., Plotkin, G.D.: A probablistic powerdomain of evaluations. In: Proceedings of Fourth Annual Symposium on Logic in Computer Science, pp. 186–195. IEEE Computer Society Press (1989)
7. Jones, N., Gomard, C., Sestoft, P.: Partial Evaluation and Automatic Program Generation. Prentice Hall (1994)
8. Kahn, K.: Partial evaluation, programming methodology, and artificial intelligence. AI Magazine **5**, 53–57 (1984)
9. Khudobakhshov, V.: Metacomputations and program-based knowledge representation. In: Kühnberger, K.-U., Rudolph, S., Wang, P. (eds.) AGI 2013. LNCS, vol. 7999, pp. 70–77. Springer, Heidelberg (2013)
10. Kowalski, J., Szykuła, M.: Game description language compiler construction. In: Cranefield, S., Nayak, A. (eds.) AI 2013. LNCS, vol. 8272, pp. 234–245. Springer, Heidelberg (2013)
11. Love, N., Hinrichs, T., Haley, D., Schkufza, E., Genesereth, M.: General game playing: game description language specification. Tech. rep., Stanford Logic Group Computer Science Department Stanford University, Technical Report LG-2006-01 (2008)
12. Potapov, A., Batischeva, V., Rodionov, S.: Optimization framework with minimum description length principle for probabilistic programming. In: These AGI-15 Proceedings (to appear)
13. Potapov, A., Rodionov, S.: Making universal induction efficient by specialization. In: Goertzel, B., Orseau, L., Snaider, J. (eds.) AGI 2014. LNCS, vol. 8598, pp. 133–142. Springer, Heidelberg (2014)
14. Wingate, D., Stuhlmüller, A., Goodman, N.D.: Lightweight implementations of probabilistic programming languages via transformational compilation. In: Proc. of the 14th Artificial Intelligence and Statistics (2011)

From Specialized Syntax to General Logic: The Case of Comparatives

Ruiting Lian[1,2], Rodas Solomon[3], Amen Belayneh[2,3], Ben Goertzel[4], Gino Yu[2], and Changle Zhou[1（⊠）]

[1] Cognitive Science Department, Xiamen University, Xiamen, China
[2] School of Design, Hong Kong Poly U, Hong Kong, China
[3] ICog Labs, Addis Ababa, Ethiopia
[4] OpenCog Foundation, Hong Kong, China
dozero@xmu.edu

Abstract. General-purpose reasoning based on knowledge encoded in natural language, requires mapping this knowledge out of its syntax-dependent form into a more general representation that can be more flexibly applied and manipulated. We have created a system that accomplishes this in a variety of cases via mapping English syntactic expressions into predicate and term logic expressions, which can then be cognitively manipulated by tools such as a probabilistic logic engine, an information-theoretic pattern miner and others. Here we illustrate the functionality of this system in the particular case of comparative constructions.

1 Introduction

In order for an AI system to reason in a general-purpose way about knowledge that comes to it in natural language form, the system must somehow transform the knowledge into a more flexible representation that is not tied to the specific linguistic syntax in which it was originally expressed. There is no consensus in the AI or computational linguistics fields on the best way to do this; various approaches are being pursued in a spirit of experimental exploration [8]. We describe here the approach we have been exploring, in which a sequence of transformations maps syntactic expressions into abstract logic expressions, in a logical language mixing predicate and term logic as specified in Probabilistic Logic Networks [2] [3]. This language comprehension pipeline has been constructed as part of a broader project aimed at Artificial General Intelligence, the open-source OpenCog initiative [4] [5]; it has been described previously in a 2012 overview paper [11], but has advanced considerably in capabilities since that time.

To illustrate the properties of this comprehension pipeline, we focus here on the case of comparative sentences. We have chosen comparatives for this purpose because they are an important yet difficult case for any NLP system to deal with, and hence a more interesting illustration of our NLP concepts and system than a standard case like SVO constructs, which essentially any reasonably sensible language processing framework can deal with acceptably in most cases. Comparatives present a diversity of surface forms, which are yet

© Springer International Publishing Switzerland 2015
J. Bieger (Ed.): AGI 2015, LNAI 9205, pp. 301–309, 2015.
DOI: 10.1007/978-3-319-21365-1_31

ultimately mappable into relatively simple logical structures. They are somewhat confusing from the perspective of modern theoretical linguistics, and also tend to be handled poorly by existing statistical language processing systems.

The language comprehension pipeline reviewed here is broadly similar in concept to systems such as Fluid Construction Grammar [14] [13]and Cycorp's [1] proprietary NLP system. However, it differs from these in important aspects. The approach given here utilizes a dependency grammar (the link grammar [12]) rather than a phrase structure grammar, and at the other end involves a customized logic system combining aspects of term logic and predicate logic. As reviewed in [11], this combination of dependency grammar and term logic allows a large amount of ambiguity to be passed through from the surface level to the logic level, which is valuable if one has a powerful logic engine with a substantial knowledge base, able to resolve ambiguities based on context in a way that earlier-stage linguistic processes could not.

2   A Deep Linguistics and Logical Inference Oriented Comprehension Pipeline

We now briefly review the language comprehension pipeline utilized in the work presented here.

2.1   Link Grammar

The initial, syntactic phase of our pipeline consists of the link grammar [12]. The essential idea of link grammar is that each word comes with a feature structure consisting of a set of typed connectors . Parsing consists of matching up connectors from one word with connectors from another. Consider the sentence:

The cat chased a snake

The link grammar parse structure for this sentence is shown in Figure 1.

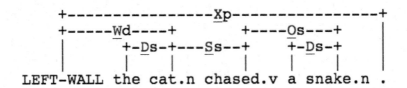

Fig. 1. Example link parse

---

[1] http://cyc.com

There is a database called the "link grammar dictionary" which contains connectors associated with all common English words. The notation used to describe feature structures in this dictionary is quite simple. Different kinds of connectors are denoted by letters or pairs of letters like S or SX. Then if a word W1 has the connector S+, this means that the word can have an S link coming out to the right side. If a word W2 has the connector S-, this means that the word can have an S link coming out to the left side. In this case, if W1 occurs to the left of W2 in a sentence, then the two words can be joined together with an S link.

The rules of link grammar impose additional constraints beyond the matching of connectors – e.g. the planarity and connectivity metarules.. Planarity means that links don't cross. Connectivity means that the links and words of a sentence must form a connected graph – all the words must be linked into the other words in the sentence via some path.

2.2 RelEx

The next phase in the pipeline under discussion is RelEx, an English-language semantic relationship extractor, designed to postprocess the output of the link parser [self-citation removed, to be inserted in the final version]. It can identify subject, object, indirect object and many other dependency relationships between words in a sentence; it generates dependency trees, resembling those of dependency grammars. The output of the current version of RelEx on the example sentence given above is:

```
singular(cat)
singular(snake)
_subj(chase, cat)
_obj(chase, snake)
past(chase)
```

Internally, RelEx works via creating a tree with a FeatureNode corresponding to each word in the sentence, and then applying a series of rules to update the entries in this FeatureNode. The rules transform combinations of link parser links into RelEx dependency relations, sometimes acting indirectly via dynamics wherein one rule changes a feature in a word's FeatureNode, and another rule then takes an action based on the changes the former rule made. Figure gives a high level overview of RelEx's internal process.

The output of RelEx is not unlike that of the Stanford parser, and indeed RelEx has a Stanford parser mode that causes it to output relations in Stanford parser compatible format. However, in our tests RelEx + link parser proved around 4x as fast as the 2012 Stanford parser [9], and qualitatively appeared to give better performance on complex constructs such as conjunctions and comparatives (which makes sense as such constructs are probably not that diversely represented in the Stanford parser's training data).

2.3   OpenCog

The next phase of the pipeline, RelEx2Logic, has the purpose of translating the output of RelEx into a format compatible with the logical reasoning component of the OpenCog AI engine. OpenCog is a high level cognitive architecture aimed at exploration of ideas regarding human-level Artificial General Intelligence, in particular the CogPrime AGI design [4] [5]. OpenCog has been used for commercial applications in the area of natural language processing and data mining , and has also been used for research involving controlling virtual agents in virtual worlds, controlling humanoid robots, genomics data analysis, and many other areas.

The centerpiece of the OpenCog system is a weighted, labeled hypergraph knowledge store called the Atomspace, which represents information using a combination of predicate and term logic formalism with neural net like weightings. The NLP comprehension pipeline described here is centrally concerned with mapping English language text into logical representations within the Atomspace.

The primary component within OpenCog that acts on the output of RelEx2Logic is Probabilistic Logic Networks (PLN) [2], a framework for uncertain inference intended to enable the combination of probabilistic truth values with general logical reasoning rules. PLN involves a particular approach to estimating the confidence values with which these probability values are held (weight of evidence, or second-order uncertainty). The implementation of PLN in software requires important choices regarding the structural representation of inference rules, and also regarding "inference control" – the strategies required to decide what inferences to do in what order, in each particular practical situation.

PLN is divided into first-order and higher-order sub-theories (FOPLN and HOPLN). FOPLN is a term logic, involving terms and relationships (links) between terms. It is an uncertain logic, in the sense that both terms and relationships are associated with truth value objects, which may come in multiple varieties. "Core FOPLN" involves relationships drawn from the set: negation; Inheritance and probabilistic conjunction and disjunction; Member and fuzzy conjunction and disjunction. Higher-order PLN (HOPLN) is defined as the subset of PLN that applies to predicates (considered as functions mapping arguments into truth values). It includes mechanisms for dealing with variable-bearing expressions and higher-order functions. We will see some simple examples of the kinds of inference PLN draws below.

2.4   RelEx2Logic

OpenCog also contains a system called RelEx2Logic, that translates RelEx output into logical relationships, utilizing the mix of predicate and term logic codified in Probabilistic Logic Networks [2]. RelEx2Logic operates via a set of rules roughly illustrated by the following example:

```
_subj(y, x)
_obj(y, z)
==>
Evaluation y x z
```

which indicates, in OpenCog/PLN syntax, that y is mapped into a PredicateNode with argument list (x, z). The above rule format is highly simplified and for illustration purposes only; the actual rule used by the system is more complex and may be found along with the rest of the current rule-base at https://github.com/opencog/opencog/tree/master/opencog/nlp/relex2logic.

So for example, for the sentence "The pig ate the tofu", the RelEx relations

```
_subj(eat, pig)
_obj(eat, tofu)
```

would result (after some simple, automated cleanup operations) in output such as

```
InheritanceLink pig_55 pig
InheritanceLink tofu_1 tofu
EvaluationLink eat pig_55 tofu_1
```

where the subscripts indicate particular definite instances of the concepts involved. On the other hand, the sentence "Pigs eat tofu" would result (after some simple, automated cleanup operations) in simply

```
EvaluationLink eat pig tofu
```

3   Handling Comparatives

Comparatives provide more interesting examples of this sort of mapping from surface form into logical expressions. Theoretical linguistics is nowhere near a consensus regarding the proper handling of comparatives in English and other languages. Some theorists posit an ellipsis theory, suggesting that comparative syntax results from the surface structure of a sentence leaving out certain words that are present in the deep structure [10] [1]. Others posit a movement theory [6] [7], more inspired by traditional generative grammar, hypothesizing that comparative syntax involves a surface structure that rearranges the deep structure.

The link grammar framework essentially bypasses this sort of issue: either ellipsis or movement would be represented by certain symmetries in the link grammar dictionary, but these symmetries don't need to be explicitly recognized or utilized by the link parser itself, though they may guide the human being (or AI system) creating the link grammar dictionary. Currently, on an empirical basis, the link parser handles comparatives reasonably well, but the relevant dictionary entries are somewhat heterogeneous and not entirely symmetrical in nature. This suggests that either

1. the syntax of English comparatives is "messy" and heterogeneous, not fitting neatly into any of the available theories; and/or
2. the link grammar dictionary can be made significantly more elegant regarding comparatives

We suspect that the truth is "a little of both", but note that this issue need not be resolved in order to deploy the link grammar as part of a practical pipeline for comprehending complex sentences, including comparatives.

As an example of how our framework, described here, deals with comparatives, one of the RelEx2Logic rules for comparatives is in compact form

```
than(w1, w2)
_comparative(ad, w)
==>
TruthValueGreaterThanLink
    InheritanceLink w1 ad
    InheritanceLink w2 ad
```

A simple example using this rule would be:

```
Pumpkin is cuter than the white dog.
==>
_predadj(cute, Pumpkin)
than(Pumpkin, dog)
_comparative(cute, Pumpkin)
_amod(dog, white)
==>
AndLink
   InheritanceLink dog_11 white
   InheritanceLink dog_11 dog
   TruthValueGreaterThanLink
        InheritanceLink Pumpkin cute
        InheritanceLink dog_11 cute
```

On the other hand, to deal with a sentence like "Amen is more intelligent than insane" we use a different rule, which in simplified form is

```
_predadj(adj1, W)
than(adj1, adj2)
_comparative(adj1, W)
==>
TruthValueGreaterThanLink
    InheritanceLink W adj1
    InheritanceLink W adj2
```

resulting in output

```
_predadj(intelligent, Amen)
than(intelligent, insane)
_comparative(intelligent, Amen)
==>
TruthValueGreaterThanLink
     InheritanceLink Amen intelligent
     InheritanceLink Amen insane
```

In cases where the link parser gives multiple parse options, the RelEx2Logic rules will provide a logic interpretation for each one. Statistical heuristics have been implemented to rank the multiple parses for plausibility based on a corpus, but these of course are not perfect. In some cases, multiple logical output options will be presented to OpenCog, and must be chosen between based on higher level contextual inference, which is a difficult topic and the subject of current research.

4   Reasoning About Comparatives

To illustrate the simplicity of reasoning about comparatives once the syntactic complexities are removed and a normalized logical form is achieved, we consider how our integrated system can take the inputs

- Bob likes Hendrix more than the Beatles
- Bob is American
- Menudo is liked less by Americans than the Beatles

and derive the conclusion that Bob likes Hendrix more than Menudo.
   For the first sentence we obtain

```
_subj(like, Bob)
_obj(like, Hendrix)
than(Hendrix, Beatles)
_comparative(like, Hendrix)
==>
TruthValueGreaterThanLink
     EvaluationLink like Bob Hendrix
     EvaluationLink like Bob Beatles
```

and for the second, correspondingly

```
_subj(like, Americans)
_obj(like, Menudo)
than(Beatles, Menudo)
_comparative(like, Beatles)
==>
TruthValueGreaterThanLink
     EvaluationLink like Americans Beatles
     EvaluationLink like Americans Menudo
```

   The logical format obtained from these sentences is quite transparent. Simply via deploying its knowledge that the TruthValueGreaterThan relationship is transitive, and that Bob is American, the PLN logic system can in two steps derive the conclusion that

```
TruthValueGreaterThanLink
     EvaluationLink like Bob Hendrix
     EvaluationLink like Bob Menudo
```

   Now that we are dealing with knowledge in logical rather than syntactic form, all sorts of manipulations can be carried out. For instance, suppose we also know that Bob likes Sinatra more than Menudo,

```
TruthValueGreaterThanLink
     EvaluationLink like Bob Hendrix
     EvaluationLink like Bob Menudo
```

PLN's abduction rule then concludes that

```
SimilarityLink
    Hendrix
    Sinatra
```

This sort of reasoning is very simple in PLN, and that's as it should be – it is also commonsensically simple for humans. A major design objective of PLN was that inferences that are simple for humans, should be relatively compact and simple in PLN. The task of the language comprehension pipeline we have designed for OpenCog is to unravel the complexity of natural language syntax to unveil the logical simplicity of the semantics underneath, which can then oftentimes be reasoned on in a very simple, straightforward way.

5   Conclusion

We have summarized the operation of a natural language comprehension system that maps English sentences into sets of logical relationships, in the logic format utilized by a probabilistic inference engine implemented within a general purpose cognitive architecture. This comprehension system is being utilized within prototype applications in multiple areas including a non-player character in a video game, a humanoid robot operating in an indoor environment, and a chat system running on a smartphone interacting with a user regarding music and media consumption.

We have focused here on the processing of comparatives, as this is a nontrivial case that is currently confusing for linguistic theory and handled suboptimally by many parsing systems. For practical cases of comparatives, as for most other cases, our system qualitatively appears to give adequate performance.

However, significant work remains before we have a generally robust comprehension system capable for use in a wide variety fo dialogue systems. Handling of conjunctions and quantifiers is one of the primary subjects of our current work, along with the use of PLN to handle commonsense inferences more subtle than the simple inference case summarized here.

6   Beyond Hand-Coded Rules

The language comprehension architecture described here is, in its current implementation, largely founded on hand-coded linguistic rules: the link-grammar dictionary, the RelEx rule-based and the RelEx2Logic rule-base. However, this is not viewed as an integral aspect of the approach pursued. In fact, research is currently underway aimed at replacing these hand-coded rules with rules automatically learned via unsupervised corpus learning; this work is overviewed in [15].

The point of the hand-coded rule-bases used in the current work is not to serve as a lasting foundation for intelligent English language processing; our view is that this would be an infeasible approach in the end, as the number of rules required would likely be infeasible to encode by hand. Rather, the point of the hand-coded rule-bases is to dissociate the problem of *language processing architecture* from the problems of *language learning* and *linguistic content*. Using the hand-coded rule-bases as a "working prototype" of linguistic content regarding the English language, we are able dissociate the architecture problem from the learning problem, and present what we propose as a general and powerful architecture for language comprehension and generation. The problem of learning more broadly functional linguistic content to operate within this architecture, is then viewed as a separate problem, we believe addressable via OpenCog learning algorithms.

References

1. Bhatt, R., Takahashi, S.: Winfried lechner, ellipsis in comparatives. The Journal of Comparative Germanic Linguistics **14**(2), 139–171 (2011). http://dx.doi.org/10.1007/s10828-011-9042-3
2. Goertzel, B., Ikle, M., Goertzel, I., Heljakka, A.: Probabilistic Logic Networks. Springer (2008)
3. Goertzel, B., Coelho, L., Geisweiller, N., Janicic, P., Pennachin, C.: Real World Reasoning. Atlantis Press (2011)
4. Goertzel, B., Pennachin, C., Geisweiller, N.: Engineering General Intelligence, Part 1: A Path to Advanced AGI via Embodied Learning and Cognitive Synergy. Springer: Atlantis Thinking Machines (2013)
5. Goertzel, B., Pennachin, C., Geisweiller, N.: Engineering General Intelligence, Part 2: The CogPrime Architecture for Integrative, Embodied AGI. Springer: Atlantis Thinking Machines (2013)
6. Grant, M.: The Parsing and Interpretation of Comparatives: More than Meets the Eye (2013). http://scholarworks.umass.edu/open_access_dissertations/689/
7. Izvorski, R.: A dp -shell for comparatives. In: Proceeding of CONSOLE III pp. 99–121 (1995)
8. Jurafsky, D., Martin, J.: Speech and Language Processing. Pearson Prentice Hall (2009)
9. Klein, D., Manning, C.: Accurate unlexicalized parsing. In: Proceedings of the 41st Meeting of the Association for Computational Linguistics, pp. 423–430 (2003)
10. Lechner, W.: Ellipsis in Comparatives. Studies in generative grammar, Moulton de Gruyter (2004). http://books.google.com.hk/books?id=JsqUHHYSXCIC
11. Lian, R., Goertzel, B., Ke, S., O'Neill, J., Sadeghi, K., Shiu, S., Wang, D., Watkins, O., Yu, G.: Syntax-semantic mapping for general intelligence: language comprehension as hypergraph homomorphism, language generation as constraint satisfaction. In: Bach, J., Goertzel, B., Iklé, M. (eds.) AGI 2012. LNCS, vol. 7716, pp. 158–167. Springer, Heidelberg (2012)
12. Sleator, D., Temperley, D.: Parsing english with a link grammar. Third International Workshop on Parsing Technologies (1993)
13. Steels, L.: Design Patterns in Fluid Construction Grammar. John Benjamins (2011)
14. Steels, L.: Modeling The Formation of Language in Embodied Agents: Methods and Open Challenges, pp. 223–233. Springer Verlag (2010)
15. Vepstas, L., Goertzel, B.: Learning language from a large unannotated corpus: A deep learning approach. Technical Report (2013)

Decision-Making During Language Understanding by Intelligent Agents

Marjorie McShane[✉] and Sergei Nirenburg

Rensselaer Polytechnic Institute, Troy, NY 12180, USA
{mcsham2,nirens}@rpi.edu

Abstract. In cognitive modeling and intelligent agent design, a widely accepted architectural pipeline is *Perception–Reasoning–Action*. But language understanding, while a type of perception, involves many types of reasoning, and can even involve action, such as asking a clarification question about the intended meaning of an utterance. In the field of natural language processing, for its part, the common progression of processing modules is *Syntax–Semantics–Pragmatics*. But this modularization lacks cognitive plausibility and misses opportunities to enhance efficiency through the timely application of knowledge from multiple sources. This paper provides a high-level description of semantically-deep, reasoning-rich language processing in the OntoAgent cognitive agent environment, which illustrates the practical gains of moving away from a strict adherence to traditional modularization and pipeline architectures.

Keywords: Natural language understanding · Intelligent agents · Reasoning · Cognitive architecture

1 Introduction

The analytic method in science prescribes decomposing problems into subproblems, finding solutions to those subproblems, then synthesizing the solutions. Despite the well-known benefits of such modularization, it has certain unfortunate consequences that have come center stage in our work on developing the cognitively modeled agents we call OntoAgents. Strict modularization of perception, reasoning and action fails to capture the rich information transfer that appears to characterize human cognition and behavior. Our current work on OntoAgents attempts to more accurately model general artificial intelligence by integrating these cognitive modules. In this paper, we discuss one aspect of this integration: *the integration of decision-making (traditionally subsumed under reasoning) into the process of natural language understanding (traditionally subsumed under perception).*

OntoAgents feature integrated physiological and cognitive simulations, modeling the body and the mind. The mind-body connection is modeled as the process of interoception, i.e., the perception of bodily signals [5], [13]. To date, the simulated minds of implemented OntoAgents have shown the capabilities

ⓒ Springer International Publishing Switzerland 2015
J. Bieger (Ed.): AGI 2015, LNAI 9205, pp. 310–319, 2015.
DOI: 10.1007/978-3-319-21365-1_32

of goal-oriented planning, decision-making influenced by personal biases and situational parameters, learning, memory management, and natural language processing (see [7], [8], [6], among others).

In this paper we present a conceptual overview of our work toward transcending the boundaries of processing modules in models of cognitive agency. Our effort addresses two separate modularizations – the traditional *Perception–Reasoning–Action* pipeline of cognitive architectures and the familiar *Syntax–Semantics–Pragmatics* pipeline of AI-oriented natural language processing.

Pipeline-oriented approaches, while differing in many respects, typically share the following two characteristics: a) the processing of an input by any module can start only after the upstream modules have finished with this input; and b) the machinery and knowledge resources of each module are typically opaque to those of other modules. There are engineering-oriented reasons for imposing these constraints. But we hypothesize that they are not optimal either as features of cognitive models or as architectural choices in computational implementations of cognitive models.

Issues of modularity and computational architectures have been amply debated in cognitive science and artificial intelligence. This paper is not meant as a contribution to those debates. Our specific objective is to enhance the efficiency and effectiveness of artificial intelligent agents by improving the ways in which they apply knowledge. This objective complements rather than competes with work on enhancing the functioning of agents through more sophisticated formalisms and improved algorithmic efficiency.

We believe that moving away from pipelines will increase verisimilitude in modeling human behavior. In this respect, we are motivated by two working hypotheses. (1) The *inclusivity hypothesis* suggests that cognitive agents, at any given time in their functioning, can apply any and all heuristics currently available to them, irrespective of the provenance of those heuristics. (2) The *least effort hypothesis* motivates agents, in well-defined aspects of their functioning, to "jump to conclusions" – i.e., to declare their current task completed and avoid exhaustive processing. Such decisions are a function of the agents' knowledge and beliefs, their personality traits, and situational constraints. This hypothesis is observationally quite plausible, as anybody who has ever been justifiably interrupted in a dialog can attest (i.e., if the interlocutor has already understood one's point well enough to respond, interrupting can be appropriate).

2   Issues with Pipelines

One insufficiency of the *Perception–Reasoning–Action* pipeline is that it obscures the fact that language understanding, a type of perception, itself routinely involves reasoning and action. Such tasks as lexical and referential disambiguation, the detection and reconstruction of elliptical gaps, and the understanding of indirect speech acts are reasoning-intensive. Moreover, if an agent is intended to model human performance, it must be able to look beyond the boundaries of the narrowly defined language understanding task to judge its confidence in the results of its language processing. If, by the time it finishes processing a language input, the agent is confident that it has understood the input, this should lead to reasoning and action. If, by contrast, the agent has not sufficiently understood the input, then it must select a recovery strategy. One such strategy is the *action* of asking its human collaborator for clarification. Incorporating such reasoning and action into the perception module, we arrive at the following, more realistic, workflow, in which parentheses show optionality: *Perception and reasoning about perception–(Reasoning about suboptimal perception processing–Recovery action)–Reasoning–Action.*

With respect to language modeling itself, the traditional, theory-driven *Syntax–Semantics–Pragmatics* pipeline fails to accommodate the large number of cross-modular methods available for treating individual linguistic phenomena. To take just one example, many instances of ellipsis – the null referring expression – can be detected and resolved *prior to* semantic analysis, with the results then being available to inform semantic analysis.[1] Therefore, just as we modified the cognitive modeling pipeline above, so must we modify the language processing pipeline, leading to the more functionally sufficient approach detailed in Section 4.

3   Pursuing Actionable Language Analyses

The goal of language understanding in OntoAgent is for the agent to arrive at an *actionable* interpretation of text input. We define as actionable those interpretations that are deemed by the agent to be sufficient to support post-perception reasoning and action. An actionable interpretation might represent a complete and correct analysis of all input strings, or it might be incomplete; it might involve only a partial analysis of the input strings, or it might invoke maximally deep reasoning; and it might be achievable by the agent alone, or it might require interactive clarifications or corrections by a human or artificial collaborator. In short, for each language input, after each stage of processing, the agent must estimate whether it has arrived at a level of input understanding sufficient for passing control to the reasoning and action modules. As soon as the answer is positive, it can proceed to post-perception reasoning and action.

This modeling strategy reflects our belief that, in order to foster the development of viable agent applications at a time when the state of the art cannot yet support full and perfect semantic analysis of unrestricted input, it is necessary to define practical halting conditions for language analysis. Consider an example from an OntoAgent prototype system called Maryland Virtual Patient [5], [13]. One of the intelligent agents in this system plays the role of a virtual patient being diagnosed and treated by a human medical trainee. During simulated office visits, the virtual patient engages in dialog with the trainee during which the latter can ask questions, suggest diagnostic and treatment protocols, provide background knowledge about the patient's disease, and answer

---

[1] If ellipsis were to be treated like other referring expressions, it would normally be subsumed under pragmatic analysis.

the patient's questions. In each of the trainee's dialog turns, the agent attempts to detect something actionable, such as a question it should answer or a recommendation it should respond to. Responding to this actionable input becomes the agent's communicative goal of choice, absolving it from the necessity of full and confident analysis of every element of input.

This type of incomplete processing is not merely an escape hatch for modeling intelligent agents in the early 21st century. We believe that it models how people naturally behave in communicative situations: they pay attention to the main point but often ignore many of the details of what others say. For example, if a doctor provides exhaustive detail about the potential side effects of a medication, do live patients pay full attention? Would they understand and remember every detail even if they did? Selective attention is a manifestation of the principle of least effort; it represents natural conservation of energy and thus protects against cognitive overload [15]. So, even though OntoAgents show "focused attention" for practical reasons, the effects of this behavior in simulation will, we hypothesize, make agents more human-like.

We will now consider, in turn, how the canonical pipelines introduced above can be modified to better serve OntoAgents in their quest for actionable language interpretations.

4   The Stages of Language Analysis

To reiterate, the agent's goal in processing language input is to arrive at a confident, actionable analysis as soon as possible. For this reason, we are working toward configuring agents that can treat phenomena as soon as the necessary heuristic evidence becomes available. At any point in language analysis, an agent should be able to decide that the current state of analysis is actionable and proceed directly to post-perception reasoning and action. We discuss the stages of language processing under development in the order presented below.

1. Perception and reasoning about perception
   (a) Exploiting situational expectations and conventions
   (b) Syntactic analysis
       i. Syntactically-informed reference resolution
       ii. Tree trimming
   (c) Semantic analysis
       i. Semantically-informed reference resolution
       ii. Semantically-informed speech act understanding
   (d) Reference resolution
   (e) Indirect speech act interpretation
   (f) Reasoning about suboptimal perception processing
       i. Recovery action
2. Post-Perception Reasoning
3. Action

Space constraints preclude a detailed description of *how* the system arrives at each type of analysis or a detailed rundown of results to date. Regarding the latter, we have recently evaluated our engines for basic semantic analysis [6], the treatment of multi-word expressions [12], verb phrase ellipsis resolution [10] and tree trimming in support of the latter [11]. The other microtheories mentioned above are at various stages of development. The rationale behind presenting this blueprint for agent functioning even before an end-to-end implementation is available is that we believe that drawing the big picture is an essential prerequisite for long-term progress on the many component challenges of configuring truly intelligent artificial agents. The modest goal of the current contribution is to motivate the reconceptualization of the traditional pipeline architectures introduced earlier.

1a. Exploiting Situational Expectations and Conventions. The first stage of language processing relies on textual string matching. The hypothesis is that some combinations of strings – which can even be entire sentences – are so frequent or expected that they are stored in memory along with their semantic analyses, thus not requiring compositional analysis at each encounter. For example, in the Maryland Virtual Patient application, we stored semantic analyses of expected formulaic inputs such as *How are you feeling?* Storing remembered analyses not only speeds up system functioning and reduces unexpected misinterpretations, it also reflects the human-oriented hypothesis that, in accordance with the principle of least effort, people store frequently encountered phrases as ready-made information bundles.

1b. Syntactic Analysis. If the agent does not treat an input "reflexively", it proceeds to syntactic analysis. Stanford CoreNLP [4] provides tokenization, sentence splitting, PoS tagging, morphological analysis, named entity recognition, syntactic immediate constituent analysis and a dependency parse. Although syntactic analysis represents only an intermediate result toward semantic analysis, it can inform certain types of decision-making. For example, an agent might choose to further process sentences only if they contain certain keywords, or combinations of keywords, of interest.

1bi. Syntactically-informed reference resolution. Next the agent engages in a series of reference resolution procedures that are undertaken at this early stage because they require as input only the results of syntactic analysis and access to the lexicon. For example, our agents can detect and resolve verb phrase ellipsis in sentences like *They attempted to **win the tournament** but couldn't [e]*, as described in [10]. Similarly, they can establish lexico-syntactically-based coreference links for a pronominal referring expressions in certain linguistically defined configurations.

The benefits of early reference processing cannot be overstated. Detecting ellipsis and reconstructing the missing string permits the meaning of the expression to be computed during basic semantic analysis. Continuing with the example from above, the agent will actually be semantically analyzing *[They]-1 attempted to [win the tournament]-2 but [they]-1 couldn't [win the tournament]-2*, in which the indices indicate coreference. Similarly, establishing high-confidence textual coreference relations for overt pronouns at this stage enhances the simultaneous disambiguation of those expressions and their selecting heads. For example, it is much easier for the agent to disambiguate both the subject and the verb in *The train stopped* than to disambiguate these strings in *It stopped*. So, coreferring *it* with *train* in a context like *The train raced toward the station then it suddenly stopped* is of great benefit to semantic analysis.

1bi. Tree Trimming. Before proceeding to semantic analysis, the agent has the option of carrying out "tree trimming," also known as syntactic pruning or sentence simplification. Tree trimming refers to automatically deleting non-core syntactic structures, such as relative clauses and various types of modification, so that the core elements can be more effectively treated.[2] It has been used in applications ranging from summarization to information extraction to subtitling. An agent's decision about whether or not to trim should be a function of (a) sentence length, (b) the constituents in the parse tree and the dependency parse, and (c) situational non-linguistic parameters, such as the agent's cognitive load and the importance of the goal being pursued through the communication.

1c. Semantic Analysis. Semantic analysis in OntoAgent is defined as generating an ontologically-grounded text meaning representation (TMR) that includes the results of lexical disambiguation and semantic dependency determination.[3] TMRs are written in a metalanguage they share with the ontology and other knowledge repositories in OntoAgent. For example, the TMR for the input *Dr. Jones diagnosed the patient* is shown in Table 1. Small caps indicate ontological concepts and numerical suffixes indicate their instances. The "textstring" and "from-sense" slots are metadata used for system debugging.

Table 1. TMR for *Dr. Jones diagnosed the patient*

DIAGNOSE-1

AGENT	HUMAN-1
THEME	MEDICAL-PATIENT-1
TIME	(before find-anchor-time) ; indicates past tense
textstring	"diagnosed"
from-sense	diagnosed-v1

HUMAN-1

AGENT-OF	DIAGNOSE-1
HAS-NAME	"Dr. Jones"
textstring	"Dr. Jones"
from-sense	*personal-name*

MEDICAL-PATIENT-1

THEME-OF	DIAGNOSE-1
textstring	"patient"
from-sense	patient-n1

---

[2] For our approach to tree trimming in service of ellipsis resolution see [11].

[3] The OntoSem process of semantic analysis is described in [6] and [14].

Every TMR produced by an agent is assigned a confidence level, which reflects the extent to which lexically and ontologically recorded expectations resulted in a single, unique analysis of the input. The more instances of residual ambiguity, the lower the overall confidence.

Although this example sketches the basic idea of semantic analysis in OntoAgent, it fails to convey that this stage of processing actually incorporates some aspects of early pragmatic analysis. For example, TMRs include the results of reference processing carried out earlier (cf. 1bi above). They also may include newly computed aspects of reference resolution as well as the treatment of indirect speech acts. We consider each of these in turn.

1ci. Semantically-informed reference resolution. The OntoSem lexicon contains lexical senses that support the detection of certain kinds of ellipsis and the resolution of certain kinds of overt referring expressions. For example, there is a sense of the verb *start* that expects its complement to be an ontological OBJECT rather than an EVENT, as in *She started the book*. This sense asserts that there is an elided event whose meaning the system should attempt to recover from the context – all during this same pass of basic semantic analysis. Other referring expressions that are treated using lexically-recorded procedural semantic routines are indexicals such as *yesterday* [9].

1cii. Semantically-informed speech act understanding. The OntoSem lexicon includes a broad range of phrasal constructions that help to reduce the ambiguity of compositional semantic analysis [12]. Among these constructions are conventionalized speech acts. For example, *Could you please tell me X* is interpreted as REQUEST-INFO THEME [the meaning of X]; *I would recommend X* is interpreted as REQUEST-ACTION [the meaning of X]; and so on. Rather than postpone indirect speech-act detection until the downstream module dedicated specifically to it, our system analyzes the semantics and the pragmatics of conventionalized indirect speech acts simultaneously.

This "Semantic Analysis" level of processing will not yet be actionable for intelligent agent applications since referring expressions have not yet been anchored in memory. However, for non-agent-oriented NLP applications, this level of output could be useful since lexical disambiguation has been carried out, the semantic dependency structure has been established, many textual *co*reference relations have been resolved, and some indirect speech acts have been detected.

1d. Reference resolution. Unlike reference resolution procedures undertaken up to this point, OntoAgent's nascent reference module (a) will have access to full semantic analysis as input, (b) will attempt ontology-based reasoning, if needed, and (c) will posit as the goal not just detecting textual *co*reference, but carrying out concept-level reference resolution, which will result in anchoring referring expressions to concept instances in agent memory. For example, given an input like *He began operating on the patient at 7 a.m.*, the system might have several males in the preceding context that could plausibly be the sponsor for the referring expression *he*. However, it is likely that only one of them is listed in the agent's fact repository with the property-value pair SOCIAL-ROLE SURGEON.

The key to selecting the correct sponsor is consulting the ontology and determining that the AGENT of the ontological concept (event) SURGERY – which was activated as the contextually appropriate meaning of *operate* – is typically a SURGEON. This is an example of "reasoning about perception." Note that if earlier reference processing had resulted in textual coreference links, true reference resolution to agent memory would still have to be undertaken at this stage. This would happen, for example, given the input, *After the surgeon completed the surgery, he changed into street clothes.* Here, the grammatical structure strongly suggests the coreference relationship between *he* and *the surgeon*, but this chain of coreference must still be anchored to the right instance of SURGEON in agent memory.

1e. Indirect speech act interpretation. In its current state, our microtheory of non-lexically-supported speech act interpretation covers exclusively application-specific cases. For example, in the MVP application, if the input includes reference to a symptom, but the input overall is not recognized as an instance of asking whether the patient is experiencing that symptom, the patient nevertheless responds as if it had been asked that question. Work is underway to extend this microtheory to cover more generic contexts.

By the time the agent reaches this point in language analysis, it will have carried out all of its basic analysis processes, constructed a TMR, and grounded concept instances in memory. Its overall analysis is associated with a cumulative confidence value that is computed as a function of its confidence about every component decision it has made: each instance of lexical disambiguation, each instance of reference resolution, etc. If the agent's overall confidence is above a threshold, the analysis is declared to be actionable. If not, the agent must decide how to proceed.

1f. Reasoning about suboptimal perception processing. If the agent chose earlier not to carry out syntactic trimming, it can choose to invoke it at this point, in hopes of being able to generate a higher-confidence TMR from a less complex input. The sequence *syntactic analysis – semantic analysis – tree trimming – semantic analysis* is another example of interleaving modules of processing beyond the rather simplistic original pipeline. If the trimming strategy is either not available (e.g., it has been carried out already) or is not favored by the agent (e.g., this is a high-risk situation with no room for error), the agent can undertake a recovery action.

1fi. Recovery action. If the agent is collaborating with a human, one recovery option is to ask a clarification question. This is particularly well-motivated in high-risk and/or time-sensitive situations. There are, however, other options as well. For example, if the analysis problem was due to "unexpected input" – e.g., an unknown word – the system can attempt learning by reading, as described in [2]. Or, the agent can decide to recover passively, by not responding and waiting for its interlocutor's next move which, in some cases, might involve linguistic clarifications, restatements, etc.

2. Post-perception reasoning & 3. Action. These modules of agent cognition take as input whatever results of language processing the agent considered an appropriate stopping condition.

5   Final Thoughts

The recognition that reasoning is needed for language processing is, of course, not novel. The idea has been addressed and debated from the early days of AI-NLP and cognitive science in works by Schank [16], Wilks [17], Woods [18], and many others. Our contribution is an attempt (a) to integrate a larger inventory of more detailed explanatory models that rely on broader and deeper knowledge bases, and (b) to arm agents with the ability to reason about their confidence in language processing and act accordingly. In this regard, it is noteworthy that a central contributor to the success of the Watson system in the *Jeopardy!* challenge was its use of confidence metrics in deciding whether or not to respond to questions [3].

The idea of interleaving processing stages is also not unknown in computational linguistics proper. For example, Agirre et al. [1] use semantic information to help determine prepositional phrase attachment, which is required for producing the correct output of syntactic analysis. Our work differs from contributions of this kind in that our ultimate goal is not success of a particular stage of language processing but, rather, deriving the semantic and discourse/pragmatic meaning of the input using all available clues.

In this space, we were able to give only a high-level overview of language understanding in OntoAgent, along with our methods of incorporating reasoning and decision-making into the process. Naturally, many aspects of this vision of agent functioning are work in progress. Our practical results, which vary across microtheories, have been reported in the cited literature. Near-term goals include both further developing the theoretical substrate of OntoAgent – continuing the genre of the current contribution – and increasing the breadth of coverage of all of the microtheories, knowledge bases and processors that contribute to the functioning of OntoAgents.

Acknowledgments. This research was supported in part by Grant N00014-09-1-1029 from the U.S. Office of Naval Research. All opinions and findings expressed in this material are those of the authors and do not necessarily reflect the views of the Office of Naval Research.

References

1. Agirre, E., Baldwin, T., Martinez, D.: Improving parsing and PP attachment performance with sense information. In: Proceedings of ACL-08: HLT, pp. 317–325, Columbus, Ohio (2008)
2. English, J., Nirenburg, S.: Striking a balance: human and computer contributions to learning through semantic analysis. In: Proceedings of ICSC-2010. Pittsburgh, PA (2010)
3. Ferrucci, D., Brown, E., et al.: Building Watson: An Overview of the DeepQA Project. Association for the Advancement of Artificial Intelligence (2010)

4. Manning, C.D., Surdeanu, M., Bauer, J., Finkel, J., Bethard, S. J., McClosky, D.: The Stanford CoreNLP natural language processing toolkit. In: Proceedings of the 52nd Annual Meeting of the Association for Computational Linguistics: System Demonstrations, pp. 55–60 (2014)

5. McShane, M., Jarrell, B., Fantry, G., Nirenburg, S., Beale, S., Johnson, B.: Revealing the conceptual substrate of biomedical cognitive models to the wider community. In: Westwood, J.D., Haluck, R.S., et al. (eds.) Medicine Meets Virtual Reality 16, pp. 281–286. IOS Press, Amsterdam, Netherlands (2008)

6. McShane, M., Nirenburg, S., Beale, S.: Language Understanding With Ontological Semantics. Advances in Cognitive Systems (forthcoming)

7. McShane, M., Beale, S., Nirenburg, S., Jarrell, B., Fantry, G.: Inconsistency as a Diagnostic Tool in a Society of Intelligent Agents. Artificial Intelligence in Medicine (AIIM) **55**(3), 137–148 (2012)

8. McShane, M., Nirenburg, S., Jarrell, B.: Modeling Decision-Making Biases. Biologically-Inspired Cognitive Architectures (BICA) Journal **3**, 39–50 (2013)

9. McShane, M., Nirenburg, S.: Use of ontology, lexicon and fact repository for reference resolution in Ontological Semantics. In: Oltramari, A., Vossen, P., Qin, L., Hovy, E. (eds.) New Trends of Research in Ontologies and Lexical Resources: Ideas, Projects, Systems, pp. 157–185. Springer (2013)

10. McShane, M., Babkin, P.: Automatic ellipsis resolution: recovering covert information from text. In: Proceedings of AAAI-15 (2015)

11. McShane, M., Nirenburg, S., Babkin, P.: Sentence trimming in service of verb phrase ellipsis resolution. In: Proceedings of EAP CogSci 2015 (forthcoming)

12. McShane, M., Nirenburg, S., Beale, S.: The Ontological Semantic Treatment of Multi-Word Expressions. Lingvisticae Investigationes (forthcoming)

13. Nirenburg, S., McShane, M., Beale, S.: A simulated physiological/cognitive "double agent". In: Beal, J., Bello, P., Cassimatis, N., Coen, M., Winston, P. (eds.) Papers from the AAAI Fall Symposium, Naturally Inspired Cognitive Architectures, Washington, D.C., Nov. 7–9. AAAI technical report FS-08-06, Menlo Park, CA: AAAI Press (2008)

14. Nirenburg, S., Raskin, V.: Ontological Semantics. The MIT Press, Cambridge, MA (2004)

15. Piantadosi, S.T., Tily, H., Gibson, E.: The Communicative Function of Ambiguity in Language. Cognition **122**, 280–291 (2012)

16. Schank, R., Riesbeck, C.: Inside Computer Understanding. Erlbaum, Hillsdale, NJ (1981)

17. Wilks, Y., Fass, D.: Preference Semantics: A Family History. Computing and Mathematics with Applications **23**(2) (1992)

18. Woods, W.A.: Procedural Semantics as a Theory of Meaning. Research Report No. 4627. Cambridge, MA: BBN (1981)

Plan Recovery in Reactive HTNs
Using Symbolic Planning

Lydia Ould Ouali[1], Charles Rich[2(✉)], and Nicolas Sabouret[1]

[1] LIMSI-CNRS, Université Paris-Sud,
UPR 3251, Orsay, France
{ouldouali,nicolas.sabouret}@limsi.fr
[2] Worcester Polytechnic Institute,
Worcester, MA, USA
rich@wpi.edu

Abstract. Building formal models of the world and using them to plan future action is a central problem in artificial intelligence. In this work, we combine two well-known approaches to this problem, namely, reactive hierarchical task networks (HTNs) and symbolic linear planning. The practical motivation for this hybrid approach was to recover from breakdowns in HTN execution by dynamically invoking symbolic planning. This work also reflects, however, on the deeper issue of tradeoffs between procedural and symbolic modeling. We have implemented our approach in a system that combines a reactive HTN engine, called Disco, with a STRIPS planner implemented in Prolog, and conducted a preliminary evaluation.

1 Introduction

Hierarchical task networks (HTNs) are widely used for controlling intelligent agents and robots in complex, dynamic environments. There are many different formalizations and graphical notations in use for HTNs. In this paper we use the simple tree notation shown in Fig. 1, which we will explain in detail in Section 4.1. HTNs are typically hand-authored and can be quite large, with five or more levels of task hierarchy and dozens or even hundreds of tasks at the leaves.

All HTNs share the basic structure of decomposing tasks into sequences (or sometimes partially ordered sets) of subtasks, with alternative decompositions (sometimes called recipes) for different situations. In addition to the decomposition tree structure, most HTNs also have conditions, such as preconditions and postconditions, associated with nodes in the tree to control execution of the HTN.

HTNs were originally a hierarchical extension of classical linear (e.g., STRIPS [4]) plans, and as in classical plans, the conditions associated with tasks were *symbolic*, i.e., they were written in some kind of formal logic and logical inference was used to reason about them. Later, in response to the difficulties of symbolic modeling (see Section 3) a variant, called *reactive* HTNs, was developed in which the conditions are *procedural*, i.e., they are written in a programming language and evaluated by the appropriate programming language interpreter. The idea

© Springer International Publishing Switzerland 2015
J. Bieger (Ed.): AGI 2015, LNAI 9205, pp. 320–330, 2015.
DOI: 10.1007/978-3-319-21365-1_33

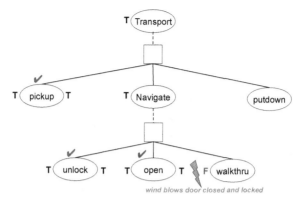

Fig. 1. Breakdown in HTN execution after wind blows door closed and locked. Check marks indicate successfully executed tasks; "T" indicates a condition that has been evaluated and returned true; "F" indicates a condition that has returned false.

of reactive HTNs has also been used in game development, where they are called behavior trees.[1]

This work is focused on reactive HTNs, and specifically on recovering from breakdowns in their execution. The basic idea is to add a small proportion of symbolic conditions to a reactive HTN in order to support a linear planner performing local plan recovery. Section 2 below starts with a simple, motivating example.

The problem of plan recovery has been studied in symbolic HTNs (see [1, 2, 7, 10]). This work is inspirational, but not directly relevant, because these plan repair techniques rely upon *all* of the conditions in the HTN being symbolically expressed, which obviates the use of a reactive HTN.

Others have proposed adding some kind of symbolic planning to reactive HTNs. For example, Firby [5] proposed using a planner to reorder tasks in the HTN execution or to help choose between alternative decompositions. Brom [3] proposed using planning to help execute tasks with time constraints. However, no one has yet developed a complete hybrid procedural/symbolic algorithm (see Section 4.2) similar to ours.

Finally, this work is preliminary because, although we have implemented and tested our algorithm on synthetically generated data (see Section 5), how well it will work in practice is still an open question.

2   A Motivating Example

To further introduce and motivate our work, we first consider a small, intuitive example of reactive HTN execution breakdown and recovery. The basic idea of this example, shown in Fig. 1 is that a robot has been programmed using an HTN to transport an object through a locked door. In this HTN, the toplevel task, Transport, is decomposed into three steps: pickup, Navigate and putdown.

---

[1] See http://aigamedev.com/open/article/popular-behavior-tree-design

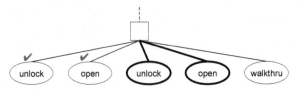

Fig. 2. Sequence of two primitive tasks (in bold) added to plan for Navigate to recover from breakdown in Fig. 1.

Navigate is further decomposed into three steps: unlock, open and walkthrough. Each of these tasks is represented by an oval in Fig. 1. (The square boxes in the HTN are there to support alternative decompositions, which can be ignored in this example.)

At the moment in time depicted in Fig. 1, the robot has successfully picked up the object, unlocked the door and opened it. However, before the precondition of the walkthru step is evaluated, the wind blows the door closed and the door locks. The walkthru precondition checks that the door is open and thus returns false. At this point, there are then no executable tasks in the HTN, which is what we call a *breakdown*.

Such breakdowns are not unusual in reactive HTNs, especially when they are executing in complex, dynamic environments. In fact, something similar to this actually happened recently to the winning robot in the prestigious DARPA Robotics Challenge[2] (emphasis added): "However, team Schaft lost points when *a gust of wind blew a door out of the robot's hand and the robot was unable to exit a vehicle* after navigated a driving course successfully." It can be hard to anticipate all possible things that can go wrong; and trying to incorporate all possible recovery plans into the HTN in advance can lead to an explosion of programming effort.

However, looking at this breakdown in particular, the recovery solution, shown in Fig. 2, is obvious, namely to unlock and open the door. Furthermore, this would be a trivial problem for a symbolic linear (e.g., STRIPS) planner to solve if only the pre- and postconditions of the relevant primitives were specified symbolically.

In a reactive HTN, pre- and postconditions are written in a procedural (programming) language and evaluated by the appropriate programming language interpreter. Fig. 3a shows the relevant procedural conditions in the Navigate plan as they might typically be written, for example, in JavaScript. For example, "isOpen()" would call code in the robot's sensory system to check whether the door is currently open. In comparison, Fig. 3b shows how the same primitive tasks would typically be formalized for a STRIPS planner using symbolic features.

Suppose that when the breakdown in Fig. 1 occurred, the HTN execution engine somehow had available the symbolic modeling knowledge shown in Fig. 3b. Recovering from the breakdown could then be formulated as a STRIPS planning problem (see Fig. 4) in which the initial state is the *current* world state, i.e., the door is not open and is locked, and the final state is the failed

---

[2] https://herox.com/news/148-the-darpa-robotics-challenge

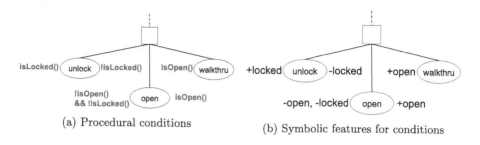

(a) Procedural conditions   (b) Symbolic features for conditions

Fig. 3. Procedural versus symbolic conditions for Navigate plan

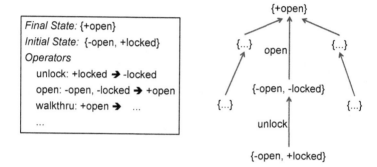

Fig. 4. Recovery from breakdown in Fig. 1 as a STRIPS planning problem

precondition of walkthru, i.e., the door is open. Simple backward-chaining would then quickly find the solution sequence of operators, namely unlock followed by open. This recovery plan could then be spliced into the HTN as shown in Fig. 2 and execution could continue.

The goal of this paper is to generalize the solution to this example problem into an application-independent plan recovery algorithm and associated modeling methodology for reactive HTNs, as described in the next two sections.

3   Procedural Versus Symbolic Modeling

A reasonable first question to ask after reading the motivating example above is why not just use a symbolic planner instead of an HTN to control the robot in the first place, and apply well-known replanning approaches when a breakdown occurs?

Answering this question leads directly to the issue of modeling. Symbolic planners, such as STRIPS, require *complete and correct* symbolic descriptions of all of the primitive tasks (operators) in the problem domain. Different planners use different symbolic formalisms to represent this knowledge, such as the add/delete lists shown in Fig. 3b, PDDL [6], and others. However, what all symbolic planners have in common is that if these symbolic descriptions are incorrect or incomplete (relative to reality), then the generated plans will fail—the poorer the correspondence to reality, the less reliable the plans will be.

Unfortunately, artificial intelligence research has shown that producing complete and correct symbolic descriptions of complex real-world domains is extremely hard and, for practical purposes, often impossible. Certainly the textbook example in Fig. 4 is easy to model symbolically, but no one participating in the DARPA Robotics Challenge seriously considered symbolically modeling the complete task domain.

The difficulty of symbolic modeling is why reactive HTNs were invented. The knowledge in a reactive HTN is encoded in two places: in the decomposition structure of the tree and in the code for the procedural conditions (especially the applicability conditions for decomposition choices, which will be explained in the next section).

So is it easier to model complex real-world domains using reactive HTNs than symbolically? As a practical matter, the answer appears to be yes, since reactive HTNs are commonly used in such applications. Our guess is that there are two main reasons for this. First, it is well known that hierarchy helps people organize their thinking to deal with complexity. Second, a procedural condition, such as a precondition, is only applied to the *current* world, whereas symbolic descriptions are essentially axioms that must be true in all possible worlds.

But of course, as we saw above, reactive HTNs can break down, which leads us to the hybrid approach, described in the next section, in which a reactive HTN is augmented with some symbolic conditions to aid specifically with recovery.

4   A Hybrid Approach

In this section we generalize the motivating example in Section 2 in two ways by considering: (1) other types of breakdowns and (2) a larger set of possible final states. We will first present a general plan recovery algorithm and then discuss the modeling methodology that goes along with it.

4.1   Reactive HTNs

For the purpose of this work, a reactive HTN, such as the general example in Fig. 5a, is formally a bipartite tree with alternating levels of *task* nodes (shown as circles or ovals) and *decomposition* (recipe) nodes (shown as squares), with a task node at the root and task nodes at the leaves. The tasks at the leaves are called *primitive*; the other tasks are called *abstract*.

Associated with the nodes of the tree are three kinds of boolean-valued procedures, each of what are evaluated in the current world state. Task nodes have an optional *precondition* and/or *postcondition*. Every decomposition node has an *applicability condition*.

Reactive HTNs are basically a kind of and/or tree, where the task nodes are "and" and the decomposition nodes are "or." Execution is a depth-first, left-to-right traversal of the tree starting at the root, with various conditions being evaluated along the way, as described below.

If the current execution node is a task, then its precondition, if any, is first evaluated. If the precondition returns false, then execution is halted (a breakdown); otherwise execution continues. If the task is primitive, then it is directly

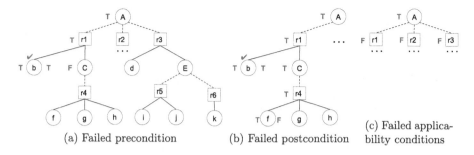

(a) Failed precondition   (b) Failed postcondition   (c) Failed applicability conditions

Fig. 5. Examples of the three types of breakdown in reactive HTN execution

executed (typically changing the world state); otherwise (i.e., for abstract tasks) the applicability conditions of the children (decomposition) nodes are evaluated in order until the first one that returns true—execution continues with this decomposition node. If all of the applicability conditions of the children return false, then execution is halted (a breakdown).

When execution of a task node is completed, its postcondition, if any, is evaluated. If the postcondition returns false, then execution is halted (a breakdown); otherwise execution continues.

If the current execution node is a decomposition, then the children (task) nodes are executed in order.

Fig. 5 summarizes the three types of execution breakdowns that are possible in reactive HTN execution. The motivating example in Section 2 was a failed precondition, as in Fig. 5a Notice that this taxonomy does not distinguish between different possible underlying causes of a breakdown. A breakdown can be caused by an external, i.e., unmodeled, agency unexpectedly changing the environment (e.g., the wind in Section 2); or it can be due to a programming bug, such as incorrect tree structure or an incorrectly coded condition. The fact these different causes are indistinguishable in the breakdown is an inherent limitation of reactive HTNs.

4.2   Plan Recovery Algorithm

The most significant generalization of the plan recovery algorithm over the motivating example in Section 2 concerns the choice of final state for the linear planning problem. In the example (see Fig. 4), the final state is the failed precondition of the walkthru primitive. However, there are other recovery possibilities that might also make sense.

For example, suppose there was a symbolic postcondition on walkthru that specified that the robot is located in the room on the other side of the door. After the breakdown, another way to recover could be for the robot to successfully find a plan (using other operators than just unlock and open) to achieve this condition, e.g., by going out another door of the current room and taking a different hallway to the original destination room. We will call this process making the postcondition of walkthru the *target* of a candidate recovery planning problem.

Continuing with this line of thought, suppose that there was no symbolic postcondition provided for walkthru, but the symbolic postcondition of Navigate specified the desired location of the robot. In that case, the postcondition of Navigate would be a good candidate recovery target.

Similarly, suppose the original breakdown in the example had instead occurred due to the postcondition of unlock failing. In this situation, the symbolic precondition of walkthru and the symbolic postconditions of walkthru and Navigate, if they are provided, are still good recovery targets.

Based on this reasoning, in the algorithm below we consider the largest possible set of pre- and postconditions in the tree as candidate recovery targets, excluding only those that have already been used in the execution process and have evaluated to true. We suspect this is an over-generalization, but need more practical experience to determine a better approach.

The recovery target issue for applicability conditions is somewhat different. The only time that an applicability condition should be a recovery target is when its and all of its siblings' conditions have evaluated to false, as in Fig. 5c.

Fig. 6 shows the pseudocode for the hybrid system we have designed. The toplevel procedure, EXECUTE, executes an HTN until either it is successfully completed, or there is a breakdown with no possible recovery. The plan recovery algorithm starts at line 5. The main subroutine, FINDCANDIDATES, recursively walks the HTN tree, accumulating candidate target conditions for the recovery planning. Notice that SYMBOLICPLANNER is not defined here, since any symbolic linear planner can be used (our implementation is described in Section 5). Notice also that since the set of operators used for symbolic planning doesn't change during execution of the HTN, it is not an explicit argument to the symbolic planner (see further discussion regarding symbolic operators in Section 4.3).

In more detail, notice on line 6 that our approach requires a method for computing from the current world state an initial state representation in the formalism used by the symbolic planner. For example, for the STRIPS planner in Section 2 this means that for every feature, such as "open," there must be an associated procedure, such as "isOpen()," to compute its value in the current world state. This association is a basic part of the hybrid modeling methodology discussed in next section.

Notice on line 8 that the candidate conditions are sorted by distance from the current node in the tree (closest first), using a simple metric such as the length of the shortest path between them in the undirected graph. The reason for this is to give preference to recovery plans that keep more closely to the structure of the original HTN. We do not yet have any experience with how well this heuristic works in practice.

Finally in EXECUTE, notice on line 12 that when a recovery plan is found, it must be properly spliced into the HTN. In the simple example in Fig. 2, this is merely a matter of inserting a sequence of nodes as children of the common parent between the initial and final nodes. However, if the initial and final nodes are more distant in the tree, more complicated changes are needed to replace the intervening tree structure with the new plan.

```
 1: procedure EXECUTE(htn)
 2:     while htn is not completed do
 3:         current ← next executable node in htn
 4:         if current ≠ null then execute current
 5:         else [breakdown occurred]
 6:             initial ← symbolic description of current world state
 7:             candidates ← FindCandidates(htn)
 8:             sort candidates by distance from current
 9:             for final ∈ candidates do
10:                 plan ← SymbolicPlanner(initial, final)
11:                 if plan ≠ null then
12:                     splice plan into htn between current and final
13:                     continue while loop above
14:             Recovery failed!

15: procedure FINDCANDIDATES(task)
16:     conditions ← ∅
17:     pre ← symbolic precondition of task
18:     if pre ≠ null ∧ procedural prec of task has not evaluated to true then
19:         add pre to conditions
20:     post ← symbolic postcondition of task
21:     if post ≠ null ∧ procedural postc of task has not evaluated to true then
22:         add post to conditions
23:     applicables ← ∅
24:     allFalse ← true
25:     for decomp ∈ children of task do
26:         for task ∈ children of decomp do FindCandidates(task)
27:         if allFalse then
28:             if procedural appl condition of decomp has evaluated to false then
29:                 app ← symbolic applicability condition of decomp
30:                 if app ≠ null then add app to applicables
31:             else allFalse ← false
32:     if allFalse then add applicables to conditions
33:     return conditions
```

Fig. 6. Pseudocode for hybrid reactive HTN execution and recovery system

The code in the definition of FINDCANDIDATES closely follows the discussion above regarding possible target conditions.

4.3 Modeling Methodology

The hybrid system described above tries to take advantage of whatever symbolic knowledge is provided by the HTN author. Notice that for the pre- or postcondition of each task node there are four possibilities: no specified condition, only a procedural condition, only a symbolic condition, or both. Since applicability conditions are not optional, there are only two possibilities for decomposition nodes: only a procedural condition, or a procedural and a symbolic condition.

As we have argued earlier, symbolic modeling is very difficult in general. The reason an author is using a reactive HTN in the first place is likely because it was not practical to fully model the domain symbolically. Two key methodological issues are therefore where to best invest whatever effort is available for symbolic modeling, and how to make the overall process of mixed procedural and symbolic modeling as convenient as possible for the HTN author. We will share some ideas below, but this is the area in which our work is also preliminary.

Our initial intuition, illustrated by the example in Section 2, is to concentrate symbolic modeling on the primitive tasks. This is because we expect symbolic plan recovery to be most successful as a local planning strategy.

Which pre- and postconditions are provided symbolically also has implications for the set of operators used by the symbolic planner. Only a task with both a symbolic precondition and postcondition can be included in the operator set. However, the planning operators need not be restricted to primitive tasks. If an abstract task is fully specified symbolically, it can in principle be included in a linear recovery plan by using its already defined decompositions (and hoping they are appropriate in the new context).

Finally, we believe there is the opportunity for tools to make the hybrid modeling process less onerous. For example, we are planning a simple design-time tool that recognizes common coding conventions, such as in Fig. 3a, and automatically produces corresponding symbolic conditions, such as in Fig. 3b. Run-time tools can also keep track of breakdowns and advise where additional symbolic knowledge may be useful.

5   Implementation and Evaluation

We have implemented the hybrid system described above in pure Java (see Fig. 7) using the ANSI/CEA-2018 standard [8] for reactive HTNs and Disco [9] as the HTN execution engine. For the symbolic planner, we have used a simple implementation of STRIPS running in a pure Java implementation of Prolog.[3] Using Prolog will facilitate adding additional symbolic reasoning rules to the planning process.

Fig. 7. Discolog implementation

The ultimate evaluation of our proposed new approach is to build several agents that operate in complex, dynamic real-world environments and to see how easy they were to build and how robustly they performed. In the meantime, however, we tested our system on synthetically generated HTNs with different levels of symbolic knowledge. Our simple hypothesis was that the more symbolic knowledge provided, the better the recovery algorithm would perform.

Fig. 8 shows the results of our experiments, which confirmed this hypothesis. We tested trees of two RxSxD sizes, 3x3x3 and 1x5x4, where R is the decomposition (recipe) branching factor, S is task (step) branching factor, and D is

---

[3] See http://tuprolog.apice.unibo.it

the task depth (see Fig. 9). For each test, we randomly sampled from the very large space (millions) of all possible combinations of symbolic knowledge at three overall levels: 25%, 50% and 75% (percentage of conditions in the tree that are symbolically specified). We did not test larger trees because the experimental running times became too long.

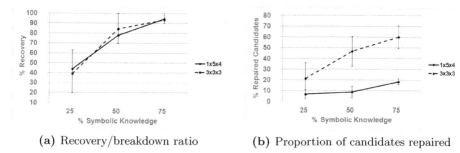

(a) Recovery/breakdown ratio   (b) Proportion of candidates repaired

Fig. 8. Results of testing on synthetically generated HTNs with different levels of symbolic knowledge.

Fig. 8a graphs how the proportion of breakdowns that are successfully recovered increases as the symbolic knowledge increases. In Fig. 8b, we were interested in the proportion of planning problems submitted to the planner which it solved, which also increased as the symbolic knowledge increased. (For this experiment, we made a small modification to the algorithm to prevent it from stopping at the first solved problem.)

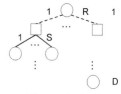

Fig. 9. RxSxD

References

1. Ayan, N.F., Kuter, U., Yaman, F., Goldman, R.: HOTRiDE: Hierarchical ordered task replanning in dynamic environments. In: Planning and Plan Execution for Real-World Systems-Principles and Practices for Planning in Execution: Papers from the ICAPS Workshop, Providence, RI (2007)
2. Boella, G., Damiano, R.: A replanning algorithm for a reactive agent architecture. In: Scott, D. (ed.) AIMSA 2002. LNCS (LNAI), vol. 2443, pp. 183–192. Springer, Heidelberg (2002)
3. Brom, C.: Hierarchical reactive planning: where is its limit. In: Proceedings of MNAS: Modelling Natural Action Selection, Edinburgh, Scotland (2005)
4. Fikes, R.E., Nilsson, N.J.: STRIPS: A new appraoch to the application of theorem proving to problem solving. Artificial Intelligence **2**, 189–208 (1971)
5. Firby, R.: An investigation into reactive planning in complex domains. In: AAAI, pp. 202–206 (1987)

6. Ghallab, M., et al.: PDDL-The planning domain definition language (1998)
7. Krogt, R.V.D., Weerdt, M.D.: Plan repair as an extension of planning. In: ICAPS, pp. 161–170 (2005)
8. Rich, C.: Building task-based user interfaces with ANSI/CEA-2018. IEEE Computer **42**, 20–27 (2009)
9. Rich, C., Sidner, C.L.: Using collaborative discourse theory to partially automate dialogue tree authoring. In: Nakano, Y., Neff, M., Paiva, A., Walker, M. (eds.) IVA 2012. LNCS, vol. 7502, pp. 327–340. Springer, Heidelberg (2012)
10. Warfield, I., Hogg, C., Lee-Urban, S., Munoz-Avila, H.: Adaptation of hierarchical task network plans. In: FLAIRS, pp. 429–434 (2007)

Optimization Framework with Minimum Description Length Principle for Probabilistic Programming

Alexey Potapov[1,2,3]($\boxtimes$), Vita Batishcheva[2,3], and Sergey Rodionov[3,4]

[1] ITMO University, St. Petersburg, Russia
pas.aicv@gmail.com
[2] St. Petersburg State University, St. Petersburg, Russia
elokkuu@gmail.com
[3] AIDEUS, Moscow, Russia
astroseger@gmail.com
[4] CNRS, LAM (Laboratoire d'Astrophysique de Marseille) UMR 7326,
Aix Marseille Université, 13388, Marseille, France

Abstract. Application of the Minimum Description Length principle to optimization queries in probabilistic programming was investigated on the example of the C++ probabilistic programming library under development. It was shown that incorporation of this criterion is essential for optimization queries to behave similarly to more common queries performing sampling in accordance with posterior distributions and automatically implementing the Bayesian Occam's razor. Experimental validation was conducted on the task of blood cell detection on microscopic images. Detection appeared to be possible using genetic programming query, and automatic penalization of candidate solution complexity allowed to choose the number of cells correctly avoiding overfitting.

Keywords: Probabilistic programming · MDL · Image interpretation · AGI

1 Introduction

Occam's razor is the crucial component of universal algorithmic intelligence models [1], in which it is formalized in terms of algorithmic information theory. In practice, Occam's razor is most widely used in the form of the Minimum Description/Message Length (MDL/MML) principles [2, 3], which can also be grounded in algorithmic information theory [4], but usually are applied loosely using heuristic coding schemes instead of universal reference machines [5].

Another form of Occam's razor is the Bayesian Occam's razor. In its simplest form, it penalizes complex models assigning them lower prior probabilities. However, these priors can be difficult to define non-arbitrarily. Some additional principles such as the maximum entropy principle were traditionally used to define priors, but algorithmic information theory providing universal priors resolves this difficulty more generally and elegantly [6] absorbing this simple form of the Bayesian Occam's razor. Real alternative to the information-theoretic interpretation of Occam's razor is 'a modern Bayesian approach to priors' [7], in which model complexity is measured by

© Springer International Publishing Switzerland 2015
J. Bieger (Ed.): AGI 2015, LNAI 9205, pp. 331–340, 2015.
DOI: 10.1007/978-3-319-21365-1_34

its flexibility (possibility to fit to or generate different data instances) estimated on the second level of inference.

Interestingly, Bayesian Occam's razor arises naturally without special implementation in probabilistic programming languages (PPLs) with posterior probability inference [8]. Programs in PPLs are generative models. They require a programmer to define prior probabilities for some basic random variables, but the total probability distribution is derived from the program. One can easily obtain universal priors by writing a function like (define (gen) (if (flip) '() (cons (if (flip) 0 1) (gen)))), where (flip) equiprobably returns #t or #f, and interpreting generated binary lists as programs for Universal Turing Machine (UTM).

Universal priors appear here from the natural structure of the program, and a concrete form of the selected distributions for the basic random choices only shifts them as the choice of a concrete UTM does. Similar situation appears in the case of models specifying Turing-incomplete spaces – higher-order polynomials with concrete coefficients will naturally have smaller prior probabilities than lower-order polynomials even if the degree of polynomials is uniformly sampled from a certain range.

Inference methods implemented in PPLs are intended for evaluating posterior probabilities incorporating priors defined by a program. Thus, instead of manually applying the MDL principle, one can simply use PPLs, which provide both the over-learning-proof criterion and automatic inference methods.

However, existing PPLs don't solve the problem of efficient inference in a general case, although they provide more efficient inference procedures than blind search. Now, different attempts to improve inference procedures are being made (e.g. [9, 10]). Most of them are done within the full Bayesian framework. The optimization framework, in which only maximum of posterior distribution (or other criterion) is sought, can be much more efficient and is enough in many practical tasks, but is much less studied in probabilistic programming.

Optimization queries require some criterion function to be defined instead of a strict condition. It is usually straightforward to define precision-based criteria. Actually, in some tasks, strict conditions are defined as stochastic equality based on likelihood (otherwise it will be necessary to blindly generate and fit noise), so the latter is more basic. Of course, if there is no appropriate quantitative criterion, the optimization framework is not applicable. However, if one uses stochastic equality, priors will be automatically taken into account by conditional sampling (since samples will be generative in accordance with prior probabilities and then kept proportionally to likelihood), while optimization queries will directly maximize the given criterion and will be prone to overfitting if this criterion is precision-based.

Thus, the necessity for MDL-like criteria arises in the optimization approach to probabilistic programming. Necessity for manual specification of such criteria, which incorporate not only precision, but also complexity, makes optimization queries much less usable and spoils the very idea of probabilistic programming. Thus, optimization queries should be designed in such a form that user-defined likelihood criteria are modified using automatically estimated priors.

In this work, we re-implement a functional PPL with optimization queries in the form of C++ library, which have been implemented in Scheme and described in the companion paper [11]. We add a wrapper for OpenCV to this library in order to deal with non-toy problems. In these settings, we develop a procedure to calculate prior probabilities of instantiations of generative models in the form of computation traces used in optimization queries, and study its applicability to avoid overlearning.

2   Background

Minimum Description Length Principle

Universal induction and prediction models are based on algorithmic complexity and probability, which are incomputable and cannot be directly applied in practice. Instead, the Minimum Description (or Message) Length principle (MDL) is usually applied. Initially, these principles were introduced in some specific strict forms [2, 3], but now are utilized in many applied methods (e.g. [5]) in the form of the following loose general definition [4]: the best model of the given data source is the one which minimizes the sum of

- the length, in bits, of the model description;
- the length, in bits, of data encoded with the use of the model.

Its main purpose is to avoid overfitting by penalizing models on the base of their complexity that is calculated within heuristically defined coding schemes. Such "applied MDL principle" is quite useful, but mostly in the context of narrow AI. Bridging the gap between Kolmogorov complexity and applications of the MDL principle can also be a step towards bridging the gap between general and narrow AI.

Probabilistic Programming

In traditional semantics, a program with random choices being evaluated many times yields different results. The main idea behind probabilistic programming is to associate the result of program evaluation not with such particular outcomes, but with the distribution of all possible outcomes. Of course, the problem is to represent and compute such distributions for arbitrary programs with random choices. It can be done directly only for some Turing-incomplete languages. In general case, the simplest way to deal with this problem is via sampling, in which a distribution is represented by the samples generated by a program evaluated many time using traditional semantics.

Crucial feature of PPLs is conditioning, which allows a programmer to impose some conditions on (intermediate or final) results of program evaluation. Programs with such conditions are evaluated to conditional (posterior) distributions, which are the core of Bayesian inference. The simplest implementation of conditional inference is rejection sampling, in which outcomes of the program evaluation, which don't meet the given condition, are rejected (not included into the generated set of outcomes representing conditional distribution). Such rejection sampling can be easily added to most existing programming languages as a common procedure, but it is highly inefficient, so it is usable only for very low-dimensional models. Consequently, more advanced inference techniques are being applied. For example, Metropolis-Hastings method is quite popular. In particular, it is used in Church [8], which extends Scheme with such sampling functions as *rejected-query*, *mh-query*, and some others.

PPLs extend traditional programming languages also adding to them some functions to sample from different distributions. In Church, such functions as *flip*, *random-integer*, *gaussian*, *multinomial*, and some others are implemented.

Bayesian Occam's Razor in Probabilistic Programming

As was mentioned, such PPLs as Church naturally support the Bayesian Occam's razor [8]. Let us consider the following very simple example.

```
(mh-query 1000 100
          (define n (+ (random-integer 10) 1))
          (define xs (repeat n (lambda () (random-integer 10))))
          n
          (= (sum xs) 12))
```

Here, we want a sum of unknown number n of random digits xs be equal to the given number, 12. Values of n belonging to the specified range are equiprobable a priori. However, the derived posterior probabilities are highly non-uniform – $P(n=2|sum=12)\approx0.9$; $P(n=3|sum=12)\approx0.09$; $P(n=4|sum=12)\approx0.009$.

Underlying combinatorics is quite obvious. However, this is exactly the effect of "penalizing complex solutions" that works in less obvious cases [8], e.g. polynomial approximation using polynomials of arbitrary degree, or clustering with unknown number of clusters.

3   Optimization Framework for Probabilistic Programming

Implemented Library

We aim at the practical, but general implementation of probabilistic programming, so we consider Turing-complete languages and optimization framework. We implemented a subset of Scheme language inside C++ using class constructors instead of function application. For example, such classes as *Define*, *Lambda*, *List*, *Cons*, *Car*, *Cdr*, *Nullp*, *ListRef*, *If*, and others with the corresponding constructors were implemented. All these classes are inherited from the *Expression* class, which has the field *std::vector<Expression *> children*, so expressions can constitute a tree. To create expressions from values, the class *Value* (with the synonym *V*) was added. This class is used for all values dynamically resolving supported types.

Also, such classes as *Add*, *Sub*, *Mult*, *Div*, *Gt*, *Gte*, *Ls*, *Lse*, etc. were added, and such operations as +, −, *, /, >, >=, <, <=, etc. were overloaded to call corresponding constructors. Consequently, one can write something like

Define(f, Lambda(xs, If(Nullp(xs), V(0), Car(xs) + f(Cdr(xs))))))

corresponding to

(define f (lambda (xs) (+ (if (null? xs) 0 (+ (car xs) (f (cdr xs))))))))

To use symbols *f* and *xs*, one needs to declare them as instances of the class *Symbol* (with the synonym *S*) or to write *S("xs")* instead of *xs*. Parentheses operator is also overloaded, so one can write *f(xs)* instead of *Apply(f, xs)*, where *Apply* is also the child of *Expression*. Similarly, one can write *xs[n]* instead of *ListRef(xs, n)*.

Classes corresponding to the basic random distributions were also added including *Flip*, *Gaussian*, *RndInt*, etc.

We also wrapped some OpenCV functions and data structures in our library. Support for *cv::Mat* as the basic type was added, so it is possible to write something like *Define(S("image"), V(cv::imread("test.jpg")))*. All basic overloaded operations with *cv::Mat* are inherited, so values corresponding to *cv::Mat* can be summed or multiplied with other values.

To avoid huge program traces while filling image pixels with random values (each such value will become a node in a program trace), we introduced such classes as *MatGaussian* and *MatRndInt* for generating random matrices as holistic values. These random matrices can be also generated as deviations from given data.

The mentioned constructors of different classes are used simply to create expressions and arrange them into trees. Evaluation of such expressions was also implemented. A given expression tree is expanded into a program trace during evaluation. This program trace is also an expression tree, but with values assigned to its nodes. Evaluation process and program traces implemented in our C++ library are similar to that implemented in Scheme and described in the companion paper [11], so we will not go into detail here. Also, we re-implemented the optimization queries based on simulated annealing and genetic programming over computation traces. For example, one can write the following program with the result of evaluation shown in Fig. 1

Symbol imr, imb;
AnnealingQuery(List()
       << Define(imr, MatRndInt(img.rows, img.cols, CV_8UC3, 256, *img))*
       << Define(imb, GaussianBlur(imr, V(11.), V(3.)))
       << imr
       *<< (MatDiff2(imb, V(img)) + MatDiff2(imb, imr) * 0.3))*;

Here, *img* is some *cv::Mat* loaded beforehand, *List() << x << y << z ...* is equivalent to (list x y z ...). Operator << can be used to put additional elements to the list on the step of expression tree creation (not evaluation). *imr* is created as the random 3-channel image with *img* as the initial value. *MatDiff2* calculates RMSE per pixel between two matrices. *AnnealingQuery* is the simulated annealing optimization query, which minimizes the value of its last child, and its return value is set to the corresponding value of its last but one child. Here, the second term in the optimization function prevents from too noisy results. Also, *GPQuery* based on genetic programming is implemented.

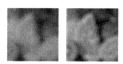

Fig. 1. The original blurred image and the result of inference

Simulated annealing is not really suitable to perform search in the space of images, but reasonable result is obtained here in few seconds. It can also be seen that general C++ code can be easily used together with our probabilistic programming library. Of course, this code is executed before or during construction of expression tree or after its evaluation, but not during the process of evaluation. The latter can be done by extending the library with new classes that is relatively simple, but slightly more involved.

Expression trees can be used not as fixed programs written by a programmer, but as dynamic data structures built automatically. So, such a library can easily be made a part of a larger system (e.g. a cognitive architecture).

Our library is under development and is used in this paper as the research tool, so we will not go into more detail. Nevertheless, the current version can be downloaded from https://github.com/aideus/prodeus

Undesirable Behavior

Optimization framework is suitable for many tasks, and optimization queries even without complexity penalty can be applied in probabilistic programming (see some examples in our companion paper [11]). However, even very simple generative models can be inappropriate in this framework. Consider the following program

> Symbol xobs, centers, sigmas, n, xgen;
> AnnealingQuery(List())
>>   << Define(xobs, V(4.))
>>   << Define(centers, List(3, -7., 2., 10.))
>>   << Define(sigmas, List(3, 1., 1., 1.))
>>   << Define(n, RndInt(Length(centers)))
>>   << Define(xgen, Gaussian(ListRef(centers, n), ListRef(sigmas, n)))
>>   << n
>>   << (xobs − xgen) * (xobs − xgen));

Intuitively, this program should simply return the number of the center closest to *xobs* since *AnnealingQuery* will minimize the distance from the generated value to the class center. However, evaluation of this program yields almost random indices of centers. The same model works fine in Church. The following query will return the distribution with $p(n=1) \approx 1$; and in the case of (define centers '(-7., -2., 10.)) it will return $p(n=1) \approx p(n=2) \approx 0.5$.

```
(define (noisy-equal? x y)
        (flip (exp (* -1 (− x y) (− x y)))))
(mh-query 100 100
        (define xobs 4)
        (define centers '(-7., 2., 10.))
        (define sigmas '(1., 1., 1.))
        (define n (random-integer (length centers)))
        (define xgen (gaussian (list-ref centers n) (list-ref sigmas n)))
        n
        (noisy-equal? xobs xgen))
```

It should be noted that noisy-equal? should apply *flip* to the correctly estimated likelihood, if one wants e.g. to get correct posterior probabilities for *xgen*. In particular, it should include such parameter as dispersion or precision. That is, these programs in C++ and Church really include the same information.

Inappropriate result of *AnnealingQuery* originates from its possibility to reduce the given criterion adjusting values of all random variables including both *n* and *xgen* in this model. It is much easier to adjust *xgen* directly since its probability is not taken into account in the criterion. This problem can be easily fixed here, if we will tell *AnnealingQuery* to minimize the distance from the n-th center to *xobs*. The program will be simpler, and its result will be correct. However, the general problem will remain. It will reveal itself in the form of overfitting, impossibility to select an appropriate number of cluster or segments in the tasks of clustering and segmentation, necessity to manually define *ad hoc* criteria, and so on. These are exactly the problems, which are solved with the use of the MDL principle.

Complexity Estimation

Apparently, if we want optimization queries to work similarly to sampling queries, we need to account for probabilities, with which candidate solutions are generated. Here, we assume that the criterion fed to optimization queries can be treated as the negative log-likelihood. Then, it will be enough to automatically calculate and add minus logarithm of prior probability of a candidate solution to achieve the desirable behavior.

We calculate these prior probabilities by multiplying probabilities in those nodes of the program trace subtree starting from *AnnealingQuery* or *GPQuery*, in which basic random choices are made. Here, we assume that the list of expressions fed to queries is relevant. As the result, each such choice is taken into account only once, even if a variable referring to this choice is used many times.

AnnealingQuery and *GPQuery* were modified and tested on the program presented above, and they returned $n=1$ in all cases, so they behave desirably. Of course, optimization queries give less information than sampling queries. For example, in the case of centers '(-7., -2., 10.) the former will return $n=1$ or $n=2$ randomly, while the latter will return their probabilities. However, optimization queries can be much more efficient, and can be used to find the first point, from which methods like *mh-query* can start.

4   Evaluation

Since we aim at practical probabilistic programming for Turing-complete languages, we consider image analysis tasks which are computationally quite heavy. To the best of our knowledge, the only example of such application is the work [12] (and unfortunately it lacks information about computation time). Thus, possibility to solve image analysis tasks in a reasonable time can be used as a sufficient demonstration of efficiency of the optimization framework. This is also our goal in addition to verification of the automatic MDL criterion calculation procedure.

Consider the task of detection of erythrocytes (our system wasn't aimed to solve this specific task, and it is taken simply as an example; other tasks could be picked). The typical image is shown in Fig. 2. The task is to detect and count cells. This task is usually solved by detecting edge pixels and applying Hough transform, or by tracking contours and fitting circles. Direct application of existing implementations of image processing methods is not enough, and application of non-trivial combinations of different processing functions or even ad hoc implementation of these functions is needed (e.g. [13]).

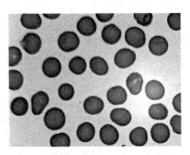

Fig. 2. The original image with red blood cells

However, an acceptable solution can be obtained using the following very small generative model:

Define(n, RndInt(20) + 10)

Define(circs, Repeat(n, Lambda0(List(RndInt(img.cols),
                                    RndInt(img.rows),
                                    RndInt(12)+6))))

Define(gen, Foldr(Lambda(circ, im,
                  DrawCircle(im, circ[0], circ[1], circ[2], V(168), V(-1))),
                  circs, V(cv::Mat::zeros(img.rows, img.cols, cv::CV_8UC1))))

circs

*Log(MatDiff2(gen, V(img))) * V(img.cols * img.rows)*

Here, *n* is the number of circles to draw, *circs* is the list of random circle centers and radii (*img* is the inverted image to be analyzed), *gen* is the generated image. It is generated starting from an empty image and consequently drawing circles from *circs*. It should be noted that since our library implements a functional quasi-language, such functions as *DrawCircle* don't modify the given image, but return a new one. The last two expressions in the model contain the resulting value and estimation of minus log-likelihood. To increase performance, we also implemented *Drawer* class. During evaluation *Drawer* processes a list of shapes and draws them using one resulting image. The program with *Drawer* instead of *Foldr* and *DrawCircle* was tested.

AnnealingQuery failed on the image with many objects, since each step of simulated annealing consists in an attempt to modify coordinates and sizes of all circles simultaneously, and successful modification becomes very unlikely for large number of variables. *GPQuery* showed acceptable results (see Fig. 3), but with some adjustment of the crossover operator.

GPQuery yields better results here, since it automatically performs "soft decomposition" of the given problem. However, its results are not optimal, and the search time is not too small (5–30 seconds on i5 2.6 GHz depending on GP parameters). Nevertheless, it is already usable for rapid prototyping.

The search problem is one of the most important problems here, and it is far from being fully solved. However, we are interested in testing the developed method for incorporating the MDL criterion into the optimization queries. Let us consider the calculated value of this criterion on different small images (Fig. 4) for different number of circles in order to ensure that the found solution is nearly optimal. Table 1 summarizes the obtained results.

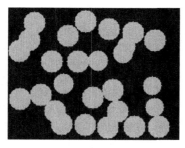

Fig. 3. The result yielded by *GPQuery* (population size = 300, number of generations = 100, mutation rate = 0.005)

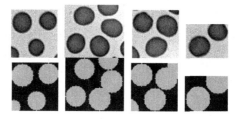

Fig. 4. Image fragments and best results for them

Table 1. Total description lengths, bits

Image #	n					
	1	2	3	4	5	6
1	14650.4	14038.0	13131.2	12687.3	12689.3	12690.0
2	20201.3	19612.1	18888.2	17955.2	17104.2	17115.2
3	14680.3	13995.2	12808.1	12391.7	12316.6	12321.0
4	9270.7	8155.1	8160.6	8162.6	8163.2	8168.5

It can be seen that the total description length starts to slowly increase from some number of circles for each image. Each circle adds around 10 bits of complexity. So, negative log-likelihood slightly decreases, but slower than increase of complexity. Actually, since blood cells are not perfectly circular, additional circles fitted to uncovered parts of cells can increase model complexity lesser than decrease of negative log-likelihood in some cases. However, in these cases, queries calculating posterior probability will also give a strong peak at the same number of circles. In other words, the origin of this result is not in query procedures or criteria, but in the model. In general, the found minima of the description length criteria correspond to the real number of blood cells, and partially presented cells are reliably detected.

5   Conclusion

The developed method for automatic usage of the Minimum Description Length principle in probabilistic programming both reduces the gap between the looselyapplied

MDL principle and the theoretically grounded, but impractical Kolmogorov complexity, and helps to avoid overfitting in optimization queries making them an efficient alternative to more traditional queries estimating conditional probabilities. Experiments conducted on the example of an image analysis task confirmed availability of this approach.

However, even optimization queries being not specialized cannot efficiently solve arbitrary induction tasks especially connected to AGI. Actually, the task of such efficient inference can itself be considered as the "AI-complete" problem. Thus, deeper connections between AGI and probabilistic programming fields are to be established.

Acknowledgements. This work was supported by Ministry of Education and Science of the Russian Federation, and by Government of Russian Federation, Grant 074-U01.

References

1. Hutter, M.: Universal Artificial Intelligence: Sequential Decisions Based on Algorithmic Probability. Springer (2005)
2. Wallace, C.S., Boulton, D.M.: An Information Measure for Classification. Computer Journal **11**, 185–195 (1968)
3. Rissanen, J.J.: Modeling by the Shortest Data Description. Automatica-J.IFAC **14**, 465–471 (1978)
4. Vitanyi, P.M.B., Li, M.: Minimum Description Length Induction, Bayesianism, and Kolmogorov complexity. IEEE Trans. on Information Theory **46**(2), 446–464 (2000)
5. Potapov, A.S.: Principle of Representational Minimum Description Length in Image Analysis and Pattern Recognition. Pattern Recognition and Image Analysis **22**(1), 82–91 (2012)
6. Solomonoff, R.: Does Algorithmic Probability Solve the Problem of Induction?. Oxbridge Research, Cambridge (1997)
7. MacKay, D.J.C.: Bayesian Methods for Adaptive Models. PhD thesis, California Institute of Technology (1991)
8. Goodman, N.D., Tenenbaum, J.B.: Probabilistic Models of Cognition. https://probmods.org/
9. Stuhlmüller, A., Goodman, N. D.: A dynamic programming algorithm for inference in recursive probabilistic programs. In: Second Statistical Relational AI Workshop at UAI 2012 (StaRAI-12), arXiv:1206.3555 [cs.AI] (2012)
10. Chaganty, A., Nori A.V., Rajamani, S.K.: Efficiently sampling probabilistic programs via program analysis. In: Proc. Artificial Intelligence and Statistics, pp. 153–160 (2013)
11. Potapov, A., Batishcheva, V.: Genetic Programming on Program Traces as an Inference Engine for Probabilistic Languages. In: LNAI (2015)
12. Mansinghka, V., Kulkarni, T., Perov, Y., Tenenbaum, J.: Approximate Bayesian Image Interpretation using Generative Probabilistic Graphics Programs. Advances in Neural Information Processing Systems, arXiv:1307.0060 [cs.AI] (2013)
13. Zhdanov, I.N., Potapov, A.S., Shcherbakov, O.V.: Erythrometry method based on a modified Hough transform. Journal of Optical Technology **80**(3), 201–203 (2013)

Can Machines Learn Logics?

Chiaki Sakama[1]([⊠]) and Katsumi Inoue[2]

[1] Department of Computer and Communication Sciences, Wakayama University,
Sakaedani, Wakayama 640-8510, Japan
sakama@sys.wakayama-u.ac.jp
[2] National Institute of Informatics,
2-1-2 Hitotsubashi, Chiyoda-ku, Tokyo 101-8430, Japan
inoue@nii.ac.jp

Abstract. This paper argues the possibility of designing AI that can learn logics from data. We provide an abstract framework for learning logics. In this framework, an agent $\mathcal{A}$ provides training examples that consist of formulas S and their logical consequences T. Then a machine $\mathcal{M}$ builds an axiomatic system that underlies between S and T. Alternatively, in the absence of an agent $\mathcal{A}$, the machine $\mathcal{M}$ seeks an unknown logic underlying given data. We next provide two cases of learning logics: the first case considers learning deductive inference rules in propositional logic, and the second case considers learning transition rules in cellular automata. Each case study uses machine learning techniques together with metalogic programming.

1 Introduction

Logic-based AI systems perform logical inferences to get solutions given input formulas. Such systems have been developed in the field of automated theorem proving or logic programming [10]. In those systems, however, a logic used in the system is specified and built-in by human engineers. Our question in this paper is whether it is possible to develop artificial (general) intelligence that automatically produces a logic underlying any given data set.

In his argument on "learning machines" in [14], Alan Turing wrote:

> Instead of trying to produce a programme to simulate the adult mind, why not rather try to produce one which simulates the child's? If this were then subjected to an appropriate course of education one would obtain the adult brain [14, p. 456].

According to Piaget's theory of cognitive development, children begin to understand logical or rational thought at age around seven [12]. If one can develop AI that automatically acquires a logic of human reasoning, it verifies Turing's assumption that a child's brain can grow into an adult's one by learning an appropriate logic. Recent advances in robotics argue possibilities of robots' recognizing objects in the world, categorizing concepts, and associating names to them (*physical symbol grounding*) [3]. Once robots successfully learn concepts

© Springer International Publishing Switzerland 2015
J. Bieger (Ed.): AGI 2015, LNAI 9205, pp. 341–351, 2015.
DOI: 10.1007/978-3-319-21365-1_35

and associate symbols to them, the next step is to learn relations between concepts and logical or physical rules governing the world.

In this study, we will capture learning logics as a problem of *inductive learning*. According to [9], "(t)he goal of (inductive) inference is to formulate plausible general assertions that explain the given facts and are able to predict new facts. In other words, inductive inference attempts to derive a complete and correct description of a given phenomenon from specific observations of that phenomenon or of parts of it" [9, p. 88]. A logic provides a set of axioms and inference rules that underlie sentences representing the world. Then given a set of sentences representing the world, one could inductively construct a logic governing the world. This is in fact a work for mathematicians who try to find an axiomatic system that is sound and complete with respect to a given set of theorems. Induction has been used as an inference mechanism of machine learning, while little study has been devoted to the challenging topic of learning logics.

In this paper, we first describe an abstract framework for learning logics based on inductive learning. Next we provide two simple case studies: learning deductive inference rules and learning cellular automata (CAs) rules. In the former case, the problem of producing deductive inference rules from formulas and their logical consequences is considered. In the second case, the problem of producing transition rules from CA configurations is considered. In each case, we use machine learning techniques together with metalogic programming. The rest of this paper is organized as follows. Section 2 introduces an abstract framework for learning logics. Section 3 presents a case of learning deductive inference rules and Section 4 presents a case of learning CA rules. Section 5 discusses further issues and Section 6 summarizes the paper.

2   Learning Logics

To consider the question *"Can machines learn logics?"*, suppose the following problem. There is an agent $\mathcal{A}$ and a machine $\mathcal{M}$. The agent $\mathcal{A}$, which could be a human or a computer, is capable of deductive reasoning: it has a set $\mathcal{L}$ of axioms and inference rules in classical logic. Given a (finite) set S of formulas as an input, the agent $\mathcal{A}$ produces a (finite) set of formulas T such that $T \subset Th(S)$ where $Th(S)$ is the set of logical consequences of S. On the other hand, the machine $\mathcal{M}$ has no axiomatic system for deduction, while it is equipped with a machine learning algorithm $\mathcal{C}$. Given input-output pairs $(S_1, T_1), \ldots, (S_i, T_i), \ldots$ (where $T_i \subset Th(S_i)$) of $\mathcal{A}$ as an input to $\mathcal{M}$, the problem is whether one can develop an algorithm $\mathcal{C}$ which successfully produces an axiomatic system $\mathcal{K}$ for deduction. An algorithm $\mathcal{C}$ is *sound* wrt $\mathcal{L}$ if it produces an axiomatic system $\mathcal{K}$ such that $\mathcal{K} \subseteq \mathcal{L}$. An algorithm $\mathcal{C}$ is *complete* wrt $\mathcal{L}$ if it produces an axiomatic system $\mathcal{K}$ such that $\mathcal{L} \subseteq \mathcal{K}$. Designing a sound and complete algorithm $\mathcal{C}$ is called a problem of *learning logics* (Figure 1). In this framework, an agent $\mathcal{A}$ plays the role of a teacher who provides training examples representing premises along with entailed consequences. The output $\mathcal{K}$ is refined by incrementally providing examples. We consider a deduction system $\mathcal{L}$ while it could be a system of

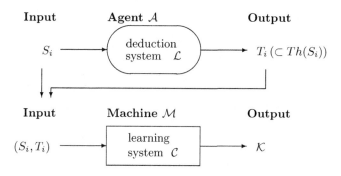

Fig. 1. Learning Logics

arbitrary logic, e.g. nonmonotonic logic, modal logic, fuzzy logic, as far as it has a formal system of inference. Alternatively, we can consider a framework in which a teacher agent $\mathcal{A}$ is absent. In this case, given input-output pairs (S_i, T_i) as data, the problem is whether a machine $\mathcal{M}$ can find an unknown logic (or axiomatic system) that produces a consequence T_i from a premise S_i.

The abstract framework provided in this section has challenging issues of AI including the questions:

1. *Can we develop a sound and complete algorithm $\mathcal{C}$ for learning a classical or non-classical logic $\mathcal{L}$?*

2. *Is there any difference between learning axioms and learning inference rules?*

3. *Does a machine $\mathcal{M}$ discover a new axiomatic system $\mathcal{K}$ such that $\mathcal{K} \vdash F$ iff $\mathcal{L} \vdash F$ for any formula F?*

The first question concerns the possibility of designing machine learning algorithms that can learn existing logics from given formulas. The second question concerns differences between learning Gentzen-style logics and Hilbert-style logics. The third question is more ambitious: it asks the possibility of AI's discovering new logics that are unknown to human mathematicians.

In this paper, we provide simple case studies concerning the first question. To this end, we represent a formal system $\mathcal{L}$ using *metalogic programming* which allows object-level and meta-level representation to be amalgamated [2].

3   Learning Deductive Inference Rules

The preceding section provided an abstract framework for learning logics. This section considers a simple case of the problem. Suppose a set S of atomic formulas which contains atoms with the predicate *hold*. Each atom in S is in the form $hold(F)$ where F is a formula in propositional logic. Hence, *hold* is a *meta-predicate*, $hold(F)$ is a *meta-atom*, while F is an *object-level* formula. A *rule* has the form:

$$A \leftarrow \Gamma \tag{1}$$

where A is a meta-atom and Γ is a conjunction of meta-atoms. Given a rule R of the form (1), A is called the *head* of R and Γ is called the *body* of R. The atom A is also represented by $head(R)$ and the set of atoms in Γ is represented by $body(R)$. In what follows, a meta-predicate or a meta-atom is simply called a predicate or an atom, and an object-level formula is called a formula as far as no confusion arises. We consider an agent $\mathcal{A}$ with an inference system $\mathcal{L}$ that performs the following inference:

$$\text{from } hold(p) \text{ and } hold(p \supset q) \text{ infer } hold(q)$$

where p and q are propositional variables. In this case, given a finite set S of atoms as an input, $\mathcal{A}$ outputs the set:

$$T = S \cup \{\, hold(q) \mid hold(p) \in S \text{ and } hold(p \supset q) \in S \,\}.$$

We now consider the machine $\mathcal{M}$ that can produce deductive inference rules from S and T as follows. Given each pair (S, T) as an input, we first consider a learning system $\mathcal{C}$ which constructs a rule:

$$A \leftarrow \bigwedge_{B_i \in S} B_i \tag{2}$$

where $A \in T \setminus S$. The rule (2) represents that an atom A in $T \setminus S$ is derived using atoms in S. For example, given the set:

$$S = \{\, hold(p),\ hold(r),\ hold(p \supset q),\ hold(p \supset r),\ hold(r \supset s) \,\},$$

two atoms $hold(q)$ and $hold(s)$ are in $T \setminus S$. Then the following two rules are constructed by (2):

$$hold(q) \leftarrow hold(p) \land hold(r) \land hold(p \supset q) \land hold(p \supset r) \land hold(r \supset s).$$
$$hold(s) \leftarrow hold(p) \land hold(r) \land hold(p \supset q) \land hold(p \supset r) \land hold(r \supset s).$$

The body of each rule contains atoms which do not contribute to deriving the atom in the head. To distinguish atoms which contribute to deriving the consequence, the agent $\mathcal{A}$ is used as follows. For a pair (S, T) from $\mathcal{A}$ such that $T \setminus S \neq \emptyset$, assume that a rule R of the form (2) is constructed. Then, select a subset S_i of S and give it as an input to $\mathcal{A}$. If its output T_i still contains the atom A of $head(R)$, replace R with

$$A \leftarrow \bigwedge_{B_i \in S_i} B_i.$$

By continuing this process, find a minimal set S_j satisfying $A \in T_j$. Such S_j contains atoms that are necessary and sufficient for deriving atoms in $T_j \setminus S_j$. In the above example, there is the unique minimal set:

$$S_1 = \{\, hold(p),\ hold(p \supset q) \,\}$$

that satisfies $hold(q) \in T_1$, and there are two minimal sets that contain the atom $hold(s)$ in their outputs:

$$S_2 = \{\, hold(r), \ \ hold(r \supset s) \,\},$$
$$S_3 = \{\, hold(p), \ \ hold(p \supset r), \ \ hold(r \supset s) \,\}.$$

Then the following three rules are obtained by replacing S with S_i in (2):

$$hold(q) \leftarrow hold(p) \wedge hold(p \supset q). \tag{3}$$
$$hold(s) \leftarrow hold(r) \wedge hold(r \supset s). \tag{4}$$
$$hold(s) \leftarrow hold(p) \wedge hold(p \supset r) \wedge hold(r \supset s). \tag{5}$$

The rules (3) and (4) represent *Modus Ponens*, and (5) represents *Multiple Modus Ponens*. As such, unnecessary atoms in the body of a rule are eliminated by the *minimization* technique.

Unnecessary atoms in the bodies are also eliminated using the *generalization* technique developed in [6].[1] Suppose an agent $\mathcal{A}$ with an inference system $\mathcal{L}$ that performs the following inference:

$$\text{from} \ \ hold(p \vee q) \ \ \text{and} \ \ hold(\neg q) \ \ \text{infer} \ \ hold(p).$$

In this case, given a finite set S of atoms as an input, $\mathcal{A}$ outputs the set:

$$T = S \cup \{\, hold(p) \mid hold(p \vee q) \in S \ \ \text{and} \ \ hold(\neg q) \in S \,\}.$$

Given a sequence of input-output pairs from the agent $\mathcal{A}$, the machine $\mathcal{M}$ constructs a rule R of the form (2) each time it receives a new pair (S_i, T_i) from $\mathcal{A}$. Suppose two rules R and R' such that (i) $head(R) = head(R')$; (ii) there is a formula F such that $hold(F) \in body(R)$ and $hold(\neg F) \in body(R')$; and (iii) $(body(R') \setminus \{hold(\neg F)\}) \subseteq (body(R) \setminus \{hold(F)\})$. Then, a generalized rule of R and R' (upon F) is obtained as

$$A \leftarrow \bigwedge_{B_i \in (body(R) \setminus \{hold(F)\})} B_i.$$

For example, given the two pairs, (S_1, T_1) and (S_2, T_2), where

$$S_1 = \{\, hold(p \vee q), \ hold(\neg q), \ hold(r) \,\},$$
$$T_1 = \{\, hold(p \vee q), \ hold(\neg q), \ hold(r), \ hold(p) \,\},$$
$$S_2 = \{\, hold(p \vee q), \ hold(\neg q), \ hold(\neg r) \,\},$$
$$T_2 = \{\, hold(p \vee q), \ hold(\neg q), \ hold(\neg r), \ hold(p) \,\},$$

the two rules are obtained as:

$$hold(p) \leftarrow hold(p \vee q) \wedge hold(\neg q) \wedge hold(r),$$
$$hold(p) \leftarrow hold(p \vee q) \wedge hold(\neg q) \wedge hold(\neg r).$$

---

[1] The technique is used for a logic with the law of excluded middle.

Then the generalization of them is:

$$hold(p) \leftarrow hold(p \vee q) \wedge hold(\neg q).$$

This rule represents *Disjunctive Syllogism*.

These procedures are applicable to learning one-step deduction rules such that

$$hold(\neg p) \leftarrow hold(\neg q) \wedge hold(p \supset q). \qquad \text{(Modus Tollens)}$$
$$hold(p \supset r) \leftarrow hold(p \supset q) \wedge hold(q \supset r). \quad \text{(Hypothetical Syllogism)}$$

We can also obtain a rule for *abductive inference* [11] by this method. For example, given the pair $(S, T) = (\{hold(q), hold(p \supset q)\}, \{hold(q), hold(p \supset q), hold(p)\})$, we can construct *the Fallacy of Affirming the Consequent*:

$$hold(p) \leftarrow hold(q) \wedge hold(p \supset q).$$

In this way, the method in this section could be used for learning non-deductive inferences.

4   Learning CA Rules

In this section, we address another example of learning logics. *Cellular automata* (CAs) [15] are discrete and abstract computational models that have been used for simulating various complex systems in the real world. A CA consists of a regular grid of *cells*, each of which has a finite number of possible *states*. The state of each cell changes synchronously in discrete time steps (or *generations*) according to a local and identical *transition rule*. The state of a cell in the next time step is determined by its current state and the states of its surrounding cells (called *neighbors*). The collection of all cellular states in the grid at some time step is called a *configuration*. An *elementary* CA consists of a one-dimensional array of (possibly infinite) cells, and each cell has one of two possible states 0 or 1. A cell and its two adjacent cells form a neighbor of three cells, so there are $2^3 = 8$ possible patterns for neighbors. A transition rule describes for each pattern of a neighbor, whether the central cell will be 0 or 1 at the next time step. Then $2^8 = 256$ possible rules are considered and 256 elementary CAs are defined accordingly. Stephen Wolfram gave each rule a number 0 to 255 (called the *Wolfram code*), and analyzed their properties [15]. The evolution of an elementary CA is illustrated by starting with the initial configuration in the first row, the configuration at the next time step in the second row, and so on. Figure 2 shows the Rule 30 and one of its evolution where the black cell represents the state 1 and the white cell represents the state 0. The figure shows the first 16 generations of the Rule 30 starting with a single black cell. It is known that the Rule 30 displays aperiodic and random patterns in a chaotic manner.

Each transition rule is considered a logic of CA, that is, every pattern appearing in a configuration is governed by one transition rule. Then we consider the

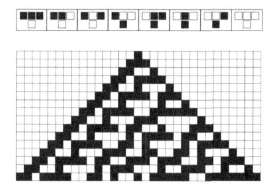

Fig. 2. Evolution of patterns by the Rule 30

problem of producing a transition rule from input configurations. Such a problem is known as the *identification problem* of CAs [1]. In what follows, we consider the problem of learning the Wolfram's Rule 30 from a series of configurations. In an elementary CA, a configuration at a time step t is represented by a (possibly infinite) sequence of cells $\langle \cdots x_{i-1}^t \, x_i^t \, x_{i+1}^t \, \cdots \rangle$ where x_i^t represents a state of a cell x_i at a time step t. For example, the initial configuration of Figure 2 is represented by

$$\langle \cdots x_{i-1}^0 \, x_i^0 \, x_{i+1}^0 \, \cdots \rangle = \langle \cdots 010 \cdots \rangle$$

where the central black cell at the time step 0 is represented by $x_i^0 = 1$. Likewise, the configuration at the time step 2 is represented by

$$\langle \cdots x_{i-3}^2 \, x_{i-2}^2 \, x_{i-1}^2 \, x_i^2 \, x_{i+1}^2 \, x_{i+2}^2 \, x_{i+3}^2 \, \cdots \rangle = \langle \cdots 0110010 \cdots \rangle.$$

We represent the state of a cell at each time step by an atom as: $hold(x_i^t)$ if $x_i^t = 1$ and $hold(\neg x_i^t)$ if $x_i^t = 0$. Then the initial configuration of Figure 2 is represented by the (infinite) set of atoms:

$$\{\ldots, hold(\neg x_{i-1}^0), \, hold(x_i^0), \, hold(\neg x_{i+1}^0), \ldots\}.$$

To cope with the problem using a finite set, we consider the five cells:

$$S^t = \langle \, x_{i-2}^t \, x_{i-1}^t \, x_i^t \, x_{i+1}^t \, x_{i+2}^t \, \rangle$$

in each time step. Table 1 represents evolution of those five cells in the first four time steps.

Corresponding to the framework provided in Section 2, an agent $\mathcal{A}$ produces S^{t+1} from an input S^t. Given input-output pairs $(S^0, S^1), \ldots, (S^t, S^{t+1}), \ldots$ of $\mathcal{A}$ as an input to a machine $\mathcal{M}$, the problem is whether $\mathcal{M}$ can identify the transition rule of this CA. For a pair of configurations (S^0, S^1), the machine $\mathcal{M}$ produces a rule R that represents the states of the cell x_j^0 $(i-1 \leq j \leq i+1)$ and its neighbors

Table 1. Evolution of $\langle\, x_{i-2}^t\, x_{i-1}^t\, x_i^t\, x_{i+1}^t\, x_{i+2}^t\,\rangle$

step	x_{i-2}^t	x_{i-1}^t	x_i^t	x_{i+1}^t	x_{i+2}^t
t=0	0	0	1	0	0
t=1	0	1	1	1	0
t=2	1	1	0	0	1
t=3	1	0	1	1	1

in the body of R and represents the state of the cell x_j^1 in the head of R. There are three such rules:

$$hold(x_{i-1}^1) \leftarrow hold(\neg x_{i-2}^0) \wedge hold(\neg x_{i-1}^0) \wedge hold(x_i^0).$$
$$hold(x_i^1) \leftarrow hold(\neg x_{i-1}^0) \wedge hold(x_i^0) \wedge hold(\neg x_{i+1}^0).$$
$$hold(x_{i+1}^1) \leftarrow hold(x_i^0) \wedge hold(\neg x_{i+1}^0) \wedge hold(\neg x_{i+2}^0).$$

Similarly, given a pair of configurations (S^1, S^2), the machine $\mathcal{M}$ produces the following three rules:

$$hold(x_{i-1}^2) \leftarrow hold(\neg x_{i-2}^1) \wedge hold(x_{i-1}^1) \wedge hold(x_i^1).$$
$$hold(\neg x_i^2) \leftarrow hold(x_{i-1}^1) \wedge hold(x_i^1) \wedge hold(x_{i+1}^1).$$
$$hold(\neg x_{i+1}^2) \leftarrow hold(x_i^1) \wedge hold(x_{i+1}^1) \wedge hold(\neg x_{i+2}^1).$$

The following two rules are respectively obtained by (S^3, S^4) and (S^6, S^7):

$$hold(\neg x_{i-1}^4) \leftarrow hold(x_{i-2}^3) \wedge hold(\neg x_{i-1}^3) \wedge hold(x_i^3).$$
$$hold(\neg x_i^7) \leftarrow hold(\neg x_{i-1}^6) \wedge hold(\neg x_i^6) \wedge hold(\neg x_{i+1}^6).$$

Since a transition rule does not change during the evolution and it is equally applied to each cell, the above eight rules are rewritten as

$$hold(x_i^{t+1}) \leftarrow hold(\neg x_{i-1}^t) \wedge hold(\neg x_i^t) \wedge hold(x_{i+1}^t). \tag{6}$$
$$hold(x_i^{t+1}) \leftarrow hold(\neg x_{i-1}^t) \wedge hold(x_i^t) \wedge hold(\neg x_{i+1}^t). \tag{7}$$
$$hold(x_i^{t+1}) \leftarrow hold(x_{i-1}^t) \wedge hold(\neg x_i^t) \wedge hold(\neg x_{i+1}^t). \tag{8}$$
$$hold(x_i^{t+1}) \leftarrow hold(\neg x_{i-1}^t) \wedge hold(x_i^t) \wedge hold(x_{i+1}^t). \tag{9}$$
$$hold(\neg x_i^{t+1}) \leftarrow hold(x_{i-1}^t) \wedge hold(x_i^t) \wedge hold(x_{i+1}^t). \tag{10}$$
$$hold(\neg x_i^{t+1}) \leftarrow hold(x_{i-1}^t) \wedge hold(x_i^t) \wedge hold(\neg x_{i+1}^{t+1}). \tag{11}$$
$$hold(\neg x_i^{t+1}) \leftarrow hold(x_{i-1}^t) \wedge hold(\neg x_i^t) \wedge hold(x_{i+1}^t). \tag{12}$$
$$hold(\neg x_i^{t+1}) \leftarrow hold(\neg x_{i-1}^t) \wedge hold(\neg x_i^t) \wedge hold(\neg x_{i+1}^t). \tag{13}$$

The eight rules (6)–(13) represent the transition rule of the Rule 30. Further, we get the following rules:

$$hold(x_i^{t+1}) \leftarrow hold(\neg x_{i-1}^t) \wedge hold(x_i^t). \quad \text{(by (7) and (9))}$$
$$hold(x_i^{t+1}) \leftarrow hold(\neg x_{i-1}^t) \wedge hold(x_{i+1}^t). \quad \text{(by (6) and (9))}$$
$$hold(\neg x_i^{t+1}) \leftarrow hold(x_{i-1}^t) \wedge hold(x_i^t). \quad \text{(by (10) and (11))}$$
$$hold(\neg x_i^{t+1}) \leftarrow hold(x_{i-1}^t) \wedge hold(x_{i+1}^t). \quad \text{(by (10) and (12))}$$

Those rules are finally summarized as:

$$hold(x_i^{t+1}) \leftarrow (hold(x_{i-1}^t) \wedge hold(\neg x_i^t) \wedge hold(\neg x_{i+1}^t))$$
$$\vee (hold(\neg x_{i-1}^t) \wedge (hold(x_i^t) \vee hold(x_{i+1}^t))). \quad (14)$$
$$hold(\neg x_i^{t+1}) \leftarrow (hold(\neg x_{i-1}^t) \wedge hold(\neg x_i^t) \wedge hold(\neg x_{i+1}^t))$$
$$\vee (hold(x_{i-1}^t) \wedge (hold(x_i^t) \vee hold(x_{i+1}^t))). \quad (15)$$

The rules (14) and (15) represent the Wolfram's Rule 30.

Learning elementary CA rules is implemented in [6]. Learning elementary CA rules is simple because it is one-dimensional, two-state, and has the fixed neighborhood size. On the other hand, identifying CA rules in practice is difficult because configurations are observed phenomena in the real-world and there is no teacher agent $\mathcal{A}$ in general.

5   Discussion

This paper argues the possibility of discovering logics using AI. Logic is considered as meta-mathematics here, so the task is to find meta-laws given pairs of premises and consequences in mathematical or physical domain. On the other hand, discovering mathematical theorems or scientific laws in the objective theories has been studied in AI. For instance, Lenat [7] develops the *automated mathematician* (AM) that automatically produces mathematical theorems including Goldbach's Conjecture and the Unique Factorization Theorem. Schmidt and Lipson [13] develop AI that successfully deduces the laws of motion from a pendulum's swings without a shred of knowledge about physics or geometry. To the best of our knowledge, however, there are few studies that aim at discovering logics or meta-theorems.

In Section 2 we address an abstract framework of learning formal systems based on logics. An interesting question is whether the same or a similar framework can be applied for learning non-logical systems. In this case, a set of input-output pairs (or premise-consequence pairs) are not given from a teacher agent $\mathcal{A}$ in general, but can be implicitly hidden in log files of dynamic systems or in dialogues with unknown agents. The machine $\mathcal{M}$ has to identify those input-output relations automatically to output a set of meta-theoretical inference rules for the domain or inference patterns of those agents. Non-logical inferences are also used in *pragmatics* [8]. In conversation or dialogue, the notion of *conversational implicature* [4] is known as a pragmatic inference to an implicit meaning of a sentence that is not actually uttered by a speaker. For instance, if a speaker utters the sentence "I have two children", it normally implicates "I do *not* have *more than* two children". This is called a *scalar implicature* which says that a speaker implicates the negation of a semantically stronger proposition than the one asserted. Given a collection of dialogues, a question is whether a machine can automatically acquire pragmatic rules of inference that interpret implicit meaning behind utterance. Once such a non-logical inference is learned, it must be refined or revised through a continuous, cyclic process between evidences and abduction on meta-theoretical relations [5]. The process would thus introduce a dynamics of incremental perfection of theories. To realize such a system, further extension and elaboration of the framework provided in this paper are needed and much work are left for future research.

6   Summary

Answering the question "can machines learn logics?" is one of the challenging topics in artificial general intelligence. We argued the possibility of realizing such AI and provided some case studies. A number of questions remain open, for instance, whether the goal is achieved using existing techniques of machine learning or AI; which logics are to be learned and which logics are not; whether non-logical rules are learned as well, etc. Exploring those issues would contribute to better understanding human intelligence and take us one step closer to realizing "strong AI." Although the abstract framework provided in this paper is conceptual and case studies are rather simple, the current study serves as a kind of base-level and would contribute to opening the topic.

References

1. Adamatzky, A.: Identification of Cellular Automata. Taylor & Francis, London (1994)
2. Bowen, K.A., Kowalski, R.A.: Amalgamating language and metalanguage in logic programming. In: Clark, K., Tarnlund, S.A. (eds.) Logic Programming, pp. 153–172. Academic Press (1983)
3. Coradeschi, S., Loutfi, A., Wrede, B.: A short review of symbol grounding in robotic and intelligent systems. KI - Kunstliche Intelligenz **27**, 129–136 (2013)
4. Grice, H.P.: Logic and conversation. In: Cole, P., Morgan, J. (eds.) Syntax and Semantics, 3: Speech Acts, pp. 41–58. Academic Press (1975)
5. Inoue, K.: Meta-level abduction. IFCoLog Journal of Logic and their Applications (in print) (2015)
6. Inoue, K., Ribeiro, T., Sakama, C.: Learning from interpretation transition. Machine Learning **94**, 51–79 (2014)
7. Lenat, D.B.: On automated scientific theory formation: a case study using the AM program. In: Hayes, J.E., Michie, D., Mikulich, O.I. (eds.) Machine Intelligence, vol. 9, pp. 251–283. Ellis Horwood (1979)
8. Levinson, S.C.: Pragmatics. Cambridge University Press (1983)

9. Michalski, R.S.: A theory and methodology of inductive learning. In: Michalski, R.S., et al. (eds.) Machine Learning: An Artificial Intelligence Approach, pp. 83–134. Morgan Kaufmann (1983)
10. Minker, J. (ed.): Logic-based Artificial Intelligence. Kluwer Academic (2000)
11. Peirce, C.S.: Elements of logic. In: Hartshorne, C., Weiss, P. (eds.) Collected Papers of Charles Sanders Peirce, vol. II. Harvard University Press (1932)
12. Piaget, J.: Main Trends in Psychology. Allen & Unwin, London (1973)
13. Schmidt, M., Lipson, H.: Distilling free-form natural laws from experimental data. Science **324** (2009)
14. Turing, A.M.: Computing machinery and intelligence. Mind **59**, 433–460 (1950)
15. Wolfram, S.: Cellular Automata and Complexity. Westview Press (1994)

Comparing Computer Models Solving Number Series Problems

Ute Schmid[1]($\boxtimes$) and Marco Ragni[2]

[1] Cognitive Systems Group, University of Bamberg, Bamberg, Germany
ute.schmid@uni-bamberg.de
[2] Foundations of AI, Technical Faculty, University of Freiburg,
Freiburg im Breisgau, Germany
ragni@cs.uni-freiburg.de

Abstract. Inductive reasoning requires to find for given instances a general rule. This makes inductive reasoning an excellent test-bed for artificial general intelligence (AGI). An example being part of many IQ-tests are number series: for a given sequence of numbers the task is to find a next "correct" successor number. Successful reasoning may require to identify regular patterns and to form a rule, an implicit underlying function that generates this number series. Number series problems can be designed along different dimensions, such as structural complexity, required mathematical background knowledge, and even insights based on a perspective switch. The aim of this paper is to give an overview of existing cognitive and computational models, their underlying algorithmic approaches and problem classes. A first empirical comparison of some of these approaches with focus on artificial neural nets and inductive programming is presented.

1 Introduction

Over the last decade, there has been growing interest in computer models solving intelligence test problems. Especially, the proposal to establish a psychometric artificial intelligence (PAI; [3,6]) with the aim to evaluate the intelligence of an artificial cognitive system based on its performance on a set of tests of intelligence and mental abilities motivated research in this domain [2].

One of the mental abilities considered by researchers as a fundamental constituent of general intelligence is inductive reasoning [22]. A well established, culture free test in this domain is Raven Progressive Matrices (RPM; [18]) where regularities have to be identified in a two-dimensional matrix of geometrical patterns. Another problem domain is inductive reasoning with numbers. In contrast to RPM, problems are represented in one dimension, that is, as a sequence, and a certain amount of mathematical knowledge is presupposed. Number series are, for example, included in two well known intelligence test batteries, namely the IST [1] and the MIT [25]. To solve RPM as well as number series problems, one has to analyze the given components, construct a hypothesis about the regularity characterizing all components, generalize this regularity and apply it to generate a solution.

© Springer International Publishing Switzerland 2015
J. Bieger (Ed.): AGI 2015, LNAI 9205, pp. 352–361, 2015.
DOI: 10.1007/978-3-319-21365-1_36

Currently, there are different proposals of computer models solving number series problems which are studied in isolation. In our opinion it would be worthwhile to compare these models to gain insight into (1) the general power of the underlying algorithmic approaches with respect to scope and efficiency, and (2) their correspondence to human cognitive processes.

In the following, we first introduce the domain of number series problems in more detail and identify characteristics to classify such problems. Afterwards, we shortly present the computer systems developed to solve number series problems within artificial intelligence and cognitive systems research. A first empirical comparison of systems concludes the article.

2   Number Series Problems

A number series can be mathematically defined by a function mapping the natural numbers into the real numbers: $f : \mathbb{N} \to \mathbb{R}$. For intelligence test problems, typically the co-domain is restricted to integers. Series used in intelligence tests are usually restricted to the four basic arithmetic operations. Furthermore, numbers are restricted to small values which allow easy mental calculations [12]. Number series problems in intelligence tests are characterized as "having a unique solution" [1]. However, in general, there do not exist unique solutions for inductive problems [11]. A more precise characterization is that it must be possible to identify a unique rule from the given pattern which captures its regularity. Whether such a rule can be found depends on the length and kind of the given sequence. In intelligence tests, often five elements of a series are given and the test person or the program has to find the next element.

A variety of number series is illustrated in Table 1. Series can be generated by applying one operation to the predecessor, resulting in a simple linear function (see E1, Table 1). There can be alternating series where a different rule applies to elements on even and odd index positions (see E2, Table 1). Series can depend on more than one predecessor, which is the case for the Fibonacci series (see E3, Table 1). Series can be composed by nesting two series (see E4, Table 1). An example for a series which has no unique solution, if only 5 elements are given is presented as E5 in Table 1: One solution can be to double the second last element and subtract 2 or, equivalently, to decrement the second last element and then double it. Alternatively, a higher order rule can explain the pattern of the first 5 elements, where 2^1 is added once, 2^2 is added twice, 2^3 is added three times, and so on. A final example presents a series containing a mathematical pattern of the index (see E6, Table 1) which has been investigated by Hofstadter [10]. This last sequence is a typical example of a problem which is simple for humans but difficult for systems based on pattern induction because it has no simple closed representation.[1] Human performance depends on the complexity of the underlying pattern but can also depend on specific background knowledge. E.g., computer science students can often easily identify Fibonacci numbers or powers of two. The examples of Table 1 show that there are simple problems for humans

---

[1] The closed representation relies on a non-primitive recursive function:
$f(n) = f(n - f(n - 1)) + 1$.

Table 1. Examples for number series problems. The numbers in brackets represent for the given series two possible successor sequences.

ID Series	General Rule $f(n)$	Type
E1 1, 4, 7, 10, 13, 16, 19, 22, ...	$= f(n-1) + 3, , f(1) = 1$	linear
E2 2, 4, 3, 5, 4, 6, 5, 7, ...	$= if(even(n), f(n-1) + 2,$ $f(n-1) - 1)$	alternating
E3 4, 11, 15, 26, 41, 67, 108, 175, ...	$= f(n-1) + f(n-2),$ $f(1) = 4, f(2) = 11$	Fibonacci
E4 5, 6, 12, 19, 32, 52, 85, 138, ...	$= f(n-1) + (f(n-2) + 1),$ $f(1) = 5, f(2) = 6$	nested
E5 8, 10, 14, 18, 26, [34, 50, 66,] ...	$= f(n-2) \times 2 - 2$ $= (f(n-2) - 1) \times 2$ $f(1) = 8, f(2) = 10$	not unique
8, 10, 14, 18, 26, [34, 42, 58,] ...	$= f(n-1) + 2^n, f(1) = 8$	
E6 1, 2, 2, 3, 3, 3, 4, 4, 4, 4, 5, ...	write each number n n-times	intuitive

(such as E6) but difficult for machines and vice versa depending on their under-lying algorithmic principles. Based on these considerations, Number series may be characterized according to the following features:

Necessary background knowledge: To solve series, only knowledge of basic arith-metic operators (or even only of the successor function) is necessary. But series can become more efficiently solvable with mathematical knowledge such as knowing the factorial or checksum-functions.

Numerical values: Numbers are typically small in the context of psychometric tests. We can assume that humans have no problems with large values if they can be represented in a simple form, such as decimal multiples and we can assume that numerical values have less impact on performance of computer systems than of humans.

Structural complexity: Series can be solvable by application of one basic operation to the predecessor or might depend on complex relations between several prede-cessors.

Existence of a closed formula: Most number series of interest can be characterized by a closed formula as given in Table 1. However, some series, such as E6 in Table 1 can be easily described verbally while a closed form is highly sophisticated or even not known. Other problems even need a switch of perspective, such as *3, 3, 5, 4, 4, 3* which gives the number of letters of the verbal representation of the index.

We assume that these features influence performance of humans as well as machines, however not necessarily in the same way. In the context of psychomet-rics, difficulty of a problem is assessed by the percentage of subjects that solve the problem at hand on a given time. This measure does not capture charac-teristics of the number series and its impact on the cognitive or computational processes involved. An empirical investigation of the cognitive determinants of number series performance was presented by Holzman *et al.* [12]. It was shown that mathematical skill has an impact on performance for more complex series. A proposal to capture difficulty of number series problems based on a resource-bounded Kolmogorov complexity was made by Strannegård *et al.* [23] with a focus on structural complexity.

Table 2. Series solved by the anti-unification approach of Burghardt [4]

0,1,4,9	$f(n) = n * n$	0,1,2,1,4,1	$f(n) = if(even, n, 1)$
0,2,4,6	$f(n) = f(n-1) + 2$	0,0,1,1,0,0,1,1	$f(n) = even(n-2)$
1,1,2,3,5	$f(n) = f(n-1) + f(n-2)$	0,1,3,7	$f(n) = 2 \times f(n-1) + 1$

3 Systems Solving Number Series

Approaches for solving number series problems can be distinguished in systems which are specifically designed to solve this type of problems and in the application of general purpose algorithms or algorithms developed for a different problem domain. For both kinds of approaches, there are computer models which aim at performance criteria such as scope and efficiency and computer models which aim at simulation of cognitive systems.

Early Systems. The earliest computational approach for a cognitively-inspired AI systems solving number series is SEEKWHENCE [10,14]. Hofstadter aimed on an expert system which depends on a set of specific rules characterizing mathematical relations. Instead, his aim was to solve sequences using general principles such as pattern recognition and analogy. The system was able to identify well known sequences appearing interleaved. For example, given *1, 1, 3, 4, 6, 9* it recognizes the square numbers *1, 4, 9* and the triangle numbers *1, 3, 6*. Hofstadter was especially interested in sequences which do not require typical mathematical operations. One example is the index number problem (see E6 in Table 1). Another example is *1, 1, 1, 2, 1, 1, 2, 1, 2, 3*. To identify the inherent pattern of this sequence, chunking is necessary: *((1)) ((1)(12)) ((1)(12)(123))*. To solve such problems Mahabal [13] developed SEQSEE influenced by the CopyCat system [10].

Sanghi and Dowe [19] presented a very simple program which was able to solve a variety of number series problems. This program was not intended as an AI or cognitive system as a demonstration that rather trivial programs can be able to pass an intelligence test. An approach developed in the context of automated theorem proving was applied to solve number series problems [4]: An algorithm for anti-unification of mathematical expressions was successfully applied to several number series, among them alternating series and Fibonacci (see Table 2).

Rule-Based Systems. In the last four years, two rule-based systems for solving number series were proposed. Siebers and Schmid [21] presented a semi-analytical approach where the term structure defining a given number series is guessed based on heuristic enumeration of term structure. To evaluate the approach, a generator of number series was realized (see also [5]) and the system was evaluated with 25,000 randomly created number series resulting in an accuracy of 93%.

A system based on similar principles is ASOLVER. However, this system takes into account plausible restrictions of working memory [23,24]. Systems

```
nat  = 0  | s(nat)          eq Plustwo((s 0) nil) = s^3 0
[nat] = [] | nat:[nat]      eq Plustwo((s^3 0) (s 0) nil) = s^5 0
                            eq Plustwo((s^5 0) (s^3 0) (s 0) nil) = s^7 0
```

Fig. 1. Representation of a simple number series for IGOR2, s is the successor function

performance was evaluated with 11 (non published) problems from the IQ test PJP and shown to outperform mathematical tools such as MAPLE and WOLFRAMALPHA.

An Inductive Programming Approach. Rule-based systems are specifically designed for solving problems from the number series domain. However, when being interested in systems which are able to general intelligent behavior, the challenge is to identify approaches which can be applied to different domains without specific adaptation and without a meta-algorithm which selects a suitable special purpose algorithm. The anti-unification approach of Burghardt [4] is a first example of a successful application of a system designed for a different domain to number series.

Another example is the inductive program system IGOR2 [9,20] which learns functional (MAUDE or HASKELL) programs from small sets of input/output examples. For instance, given examples for reversing a list with up to three elements, IGOR2 generalizes the recursive *reverse* function together with helper functions *last* and *init*. IGOR2 is based on constructor-term rewriting and therefore, besides the examples for the target function, the data types have to be declared. For lists, the usual algebraic data type [a] = [] | a:[a] is used. To apply IGOR2 for induction of a constructor-function which correctly describes and continues a given number series, as a crucial first step, we have to decide how to represent the needed data types, equations, and background knowledge.

In a first investigation the effect of different representations on IGOR2's performance was investigated with 100 number series varied with respect to size of numerical values and structural complexity [8]. It turned out that the system performed comparably with all representation formats tested, in the following we only consider the format given in Figure 1: The system needs the data types for list and natural number as input. A number series problem is represented as a set of example equations. For instance, the sequence *1, 3, 5* is represented as three examples giving the sequence up to a given length as input and the next element as output.

IGOR2 can induce functions characterizing the infinite sequence without background knowledge, for series which can be characterized by incrementing or decrementing values of predecessors. For more complex series, more specialized mathematical operations can be pre-defined and the system can use them for rule construction. However, while the availability of mathematical knowledge typically will improve human performance [12], IGOR2' performance time and memory requirements increase when background knowledge is given.

A Neural Network Approach. All approaches introduced so far are based on symbolic computation. Such systems generate the solution of a number series problem by identifying the underlying regularity. The generalized rule to characterize the infinite sequence is explicitly constructed. That is, the symbolic systems are not only able to produce the next number, but to "explain" by the given function why this number was given. A limitation is that the set of functions that can be computed is rather restricted. In contrast, artificial neural networks (ANNs) are in principle able to approximate arbitrary functions. Ragni and Klein [16] investigated number series prediction with three-layered networks with error back-propagation and the hyperbolic tangent as activation function. The approach uses a dynamic learning approach: An ANN was trained on the given numbers and the missing number was the target value to be predicted. The number of training values of a pattern is equivalent to the number of input nodes i of the network used. Starting with the first number, a sub-sequence of training values was shifted through the number series. As corresponding target value, the next number of the sub-sequence was used. Since the last given value of the number series with length n remains as target value and at least one training and one test pattern is needed, the maximum length of a subsequence of training values is $n - 2$. Hence, for a network configuration with m input nodes $n - m$ patterns were generated. The first $(n - m) - 1$ patterns were used for training, while the last one remained for testing and thus predicting the last given number of the sequence.

4 Performance Comparison: Igor2, ANNs, and Humans

IGOR2's performance was tested with the series presented in [4] (see Table 2) and could generate correct solutions for all of them. We did not systematically evaluate performance time, since performance was very fast (some milliseconds) for all problems. Most series could be solved without background knowledge with the following exceptions: For Fibonacci, addition had to be pre-defined, for the square function, the square function had to be pre-defined, and for the series $f(n) = 2 \times f(n - 1) + 1$, multiplication had to be pre-defined. IGOR2 could not solve problem E6 from Table 1 since it depends on identifying a pattern in form of a recursive function which is μ-recursive for this problem.

Furthermore, IGOR2's performance was tested against human performance on 20 series systematically varied with respect to structural complexity and numerical values [15]. Based on results of 46 subjects who participated in an online experiment, it showed that indeed, a lesser number of humans (34 out of 46) succeeded for number series with high numbers, such as *237, 311, 386, 462, 539*, characterizable as $f(n) = f(n - 1) + n + 73$. Furthermore, due to the constructive representation of numbers, IGOR2 failed to solve this series. The largest constant for which IGOR2 could produce a result was for with problem was 36. Details of the study are given in [15],

The ANN approach was applied to the 73 SEQSEE number series problems described in section 3 and presented in [13]. As in a previous investigation [17] settings were systematically varied from $500, 1000, 5000, 10000, 15000$, each with a learning rate ranging from .125 up to .875 with a step width of .125.

Table 3. Empirical comparison of human performance ($n = 17$) with ANNs and IGOR2 (ID based on the order of the series as reported in [16]; results for humans are correct/incorrect/no answer)

		Responses		
ID Number Series	Rule $f(n) =$	Human	IGOR2	ANN
05 2,5,8,11,14,17,20,23	$f(n-1)+3$	9/3/5	+	+
07 25,22,19,16,13,10,7,4	$f(n-1)-3$	16/0/1	+	+
19 8,12,16,20,24,28,32,36	$f(n-1)+4$	15/0/2	+	+
13 54,48,42,36,30,24,18	$f(n-1)-6$	16/1/0	+	+
08 28,33,31,36,34,39,37	$f(n-2)+3$	17/0/0	+	+
14 6,8,5,7,4,6,3,5	$f(n-2)-1$	16/0/1	+	+
20 9,20,6,17,3,14,0,11	$f(n-2)-3$	16/0/1	-	+
01 12,15,8,11,4,7,0,3	$f(n-2)-4$	15/0/2	+	+
11 4,11,15,26,41,67,108	$f(n-1)+f(n-2)$	8/1/8	+	+
09 3,6,12,24,48,96,192	$f(n-1) \times 2$	13/1/3	+	-
16 7,10,9,12,11,14,13,16	$if(even, f(n-1)+3, f(n-1)-1)$	14/0/3	+	+
18 8,12,10,16,12,20,14,24	$if(even, f(n-2)+4, f(n-2)+2)$	17/0/0	+	+
15 6,9,18,21,42,45,90,93	$if(even, f(n-1)+3, f(n-1) \times 2)$	14/1/2	-	+
17 8,10,14,18,26,34,50,66	$if(even, f(n-2)+6 \times 2^i, f(n-2)+8)$	13/1/3	-	+
10 3,7,15,31,63,127,255	$f(n) = 2 \times f(n-1)+1$	12/3/2	+	-
04 2,3,5,9,17,33,65,129	$f(n-1)+f(n-1)-1$	13/1/3	+	+
03 2,12,21,29,36,42,47,51	$f(n-1)+12-n$	14/1/2	-	+
02 148,84,52,36,28,24,22	$(f(n-1)/2)+10$	12/2/3	+	+
06 2,5,9,19,37,75,149,299	$f(n-1) \times 2+(-1)^n$	6/4/7	-	-
12 5,6,7,8,10,11,14,15	*no squares*	10/1/6	-	+

The number of input nodes from 1 to 3 are varied, but the number of nodes within the hidden layer from 1 to 20. On average, over all number series, an increasing number of training iterations was counter-effective, that is, the number of solvable series was reduced. For 500 iterations 19 number series could not be solved by any configuration. For 15 000 iterations this number rose to 22. Over all types of configurations there remain 13 number series unsolved. Furthermore, the ANN approach was applied to number series given in intelligence tests: the 20 problems of IST, also investigated by Strannegård *et al.* [23] and the 14 problems of the MIT. Again number of input nodes, hidden layers, and learning rate were varied as above. Over all configurations 19 out of the 20 IST number series could be solved, one remains unsolved. For the MIT over all configurations 12 out of the 14 number series could be solved, two remain unsolved. Analyzing the networks show again, that 3 input nodes and about 5-6 hidden nodes with a low learning rate are the most successful ones. This pattern appears in all our benchmarks. Ragni and Klein [16] developed 20 number series as a benchmark for the ANN approach given in Table 3. The problems differed in the underlying construction principle and varied from simple additions and multiplications to combinations of these operations. One series (S12) is of the type studied by Hofstadter [10]: it is composed of the numbers which are not squares.

An empirical study with 17 human subjects was conducted[2]. Subjects received the series in randomized order on paper and had to fill in the last number of the series. With the exception of the low performance for the simple series S05, the empirical results support our assumptions: While humans deal easily with series based on a simple operation on the immediate predecessor, they have problems with series depending on more than one predecessor number (as the Fibonacci variant S11). Although humans can deal with alternating series for simple operations, they have problems if these series involve multiplications (S15) or a nested series depending on the index (S17). IGOR2 and the ANN approach were tested with the same problems. However, IGOR2 did only receive the first 5 elements of a series as input, the ANN was trained with 7 inputs and had to predict the 8th value. For some of the series, solution success of IGOR2 did depend on the chosen representation for the series. For some of the series, mathematical background knowledge was given to IGOR2 as described in section 3. Details of the empirical results for IGOR2 are given in [7]. Overall, there are six number series which could not be solved by IGOR2 and three number series which could not be solved by the ANNs. Among them is only one series (S06) which could be solved by neither approach.

5   Conclusions and Further Work

Number series form an excellent testbed for AGI-systems. An overview of systems solving number series problems show that some systems are designed to model human cognitive processes while others aim at high performance. We introduced two approaches: The inductive programming system IGOR2 is a symbolic approach to learning declarative rules from examples and a sub-symbolic approach using ANNs to function estimation. We compared both approaches with human performance. It showed that the ANN approach could solve more problems than IGOR2. However, each ANNs must be trained for each series taking several thousand training iterations while IGOR2 could be applied to all series without adaptation. Furthermore, IGOR2 not only returns the next number but also the function which explains how the solution was generated. This is more similar to humans that can justify a given solution. This approach shows that there are many interesting questions left. To compare systems systematically, a benchmark set – a repository of problems with a difficulty measure independent of a specific systems might be necessary. A first step into this direction was made by Strannegård *et al.* [23] who characterized problem difficulty by bounded Kolmogorov complexity, but depending on a specific algorithm. Alternatively, human performance could be used as a guideline. Given the 20 series investigated, IGOR2 as well as the ANN could not solve all problems and they differed from human performance. However, the 20 series do not represent a systematic variation over the features characterizing problems as described in section 2. As a next step, we plan to compose a more systematic repository of

---

[2] For more information please refer to [16]

problems and to invite researchers to discuss and propose other number series problems – towards a systematic competition in this domain.

Acknowledgments. This work has been supported by a Heisenberg-fellowship to the second author and a grant within the SPP 1516 "New Frameworks of Rationality". The authors are grateful to Andreas Klein for helping in evaluating the ANNs.

References

1. Amthauer, R., Brocke, B., Liepmann, D., Beauducel, A.: Intelligenz-Struktur-Test 2000 (I-S-T 2000). Hogrefe, Goettingen (1999)
2. Besold, T., Hernández-Orallo, J., Schmid, U.: Can machine intelligence be measured in the same way as human intelligence? KI - Künstliche Intelligenz (2015)
3. Bringsjord, S.: Psychometric artificial intelligence. Journal of Experimental & Theoretical Artificial Intelligence **23**(3), 271–277 (2011)
4. Burghardt, J.: E-generalization using grammars. Artificial Intelligence **165**, 1–35 (2005)
5. Colton, S., Bundy, A., Walsh, T.: Automatic invention of integer sequences. In: AAAI/IAAI, pp. 558–563 (2000)
6. Hernández-Orallo, J., Dowe, D.L., Hernández-Lloreda, M.V.: Universal psychometrics: Measuring cognitive abilities in the machine kingdom. Cognitive Systems Research **27**, 50–74 (2014)
7. Hofmann, J.: Automatische Induktion über Zahlenreihen - Eine Fallstudie zur Analyse des induktiven Programmiersystems IGOR2 (Automated induction of number series - A case study analysing the inductive programming system IGOR2). Master's thesis, University of Bamberg (December 2012)
8. Hofmann, J., Kitzelmann, E., Schmid, U.: Applying inductive program synthesis to induction of number series a case study with IGOR2. In: Lutz, C., Thielscher, M. (eds.) KI 2014. LNCS, vol. 8736, pp. 25–36. Springer, Heidelberg (2014)
9. Hofmann, M., Kitzelmann, E., Schmid, U.: A unifying framework for analysis and evaluation of inductive programming systems. In: Goerzel, B., Hitzler, P., Hutter, M. (eds.) Proceedings of the Second Conference on Artificial General Intelligence (AGI-09, Arlington, Virginia, March 6–9 2009), pp. 55–60. Atlantis Press, Amsterdam (2009)
10. Hofstadter, D.: Fluid Concepts and Creative Analogies. Basic Books, New York (1995)
11. Holland, J., Holyoak, K., Nisbett, R., Thagard, P.: Induction - Processes of Inference, Learning, and Discovery. MIT Press, Cambridge (1986)
12. Holzman, T.G., Pellegrino, J.W., Glaser, R.: Cognitive variables in series completion. Journal of Educational Psychology **75**(4), 603–618 (1983)
13. Mahabal, A.A.: Seqsee: A concept-centred architecture for sequence perception. Ph.D. thesis, Indiana University Bloomington (2009)
14. Meredith, M.J.E.: Seek-whence: a model of pattern perception. Tech. rep., Indiana Univ., Bloomington (USA) (1986)
15. Milovec, M.: Applying Inductive Programming to Solving Number Series Problems - Comparing Performance of IGOR with Humans. Master's thesis, University of Bamberg (September 2014)

16. Ragni, M., Klein, A.: Predicting numbers: an AI approach to solving number series. In: Bach, J., Edelkamp, S. (eds.) KI 2011. LNCS, vol. 7006, pp. 255–259. Springer, Heidelberg (2011)
17. Ragni, M., Klein, A.: Solving number series - architectural properties of successful artificial neural networks. In: Madani, K., Kacprzyk, J., Filipe, J. (eds.) NCTA 2011 - Proceedings of the International Conference on Neural Computation Theory and Applications, pp. 224–229. SciTePress (2011)
18. Raven, J., et al.: Raven progressive matrices. In: Handbook of nonverbal assessment, pp. 223–237. Springer (2003)
19. Sanghi, P., Dowe, D.L.: A computer program capable of passing I.Q. tests. In: Slezak, P.P. (ed.) Proc. Joint 4th Int. Conf. on Cognitive Science, & 7th Conf. of the Australasian Society for Cognitive Science (ICCS/ASCS-2003), pp. 570–575. Sydney, NSW, Australia (2003)
20. Schmid, U., Kitzelmann, E.: Inductive rule learning on the knowledge level. Cognitive Systems Research **12**(3), 237–248 (2011)
21. Siebers, M., Schmid, U.: Semi-analytic natural number series induction. In: Glimm, B., Krüger, A. (eds.) KI 2012. LNCS, vol. 7526, pp. 249–252. Springer, Heidelberg (2012)
22. Sternberg, R.J. (ed.): Handbook of Intelligence. Cambridge University Press (2000)
23. Strannegård, C., Nizamani, A.R., Sjöberg, A., Engström, F.: Bounded Kolmogorov complexity based on cognitive models. In: Kühnberger, K.-U., Rudolph, S., Wang, P. (eds.) AGI 2013. LNCS, vol. 7999, pp. 130–139. Springer, Heidelberg (2013)
24. Strannegård, C., Amirghasemi, M., Ulfsbäcker, S.: An anthropomorphic method for number sequence problems. Cognitive Systems Research **22–23**, 27–34 (2013)
25. Wilhelm, O., Conrad, W.: Entwicklung und Erprobung von Tests zur Erfassung des logischen Denkens. Diagnostica **44**, 71–83 (1998)

Emotional Concept Development

Claes Strannegård[1,2](✉), Simone Cirillo[2], and Johan Wessberg[3]

[1] Department of Philosophy, Linguistics and Theory of Science,
University of Gothenburg, Gothenburg, Sweden
claes.strannegard@gu.se
[2] Department of Applied Information Technology,
Chalmers University of Technology, Göteborg, Sweden
simone.cirillo@alumni.chalmers.se
[3] Institute of Neuroscience and Physiology,
University of Gothenburg, Gothenburg, Sweden
johan.wessberg@gu.se

Abstract. Artificial emotions of different varieties have been used for controlling behavior, e.g. in cognitive architectures and reinforcement learning models. We propose to use artificial emotions for a different purpose: controlling concept development. Dynamic networks with mechanisms for adding and removing nodes are more flexible than networks with a fixed topology, but if memories are added whenever a new situation arises, then these networks will soon grow out of proportion. Therefore there is a need for striking a balance that ideally ensures that only the most useful memories will be formed and preserved in the long run. Humans have a tendency to form and preserve memories of situations that are repeated frequently or experienced as emotionally intense (strongly positive or strongly negative), while removing memories that do not meet these criteria. In this paper we present a simple network model with artificial emotions that imitates these mechanisms.

Keywords: Autonomous agent · Concept development · Emotion

1 Introduction

One strategy toward artificial general intelligence (AGI) uses mathematical methods developed without regard to natural intelligence [23]. A second strategy imitates the mechanisms of human psychology [3,18]. A third tries to simulate the human brain at the neural level – as attempted in the BRAIN Initiative and the Human Brain Project. A fourth tries to imitate computational mechanisms that are present in nervous systems across the animal kingdom [1,6].

Bees have less than a million neurons in their brains, yet they are able to learn new concepts with the help of reward and punishment and adapt to a wide range of environments [9,24]. Bees are arguably more flexible and better at adapting to new environments than present-day AI systems, so it might be possible to create more flexible AI systems by mimicking certain of their computational mechanisms.

© Springer International Publishing Switzerland 2015
J. Bieger (Ed.): AGI 2015, LNAI 9205, pp. 362–372, 2015.
DOI: 10.1007/978-3-319-21365-1_37

In this paper, we present a simple graphical model for network-based computation and an algorithm for developing such networks – one that uses emotional factors to guide their development. Thus we tackle the problem of novelty-driven concept-formation, which easily leads to explosive memory formation [20]. Although our model was inspired by mechanisms described in neuroscience, we have made no attempt to model any particular biological system. Because our research focus is on AGI, we have felt free to mix biologically realistic features with more strictly pragmatically motivated ones.

Bees are capable of forming memories, reflecting capacities that cannot possibly be innate. In one revealing study [9], bees learned to differentiate between vowels and consonants of the Latin alphabet with the help of bowls of water containing or not containing sugar – placed next to the letters. The bees learned the two concepts robustly despite large variations in color, font, size, and mode of presentation. Bees have only about 950,000 neurons in their brains, implying that they can only form a limited number of memories [24]. This raises the obvious question of which memories would be most useful from the perspective of survivability.

Contemporary research has emphasized the importance of emotions to memory formation [13] and the role of emotional systems in decision making [4]. Sensory events can trigger reward signals (e.g., food) or indicate danger (e.g., an approaching predator). The emotional circuits receive sensory information from both lower and higher (i.e., cortical) levels; in mammals, they include the amygdala (for punishment) and the dopaminergic and opioid systems – such as the ventral tegmental area and periaqueductal gray (for reward). Their activation affects memory formation via several mechanisms: e.g., by directing attention towards the stimulus and then activating the brain's arousal systems [12]. Emotions can act directly on memory circuits in the hippocampus to sort more from less relevant memories: so-called emotional tagging [17]. It has recently been shown how repetitive or iterative mechanisms for memory formation – the classical Hebbian view – interact critically with emotion-driven mechanisms in the formation of behaviorally useful long-term memories [10].

Automatic-concept-formation techniques have been used for categorization [16,21], clustering [11], and automatic theorem proving [8]. Blum and colleagues [7] survey several concept-formation techniques for machine-learning. Concept formation is a central component of such cognitive architectures as Sigma [18] and MicroPsi [2].

Concept formation finds a close statistical analogue in learning the structure of graphical models [19]: e.g., variable-order Markov models (VMMs: see [5]), which can be used for sequential prediction. The main difficulty with learning such models is discovering which parts of the past are useful for predicting the future. VMMs make predictions based on variable-length history windows; they are very efficient to learn, given that they can be described in terms of nonparametric tree distributions. Consequently, VMMs – and other tree models – have been used in reinforcement learning for some time. One of the first successful models was the U-tree [15], which adds leaf nodes to a VMM tree only when the new nodes' utility predictions are statistically different from the current ones. This and similar models are not limited to sequential partitions of observations: it is possible to generate trees using an arbitrary metric, to compare histories [22] within a fully Bayesian framework.

Marsella and colleagues [14] survey computational models of emotion, including models based on appraisal theory; while Bach [2] offers a framework for modeling emotions.

Section 2 presents our network model and Section 3 describes computations in such models. Section 4 offers an algorithm for developing these networks automatically. Section 5 presents results. Section 6 draws some preliminary conclusions.

2   Transparent Networks

Definition 1 (Network). *A (transparent) network is a finite, labeled, directed, and acyclic graph (V, E) where nodes $a \in V$ may be labeled:*

- *$SENSOR_i$, where $i \in \omega$ (fan-in 0)*
- *$MOTOR$ (fan-in 1, fan-out 0)*
- *AND (fan-in 2)*
- *OR (fan-in 2)*
- *$DELAY$ (fan-in 1)*
- *$REVERB$ (fan-in 1)*

The fan-in and fan-out conditions in parentheses are restrictions on E. Each $(a, b) \in E$ has an associated weight $w(a, b) \in [0, 1]$.

Nodes labeled $SENSOR_i$ model sensors of modality i. $SENSOR_i$ could e.g. model a receptor cell with ion channels sensitive to cold temperature, mechanical pressure, or acidity. Nodes labeled $MOTOR$ model muscle-controlling motor neurons. Nodes labeled AND and OR model nerve cells with high and low thresholds respectively. Nodes labeled $DELAY$ model nerve cells that retransmit action potentials with a delay. Nodes labeled $REVERB$ model nerve cells or nerve-cell clusters that stay active (i.e., reverberate) for some time after they have been excited. Figure 1 provides example networks. Note that some nodes that appear in figures throughout this paper have labels that do not appear in Definition 1. They represent sensors or more complex networks computing the concept indicated by the label.

3   Network Computation

Definition 2 (Stimulus). *Let $G = (V, E)$ be a network and let $S(V)$ consist of the sensors of V, i.e. those nodes that are labeled $SENSOR_i$, for some i. A stimulus for G is a function $\sigma : S(V) \rightarrow \{0, 1\}$.*

Stimuli model the presence or absence of action potentials on receptors.

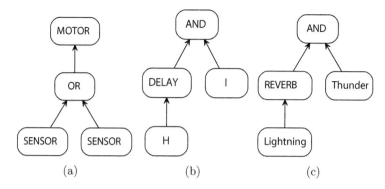

Fig. 1. Examples of transparent networks. (a) The tentacle of an anemone that retracts upon being touched. (b) The letter *H* immediately followed by the letter *I*. (c) Lightning followed by thunder (within ten time steps of the system).

Definition 3 (Input Stream). *Let $G = (V, E)$ be a network. An input stream for G is a sequence $\sigma_1, \sigma_2, \ldots$, where each σ_i is a stimulus for G.*

Input streams give rise to two types of activity that propagate through the networks: perception and imagination. We chose to model perception and imagination separately, thus distinguishing clearly between exogenous perception and endogenous imagination.

Definition 4 (Time). *Let T be the set of natural numbers, modeling time.*

Input streams give rise to two types of activity that propagate through the networks: perception and imagination. We chose to model perception and imagination separately, thus distinguishing clearly between exogenous perception and endogenous imagination.

Definition 5 (Perception). *Let $G = (V, E)$ be a network and let $L(a)$ be the label of node $a \in V$. The perception $p_G : V \times T \to \{0, 1\}$ generated by the input stream $\sigma_1, \sigma_2, \ldots$ is defined as follows. Let $p_G(a, 0) = 0$ for all $a \in V$. Let*

$$p_G(a, n + 1) = \begin{cases} \sigma_{n+1}(a) & \text{if } L(a) = SENSOR_i \\ p_G(a', n + 1) & \text{if } L(a) = MOTOR, (a', a) \in E \\ \min\{p_G(a', n + 1) : (a', a) \in E\} & \text{if } L(a) = AND \\ \max\{p_G(a', n + 1) : (a', a) \in E\} & \text{if } L(a) = OR \\ p_G(a', n) & \text{if } L(a) = DELAY, (a', a) \in E \\ 1 & \text{if } L(a) = REVERB, (a', a) \in E, \exists n' \in [n - 10, n] p_G(a', n') = 1 \\ 0 & \text{if } L(a) = REVERB, (a', a) \in E, \nexists n' \in [n - 10, n] p_G(a', n') = 1 \end{cases}$$

Given a certain input sequence, node a is *active* at step n in G if $p_G(a, n) = 1$. A DELAY node is active at n *iff* its parent node was active at $n - 1$. A REVERB node is active at n *iff* its parent node was active at some point during the last ten time steps. Figure 2 offers examples of perception, where perceptual activity is indicated by boldface node borders.

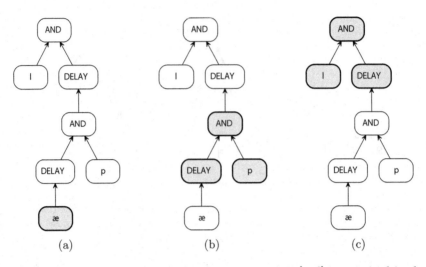

Fig. 2. Propagation of perception. The phonetic sequence [æpl] is perceived in three consecutive steps.

Definition 6 (Imagination). *Imagination* $i : V \times T \rightarrow [0,1]$ *is defined as follows. Let* $i(a,n) = max\{p(a',n) \cdot w(a',b,n) : E(a',b) \text{ and } E(a,b)\}$, *where* $w(a',b,n)$ *is the label on edge* $(a',b) \in E$ *at time* n.

Figure 3 offers examples of imagination, where imagination is indicated by dashed-line node borders. The darker the interior of the node, the more intense the imagination.

4 Network Development

Next, we define the network-development mechanism that generates a sequence of networks $G_0, G_1, \ldots$ from input stream $\sigma_0, \sigma_1, \ldots$ and initial network G_0. The initial graph G_0 is called the *genotype*; all graphs G_{n+1} are *phenotypes*. For each n, G_{n+1} is obtained either by extending G_n or trimming G_n. As in natural nervous systems, activity continues to flow in the networks while they are being modified. The definitions of activity propagation can be taken directly from fixed graphs and applied to graph sequences. First, we must introduce some basic concepts pertaining to networks.

Definition 7 (Reward Signal). *A reward signal is a function* $r : T \rightarrow [-1,1]$, *where* $[-1,1]$ *is the real interval between -1 and 1.*

Positive reward signals model reward; negative reward signals model punishment.

Definition 8 (Arousal). *Let* $arousal(n) = abs(r(n))$, *where abs means absolute value.*

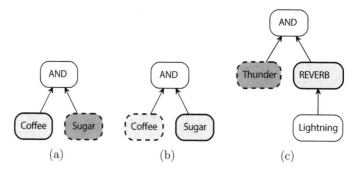

Fig. 3. Propagation of imagination. (a) Perceiving coffee, while imagining sugar strongly. (b) Perceiving sugar, while imagining coffee weakly. (c) Expecting thunder after lightning.

Definition 9 (Birth). *Let $G_0, G_1, \ldots$ be a sequence of networks. Suppose node a appears in some G_i. Then $birth(a)$ is the smallest n such that $a \in G_n$.*

Definition 10 (Relative Frequency). *Let $RF(a, n) = card\{m \in [birth(a), n] : p(a, m) = 1\}/(n - birth(a))$, where card is the cardinality function.*

Definition 11 (Closure). *Let E^* be the reflexive and transitive closure of E.*

Definition 12 (Learning Parameters). *The following parameters regulate the network development process:*

- *$p_0 \in \omega$ (size parameter)*
- *$p_1 \in [0, 1]$ (construction parameter)*
- *$p_2 \in [0, 1]$ (viability parameter)*
- *$p_3 \in [0, 1]$ (destruction parameter)*
- *$p_4 \in [0, 1]$ (multimodality parameter)*

Next, we will introduce a number of notions that trigger extensions (14-17) or trimming (18-19) of the network. We begin with a local notion of emotionality.

Definition 13 (Emotionality). *Let $emo(a, n) = avg\{r(n') : p_{G_{n'}}(a, n') = 1 : n' \in [birth(a), n]\}$, where avg means average.*

Example 1. Here are examples of how emotionality might be computed:

- $emo(cake, t) = avg\{0.7, 0.8, 0.3\} = 0.6$
- $emo(snake, t) = avg\{-0.5, -0.7, -0.9\} = -0.7$

Definition 14 (Top Active Node). *Suppose $G = (V, E)$ is a graph and $\sigma_0, \sigma_1, \ldots$ a sequence of stimuli: $a \in V$ is top active in G at n if $p_G(a, n) = 1$ and there is no $b \neq a$ such that $(a, b) \in E^*$ and $p_G(b, n) = 1$.*

Definition 15 (Surprise). *Let $surprise(n) = min\{abs(r(n) - emo(a, n)) : a$ is top active at $n\}$.*

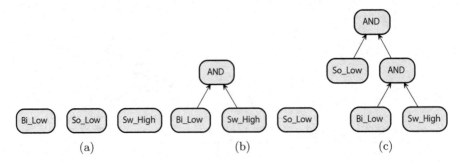

Fig. 4. Unimodal spatial construction: formation of a memory structure for the taste of a certain apple. (a) The sensors for low bitterness, low sourness, and high sweetness are activated. (b) Two of the top active nodes are randomly selected and joined. (c) The only top active nodes are joined.

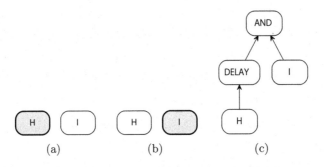

Fig. 5. Unimodal temporal construction: formation of a memory structure for the written word "HI" takes place in three steps.

Definition 16 (Learning Rate). *Let* $LR(n) = p_1 \cdot surprise(n) + (1 - p_1) \cdot arousal(n)$.

Definition 17 (Modality). *Suppose* $G = (V, E)$ *is a network and* $b \in V$. *Modality* $mod(b, G)$ *is defined as* $\{i : E^*(a, b)$ *and* $L(a) = SENSOR_i\}$.

Definition 18 (Emotional Importance). *Let* $EI(a, n) = max\{abs(emo(b, n)) : E^*(a, b)\}$.

Definition 19 (Viability). *Let* $via(a, n) = p_2 \cdot EI(a, n) + (1 - p_2) \cdot RF(a, n)$.

Finally we are ready to introduce our operations: Two that extend the networks and one that trims them.

Definition 20 (Spatial Construction). *Suppose* $G = (V, E)$ *is a graph and* $a, b \in V$. *Then* $spatial(G, a, b)$ *is the graph* (V', E'), *where* $V' = V \cup \{c\}$, c *is a new node labeled* AND, *and* $E' = E \cup \{(a, c), (b, c)\}$, *with the weights of both new edges set to* 1.

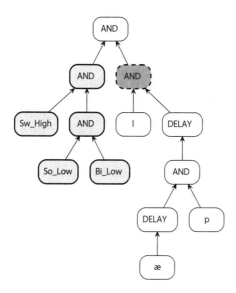

Fig. 6. Multimodal spatial construction: when the top node was formed, the two nodes representing apple taste and the phonetic sequence [æpl] were active and the level of arousal was sufficiently high. At present, only apple taste is active, giving rise to imagination in the form of the word [æpl].

Definition 21 (Temporal Construction). *Suppose $G = (V, E)$ is a graph and $a, b \in V$. Then $temporal(G, a, b)$ is the graph (V', E'), where $V' = V \cup \{c, d\}$, c is a new node labeled $DELAY$, d is a new node labeled AND, and $E' = E \cup \{(a, c), (c, d), (b, d)\}$, with the weights of the three new edges set to 1.*

Definition 22 (Destruction). *Suppose $G = (V, E)$ is a graph and $a \in V$. Then $forget(G, a)$ is the graph (V', E'), where $V' = V - V''$, $V'' = \{b \in V : E^*(a, b)\}$ and $E' = E - \{(b, c) \in E : b \in V'' \text{ or } c \in V''\}$.*

Definition 23 (Admissibility). *Let $G_0, G_1, \ldots$ be a sequence of networks and $\sigma_0, \sigma_1, \ldots$ a sequence of stimuli. $Spatial(G_n, a, b)$ is admissible at n if both a and b are top active in G_n at n. $Temporal(G_n, a, b)$ is admissible at n if a is top active in G_{n-1} at $n - 1$ and b is top active in G_n at n.*

With the terminology in place, we are ready to define the network development algorithm: see Algorithm 1, where $flip(p)$ is the result of flipping a weighted coin that produces outcome 1 with probability p.

Figures 4 and 6 offer examples of network development processes generated by Algorithm 1. Figure 4 shows the formation of a memory of apple taste. Figure 5 shows the formation of a memory of the written word "HI". A memory of the spoken word [æpl], shown in Figure 2 (a), can be formed analogously, but it requires one repetition of the sequence [æpl]. Figure 6, finally, shows how the apple taste and apple word networks are joined.

Algorithm 1. Network development algorithm

---

  loop
    if $card(V_n) < p_0$ **and** $flip(LR(n)) = 1$ **then**
      if there are preferred a, b s.t. $spatial(G_n, a, b)$ is admissible at n
      and $mod(a, G_n) = mod(b, G_n) = \{i\}$, for some i **then**
        Let $G_{n+1} = spatial(G_n, a, b)$.
      else if there are preferred a, b s.t. $temporal(G_n, a, b)$ is admissible at n
      and $mod(a, G_n) = mod(b, G_n) = \{i\}$, for some i **then**
        Let $G_{n+1} = temporal(G_n, a, b)$.
      else if $arousal(G_n) > p_4$
        if there are preferred a, b s.t. $spatial(G_n, a, b)$ is admissible at n
          Let $G_{n+1} = spatial(G_n, a, b)$.
        else if there are preferred a, b s.t. $temporal(G_n, a, b)$ is admissible at n
          Let $G_{n+1} = temporal(G_n, a, b)$.
        end if
      end if
    else if $via(a, n) < p_3$ for some $a \in V_n$ **then**
      Let $G_{n+1} = forget(G_n, a)$, where $via(a, n)$ is minimal.
    end if
    Compute the edge weights $w(a, b, n+1)$ reflecting $Pr(b|a)$.
    Compute the learning rate $LR(n+1)$.
    Compute the viabilities $via(a, n+1)$.
  end loop

---

5   Results

Algorithm 1 was implemented in Python 2.7 using the graphic package Graphviz for visualization. All of the development processes described in this paper were obtained using this program and straightforward input streams.

Figures 1–6 illustrate how networks are formed by the algorithm. In this case the algorithm develops exactly the desired memory structures with no undesirable structures as side effects. The algorithm gravitates toward memories that are emotionally intense, frequently repeated, or both.

6   Conclusion

Our study indicates that artificial emotions are well suited for guiding the development of dynamic networks by regulating the quality and quantity of memories formed and removed. The presented network model and network development mechanism are relatively simple and were mainly devised for presenting the idea of emotional concept development. Both can clearly be improved and elaborated in several directions. We conclude that artificial emotions can be fruitful, not only for guiding behavior, but also for controlling concept development.

Acknowledgments. This research was supported by The Swedish Research Council, grants 2012-1000 and 2013-4873. We would like to thank Christos Dimitrakakis for many helpful suggestions.

References

1. Abbeel, P., Coates, A., Quigley, M., Ng, A.Y.: An application of reinforcement learning to aerobatic helicopter flight. Advances in Neural Information Processing Systems **19**, 1 (2007)
2. Bach, J.: A framework for emergent emotions, based on motivation and cognitive modulators. International Journal of Synthetic Emotions (IJSE) **3**(1), 43–63 (2012)
3. Bach, J.: MicroPsi 2: The Next Generation of the MicroPsi Framework. In: Bach, J., Goertzel, B., Iklé, M. (eds.) AGI 2012. LNCS, vol. 7716, pp. 11–20. Springer, Heidelberg (2012)
4. Bechara, A., Damasio, H., Damasio, A.R.: Role of the amygdala in decision-making. Annals of the New York Academy of Sciences **985**(1), 356–369 (2003)
5. Begleiter, R., El-Yaniv, R., Yona, G.: On prediction using variable order markov models. Journal of Artificial Intelligence Research, 385–421 (2004)
6. Bengio, Y.: Learning deep architectures for ai. Foundations and trends in Machine Learning **2**(1), 1–127 (2009)
7. Blum, A.L., Langley, P.: Selection of relevant features and examples in machine learning. Artificial Intelligence **97**(1), 245–271 (1997)
8. Colton, S., Bundy, A., Walsh, T.: Automatic concept formation in pure mathematics (1999)
9. Gould, J.L., Gould, C.G., et al.: The honey bee. Scientific American Library (1988)
10. Johansen, J.P., Diaz-Mataix, L., Hamanaka, H., Ozawa, T., Ycu, E., Koivumaa, J., Kumar, A., Hou, M., Deisseroth, K., Boyden, E.S., et al.: Hebbian and neuromodulatory mechanisms interact to trigger associative memory formation. Proceedings of the National Academy of Sciences **111**(51), E5584–E5592 (2014)
11. Lebovitz, M.: Experiments with incremental concept formation. Machine Learning **2**, 103–138 (1987)
12. LeDoux, J.: Emotion circuits in the brain (2003)
13. LeDoux, J.E.: Emotional memory systems in the brain. Behavioural Brain Research **58**(1), 69–79 (1993)
14. Marsella, S., Gratch, J., Petta, P.: Computational models of emotion. A Blueprint for Affective Computing-A sourcebook and Manual, 21–46 (2010)
15. McCallum, R.A.: Instance-based utile distinctions for reinforcement learning with hidden state. In: ICML, pp. 387–395 (1995)
16. Pickett, M., Oates, T.: The Cruncher: Automatic Concept Formation Using Minimum Description Length. In: Zucker, J.-D., Saitta, L. (eds.) SARA 2005. LNCS (LNAI), vol. 3607, pp. 282–289. Springer, Heidelberg (2005)
17. Richter-Levin, G., Akirav, I.: Emotional tagging of memory formationØl' the search for neural mechanisms. Brain Research Reviews **43**(3), 247–256 (2003)
18. Rosenbloom, P.S.: The sigma cognitive architecture and system. AISB Quarterly **136**, 4–13 (2013)
19. Schmidt, M., Niculescu-Mizil, A., Murphy, K., et al.: Learning graphical model structure using l1-regularization paths. In: AAAI. vol. 7, pp. 1278–1283 (2007)

20. Strannegård, C., von Haugwitz, R., Wessberg, J., Balkenius, C.: A Cognitive Architecture Based on Dual Process Theory. In: Kühnberger, K.-U., Rudolph, S., Wang, P. (eds.) AGI 2013. LNCS, vol. 7999, pp. 140–149. Springer, Heidelberg (2013)

21. Tenenbaum, J.B., Kemp, C., Griffiths, T.L., Goodman, N.D.: How to grow a mind: Statistics, structure, and abstraction. Science **331**(6022), 1279–1285 (2011)

22. Tziortziotis, N., Dimitrakakis, C., Blekas, K.: Cover tree bayesian reinforcement learning. The Journal of Machine Learning Research **15**(1), 2313–2335 (2014)

23. Veness, J., Ng, K.S., Hutter, M., Uther, W., Silver, D.: A monte-carlo aixi approximation. Journal of Artificial Intelligence Research **40**(1), 95–142 (2011)

24. Witthöft, W.: Absolute anzahl und verteilung der zellen im him der honigbiene. Zeitschrift für Morphologie der Tiere **61**(1), 160–184 (1967)

The Cyber-Physical System Approach Towards Artificial General Intelligence: The Problem of Verification

Zoltán Tősér and András Lőrincz[✉]

Faculty of Informatics, Eötvös Loránd University, Budapest, Hungary
lorincz@inf.elte.hu

Abstract. Cyber-Physical Systems have many components including physical ones with heavy demands on workflow management; a real-time problem. Furthermore, the complexity of the system involves some degree of stochasticity, due to interactions with the environment. We argue that the factored version of the event-learning framework (ELF) being able to exploit robust controllers (RCs) can meet the requirements. We discuss the factored ELF (fELF) as the interplay between episodic and procedural memories, two key components of AGI. Our illustration concerns a fELF with RCs and is a mockup of an explosive device removal task. We argue that (i) the fELF limits the exponent of the state space and provides solutions in polynomial time, (ii) RCs decrease the number of variables and thus decrease the said exponent further, while the solution stays ε-optimal, (iii) solutions can be checked/verified by the execution being linear in the number of states visited, and (iv) communication can be restricted to instructions between subcomponents of an AGI system.

1 Introduction

Cyber-physical systems (CPSs) are in the forefront of algorithmic, software, and hardware developments. They are goal oriented. In the typical setting they are distributed, have physical components, and can include e.g., sensory, computational and robotic units. Given their complexity, testing may become the bottleneck, especially for safety- and time-critical applications. In case of any unexpected event or anomaly in the behavior, fast workflow management may become a necessity and might involve changes of the plan and thus communication of new subtasks, new roles, and new methods of communication, among other things. We say that a simple instruction or a more complex subtask make sense in a given context, if the responsible actors can execute them given the information provided. Successful completion of an instruction or a subtask verifies a portion of a larger plan. The larger the plan and the more complex the system, the more serious anomalies may occur. In turn, stochastic formulation is required.

We shall put forth the factored event-learning framework (fELF), a special form of reinforcement learning (RL), that has polynomial time learning characteristics and the maximal number of concurrent and dependent factors limits

© Springer International Publishing Switzerland 2015
J. Bieger (Ed.): AGI 2015, LNAI 9205, pp. 373–383, 2015.
DOI: 10.1007/978-3-319-21365-1_38

the exponent of the state space (Sect. 2). We illustrate fELF via a toy mockup explosive device (ED) removal task (Sect. 3). Up to the number of variables, the solution is '*hard to find*'. In the discussion section (Sect. 4) we will argue that this problem is '*easy to verify*' by following the steps in time as prescribed by the *solution*. Such solutions are worth to communicate. We conjecture that IQ tests are of similar nature. Conclusions will be drawn in Sect. 5.

2   Theoretical Background

We propose the MDP framework for CPSs. We utilize the generalized MDP (gMDP) formulation. Its ε-gMDP extension concerns ε-precise quantities and can exploit robust controllers if they meet the ε-precise condition. We review the event-learning framework (ELF) [8,16] that breaks tasks into subtasks, can admit ε-precise robust controllers and can hide some of the variables. An ELF extended with robust controllers is an ε-gMDP. The factored formulation of MDP gives rise to polynomial time optimization. Taken together, a factored generalized ELF with a robust controller is an ε-gMDP with polynomial time optimization. Execution requires the communication of instructions to the subcomponents making verification linear in time for deterministic systems.

2.1   Markov Decision Processes

A (finite) MDP [10] is defined by the tuple $\langle X, A, R, P \rangle$. X and A denote the finite set of states and actions, respectively. $P : X \times A \times X \rightarrow [0,1]$ is the transition function, the probability of arriving at state y after executing action a in state x. $R : X \times A \times X \rightarrow \mathbb{R}$ is the reward function: $R(x,a,y)$ is the immediate reward for transition (x,a,y).

Decision making aims at finding the optimal behavior subject to some optimality criterion, e.g., to infinite-horizon expected discounted total reward, when we want to find a policy $\pi : X \times A \rightarrow [0,1]$ that maximizes the expected value of $\sum_{t=0}^{\infty} \gamma^t r_t$, where r_t is the immediate reward in time step t and $0 \leq \gamma < 1$ is the discount factor.

A standard way to find an optimal policy is to estimate the optimal value function $V^* : X \rightarrow \mathbb{R}$, which gives the value (the expected cumulated discounted reward with the given starting state) of each state. From this, the optimal policy is the 'greedy' policy with respect to the optimal value function, i.e., the following Bellman equation:

$$V^*(x) = \max_a \sum_y P(x,a,y)\left(R(x,a,y) + \gamma V^*(y)\right), \quad \text{for all } x \in X. \quad (1)$$

2.2   Generalized MDP (gMDP) and ε-gMDPs

Operations $\sum_y P(x,a,y) \ldots$ and $\max_a \ldots$ can be extended, e.g., with risk considerations. Joint formalism for the different Bellman equiations has been constructed in [13]: a generalized MDP is defined by the tuple $\langle X, A, R, \bigoplus, \bigotimes \rangle$, where X, A, R are defined as above; $\bigoplus : (X \times A \times X \to \mathbb{R}) \to (X \times A \to \mathbb{R})$ is an 'expected value-type' operator and $\bigotimes : (X \times A \to \mathbb{R}) \to (X \to \mathbb{R})$ is a 'maximization-type' operator. We want to find the value function V^*, where

$$V^*(x) = \bigotimes\bigoplus(R(x,a,y) + \gamma V^*(y)), \quad \text{for all } x \in X.$$

or in short form $V^* = \bigotimes\bigoplus(R + \gamma V^*)$. The optimal value function can be interpreted as the total reward received by an agent behaving optimally in a non-deterministic environment. The operator $\bigoplus$ describes the effect of the environment. The operator $\bigotimes$ describes the action-selection of an optimal agent. When $0 \le \gamma < 1$, and both $\bigoplus$ and $\bigotimes$ are non-expansions, the optimal solution V^* of the equations exists and it is unique.

Generalized ε-MDP (ε-gMDP) assumes a prescribed $\varepsilon > 0$ and is defined by the tuple $\langle X, A, R, \{\bigoplus_t\}, \{\bigotimes_t\}\rangle$, with $\bigoplus_t : (X \times A \times X \to \mathbb{R}) \to (X \times A \to \mathbb{R})$ and $\bigotimes_t : (X \times A \to \mathbb{R}) \to (X \to \mathbb{R})$, $t = 1, 2, 3, \ldots$, if there exists a generalized MDP $\langle X, A, R, \bigoplus, \bigotimes\rangle$ such that $\limsup_{t\to\infty} \|\bigotimes_t\bigoplus_t - \bigotimes\bigoplus\| \le \varepsilon$. ε-MDPs have been first introduced in [7].

2.3 The Event-Learning Framework (ELF)

Event learning turns the MDP into a hierarchical problem via the *event-value function* $E : X \times X \to \mathbb{R}$ [16]. Pairs of states (x, y) and (x, y^d) are called *events* and *desired events*, respectively: for a given initial state x, y^d denotes the desired next state. The formalism remains the same, but any event can be seen as an *MDP subtask*: the $e_d = (x, y^d)$ state sequence can be a *subtask* to be optimized. $E(x, y^d)$ is the value of trying to get from actual state x to next state y^d. Note that state y reached could differ from desired state y^d.

2.4 Robust Controller

Assume that a state space X and a velocity field $v^d : X \to \dot{X}$ are given. At time t, the system is in state x_t with velocity v_t. We are looking for a control action that modifies the actual velocity to $v^d(x_t)$ with maximum probability:

$$u_t(x_t, v_t^d) = \Phi(x_t, v_t^d),$$

$\Phi(x_t, v_t^d)$ is called the inverse dynamics and it can be approximated. Under certain conditions, one can bound the tracking error to the desired level (see [16] and the references therein).

If time is discrete, like here, then prescribing the desired velocity v^d is equivalent to prescribing the desired successor state y^d. The controller can be directly inserted into an ELF by setting $\pi_t^A(x_t, y_t^d, a) = 1$ if $a = u_t(x_t, y_t^d)$ and 0 otherwise (Fig. 1).

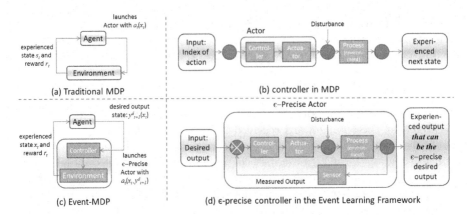

Fig. 1. MDP models. (a): MDP, (b): One step. Input: index of the action, output: experienced next state, (c): ELF, (d): One step. Input: desired output and the output can be the ε-precise version of the desired output.

2.5   Event-Learning with Robust Controller Belongs to the ε-gMDP Family

In the generalized ε-MDP, X denotes the set of states and the action corresponds to selecting a new desired state; the set of actions A is also equal to X. Reward function R is $R(x, y^d, y)$ and it gives the reward for arriving at y from x, when the desired state was y^d. Now, $(\bigotimes_t E)(x) = \max_{y^d} E(x, y^d)$, independently of t, and $(\bigoplus_t E)(x, y^d) = \sum_y p_t(y|x, y^d) E(x, y^d, y)$, where $p_t(y|x, y^d) = \sum_u \pi_t^A(x, y^d, u) P(x, u, y)$. Finally, we define the operators $\bigoplus$ and $\bigotimes$ as $(\bigotimes E)(x) = \max_{y^d} E(x, y^d)$ and $(\bigoplus E)(x, y^d) = \sum_y \sum_u \pi^A(x, y^d, u) P(x, u, y) E(x, y^d, y)$. In turn, if robust controllers are introduced into an ELF, then we still have an ε-gMDP problem with errors that can be bounded.

2.6   Factored Markov Decision Processes (fMDPs)

In CPS, naïve tabular representation of the transition probabilities requires a state space exponential in the number of variables. However, ongoing processes typically exclude other ones and a much smaller number of variables may be sufficient at any given time instant. Let $\mathbf{X}$ be the Cartesian product of m smaller state spaces (corresponding to individual variables), i.e., $\mathbf{X} = X_1 \times X_2 \times \ldots \times X_m$. Each X_i has size $|X_i| = n_i$ and the size of the state space is $N = |\mathbf{X}| = \prod_{i=1}^m n_i$.

In this case, the next-step value of a state variable depends only on a few other variables, so the full transition probability can be obtained as the product of several simpler factors. Formally, for any subset of variable indices $Z \subseteq \{1, 2, \ldots, m\}$, $\mathbf{X}[Z]$ denotes $\underset{i \in Z}{\times} X_i$ and for any $\mathbf{x} \in \mathbf{X}$, $\mathbf{x}[Z]$ denotes the value of the variables with indices in Z. Below, we shall use the shorthand $\mathbf{x}$ for the sake of simplicity. FMDPs were first introduced in [3].

2.7   Polynomial Time Learning

An fMDP with a factored optimistic initialization model (fOIM) – defined below – has a polynomial per-step computational complexity. FOIM gets ε-close to the value function of factored value iteration (which could be suboptimal) in polynomial time [15]:

Theorem 1 (fOIM). *Suppose that an agent is following factored value iteration in an unknown fMDP, where all reward components fall into the interval $[0, R_{\max}]$, there are m state factors, and all probability- and reward-factors depend on at most m_f factors. Let $E^\times(\mathbf{x}_t, \mathbf{y}_t^d)$ denote the value function of the approximate value iteration exploiting function approximations. Let $N_f = n^{m_f}$ and let $\varepsilon > 0$ and $\delta > 0$. If we set*

$$R_E = c \cdot \frac{mR_{\max}^2}{(1-\gamma)^4 \varepsilon} \left[\log \frac{mN_f|A|}{(1-\gamma)\varepsilon\delta} \right],$$

as the initial values of the MDP, then the number of time steps when the agent makes non-near-optimal moves, i.e., when $E^{fOIM}(\mathbf{x}_t, \mathbf{y}_t^d) < E^\times(\mathbf{x}_t, \mathbf{y}_t^d) - \varepsilon$, is bounded by

$$O\left(\frac{R_{\max}^2 m^4 N_f |A|}{\varepsilon^4 (1-\gamma)^4} \log^3 \tfrac{1}{\delta} \log^2 \frac{mN_f|A|}{\varepsilon} \right)$$

with probability at least $1 - \delta$.

3   Illustrative Experiment and the CPS Connection

For the sake of a fELF illustration we show an experiment with a WheelPhone (WP) and with a Lego NXT, both equipped with Android phones, image processing, QR code reading (not detailed here), and work sharing on a mockup explosive device (ED) removal task. This illustration gives us the opportunity to explain the concept of events, event hierarchy, desired states, episodes, robust controllers and procedures, cost and risk sensitive decision making, meta-level communication and finally, *the problem of verification.*

The illustration is by no means at the level of true cyber-physical systems, although it is a high-risk analogue of a smart factory shop-floor task [11] and has the relevant issues, such as work sharing, path planning, and execution time. The goal of the robots is to find explosive devices and transport them to a given safe location. The terrain contains several obstacles, which may be pushed aside to give way to the ED-carrying robot – but this takes time. Robots used the fELF method for decision making.

The two robots have different capabilities, their control precisions also differ and they share the work. One robot has chances to remove the ED, the other can clear the terrain. We used different number of obstacles and starting points and estimated the distributions of the execution times of the subtasks and their success rates. Each subtask is a desired event given by the actual state and the desired state of the event may become the experienced state later. Desired states include: 'ED found', 'obstacles found', 'path planned', 'first obstacle probably cleared', 'ED collected', 'terrain cleared', 'track is left', 'ED removed', among a few others. Some tasks are concurrent. The low-complexity RL task in [14] is similar and thus direct policy optimization is also possible, in case if the Markov property is questionable. FMDP description is like in [6]: transitions are limited to the possible ones.

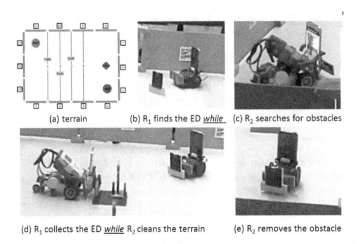

(a) terrain   (b) R_1 finds the ED *while*   (c) R_2 searches for obstacles

(d) R_1 collects the ED *while* R_2 cleans the terrain   (e) R_2 removes the obstacle

Fig. 2. Experimental arrangement with subtasks. Some of them, including subfigure (d), can be concurrent.

Explosion time has a distribution. The fELF makes decisions at discrete time steps according to the time elapsed, the subtasks executed, the ongoing subtasks, and the time-discretized distributions.

3.1   Results

According to the results (Fig. 3), there are three typical groups in the time variable: execution time is shorter than 2 min, it is longer than 2 min 20 sec and it is between these two values. We used these values for the discretization of the execution time.

The size of the state space in the fMDP depends on the number of factored variables at decision points. This number can be decreased if controllers are precise. For example, the NXT robot is sufficiently precise and direction uncertainties are neglected. NXT can clear away obstacles with certain probabilities, but it remains uncertain if it succeeded to move an obstacle out of the way of the WP robot or not. The motion of the WP robot is straight, but its direction is somewhat imprecise. We left it like this and that made uncertain the success of each obstacle clear-away subtask. Uncertainties measured experimentally and the computed direction uncertainties are used in decision making. The number of obstacles is randomly chosen from 2, 3 and 4 and are placed quasi-randomly over the terrain.

Nr	1	2	3	4	5	6	7	8	9	10	11	12	13	14	15
Time (min:sec)	2:16	2:19	2:25	2:14	2:21	2:33	2:28	1:57	2:15	2:14	1:49	2:19	2:18	2:06	2:12
Outcome	S	S	S	S	S	S	S	F	F	S	F	S	S	S	S
Trash location	1,2,4	1,3,4	1,2,3	1,2	1,2,3	1,3,4	1,2,3	1,2,4	1,3,4	1,2,4	2,3,4	2,3,4	1,3,4	1,4	2,3
NXT start position	12	11	14	12	11	14	12	14	14	1	12	12	11	12	1
WheelPhone start position	5	6	8	4	6	4	7	4	4	4	4	4	7	6	8

Fig. 3. Examples for estimating distributions. Green S: success. Red F: failure. For start positions, see Fig. 2(a). Failures in order: obstacle 1 is not cleared away, NXT-WP crashed, obstacles 3 and 4 are not cleared away.

3.2 Outlook to General Cyber-Physical Systems

Components of a real CPS task are similar to a large extent. Tools, computers, robots — that take part in the task hierarchy — all have capabilities that can be characterized by the complexity of the subtasks they can execute, the belonging success rates, and execution time distribution, for example. Subtasks may be sequential or concurrent according to causal relationships and urgency. Spatio-temporal dependencies of the processes in a complex CPS constrain possible state–desired state pairs of fMDP events. Depending on the type of the ask, e.g., if it is a smart factory, or an emergency situation [9], stochastic environmental disturbances may occur with different probabilities and they may require frequent real-time workflow management. Decision making about the changes of the workflow may not take considerable time even for complex systems and the lowering of the number of variables is highly desired due to the exponential dependence of the state space on those. This is a crucial problem and robust controllers can help in saving time, since such controllers support module construction that may span longer time intervals. For example, the controller of the NXT is more precise than that of the WP and the number of states that may occur and the required frequency of decision making is smaller for the NXT robot than for the WP one. Note that control precision could be increased for the WP robot using its high quality camera. The image processing, however, may increase energy consumption, the need for recharging, and thus the execution time. Plans and workflow management depend on the actual ED and the related risk and cost considerations.

4 Discussion: The Problem of Verification

In the ED removal problem we used higher order concepts (factors) for decision making. Such concepts include 'explosive', 'device', 'time', and alike, instead of raw visual, acoustic, and motor information. Furthermore, we could neglect some of these factors in the description of the situation if those factors were not relevant at that time of decision making. Such simplifications suit factored RL. The problem of forming higher order concepts — that fits the task to be solved and decreases the state space of decision making — falls outside of our considerations.

Problem solving is combinatorial in terms of the selection of the relevant factors, the order of actions to be executed, and the selection of the agent that should execute the action. If a decision is made then it should be communicated to the partners and they must *make sense* of the messages by verifying that the attempt towards the execution of the sub-task is feasible. This procedure of making sense is typical: intelligence proves the solution by means of verification. In general, intelligent verification is a pro-active mental step that exploits an approximate an sufficiently detailed model of the world. Evolution also verifies, but in a different way: evolution finds solutions by their success rates and without any mental model. We take a closer look to the issue of verification below. We note that model based verification is not part of our illustration, but the mockup itself or its computer model can serve as tools for such verification.

4.1 Verification in the Context of Intelligence

There are at least three types of knowledge transfer:

Supervised training. concerns the agreement about concepts (or categories) and can serve meta-level communication after the training phase.

Observations. are important pieces for decision making. However, the world is typically partially observed and distributed observation by many agents can help in solving the problems in due course, e.g., in the case of danger. This knowledge transfer happens at the meta level.

Solutions to problems. include concept forming, procedures, tricks, quizzes, mathematical proofs that exploit the formed concepts, among other things. Many of these procedures (problems) are hard to find (solve), but the verification of the solution can be easy.

Out of the ten broad abilities underpinning the g factor of intelligence [4], only fluid intelligence is connected to the third item, i.e., to concept forming, solving problems, and reasoning abilities. The other nine features of intelligence include reading and writing abilities, quantitative reasoning abilities, speed of decision making and alike. They are of high importance, but we believe that — from point of view of AGI and cyber-physical systems — they are either *solved* or can be solved by available technologies since efficient algorithms can reach superhuman performance if sufficiently large training samples are made available to them [12].

Fluid intelligence seems to differ: it shows up in two steps. One step is concept formation and the other one is solving the problem by means of those new concepts. These two processes are interlinked. The solution can be checked by means of verification using the formed concepts. One may say that if concept formation and problem solving are the core problems of general intelligence then model based verification is the tool for the appreciation of the solution.

4.2 'Verification' is the Goal of Intelligent Communication

There are four categories according to the complexity of solving problems and the complexity of the verification of the solution since both can be 'hard', or 'easy'. Tasks can be hard or easy if they scale exponentially or polynomially with the number of variables, respectively. Out of the four cases, problems belonging to the hard to solve, but easy to verify category are particularly worth to communicate. Such solutions can provide large savings in time and efforts for teammates.

4.3 Interplay Between Procedural and Episodic Memories

Our example has both procedural and episodic components. Any event is an episode and it can be saved in episodic memory for data mining, anomaly detection, model construction, and for learning to predict and control the event. The method of dealing with an ongoing event is the procedure. It is made of actions and sub-events. The 'ED removal story' is an 'ED removal event' brought off by the 'ED removal procedure'. This event may be concurrent with other events and it is probably embedded into a larger one. The event, as described here is independent from the other ongoing concurrent events, which in principle, could disturb it. However, such disturbance is also an event and it is limited in space and time. New concepts, new sensors and additional control tools can be introduced to overcome disturbances of the events provided that the details of the event are knowable, time is available and if the related costs and savings justify the effort.

From the point of view of a larger system, 'ED removal' could be one of its capabilities. Capabilities, i.e., the number of different events that can be invoked by the agent, correspond to desired states in a fELF and they make the variables of decision making. The number of events that can be invoked in a given state enters exponent of state space. The size of the state space can be decreased by learning and optimizing new capabilities made of smaller ones. The number of variables can be decreased by introducing robust controllers. For example, the measurement of the weight of the load can be neglected by adding a robust controller to increase the range of the capability, see. e.g. the example presented in [16]. Communication towards the decision making unit can be limited to the experienced state after execution of a sub-task and to an instruction towards the unit that has the capability to execute the next step. Such instruction contains the desired state and possibly (some of) the steps towards the desired state, i.e., (part of) the 'solution' .

In turn, a fELF with robust controllers efficiently decreases both the number of variables and the data to be communicated. From the point of view of verification, deterministic solutions are easy to verify if a model of the environment is available. For stochastic problems, stochasticity indicates limited knowledge about a knowable universe and may call for further exploration and learning. If more knowledge cannot be acquired in due course or if the collection of such information is costly, then solutions and verifications may require high costs since risks can be overestimated. Model based experimental methods of risk estimation are in the focus of ongoing research [1].

5   Conclusions

We have used an illustrative CPS mockup experiment in the factored event learning framework (fELF). The problem involved recognition, planning, decision making, work sharing, and risk estimation. We included distributions of execution times and success rates either via computational estimations or by measuring those experimentally.

We have argued that a fELF with a robust controller decreases combinatorial explosion. From the point of view of deterministic CPS problems, verification is polynomial *in the number of states* [2]. If we can afford non-tight bounds and additional resources, then experimental verification can be fast, if a model of the environment is available [1].

It has been noted that the problem of verification is alleviated by subtask construction provided that the subtasks can be executed with high fidelity. Robust controllers suit such demands and can save task execution even in the case of environmental disturbances. Any subtask can be viewed as a fELF problem and as such, it can be the subject of optimization. In the same vein, optimized fELF solutions can be embedded into larger tasks. In turn, fELF makes a partially ordered hierarchical RL in a natural fashion.

We note that time critical cyber-physical systems require easy to verify solutions. Such solutions are of high importance for interacting intelligences, since they offer combinatorial gains for teammates. Furthermore, communication can be limited to meta-level instructions about the states to be reached and meta-level information about the states that have been reached upon the execution of the instructions. CPS verification assumes approximately non-interacting sub-events that can run concurrently or may follow each other.

We conclude that CPS tasks concern fluid intelligence and — for large distributed systems — model based real-time verification is required and the time of verification is critical. Finding and learning potentially concurrent, but barely interacting, i.e., *independently and robustly executable* sub-tasks derived from the task space itself offer both exponential gains in the state space and flexibility in multi-tasking. Evolution demonstrates the feasibility of such constructs [5] and engineered solutions may follow similar routes. However, from the point of view of artificial general intelligence this is an unsolved problem. This problem is closely related to task oriented episodic and procedural memories and it deserves further investigations.

Acknowledgments. Thanks are due to Richárd Bellon, Dávid Hornyák, Mike Olasz, and Róbert Rill for running the experiments. Research was supported by the European Union and co-financed by the European Social Fund (grant no. TÁMOP 4.2.1./B-09/1/KMR-2010-0003) and by the EIT ICTLabs grant on *CPS for Smart Factories*.

References

1. Altmeyer, S., Cucu-Grosjean, L., Davis, R.I.: Static probabilistic timing analysis for real-time systems using random replacement caches. Real-Time Systems **51**(1), 77–123 (2015)
2. Angluin, D.: A note on the number of queries needed to identify regular languages. Information and Control **51**(1), 76–87 (1981)
3. Boutilier, C., Dearden, R., Goldszmidt, M., et al.: Exploiting structure in policy construction. IJCAI **14**, 1104–1113 (1995)
4. Carroll, J.B.: The higher-stratum structure of cognitive abilities. In: The Scientific Study of General Intelligence, ch., pp. 5–21. Pergamon (2003)
5. Graziano, M.: The organization of behavioral repertoire in motor cortex. Annu. Rev. Neurosci. **29**, 105–134 (2006)
6. Gyenes, V., Bontovics, Á., Lőrincz, A.: Factored temporal difference learning in the New Ties environment. Acta Cybern. **18**(4), 651–668 (2008)
7. Kalmár, Z., Szepesvári, C., Lőrincz, A.: Module-based reinforcement learning: Experiments with a real robot. Machine Learning **31**, 55–85 (1998)
8. Lőrincz, A., Pólik, I., Szita, I.: Event-learning and robust policy heuristics. Cognitive Systems Research **4**(4), 319–337 (2003)
9. Orlosky, J., Toyama, T., Sonntag, D., Sárkány, A., Lőrincz, A.: On-body multi-input indoor localization for dynamic emergency scenarios. In: IEEE Int. Conf. on Pervasive Comp. Comm. Workshop, pp. 320–325. IEEE (2014)
10. Puterman, M.: Markov decision processes. John Wiley & Sons, New York (1994)
11. Ribeiro, L., Rocha, A., Veiga, A., Barata, J.: Collaborative routing of products using a self-organizing mechatronic agent framework - a simulation study. Comp. Ind. **68**, 27–39 (2015)
12. Schmidhuber, J.: Deep learning in neural networks: An overview. Neural Networks **61**, 85–117 (2015)
13. Szepesvári, C., Littman, M.L.: Generalized Markov decision processes. In: Proceedings of International Conference of Machine Learning 1996, Bari (1996)
14. Szita, I., Lőrincz, A.: Learning to play using low-complexity rule-based policies. J. Artif. Int. Res. **30**, 659–684 (2007)
15. Szita, I., Lőrincz, A.: Optimistic initialization and greediness lead to polynomial time learning in factored MDPs. In: Int. Conf. Mach. Learn., pp. 1001–1008. Omnipress (2009)
16. Szita, I., Takács, B., Lőrincz, A.: Epsilon-MDPs. J. Mach. Learn. Res. **3**, 145–174 (2003)

Analysis of Types of Self-Improving Software

Roman V. Yampolskiy[✉]

Computer Engineering and Computer Science, Speed School of Engineering,
University of Louisville, Louisville, USA
roman.yampolskiy@louisville.edu

Abstract. Software capable of improving itself has been a dream of computer scientists since the inception of the field. In this work we provide definitions for Recursively Self-Improving software, survey different types of self-improving software, and provide a review of the relevant literature. Finally, we address security implications from self-improving intelligent software.

Keywords: Recursive self-improvement · Self-modifying code · Self-modifying software · Self-modifying algorithm · Autogenous intelligence · Bootstrap fallacy

1   Introduction

Since the early days of computer science, visionaries in the field anticipated creation of a self-improving intelligent system, frequently as an easier pathway to creation of true artificial intelligence[1]. As early as 1950 Alan Turing wrote: "Instead of trying to produce a programme to simulate the adult mind, why not rather try to produce one which simulates the child's? If this were then subjected to an appropriate course of education one would obtain the adult brain. Presumably the child-brain is something like a notebook as one buys from the stationers. Rather little mechanism, and lots of blank sheets... Our hope is that there is so little mechanism in the child-brain that something like it can be easily programmed. The amount of work in the education we can assume, as a first approximation, to be much the same as for the human child" [1].

Turing's approach to creation of artificial (super)intelligence was echoed by I.J. Good, Marvin Minsky and John von Neumann, all three of whom published on it (interestingly in the same year, 1966): Good - "Let an ultraintelligent machine be defined as a machine that can far surpass all the intellectual activities of any man however clever. Since the design of machines is one of these intellectual activities, an ultraintelligent machine could design even better machines; there would then unquestionably be an 'intelligence explosion,' and the intelligence of man would be left far behind. Thus the first ultraintelligent machine is the last invention that man need ever make" [2]. Minsky - "Once we have devised programs with a genuine capacity for self-improvement a rapid evolutionary process will begin. As the machine improves both itself and its model of itself, we shall begin to see all the phenomena associated

---

[1]This paper is based on material excerpted, with permission, from the book - Artificial Superintelligence: a Futuristic Approach © 2015 CRC Press.

© Springer International Publishing Switzerland 2015
J. Bieger (Ed.): AGI 2015, LNAI 9205, pp. 384–393, 2015.
DOI: 10.1007/978-3-319-21365-1_39

with the terms "consciousness," "intuition" and "intelligence" itself. It is hard to say how close we are to this threshold, but once it is crossed the world will not be the same" [3]. Von Neumann - "There is thus this completely decisive property of complexity, that there exists a critical size below which the process of synthesis is degenerative, but above which the phenomenon of synthesis, if properly arranged, can become explosive, in other words, where syntheses of automata can proceed in such a manner that each automaton will produce other automata which are more complex and of higher potentialities than itself" [4]. Similar types of arguments are still being made today by modern researchers and the area of RSI research continues to grow in popularity [5-7], though some [8] have argued that recursive self-improvement process requires hyperhuman capability to "get the ball rolling", a kind of "Catch 22"

2 Taxonomy of Types of Self-Improvement

Self-improving software can be classified by the degree of self-modification it entails. In general we distinguish three levels of improvement – modification, improvement (weak self-improvement) and recursive improvement (strong self-improvement). However, it is easy to see that recursive improvement is a type/subset of improvement which is a subset of modification. For the purposes of this paper we will treat them as separate classes.

2.1 Self-Modification

Self-Modification does not produce improvement and is typically employed for code obfuscation to protect software from being reverse engineered or to disguise self-replicating computer viruses from detection software. While a number of obfuscation techniques are known to exist [9], ex. self-modifying code [10], polymorphic code, metamorphic code, diversion code [11], none of them are intended to modify the underlying algorithm. The sole purpose of such approaches is to modify how the source code looks to those trying to understand the software in questions and what it does [12].

2.2 Self-Improvement

Self-Improvement or Self-adaptation [13] is a desirable property of many types of software products [14] and typically allows for some optimization or customization of the product to the environment and users it is deployed with. Common examples of such software include evolutionary algorithms such as Genetic Algorithms [15-20] or Genetic Programming which optimize software parameters with respect to some well understood fitness function and perhaps work over some highly modular programming language to assure that all modifications result in software which can be compiled and evaluated. The system may try to optimize its components by creating internal tournaments between candidate solutions. Omohundro proposed the concept of efficiency drives in self-improving software [21]. Because of one of such drives, balance drive, self-improving systems will tend to balance the allocation of resources between their different subsystems. If the system is not balanced overall performance of the system could be increased by shifting resources from subsystems with small marginal improvement to those with larger marginal increase [21]. While performance of the software as a result of such optimization may be improved the overall algorithm is unlikely to be modified to a fundamentally more capable one.

Additionally, the law of diminishing returns quickly sets in and after an initial significant improvement phase, characterized by discovery of "low-hanging fruit", future improvements are likely to be less frequent and less significant, producing a Bell curve of valuable changes. Metareasoning, metalearning, learning to learn, and lifelong learning are terms which are often used in the machine learning literature to indicate self-modifying learning algorithms or the process of selecting an algorithm which will perform best in a particular problem domain [22]. Yudkowsky calls such process *non-recursive optimization* – a situation in which one component of the system does the optimization and another component is getting optimized [23].

In the field of complex dynamic systems, aka chaos theory, positive feedback systems are well known to always end up in what is known as an *attractor*- a region within system's state space that the system can't escape from [24]. A good example of such attractor convergence is the process of Metacompilation or Supercompilation [25] in which a program designed to take source code written by a human programmer and to optimize it for speed is applied to its own source code. It will likely produce a more efficient compiler on the first application perhaps by 20%, on the second application by 3%, and after a few more recursive iterations converge to a fixed point of zero improvement [24].

2.3   Recursive Self-Improvement

Recursive Self-Improvement is the only type of improvement which has potential to completely replace the original algorithm with a completely different approach and more importantly to do so multiple times. At each stage newly created software should be better at optimizing future version of the software compared to the original algorithm. As of the time of this writing it is a purely theoretical concept with no working RSI software known to exist. However, as many have predicted that such software might become a reality in the 21st century it is important to provide some analysis of properties such software would exhibit.

Self-modifying and self-improving software systems are already well understood and are quite common. Consequently, we will concentrate exclusively on RSI systems. In practice performance of almost any system can be trivially improved by allocation of additional computational resources such as more memory, higher sensor resolution, faster processor or greater network bandwidth for access to information. This linear scaling doesn't fit the definition of recursive-improvement as the system doesn't become better at improving itself. To fit the definition the system would have to engineer a faster type of memory not just purchase more memory units of the type it already has access to. In general hardware improvements are likely to speed up the system, while software improvements (novel algorithms) are necessary for achievement of meta-improvements.

It is believed that AI systems will have a number of advantages over human programmers making it possible for them to succeed where we have so far failed. Such advantages include [26]: longer work spans (no breaks, sleep, vocation, etc.), omniscience (expert level knowledge in all fields of science, absorbed knowledge of all published works), superior computational resources (brain vs processor, human memory vs RAM), communication speed (neurons vs wires), increased serial depth (ability to perform sequential operations in access of about a 100 human brain can manage), duplicability (intelligent software can be instantaneously copied), editability (source code unlike DNA can be quickly modified), goal coordination (AI copies can work towards a common goal without much overhead), improved rationality (AIs are likely to be free from human cognitive biases) [27], new sensory modalities (native sensory hardware for source code), blending over of deliberative and automatic processes (management of computational resources over multiple tasks), introspective perception and manipulation (ability to analyze low level hardware, ex. individual neurons), addition of hardware (ability to add new memory, sensors, etc.), advanced communication (ability to share underlying cognitive representations for memories and skills) [28].

Chalmers [29] uses logic and mathematical induction to show that if an AI_0 system is capable of producing only slightly more capable AI_1 system generalization of that process leads to superintelligent performance in AI_n after n generations. He articulates, that his proof assumes that the *proportionality thesis,* which states that increases in intelligence lead to proportionate increases in the capacity to design future generations of AIs, is true.

Nivel et al. proposed formalization of RSI systems as autocatalytic sets – collections of entities comprised of elements, each of which can be created by other elements in the set making it possible for the set to self-maintain and update itself. They also list properties of a system which make it purposeful, goal-oriented and self-organizing, particularly: *reflectivity* – ability to analyze and rewrite its own structure; *autonomy* – being free from influence by system's original designers (*bounded autonomy* – is a property of a system with elements which are not subject to self-modification); *endogeny* – an autocatalytic ability [30]. Nivel and Thorisson also attempt to operationalize autonomy by the concept of *self-programming* which they insist has to be done in an experimental way instead of a theoretical way (via proofs of correctness) since it is the only tractable approach [31].

Yudkowsky writes prolifically about recursive self-improving processes and suggests that introduction of certain concepts might be beneficial to the discussion, specifically he proposes use of terms - Cascades, Cycles and Insight which he defines as: Cascades – when one development leads to another; Cycles – repeatable cascade in which one optimization leads to another which in turn benefits the original optimization; Insight – new information which greatly increases one's optimization ability [32]. Yudkowsky also suggests that the goodness and number of opportunities in the space of solutions be known as *Optimization Slope* while *optimization resources* and *optimization efficiency* refer to how much of computational resources an agent has access to and how efficiently the agent utilizes said resources. An agent engaging in an *optimization process* and able to hit non-trivial targets in large search space [33] is described as having significant optimization power [23].

3   RSI Software Classification

RSI software could be classified based on the number of improvements it is capable of achieving. The most trivial case is the system capable of undergoing a single fundamental improvement. The hope is that truly RSI software will be capable of many such improvements, but the question remains open regarding the possibility of an infinite number of recursive-improvements. It is possible that some upper bound on improvements exists limiting any RSI software to a finite number of desirable and significant rewrites. Critics explain failure of scientists, to date, to achieve a sustained RSI process by saying that RSI researchers have fallen victims of the *bootstrap fallacy* [34].

3.1   How Improvements are Discovered

Another axis on which RSI systems can be classified has to do with how improvements are discovered. Two fundamentally different approaches are understood to exist. The first one is a brute force based approach [35] which utilizes Levin (Universal [36]) Search [37]. The idea is to consider all possible strings of source code up to some size limit and to select the one which can be proven to provide improvements. While theoretically optimal and guaranteed to find superior solution if one exists this method is not computationally feasible in practice. Some variants of this approach to self-improvement, known as Gödel Machines [38-43], Optimal Ordered Problem Solver (OOPS) [44] and Incremental Self-Improvers [45, 46], have been thoroughly analyzed by Schmidhuber and his co-authors. Second approach assumes that the system has a certain level of scientific competence and uses it to engineer and test its own replacement. Whether a system of any capability can intentionally invent a more capable and so a more complex system remains as the fundamental open problem of RSI research.

It is important to note that the first concrete algorithms for RSI were all by Schmidhuber. His diploma thesis from 1987 already was about an evolutionary system that learns to inspect and improve its own learning algorithm, where Genetic Programming (GP) is applied to itself, to recursively evolve better GP methods. His RSI based on the self-referential Success-Story Algorithm for self-modifying probabilistic programs was already able to solve complex tasks [47]. And finally, his self-referential recurrent neural networks run and inspect and change their own weight change algorithms [48]. In 2001, his former student Hochreiter had actually a practical implementation of such an RNN that learns an excellent learning algorithm, at least for the limited domain of quadratic functions [49, 50].

3.2   Hybrid Systems

Finally, we can consider a hybrid RSI system which includes both an artificially intelligent program and a human scientist. Mixed human-AI teams have been very successful in many domains such as chess or theorem proving. It would be surprising if having a combination of natural and artificial intelligence did not provide an advantage in designing new AI systems or enhancing biological intelligence. We are currently experiencing a limited version of this approach with human computer scientists developing progressively better versions of AI software (while utilizing continuously improving software tools), but since the scientists themselves remain unenhanced we can't really talk about self-improvement. This type of RSI can be classified as Indirect recursive improvement as opposed to Direct RSI in which the system itself is responsible for all modifications. Other types of Indirect RSI may be based on collaboration between multiple artificial systems instead of AI and human teams [51].

3.3   Other Properties

In addition to classification with respect to types of RSI we can also evaluate systems as to certain binary properties. For example: We may be interested only in systems which are guaranteed not to decrease in intelligence, even temporarily, during the improvement process. This may not be possible if the intelligence design landscape contains local maxima points.

Another property of any RSI system we are interested in understanding better is necessity of unchanging source code segments. In other words must an RSI system be able to modify any part of its source code or are certain portions of the system (encoded goals, verification module) must remain unchanged from generation to generation. Such portions would be akin to ultra-conserved elements or conserved sequences of DNA [52, 53] found among multiple related species. This question is particularly important for the goal preservation in self-improving intelligent software, as we want to make sure that future generations of the system are motivated to work on the same problem [29]. As AI goes through the RSI process and becomes smarter and more rational it is likely to engage in a de-biasing process removing any constraints we programmed into it [8]. Ideally we would want to be able to prove that even after recursive self-improvement our algorithm maintains the same goals as the original. Proofs of safety or correctness for the algorithm only apply to particular source code and would need to be rewritten and re-proven if the code is modified, which happens in RSI software many times. But we suspect that re-proving slightly modified code may be easier compared to having to prove safety of a completely novel piece of code.

We are also interested in understanding if RSI process can take place in an isolated (leakproofed [54]) system or if interaction with external environment, internet, people, other AI agents is necessary. Perhaps access to external information can be used to mediate speed of RSI process. This also has significant implications on safety mechanisms we can employ while experimenting with early RSI systems [55-63]. Finally, it needs to be investigated if the whole RSI process can be paused at any point and for any specific duration of time in order to limit any negative impact from potential intelligence explosion. Ideally we would like to be able to program our Seed AI to RSI until it reaches certain level of intelligence, pause and wait for further instructions.

4   Conclusions

Recursively Self-Improving software is the ultimate form of artificial life and creation of life remains one of the great unsolved mysteries in science. More precisely, the problem of creating RSI software is really the challenge of creating a program capable of writing other programs [64], and so is an AI-Complete problem as has been demonstrated by Yampolskiy [65, 66]. AI-complete problems are by definition most difficult problems faced by AI researchers and it is likely that RSI source code will be so complex that it would be difficult or impossible to fully analyze [51]. Also, the problem is likely to be NP-Complete as even simple metareasoning and metalearning [67] problems have been shown by Conitzer and Sandholm to belong to that class. In particular they proved that allocation of deliberation time across anytime algorithms running on different problem instances is NP-Complete and a complimentary problem of dynamically allocating information gathering resources by an agent across multiple actions is NP-Hard, even if evaluating each particular action is computationally simple. Finally, they showed that the problem of deliberately choosing a limited number of deliberation or information gathering actions to disambiguate the state of the world is PSPACE Hard in general [68].

This paper is a part of a two paper set presented at AGI2015 with the complementary paper being: "On the Limits of Recursively Self-Improving AGI" [69].

References

1. Turing, A.: Computing Machinery and Intelligence. Mind **59**(236), 433–460 (1950)
2. Good, I.J.: Speculations Concerning the First Ultraintelligent Machine. Advances in Computers **6**, 31–88 (1966)
3. Minsky, M.: Artificial Intelligence. Scientific American **215**(3), 257 (1966)
4. Burks, A.W., Von Neumann, J.: Theory of Self-Reproducing Automata. University of Illinois Press (1966)
5. Pearce, D.: The biointelligence explosion. In: Singularity Hypotheses, pp. 199–238. Springer (2012)
6. Omohundro, S.M.: The nature of self-improving artificial intelligence. In: Singularity Summit, San Francisco, CA (2007)
7. Waser, M.R.: Bootstrapping a structured self-improving & safe autopoietic self. In: Annual International Conference on Biologically Inspired Cognitive Architectures, Boston, Massachusetts, November 9, 2014
8. Hall, J.S.: Engineering utopia. Frontiers in Artificial Intelligence and Applications **171**, 460 (2008)
9. Mavrogiannopoulos, N., Kisserli, N., Preneel, B.: A taxonomy of self-modifying code for obfuscation. Computers & Security **30**(8), 679–691 (2011)
10. Anckaert, B., Madou, M., De Bosschere, K.: A model for self-modifying code. In: Camenisch, J.L., Collberg, C.S., Johnson, N.F., Sallee, P. (eds.) IH 2006. LNCS, vol. 4437, pp. 232–248. Springer, Heidelberg (2007)
11. Petrean, L.: Polymorphic and Metamorphic Code Applications in Portable Executable Files Protection. Acta Technica Napocensis, **51**(1) (2010)
12. Bonfante, G., Marion, J.-Y., Reynaud-Plantey, D.: A computability perspective on self-modifying programs. In: Seventh IEEE International Conference on Software Engineering and Formal Methods, pp. 231–239. IEEE (2009)
13. Cheng, B.H., et al.: Software engineering for self-adaptive systems: a research roadmap. In: Cheng, B.H., de Lemos, R., Giese, H., Inverardi, P., Magee, J. (eds.) Software Engineering for Self-Adaptive Systems. LNCS, vol. 5525, pp. 1–26. Springer, Heidelberg (2009)

14. Ailon, N., et al.: Self-improving algorithms. SIAM Journal on Computing **40**(2), 350–375 (2011)
15. Yampolskiy, R., et al.: Printer model integrating genetic algorithm for improvement of halftone patterns. In: Western New York Image Processing Workshop (WNYIPW). IEEE Signal Processing Society, Rochester, NY (2004)
16. Yampolskiy, R.V., Ashby, L., Hassan, L.: Wisdom of Artificial Crowds—A Metaheuristic Algorithm for Optimization. Journal of Intelligent Learning Systems and Applications **4**(2), 98–107 (2012)
17. Yampolskiy, R.V., Ahmed, E.L.B.: Wisdom of artificial crowds algorithm for solving NP-hard problems. International Journal of Bio-Inspired Computation (IJBIC) **3**(6), 358–369
18. Ashby, L.H., Yampolskiy, R.V.: Genetic algorithm and wisdom of artificial crowds algorithm applied to light up. In: 16th International Conference on Computer Games: AI, Animation, Mobile, Interactive Multimedia, Educational & Serious Games, Louisville, KY, USA, pp. 27–32, July 27–30, 2011
19. Khalifa, A.B., Yampolskiy, R.V.: GA with Wisdom of Artificial Crowds for Solving Mastermind Satisfiability Problem. International Journal of Intelligent Games & Simulation **6**(2), 6 (2011)
20. Port, A.C., Yampolskiy, R.V.: Using a GA and Wisdom of Artificial Crowds to solve solitaire battleship puzzles. In: 17th International Conference on Computer Games (CGAMES), pp. 25–29. IEEE, Louisville (2012)
21. Omohundro, S.: Rational artificial intelligence for the greater good. In: Singularity Hypotheses, pp. 161–179. Springer (2012)
22. Anderson, M.L., Oates, T.: A review of recent research in metareasoning and metalearning. AI Magazine **28**(1), 12 (2007)
23. Yudkowsky, E.: Intelligence explosion microeconomics. In: MIRI Technical Report. www.intelligence.org/files/IEM.pdf
24. Heylighen, F.: Brain in a vat cannot break out. Journal of Consciousness Studies **19**(1–2), 1–2 (2012)
25. Turchin, V.F.: The concept of a supercompiler. ACM Transactions on Programming Languages and Systems (TOPLAS) **8**(3), 292–325 (1986)
26. Sotala, K.: Advantages of artificial intelligences, uploads, and digital minds. International Journal of Machine Consciousness **4**(01), 275–291 (2012)
27. Muehlhauser, L., Salamon, A.: Intelligence explosion: evidence and import. In: Singularity Hypotheses, pp. 15–42. Springer (2012)
28. Yudkowsky, E.: Levels of organization in general intelligence. In: Artificial General Intelligence, pp. 389–501. Springer (2007)
29. Chalmers, D.: The Singularity: A Philosophical Analysis. Journal of Consciousness Studies **17**, 7–65 (2010)
30. Nivel, E., et al.: Bounded Recursive Self-Improvement. arXiv preprint arXiv:1312.6764 (2013)
31. Nivel, E., Thórisson, K.R.: Self-programming: operationalizing autonomy. In: Proceedings of the 2nd Conf. on Artificial General Intelligence (2008)
32. Yudkowsky, E., Hanson, R.: The Hanson-Yudkowsky AI-foom debate. In: MIRI Technical Report (2008). http://intelligence.org/files/AIFoomDebate.pdf
33. Yampolskiy, R.V.: The Universe of Minds. arXiv preprint arXiv:1410.0369 (2014)
34. Hall, J.S.: Self-improving AI: An analysis. Minds and Machines **17**(3), 249–259 (2007)

35. Yampolskiy, R.V.: Efficiency Theory: a Unifying Theory for Information, Computation and Intelligence. Journal of Discrete Mathematical Sciences & Cryptography **16**(4–5), 259–277 (2013)
36. Gagliolo, M.: Universal search. Scholarpedia **2**(11), 2575 (2007)
37. Levin, L.: Universal Search Problems. Problems of Information Transmission **9**(3), 265–266 (1973)
38. Steunebrink, B., Schmidhuber, J.: A Family of Gödel Machine implementations. In: Fourth Conference on Artificial General Intelligence (AGI-11), Mountain View, California (2011)
39. Schmidhuber, J.: Gödel machines: fully self-referential optimal universal self-improvers. In: Artificial General Intelligence, pp. 199–226. Springer (2007)
40. Schmidhuber, J.: Gödel machines: towards a technical justification of consciousness. In: Adaptive Agents and Multi-Agent Systems II, pp. 1–23. Springer (2005)
41. Schmidhuber, J.: Gödel machines: self-referential universal problem solvers making provably optimal self-improvements. In: Artificial General Intelligence (2005)
42. Schmidhuber, J.: Ultimate cognition à la Gödel. Cognitive Computation **1**(2), 177–193 (2009)
43. Schmidhuber, J.: Completely self-referential optimal reinforcement learners. In: Duch, W., Kacprzyk, J., Oja, E., Zadrożny, S. (eds.) ICANN 2005. LNCS, vol. 3697, pp. 223–233. Springer, Heidelberg (2005)
44. Schmidhuber, J.: Optimal ordered problem solver. Machine Learning **54**(3), 211–254 (2004)
45. Schmidhuber, J., Zhao, J., Wiering, M.: Shifting inductive bias with success-story algorithm, adaptive Levin search, and incremental self-improvement. Machine Learning **28**(1), 105–130 (1997)
46. Schmidhuber, J.: A general method for incremental self-improvement and multiagent learning. Evolutionary Computation: Theory and Applications, 81–123 (1999)
47. Schmidhuber, J.: Metalearning with the Success-Story Algorithm (1997). http://people.idsia.ch/~juergen/ssa/sld001.htm
48. Schmidhuber, J.: A neural network that embeds its own meta-levels. In: IEEE International Conference on Neural Networks, pp. 407–412. IEEE (1993)
49. Younger, A.S., Hochreiter, S., Conwell, P.R.: Meta-learning with backpropagation. In: International Joint Conference on Neural Networks (IJCNN 2001). IEEE (2001)
50. Hochreiter, S., Younger, A., Conwell, P.: Learning to learn using gradient descent. In: Artificial Neural Networks—ICANN 2001, pp. 87–94 (2001)
51. Osterweil, L.J., Clarke, L.A.: Continuous self-evaluation for the self-improvement of software. In: Robertson, P., Shrobe, H.E., Laddaga, R. (eds.) IWSAS 2000. LNCS, vol. 1936, pp. 27–39. Springer, Heidelberg (2001)
52. Beck, M.B., Rouchka, E.C., Yampolskiy, R.V.: Finding data in DNA: computer forensic investigations of living organisms. In: Rogers, M., Seigfried-Spellar, K.C. (eds.) ICDF2C 2012. LNICST, vol. 114, pp. 204–219. Springer, Heidelberg (2013)
53. Beck, M., Yampolskiy, R.: DNA as a medium for hiding data. BMC Bioinformatics **13**(Suppl. 12), A23 (2012)
54. Yampolskiy, R.V.: Leakproofing Singularity - Artificial Intelligence Confinement Problem. Journal of Consciousness Studies (JCS) **19**(1–2), 194–214 (2012)
55. Majot, A.M., Yampolskiy, R.V.: AI safety engineering through introduction of self-reference into felicific calculus via artificial pain and pleasure. In: 2014 IEEE International Symposium on Ethics in Science, Technology and Engineering. IEEE (2014)
56. Yampolskiy, R., Fox, J.: Safety Engineering for Artificial General Intelligence, pp. 1–10. Topoi (2012)

57. Yampolskiy, R.V., Fox, J.: Artificial general intelligence and the human mental model. In: Singularity Hypotheses: A Scientific and Philosophical Assessment, p. 129 (2013)
58. Sotala, K., Yampolskiy, R.V.: Responses to catastrophic AGI risk: A survey. Physica Scripta. **90**, December 2015
59. Yampolskiy, R.V.: What to do with the singularity paradox? In: Müller, V.C. (ed.) Philosophy and Theory of Artificial Intelligence. SAPERE, vol. 5, pp. 397–413. Springer, Heidelberg (2012)
60. Yampolskiy, R., Gavrilova, M.: Artimetrics: Biometrics for Artificial Entities. IEEE Robotics and Automation Magazine (RAM) **19**(4), 48–58 (2012)
61. Yampolskiy, R., et al.: Experiments in Artimetrics: Avatar Face Recognition. Transactions on Computational Science XVI, 77–94 (2012)
62. Ali, N., Schaeffer, D., Yampolskiy, R.V.: Linguistic profiling and behavioral drift in chat bots. In: Midwest Artificial Intelligence and Cognitive Science Conference, p. 27 (2012)
63. Gavrilova, M., Yampolskiy, R.: State-of-the-Art in Robot Authentication [From the Guest Editors]. Robotics & Automation Magazine, IEEE **17**(4), 23–24 (2010)
64. Hall, J.S.: VARIAC: an Autogenous Cognitive Architecture. Frontiers in Artificial Intelligence and Applications **171**, 176 (2008)
65. Yampolskiy, R.V.: Turing test as a defining feature of ai-completeness. In: Yang, X.-S. (ed.) Artificial Intelligence, Evolutionary Computing and Metaheuristics. SCI, vol. 427, pp. 3–17. Springer, Heidelberg (2013)
66. Yampolskiy, R.V.: AI-Complete, AI-Hard, or AI-Easy–Classification of problems in AI. In: The 23rd Midwest Artificial Intelligence and Cognitive Science Conference, Cincinnati, OH, USA (2012)
67. Schaul, T., Schmidhuber, J.: Metalearning. Scholarpedia **5**(6), 4650 (2010)
68. Conitzer, V., Sandholm, T.: Definition and complexity of some basic metareasoning problems. In: Proceedings of the Eighteenth International Joint Conference on Artificial Intelligence (IJCAI), Acapulco, Mexico, pp. 1099–1106 (2003)
69. Yampolskiy, R.V.: On the limits of recursively self-improving AGI. In: The Eighth Conference on Artificial General Intelligence, Berlin, Germany, July 22–25, 2015

On the Limits of Recursively Self-Improving AGI

Roman V. Yampolskiy[(✉)]

Computer Engineering and Computer Science, Speed School of Engineering,
University of Louisville, Louisville, USA
`roman.yampolskiy@louisville.edu`

Abstract. Self-improving software has been a goal of computer scientists since
the founding of the field of Artificial Intelligence. In this work we analyze limits on computation which might restrict recursive self-improvement. We also introduce Convergence Theory which aims to predict general behavior of RSI
systems.

Keywords: Recursive self-improvement · Convergence theory · Bootstrapping

1 Introduction

Intuitively most of us have some understanding of what it means for a software system to be self-improving, however we believe it is important to precisely define such
notions and to systematically investigate different types of self-improving software[1].
First we need to define the notion of improvement. We can talk about improved efficiency – solving same problems faster or with less need for computational resources
(such as memory). We can also measure improvement in error rates or finding closer
approximations to optimal solutions, as long as our algorithm is functionally equivalent from generation to generation. Efficiency improvements can be classified as either producing a trivial improvement as between different algorithms in the same
complexity class (ex. NP), or as producing a fundamental improvement as between
different complexity classes (ex. P vs NP) [1]. It is also very important to remember
that complexity class notation (Big-O) may hide significant constant factors which
while ignorable theoretically may change relative order of efficiency in practical applications of algorithms.

This type of analysis works well for algorithms designed to accomplish a particular
task, but doesn't work well for general purpose intelligent software as an improvement in one area may go together with decreased performance in another domain.
This makes it hard to claim that the updated version of the software is indeed an improvement. Mainly, the major improvement we want from self-improving intelligent
software is higher degree of intelligence which can be approximated via machine
friendly IQ tests [2] with a significant G-factor correlation.

---

[1] This paper is based on material excerpted, with permission, from the book - Artificial Superintelligence:
a Futuristic Approach © 2015 CRC Press.

© Springer International Publishing Switzerland 2015
J. Bieger (Ed.): AGI 2015, LNAI 9205, pp. 394–403, 2015.
DOI: 10.1007/978-3-319-21365-1_40

A particular type of self-improvement known as Recursive Self-Improvement (RSI) is fundamentally different as it requires that the system not only get better with time, but that it gets better at getting better. A truly RSI system is theorized not to be subject to diminishing returns, but would instead continue making significant improvements and such improvements would become more substantial with time. Consequently, an RSI system would be capable of open ended self-improvement. As a result, it is possible that unlike with standard self-improvement, in RSI systems from generation-to-generation most source code comprising the system will be replaced by different code. This brings up the question of what "self" refers to in this context. If it is not the source code comprising the agent then what is it? Perhaps we can redefine RSI as Recursive Source-code Improvement (RSI) to avoid dealing with this philosophical problem. Instead of trying to improve itself such a system is trying to create a different system which is better at achieving same goals as the original system. In the most general case it is trying to create an even smarter artificial intelligence.

2   On the Limits of Recursively Self-Improving AGI

The mere possibility of recursively self-improving software remains unproven. In this section we present a number of arguments against such phenomenon. First of all, any implemented software system relies on hardware for memory, communication and information processing needs even if we assume that it will take a non-Von Neumann (quantum) architecture to run such software. This creates strict theoretical limits to computation, which despite hardware advances predicted by Moore's law will not be overcome by any future hardware paradigm. Bremermann [3], Bekenstein [4], Lloyd [5], Anders [6], Aaronson [7], Shannon [8], Krauss [9], and many others have investigated ultimate limits to computation in terms of speed, communication and energy consumption with respect to such factors as speed of light, quantum noise, and gravitational constant. Some research has also been done on establishing ultimate limits for enhancing human brain's intelligence [10]. While their specific numerical findings are outside of the scope of this work, one thing is indisputable: there are ultimate physical limits to computation. Since more complex systems have greater number of components and require more matter, even if individual parts are designed at nanoscale, we can conclude that just like matter and energy are directly related [11] and matter and information ("it from bit") [12] so is matter and intelligence. While we are obviously far away from hitting any limits imposed by availability of matter in the universe for construction of our supercomputers it is a definite theoretical upper limit on achievable intelligence.

In addition to limitations endemic to hardware, software-related limitations may present even bigger obstacles for RSI systems. Intelligence is not measured as a standalone value but with respect to the problems it allows to solve. For many problems such as playing checkers [13] it is possible to completely solve the problem (provide an optimal solution after considering all possible options) after which no additional performance improvement would be possible [14]. Other problems are known to be unsolvable regardless of level of intelligence applied to them [15]. Assuming separation of complexity classes (such as P vs NP) holds [1], it becomes obvious that certain classes of problems will always remain only approximately solvable and any improvements in solutions will come from additional hardware resources not higher intelligence.

Wiedermann argues that cognitive systems form an infinite hierarchy and from a computational point of view human-level intelligence is upper-bounded by the Σ_2 class of the Arithmetic Hierarchy [16]. Because many real world problems are computationally infeasible for any non-trivial inputs even an AI which achieves human level performance is unlikely to progress towards higher levels of the cognitive hierarchy. So while theoretically machines with super-Turing computational power are possible, in practice they are not implementable as the non-computable information needed for their function is just that – not computable. Consequently Wiedermann states that while machines of the future will be able to solve problems, solvable by humans, much faster and more reliably they will still be limited by computational limits found in upper levels of the Arithmetic Hierarchy [16, 17].

Mahoney attempts to formalize what it means for a program to have a goal G and to self-improve with respect to being able to reach said goal under constraint of time, t [18]. Mahoney defines a goal as a function $G: N \rightarrow R$ mapping natural numbers N to real numbers R. Given a universal Turing machine L, Mahoney defines $P(t)$ to mean the positive natural number encoded by output of the program P with input t running on L after t time steps, or 0 if P has not halted after t steps. Mahoney's representation says that P has goal G at time t if and only if there exists $t' > t$ such that $G(P(t')) > G(P(t))$ and for all $t' > t$, $G(P(t') \geq G(P(t))$. If P has a goal G, then $G(P(t))$ is a monotonically increasing function of t with no maximum for $t > C$. Q improves on P with respect to goal G if and only if all of the following condition are true: P and Q have goal Q. $\exists t, G(Q(t)) > G(P(t))$ and $\sim\exists t, t' > t, G(Q(t)) > G(P(t))$ [18]. Mahoney then defines an improving sequence with respect to G as an infinite sequence of program $P_1, P_2, P_3, \ldots$ such that for $\forall i, i > 0, P_{i+1}$ improves P_i with respect to G. Without the loss of generality Mahoney extends the definition to include the value -1 to be an acceptable input, so $P(-1)$ outputs appropriately encoded software. He finally defines P_1 as an RSI program with respect to G iff $P_i(-1) = P_{i+1}$ for all $i > 0$ and the sequence $P_i, i = 1, 2, 3 \ldots$ is an improving sequence with respect to goal G [18]. Mahoney also analyzes complexity of RSI software and presents a proof demonstrating that the algorithmic complexity of P_n (the nth iteration of an RSI program) is not greater than $O(log\ n)$ implying a very limited amount of knowledge gain would be possible in practice despite theoretical possibility of RSI systems [18]. Yudkowsky also considers possibility of receiving only logarithmic returns on cognitive reinvestment: $log(n) + log(log(n)) + \ldots$ in each recursive cycle [19].

Other limitations may be unique to the proposed self-improvement approach. For example Levin type search through the program space will face problems related to Rice's theorem [20] which states that for any arbitrarily chosen program it is impossible to test if it has any non-trivial property such as being very intelligent. This testing is of course necessary to evaluate redesigned code. Also, universal search over the space of mind designs which will not be computationally possible due to the No Free Lunch theorems [21] as we have no information to reduce the size of the search space [22]. Other difficulties related to testing remain even if we are not taking about arbitrarily chosen programs but about those we have designed with a specific goal in mind and which consequently avoid problems with Rice's theorem. One such difficulty is determining if something is an improvement. We can call this obstacle – "multi-dimensionality of optimization".

No change is strictly an improvement; it is always a tradeoff between gain in some areas and loss in others. For example, how do we evaluate and compare two software systems one of which is better at chess and the other at poker? Assuming the goal is increased intelligence over the distribution of all potential environments the system would have to figure out how to test intelligence at levels above its own a problem which remains unsolved. In general the science of testing for intelligence above level achievable by naturally occurring humans (IQ < 200) is in its infancy. De Garis raises a problem of evaluating quality of changes made to the top level structures responsible for determining the RSI's functioning, structures which are not judged by any higher level modules and so present a fundamental difficulty in accessing their performance [23].

Other obstacles to RSI have also been suggested in the literature. Löb's theorem states that a mathematical system can't assert its own soundness without becoming inconsistent [24], meaning a sufficiently expressive formal system can't know that everything it proves to be true is actually so [24]. Such ability is necessary to verify that modified versions of the program are still consistent with its original goal of getting smarter. Another obstacle, called *procrastination paradox* will also prevent the system from making modifications to its code since the system will find itself in a state in which a change made immediately is as desirable and likely as the same change made later [25, 26]. Since postponing making the change carries no negative implications and may actually be safe this may result in an infinite delay of actual implementation of provably desirable changes.

Similarly, Bolander raises some problems inherent in logical reasoning with self-reference, namely, self-contradictory reasoning, exemplified by the Knower Paradox of the form - "This sentence is false" [27]. Orseau and Ring introduce what they call "Simpleton Gambit" a situation in which an agent will chose to modify itself towards its own detriment if presented with a high enough reward to do so [28]. Yampolskiy reviews a number of related problems in rational self-improving optimizers, above a certain capacity, and concludes, that despite opinion of many, such machines will choose to "wirehead" [29]. Chalmers [30] suggests a number of previously unanalyzed potential obstacles on the path to RSI software with *Correlation obstacle* being one of them. He describes it as a possibility that no interesting properties we would like to amplify will correspond to ability to design better software.

Yampolskiy is also concerned with accumulation of errors in software undergoing an RSI process, which is conceptually similar to accumulation of mutations in the evolutionary process experienced by biological agents. Errors (bugs) which are not detrimental to system's performance are very hard to detect and may accumulate from generation to generation building on each other until a critical mass of such errors leads to erroneous functioning of the system, mistakes in evaluating quality of the future generations of the software or a complete breakdown [31].

The self-reference aspect in self-improvement system itself also presents some serious challenges. It may be the case that the minimum complexity necessary to become RSI is higher than what the system itself is able to understand. We see such situations frequently at lower levels of intelligence, for example a squirrel doesn't have mental capacity to understand how a squirrel's brain operates. Paradoxically, as the system becomes more complex it may take exponentially more intelligence to understand itself and so a system which starts capable of complete self-analysis may lose that ability as it self-improves. Informally we can call it the Munchausen obstacle, inability of a system to lift itself by its own bootstraps. An additional problem may be that the system in question is computationally irreducible [32] and so can't simulate running its own source code. An agent cannot predict what it will think without thinking it first. A system needs 100% of its memory to model itself, which leaves no memory to record the output of the simulation. Any external memory to which the system may write becomes part of the system and so also has to be modeled. Essentially the system will face an infinite regress of self-models from which it can't escape. Alternatively, if we take a physics perspective on the issue, we can see intelligence as a computational resource (along with time and space) and so producing more of it will not be possible for the same reason why we can't make a perpetual motion device as it would violate fundamental laws of nature related to preservation of energy. Similarly it has been argued that a Turing Machine cannot output a machine of greater algorithmic complexity [14].

We can even attempt to formally prove impossibility of intentional RSI process via proof by contradiction: Let's define RSI R_1 as a program not capable of algorithmically solving a problem of difficulty X, say X_i. If R_1 modifies its source code after which it is capable of solving X_i it violates our original assumption that R_1 is not capable of solving X_i since any introduced modification could be a part of the solution process, so we have a contradiction of our original assumption, and R_1 can't produce any modification which would allow it to solve X_i, which was to be shown. Informally, if an agent can produce a more intelligent agent it would already be as capable as that new agent. Even some of our intuitive assumptions about RSI are incorrect. It seems that it should be easier to solve a problem if we already have a solution to a smaller instance of such problem [33] but in a formalized world of problems belonging to the same complexity class, re-optimization problem is proven to be as difficult as optimization itself [34-37].

3   Analysis

A number of fundamental problems remain open in the area of RSI. We still don't know the minimum intelligence necessary for commencing the RSI process, but we can speculate that it would be on par with human intelligence which we associate with universal or general intelligence [38], though in principal a sub-human level system capable of self-improvement can't be excluded [30]. One may argue that even human level capability is not enough because we already have programmers (people or their intellectual equivalence formalized as functions [39] or Human Oracles [40, 41]) who have access to their own source code (DNA), but who fail to understand how DNA (nature) works to create their intelligence. This doesn't even include additional complexity in trying to improve on existing DNA code or complicating factors presented by the impact of learning environment (nurture) on development of human intelligence. Worse yet, it is not obvious how much above human ability an AI needs to be to begin overcoming the "complexity barrier" associated with self-understanding. Today's AIs can do many things people are incapable of doing, but are not yet capable of RSI behavior.

We also don't know the minimum size of program (called Seed AI [42]) necessary to get the ball rolling. Perhaps if it turns out that such "minimal genome" is very small a brute force [43] approach might succeed in discovering it. We can assume that our Seed AI is the smartest Artificial General Intelligence known to exist [44] in the world as otherwise we can simply delegate the other AI as the seed. It is also not obvious how the source code size of RSI will change as it goes through the improvement process, in other words what is the relationship between intelligence and minimum source code size necessary to support it. In order to answer such questions it may be useful to further formalize the notion of RSI perhaps by representing such software as a Turing Machine [45] with particular inputs and outputs. If that could be successfully accomplished a new area of computational complexity analysis may become possible in which we study algorithms with dynamically changing complexity (Big-O) and address questions about how many code modification are necessary to achieve certain level of performance from the algorithm.

This of course raises the question of speed of RSI process, are we expecting it to take seconds, minutes, days, weeks, years or more (hard takeoff VS soft takeoff) for the RSI system to begin hitting limits of what is possible with respect to physical limits of computation [46]? Even in suitably constructed hardware (human baby) it takes decades of data input (education) to get to human-level performance (adult). It is also not obvious if the rate of change in intelligence would be higher for a more advanced RSI, because it is more capable, or for a "newbie" RSI because it has more low hanging fruit to collect. We would have to figure out if we are looking at improvement in absolute terms or as a percentage of system's current intelligence score.

Yudkowsky attempts to analyze most promising returns on cognitive reinvestment as he considers increasing size, speed or ability of RSI systems. He also looks at different possible rates of return and arrives at three progressively steeper trajectories for RSI improvement which he terms: "fizzle", "combust" and "explode" aka "AI go FOOM" [19]. Hall [47] similarly analyzes rates of return on cognitive investment and derives a curve equivalent to double the Moore's Law rate. Hall also suggest that an AI would be better of trading money it earns performing useful work for improved hardware or software rather than attempt to directly improve itself since it would not be competitive against more powerful optimization agents such as Intel corporation.

Fascinatingly, by analyzing properties which correlate with intelligence, Chalmers [30] is able to generalize self-improvement optimization to properties other than intelligence. We can agree that RSI software as we describe it in this work is getting better at designing software not just at being generally intelligent. Similarly other properties associated with design capacity can be increased along with capacity to design software for example capacity to design systems with sense of humor and so in addition to intelligence explosion we may face an explosion of funniness.

4   RSI Convergence Theorem

A simple thought experiment regarding RSI can allow us to arrive at a fascinating hypothesis. Regardless of the specifics behind the design of the Seed AI used to start an RSI process all such systems, attempting to achieve superintelligence, will converge to the same software architecture. We will call this intuition - RSI Convergence Theory. There is a number of ways in which it can happen, depending on the assumptions we make, but in all cases the outcome is the same, a practically computable agent similar to AIXI (which is an incomputable but superintelligent agent [48]).

If an upper limit to intelligence exists, multiple systems will eventually reach that level, probably by taking different trajectories, and in order to increase their speed will attempt to minimize the size of their source code eventually discovering smallest program with such level of ability. It may even be the case that sufficiently smart RSIs will be able to immediately deduce such architecture from basic knowledge of physics and Kolmogorov Complexity [49]. If, however, intelligence turns out to be an unbounded property RSIs may not converge. They will also not converge if many programs with maximum intellectual ability exist and all have the same Kolmogorov complexity or if they are not general intelligences and are optimized for different environments. It is also likely that in the space of minds [50] stable attractors include sub-human and super-human intelligences with precisely human level of intelligence being a rare point [51].

In addition to architecture convergence we also postulate goal convergence because of basic economic drives, such as resource accumulation and self-preservation. If correct, predictions of RSI convergence imply creation of what Bostrom calls a Singleton [52], a single decision making agent in control of everything. Further speculation can lead us to conclude that converged RSI systems separated by space and time even at cosmological scales can engage in acausal cooperation [53, 54] since they will realize that they are the same agent with the same architecture and so are capable of running perfect simulations of each other's future behavior. Such realization may allow converged superintelligence with completely different origins to implicitly cooperate particularly on meta-tasks. One may also argue that humanity itself is on the path which converges to the same point in the space of all possible intelligences (but is undergoing a much slower RSI process). Consequently, by observing a converged RSI architecture and properties humanity can determine its ultimate destiny, its purpose in life, its Coherent Extrapolated Volition (CEV) [55].

5   Conclusions

Intelligence is a computational resource and as with other physical resources (mass, speed) its behavior is probably not going to be just a typical linear extrapolation of what we are used to, if observed at high extremes (IQ > 200+). It may also be subject to fundamental limits such as the speed limit on travel of light or fundamental limits we do not yet understand or know about (unknown unknowns). In this work we reviewed a number of computational upper limits to which any successful RSI system will asymptotically strive to grow, we can note that despite existence of such upper bounds we are currently probably very far from reaching them and so still have plenty of room for improvement at the top. Consequently, any RSI achieving such significant level of enhancement, despite not creating an infinite process, will still seem like it is producing superintelligence with respect to our current state [56].

The debate regarding possibility of RSI will continue. Some will argue that while it is possible to increase processor speed, amount of available memory or sensor resolution the fundamental ability to solve problems can't be intentionally and continuously improved by the system itself. Additionally, critics may suggest that intelligence is upper bounded and only differs by speed and available info to process [57]. In fact they can point out to such maximum intelligence, be it a theoretical one, known as AIXI, an agent which given infinite computational resources will make purely rational decisions in any situation.

Others will say that since intelligence is the ability to find patterns in data, intelligence has no upper bounds as the number of variables comprising a pattern can always be greater and so present a more complex problem against which intelligence can be measured. It is easy to see that even if in our daily life the problems we encounter do have some maximum difficulty it is certainly not the case with theoretical examples we can derive from pure mathematics. It seems likely that the debate will not be settled until a fundamental unsurmountable obstacle to RSI process is found or a proof by existence is demonstrated. Of course the question of permitting machines to undergo RSI transformation is a separate and equally challenging problem.

This paper is a part of a two paper set presented at AGI2015 with the complementary paper being: "Analysis of Types of Self-Improving Software" [58].

References

1. Yampolskiy, R.V., Construction of an NP Problem with an Exponential Lower Bound (2011). Arxiv preprint arXiv:1111.0305
2. Yonck, R.: Toward a Standard Metric of Machine Intelligence. World Future Review 4(2), 61–70 (2012)
3. Bremermann, H.J.: Quantum noise and information. In: Proceedings of the Fifth Berkeley Symposium on Mathematical Statistics and Probability (1967)
4. Bekenstein, J.D.: Information in the holographic universe. Scientific American 289(2), 58–65 (2003)
5. Lloyd, S.: Ultimate Physical Limits to Computation. Nature 406, 1047–1054 (2000)
6. Sandberg, A.: The physics of information processing superobjects: daily life among the Jupiter brains. Journal of Evolution and Technology 5(1), 1–34 (1999)
7. Aaronson, S.: Guest column: NP-complete problems and physical reality. ACM Sigact News 36(1), 30–52 (2005)
8. Shannon, C.E.: A Mathematical Theory of Communication. Bell Systems Technical Journal 27(3), 379–423 (1948)
9. Krauss, L.M., Starkman, G.D.: Universal limits on computation (2004). arXiv preprint astro-ph/0404510
10. Fox, D.: The limits of intelligence. Scientific American 305(1), 36–43 (2011)
11. Einstein, A.: Does the inertia of a body depend upon its energy-content? Annalen der Physik 18, 639–641 (1905)

12. Wheeler, J.A.: Information, Physics, Quantum: The Search for Links. Univ. of Texas (1990)
13. Schaeffer, J., et al.: Checkers is Solved. Science **317**(5844), 1518–1522 (2007)
14. Mahoney, M.: Is there a model for RSI?. In: SL4, June 20, 2008. http://www.sl4.org/archive/0806/19028.html
15. Turing, A.: On computable numbers, with an application to the Entscheidungsproblem. Proceedings of the London Mathematical Society **2**(42), 230–265 (1936)
16. Wiedermann, J.: A Computability Argument Against Superintelligence. Cognitive Computation **4**(3), 236–245 (2012)
17. Wiedermann, J.: Is There Something Beyond AI? Frequently Emerging, but Seldom Answered Questions about Artificial Super-Intelligence, p. 76. Artificial Dreams, Beyond AI
18. Mahoney, M.: A Model for Recursively Self Improving Programs (2010). http://mattmahoney.net/rsi.pdf
19. Yudkowsky, E., Intelligence Explosion Microeconomics. In: MIRI Technical Report. www.intelligence.org/files/IEM.pdf
20. Rice, H.G.: Classes of recursively enumerable sets and their decision problems. Transactions of the American Mathematical Society **74**(2), 358–366 (1953)
21. Wolpert, D.H., Macready, W.G.: No free lunch theorems for optimization. IEEE Transactions on Evolutionary Computation **1**(1), 67–82 (1997)
22. Melkikh, A.V.: The No Free Lunch Theorem and hypothesis of instinctive animal behavior. Artificial Intelligence Research **3**(4), p43 (2014)
23. de Garis, H.: The 21st. Century Artilect: Moral Dilemmas Concerning the Ultra Intelligent Machine. Revue Internationale de Philosophie **44**(172), 131–138 (1990)
24. Yudkowsky, E., Herreshoff, M.: Tiling agents for self-modifying AI, and the Löbian obstacle. In: MIRI Technical Report (2013)
25. Fallenstein, B., Soares, N.: Problems of self-reference in self-improving space-time embedded intelligence. In: MIRI Technical Report (2014)
26. Yudkowsky, E.: The Procrastination Paradox (Brief technical note). In: MIRI Technical Report (2014). https://intelligence.org/files/ProcrastinationParadox.pdf
27. Bolander, T.: Logical theories for agent introspection. Comp. Science **70**(5), 2002 (2003)
28. Orseau, L.: Ring, M.: Self-modification and mortality in artificial agents. In: 4th international conference on Artificial general intelligence, pp. 1–10. Mount. View, CA. (2011)
29. Yampolskiy, R.V.: Utility Function Security in Artificially Intelligent Agents. Journal of Experimental and Theoretical Artificial Intelligence (JETAI), 1–17 (2014)
30. Chalmers, D.: The Singularity: A Philosophical Analysis. Journal of Consciousness Studies **17**, 7–65 (2010)
31. Yampolskiy, R.V.: Artificial intelligence safety engineering: Why machine ethics is a wrong approach. In: Philosophy and Theory of Artificial Intelligence, pp. 389–396, Springer (2013)
32. Wolfram, S.: A New Kind of Science. Wolfram Media, Inc., May 14, 2002
33. Yampolskiy, R.V.: Computing Partial Solutions to Difficult AI Problems. In: Midwest Artificial Intelligence and Cognitive Science Conference, p. 90 (2012)
34. Böckenhauer, H.-J., Hromkovič, J., Mömke, T., Widmayer, P.: On the hardness of reoptimization. In: Geffert, V., Karhumäki, J., Bertoni, A., Preneel, B., Návrat, P., Bieliková, M. (eds.) SOFSEM 2008. LNCS, vol. 4910, pp. 50–65. Springer, Heidelberg (2008)
35. Ausiello, G., Escoffier, B., Monnot, J., Paschos, V.T.: Reoptimization of minimum and maximum traveling salesman's tours. In: Arge, L., Freivalds, R. (eds.) SWAT 2006. LNCS, vol. 4059, pp. 196–207. Springer, Heidelberg (2006)

36. Archetti, C., Bertazzi, L., Speranza, M.G.: Reoptimizing the traveling salesman problem. Networks **42**(3), 154–159 (2003)
37. Ausiello, G., Bonifaci, V., Escoffier, B.: Complexity and approximation in reoptimization. Imperial College Press/World Scientific (2011)
38. Loosemore, R., Goertzel, B.: Why an intelligence explosion is probable. In: Singularity Hypotheses, pp. 83–98. Springer (2012)
39. Shahaf, D., Amir, E.: Towards a theory of AI completeness. In: 8th International Symposium on Logical Formalizations of Commonsense Reasoning. California, March 26–28, 2007
40. Yampolskiy, R.V.: Turing test as a defining feature of AI-completeness. In: Yang, X.-S. (ed.) Artificial Intelligence, Evolutionary Computing and Metaheuristics. SCI, vol. 427, pp. 3–17. Springer, Heidelberg (2013)
41. Yampolskiy, R.V.: AI-complete, AI-hard, or AI-easy–classification of problems in AI. In: The 23rd Midwest Artificial Intelligence and Cognitive Science Conference, OH, USA (2012)
42. Yudkowsky, E.S.: General Intelligence and Seed AI (2001). http://singinst.org/ourresearch/publications/GISAI/
43. Yampolskiy, R.V.: Efficiency Theory: a Unifying Theory for Information, Computation and Intelligence. J. of Discrete Math. Sciences & Cryptography **16**(4–5), 259–277 (2013)
44. Yampolskiy, R.V.: AI-Complete CAPTCHAs as Zero Knowledge Proofs of Access to an Artificially Intelligent System. ISRN Artificial Intelligence **271878** (2011)
45. Turing, A.M.: On Computable Numbers, with an Application to the Entscheidungsproblem. Proceedings of the London Mathematical Society **42**, 230–265 (1936)
46. Bostrom, N.: Superintelligence: Paths, dangers, strategies. Oxford University Press (2014)
47. Hall, J.S.: Engineering utopia. Frontiers in AI and Applications **171**, 460 (2008)
48. Hutter, M.: Universal algorithmic intelligence: A mathematical top$\rightarrow$ down approach. In: Artificial general intelligence, pp. 227–290. Springer (2007)
49. Kolmogorov, A.N.: Three Approaches to the Quantitative Definition of Information. Problems Inform. Transmission **1**(1), 1–7 (1965)
50. Yampolskiy, R.V.: The Universe of Minds (2014). arXiv:1410.0369
51. Yudkowsky, E.: Levels of organization in general intelligence. In: Artificial general intelligence, pp. 389–501. Springer (2007)
52. Bostrom, N.: What is a Singleton? Linguistic and Philosophical Invest. **5**(2), 48–54 (2006)
53. Yudkowsky, E.: Timeless decision theory. The Singularity Institute, San Francisco (2010)
54. LessWrong: Acausal Trade, September 29, 2014. http://wiki.lesswrong.com/wiki/Acausal_trade
55. Yudkowsky, E.S.: Coherent Extrapolated Volition. Singularity Institute for Artificial Intelligence, May 2004. http://singinst.org/upload/CEV.html
56. Yudkowsky, E.: Recursive Self-Improvement. In: Less Wrong, December 1, 2008. http://lesswrong.com/lw/we/recursive_selfimprovement/, September 29, 2014
57. Hutter, M.: Can Intelligence Explode? J. of Consciousness Studies **19**(1–2), 1–2 (2012)
58. Yampolskiy, R.V.: Analysis of types of self-improving software. In: The Eighth Conference on Artificial General Intelligence, Berlin, Germany, July 22–25, 2015

Gödel Agents in a Scalable Synchronous Agent Framework

Jörg Zimmermann(✉), Henning H. Henze, and Armin B. Cremers

Institute of Computer Science, University of Bonn, Bonn, Germany
{jz,abc}@iai.uni-bonn.de

Abstract. A synchronous framework for the interaction of an agent and an environment based on Moore machines is introduced. Within this framework, the notion of a Gödel agent is defined relative to a family of agents and environments and a time horizon T. A Gödel agent is the most flexible, adapting and self-improving agent with regard to the given environment family. It scores well across many environments, and not only in a selected few. Ideas from infinite game theory and ruin theory are used to get well-defined limits for $T \to \infty$ by introducing negative goals or repellors. This allows to score actions of the agent by how probable an action makes the survival of the agent till the end of time. Score functions of this type will be called "liveness" scores, and they provide a solution to the horizon problem from a foundational point of view. Additionally, by varying the agent and environment families, one gets a scalable and flexible testbed which could prove to be well-suited for analyzing phenomena of adaptation and self-improvement, both theoretically and empirically.

1 A Scalable Synchronous Agent Framework

Theoretical investigations have to be conducted within a conceptual framework. The process of taking a notion of colloquial language and turn it into a formal, precisely defined one often is not a straight path from the colloquial notion to the formal one, but a long and intertwined development resulting in several precise, but different versions of the colloquial term. These differences often are very subtle, but can have profound implications for the results obtainable within the respective frameworks. This conceptual dynamics also holds for the notion of an agent, which plays a central role in computer science, but especially in artificial intelligence. The agent concept underlying much of the research in foundations of artificial intelligence is, for example, defined by M. Hutter in [5], p. 126. It consists of two interacting Turing machines, one representing the agent and one representing the environment. If the environment produces an output, it is written on the percept tape of the agent. Then the agent starts its computations, deliberating the new percept, and finally produces an action as output, which is written on the action tape of the environment. While one machine is computing its next output, the other one is effectively suspended.

© Springer International Publishing Switzerland 2015
J. Bieger (Ed.): AGI 2015, LNAI 9205, pp. 404–413, 2015.
DOI: 10.1007/978-3-319-21365-1_41

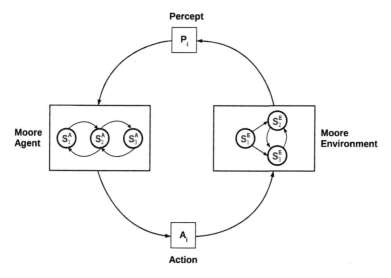

Fig. 1. Two Moore machines, agent and environment, interacting in a synchronous manner. The output of the environment at time i is the input of the agent at time $i+1$ and vice versa.

We call this agent framework *locally synchronous*, because the time structures of the agent and the environment are independent, as if they would exist in different universes, but are locally interconnected via percepts and actions. For a detailed discussion of local synchrony, which lies between global synchrony and asynchrony, see [3]. The locally synchronous framework was also used by R. Solomonoff in his seminal articles on universal induction [12,13]. Full Solomonoff induction is incomputable, but in [14] it is outlined how *effective and universal induction* is possible when the agent and the environment are embedded into a synchronous time structure. This is one example for surprising implications resulting from seemingly small changes to a conceptual framework, stressing the point that some results are not as absolute as they might appear, but depend crucially on the details of the chosen framework.

Here we want to modify the locally synchronous framework in two ways, calling the new framework *globally synchronous* or just synchronous: First we replace Turing machines by Moore machines (see below), and second we do not assume the agent or environment are suspended while the other one is computing, but the Moore agent and the Moore environment are interacting in a simultaneous fashion: their transitions are synchronized, the output of one machine is the input of the other, and the output is generated and read in each cycle (see figure 1). A Moore agent can conduct complex calculations using its internal states and multiple cycles, but during these calculations the last output (or whatever the Moore agent produces as preliminary output while the complex calculation is running) of the Moore agent is used as input for the environment. Thus the Moore agent has to act in real-time, but on the other hand the environment is scanned in real-time, too, excluding the possibility that the environment takes more and more time to generate the next percept. In fact, in the locally synchronous framework, the agent does not know whether the current percept was generated within a second or one billion years.

Moore machines are finite state machines which read in an input symbol and generate an output symbol in each cycle. They do not terminate, but translate a stream of input symbols into a stream of output symbols, accordingly they are also called finite state transducers. Moore machines are named after E. F. Moore, who introduced the concept in 1956 [8].

A Moore machine is a 6-tuple $(S, S_0, \Sigma, \Lambda, T, G)$ where:

- S is a finite set of states,
- $S_0 \in S$ is a start state,
- Σ is a finite set called the input alphabet,
- Λ is a finite set called the output alphabet,
- $T : S \times \Sigma \to S$ is a transition function mapping a state and an input symbol to the next state,
- $G : S \to \Lambda$ is an output function mapping each state to an output symbol.

We replace Turing machines by Moore machines in order to have a better control of the complexity of the agents and environments, where the number of states of a Moore machine provide a natural complexity measure. This enables us to investigate notions of learning, adapting, and self-improving in scaled-down versions of the full Turing model, simplifying theoretical and empirical analysis. Furthermore, the synchronous agent framework is not only closer to real world applications than the locally synchronous one (the world doesn't stop while we are thinking, unfortunately), but also allows the distinction between adaptability and self-improvement within the framework. This distinction follows when one basically defines adaptability as *finding better actions for the same situation*, driven by past observations (which can be modeled in the locally synchronous framework), and self-improvement as *finding the same action, but quicker*, driven by internal self-modification (which doesn't count in the locally synchronous framework, but in the synchronous one).

2   Gödel Agents

An *arena* is a triple $(\mathcal{A}, \mathcal{E}, S)$, where $\mathcal{A}$ is a family of agents, $\mathcal{E}$ is a family of environments, and $S : \mathcal{A} \times \mathcal{E} \to \mathbf{R}$ is a score function assigning every pair of agent A and environment E a real number measuring the performance of agent A in environment E. First we assume that the agent and the environment families are finite, the cases where agent or environment families or both become infinite is discussed in section 4. In the finite case, the following notions are well-defined:

Definition 1. *For all environments $E \in \mathcal{E}$ the score $S^{pre}(E) = \max_{A \in \mathcal{A}} S(A, E)$ is called the* pre-established score *of E. An agent $A \in \mathcal{A}$ is called an* pre-established agent *of E if $S(A, E) = S^{pre}(E)$.*

So pre-established agents a priori fit best into a given environment, so there is no need for adaptation or self-improvement, but in general a pre-established agent for environment E_1 will fail miserably for environment E_2. The term "pre-established" is borrowed from Leibnizian philosophy. Gottfried W. Leibniz introduced the concept of "pre-established harmony" to describe that there is no need for "substances" (especially mind and body) to interact or adapt because God has them programmed in advance to "harmonize" with each other ([4], p. 197).

Definition 2. *The* loss *of agent A wrt. environment E is defined as: $L(A, E) = S^{pre}(E) - S(A, E)$.*

Definition 3. *A Gödel agent wrt. agent family $\mathcal{A}$ and environment family $\mathcal{E}$ is defined as an agent minimizing the maximal loss, i.e., as an element of the set $G(\mathcal{A}, \mathcal{E}, S) = argmin_{A \in \mathcal{A}} \max_{E \in \mathcal{E}} L(A, E)$.*

Definition 4. *The maximal loss of an agent is called its* global loss. *The global loss of a Gödel agent is called* Gödel loss.

In our case of finite agent and environment families, G contains at least one element, i.e., one or more Gödel agents exist. In section 4 we will see that this is also the case when the environment family becomes infinite but the agent family stays finite.

A Gödel agent can be seen as an agent which is most flexible, adapting and self-improving with regard to the given environment family. It scores well across the whole set of environments, and not only in a selected few. Thus a Gödel agent can be regarded as intelligent (at least wrt. the given environment family) in the sense introduced by S. Legg and M. Hutter in [7], where intelligence is defined as "the ability to achieve goals in a wide range of environments". Additionally, a Gödel agent operates within the real-time restrictions of the synchronous agent framework. If the environment family is diverse and complex, a Gödel agent has to be extremely adaptive and, driven by real-time pressure, self-improving. In this regard, Gödel agents are closely related to Gödel machines, which were introduced by J. Schmidhuber [11], and which represent self-improving and, in a certain sense, optimally efficient problem solvers. While Schmidhuber describes in detail the internal structure of Gödel machines, we try to characterize Gödel agents by their externally observable behavior. To elucidate the exact relationship between Gödel agents and Gödel machines is the topic of ongoing investigations.

If the loss is interpreted as a distance measure between an agent and an environment, then a Gödel agent would be located at the place which minimizes the maximal distance. In this sense Gödel agents are located in the center of the environment family.

3   Infinite Games, Ruin Theory, and the Horizon Problem

One goal of foundational investigations is to reduce contingent aspects like arbitrary parameters, often called "magic numbers", or reasonable but not necessary design decisions. One such parameter is the "horizon", a finite lifespan or maximal planning interval often necessary to define for an agent in order to get well-defined reward-values for agent policies. But especially in open environments existing for an indefinite timespan, this is an ad hoc parameter containing contingent aspects which may prevent the agent from optimal behavior. To stress this point, we quote M. Hutter ([5], p. 18):

"The only significant arbitrariness in the AIXI model lies in the choice of the lifespan m."

where AIXI is a learning agent aiming to be as general as possible.

In order to eliminate this parameter and to tackle the horizon problem from a foundational point of view, we will look into the notion of an infinite game, and, in a probabilistic context, into ruin theory.

An infinite game is a game which potentially has no end, but could go on forever. And for at least one of the players this is exactly the goal: to stay in the game till the end of time. A good illustration of this abstract concept is the Angel and Devils Game, introduced by J. H. Conway in 1982 [2]. The game is played by two players called the angel and the devil. The playground is $\mathbf{Z} \times \mathbf{Z}$, an infinite 2D lattice. The angel gets assigned a power k (a natural number 1 or higher), which is fixed before the game starts. At the beginning, the angel is located at the origin. On each turn, the angel has to jump to an empty square which has at most a distance of k units from the angel's current square in the infinity norm. The devil, on its turn, can delete any single square not containing the angel. The angel can jump over deleted squares, but cannot move to them. The devil wins if the angel cannot move anymore. The angel wins by moving, i.e., surviving, indefinitely. In [2] it was proved that an angel of power 1 can always be trapped by the devil, but it took 25 years to show that an angel of power 2 has a winning strategy [6], i.e., an angel of power 2 using the right strategy can survive forever.

This game nicely illustrates that the angel has not a definite or finite goal it wants to reach, but aspires to *avoid* certain states of the world. This seemingly innocuous transition from a positive goal, an attractor, to a negative goal, a repellor, solves the horizon problem from a foundational point of view, avoiding the introduction of arbitrary parameters. Now actions do not have to be scored with regard to the positive goals they can reach within a certain time frame, but according to the probability they entail for avoiding the repellor states forever.

A classical probabilistic example to illustrate the concept of an infinite horizon is from ruin theory. Ruin theory was developed as a mathematical model for the problem an insurance company is typically facing: there is an incoming flow of premiums and an outgoing flow of claims [1]. Assuming that the flow of premiums is constant and the time and size of claims is exponentially distributed, the net capital position of an insurance company can be modeled as a biased random walk. Ruin is defined as a negative net capital position. Now the maybe surprising fact is that there are parameter values for which ruin probability even for an infinite time horizon stays below 1, i.e., an indefinite survival has a positive probability. For the above model of exponentially distributed claims and

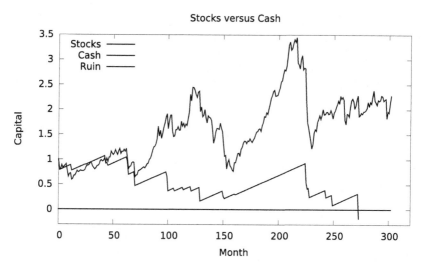

Fig. 2. In the insurance example, different actions (investing in either stocks or cash) lead to different capital position outcomes (survival or ruin) while getting the same premiums and the same claims occur in both scenarios. The safer cash investment scenario initially fares better but in the end ruin occurs (in month 273), while the riskier stock investment scenario is able to accumulate enough reserves over a longer horizon to survive. The simulation uses 302 monthly periods from 1990 to 2015, an initial capital of 1, a constant premium of 0.01 per month, exponentially distributed claim sizes ($\lambda = 5$) occurring with a probability of 0.10 per period and investment in either a stock performance index (DAX) or interest-free cash.

interclaim times, there is an analytical formula for the ruin probability ψ with infinite time horizon [9]:

$$\psi(u) = \frac{\mu}{c\lambda} \exp((\frac{\mu}{c} - \lambda)u),$$

where $u > 0$ is the initial capital, $c > 0$ is the premium received continuously per unit time, interclaim times T_i are distributed according to $Exp(\mu), \mu > 0$ and the sizes of claims Y_i according to $Exp(\lambda), \lambda > 0$. For example, if the initial capital is $u = 1$, premium rate is $c = 0.2$, the expected interclaim time $E(T_i) = 2$ ($\mu = 0.5$), and the expected size of claims $E(Y_i) = 0.2$ ($\lambda = 5$), we get an infinite horizon ruin probability of $\psi = 0.04$, i.e., in this case the probability to stay in business forever, the *liveness*, is $1 - \psi = 96\%$.

In a more general example one can imagine that the insurance company can invest its capital in stocks. In figure 2, beginning from the same initial capital, two scenarios for the development of the net capital are shown: one conservative, where all the capital is kept as cash, and one aggressive, where all the capital is invested in stocks. In this case, the risky strategy prevails over the less risky one, but the best strategy is probably a smart mix of cash and stocks which is reallocated periodically, i.e., the investment strategy of the insurance company would decide on ruin or indefinite survival.

Both examples, the angel problem and the insurance problem, show how to avoid the horizon problem by switching the definition of goal from *reaching a world state* to *avoiding a world state*. In this sense, the accumulation of reward is only relevant as long as it helps to stay away from the repellor.

The above discussion of negative goals or repellors should serve as an illustration of a principled solution of the horizon problem and should inspire to search for new goal systems of agents. We do not claim that all agent policies should strive to avoid repellors. Negative goals should be seen as complementing, not replacing positive goals.

4   Gödel Agents in Infinite Arenas

Here we discuss the cases when one or both of the agent and environment families become infinite. This is especially relevant for theoretical investigations, because in most settings in machine learning or statistics the set of models assumed to generate the observations is infinite.

First we assume that only the environment family is infinite. The pre-established score is still well-defined wrt. each single environment, because the agent family is finite and thus the maximum in definition 1 exists. The same is true for the loss, so we arrive at an infinite number of losses wrt. one agent. Now this infinite number of losses may have no maximum, but they still have a supremum. In case of unbounded score functions, this supremum could be infinite, but for bounded score functions (which is the case for liveness scores, as a probability they lie in the $[0, 1]$-interval), we will get a finite number. So we can assign this finite supremum to the agents as the loss wrt. to the whole environment family, now calling this the global loss of the agent. This results in a finite family of agents each getting assigned a global loss number. Then there is at least one agent in this finite family having a minimal global loss, i.e., there is at least one Gödel agent.

The situation becomes more complicated if there are infinitely many agents, too. Then we can still define the infimum of all the global losses of all agents, but there does not have to be an agent assuming this infimum as its global loss. But in the case of bounded score functions, there is at least for every $\epsilon > 0$ an agent whose global loss exceeds the infimum less than ϵ, because in every neighborhood of the infimum has to be a global loss value assumed by an agent from the agent family. If we call such agents ϵ-Gödel agents, than we have just proved that for bounded score functions (and, as mentioned above, liveness scores are bounded), even when both agent and environment families are infinite, there are ϵ-Gödel agents for all $\epsilon > 0$.

An even more realistic agent framework should also address spatial aspects of Moore agents, like states per volume or access times for large storage devices, which become relevant when dealing with infinite agent families. A thorough analysis of the spatial aspects may imply the general existence of genuine Gödel agents even in the infinite family case, because minor decreases of global loss by using more states are offset by the associated costs caused by these additional states. This will be the topic of future research.

The above discussion addresses only the existence of Gödel agents in certain situations, not how to construct or approximate them. At least we now know that there is something worthwhile to search for.

5   A Scalable Testbed for Self-Improving Agents

As mentioned in section 1, one motivation for using Moore machines is their scalable complexity. In addition to the synchrony condition, this enables to investigate phenomena of adaptability and self-improvement in a wide range of different agent and environment families, providing a flexible and scalable testbed with regard to available agent resources and environment complexities.

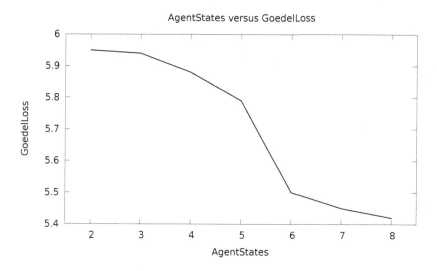

Fig. 3. Increasing agent complexity leads to lower Gödel losses as seen in these preliminary results from a simulation performed with 500 fixed Moore environments (having 5 states, 4 inputs and 6 outputs with random transition tables and random outputs), a fixed score function (using random scores in [0-10] depending on the environment state, the final score is given as average score per simulation step), and 100000 random Moore agents drawn per agent state number, all evaluated for 100 steps per environment-agent pair.

Our working hypothesis is that many aspects of adaptation and self-improvement occur already in scaled-down versions of the full Turing model. The detailed investigation of these questions, both theoretically and empirically, has just started and is the topic of ongoing research. Here we can present only a small, preliminary result, which nevertheless provides an indication of the fruitfulness and power of the proposed framework. Especially, it inspires to ask new questions which otherwise may have stayed unasked.

For example, we want to know how the Gödel loss varies if we increase the number of states in the agent family. Is there a "bang per state" effect and how large is it? In figure 3 the estimated Gödel losses for a fixed environment family, fixed score function, and increasing number of agent states are displayed. We can see a "bang per state" effect, but, like in many saturation phenomena, it finally gets smaller for every added state. Of course these phenomena have to be investigated much more extensive, both theoretically and empirically, but that is exactly what we hope for: that the proposed framework is the starting point for the detailed exploration of the landscape of arenas, adaptability, and self-improvement.

6   Discussion and Outlook

This is primarily a conceptual paper. A crucial part of theoretical investigations, aimed at solving real world questions, is to create a conceptual framework which is a good mix of abstracting away irrelevant or subrelevant details on the one side, but keeping enough structure so that vital aspects of the real world problem are still present on the other side. The scalable synchronous agent framework introduced in this article tries to offer such a good mix between structure and abstraction, hopefully leading to a fruitful testbed for theoretical and empirical investigations into phenomena of adapting and self-improving agents across a wide range of environments.

Especially the synchronization of agent and environment time allows to investigate phenomenons of self-improvement which is not possible in the locally synchronous framework. Our framework allows to explicitly, systematically and quantitativly analyze the trade-off between action quality and action time, which in other frameworks cannot even be formulated and hence has to be dealt with in an implicit and often ad hoc fashion.

This may lead to a new discovery process for agent policies by just looking at their performance with regard to the quality-time trade-off, without the need for a conceptual understanding of how they achieve this performance. From the outside, a Gödel agent for given agent and environment families is just a "bit mixer", and describing its inner workings by stating that it builds models or makes inferences is just a way to try to understand what is going on inside the agent, but is not necessary for its discovery or implementation.

By following this approach, we lose transparency, but we gain access to the whole agent space. In fact, concepts for designing the cognitive structure of an agent like logical inference, probabilistic inference, or utility, can be seen as specific *search biases* in exploring the agent space. But these biases are very focused, leading to the exploration of only some archipelagos, while leaving the great ocean of nonconventional cognitive architectures invisible and undiscovered. Of course, that does not mean that we aim for a bias-free, totally random discovery process for agent policies, but that the search biases should emerge as a result of a self-improving cognitive dynamics, rather than to be hardwired into the agent policy.

Generally, we advocate a change in perspective with regard to agent concepts from defining them via their inner structure (like this is done, for example, in [10]) to characterizing them from the outside using observable properties. This can be seen in analogy to the development in many mathematical areas, where first a "coordinate-dependent" description was introduced and then gradually replaced by a "coordinate-independent" one, often leading to general, elegant and powerful theories.

References

1. Asmussen, S.: Ruin Probabilities. World Scientific (2000)
2. Berlekamp, E.R., Conway, J.H., Guy, R.K.: Winning Ways for your Mathematical Plays. Academic Press (1982)
3. Cremers, A.B., Hibbard, T.H.: A programming notation for locally synchronized algorithms. In: Bertolazzi, P., Luccio, F. (eds.) VLSI: Algorithms and Architectures, pp. 341–376. Elsevier (1985)
4. Garber, D.: Body, Substance, Monad. Oxford University Press, Monad (2009)
5. Hutter, M.: Universal Artificial Intelligence. Springer (2005)
6. Kloster, O.: A solution to the angel problem. Theoretical Computer Science **389**(1–2), 152–161 (2007)
7. Legg, S., Hutter, M.: Universal intelligence: A definition of machine intelligence. Minds & Machines **17**(4), 391–444 (2007)
8. Moore, E.F.: Gedanken-experiments on sequential machines. Automata Studies **34**, 129–153 (1956)
9. Rongming, W., Haifeng, L.: On the ruin probability under a class of risk processes. Astin Bulletin **32**(1), 81–90 (2002)
10. Russell, S., Norvig, P.: Artificial Intelligence: A Modern Approach, 3rd edn. Prentice Hall (2009)
11. Schmidhuber, J.: Gödel machines: Fully self-referential optimal universal self-improvers. In: Goertzel, B., Pennachin, C. (eds.) Artificial General Intelligence. Springer (2007)
12. Solomonoff, R.: A formal theory of inductive inference, part I. Information and Control **7**(1), 1–22 (1964)
13. Solomonoff, R.: A formal theory of inductive inference, part II. Information and Control **7**(2), 224–254 (1964)
14. Zimmermann, J., Cremers, A.B.: Making Solomonoff Induction Effective. In: Cooper, S.B., Dawar, A., Löwe, B. (eds.) CiE 2012. LNCS, vol. 7318, pp. 745–754. Springer, Heidelberg (2012)

Author Index

Printed in the United States
By Bookmasters